Theory as History

Historical Materialism Book Series

More than ten years after the collapse of the Berlin Wall and the disappearance of Marxism as a (supposed) state ideology, a need for a serious and long-term Marxist book publishing program has risen. Subjected to the whims of fashion, most contemporary publishers have abandoned any of the systematic production of Marxist theoretical work that they may have indulged in during the 1970s and early 1980s. The Historical Materialism book series addresses this great gap with original monographs, translated texts and reprints of "classics."

Editorial board: Paul Blackledge, Leeds; Sebastian Budgen, London; Jim Kincaid, Leeds; Stathis Kouvelakis, Paris; Marcel van der Linden, Amsterdam; China Miéville, London; Paul Reynolds, Lancashire.

Haymarket Books is proud to be working with Brill Academic Publishers (http://www.brill.nl) and the journal *Historical Materialism* to republish the Historical Materialism book series in paperback editions. Current series titles include:

Alasdair MacIntyre's Engagement with Marxism: Selected Writings 1953–1974, edited by Paul Blackledge and Neil Davidson

Althusser: The Detour of Theory, Gregory Elliott

Between Equal Rights: A Marxist Theory of International Law, China Miéville

The Capitalist Cycle, Pavel V. Maksakovsky, translated with introduction and commentary by Richard B. Day

The Clash of Globalisations: Neo-Liberalism, the Third Way, and Anti-Globalisation, Ray Kiely

Critical Companion to Contemporary Marxism, edited by Jacques Bidet and Stathis Kouvelakis

Criticism of Heaven: On Marxism and Theology, Roland Boer

Criticism of Religion: On Marxism and Theology II, Roland Boer

Exploring Marx's Capital*: Philosophical, Economic, and Political Dimensions*, Jacques Bidet, translated by David Fernbach

Following Marx: Method, Critique, and Crisis, Michael Lebowitz

The German Revolution: 1917–1923, Pierre Broué

Globalisation: A Systematic Marxian Account, Tony Smith

The Gramscian Moment: Philosophy, Hegemony and Marxism, Peter D. Thomas

Impersonal Power: History and Theory of the Bourgeois State, Heide Gerstenberger, translated by David Fernbach

Lenin Rediscovered: What Is to Be Done? in Context, Lars T. Lih

Making History: Agency, Structure, and Change in Social Theory, Alex Callinicos

Marxism and Ecological Economics: Toward a Red and Green Political Economy, Paul Burkett

A Marxist Philosophy of Language, Jean-Jacques Lecercle, translated by Gregory Elliott

Politics and Philosophy: Niccolò Machiavelli and Louis Althusser's Aleatory Materialism, Mikko Lahtinen, translated by Gareth Griffiths and Kristina Köhli

The Theory of Revolution in the Young Marx, Michael Löwy

Utopia Ltd.: Ideologies of Social Dreaming in England 1870–1900, Matthew Beaumont

Western Marxism and the Soviet Union: A Survey of Critical Theories and Debates Since 1917, Marcel van der Linden

Witnesses to Permanent Revolution: The Documentary Record, edited by Richard B. Day and Daniel Gaido

Theory as History

Essays on Modes of Production and Exploitation

Jairus Banaji

Haymarket Books
Chicago, Illinois

First published in 2010 by Brill Academic Publishers, The Netherlands
© 2010 Koninklijke Brill NV, Leiden, The Netherlands

Published in paperback in 2011 by
Haymarket Books
P.O. Box 180165
Chicago, IL 60618
773-583-7884
www.haymarketbooks.org

ISBN: 978-1-60846-143-1

Trade distribution:
In the US, Consortium Book Sales, www.cbsd.com
In Canada, Publishers Group Canada, www.pgcbooks.ca
In the UK, Turnaround Publisher Services, www.turnaround-psl.com
In Australia, Palgrave Macmillan, www.palgravemacmillan.com.au
In all other countries, Publishers Group Worldwide, www.pgw.com

Cover image of *Composition for Elena Guro's Death*, 1918, by Mikhail Matiushin.

This book was published with the generous support of Lannan Foundation and the Wallace Global Fund.

Printed in the United States.

10 9 8 7 6 5 4 3 2

Library of Congress Cataloging-in-Publication data is available.

To the memory of
Evgeny Preobrazhensky
(1886–1937)

Contents

Foreword xi
Marcel van der Linden
Acknowledgements xvii

Chapter One   Introduction: Themes in Historical Materialism 1
1.1. Questions of theory 4
1.2. A Marxist characterisation of 'Asiatic' régimes 15
    1.2.1. From the Asiatic to the tributary mode: Marx, Haldon and beyond 17
    1.2.2. Ruler and ruling class: configurations of the tributary mode 23
1.3. Some general conclusions 41

Chapter Two   Modes of Production in a Materialist Conception of History 45
2.1. The retreat into historical formalism 45
2.2. *Produktionsweise* as 'labour-process' and 'epoch of production' 50
2.3. Levels of abstraction in historical materialism 52
    2.3.1. Wage-labour as abstract determination and determinate abstraction 52
    2.3.2. Serf-owning capital 55
    2.3.3. The defining role of the laws of motion 58
    2.3.4. The failure of abstraction in vulgar Marxism 61
2.4. Reading history backwards 65
2.5. Slavery and the world-market 67
    2.5.1. 'Slavery' 67
    2.5.2. The nascent world-market 71

2.6. Feudal production 72
   2.6.1. The estate 72
   2.6.2. Peculiarities of the 'second serfdom' 79
   2.6.3. Commodity-feudalism as the pure form 82
   2.6.4. Modes of production as objects of long duration 87
   2.6.5. Two brief conclusions 92
2.7. Simple-commodity production: a 'determination of form' 94
   2.7.1. The peasant mode of production 94
   2.7.2. The simple-commodity producer as wage-slave 95

Chapter Three Historical Arguments for a 'Logic of Deployment'
  in 'Precapitalist' Agriculture 103
3.1. Part I 104
3.2. Part II 107
3.3. Part III 111

Chapter Four Workers Before Capitalism 117

Chapter Five The Fictions of Free Labour: Contract, Coercion and
  so-called Unfree Labour 131
5.1. Premises: the elusive reality of consent 131
5.2. A Marxism of liberal mystifications? 134
5.3. Forms of exploitation based on wage-labour 143
5.4. 'Free contract' in Sartre's *Critique* 150
5.5. Summary 153

Chapter Six Agrarian History and the Labour-Organisation of
  Byzantine Large Estates 155
6.1. Introduction 155
6.2. A historiography of abstractions 157
6.3. Rural stratification: *geouchountes*, *ktetores* and *ergatai* 159
6.4. The case for permanent labour 161
6.5. Restructuring in the later empire 166
6.6. The new estates 168
6.7. The labour-organisation of sixth-century estates 173
6.8. Conclusion 177

Chapter Seven Late Antiquity to the Early Middle Ages: What Kind
   of Transition? 181
7.1. Introduction: Marxist uncertainties 181
7.2. Background to the late empire 185
7.3. Unresolved issues 188
7.4. The reshaping of relations of production 190
   7.4.1. The legacy of the colonate 191
   7.4.2. Slavery and the post-Roman labour-force 198
   7.4.3. The legacy of direct management 203
   7.4.4. What happened to the aristocracy? 208
7.5. Final comments: Wickham and modes of production 210

Chapter Eight Aristocracies, Peasantries and the Framing of the
   Early Middle Ages 215
8.1. Introduction 215
8.2. Aristocracies 219
8.3. The agrarian watershed of the seventh century 224
8.4. Critique of Wickham 231
8.5. The East: vulnerability 240

Chapter Nine Islam, the Mediterranean and the Rise of
   Capitalism 251
9.1. Historiographies of capital 251
9.2. Towards a Marxist theory of commercial capitalism 255
9.3. From corporate capitalism to the earliest capitalist forms of
   association 258
9.4. The Arab trade-empire 262
9.5. From Genoa to Portugal 268
9.6. Company-capitalism and the advance system 270
9.7. Concluding note: merchant-capitalism and labour 273

Chapter Ten Capitalist Domination and the Small Peasantry:
   The Deccan Districts in the Late Nineteenth Century 277
10.1. The 'subordination of labour to capital' 277
10.2. Commodity-expansion in the Deccan districts, 1850–90 283
10.3. Structure of capital in the Deccan 292

10.4. 'Interest' as surplus-value: increasing formal subsumption of
    labour into capital 301
10.5. The big peasantry of the Deccan 310
10.6. Peasant-differentiation 317
10.7. The stage of evolution of capitalism in the nineteenth-century
    Deccan 324

Chapter Eleven   Trajectories of Accumulation or 'Transitions' to
    Capitalism? 333

Chapter Twelve   Modes of Production: A Synthesis 349
12.1. Marxists and feudalism 353
12.2. The tributary mode 354
12.3. Periodising capitalism 356
12.4. Articulation? 359

Publications of Jairus Banaji 361

References 365

Index 393

Foreword

'The concrete is concrete because it is the concentration of many determinations, hence unity of the diverse.'[1] These words, penned by Karl Marx in his *Grundrisse* manuscript when he considered how the analysis of bourgeois society should proceed, are in my view a fitting motto for Jairus Banaji's learned work. If we are to understand historical processes truly and in depth, then we ought to do full justice to the empirical record. But that is not all. We also have to reveal the abstract determinations which are hidden 'behind' the concrete, and which 'lead towards a reproduction of the concrete by way of thought.'[2] If we disregard this necessary dialectic of the abstract and the concrete, one of two kinds of errors is likely to result. Either we remain entrapped in a descriptive narrative of a mass of empirical details, failing to reach the abstract determinations that identify and convincingly *explain* the real nature of a historical process in its totality. Or, we superimpose 'forced abstractions' on history, which are not grounded in a thorough analysis of its concrete specificities, and which, therefore, are to a large degree arbitrary and superficial, or even purely subjective preferences. Unfortunately, both errors occur all too frequently in Marxist historiography. Many so-called 'Marxist' studies of concrete structures and processes can be regarded as nothing more than applications of academic political or economic history to a different subject area, with a different political perspective. Also, most of the contributions to the Marxist philosophy of history have been written by Marxists who never consulted primary sources themselves, and base their knowledge only on handbooks and already published historical surveys. Exceptions to the rule can certainly be found; empirical studies of history have been written which, despite their appearance as narratives, are deeply theoretical (see, for example, Leon

---

[1] Marx 1973, p. 101.
[2] Ibid.

Trotsky's *History of the Russian Revolution*) and there are also philosophical works which obtain important abstractions from the empiria (for example, Alex Callinicos's *Making History*). But the number of such works is unfortunately rather small.

Serious, comprehensive attempts to integrate the 'concrete' and the 'abstract' are, quite simply, scarce. Some notable examples are Karl August Wittfogel's monumental early treatise on China's economy and society, Perry Anderson's analysis of the nomadic mode of production in his *Passages from Antiquity to Feudalism*, Robert Brenner's contributions to the debate about the origins of capitalism (known as the 'Brenner debate'), and Chris Wickham's large study of the early middle ages in Europe.[3] Obviously, all of these works can be criticised retrospectively for their shortcomings, but they remain landmarks of scholarship which, by digging deeper, will continue to provide direction for research. The writings of Jairus Banaji belong to this genre. Yet they also deviate from tradition and conventions; not only is Banaji more 'heterodox' in his approach than comparable authors, but with admirable zest and energy he also covers a much larger temporal and geographic terrain.

From the very start, Jairus Banaji endeavoured to derive his abstractions from the historical facts, in such a way that the abstractions do not end up by denying the facts. In this way, he has aimed to 'reproduce by way of thought' their true significance and coherence. It all began forty years ago, when he published his first scholarly article – an essay in the *New Left Review* about the disintegration of British functionalist anthropology. He was only twenty-three years of age at the time, but the article already displayed all the themes to which he would return in his later writings. It concerned the analysis of social formations, and was both deeply historical and theoretical, demonstrating a razor-sharp intelligence.[4] In the subsequent decade, the youthful Indian Marxist made himself heard in many interconnected areas of research. He intervened explicitly in the 'modes of production controversy' in his country – a debate about the specificities of the relations of production in Indian

---

[3] Wittfogel 1931 – this book is best read together with Wittfogel 1929 and Wittfogel 1932; Anderson 1974, Part Two, Ch. II/2; Aston and Philpin (eds.) 1985; Wickham 2005.
[4] Banaji 1970.

agriculture.⁵ Beyond this, he provided more general contributions about modes of production, in which he insistently countered the prevailing opinion that modes of production are 'in essence' driven by specific forms of exploitation: it does not make sense, he argued, to speak of 'slave mode of production', and even less can capitalism be reduced to the compulsion to perform wage-labour.

A second terrain which Banaji researched is agrarian history – the empirical test, as it were, of his theoretical arguments. An important contribution in this area was his study of the small peasantry in the Deccan during the nineteenth century, included in this book. Especially using official reports, Banaji argued that the small peasants in this Western part of India were not dominated under 'semi-feudalism' or 'semi-feudal relations', but that they, due to their debts to professional moneylenders and rich peasants who engaged in moneylending, were integrated in capitalist relations – a variant of what Marx called the 'formal subsumption' under capital.⁶ The third terrain Banaji researched in the 1970s was Marx's theory of value. Through a careful reading of Hegel's Preface to the *Phenomenology of Spirit* and, especially, his *Science of Logic*, Banaji tried to clarify that Marx's *Capital* can only be understood profoundly if one takes the Hegelian background of the book seriously. In so doing, he contributed to a scholarly discussion, which continues to this day.⁷

After such a flying start, a brilliant intellectual like Jairus Banaji could easily have pursued a glamorous academic career. But he considered other matters more important. He became politically active, together with his companion Rohini Hensman and with Praful Bidwai, Dilip Simeon and other comrades in the 'Platform Tendency', a grouping opposed to the Stalinist orthodoxies of the Indian Left. By the early eighties, some of them had built a wide range of contacts and solidarity among the unions around industrial issues. Banaji's interest in agrarian history moreover led him to explore a completely new terrain, namely the social and economic relations in the late-Roman empire. The first pursuit resulted in a study, co-authored by Rohini Hensman, with the title *Beyond Multinationalism: Management Policy and Bargaining Relationships in International Companies* (1990). The second pursuit culminated, after various

---

⁵ The most important contributions to the controversy are collected in Patnaik (ed.) 1990.
⁶ This volume, Chapter 10.
⁷ Banaji 1979.

prologues, in the monograph *Agrarian Change in Late Antiquity: Gold, Labour and Aristocratic Dominance* (2001), which is considered authoritative also by non-Marxists, and of which a second, revised edition was subsequently published. Beyond this, Banaji remained interested in general theoretical questions. In 1992, he published an abridged English edition of Henryk Grossmann's *Law of Accumulation and Breakdown*, which he had first translated in the late 1970s. He also published more articles about the analysis of precapitalist and early capitalist social formations.

The present collection brings together eleven important and provocative historical contributions by Banaji which are of enduring value – the majority have appeared earlier in various journals, but some of them are previously unpublished. *All* chapters in this book are 'empirical' and 'theoretical' at the same time, and draw inspiration not just from Marx and some Marxists, but often also from non-Marxist authors. The reason, as Banaji tersely noted in his classic essay written in 1977 (reprinted in this volume), is that, in some cases, strictly professional historians, 'not known for purely scholastic disquisitions on "modes of production" and "social formations", came far closer to the conceptions of Marx than the whole tradition of abstract historical formalism which passed for "Marxism"'.[8]

Banaji's extensive studies of European, Asian and African history, and of the relevant literatures in many languages, have constantly enriched and deepened his insights. From numerous different angles, he returns constantly to core questions which have preoccupied historians, anthropologists and archaeologists, such as: what explains the internal dynamics of modes of production? How are modes of production and forms of exploitation related? Under what circumstances are given forms of exploitation more or less often present? What is the historical meaning of simple-commodity production? What is capitalism, and how did it originate? What is the relationship between legal systems and capitalist development? Can only wage-labour be capital-positing, or can chattel-slavery also function in this way?

To these and related questions, Banaji has typically answered with heterodox, and therefore controversial, replies – and he arrives at conclusions which will no doubt surprise and provoke many. He concludes, for example,

---

[8] This volume, Chapter 2.

that there are no linear transitions from one mode of production to another, that 'Marxists have radically underestimated the extent of wage-labour in so-called "precapitalist" societies';[9] and also, that we should reject the free/unfree labour dichotomy as a legacy of mainstream liberal legalism, an ideological construct. Banaji's seemingly idiosyncratic but in fact highly sophisticated and original approach to historical analysis provides, I think, not only a welcome stimulus and a challenge for scholars today, but also will give them plenty to think about for many years to come.

Marcel van der Linden
Amsterdam, November 2009

---

[9] This volume, Chapter 4.

Acknowledgements

The essays brought together in this volume propound a more complex vision of historical materialism than the standard fare doled out to Marxist novices in hundreds of study-circles over the past few decades and reiterated, still, in the potted versions of Marx that grace the lecture-lists of countless universities. Historiography in the modern sense barely existed when Marx and Engels forged the outlines of a profoundly subversive vision of history and the forces shaping its development at different levels, roughly in the 1840s and 1850s. And although some of that historiography since has been shaped by Marxism itself, in more far-reaching ways than most historians would care to admit, the greater part of it remains curiously excluded and unexploited by historical materialists themselves. The reason for this of course is not just the deluded notion that Marxism (in at least one of its many varieties) remains superior to everything else that has ever been thought or written in human history, but, more insidiously, the timid attachment to orthodoxies that continues to sap the astonishing energies unleashed by Marx's own work. Engels himself was aware of this impending stagnation, complaining famously, in 1890, 'Our conception of history is above all a guide to study, not a lever for construction after the manner of the Hegelians. All history must be studied afresh.... But instead of this too many of the younger Germans simply make use of the phrase historical materialism (and *everything* can be turned into a phrase) only in order to get their own relatively scanty historical knowledge... constructed into a neat system as quickly as possible' (letter to Conrad Schmidt, August 1890). And, when Trotsky wrote, 'Where there are no "special features", there is no history, but only a sort of pseudo-materialistic geometry. Instead of studying the living and changing matter of economic development it is enough to notice a few outward symptoms and adapt them to a few ready-made clichés', he was effectively driving home the same point.

The renewal of historical materialism and of theory more generally will thus require a transformation of attitudes *in the first instance*, a vigorous iconoclasm that can prise Marxists away from their obsession with orthodoxy, so that a left that was never attached to Stalinism and felt profoundly humiliated and defeated by it can finally break with the residues of that terrifying conservatism of which Sartre's *Questions de méthode* (1960) still remains the most trenchant critique. The best work in the Marxist tradition has always been done by revolutionaries who took Marx seriously but doctrinalism not at all.

Since the essays collected here span a period of some thirty years, I have numerous friends to thank: in India, my friends Dilip Simeon, Neeladri Bhattacharya and Mukul Mangalik, all historians and all 'committed', also Praful, Javed, Rohini, Kannan, Mihir, and M.J. Pandey, all of whom are embodiments in their own way of a 'New-Left' culture in India that is sharply distinct from the dominant Stalinist formations; elsewhere, Jan Breman, Terry Byres, John Haldon, Barbara Harriss-White, Harsh Kapoor, Elio Lo Cascio, Mahmood Mamdani, Sughosh Mazmundar, Peter Sarris, Marcel van der Linden, and Gavin Williams. I am grateful to Chris Arthur, Robert Brenner, Peter Brown, Andrea Giardina, Karl Klare, Juan Martínez-Alier, Michael Krätke, Alfredo Saad Filho, and Brent Shaw for gifting substantial pieces of their work at various times, particularly grateful to Romila Thapar for making it possible for me to settle back in India in the early 1970s, and conscious of the debt I owe to Maurice Aymard (Paris) and Fergus Millar (Oxford) for the chance to resume academic work in the late 1980s. Rana Sen and Dave Rosenberg have been sorely missed for the greater part of my intellectual life, so infectious was the warmth of their personalities and the stimulation of their ideas. It was Sebastian Budgen who first mooted the idea of this collection and Henry Bernstein who sustained my access to the libraries in London. I am deeply indebted to them for their encouragement and solidarity.

Seven of the chapters that follow reprint papers published elsewhere over the past three decades: Chapter 2 is reprinted from *Capital & Class*, 3 (1977) pp. 1–44; Chapter 3 from *Journal of Historical Sociology*, 5/4 (1992) pp. 379–91; Chapter 5 from *Historical Materialism*, 11/3 (2003) pp. 69–95; Chapter 6 from *Agriculture in Egypt from Pharaonic to Modern Times*, edited by Alan K. Bowman and Eugene Rogan, Proceedings of the British Academy 96 (Oxford University Press, 1999); Chapter 8 from *Journal of Agrarian Change*, 9/1 (2009) pp. 59–91; Chapter 9 from *Historical Materialism*, 15/1 (2007) pp. 47–74; Chapter

10 from *Economic and Political Weekly*, 12/33–4 (1977) pp. 1375–404. None of these papers have been modified in any way except for the last one (the one from *EPW*) which is reprinted here in a shorter and slightly revised version with no change to the content of the original article. Chapter 4 was first written for a workshop organised by the International Institute of Social History, Amsterdam, in April 2006, on the general theme 'What Is the Working Class?'. Chapter 11 is a revised version of part of a paper presented to the *Journal of Agrarian Change* conference in London in May 2008. Finally, Chapter 12 is an expanded version of an entry scheduled to appear in the *Elgar Companion to Marxist Economics*, edited by Ben Fine and Alfredo Saad Filho.

Chapter One
Introduction: Themes in Historical Materialism

By 'modes of production', Marx meant forms of domination and control of labour bound up with a wider set of class-relations expressive of them and of the social functions implied in them. He saw these general 'forms' and the class-divisions grounded in them as 'historically created', that is, specific to the period they belonged to, yet capable of subsuming often much earlier forms as an intrinsic part of their own (form of) development, as, for example, in 'the connection between Roman civil law and modern production' (*Grundrisse*).[1] Marx also believed that these general configurations ('totalities of production relations') were defined by an inherent dynamic that worked itself out in the eventual dissolution of existing relations. *How* this happened, or could happen, was, of course, best described in his description of capitalism and its general 'laws of motion'.

The essays published in this collection span a period of just over thirty years (from debates in the late 1970s down to 2009) and set out first to map a general conception of modes of production as *historical characterisations* of whole epochs, in other words, to restore a sense a historical complexity to them, and then to illustrate/explore *some* of that complexity in detailed studies based as far as possible on primary-source material.

---
[1] Marx 1973, p. 109; using McLellan's translation in McLellan 1971, p. 132.

Marx himself was opposed to a 'supra-historical' approach that simply reduced historical characterisations to formulae. It was obvious to him that historical materialists would have to 'study the different forms of evolution' and 'compare them' *before* a workable characterisation was available for any period. He said as much in his reply to Mikhailovsky.[2] By contrast, most Marxist historiography of the precapitalist period tends to assume we already know the different modes of production from the labels attached to them, and *lacks any sustained attempt to grasp (explore, construct) their complexity*. Kula's study of feudal economy had a considerable impact precisely because he broke with this method of 'formal abstraction'.[3]

The challenge is formidable. We shall almost certainly never be able to replicate the rigour that Marx could demonstrate in his analysis of capitalism for any comparable epoch before it. But historical materialism establishes an element of continuity between that analysis and attempts to understand earlier periods. That Marx conceived the complexity of historical modes of production in *law-like terms* is clear from the famous citation in the 'Nachtrag' to the second edition of *Capital*, where the Russian reviewer's description of his 'method' claimed, *to Marx's approval*, that what chiefly interested him (Marx) were 'the special laws that regulate the origin, existence, development and death of a given social organism and its replacement by another, higher one'. That 'social organism' was Kaufman's peculiarly biological way of referring to the general form of society characteristic of the main historical periods in Europe's development is clear from his statement elsewhere that, for Marx, 'every historical period possesses its own laws'.[4]

After this introductory essay, Chapter 2 develops this theme (of the *complexity* and *law-like nature* of modes of production as Marx understood these) against the background of literature and debates that were current in the 1970s. That its central arguments are still relevant today is shown by the present state of discussion of these issues. One of the key distinctions suggested there was between 'relations of production' and 'forms of exploitation', yet the conflation of these categories is still endemic to a whole form of Marxism and runs through even some of the best historical work, such as Chris Wick-

---

[2] Marx 1877a; Marx 1877b.
[3] Kula 1970.
[4] Marx 1976, p. 100ff., citing the review by the Russian economist I. Kaufman.

ham's recent book, where (Marxist) feudalism is seen simply as coercive rent-taking and lacks any historical depth beyond that.[5] Wickham's conception of what constitutes a feudal mode of production is so general that even the Roman empire finally contains at least two versions of it! Again, Pierre Bonnassie's contention that a 'slave economy' persisted down to the aristocratic upsurge or 'feudal revolution' of the eleventh century is a classic instance of the same confusion: the widespread use of slaves in the early middle ages certainly implies a continuance of slavery as a form of *exploitation* but surely not the survival or persistence of a slave *mode of production*, however that is construed.[6] Another example: in one of the few recent attempts to return to these issues in a more theoretical way, John Haldon ends up recommending a conception of modes of production that denies that we can sensibly speak of them containing tendencies, much less laws of any sort.[7]

The essays collected in this book range widely across historical periods. They strike a balance between theory and history, suggesting that historians cannot construct viable models of the periods they deal with without a grasp of theory and without attempts to use it creatively. They discuss themes that are basic to Marxism but do so in ways subversive of existing orthodoxies. To take just one example of this, at least three of the papers address the issue of 'historical capitalism' in one way or another.[8] In the *Grundrisse*, Marx implied an interesting distinction between 'forms such as capital which belong to a specific epoch of history' and 'categories which belong more or less to all epochs, such as e.g. money'.[9] Since capital presupposes money and emerges out of its circulation, the emergence of capitalism, conceived historically, presumes a necessary connection between these two sorts of 'forms'. In other words, the contrast between them cannot be a historical gap separating one from the other. Marx was clearly aware of this because, unlike the widespread dogma that locates capitalist origins in a largely English and agrarian context,

---

[5] Wickham 2005; cf. Wickham 1985, p. 170, 'Coercive rent-taking is the feudal mode of production' (!); Wickham 1984, p. 6, 'feudal relations are represented *simply* by tenants paying rent to (or doing labour service for) a monopolistic landowner class'; my italics.
[6] Bonnassie 1991.
[7] Haldon 1993.
[8] Chapters 4, 9 and 12 (most substantially Chapter 9); also the allusion to this theme towards the end of Chapter 6.
[9] Marx 1973, p. 776.

the famous chapter on primitive accumulation ends with a note that tells us that Italy was where 'capitalist production developed earliest'.[10] A Mediterranean location for early capitalism shows how flexible Marx himself was in the understanding of capitalism's history and the great possibilities that can be opened up for 'scientific research programmes' based on a flexible and rather more sophisticated grasp of historical materialism.

1.1. Questions of theory

To take modes of production first, these, for Marx, comprised the 'relations of production *in their totality*' (as he says in *Wage Labour and Capital*),[11] a nuance completely missed by Marxists who simply reduce them to historically dominant forms of exploitation or forms of labour, for example, positing a slave mode of production wherever slave-labour is used or ruling out capitalism if 'free' labour is absent. The underlying assumption here is that Marx means by relations of production the relations of the immediate process of production, or what, in a perfectly nebulous expression, some Marxists call the 'method of surplus-appropriation'. But the immediate process of production can be structured in all sorts of ways, even under capitalism. This was a point that was probably better understood in the 1980s than it is today. For example, when Lewis Taylor described early twentieth-century changes on the haciendas of Cajamarca in Peru, he stated, quite rightly, that, according to Lenin, 'a Marxist analysis of rural society cannot mechanically identify forms of exploitation and relations of production'.[12] The distinction drawn there between (capitalist) relations of production and (precapitalist) forms of exploitation permeated much of the historical work on South African agriculture, such as when Helen Bradford in a general review of this literature noted that '"quasi-feudal" relations of exploitation, and racist relations of oppression, were created in the very course of capitalist penetration' in South Africa's countryside.[13] The general distinction here is one between *relations of production* and *forms of*

---

[10] Marx 1976, p. 876, note 1.
[11] Cited McLellan 1971, p. 131.
[12] Taylor 1984, p. 97, 'un análisis marxista de la sociedad rural no puede identificar mecánicamente formas de explotación y relaciones de producción'; about the use of precapitalist relations on the Gildemeister estates.
[13] Bradford 1990, p. 81.

exploitation, and Marxist theory would advance considerably if more Marxists took this on board (see Chapter 2). The point here is not just that relations of production include vastly more than the labour-process and the forms in which it is organised and controlled (the *immediate* process of production, as Marx called it), such as when Marx calls money a relation of production (in the *Grundrisse*)[14] or suggests in *The Poverty of Philosophy* that a relation of production is 'any economic relation',[15] but that labour itself, the *exploitation* of labour, breaks down into comparable dimensions of complexity. This is best illustrated by contrasting the general forms of domination of the peasantry with the concrete or specific ways in which landowners dominate, control and deploy peasant labour. When Carlo Poni described the struggle of the Bologna landowners to impose new methods of ploughing on their *mezzadri* and the different ways in which the peasants thwarted or circumvented those methods because they involved considerably more effort, this was not a statement about the 'mode of production' that prevailed in northern Italy in the seventeenth century.[16] Sharecropping or labour-tenancy or even the forms of labour-service described by Lenin in *The Development of Capitalism in Russia*[17] lie at a very different level of abstraction from serfdom, *peonaje*, etc. conceived as historical categories. Yet all these categories (at both levels) are about ways of controlling and exploiting living labour. The historical forms of exploitation of labour (slavery, serfdom, wage-labour is the usual trinity in most discussions; Marx tended to add 'Asiatic production') cannot be assimilated to the actual deployment of labour, as if these were interchangeable levels of theory. Since the latter is defined by immensely greater complexity, a conflation of these levels would mean endless confusion in terms of a strictly Marxist characterisation, the kind of confusion attacked by Taylor and by Bradford.

The conclusion here can be stated quite simply by saying that the *deployment of labour is correlated with modes of production in complex ways*. Not only are modes of production *not* reducible to forms of exploitation, but the *historical* forms of exploitation of labour (relations of production in the conventional

---

[14] Marx 1973, p. 123; so too in *The Poverty of Philosophy*, where credit, money, the division of labour, the modern workshop based on machinery are all called relations of production, Marx 1975, pp. 97, 124.
[15] Marx 1975, p. 76, saying that money is a production relation 'like any other economic relation'.
[16] Poni 1963.
[17] Lenin 1956, p. 198ff.

sense) lie at a completely different level of abstraction from the numerous and specific ways in which labour is or can be deployed. Chapter 3 lays out a general argument suggesting that in agriculture especially 'a much wider range of relationships of exploitation on the land is revealed than is suggested' by some Marxists.[18] Indeed, the logic that regulates the combination and use of different categories and forms of labour in the agrarian sector is one that *cuts across historical periods*, so that similar forms of labour-use can be found in very different modes of production.

In short, given the argument above, modes of production have to be constructed as objects of much greater complexity and a different sort of complexity. The theory has to be *stripped of its evolutionism* and refurbished to allow for more *complex trajectories*. For example, transitions to capitalism do not simply replicate some universal model or fixed sequence such as the one implied in the canonical genealogy of European culture (slavery → feudalism → capitalism). There were whole parts of the world where forms of capitalism evolved *without* the canonical antecedents of slavery and feudalism (the most obvious being the Islamic world). (See Chapter 9; also the next section of this chapter.) As Marx's reviewer said, 'every historical period possesses its own laws'.[19] But, certainly by the sixteenth century, those *endogenous* developments were soon bound up with the dynamics of an expanding international capitalism ('several European capitalisms, each with its zone and its circuits'),[20] so that there least of all could one study the indigenous expansion of capital 'in its pure state', unaffected by 'disturbing influences'.[21] Again, the transition from 'slavery' to 'feudalism' was scarcely driven by some spurious logic that led ineluctably from one to the other. Serfdom was not 'caused' by the decline of slavery (indeed, Marc Bloch himself pointed to the renewed vigour of slavery between the late empire and the ninth century), and the subjection of the peasantry through most of the middle ages but especially after the 'year 1000' 'needs other explanations'.[22]

---

[18] Beinart and Delius 1986, p. 33.
[19] Marx 1976, p. 101.
[20] Braudel cited Wallerstein 1974, p. 77.
[21] Marx 1976, p. 90.
[22] Bloch 1975, pp. 2–3; Davies 1996, p. 242, who says, 'there remains good reason to agree with Bloch that the decline of ancient slavery did not *cause* medieval serfdom'. Davies's italics.

At another, less obvious level, perhaps, the theory also needs *depth*. For example, how do we integrate the expansion of monetary economy into a theory of modes of production? The idea that precapitalist economies were based (universally) on natural economy is no longer tenable. Marx himself knew enough Roman history to know that the steady decline of the peasantry in the last two centuries of the Republic was bound up with the enrichment of the nobility and the formation of huge slave-run estates. 'The same movement which divorced them [the free peasants] from their means of production and subsistence involved the formation not only of big landed property *but also of big money capital.*'[23] Indeed, by the last decades of the Republic, the Roman monetary system had evolved sufficiently for one scholar to refer recently to the 'complexity and sophistication of late republican and high imperial finance'.[24] Credit was 'pervasive and institutionalized and *added enormously to the money supply*'.[25] Roman money was, in other words, more than coinage and there were financiers who held their entire capital in outstanding loans [*nomina*].[26] Again, in the *Grundrisse*, Marx writes, 'it is clear that the changes in the value of the material in which (money) represents itself (directly, as in gold, silver, or indirectly, as claims, in notes, on specific quantity of gold, silver etc.) must bring about *great revolutions between the different classes of a state*'.[27] If so, where in the theoretical space that surrounds our notions of a mode of production do these 'great revolutions' come? How do we account for them in terms of the theory itself? Unless 'relations of production' are constructed and defined to have the sort of reach and conceptual power that can 'integrate' all the fundamental phenomena or movements that social and economic historians deal with as their staple (conquests, demography, monetary expansion, historical ruptures like the great transition from T'ang to Sung, crises within régimes such as the state of Russia at the death of Ivan the Terrible in 1585, major ecological changes, etc.), Marxist historians who work on anything other than capitalism will simply continue to pay lip service to historical materialism, as Anderson does in *Passages from Antiquity to Feudalism* in some striking demonstrations of bad theory. By 'bad theory' I mean the

---

[23] Marx 1877a, p. 136; my emphasis.
[24] Harris 2006, p. 13.
[25] *Ibid.*, my emphasis.
[26] Harris 2006, p. 6.
[27] Marx 1973, p. 805; emphasis mine.

substitution of *purely* theoretical explanations for historical research and/or recourse to a theory that is itself simply a string of abstractions.

If the breathtaking formalism of *Pre-Capitalist Modes of Production* drove Hindess and Hirst into a wholesale repudiation of the theory of modes of production within two years of its publication,[28] Anderson at least pulled off a major *tour de force*, certainly with the longer of his two volumes. *Lineages of the Absolutist State* was a striking piece of comparative history, and it is hard to see how anyone could have covered so much ground (especially in the two 'essays' taken together) without relying largely or entirely on the work of other historians and no special grasp of any of the sources. The issue here, however, is Anderson's use of Marxist categories, ostensibly as the scaffolding of the whole panoramic edifice. If bad theory in *Pre-Capitalist Modes of Production* was an extreme but ultimately positivistic formalism that destroyed itself in its rapid 'auto-critique',[29] in *Passages from Antiquity to Feudalism* it surfaced sporadically as a metaphysical mode of reasoning that is best exemplified, perhaps, in the following excerpts. In the first, Anderson writes:

> The fall of the Roman Empire in the West was fundamentally determined by the dynamic of *the slave mode of production and its contradictions*, once imperial expansion was halted...it was always in the Western provinces that the *remorseless logic of the slave mode of production* achieved its fullest and most fatal expression[30]

The second passage tells us

> The Byzantine Empire, in effect, unloaded enough of the burden of Antiquity to survive into a new epoch, but not enough to develop dynamically across it. It remained *transfixed between slave and feudal modes of production*, unable

---

[28] Hindess and Hirst 1977, rejecting the argumentation in Hindess and Hirst 1975. Here they start by stating 'The present text rejects the pertinence of the concept of mode of production. *The effect of concentration on the conceptualisation of modes of production is the restriction of analysis to an extremely limited range of economic class relations* and the consequent neglect of the problems of conceptualising more complex forms of class relations' (p. 2; my italics). In other words, having discussed the issue with little sense of the centrality of class (having *banished* history!) and with the 'theoretical bubble-blowing' that was fashionable in the 1970s, they concluded that it was the 'concept' itself that was faulty, not just their approach to it.
[29] Cf. Thompson 1978, esp. pp. 205ff., 386 n. 21.
[30] Anderson 1974b, p. 266; italics mine.

either to return to the one or advance to the other, in a social deadlock that could only eventually lead to its extinction[31]

But no historians of late antiquity have ever invoked slavery as the fundamental reason for the fall of the western empire, at least not since Anderson published *Passages*. Indeed, slavery remained widespread in the late empire and has little to do with the crisis of the fifth century. And the second passage presents us with the image of a society transfixed between modes of production for centuries together (for some 900 years!), which must leave any reader wondering what Marx himself would have made of this historically interminable 'deadlock' of 'rural modes of production'.[32] In *both* cases (Anderson as well as Hindess and Hirst) it is the lack of complexity that undermines a credible use of categories which are, potentially, the bedrock of any materialist conception of history.

What sort of complexity, then? One form of this has been outlined briefly in the distinction I drew earlier between relations of production and forms of exploitation as well as the different levels at which we have to construe or grasp exploitation itself. These distinctions generate another (a second level of complexity) because if, say, the accumulation of capital, that is, *capitalist* relations of production, can be based on forms of exploitation that are typically *precapitalist*, then clearly there is not one ostensibly unique configuration of capital but a series of *distinct configurations*, forms of the accumulation-process, implying other combinations. Chapters 9–10 are about configurations of this sort, dealing with commercial and moneylending capitalism respectively; configurations of capital which, like commercial capitalism in particular, comprised a *rich variety of forms* from the peculiar domination of small producers by merchants discussed by Marx in the *Grundrisse*,[33] widespread not just in the European middle ages but throughout the Muslim world, to the large-scale Havana merchant-houses who controlled the smaller Cuban planters through *refacción* contracts and were themselves 'intimately

---

[31] Anderson 1974b, p. 270; italics mine.
[32] Anderson 1974b, p. 274.
[33] Marx 1973, p. 510, which starts 'The way in which money transforms itself into capital often shows itself quite tangibly in history'; Marx 1981, pp. 452–3, here contrasted with the 'genuine capitalist mode of production'.

linked' with US merchant-houses and British banking institutions,[34] or the London financiers, West-India merchants like the Lascelles, who underwrote the 'expansion of sugar and slavery' in the English-speaking West Indies and eventually took over the management of plantations 'formerly under the control of their business associates', becoming large-scale planters by the 1780s.[35] The paper reprinted here as Chapter 2 argued years ago that Marxists had no good grounds for resisting the idea of a *slaveholding capitalism* of the kind that dominated the economies of the American South and the Caribbean more generally. In a brilliant paper published in *New Left Review* at the end of the 1970s, Orlando Patterson had already noted in passing that 'for all its eloquence, Genovese's pre-capitalist conception of the Old South *is no longer tenable*'.[36] He referred to the 'essentially capitalistic nature' of modern slave-formations such as those of the British and French Caribbean,[37] and contrived the more general expression 'American slave capitalisms', arguing that, in the context of modern capitalism, slavery was simply a 'variant' of the capitalist system.[38] It is these ideas and premises that have gained much wider support among historians of the Old South today than the traditional dogma that slavery could not possibly form a configuration of capital (a form of capitalism) because it was the most extreme antithesis of free labour. Historians have, happily, broken out of this tautology.

Patterson's assessment of the mood among historians of the Old South was remarkably accurate. In the introduction to *The Ruling Race* James Oakes declared, 'I agree with those (historians)...who stress the capitalist nature of the slave system in the Old South'[39] and went on to explain,

> [i]mplicitly equating capitalism with free labor, Genovese argues that slavery was a pre-capitalist form of social organization whose 'logical outcome' was a paternalistic world view. And it was the slaveholders' paternalism, as he sees it, that created a constant tension between the slaveholders and the capitalist world market in which they conducted their business. But

---

[34] Bergad 1990, Chapter 10, esp. pp. 174ff., 178.
[35] Smith 2006, pp. 7ff., 186, 189, 'by 1787 a total of twenty-four Caribbean properties were directly owned or controlled by the Lascelles, covering 27,055 acres'.
[36] Patterson 1979, p. 54, n. 26; my italics.
[37] Patterson 1979, p. 52.
[38] Patterson 1979, p. 49ff. Note that Patterson also took the stand that 'no such thing as a slave mode of production exists' (p. 52), a position with which I agree.
[39] Oakes 1982, p. xi.

Genovese does not explore the nature of this tension, nor does he examine in any detail its manifestations *within* the Old South.[40]

A 1988 paper by Ransom and Sutch began with the vigorous assertion 'Karl Marx recognized the capitalist nature of American slavery long before American historians'.[41] They went on to state '[t]he discovery, or rediscovery, of the capitalist nature of slavery has proven to be a significant development. This breakthrough not only has prompted a complete and far-ranging reexamination of racial slavery in the Americas, it has also stimulated a renaissance in the field of American economic history more generally'.[42] And, by the mid nineties, the historiography of the South threw up its first 'revisionist' micro-history, William Dusinberre's now classic first volume on the massive rice-plantations of South Carolina and Georgia, with the bulk of their capital invested in slaves, in enormous irrigation-schemes and pounding and threshing mills, and with marked economies of scale and a remorseless control of workers stripped of any paternalism.[43] Dusinberre's description of low-country slavery is the best critique to date of Genovese's paternalism (or 'precapitalist') thesis and demonstrates how little of that there was in the vigorous agricultural capitalism that dominated the rice-swamps.[44] The idea that the history of capitalism comprises a series of *configurations* of capital helps to resolve the dilemmas and paradoxes behind much of this debate, and others like it, since historians like Dusinberre insist that they are describing a 'variant' of capitalism, not some featureless abstract model, and that a slave-based capitalism was bound to display features specific to this variant (planter-capitalism).[45]

Now, what this 'variant' does demonstrate is that free labour, so-called, *cannot* be an essential moment of capital,[46] not if the self-expansion of value is intrinsically indifferent to the forms in which it dominates labour, as

---

[40] Oakes 1982, p. xiii, followed by a citation of the famous passage in *Capital* where Marx describes Southern slavery as a 'calculated and calculating system' geared to the production of *surplus-value*. Oakes quotes from Moore and Aveling, so the citation has 'surplus-labour', which is wrong.
[41] Ransom and Sutch 1988, p. 133, prefaced by a master quote from *Capital*, Volume III.
[42] Ransom and Sutch 1988, p. 135.
[43] Dusinberre 1996.
[44] Dusinberre 1996, p. 201ff.
[45] For an introduction to the main themes in this debate, see Smith 1998.
[46] So too Patterson 1979, pp. 53–4.

Marxists such as Rosa Luxemburg and Henryk Grossmann surely understood. Luxemburg herself referred to 'capitalist accumulation with forms of slavery and serfdom'[47] ('with' meaning 'based on') and Grossmann suggested that the whole character of the Spanish and Portuguese colonisation was capitalist from its inception even if the plantations were based on *slave*-labour, accepting Sombart's description of the plantations as the 'first truly large-scale capitalist organisations' in history.[48]

The argument developed so far has at least two major implications for theory. *In the first place*, it frees up conceptual space for rethinking the history of capitalism as a much richer and more complex set of trajectories than the conventional stereotype of capitalist history as a history of the first capitalist nation. A small part of this richness and complexity is indicated in Chapter 9 by showing how one of the key institutions in the emergence of capitalism, the 'form' of the partnership, may well have been the Muslim world's major contribution to the business culture of the Mediterranean in the central middle ages. Marx tended to periodise capitalism into 'manufacture' and 'large-scale industry', ignoring merchant-capital as an antediluvian form. But it was through the rapidly expanding commercial world of the middle ages that capitalism emerged in a more systematic guise. Marx had a sense of this because, in Volume I, he admits, 'we come across the *first sporadic traces of capitalist production* as early as the fourteenth or fifteenth centuries in certain towns of the Mediterranean',[49] and, in Volume III, he allows for the direct domination of production by commercial capital, citing the colonial trades.[50] The claim that Holland was 'the model capitalist nation of the seventeenth century'[51] was not a claim about internal transformations in the Dutch economy in the early-modern period so much as a statement about the Dutch colonial empire and

---

[47] Luxemburg 1972, p. 56, 'we could discern capitalist accumulation with forms of slavery and serfdom up until the sixties of the last century in the United States, still today in Rumania and various overseas colonies'.

[48] Grossmann 1970, pp. 406ff., esp. 408.

[49] Marx 1976, pp. 875–6. How sporadic? That surely was a matter for historical investigation and today we know from some of the best work in European economic history just how pervasive commercial capitalism was. And, of course, the 'first sporadic traces of capitalist production' can be found much earlier than the fourteenth century if we look outside Europe, e.g., Hartwell 1966 on the foundries of northern Kiangsu or Johansen 2006 analysing the *salam* contract as a circulation of *capital* but one based, in legal theory at least, on the formal economic independence of the producer.

[50] Marx 1981, pp. 446–7.

[51] Marx 1976, p. 916.

the forms in which the VOC secured that country's commercial supremacy. In the essay that concludes this collection (Chapter 12) I have suggested tentatively that we might mark the historical distinction between these early forms of capitalism, dominated by merchants and bankers and the international syndicates they formed, and the developed form of capitalism analysed by Marx in *Capital*, by describing the former, quite simply, as capitalism or 'historical capitalism' and reserving the term 'capitalist mode of production' for the latter. But this is largely a matter of terminology, the more substantial point is to retain some sense of the richness of the history of capitalism.

The *second* implication relates to the issue of labour. If free labour is not a precondition for the accumulation of capital or even for whole forms of capitalist economy but the contingent outcome of struggles to shape the law and the social relations behind it, no more is the absence of coercion a precondition for the deployment of free labour itself. It is crucial to think all this through dialectically, because capitalist relations of exploitation are being construed increasingly by a seductive dichotomy between 'free' and 'unfree' labour, *as if these categories were actually opposites*! That was certainly not how Marx understood free labour. When he wrote, 'A presupposition of wage labour, and one of the historic preconditions for capital, is free labour and the exchange of this free labour for money',[52] or that 'With free labour, wage labour is not yet completely posited' since wages might still be regulated by statute,[53] 'free' simply meant dispossessed, divorced from the means of production. Indeed, this was generally true of the way 'free' labour was understood in the nineteenth century. As Hay and Craven state, '"free labour" emphatically was not understood to be labour free of penal coercion in the colonies, *as it was not in England itself*'.[54] Blackstone's *Commentaries*, the dominant textbook of English law between 1770 and 1850, still embodied a feudal model of wage-labour where the master-servant relation was based on status and not on contract, in other

---

[52] Marx 1973, p. 471; 'one of the historic preconditions for capital' *because Marx assumes* that the exchange of money for labour-power occurs only as a transaction between worker and capitalist, which is manifestly false, since the buying and selling of enslaved labour (or of the labour-power of children for that matter) is not a transaction between *worker* and capitalist.
[53] Marx 1973, p. 736.
[54] Hay and Craven 2004, p. 29; my emphasis.

words, discussed under the Law of Persons.⁵⁵ It is a supreme paradox that the first country of industrial capitalism was also the one most sharply characterised by what Kahn-Freund called an 'atrophy of the contract of employment' for most of the nineteenth century!⁵⁶ It was the lingering strength of the feudal model of wage-labour in England that explains the anomalous structuring of the English labour-market discussed by Steinfeld, viz. that as the market for labour expanded criminal sanctions for contract breaches proliferated.⁵⁷ Penal sanctions for contract breach were only abolished in 1875.⁵⁸ In other words, when Marx was writing *Capital*, English workers were still not 'formally free'. They laboured in the shadow of a legal régime that could compel the performance of contracts by the threat of criminal sanctions. It was not the repeal of the law of apprenticeship that formed the true watershed, as Marx himself seemed to think,⁵⁹ but the abolition of penal sanctions for breach of contract in 1875.

The further consequences of all this are, first, that the 'formal' freedom of wage-labour, this 'essential formality' as Marx calls it in the famous appendix to *Capital*, Volume I,⁶⁰ is not, in Marx's view, its essential characteristic but merely the 'deceptive appearance' that mediates its essential nature as a form of subjugation by capital. The voluntarist model of wage-labour that was constructed in the nineteenth century under the will-theory of contracts⁶¹ was not one that Marx himself accepted, at least not as an *essential* determination of capital, although it still remains the most widespread delusion people have about modern capitalist economy. The argument is propounded in Chapter 5 below and has received a thunderous response from Tom Brass, who continues to believe that the dichotomy between free and unfree labour

---

⁵⁵ Kahn-Freund 1977, esp. p. 514, 'Blackstone's concept of the employment relation is redolent of serfdom'.
⁵⁶ Kahn-Freund 1977, p. 524, after noting that it was Pottier's contract for the hire of services as the universal basis of employment that 'became the foundation of a modern system of labour law'.
⁵⁷ Steinfeld 2001, p. 46; 'employers commonly used criminal sanctions to hold skilled workers to long contracts' (p. 59) as late as the 1860s.
⁵⁸ Steinfeld 2001, p. 47.
⁵⁹ Marx 1973, p. 770, 'Only at a certain stage of the development of capital does the exchange of capital and labour become in fact formally free. One can say that wage labour is *completely realized in form in England only at the end of the eighteenth century, with the repeal of the law of apprenticeship*'; my emphasis and removing Marx's.
⁶⁰ Marx 1976, p. 1064.
⁶¹ Marx 1976, p. 280.

is a meaningful one,⁶² whereas to my mind this contrast, taken literally, only makes sense as a reference to the legal and social status of workers who are, as individuals, free, enslaved, or held in some form of legal bondage. Under capitalism, *all* workers are subject to *some* form and degree of domination and it is profoundly misleading to forge categories like 'unfree labour' in some diffuse sense that implies the construction of free labour as its alleged opposite, thus undermining the basis of Marx's critique of wage-labour and its legal mystification.

In the second place, the forcible creation and regulation of labour-markets are an intrinsic feature of capitalism and Marxists need to abandon the naïve view that law somehow stands 'outside' this process and is not intrinsic to it. Duncan Kennedy and his colleagues in 'Critical Legal Studies' demonstrated as much in the 1980s,⁶³ and Thompson had to remind Althusser that he, as a historian, found that 'law did not keep politely to a "level" but was at *every* bloody level; it was imbricated within the mode of production and productive relations themselves (as property-rights, definitions of agrarian practice) and it was simultaneously present in the philosophy of Locke' etc.⁶⁴ The labour-market has never been a purely economic phenomenon, and the relative freedom of workers, the fact that some are 'freer' than others, is entirely a matter of struggle and of the plasticity of legal reasoning.

A final issue: what about the 'Asiatic mode of production'? How do we deal with that today? Since none of the essays in this collection address the issue in any way, the section that follows is an attempt to map out a possible way of both discarding Marx's formulation *and* retaining the essential element within it.

1.2. A Marxist characterisation of 'Asiatic' régimes

It goes without saying that 'Asiatic' is a misleading description on several counts, not least for its Orientalist baggage. It is retained here to project continuity with Marx's discussion of the Asiatic mode and to expand on a

---

⁶² Brass 2003.
⁶³ Kennedy 1998 is the best introduction.
⁶⁴ Thompson 1978, p. 288, a scintillating passage that ends '(law) contributed to the definition of the self-identity both of rulers and of ruled; above all, it afforded an arena for class struggle, within which alternative notions of law were fought out'.

central theme in Oriental despotism, namely, the peculiar absence of a ruling class that emerges *organically* from the depths of society and achieves sufficient stature to control and dominate the state. The tradition that influenced Marx in the 1850s (long before he read Kovalevsky) maintained that 'Asiatic despotism' lacked 'intermediate and independent classes' between the sovereign and the mass of the subject population,[65] or, more realistically, that the aristocracy, such as it was, was a creature of the sovereign and completely unlike any equivalent group in Europe.[66] What the 'unbroken despotism of the Eastern world'[67] had 'lost respect for' (!) was of course the 'right of property, which is the basis of all that is good and useful in the world', as Bernier exclaimed in a hugely influential description of Aurangzeb's empire.[68] 'Bernier correctly discovers the basic form of all phenomena in the East – he refers to Turkey, Persia, Hindostan – to be the *absence of private property* in land. This is the real key even to the Oriental heaven', Marx famously told Engels in a letter dated June 1853.[69] Bernier was, of course, aware of the existence of a nobility in the Mughal state. 'It should be borne in mind, that the *Great Mogol* constitutes himself heir of all the *Omrahs*, or lords, and likewise of the *Mansebdars*, or inferior lords, who are in his pay', he wrote, adding, 'and, what is of the utmost importance, that he is proprietor of every acre of land in the kingdom, excepting, perhaps, some houses and gardens which he sometimes permits his subjects to buy, sell, and otherwise dispose of, among themselves'.[70] 'The King being proprietor of all the lands in the empire, there can exist neither Dukedoms nor Marquisates; nor can any family be found possessed of wealth arising from a domain, and living upon its own patrimony…no family can long maintain its distinction, but, after the *Omrah's* death, is soon extinguished'.[71] In other words, the *amirs*, or *Omrahs* as he called them, lacked any significance because, unlike the nobility in

---

[65] Jones 1831, p. 113, where he says, 'intermediate and independent classes there are none'.

[66] Campbell 1852, p. 75, '[the Mahommedan] tendency has always been to the formation of great empires, having nothing feudal in their composition, but everything centralized – *the only aristocracy being official, and the officials the creatures of the sovereign…*'; emphasis mine.

[67] Jones 1831, p. 8.

[68] Bernier 1916, p. 232.

[69] Marx to Engels, 2 June, 1853 (in Avineri 1969, p. 451).

[70] Bernier 1916, p. 204.

[71] Bernier 1916, p. 211.

France, they lacked the stability of a hereditary class. Yet Bernier was willing to acknowledge that the *jagirdars* enjoyed 'an authority almost absolute over the peasantry',[72] a nuance Marx ignored in reducing Asiatic régimes to the bipolar simplicity of a mass of village-communities on one side and an all-powerful sovereign on the other.

1.2.1. *From the Asiatic to the tributary mode: Marx, Haldon and beyond*

This bipolar model of isolated village-communities and an all-powerful state fails as a description of 'Asiatic' régimes for at least three substantial reasons. To take the least interesting of these first, Marx's characterisation of isolated and self-sufficient village-communities was drawn from English accounts of the early nineteenth century that were both embroiled in actual controversies regarding the best kind of revenue-system to introduce in various parts of India *and* far removed from the reality of most Indian villages, which were scarcely the 'little republics' Sir Charles Metcalfe imagined them to be.[73] Certainly, the self-sufficiency of the Indian village was a myth. 'There was nothing more remarkably autarkic about the Indian by comparison with the European village.'[74] Indeed, the 'scale, range and penetration of exchange relations in urban and rural Mughal India were so extensive' that they are simply incompatible with Marx's description of the Asiatic mode of production. And Athar Ali makes the point that Marx's village-community model 'could hardly apply to the Ottoman Empire and Iran which has no caste system to supply a hereditary, fixed division of labour'.[75] A second, more substantial reason for rejecting the way Marx construes the Asiatic mode is that it is simply not true, as Richard Jones claimed and Marx himself implied, that 'the Asiatic sovereign [had] no body of powerful privileged landed proprietors to contend with',[76] and that the régimes of 'Asiatic despotism' lacked any significant types of class-formation. In fact, it should be possible to argue

---

[72] Bernier 1916, p. 225.
[73] See Dumont 1966 on the recycling of the same 'stereotyped formulas' from one report to another and the literal source of some of Marx's formulations. For what the North-Indian village actually looked like in the nineteenth century, see Metcalf 1979.
[74] O'Leary 1989, p. 292.
[75] Athar Ali 2006, p. 102.
[76] Jones 1831, p. 139.

that a comparative political economy of Asiatic régimes, or of the tributary mode of production on which they were founded, is best constructed along the kinds of ruling class that the sovereign had to contend with and the *historically distinct ways in which the relationship between ruler and ruling class was configured*. This is something I shall attempt, briefly, below. Third, and finally, Marx's handling of the claim that (in Jones's words) 'Throughout Asia, the sovereigns have ever been in the possession of an exclusive title to the soil of their dominions',[77] or, as he himself put it, the claim about the 'absence of private property in land' (a notion which made its way into the draft pages of *Capital*, Volume III),[78] was thoroughly uncharacteristic for the uncritical way in which he simply repeated the core doctrine of the Orientalist tradition with no further penetration of the issue.

The point here is not that Asiatic régimes (Muscovy included) were not typically defined by their own doctrines to the effect that the entire territory of a sovereign was in some sense his or her property but that this claim took very different forms in different régimes, was asserted to unequal degrees and, most crucially from a Marxist perspective, was largely a legal or political fiction or at least is best construed as such. Thus in China, Twitchett states that 'Traditionally, all the lands of the empire were considered theoretically as belonging to the emperor, but by the beginning of the T'ang dynasty there was a strong and ever-increasing movement towards the recognition of the right of private possession of landed property'.[79] The T'ang 'seem simply to have accepted the growth of such great holdings and recognised the principle of private ownership of land.... But in law the the rules of the *chün-t'ien* [land-allotment] system remained in force and the doctrine of the emperor's ownership of all land remained unquestioned'.[80] There could scarcely be a better expression of the largely doctrinal nature of the ruler's claims.[81] Roughly analogous to this was the position under the Ṣafavids, when, as Lambton argues, 'the theory of the ruler as the sole landowner did not receive in practice complete and unqualified acceptance... in practice private persons enjoyed full

---

[77] Jones 1831, p. 7.
[78] Marx 1981, p. 927.
[79] Twitchett 1963, p. 1.
[80] Twitchett 1963, pp. 21–2.
[81] Cf. Twitchett 1962, p. 17, referring to the 'Confucian dogma that all land was the Emperor's'.

rights of ownership over land'.⁸² Again, in the Mughal case, Athar Ali suggests that 'The doctrine of state property could seldom be distinctly enunciated, in view of the lack of its reconcilability with Islamic law'.⁸³ In Byzantium, as Oikonomidès points out, 'The state was the largest landowner of all. To it belonged all the land *that was not owned by private individuals or institutions*'.⁸⁴ Thus, here the principle existed in a much less absolute form, and Aleksandr Kazhdan was always in a minority among Byzantinists in his view that ownership of all land vested in the emperor. The one 'Asiatic' régime where the doctrine was asserted in its purity was the Ottoman Empire, the primordial instance of Oriental despotism and the closest 'Eastern' parallel to the autocracy of the Muscovite state.⁸⁵ Needless to say, the actual arrangements under which land was held were more complex and subject to variation, and what really impressed travellers to the East, both in Turkey and in Russia, was the peculiar servility of the ruling class, a theme I shall come to in a moment. Yet even these broadly comparable autocracies reflected so-called 'state-property' in radically different ways. As Richard Pipes says, 'The Great Princes of Vladimir...regarded their realm as their *votchina*, that is outright property'.⁸⁶ Muscovy was the purest example, historically, of a patrimonial régime, *one in which there was no notion of a public order distinct from the rights and claims of the sovereign*, so that the kingdom was literally the 'personal patrimony of the prince'.⁸⁷ The Islamic model was a very different one, by contrast. Conquered territories were retained in the public ownership of the Muslim community,⁸⁸ and the underlying principle was that 'public revenues should be spent in the interests of all [Muslims], not of rulers or privileged groups'.⁸⁹ This was a legal fiction, of course, and one that allowed for developed notions of private property in land.⁹⁰

Having said this, there is in Marx's fascination with the absence of private property in land an important clue to a different mode of production from

---

⁸² Lambton 1953, p. 106.
⁸³ Athar Ali 2006, p. 97, adding 'but it came to arise in practice nevertheless'.
⁸⁴ Oikonomidès 2002, p. 1005.
⁸⁵ E.g., Mill 1820, Volume 1, p. 259, 'Throughout the Ottoman dominions, the Sultan claims to himself the sole property in land'; and see Anderson 1974a, p. 398f.
⁸⁶ Pipes 1995, p. 64.
⁸⁷ Pipes 1995, p. 65.
⁸⁸ Coulson 1978, p. 23.
⁸⁹ Crone 2004, pp. 304–5.
⁹⁰ Cf. Lambton 1953, p. 30.

that which came to define a small if dynamic sector of Europe in the middle ages. Marx himself was clearly reluctant to accept 'feudalism' as a sensible or historically accurate characterisation of large parts of the world where class-relations and production were structured so differently. It was the peculiar dominance of the *state* that set these régimes apart from Western Europe, and, of course, Marx expressed his aversion to the idea of an all-encompassing feudalism in the excerpts from Kovalevsky's book which he made in 1879.[91] There is no dearth of reference to these famous passages. It is clear that by the 1870s, when he read Kovalevsky he had *abandoned his earlier view about the government as the original owner of all the land*, denouncing its doctrinal character and the role it played in legitimating the dispossession of indigenous communities by the French (in Algeria) and the British (in northern India).[92] 'The lousy "Orientalists" etc., have recourse in vain to the passages in the Koran where it is said of the earth that it belongs "to the property of God"', he comments acerbically, after noting, '[There is] no trace of *conversion of the entire conquered land into "domanial property"'* in the *Multequa-ul-Ubhur* of Ibrahim Halebi (d. 1549), the massive legal compilation that formed the basis of Ottoman law.[93] This was a major shift of perspective but one which Marx never theorised in the sense that he seems never to have returned to the Asiatic mode of production and may just have quietly buried it.

The crucial difference between the abstraction of an Oriental despotism founded on the possession by the sovereign of an 'exclusive title' to the soil (Marx's Asiatic mode of production) and the more densely textured and complex picture that emerges in the notes from Kovalevsky is the completely fictitious idea, in the orientalist model, that 'Asiatic despotism' was marked by an absence of classes between the sovereign and the mass of village-communities. In reading Kovalevsky, but also some of the sources he used, Marx would have realised how distant his formulation of the Asiatic mode was from the actual history of countries such as India where, in Kovalevky's description, much of the conflict centred on the aspirations of the *muqta's* (Kovalevsky's *iktadars*) to make their assignments of revenue or *iqtā's* 'hereditary and inde-

---

[91] See the criticism of Kovalevsky in Marx 1879, pp. 373, 383.
[92] Cf. Krader 1975, pp. 203–4.
[93] Marx 1879, pp. 369–70; by 'domanial property' Marx meant land over which the Imam had full rights of disposal, i.e. the public property of the Muslim community.

pendent of the sultan'. (The reference here is to the thirteenth-century Delhi Sultanate.)

> The *iktadari* (military aristocracy) sought *to make their prerogatives hereditary and independent of the sultan*, as the beneficarii in western Europe. (133, 134). The Persian Barani, according to Kovalevsky, said that Ghiyas-ad-Din Balban had found the monarchy shattered to the ground because the *iktadars of his father* [*the father of the slave Ghiyas-ad-Din Balban, later Vizier of the Sultan Nasir ud-Din Muhammed ?!*], who appropriated the title of *Khan*, strove for independence and divided among themselves the wealth of the state treasury. Instead of appearing at military reviews they *excused themselves for not appearing and secured their usurpation each time by bribing officials*. The majority of the iktadars *directly renounced the military service*, on the grounds that the *ikta* had been given them not as *conditioned but as unconditioned property*, so-called '*in'am*'. (134). 'Thus already in the 13th century the iktadars strove towards '*mulk*' or '*milk*', *complete property*, which the Sultan could only give and gave *only* in reality, *from the domanial estates*, and the *waste land* that was reckoned thereto, – usually to worthy officials and courtiers. (l.c.)[94]

These remarkable pages on the Delhi Sultanate could well have formed the basis for a more complex and sophisticated description of Asiatic régimes, had Marx had the inclination. Kovalevsky described a form of class-struggle that pitted *ruler against ruling class* and (in his pages on the Mughals) the gradual consolidation of a subversive rural aristocracy, the *zamindars*, whose relation to the state had always been fraught with tension. This, for Marx, was not feudalism of any variety but nor could it have seemed even remotely comparable to the way he and Engels had construed the Asiatic mode of production in the 1850s.

Lenin's characterisation of Russia as an 'Asiatic state'[95] and Trotsky's repeated insistence on the 'peculiarities' of Russia's historical development[96] are, I suggest, best understood, in materialist terms, as the expression of a historical dynamic and of class-relations founded on a mode of production that

---

[94] Marx 1879, p. 376; the figures in brackets refer to the pages in Kovalevsky.
[95] Cf. Bahro 1978, p. 54, citing Lenin, 'The War in China' (1900), but also the remarks on Lenin's use of the term at pp. 85ff.
[96] Trotsky 1972, Chapter 27; the response to Pokrovsky.

was neither some exotic variant of feudalism nor, certainly, an inert replica of the Asiatic mode. But 'If not feudalism, or the Asiatic mode, then what?', as Terry Byres asked, with evident bafflement, when summarising a collection of papers on the theme in 1985.[97] The tributary mode of production now looks to me like the best contender for a Marxist characterisation of 'Asiatic' régimes and has both attracted support from leading currents in the Spanish historiography of al-Andalus and been discussed at length by John Haldon.[98] The strength of Haldon's analysis is the focus on imperial states, late Rome and Byzantium included (these, strangely, were never discussed by Marx, who showed little interest in late antiquity), and the perception that 'tributary' is a much better characterisation of these states and their economic régimes than the description of them as 'feudal'. But Haldon jeopardises this insight by suggesting that the distinction between 'tax' and 'rent' is purely formal since they are both charges on peasant-labour, or 'modes of surplus appropriation' as he calls them, *so that* feudal and tributary economic régimes are ultimately simply variants of a common (and, indeed, *universal* precapitalist) mode of production. This makes little sense to me *historically* (as to Marx as well) and differentiates Haldon's understanding of the tributary mode sharply from that of his Spanish colleagues, for whom the whole point of a *different* characterisation is to retain the historical peculiarities of (in their case) Islamic economic régimes (the economic régimes bound up with the military expansion of Islam) in contrast to developments in most of Western Europe.[99] Unlike Haldon, and with Pierre Guichard and Manuel Acién, I believe it is crucial not to minimise the historical difference between European feudalism and Asiatic-style economic régimes (this vindicates Marx) but unlike Acién and his use of the expression 'Islamic social formation', the historical complexity of the tributary mode is, I feel, best restored to it by abandoning the positivist distinction between 'modes of production' and 'social formations' (in fact, in Acién the distinction is residual, since he speaks of 'social formations' *tout court*)[100] and speaking instead of the possible ways in which a mode of

---

[97] Byres 1985, p. 13.
[98] The leading Spanish contributions that I am familiar with are Guichard 1990 and Acién Almansa 1997; the seminal discussion is Haldon 1993.
[99] This at least is how Manzano 1998b frames the issue, correctly in my view; see esp. pp. 894ff.
[100] See Turner 1978, p. 35ff. for an early critique.

production can be configured historically. Capitalism is a good example of this sort of historical complexity, as I suggested earlier, but so, in fact, is the tributary mode, as I shall now try and show.

1.2.2. *Ruler and ruling class: configurations of the tributary mode*

The tributary mode of production may be defined as a mode of production where the state controls *both the means of production and the ruling class*, and has 'unlimited disposal over the total surplus labour of the population'.[101] This is bound to strike many Marxists as an anomalous formulation, but that is because the theoretical issue here is one that has hardly ever been discussed in historical materialism, chiefly because Marxist debates on the nature of the state have focused very largely on the capitalist state, framing the issue in terms of the state's autonomy and thus *starting* from the presupposition that state-power and class-interests are analytically distinct.[102] But formulations like Miliband's 'partnership of state and capital'[103] will simply not work for tributary régimes, where, as Trotsky understood in his brilliant pages on the peculiarities of Russia's historical development, the Muscovite state shaped the evolution of the possessing classes in a fundamental way and quite unlike anything seen in the West.[104] Trotsky himself preferred to speak of the 'incompleteness of Russian feudalism, its formlessness'.[105] This, like the recurrent image of Russia standing 'between Europe and Asia',[106] left the issue of theory open. The 'profound differences between the whole of Russia's development and that of other European countries'[107] was a challenge for historical materialism that might well have been met had the circumstances of the revolutionary movement been less fraught with tragedy. But to round off the point I want to make here, even Theda Skocpol when dealing with imperial states such as Russia and China automatically assumes that we can sensibly posit a dominant class that is distinct from the state. To describe the

---

[101] 'Unlimited disposal, etc.' from Bahro 1978, p. 73.
[102] E.g., Miliband 1983; Bahro 1978 is an exception and has some fine passages, especially on the 'Tsarist state machine'.
[103] Miliband 1983, p. 65.
[104] Trotsky 1967, pp. 23–4.
[105] Trotsky 1967, p. 22.
[106] Trotsky 1967, p. 22; 1972, p. 8.
[107] Trotsky 1972, p. 331.

Russian nobility as 'politically dependent vis-à-vis the Imperial authorities' is a bizarre understatement for anyone with a sense of the history of the Muscovite absolutism![108]

In the *Grundrisse*, Marx treats 'oriental despotism' as a form of communal property whose real foundation is the inert multiplicity of stable agrarian communities that 'vegetate independently alongside one another'.[109] This 'communal' mediation of production – of the *community* as a 'presupposition of labour'[110] – undermines the separability of the economic from other levels of social reality in any characterisation of precapitalist modes of production, and certainly of the Asiatic mode.[111] Paul Frölich's image of a ruling bureaucratic caste superimposed on a peasant economic base (this about China)[112] is not a sufficiently integrated image of the relations of production of the tributary mode, which involved *both* the control of peasant-labour by the state (the state-apparatus as the chief instrument of exploitation) *and* the drive to forge a unified imperial service based on the subordination of the ruling class to the will of the ruler. The leitmotif of much of the historical writing on tributary régimes is the paramount importance for the ruler of a disciplined ruling class. The bond between the ruler and the ruling élite within the wider circles of the ruling class was the basis on which *new* states were constructed[113] and the state itself bureaucratised to create an efficient tool of administration. The autocratic centralism of the tributary mode and its backbone in the recruitment of a pliant nobility were not just 'political superstructures' to some self-contained economic base, they were essential moments of the structuring and organisation of the economy (*of the relations of production*). Moreover, tributary economies had considerably more vitality than Marx ever attributed to the Asiatic mode. Late Rome in the fourth century, the eastern empire under Justinian, China in the expansive phase of the Southern Sung and Mughal India

---

[108] Skocpol 1979, p. 85.
[109] Marx 1973, p. 471ff., at 473.
[110] Marx 1973, p. 495.
[111] Sayer made the point in *Violence of Abstraction*, cf. Sayer 1987, p. 69, 'There is simply no way, for any of these pre-capitalist socio-economic formations, that we can even begin to exclude "superstructural" terms from the very definition of "economic structures". To do so would make nonsense of Marx's entire analysis' in the *Grundrisse*.
[112] Frölich 1976, p. 149ff.; cf. van der Linden 2007, p. 134ff.
[113] Cf. Constantine in the fourth century, T'ai-tsu in the tenth, Akbar in the sixteenth!

in the seventeenth century were prosperous powerful states with a vast financial capacity.[114] They were scarcely exemplars of a 'stagnant Asiatic despotism'. On the contrary, the financial drive was always paramount. 'The entire government apparatus was built, and constantly rebuilt, in the interests of the treasury', as Trotsky said about Russia's state-economy.[115] The late Sasanian, late Roman and Mughal states had staggering levels of monetary circulation which were bound up with the assessment and collection of the land-tax in cash. In some ways, that was even more true of the Umayyads and 'Abbasids. As for China, 'the achievements of late sixteenth- and early seventeenth-century England...were in many respects even *exceeded by the impressive expansion of mining and manufacturing in eleventh-century China*'.[116]

Max Weber's discussion of 'patrimonial domination' in *Economy and Society* is a useful starting point because it works, at least implicitly, in terms of the distinction between 'landed nobility' and 'patrimonial officialdom', or landowner and bureaucrat, land and office, as radically different types and sources of power. It is the variant combination of these 'elements', as I shall call them, that structures his description of the leading patrimonial states and even if some of those descriptions are simply wrong or inaccurate, the following discussion of the crucially different ways in which the tributary mode was *historically configured* retains the distinction and varying articulations of his 'elements'. To start with one of Weber's more schematic and certainly less accurate descriptions, the late Roman empire is characterised in the striking image of a 'disconnected juxtaposition of landed nobility and patrimonial officialdom'. 'In the late Roman empire the increasingly important land-owning class of the *possessores* confronted a socially quite distinct stratum of officials', he writes.[117] But the hallmark of the late empire was precisely Constantine's creation of what Santo Mazzarino called a 'unitary bureaucratic organism' based on a fusion between senators and bureaucrats.[118] Constantine restructured the aristocracy to produce a tighter integration of the senatorial clans with the new imperial administration and expand the governing class

---

[114] The cash treasury contained well over a thousand metric tons of silver on Akbar's death in 1605. When Anastasius died in 518, the reserves stood at 23 million *solidi*.
[115] Trotsky 1972, p. 5.
[116] Hartwell 1966, p. 29.
[117] Weber 1968, Volume 2, p. 1067.
[118] Mazzarino 1980, Volume 3, p. 695, 'organismo unitario burocratico'.

as a whole by the induction of new elements. And, if Weber's disconnected juxtaposition remained only partially true of the western provinces where the senatorial clans had a greater freedom of action and would eventually undermine the survival of the Imperial state, it was the opposite of the truth in the East, where, on the contrary, it was the bureaucracy that threw up a powerful new class of landowners in the main part of the fifth century.[119] The renewed growth of a Byzantine aristocracy from the eighth century (following the Imperial crisis of the seventh) did not fundamentally modify its sixth-century character as a class that dominated the key offices of state as a bureaucratic élite with substantial landholdings in the provinces. The key difference was that now the more purely bureaucratic element, the civilian aristocracy of Constantinople, remained sharply distinct from the military aristocracy or powerful aristocratic clans based in the provinces.[120] The *continuity* of these great clans (the Phocades, Maleïnoi, Skleroi, etc.) sets them apart from Bernier's stereotype of the ephemeral ruling class of Asiatic despotism, but though Ostrogorsky saw them essentially as feudal magnates out to destroy the central power (the theory of a 'Byzantine feudalism'), it is crucial to see that this 'now-overmighty landed aristocracy' *remained* part of the Byzantine bureaucratic hierarchy in Ostrogorsky's own expression,[121] and that 'even for the families most solidly established in the provinces, *the emperor's service was the main means of acquiring wealth*'.[122] The conflict between ruler and individual factions of the (mainly) military aristocracy – especially in the tenth century – was one that typified all 'Asiatic' régimes and was a struggle not primarily for control of the peasantry but for power, waged not by a monolithic and unified class of aristocrats on one side against absolutism on the other, but by factions or alliances among magnate families who were themselves divided, and where individual rulers could always count on the support of leading aristocrats.[123] As Cheynet remarks, 'This aristocracy, which becomes stronger during the following centuries [that is, after the eighth century – JB] … has nothing "feudal" about it, since until the eleventh century, the imperial

---

[119] Banaji 2007, p. 130 and Chapter 6 there.
[120] Cheynet 1990; a superb study.
[121] Ostrogorsky 1968, pp. 306, 252.
[122] Cheynet 2006, I, p. 25.
[123] Sifonas 1994, against Ostrogorsky's conception of an endemic conflict between the central power and the aristocracy as a class.

authorities always controlled it, *forbidding its members any real autonomy in the provinces where they resided*'.[124] 'Born out of service to the sovereign, [it] never ceased to be linked to him, even during the period of the Komnenoi'.[125]

If this essentially *integrated* model of a bureaucratic élite extending its sway over landholding without ever establishing the kind of autonomy that might have effected its emancipation from the clutches of autocracy is one – quintessentially *late antique* – configuration of the tributary mode, China represents another more purely bureaucratic version. Weber suggested that here, in China, 'the patrimonial bureaucracy benefited from the even more complete absence of a landed nobility than was the case in [Ptolemaic] Egypt',[126] but this is simply not true. As Naitō Torajirō argued in a series of brilliant pieces contemporary with Weber, the evolution of a modern-style autocracy in China followed a long period, many centuries, of aristocratic dominance. During those centuries, though China was formally ruled by a monarchy, 'the monarch was [simply] the common property of the aristocratic class', 'merely a representative of the aristocracy' which dominated the leading organs of the state down to later T'ang.[127] 'Aristocratic government reached its zenith between the Six Dynasties and the mid-T'ang', declining in the 'transitional era from the late Ta'ng to the Five Dynasties' till its final and rapid dissolution in the turmoil and civil wars between 880 and 960.[128] From the Sung dynasty on (the period Naitō identified as the 'start of the modern era' in China's history), 'the power of the sovereign developed without limitation' based on a new class of professional bureaucrats drawn from a much wider social base, who now 'became the agents of the ruling dynasty'.[129] As Twitchett says, 'Naitō's theory was stated in very general terms'. But the 'general outline which Naitō perceived – largely by intuitive understanding – has stood up remarkably well to the progress of modern research'.[130] Implicit in the outline is a *sequential* model where, unlike Byzantium, the T'ang-Sung transition that straddles the same centuries sees a radical restructuring of the ruling class as a 'small group of extremely powerful lineages' who had 'completely domi-

---

[124] Cheynet 2006, I, p. 41.
[125] Cheynet 2006, I, p. 42.
[126] Weber 1968, Volume 2, p. 1047.
[127] Naitō 1983, p. 90.
[128] Naitō 1983, pp. 88–9.
[129] Naitō 1983, p. 92; Twitchett 1979, pp. 8–9.
[130] Twitchett 1979, pp. 9–10.

nated the political scene' and 'monopolized highest offices of state through their rights to hereditary employment' are displaced by a 'new class of professional bureaucrats',[131] completely different in character from the Kuan-chung aristocracy and other great regional groups and the enduring base of the autocratic régimes that would henceforth rule China into the modern world. It was the great historian Ch'en Yin-k'o who analysed the class-dynamics of this transition in detail, showing how, during the T'ang, 'the ruling house, itself a member of the close-knit north-western aristocracy, presided over a court' divided by a 'constant tension between the old aristocracy and a new class of professional bureaucrats recruited through the examination system'. 'The examination system was in his view a means of providing the dynasty with a bureaucratic elite dependent upon the dynasty for its position and authority rather than upon' lineage and hereditary privilege.[132] 'When the T'ang fell, not a single one of the regimes of the succeeding Five Dynasties period...was ruled by one of the great clans of the early T'ang "national aristocracy"'.[133]

Thus, here, the bureaucratic élite was precisely *not* the aristocracy but its historical successor, the instrument of a new autocracy, dominated, under T'ang, by a permanent conflict of these very social forces[134] that was resolved increasingly in favour of the officials who had come up through the examination-system.[135] The late T'ang was the 'beginning of a major transformation of the economy which continued until the Mongol invasion'.[136] The economic expansion of the late T'ang, Five Dynasties, and early Sung period involved such dramatic economic and social changes, and the 'Chinese economy began to grow at such a rate', that some historians 'have seriously suggested that by late Sung times the conditions were ripe for the emergence of a modern capitalist society'.[137] The vast reaches south of the Yangtze River with their

---

[131] Twitchett 1973, pp. 47–8.
[132] Twitchett 1979, p. 10.
[133] Twitchett 1979, p. 22.
[134] Cf. Pulleyblank 1955, p. 47, 'certainly for the first century and a half of the T'ang dynasty the two groups were far from identical in outlook and were often in sharp conflict'.
[135] Pulleyblank 1955, p. 48; based on Ch'en.
[136] Twitchett 1979, p. 31.
[137] Twitchett 1979, p. 31; cf. Hartwell 1982, p. 366, 'Quantitative and qualitative changes in the Chinese economy during the first five hundred years of this period – the T'ang-Five Dynasties-early Sung demographic and agricultural transition – were so remarkable that some scholars refer to the era as one of economic revolutions and others view it as an early stage of protocapitalism'.

'massive infusion of newcomers from the north',[138] the renewed expansion of large estates now linked to a new, more rapacious class of officials (the 'scholar-gentry'), the substantial pool of dispossessed labour driven from the land by political turmoil and land-grabbing, with *up to* seventy per cent of *registered* households dependent on landlords for their survival,[139] and the role played by the large landed interests in the 'reclamation of farm lands from river-bottoms, lake-beds, swamps, sandbanks and coastal flats' with rapid improvements in agricultural techniques and the invention of new implements,[140] were *part* of the major transformations that lie at the back of the surge of commercial capitalism that swept through China in the Sung period. Cities such as Hang-chou and K'ai-feng[141] were the most populous the world would see for centuries, the former concentrating a population of well over a million in an area of some eight square miles![142] By the mid-tenth century (in 955), the bells and statues from thousands of Buddhist monasteries had to be 'melted down and cast into coins to feed the rapidly expanding money economy',[143] and, by the mid-eleventh, money-taxes amounted to over fifty per cent of fiscal income, the bulk of this from the state-monopolies on salt, tea and alcohol and from the taxation of trade.[144] 'Huge sums of money were in circulation, available for investment in commerce and industry.'[145] For example, the colossal flow of Chinese ceramics to the west is a good example of a purely capitalist industry with factories located close to the major ports, often sprawling over entire valleys, and controlled no doubt by the business-magnates of the southeastern coastal cities.[146] Quanzhou was the base of a regulated private capitalism geared to international markets. And, further north, the iron- and steel-industry of northern Kiangsu was also privately owned and operated, with some 'thirty-six complex and costly mining and

---

[138] Clark 2009, p. 134ff.
[139] Elvin 1973, pp. 78–9.
[140] Twitchett 1979, pp. 30–1.
[141] E.g., Kuhn 2009, p. 195.
[142] Tuan 1970, pp. 132ff.
[143] Lau and Huang 2009, p. 208.
[144] Lo 1969, p. 61; Kreifelts 1995, p. 210.
[145] Lo 1969, p. 61.
[146] On the volume of ceramic exports cf. Bivar 1976, p. 8, 'A fascinating text, the *Kitab al-Dhaka'ir wal-tuḥaf*...describes the seven rooms filled with Chinese porcelain in the treasury of the Fāṭimid al-Mustanṣir at Cairo'; on the organisation of the industry, cf. Ho 2001, p. 268ff.

metallurgical establishments of Li-kuo *chien'* employing over 3,600 full-time wage-labourers. 'According to a memorial presented by Su Tung-p'o in the 1070s, each of the thirty-six great houses (*ta-chia*) possessed tens of thousands of strings of cash in liquid capital in addition to their investments in mines, land, plant and equipment.'[147]

The vitality of the tributary mode could scarcely be more strikingly demonstrated than by the example of China. The state both encouraged and regulated foreign trade, it 'opened harbors and dredged canals, built breakwaters and warehouses', and encouraged merchant involvement in the management of state-enterprises.[148] It was also state-demand for iron (for armaments, coinage, agricultural tools, etc.) that fuelled the expansion of the metal industry, and, on a more general level, in terms of the *dynamic* at work, 'The location of the central government in an area almost always generated a period of intraregional development, and its removal, an era of systemic decline'.[149]

> [T]he Southern Sung capital Hang-chou helped stimulate a period of rapid growth in the Lower Yangtze during the twelfth and thirteenth centuries.... Development was the result of interregional integration brought about by a fiscal system which artificially reduced freight costs by subsidizing the transport of tax revenues and state purchases...[150]

To finish with China; the powerful landed interests behind the creation of so-called Wei-land, that is, the reclamation of lake-bottoms and river-beds that became widespread in the twelfth century, were 'actually the most powerful personages in the government'.[151] 'This was true not only of the local government, but also true with regard to the central government. The Sung scholar, Ma Twan-lin, indignantly refers to the fact that east of the Yangtze, Tsai Ching and Ch'in Kuei, notorious leading ministers at the Sung court, successively owned the Wei-lands'.

> The lands of today are mostly the lakes of yesterday. Those who are responsible for the Wei-land seem only to know that the lakes can be drained and reclaimed for cultivation, but do not seem to realize that land

---

[147] Hartwell 1966, p. 45.
[148] Lo 1969, pp. 64, 61.
[149] Hartwell 1982, p. 386.
[150] Hartwell, 1982, p. 386.
[151] Chi 1963, p. 137.

outside the lake will thus be flooded. This is because *the responsible parties are court favourites and powerful officials*; hence they can, without fearing any interference, condemn the neighbouring land to the fate of a water-shed and thus benefit themselves by hurting the people.[152]

In other words, the rapacious landed interests of these expansive centuries were an inextricable part of the Sung bureaucracy, in a pattern peculiar to China's configuration of the tributary mode. This can be described either as collusion between the bureaucracy and the landed élite ('powerful families whose words and influence could dominate the government', as an official of the Southern Sung put it)[153] or as 'court favourites and powerful officials' grabbing land on a model of estate-building especially characteristic of the official class. In short, China represented a *fusion* of landed and bureaucratic interests where no aristocracy in any conventional sense was involved, at least not by this stage, and the autocracy was rarely strong enough to defend the financial interests of the government by opposing its own officials.

Russian absolutism, from the period of Muscovite consolidation in the late fourteenth century on, was almost the opposite of this, and here Weber's intuition is more accurate than Anderson's. Anderson reads Russian absolutism on a European model, assimilating the *boyars* to the feudal aristocracies of Western Europe and describing the Russian autocracy itself as an 'Absolutist State *of a type which was common to most European countries in the same epoch*'.[154] This essentially feudal reading of tsarism contrasts sharply with Trotsky's repeated emphasis on the 'historical peculiarities' of Russia's development and fails to explain why Trotsky himself characterised the Russian state as a 'bureaucratic autocracy'[155] or 'bureaucratic absolutism',[156] an 'intermediate form between European absolutism and Asian despotism' and one that was

---

[152] Chi 1963, pp. 137–8; italics mine.
[153] Chi 1963, p. 136, citing Wei Chin: 'It was the powerful families, whose words and influence could dominate the government, that created the Wei-land'.
[154] Anderson 1974a, p. 336 (feudal aristocracy), 334–5 (European-style state, but adding 'which assumed peculiar features in the more backward Eastern environment'); my italics.
[155] Trotsky 1972, p. 8.
[156] Trotsky 1967, p. 25.

'possibly' 'closer to the latter of these two'.[157] The Russian nobility was, as Weber described it, 'entirely powerless in relation to the ruler'.[158]

> The Crown could indeed risk a behavior toward the nobility, even toward the bearers of the most famous names and owners of the largest properties, which no Occidental ruler, no matter how great a potentate, could have permitted himself toward the lowliest of his legally unfree *ministeriales*.[159]

The conducting wire that runs through the early history of the Muscovite state is the subordination of the aristocracy (the *boyars* and the Moscow nobility)[160] and their integration into a class of servitors who, as Andrej Pavlov notes, lacked not only political freedom but even the last vestiges of economic independence in relation to the ruler.[161] During the fifteenth and sixteenth centuries, 'the Moscow monarchy succeeded in eliminating alodial holdings and making secular land tenure a form of possession conditional on state service'.[162] The principle of compulsory service, namely that 'all land must serve', formally introduced in 1556, would effectively mean that 'private property of the means of production became virtually extinct'.[163] The *oprichnina* uprooted boyars holding large *vótchina* estates in the central regions of Muscovy[164] and led, in the end, to a 'profound transformation of the aristocracy that rendered it entirely dependent on the monarchy'.[165] 'The future belonged not to the boyars but to the dvoriane.'[166] 'During the three centuries separating the reign of Ivan III from that of Catherine II the Russian equivalent of the nobility held its land on royal sufferance'.[167] This was the feature of Russian despotism that struck every observer from the West and, of course, the Russian intelligentsia itself of the nineteenth century. When Trotsky wrote of the Russian state and its possessing classes that it 'forced and regimented their growth'

---

[157] Trotsky 1972, p. 8; written in 1907.
[158] Weber 1968, Volume 2, p. 1066.
[159] Weber 1968, Volume 2, p. 1065.
[160] On these definitions see Meehan-Waters 1982, Chapter 1.
[161] Pavlov 2005, p. 92, in a paper that discusses the abortive consequences of a restructuring of the Court nobility in the sixteenth century that might have led to stronger regional links in the ruling class.
[162] Pipes 1995, p. 69.
[163] Pipes 1995, pp. 93–4.
[164] Pipes 1995, pp. 94–5.
[165] Pavlov 2005, pp. 105–6.
[166] Pipes 1995, p. 95.
[167] Pipes 1995, p. 172; scarcely a feudal aristocracy then!

and compared tsarism to an 'Asiatic despotism',[168] he drew on a long tradition within that intelligentsia. Romanovich-Slavatinsky had argued in 1870 that the Russian nobility was, fundamentally, a creation of the state ('This is the fundamental difference which separates our "service nobility" from the feudal landowning aristocracy of Western Europe'),[169] and Miliukov, who saw the *pomest'ye* system as a Muscovite borrowing from the 'oriental states',[170] explained how the 'final forming of the landed aristocracy' took place in Russia, as in Turkey, on the foundation of autocratic power, that is, when the 'national state was already founded'. 'In all these cases[171] the appropriation of state lands by private owners did not lead to the feudal organization of society, because the central power was already too strong to be dispossessed of its superior rights in the land'.[172]

Thus, the conflict peculiar to China between a hereditary aristocracy (the great aristocratic clans that disintegrated in the late ninth and early tenth centuries) and the new class of professional bureaucrats that formed the backbone of the autocracy has no Russian counterpart, both because the aristocracy inherited from the appanage period survived but was ruthlessly subordinated, certainly by the sixteenth century, and because the Russian monarchy 'never allowed its service class to sink roots in the countryside'.[173] Both aristocrats and the mass of *dvoriane* were simply elements of a unified service class, and, here, it would be more true to speak of the *bureaucratisation* of the nobility, certainly by the eighteenth century when Peter the Great set out to modernise this class.[174] The 'noble bureaucrats' of Peter's reign were state-servitors first and landowners second,[175] reflecting the deep-rooted traditions of the pre-imperial Muscovite state which Weber correctly characterised as 'patrimonial'.[176] Although Russia was the one tributary (non-feudal) régime that saw the

---

[168] Trotsky 1967, pp. 23–4.
[169] Madariaga 1995, p. 223, citing Slavatinsky's preface to *Dvoryanstvo v Rossii*.
[170] Miliukov 1962, p. 119 ('this eastern system of military holdings was borrowed by the Muscovite princes') and 120 ('Dependent military tenure of the oriental states was always founded on the idea of the superior property rights of the prince in the whole land').
[171] Miliukov includes British policy in India, possibly misconstruing the *zamindars* as 'military landholders'.
[172] Miliukov 1962, p. 118.
[173] Pipes 1995, pp. 172–3.
[174] Meehan-Waters 1982, p. 62ff.
[175] Meehan-Waters 1982, p. 64.
[176] Weber 1968, Volume 2, p. 1066 ('the Muscovite patrimonial state').

widespread emergence of serfdom, the peculiarity of Russian serfdom was that the 'peasants fixed to the land did not belong to their landlords'.[177] The model is a late Roman one, where the tying of the peasantry to the land reflects a more widespread bondage driven by the needs of the treasury. And so it was in Russia.[178] But perhaps the best analogy for Russian serfdom comes from the Rumanian principalities, where the enserfment of the peasantry was fiscally driven (this at the very end of the sixteenth century) and the similarity with Russia argued, persuasively and decades ago, by Brătianu.[179]

The ferocious domination that held the Russian upper classes in the vice of tsarism meant both a pliant aristocracy, and one that was committed to a strong monarchy,[180] *and* the 'absence in tsarist and imperial Russia of any effective regional loci of power, able to stand up to central authority'.[181] *Mughal India differed profoundly in both respects*, and, of the four configurations described here, was the tributary mode with the *least* integration between its 'elements'. The provincial magnates of Byzantium were part of the bureaucratic hierarchy, an administrative élite subservient to the emperor despite the 'dissensions' Basil II (976–1025) complained about[182] and the aristocracy's potential for subversion. There was no distinction here between a service-nobility and a rural aristocracy. China, too, lacked any 'disconnected juxtaposition' of elements, once the Chinese state was rid of the powerful aristocratic clans that had dominated the administration during T'ang and all previous régimes. The dominance of a sophisticated literate bureaucracy was the hallmark of China's modernity, and conflicts within the state were largely conflicts within that class and its rival factions. And in Russia (again!) aristocratic subservience to the Crown would only weaken significantly in the last decades of the eighteenth century,[183] yet, even then, the Russian nobility was never a threat to the state.[184]

Thus, India under the Mughals was totally exceptional in evolving a model that *juxtaposed* a service-élite with powerful *regional* aristocracies, the discor-

---

[177] Pipes 1995, p. 103, adding 'they were *glebae adscripti*'.
[178] Pipes 1995, p. 105.
[179] Brătianu 1933, esp. p. 452ff.
[180] Pavlov 2005, p. 104.
[181] Pipes 1995, p. 67.
[182] Psellus 1966, p. 43.
[183] Blum 1968, p. 351ff.
[184] Pipes 1995, p. 183ff.

nected juxtaposition of a subversive rural aristocracy with a tightly disciplined class of administrators, the *mansabdars*, who formed the service-nobility and the backbone of the state.[185] If the late fifteenth-century Ottoman expansion had successfully integrated 'members of the Byzantine and Balkan nobility into the highest reaches of [the Ottoman] administration',[186] neither the Sultanate nor even Akbar would ever succeed in achieving anything remotely comparable. The Ghurid conquests had 'established a basis for Muslim rule in the north Gangetic plain, while leaving certain Hindu rulers on their thrones in return for the payment of tribute'.[187] A century later, under 'Alā' al-Dīn Khaljī and his imposition of *kharāj* over a considerable part of northern India, the subjection of this rural aristocracy, more advanced now, meant the transfer of a 'significantly larger share of the agricultural surplus from the countryside to the towns and from the Hindu chiefs to the Muslim governing class'.[188] But, of course, the 'Hindu chiefs', 'powerful, independent and autonomous chieftains', as Nurul Hasan described them,[189] were never completely subordinated, much less exterminated, and every succeeding dynasty and régime had to contend with them. Akbar is justly praised for recruiting the Rajput chiefs into the Mughal ruling hierarchy and for giving a 'radical turn to the relationship between the centre and the landed magnates'.[190] Yet even after the huge expansion of the Mughal governing class between the fortieth year of Akbar (1595–6) and the early part of Aurangzeb's reign, these powerful Hindu chieftains remained barely 15 per cent of the official ruling élite.[191] The fact is that 'disarming and subduing regional aristocracies, or converting them into officials was a formidable task that was rarely accomplished by early modern states'.[192] The *zamindars*, as the Mughals now came to call these local *rajas* and regional aristocracies, were bastions of endemic rural resistance. 'It was

---

[185] The best case study by far remains Richards 1975.
[186] The argument is developed in Lowry 2003, Chapter 7. He suggests that 'following the ultimate defeat of Byzantium, the confidence of the Ottoman rulers Mehmed II (1451–1481), Bayezid II (1481–1512), and Selim I (1512–1520), was such that they felt able to to subsume even members of the defeated ruling dynasty into the highest levels of their own state's elite'.
[187] Jackson 1999, p. 124.
[188] Jackson 1999, pp. 242 (*kharāj* set at 50 per cent), 247 (Hindu chiefs).
[189] Hasan 1969, p. 18.
[190] Zaidi 1997, pp. 16–17.
[191] Athar Ali 1997, pp. 9, 12–13.
[192] Richards 1993a, p. 87.

precisely from the *zamindars* that they [the *jagirdars*][193] met with the greatest opposition and hostility'.[194] There was always, as Manucci said, 'some rebellion of the *rajahs* and *zamindars* going on in the Mogul Kingdom'.[195] The widespread agrarian uprisings of the eighteenth century,[196] led by the *zamindars*, were the key symptom that the 'Mughal effort at internal consolidation of power' had simply failed.[197]

The drastic loosening of the imperial structure that came by the eighteenth century was driven as much by these political factors, *the way its tributary mode was configured in class-terms*, as by the enormous economic expansion that reconfigured the relationship between the centre and the regions throughout India. That expansion was, to a great degree, a legacy of the Mughal state itself and of the peculiar dynamism of the tributary mode in stimulating monetary growth. By the 1580s, 'the Mughal "regulation" (*zabt*) revenue system funnelled huge sums in copper coin and silver rupee into the hierarchy of imperial treasuries'.[198] 'Foodgrains and other crops, sold for cash in a network of rural and urban markets, moved from the countryside to the cities in an annual rhythm in response to this state demand for payment of its tax levies in cash'.[199] 'Akbar's empire maintained large and growing reserves' of both gold and silver,[200] showing that the Mughal fiscal dynamic was *inextricably* bound up with the world-economy and India's ability to attract substantial flows of bullion and foreign specie through an expanding international trade that was vital to the fortunes of European commercial capitalism in the seventeenth century.[201] As John Richards argued, 'the vast currency of the empire

---

[193] That is, nobles who held salary-assignments in the form of *jagirs*, i.e. assignments of revenue on specified lands, with a 'temporary authority to make land-tax collections', Richards 1975, p. 21. As Athar Ali notes, 'By far the larger part of the Empire was assigned in *jagirs*', Athar Ali 1997, p. 74.
[194] Athar Ali 1997, p. 85.
[195] Cited Athar Ali 1997, p. 87.
[196] Alam 1986.
[197] Richards 2004, p. 397. '[O]ne of the most important goals for successive Mughal rulers was to penetrate the defenses of the countryside. Mughal imperial officials tried to weaken and bypass the hard shells of localized *zamīndārī* power embedded in each pargana.... However, the Mughal effort at internal consolidation of power failed' (pp. 396–7).
[198] Richards 1993b, VI, p. 627.
[199] Ibid.
[200] Ibid.
[201] Richards 1993b, VI, p. 634ff.; Prakash 1994, VI; Haider 1996.

depended on rising European silver and gold imports'.[202] 'The deluge of New World silver carried to India was of direct benefit to Akbar's construction of the empire in the latter half of the sixteenth century'.[203]

To sum up, tributary modes of production were class-régimes characterised, in their developed forms, by a powerful monetary economy and considerable economic dynamism. They were 'world-scale economies'[204] constructed on imperial foundations, that is, *installed* through conquest and expansion and built on centralising administrations 'capable of steady expansion as new provinces were added to the empire'.[205] Moscow's expansion in the late fifteenth and sixteenth centuries was gigantic and yet the 'greatest conquests were still to come'. By the middle of the seventeenth century, the tsars of Russia 'ruled over the largest state in the world'.[206] Byzantium, too, was the legacy of an empire that had expanded over centuries, then contracted sharply in the fifth to seventh centuries, to reconstruct itself later. That reconstruction involved renewed expansion. The Muslim states in India expanded over centuries, from the Ghurid conquests at the end of the twelfth century to Aurangzeb's campaigns in the Deccan at the end of the seventeenth. If the eighteenth century saw the final dissolution of central power behind the façade of autocracy, this was due not to stagnation but to the forces of economic expansion unleashed by the tributary régimes themselves, from the longer cycles of demographic and commercial growth to the evolution of indigenous networks of commercial capitalism dominated by 'commercial classes at every level' starting with the great banking houses.[207] The fiscal expansion of the Mughal régime between Akbar and Aurangzeb was a formidable achievement[208] and, as Richards notes, 'peace, order, and new market opportunities, as well as state encouragement, increased the surplus to be shared between producer, middlemen (traders, brokers, moneylenders), zamindars, and the

---

[202] Richards 1993b, V, p. 307; the best study of this issue is Haider 1996.
[203] Richards 1993b, V, p. 308.
[204] Bayly 1986, p. 71, describing 'the later eighteenth century China, India and the Arab world'.
[205] Richards 1993a, p. 58.
[206] Pipes 1995, p. 83. The land seized from Poland in the eighteenth century was handed out in massive grants to select members of the nobility, 'favourites and prominent public servants', cf. Madariaga 1974, pp. 58–61.
[207] Bayly 1983, esp. Chapter 4; Subrahmanyam and Bayly 1988, pp. 413–18.
[208] Richards 1993a, p. 186ff.

state'.[209] 'Indian peasants in the seventeenth century grew a large number of food and industrial crops efficiently and well', and by the 1680s 'hundreds of prosperous market towns (*qasbas*) had proliferated in northern India'.[210] The import of large quantities of precious metals by the Companies contributed to the expansion of the Mughal régime,[211] with Bengal offering the 'most dramatic example of export-stimulated economic growth'.[212] In short, the 'secular trend for Mughal India was that of economic growth and vitality',[213] but, with the counterfinality characteristic of the dissolution of *all* modes of production, 'it was precisely the wealthy and more prosperous parts of all the great empires...which in various ways and at various rates seceded from, ignored or revolted against the fragile imperial hegemonies'.[214] As Bayly says, 'The decline of the great empires...now appears more like a consequence of their very success, the price of their earlier rapid expansion',[215] which is a way of saying that the trajectories of the tributary régimes were driven by an internal logic or what Marx called a 'law of motion'.

Finally, what about relations of production in the narrower sense? Marx argued that in tributary modes of production (in contrast to feudalism and its tradition of bondage) 'the relationship of dependence *does not need to possess any stronger form, either politically or economically, than that which is common to all subjection to*' the state.[216] In other words, the general form of exploitation was simply one that subjected the peasantry to taxation by the state. To this we can now add that this general form of domination of the peasantry, the 'same' general 'economic basis', could display 'endless variations and gradations in its appearance' not so much, as Marx himself seemed to think, 'as the result of innumerable different empirical circumstances, natural conditions' and so on,[217] i.e. not just for purely contingent reasons, but *because of the way tributary modes were configured in class-terms*. In the model of the tributary mode described by Guichard for Valencia, a relatively weak state-apparatus and

---

[209] Richards 1993a, pp. 189–90.
[210] Richards 1993a, pp. 190, 194.
[211] Prakash 1985, p. 222.
[212] Richards 1993a, p. 202.
[213] Richards 1993a, p. 204.
[214] Bayly 1986, p. 74, about the Ottoman and Mughal Empires mainly.
[215] Bayly 1986, p. 75.
[216] Marx 1981, p. 927.
[217] Marx 1981, pp. 927–8.

the ruling 'aristocracy' linked to it confronted strong rural communities.[218] Ironically, this is the configuration closest to Marx's own conception of the Asiatic state. In contrast, in the Byzantine model, rulers would periodically have to defend a *more* vulnerable peasantry against the depredations of the 'powerful',[219] and, here, *paroikoi* were widespread on private estates.[220] In an even more extreme and probably exaggerated contrast, Bernier emphasised the oppression of the Mughal peasantry,[221] blaming the *jagirdars* for a hurried rapacity and constructing a whole explanation of the 'rapid decline of the Asiatic states' on this basis.[222] But, here even more than in Byzantium, rulers showed a manifest interest in curbing the oppression of the peasantry, and it was almost certainly the eventual dissolution of central power and of the imperial authority that went with it that left the villages to the mercy of *zamindars* and capitalists,[223] transforming the *ryot* into 'a field-labourer, living from hand to mouth'.[224] By the 1880s, Marx was fully aware of the 'complexity of landed interests' in regions such as Bengal,[225] an evolution that had come about 'long before the English'[226] and one that, for him at least, had nothing to do with feudalism ('This ass Phear calls the Constitution of the village *feudal*.')[227] The endless British confusion about whether the *zamindars* were revenue-collectors or landlords[228] reflected the agrarian conditions of a disintegrating tributary mode of production where the early-eighteenth-century

---

[218] Guichard 1990–1, p. 474; also p. 20.
[219] See the novels translated in McGeer 2000.
[220] I take the *paroikoi* to be a form of bound tenantry, the permanent labour-force of estates like the Anglo-Saxon *geburs*.
[221] Bernier 1916, p. 225, 'The persons thus put in possession of the land...have an authority almost absolute over the peasantry...and nothing can be imagined more cruel and oppressive than the manner in which it is exercised'.
[222] Bernier 1916, p. 227.
[223] Cf. Athar Ali 1997, p. 90ff. for this perspective, one with which I completely agree.
[224] Marx 1972, p. 256, where he also describes the *mahajan* as 'the village capitalist'.
[225] Marx 1972, p. 264, referring to sub-infeudation and its consequences, viz. 'Daher beispiellose complexity of landed interests u. keiner hat ein Interesse improvements d. land zu machen'.
[226] Marx 1972, p. 262, 'Lang vor d. Engländern the original simplicity of the zemindari system lost; there were *Zemindaris* u. *taluqs* of several orders and designations *paying revenue directly to Gvt*; innerhalb derselben wieder subordinate *taluqs u. tenures* converted from the condition of being parts of a homogeneous collecting machine into semi-indepedence'; Marx's emphases.
[227] Marx 1972, p. 256; Marx's emphasis.
[228] See the classic study by Ranajit Guha, reissued as Guha 1996.

drive to expand revenue in distant provinces such as Bengal had led to a massive concentration of *zamindari* rights[229] and the *zamindars* were beginning to look more like landlords than revenue-collectors. But they were essentially fiscal intermediaries and, as John Shore alone among British officials pointed out, 'A property in the soil must not be understood to convey the same rights in India as in England'.[230] When the British made the *zamindars* into proper landowners, transforming their tributary jurisdictions into estates, they simply ignored the reality of the Bengal village where 'respectable agricultural castes', the 'backbone of the *jotedar* tenantry', with holdings that could run up to 6000 acres, exploited a largely 'untouchable' mass of sharecroppers, tenants-at-will and hired labourers.[231] The distinction implied here is easier to track from the last decades of the eighteenth century, and certainly in the nineteenth, when emerging capitalist relations of production, tributary and colonial in form, were mediated through an endlessly complex 'range of relationships of exploitation on the land';[232] in the United Provinces, the reclassification of whole masses of the population as 'tenants' and the domination of most cultivators by a controlling minority of traders and *zamindars*,[233] in Bengal the emergence of a substantial peasantry and its control of the rural credit-market, *and so on*. And, finally, of course, Russia was the one tributary régime where 'Asiatic despotism' would eventually subject its peasantry to *forms of exploitation* typical of the feudal mode of production. A widespread Marxist view that lacks any sophistication works back from the form of exploitation to the mode of production and concludes that 'therefore' Russia under tsarism was a feudal society with typically feudal relations of production. One hopes that this introductory essay and the chapters that follow will show why we need to abandon this way of thinking and restore a sense of complexity to the theory of historical materialism.

---

[229] Calkins 1970, pp. 802–3.
[230] Guha 1996, p. 207, citing a minute dated June 1789.
[231] Ray and Ray 1975, pp. 82–4.
[232] Beinart and Delius 1986, p. 33, cf. n. 33.
[233] Whitcombe 1971, pp. 123, 178.

1.3. Some general conclusions

When Marx wrote that with the expansion of a world-market dominated by the capitalist mode of production 'the civilized horrors of over-work are grafted onto the barbaric horrors of slavery, serfdom, etc.',[234] he was half-suggesting that forms of exploitation that were typically precapitalist *could* be integrated into capitalism (the production and accumulation of surplus-value). Rosa Luxemburg referred to the 'most peculiar combinations between the modern wage system and primitive authority in the colonial countries' and used the example of the closed compounding of workers in the De Beers diamond mines at Kimberley to illustrate this.[235] But the forced recruitment of wage-labour in the colonies[236] or the outright use of forced labour in German mining, construction and metals under fascism[237] are but one sort of indication of the complex ways in which *capitalist* relations of production (the accumulation and competition of capitals) can be structured in terms of the actual exploitation of labour. Relations of production are simply not reducible to forms of exploitation, *both* because modes of production embrace a wider range of relationships than those in their immediate process of production *and* because the deployment of labour, the organisation and control of the labour-process, 'correlates' with historical relations of production in complex ways.[238] Lenin's pages on the labour-service system in Russia, with their fine distinctions between 'bonded hire' and 'purely capitalist wage-labour', and between the leasing of land and the allotment of land to workers as a 'method of providing the estate with manpower',[239] are a model of how Marxists can restore a sense of complexity to their analysis of exploitation (the deployment of labour). The 'capitalist system of providing the estate with agricultural workers by alloting patches of land to them'[240] was widespread in Latin America and parts of Europe, the Middle East, India, South Africa and so on, but, of course, just as systematically misconstrued as the residues of 'feudal' or 'semi-feudal' modes of production to justify political interventions that

---

[234] Marx 1976, p. 345.
[235] Luxemburg 1963, pp. 362–4; on the compounds see Worger 1987.
[236] Cooper 1996.
[237] Herbert 1997.
[238] 'Historical relations of production': Marx 1981, p. 957.
[239] Lenin 1956, pp. 198–209.
[240] Lenin 1956, p. 200.

stopped short of confronting capitalism. Marx himself was certainly aware of the complexities peculiar to this level of abstraction. Engels tells us that in the 1870s, Marx began to study sources in Russian by way of work towards a final draft of his section on ground-rent.

> Given the manifold diversity of forms of landed property and exploitation of the agricultural producers in Russia, this country was to play the same role in the Part on ground-rent as England had done for industrial wage-labour in Volume 1. Unfortunately Marx was never able to carry out this plan.[241]

Had Marx lived to complete the new version of this section, we would no doubt have had an even more powerful demonstration of what it meant to study the 'more concrete forms', the 'manifold diversity of forms of exploitation', in this instance of the peasantry in Russia.

Again, when Marx writes that 'the legal forms in which these economic transactions[242] appear as voluntary actions of the participants, as the expressions of their common will and as contracts that can be enforced on the parties concerned by the power of the state, *are mere forms that cannot themselves determine this content*',[243] the argument is not that law is irrelevant to production or an excrescence on the 'economy'. On the contrary, Marx's whole 'definition of commodity production...presupposes the legal concepts of private property and contract'. As Duncan Kennedy argued in the 1980s, 'the legal categories are built into the definition of the..."mode of production"'; 'legal *concepts* are built into the base itself',[244] or, in a later formulation, 'legal rules define the "base"'.[245] In Kelman's words, 'the determining structural base *includes* vital legal elements (for example, a competitive market, "free" labor)'.[246] However, this conception of the interpenetration of 'law' and 'society' undermines the base/superstructure distinction, at least in the conventional form in which it has been upheld in some versions of Marxism. *There are no prelegal relations of production*, just as there are 'many different regimes of specific legal subrules

---

[241] Engels in Marx 1981, pp. 96–7, from the Preface to Volume III, dated 1894.
[242] Marx is referring to transactions between capitalists.
[243] Marx 1981, pp. 460–1; my emphasis.
[244] Kennedy 1985, pp. 978, 993.
[245] Kennedy 1998, p. 287.
[246] Kelman 1987, p. 254; 'we can no longer speak coherently of law *responding* to distinct prelegal interests once we see how much these interests are defined by law' (p. 243).

that are consistent with the indeterminate general notions of property and free contract'.[247] The more general point here is that 'markets are always constituted by the law that enforces the bargains made in them'.[248] Master-and-servant régimes constructed the labour-markets of the nineteenth century as much as they regulated the relations between wage-labour and capital. These are insights of critical legal theory that can surely only strengthen the perspectives of historical materialism.

Finally, primitive accumulation is no longer the best way to frame the early history of capitalism, and this *not* because the epoch of commercial capitalism did not contribute decisively to the rise of modern production[249] – it obviously did – but because that remains a *purely teleological perspective* and one that diverts attention from the real lacuna in materialist historiography, which is the study and, one hopes, ultimately a synthesis of the emergence of capitalism, which in the sporadic form that Marx described it as having was certainly in place by the thirteenth century. If the obscure early centuries of capitalism were defined by the 'sporadic existence of capitalist production',[250] this was much less true of the fifteenth century, when a sort of merchant-controlled industrial capitalism was widespread in centres such as Genoa[251] and led the way into the great watershed of the sixteenth century.[252] The section on primitive accumulation sums up much of the history it deals with as the 'period of manufacture', but manufacture, as Marx knew, was a legacy of commercial capitalism,[253] of the fusion of commercial capital with production,[254] as indeed were the slave plantations.[255] The 'forms' thrown up by the early capitalism of the Mediterranean were *essentially those that continued to drive global history*

---

[247] Kennedy 1985, p. 995, who goes on to suggest that 'Marx was a formalist' in his understanding of the implicit legal background, adding 'it's hard to see how he could have been otherwise, given the time at which he wrote'.

[248] Hay and Craven 2004, p. 26.

[249] E.g., Marx 1981, p. 455.

[250] Marx 1976, p. 949, cf. p. 876.

[251] Heers 1961, p. 251, with his excellent discussion of the silk industry at pp. 242–51.

[252] Braudel 1975, Volume 1, p. 430ff.

[253] Marx 1973, pp. 510–11.

[254] Marx 1971b, p. 469, where he says, 'commercial capital thereby loses the fixed form which it previously possessed in contrast to production'.

[255] Pares 1960. Note Thomas Jefferson's description of the American planters as 'a species of property annexed to certain mercantile houses in London', cited Oakes 1990, p. 55. Other plantations: Antrobus 1957, p. 36ff. (the Assam Company formed at a meeting of merchants in London in 1839).

down to the expansion of large-scale industry and its revolutionary mode of production in the nineteenth century, so that the history of commercial capitalism is no longer simply a prelude to industrial capital but more like an act (to retain the operatic metaphor), something that is best seen as a *totality*, a narrative with its own coherence, forms, internal periodisation, and conceptions of empire.[256] Marx was right, 'the different moments of primitive accumulation can be assigned in particular to Spain, Portugal, Holland, France, and England, in more or less chronological order',[257] only today, with so much more historiography before us, there is no compelling reason why this whole swathe of history should remain the compressed if brilliant *histoire raisonnée* Marx inserted into Volume I and not acquire the expansion of content it deserves.[258]

---

[256] The 'forms' included large-scale enterprises with huge concentrations of labour, and one decisive innovation, the factory system which was widely diffused in the silk-mills of northern Italy by the seventeenth century, ahead of England 'by some two centuries', as Carlo Poni remarked in a classic paper, Poni 1976, esp. p. 491.

[257] Marx 1976, p. 915.

[258] Krätke 2007, p. 121ff., esp. note 41 where he notes that historical digressions like the one on primitive accumulation 'were never meant to be more than sketches of the logic of a historical process and *could never replace a history of capitalism*'; my emphasis.

Chapter Two
Modes of Production in a Materialist Conception of History

> ...the extremely dubious speculative juggling, with the concepts and terms of the materialist method, which has under the pens of some of our Marxists transplanted the methods of formalism into the domain of the materialist dialectic; which has led to reducing the task to rendering definitions and classifications more precise and to splitting empty abstractions into four equally empty parts; in short, has adulterated Marxism by means of the indecently elegant mannerisms of Kantian epigones. It is a silly thing indeed endlessly to sharpen or resharpen an instrument, to chip away Marxist steel when the task is to apply the instrument in working over the raw material! (Leon Trotsky)

2.1. The retreat into historical formalism*

In his polemic with Dühring, Engels described the theory of surplus-value and the materialistic conception of history as the 'two great discoveries' of Marx,

---

* Some of the positions proposed in this essay will be argued more extensively in a forthcoming book on *Modes of Production and the Peasantry*. Parts of the section on Feudal Production have appeared in an article in the *Journal of Peasant Studies*, April, 1976. It was written before Anderson's two recent volumes appeared, and therefore contains no reference to them. Although Laclau's article on Frank is criticised at various points in the essay, my own train of thought derived much of its impetus from the directions of that critique.

through which were established the scientific foundations of socialism. Modern materialism, wrote Engels, characterised history as a 'process of evolution' and set itself the task of discovering its 'laws of motion'.[1] In one of the best reviews of *Capital* to appear at that time, a bourgeois economist Kaufmann repeated the point to Marx's approval: Marx treats the social movement 'as a process of natural history governed by laws'.[2] In a famous resumé of his conception of history, written closer to our time, Braudel describes Marx as the originator of 'historical models'.[3] In their own way, these writers implied, in a language borrowed from the sciences of their time, that social phenomena like the phenomena of nature are scientifically penetrable, and that we owe the recognition of this fact to the work of Marx. Between the period from which this discovery dates and our own period, roughly in the last hundred years, the foundations of the older traditional conceptions of history collapsed as rapidly as the inherited conceptions of matter. But there the analogy ends. On the ruins of substantialism, a new physics evolved at rapid speed, whereas the 'programme of a fully scientific history remains not merely to be realized, but even to be drafted'.[4] In short, the materialist conception of history did not actually produce a specifically materialist history.

In a sense, this abortion is not difficult to understand. Later in his life, Engels repeatedly noted in his correspondence[5] that the younger elements attracted to Marxism saw in its theory, 'historical materialism', the summary of established results or points of arrival. In their conception, between historical materialism and materialist history there was a relation of immediate identity or implicit spontaneous derivation. Liberal-bourgeois historiography of that time and later proceeded as if theory could be derived from 'facts'; in this positivist conception, 'facts' were objects outside theory, constituted, like matter, independently of consciousness. For vulgar Marxism, infected by the illusion which Engels noted, history, already endowed with its theory ('historical materialism'), consisted in the application of this theory to 'facts'. By its vulgar conception of historical materialism this tendency implicitly threat-

---

[1] Engels 1959, pp. 39, 43.
[2] Marx 1971a, Volume 1, p. 27; Marx 1976, p. 101, from the 'Afterword' to the Second German edition.
[3] Braudel 1972.
[4] Vilar 1973, p. 67.
[5] E.g., letter to Schmidt, 5 August, 1890 (Marx and Engels 1934, pp. 496–7).

ened to submerge the scientific possibilities contained in Marx's conception of history in a quasi-positivism for which theory was latent in an objective succession of immutable facts. If such a premise were accepted, only minor differences remained: for positivism, the collection of those facts would lead spontaneously to the framing of general 'laws'; for the vulgar tendencies in Marxism these 'laws' were already known, and the task of history lay in their verification by 'facts'.[6]

In fact, as we know,[7] it was this convergence which became central to the Marxism of that period. For Marx himself, the task of scientific history consisted in the determination of the laws regulating the movement of different epochs of history, their 'laws of motion' as they were called after the example of the natural sciences. Vulgar Marxism abdicated this task for a less ambitious programme of verifying 'laws' already implicit, as it supposed, in the materialist conception of history. Whereas Marx had noted, as one of the points 'not to be forgotten', that is, to be investigated in future by him or others, the 'dialectic of the concepts productive force and relation of production, a dialectic whose boundaries are to be determined',[8] a whole tradition from Plekhanov to Stalin argued with more assurance. Reverting to a naturalistic conception of history that Engels himself had explicitly rejected in the *Dialectics of Nature* (see the note on 'causality'), Plekhanov wrote: '*We now know* that the development of the productive forces, which in the final analysis determines the development of all social relations, is determined by the properties of the geographical environment'.[9] Reared in a Plekhanovist tradition, as so many of the other Bolsheviks were, but with a singular capacity for vulgarisation, Stalin would tell the party-cadre many years later, 'first the productive forces of society change and develop, and then, depending on these changes and in conformity with them, men's relations of production, their economic relations change'. Marx had been emphatic that abstract laws do not exist in history,

---

[6] That this conception underlay most Marxist historiography after the twenties is evident from Pecirka 1967. Practically every essay in this collection, for example, or in the CERM collection (1969) proceeds from the premise of verification. Yet these essays were characterized recently as 'important articles' (by Samir Amin). Only one of the essays in fact showed a definitely critical and scholarly tendency: Antoniades-Bibicou 1969.
[7] Cf. Colletti 1972.
[8] Marx 1973, p. 109.
[9] Plekhanov 1969.

that the laws of motion which operate in history are historically determinate laws. He indicated thereby that the scientific conception of history could be concretised only through the process of establishing these laws, specific to each epoch, and their corresponding categories. In other terms, through a process of producing concepts on the same level of historical 'concreteness' as the concepts of 'value', 'capital' and 'commodity-fetishism'. The 'laws' which Plekhanov and Stalin proposed were laws of the historical process *in general*.

The tradition of vulgar Marxism which drew its earliest sources of energy from the Marxism of the Second International, crystallised only under the domination of Stalin. Stalinism uprooted not only the proletarian orientations of Marxism, but its scientific foundations as well. For the dialectic as the principle of rigorous scientific investigation of historical processes – it was, after all, this *rational* dialectic that was 'a scandal and abomination to bourgeoisdom and its doctrinaire professors'[10] – Stalinism substituted the 'dialectic' as a cosmological principle prior to, and independent of, science. For the materialist conception of history, it substituted a theory of history 'in general', 'converting historical epochs into a logical succession of inflexible social categories'.[11] Finally, this rubber-stamp conception of history it represented as a history *déjà constituée*, open therefore only to the procedures of verification. This lifeless bureaucratic conception, steeped in the methods of formalism, produced a history emptied of any specifically historical content, reduced by the forced march of *simple formal abstractions* to the meagre ration of a few volatile categories. Within five decades of Marx's death, the history written by the Stalinists became as opaque and dream-like, and hardly as exciting, as the fantasies of surrealism.

Superficially these conceptions seemed to conflict, to clash sharply: the cosmological dialectic asserted a principle of *continuous flux* in the vast ambit of the Universe; 'historical materialism', by contrast, proposed a principle of *eternal recurrence*, of the endless repetition of essentially identical mechanisms. Yet beneath this apparent conflict, idealism provided the deeper connection between these conceptions, in the idea, found both in the Academy's conception of history[12] and, much later, in abstract, systematising rationalism,[13] that

---

[10] Marx 1971a, Volume 1, p. 29, from the 'Afterword'; Marx 1976, p. 103.
[11] Trotsky 1967, Appendix I, p. 428.
[12] See Toulmin and Goodfield 1967.
[13] Lukács 1968.

reason abolishes the chaotic flux of the empirical order when it grasps those abstract principles of necessity which are its deeper rational foundations. The Academy sought these principles in the geometric layout of the heavens and in the mathematical forms associated with the different material elements. At a certain stage in its evolution, Greek thought deprived history of any intrinsic significance. 'It became interested only to the extent that history offered clues to the nature of the enduring realities'.[14] To its cosmological conception of the dialectic Stalinism thus welded a cosmological conception of history, the ancestry of which lay not in Marx but in the whole tradition of metaphysics beginning with the Academy.

In their Stalinist determination, the basic categories of the materialist conception functioned as abstractions akin to Platonic Ideas.[15] The full impact of this paradox is driven home when we compare this formalist construction of history, entirely metaphysical in character, to the real, if limited, progress of the politically domesticated currents of 'academic' history. The pioneers who explored, colonised and subjugated the 'continent' of history discovered by Marx were not Marxists, by and large: Rostovtzeff, Mickwitz, Ostrogorsky, Pirenne, Kato Shigeshi, Hamilton, Goitein.[16] Moreover, the 'most successful revolutionary group of modern historians'[17] around *Annales* bore only a marginal and indirect relation to Marxism. On this current, Marxism exerted its influence only at a distance, through the sociology of Weber and the writings of Sombart and Henri Sée.[18] In fact, the reverse was true: the few consciously Marxist historians who grew up in this period were largely formed, to one degree or another, in connection with *Annales*: notably, Labrousse, Lefebvre, Vilar, Pach, Kula.[19] This strictly professional history, not known for purely scholastic disquisitions on 'modes of production' and 'social formations', came far closer to the conceptions of Marx than the whole tradition of abstract historical formalism which passed for 'Marxism' and which, in the period of

---

[14] Toulmin and Goodfield 1967.
[15] Sartre 1960, p. 36.
[16] Some of their key works are listed in the bibliography.
[17] Stedman Jones 1972, p. 115.
[18] In 1927 Henri Sée published a work entitled *Matérialisme historique et interprétations économiques de l'histoire*.
[19] There were, of course, exceptions to this generalisation, e.g., E.A. Kosminsky, Rodney Hilton. No detailed studies exist of the evolution of *Annales* and its relationship to Marxism.

its confident domination, decisively shaped all later discussions of the 'mode of production'.

2.2. *Produktionsweise* as 'labour-process' and 'epoch of production'

A summary glance at the *Grundrisse* or *Capital* would show that Marx ascribed two distinct meanings to *'Produktionsweise'* [mode of production]. According to one of these, it was indistinguishable from the 'labour-process [*Arbeitsprozess*]', or what Lenin would sometimes call the 'technical process of production'. For example, in a brief reference to the domestic system, Marx writes:

> The manufacturer in the French silk industry and in the English hosiery and lace industries was mostly but nominally a manufacturer until the middle of the nineteenth century. In point of fact, he was merely a merchant, who let the weavers carry on in their old unorganised way and exerted only a merchant's control, for that was for whom they really worked. This system presents everywhere an obstacle to the real capitalist mode of production and goes under with its development. Without revolutionising the *mode of production*, it only worsens the condition of the direct producers, turns them into mere wage-workers and proletarians under conditions worse than those under the immediate control of capital, and appropriates their surplus-labour on the basis of the old *mode of production*.[20]

When capital concentrates these scattered producers into one manufactory, it 'no longer leaves them in the *mode of production* found already in existence, establishing its power on that basis, but rather creates a *mode of production* corresponding to itself, as its basis. It posits the concentration of the workers in production...'.[21] When Lenin describes this process of the subordination of the simple-commodity producer by capital, his vocabulary is more precise: 'The subordination begins with merchant's and usury capital, then grows into industrial capitalism, which in its turn is at first technically quite primitive, and does not differ in any way from the old *systems of production* – which is

---

[20] Marx 1971a, Volume 3, pp. 334–5; Marx 1981, p. 452; all italics mine.
[21] Marx 1973, p. 587.

still based on hand labour and on the dominant handicraft industries...'.[22] For Lenin, this incipient 'industrial capitalism' which evolves out of the merchant's domination over the small producer is quite compatible with the 'system of production' inherited from small-scale handicraft industries. In this form of incipient capitalism, capital operates on an inherited labour-process. When he describes this phenomenon, Marx writes: 'Here then the *mode of production* is not yet determined by capital, but rather found on hand by it';[23] whereas Lenin prefers to say, 'Capital always takes the *technical process of production* as it finds it, and only subsequently subjects it to technical transformation'.[24] Again, in the sections dealing with relative surplus-value in *Capital*, Volume I, we find Marx writing: 'With regard to the *mode of production* itself, manufacture, in its strict meaning, is hardly to be distinguished, in its earliest stages, from the handicraft trades of the guilds, otherwise than by the greater number of workmen simultaneously employed by one and the same individual capital'.[25]

> When surplus-value has to be produced by the conversion of necessary labour into surplus-labour, it by no means suffices for capital to take over the *labour-process* in the form under which it has been historically handed down.... The technical and social conditions of the process, and consequently the very *mode of production* must be revolutionised before the productiveness of labour can be increased.[26]

Elsewhere in these sections, he writes that an increase in the productivity of labour posits as its condition a revolution in the 'mode of production and the labour-process itself'. When he says in the *Grundrisse* that 'agriculture forms a *mode of production* sui generis...',[27] he means that it is defined by technical conditions peculiar to itself.

In various other passages where Marx made more general statements about the various stages of social development, '*Produktionsweise*' figured in a broader and more specifically historical meaning. Modes of production are variously

---

[22] Lenin 1963a, p. 438.
[23] Marx 1973, p. 586.
[24] Lenin 1963a, p. 466.
[25] Marx 1971a, Volume 1, p. 305; Marx 1976, p. 439.
[26] Marx 1971a, Volume 1, pp. 298–9; Marx 1976, p. 432.
[27] Marx 1973, p. 726.

called: 'forms of production';[28] 'forms of the social process of production'; 'epochs in the economic development of society';[29] 'epochs of production';[30] 'periods of production'[31] or, finally, 'historical organizations of production'.[32] Here, the 'mode of production' figures as a 'social form of production' or 'social form of the production process'.[33]

2.3. Levels of abstraction in historical materialism

2.3.1. *Wage-labour as abstract determination and determinate abstraction*

All the various tendencies of that abstract scholastic formalism which dominated Marxist theory much later accepted the implicit premise that a scientific history could be derived spontaneously from the materialist conception. In other words, the unity of these various currents lay essentially in a Ricardian methodology of 'forced abstractions'.[34]

The definition of the different epochs of production distinguished by Marx required only a closer examination of their specific 'relations of production', which were nothing else than the various forms which the subjugation of labour assumed historically. 'Our definition will characterize feudalism primarily as a "mode of production"', wrote Dobb in his major work of historical interpretation. 'As such it will be virtually identical with what we generally mean by serfdom...'.[35] As he would explain later in his debate with Sweezy, by 'serfdom' was meant 'exploitation of the producer by virtue of direct polit-

---

[28] Marx 1971b, pp. 55, 430.
[29] Marx 1970, p. 21 (from the 'Preface').
[30] Marx 1973, p. 85.
[31] Marx 1973, p. 98.
[32] Marx 1973, p. 105.
[33] Marx 1971a, Volume 2, pp. 36, 114; Marx 1978, pp. 120, 190. The fact that Marx tended to use *Produktionsweise* and *Arbeitsprozess* more or less interchangeably would partly explain why the 'naturalist' conception of production which became widespread in the Second International and which passed, through Plekhanov, into Bukharin, for example, was hardly ever directly challenged by those Marxists who assaulted its underlying philosophical premises, e.g., Gramsci. Lukács provides a partial exception in his critique of Bukharin, Lukács 1966.
[34] Marx 1968, p. 437.
[35] Dobb 1963 [1946], p. 35.

ico-legal compulsion', or 'coercive extraction of surplus labour'.[36] According to this formal abstractionism, modes of production were deducible, by a relation of 'virtual identity', from the given forms of exploitation of labour. These forms of exploitation, the so-called 'relations of production', were the independent variables of the materialist conception of history.

This conception, quite unexceptionable as it appears, became one of the most widespread and persistent illusions of vulgar Marxism. Although neither Marx nor Engels ever consciously reflected on the nature of their categories – the fact that Marx distinguished implicitly between 'simply formal abstractions' and 'true abstractions', that he saw in his failure to carry abstraction 'far enough' the secret of Ricardo's confusions on 'value', that he himself subjected 'wage-labour' to a careful and painstaking analysis – all go to indicate that, in the materialist conception, the process of investigating and defining the 'relations of production' in any given epoch was far more complicated that Dobb seemed to imagine.

To begin with 'wage-labour': in the dominant inherited notion, a wage-labourer is one who, divorced from any means of subsistence, is forced to sell her labour-power to others. 'Wage-labour', in this vulgar definition, is dispossessed labour, labour divorced from the means of production, with labour-power as a commodity. When Dobb defined capitalism on a model symmetrical to his definition of feudalism, he called it 'a system under which labour-power has itself become a commodity, bought and sold on the market like any other object of exchange'.[37] In this definition of capitalist production, 'wage-labour' figures as the commodity labour-power, that is, as a *simple category*.

---

[36] Dobb 1954, pp. 21, 24. As some of Sweezy's comments indicate, a certain confusion prevailed in the debate about the content of the term 'serfdom'. (i) Marx himself tended to identify 'serfdom' specifically with the performance of labour-services, e.g., *Theories of Surplus Value*, pt. 3, p. 401. (ii) Historically, *servage* and *villeinage* were not organically linked to labour-services and only became so when the estates turned to commodity production (cf. Hilton 1969, p. 30). (iii) Dobb made the term sufficiently elastic to mean by it not only labour services as such but 'the appropriation of tribute either in kind or in money' (Dobb in Sweezy *et al.* 1954). This confusing and historically illegitimate conception of 'serfdom' directly contradicted Marx's conception, e.g., in the following statement from *Theories of Surplus-Value*: 'Serf-labour has this in common with wage labour, in respect of rent, that the latter (rent) is paid *in labour, not in products, still less in money*', Marx 1971b, p. 401. (my emphasis)

[37] Dobb 1963 [1946], p. 7.

Marx defined 'simple categories' as those which were common to several epochs of production. In this simple determination, 'wage-labour', that is, the commodity labour-power, was known under various forms of social production before the capitalist epoch. Duby tells us that 'from the very earliest years of the thirteenth century, the administrators of the estates of the bishops at Winchester spent hundreds of pounds every year on wages'. Moreover, 'on the lands of Worcester Abbey the growth of the demesne economy was entirely achieved...by taking on wage labour'. 'The accounts of Henry de Bray, a knight of no great wealth, show that men subject to labour service played hardly any part in the cultivation of the demesne, which was wholly worked by hired labour'.[38]

In accordance with the requirements of capitalist production, 'wage-labour', in this simple determination as the commodity labour-power, was the necessary basis of capitalism as the generalised form of social production. Within certain limits, the mobility of labour-power became as essential to the laws of motion of capital as the ability of capital itself to operate on a world-scale. But the historical specificity of wage-labour, its character as a specifically bourgeois relation of production, its position as a historically determinate abstraction equivalent to the abstractions 'capital' and 'commodity-fetishism' – derived from quite other mechanisms than this mere generalisation of the labour-power commodity. At this deeper level of abstraction, where it now figured, in the process of Marx's analysis, as a 'concrete' category,[39] wage-labour was, for Marx, capital-positing, capital-creating labour. 'Wage labour, here, *in the strict economic sense*,' Marx wrote, 'is capital-positing, capital-producing labour'.[40] In a methodology of forced abstractions, which identified relations of production with particular forms of exploitation, the concept of 'historical specificity' was radically impoverished. Sweezy, for example, found Dobb's position unacceptable; he argued that there was nothing specifically feudal in the 'exploitation of producers by virtue of direct politico-legal compulsion'.[41] To this, Dobb replied that the elements of such compulsion do occur in a subordinate and incidental role in various other forms of economy: 'if [these elements] are merely incidental and subordinate, their presence no more suffices

---

[38] Duby 1968, pp. 262–3.
[39] Marx 1973, p. 100.
[40] Marx 1973, p. 463 (emphasis added).
[41] Sweezy 1954, p. 1.

to constitute [the form of economy in question] as feudal than does the incidental existence of hired wage-labour suffice to constitute a particular society capitalist'.[42] In other terms, if we follow through the logic of this argument, what makes an economy 'capitalist' is the statistical preponderance of the simple abstraction 'labour-power as a commodity'. A simple category becomes a historically determinate category when it becomes historically preponderant.

This failure to understand 'wage-labour' at the same level of abstraction as Marx, in the 'strict economic sense' which Marx gave it, that is, as *abstract, value-producing* labour, hence as labour which already posits the elements of capitalist production, would lead Dobb to quite absurd positions. He would be compelled to argue, for example, that when some of the most deeply entrenched feudal estates of thirteenth-century England often based their production mainly or entirely on paid labour ('wage-labour' in Dobb's sense), specifically capitalist relations of production were established.[43] He would have to hold that the Russian feudal estates which utilised slave-labour in the sixteenth and seventeenth centuries[44] operated within the framework of a 'slave mode of production'. He would have to hold that wherever in history the extraction of surplus-labour was based on 'coercion', feudal relations of production predominated, or 'coexisted' according to the currently fashionable conceptions.

2.3.2. *Serf-owning capital*

In fact, Dobb himself might have found several clear indications in the revolutionary-Marxist tradition refuting his law of the 'virtual identity' of forms of exploitation and relations of production. Analysing the pottery industry of Moscow *gubernia*, characterised by the Narodniks as a 'purely domestic' industry, Lenin wrote:

> The relations in this industry are bourgeois.... We see how a minority, owning larger and more profitable establishments, accumulate 'savings',

---

[42] Dobb 1954, p. 21, n. 1.
[43] In *Studies*, he does characterise the increasing use of hired labour by such estates as the emergence of a 'new mode of production', i.e., capitalism (Dobb 1963 [1946], p. 55).
[44] Cf. Blum 1968, pp. 271–2. According to Bloch 1963, p. 214, slaves were a 'normal element of nearly every seigneurie' in the early feudal period.

while the majority are ruined.... It is obvious and inevitable that the latter should be enslaved to the former – inevitable precisely because of the *capitalist character of the given production relations*.... Do not think that this exploitation, this oppression is any less marked because relations of this kind are still poorly developed, because the accumulation of *capital*, accompanying the ruination of the producers, is negligible. Quite the contrary. This only leads to *cruder, serf forms of exploitation*, to a situation where capital, not yet able to subjugate the worker directly, by the mere purchase of his labour-power at its value, enmeshes him in a veritable net of usurious extortion, binds him to itself by kulak methods, and as a result robs him not only of the surplus-value, but of an enormous part of his wages too....[45]

In this industry, then, specifically capitalist relations of production were expressed and mediated through 'serf forms of exploitation'. Against Struve, Lenin wrote elsewhere:

> The argument is based on extremely strange methods that are not Marxist at all. A comparison is made between 'bondage' and 'differentiation' as between two independent special 'systems'.... This *bondage* which he has now demolished as retrogressive is nothing but the initial manifestation of *capitalism* in agriculture.... It is purely *capitalist* in essence, and the entire peculiarity consists in the fact that this initial, embryonic form of capitalist relations is totally enmeshed in the *feudal* relations of former times: here there is no free contract, but a forced deal....[46]

In these passages, Lenin argued, in other words, that as simple-commodity producers are subordinated to the power of capital, in town or village, and specifically bourgeois relations of production develop, far from transforming bondage and serf-forms of exploitation into specifically capitalist forms of exploitation, i.e., those forms which correspond to the 'classical, adequate mode of production of capital', these new relations of production, founded on capital, intensify the existing backward forms of exploitation: these forms remain 'feudal' or 'semi-feudal' in character, while the relations of production acquire a bourgeois character.[47] Because Lenin understood this mechanism,

---

[45] Lenin 1963b, p. 216; italics mine.
[46] Lenin 1963a, p. 484; italics mine.
[47] Palloix 1971, pp. 74–5 simply fails to understand this process when he argues that, as long as the peasant remains tied to the means of production, capital appropriates

he could refer elsewhere to 'semi-feudal forms of appropriation of surplus-value',[48] just as Kautsky refers, in the *Agrarfrage*, to the fact that in the early growth of capitalism in European silviculture, 'surplus-value' was produced by exploiting a feudally-subjugated labour-force [*travail forcé de nature féodale*].[49] Earlier than either Lenin or Kautsky, Marx himself spoke of the production of 'surplus-value' in the cotton-plantations of the American South.[50] Although the translation of Moore and Aveling distorted the sense of this passage when it used 'surplus-labour' for *Mehrwert*, the meaning was abundantly clear to both Rosa Luxemburg and Preobrazhensky. Luxemburg, with this passage in mind, spoke of 'capitalist accumulation with forms of slavery and serfdom' persisting down to the 1860s in the American South, and, as late as her own day in Rumania, 'and various overseas colonies'.[51] In his own commentary, Preobrazhensky wrote, 'the important thing is that there are present all the prerequisites of surplus-value, except the last, which is characteristic of the development of capitalism – the transformation of labour-power into a commodity'; he proposed 'transitional forms of surplus-value' as a more precise characterisation.[52] Again, in *Capital* Volume III, Marx referred to the evolution of merchant-capital in the ancient world transforming 'a patriarchal slave-system devoted to the production of immediate means of subsistence into one devoted to the production of surplus-value'.[53] According to an edict of 1721, Peter the Great had allowed the Russian factory-owners to utilise serf-labour. 'But if the factory-owner could now carry on his business with the labour of

---

his surplus-labour on the basis of the old feudal *relations of production*: 'le processus de quasi-intégration de l'atelier agricole par le marchand drapier laisse subsister des anciens rapports féodaux tant que ce procès n'aboutit pas à la prolétarisation du paysan'. On the contrary, Marx spoke of the artisans being 'turned into mere wage-workers and proletarians', and referred, elsewhere, to the means of production which were left to the small producer by capital as 'sham property'. Palloix cites *Capital*, Volume III, (Marx 1981, pp. 452–3) to substantiate his view, thus ignoring the fact that, in this passage, as in so many others, Marx meant by 'mode of production' only the labour-process of the small producer. (See Section 7 below for a fuller analysis.) Amin 1976, is correct to point out that peasants who produced under these conditions were wage-workers, but he abolishes this insight in Amin 1974, when, in the short chapter on 'modes of production', he writes that the internal disintegration of simple-commodity production into capitalism was an 'absolute law' of this form of economy.

[48] Lenin 1963a, p. 414.
[49] Kautsky 1970, p. 25.
[50] Marx 1971a, Volume 1, pp. 226–7; Marx 1976, p. 345.
[51] Luxemburg 1972, pp. 55–6.
[52] Preobrazhensky 1965, p. 185.
[53] Marx 1971a, Volume 3, p. 332; Marx 1981, p. 449.

serfs', wrote Pokrovsky, 'who prevented the serf-holder from establishing a factory?' To Pokrovsky the edict was one of the forerunners of 'bondage or landlord capitalism'.[54] Analysing the land-question in Peru, Mariátegui wrote about the technically advanced capitalist latifundia on the coast, owned by US and British business, in which 'exploitation still rests on feudal practices and principles'.[55] In its *Theses on the Eastern Question* adopted at the Fourth Congress, the colonial commission of the Comintern spoke of capitalism arising in the colonies 'on feudal foundations' and developing 'in distorted and incomplete transitional forms which give commercial capital predominance'.[56] Finally, outside the Marxist tradition, Hobson could refer to industrial profits which 'represented the "surplus-value" of slave or forced labour',[57] and Barrington Moore to 'labor-repressive forms of capitalist agriculture'.[58] In all these varied instances – the subordination of the potters of Moscow province to merchant-capital, the production of cotton in the slave South, the expansion of landlord-capitalism in Rumanian agriculture or Petrine industry, the sugar-latifundia of coastal Peru – there was no question of identifying the 'mode of production' according to the character of the given forms or relations of exploitation. Nor did any of these instances involve a 'coexistence' of modes of production.

2.3.3. *The defining role of the laws of motion*

> To identify the different kinds of motion is to identify the bodies themselves.
>
> (Engels to Marx 1873)

---

[54] Pokrovsky 1931, p. 287.

[55] Mariátegui 1971, p. 55, 'But on the coast, the latifundium has reached a fairly advanced level of capitalist technique, although its exploitation still rests on feudal practices and principles. The yields of cotton and sugar cane are those of the capitalist system. Enterprises are heavily financed and land is worked with modern machines and methods'.

[56] Degras 1971, Volume 1, p. 384; Carrère d'Encausse and Schram 1969, p. 194, with a slightly different translation: 'To the extent that capitalism in the colonial countries arises on feudal foundations, and develops in distorted and incomplete transitional forms, which give predominance to commercial and usurious capital (the Muslim East, China)...'.

[57] Hobson 1917, p. 13, where he states that, under colonial economy, '[t]rading profits were supplemented by the industrial profits representing the "surplus-value" of slave or forced labour'.

[58] Moore 1966, p. 495.

Engels defined the dialectic as the 'science of the general laws of motion of the external world'.⁵⁹ But the abstractness of the dialectic in this definition deprived it of its specifically revolutionary function in Marx. For Marx, as his approval of Kaufman's review indicates, the dialectic was, more specifically, a science of the laws of motion of the 'social process', profoundly historical by its very nature, not only in that it guided only the investigation of social (or historical) phenomena, but insofar as it denied that such phenomena could be understood according to abstract or historically indeterminate (social or historical) laws: 'in Marx's opinion', Kaufman wrote, 'every historical period has laws of its own'.⁶⁰ The dialectic in *Capital* was thus nothing else than the rigorous, systematic investigation of the laws of motion of capitalist production, in the course of which a series of simple abstractions ('wage-labour', money, etc.) were historically concretised as bourgeois relations of production, or abstractions determinate to capitalism as a mode of production; that is, reconstituted as 'concrete categories', as historically determinate social forms. It follows that modes of production are impenetrable at the level of simple abstractions. The process of 'true abstraction' is simultaneously a process of 'concretisation', of the definition of specific historical laws of motion. Isolating the enterprise of production under capitalism, Marx analysed these laws at two levels: at the level of each enterprise (or 'economic unit': Lenin) and at the level of the social totality of enterprises. If we generalise from this analysis, at its first level, the enterprise, an isolated entity, figures as a unit of production governed by specific laws which impose on it a determinate mode of economic behaviour, converting the given inherited forms of the labour-process into the form posited by their own motion. It follows that the different types of enterprise which form the basic cell of production in a given social form of economy are determined, in the first instance, as *units of production*, and only crystallise (that is, acquire their classical developed structure) in the determinate form of historically specific modes of organisation of the labour-process which posit a particular level of technique and specific historical forms of appropriation of the objective conditions of labour. At the level of the economy of enterprises, the process of investigation

---
⁵⁹ Engels 1968.
⁶⁰ Marx 1971a, Volume l, p. 28; Marx 1976, p. 101. This principle of 'historical specificity' was central to Korsch's interpretation of Marx, cf. Korsch 1963.

traces those tendencies which derive from the behaviour of each enterprise at the level of all enterprises. In Marx, *Capital*, Volume I comprises the analysis of the enterprise (of capitalist production) as an *isolated entity*, as individual capital – of the production and accumulation of surplus-value and of the labour-process as a value-producing process, which Marx characterises as the 'direct process of the production of capital' or the 'immediate productive process'. The laws of the rising organic composition of capital and of the concentration and centralisation of capital are already implied in the motion of individual capital (of capital as an isolated enterprise). Volumes II and III derive the laws of motion of capital at higher levels of integration (social capital, many capitals) from the laws of motion of capital as an isolated entity, arriving finally at the transformation of surplus-value into profit and the law of the falling rate of profit. The first three parts of Volume III complete the definition of capitalism as a mode of production. Taken as a whole, across its various stages, the substance of Marx's analysis lies in its definition of the laws of motion of capitalist production: the production and accumulation of surplus-value, the revolutionisation of the labour-process, the production of relative surplus-value on the basis of a capitalistically-constituted labour-process, the compulsion to increase the productivity of labour, etc. The 'relations of capitalist production' are the relations which express and realise these laws of motion at different levels of the social process of production. They are, as Marx calls them in a polemic against Proudhon, 'all the economic relations which are merely the necessary relations of the particular mode of production'. As modes of production are only a definite totality of historical laws of motion, relations of production thus become a *function of the given mode of production*. The character of any definite type of production relations, is, in short, impossible to determine until these laws of motion are themselves determined.

Finally, apart from *deriving* the nature of production relations of a given type from the mode of production as such, the defining role of the laws of motion implies that the specific *economic rhythms* through which these laws become at once historically effective and verifiable are themselves purely derivative economic phenomena. Although phenomena of this order (trends, cycles, intercycles) are in some sense perceptible and open to statistical determination independently of any conception of those laws, of which they are simply the expression, their historical content remains indeterminate without a prior conceptualisation in economic theory.[61] Lacking any determination in theory, they retain their character as empirical (quantitative) facts: on certain epistemological premises – observation as the origin of theory – they become therefore the basis for positing 'laws' of a purely fictitious nature, e.g., the 'acceleration principle' of neoclassical economic theory.

2.3.4. *The failure of abstraction in vulgar Marxism*

Even when the later Marxism broke with Stalinism politically, its theoretical conceptions were to a large extent still imprisoned in the deeper framework of a metaphysical-scholastic formalism, which deduced its 'modes of production' by forced abstraction from the simple categories present in various epochs of production. The classification of 'modes of production' which came to prevail on this basis resembled nothing so much as the Periodic Table of Mendeleiev, when the discovery of the structure of the atom had yet to explain the physical basis of that Table. The simple abstractions of Stalinist history, its 'inflexible social categories', functioned in the historical process as social *substances*, and this Newtonian conception of history was absorbed into the later Marxism, even when it modified or rejected the established sequence of those elements. (In this sense, the 'linear notion of historical time' had always been a purely subsidiary characteristic of vulgar historical materialism.) In short, the naïve conception of 'relations of production' as forms of exploitation of labour, and the classification of 'modes of production' according to the *simple formal identities* which this equation yielded, remained essential links of continuity between the ossified pseudo-Marxism of the Stalinists and the 'critical' tendencies of modern Marxism.

The persistent underlying confusion between 'relations of production' and therefore, in this conception, 'modes of production', with the different mechanisms of surplus-labour extraction became the most characteristic symptom of this continuity of problematics in the more recent debates on the 'transition' and on the nature of imperialist world-economy. Despite their critical character, these debates produced no breakthroughs by way of a specifically Marxist analysis either of the decline of feudalism or of colonial history.

---

[61] Thus Marx wrote of Sismondi that he 'forcefully criticizes the contradictions of bourgeois production, but does not understand them...' (1971b, p. 56).

It was precisely in the backward countries subjugated to world-economy as colonies that the process of the *mediation of capitalist (value-producing) relations of production by archaic ('precapitalist') forms of subjection of labour* assumed historically unprecedented dimensions, while *feudal relations of production figured predominantly in their pure form of commodity-feudalism*. Insofar as these relationships were perceived by them, a number of Marxists conceptualised them, completely wrongly, as the structure of the 'social formations' themselves. The chaos of simple abstractions was overcome by them through the simple notion, today commonplace to the point of banality, that the colonial 'social formations' typically 'combined' a number of 'modes of production' (which was true, of course, but *not at this level of abstraction*).

The colonial countries were mainly dominated by two distinct forms of enterprise, radically different in their specific laws of motion and characteristic preoccupations, but converging in their external forms: on one side, in most of Latin America and parts of South-East Asia, feudal estates integrated into the network of world commodity-exchanges, estates which, in their external attributes, resembled capitalist enterprises insofar as the major share of their output was produced for national and international markets; on the other, in the West Indies, most of Africa and large sectors of Asia, capitalist firms operating mainly through archaic ('precapitalist') modes of labour-organisation at low and generally stagnant levels of technique. Isolated from their specific laws of motion, these enterprises disintegrate analytically into a single type, 'capitalist' or 'precapitalist' according to the specific formal appearances collapsing them together (for Frank, commodity-production; for Laclau, the prevalence of servitude of various forms).[62] This collapsing together, from which followed the false conception of the colonial world as a 'sector', or unified totality of production-relations of one type, became one of the common premises in the debate started by the publication of Frank's book.

The whole challenge which the 'colonial question' poses for historical materialism lies in establishing these distinct economic rhythms and movements, in tracing their specific origins according to the conjuncture of world-economy, and finally in grasping their deeper connections. If the feudal enterprises of the colonial world functioned as commodity-producers, the explanation lies basically not in their historical position as colonial enterprises (that is,

---

[62] Frank 1969; Laclau 1971.

not in their determinate form and function as elements in a specific type of social formation), but in their specifically feudal character; and, if the capitalist enterprises which dominated most of colonial Africa and large parts of Asia utilised coercive forms of exploitation, we must ask whether the laws of motion of capital are not, within certain limits, compatible with 'barbarous forms of labour'.

Thus, neither the phenomena of colonial history nor the disintegration of feudalism could be subjected to a specifically Marxist analysis as long as relations of production were conceived in their abstract, one-sided determination as 'forms of exploitation'. For, on this premise, Marxists consciously or unconsciously denied the intrinsic connection between feudalism and commodity-production, or between bondage and capitalism, which was established in given historical conditions. Once currency began to circulate on an expanding scale, the whole tendency of feudal production lay in the direction of its integration into circuits of commodity-exchange. Moreover, the whole history of colonialism in Africa was basically a history of capitalist enterprises subjugating peasant labour on specifically non-capitalist foundations. Both these phenomena, characterised by Marx as 'intermediate, hybrid forms [*Mittelgattungen, Zwittergattungen*]'[63] were historically never of purely limited scope or passing significance. The 'second serfdom' engulfed most of Eastern Europe and large areas of Latin America, where it persisted for well over four centuries, longer than capitalism has existed in its classical form of large-scale socialised production; and the archaic barbarous forms of capitalist production itself appeared sporadically over a similar historical span – from the early origins of the 'domestic system' in medieval Europe, through the sugar plantations of Barbados in the seventeenth century, to the gold-mines of South Africa in the nineteenth, the agrarian colonate of Algeria, the Junker estates of Prussia, the tea plantations of Assam and sugar centrales of Cuba, or, finally, in our own century, the processing factories of coastal Peru, cotton fields of northern Mozambique or white settler-farms of Kenya.[64]

Constricted by their problematic of characterisation (of simple formal abstraction), the debates among Marxists perceived these facts in a purely one-sided, distorted way: that is, the facts were 'formulated' incorrectly even

---

[63] Marx 1973, p. 512.
[64] E.g., Trapido 1971; Van Zwanenberg 1971.

when they were perceived. Sweezy perceived a certain connection between the decay of feudalism and expanding commodity-relationships, but formulated the connection as a collapse of feudal economy. Dobb, and later, in Dobb's tradition, Laclau, perceived the link between commodity-production and the intensification of servitude, but concluded, from their famous 'virtual identity', that the market 'consolidated' the feudal economy.[65] Frank perceived the intrinsic bond which tied the feudal haciendas to the market, only to dissolve it immediately by defining them as 'capitalist'.[66] Bettelheim argued, correctly, that the exploitation of colonial peasants by capitalist firms had to be 'rooted at the level of production', only to reconstitute the relation at the level of exchange in saying that these peasants sold not their labour-power but their products.[67] The new currents of 'political economy' influenced by Arrighi and Amin correctly defined the role of the 'labour-reserves' in Africa in relation to the needs of capital accumulation, only to characterise them as distinct 'modes of production' perpetuated by capital.[68]

Marx himself had proposed the view that 'commerce has a more or less dissolving influence everywhere on the producing organization, which it finds at hand and whose different forms are mainly carried on with a view to use-value'.[69] When the world-market crystallised after the revolution of the sixteenth century, these 'producing organizations' or enterprises, as we have called them, consisted mainly of two types: feudal estates and independent peasant family-labour farms. The progressive integration of these types of enterprise into commodity-circuits convulsed both, but only on the longer historical scale of several centuries. Both the feudal estates and the peasant farms entered a process of dissolution, but neither 'collapsed' or disappeared immediately. Moreover, this process of dissolution acquired, in the case of feudalism, a 'combined' character. Feudal production (the feudal *mode of production*) *both crystallised and decayed* within the framework of expanding market-relations: the feudal estate both acquired its 'classical', fully developed, structure and reached its inherent limits as a commodity-producing enter-

---

[65] Dobb 1954, p. 24; Laclau 1971.
[66] Frank 1969.
[67] Bettelheim 1972, p. 300.
[68] Arrighi 1970; Amin 1974; Amin 1976.
[69] Marx 1971a, Volume 2, p. 36; Marx 1978, pp. 119–20; Marx 1971a, Volume 3, p. 331f.; Marx 1981, p. 449.

prise. By contrast to both forms, the slave-plantations, normally regarded as 'precapitalist', disintegrated by an entirely different process, not immediately connected with the expanding volume of exchanges in whose vortex they were, in fact, born as 'centres of commercial speculation'.

2.4. Reading history backwards

When the revolutionary-Marxist tradition took up the analysis of the world-economy early in the present century, the context was set by an international division of labour centred on the requirements of capital-reproduction on the basis of large-scale industrial enterprises. The classical conception which now evolved in the writings of Lenin, Luxemburg and Bukharin saw in the major tendencies of evolution of the world economy the separate phases of the reproduction-process of capital: the conversion of value into money and of money, as the pure form of value, into capital. The debate which began closer to our own period about the early phases of evolution of the world-economy inherited this classical conception and converted its points of arrival into points of departure. If, to the Marxists of the Second and Third Internationals, the contemporary world-market was an entirely capitalist phenomenon, it seemed evident to Frank that the world-economy had been capitalist from its inception. So deeply entrenched was this notion, that, even when he disputed Frank's position that capitalism prevailed in Peru or Chile from the earliest stages of the Spanish colonisation, Laclau accepted his premise that metropolitan-industrial capital provided the major impulse behind this process of colonisation. For Frank, colonisation converted the countries of Latin America into 'sources for metropolitan capital accumulation and development'; for Laclau, too, the world-economy was, from its inception, an expression of the accumulation-process: 'the growth of the system depends on the accumulation of capital, the rhythm of this accumulation depends on the average rate of profit, and the level of this rate depends in its turn on the consolidation and expansion of pre-capitalist relationships in the peripheral areas'.[70] Behind their formal dispute about 'characterisation', the two arguments shared this single premise: whether one characterised the forms of economy in Latin America as 'feudal' or as 'capitalist' – that is, whether one 'deduced' their

---

[70] Laclau 1971, p. 37; Laclau 1977, p. 40.

character from one or other of the two simple abstractions specified earlier – the point was that the world-economy evolved in this period as a response to the expansion of industrial capitalism. If this was so evident both to Frank and Laclau, the only 'problem' which remained was the formal problem of characterisation: 'the problem is to define in each case the specificity of the exploitative relationship in question' – which was no different from saying that there was in fact no problem at all, or that the problem was purely formal, because this so-called 'specificity' was already self-evident at the level of the simple abstraction. For example, for the plantations, it required literally only a single sentence to establish this 'specificity': 'in the plantations of the West Indies', Laclau wrote, 'the economy was based on a mode of production constituted by slave labour'.[71] It was as simple as that.

Inherent in this form of argument – not peculiar to Laclau or Frank, but deeply entrenched in the whole tradition of 'Marxism' inherited from the 1920s – is the following underlying premise, which is inseparably bound up with the formal problematic of 'characterisation': in all phases of its evolution, the structure of the world-economy posits only one element of explanation, namely, the demands of capital-reproduction. From this, it follows that modes of production other than capital which coexist within the structure of that economy figure only as 'specific' forms of subjugation of labour perpetuated over time by the requirements of industrial accumulation. These are 'modes of production' entirely deprived of their own laws of motion, vegetating on the periphery of an industrialising Europe like a vast reserve of labour-power periodically called into action by the spasmodic expansions of metropolitan capital. For purposes of propaganda, it would be entirely adequate to relate the existence of slavery in the cotton plantations to the requirements of the English textile industry, or the intensified exploitation of serf-labour in the grain-exporting nations of Eastern Europe to the fact that capital requires a large volume of grain at low prices. But Marx was aware that a scientific enquiry was an entirely different sort of exercise to a propagandistic tract, and it was this awareness that initially distinguished Marxism from Ricardian and petit-bourgeois socialism.

---

[71] Laclau 1971, p. 30; Laclau 1977, p. 30.

2.5. Slavery and the world-market

2.5.1. 'Slavery'

To start with this 'mode of production constituted by slave labour', it is a striking fact, impossible to ignore, that within the Marxist tradition, as outside it, the slave-plantations of the American South were never always as simply characterised as Laclau imagines. For example: Marx wrote that in the English colonies which produced tobacco, cotton, sugar, the colonists acted 'like people, who, driven by motives of bourgeois production, wanted to produce commodities...'.[72] He described these plantations as enterprises of 'commercial speculation' in which 'a capitalist mode of production exists, if only in a formal sense.... The business in which slaves are used is conducted by capitalists'.[73] He described the exploitation of slave-labour as a 'factor in a calculated and calculating system', driven by the compulsion to produce 'surplus value'.[74] Commenting on this passage, Preobrazhensky spoke of 'undeveloped, transitional forms of surplus-value, which are not completely characteristic of a developed capitalist mode of production'.[75] On the other hand, for Kautsky, the slave-plantations of America were a form of 'large-scale production of a pre-capitalist type'.[76] Lenin, who accepted this characterisation directly under Kautsky's influence, later argued, in a polemic on American agriculture, that there was really 'no foundation for the common practice [sic.] of classifying the [slave] latifundia as *capitalist* enterprises', that these latifundia were 'frequently [sic.] survivals of pre-capitalist relationships – slave-owning, feudal or patriarchal' which typically manifested the lowest percentages of 'improved acreage'.[77] Much more recently, in one of his books, Genovese argues that the 'slave regime in the British Caribbean bore the clear stamp of capitalist enterprise', and that sugar was grown on 'large plantations of a decidedly bourgeois type' run by 'capitalist slaveholders'.[78] But earlier, in his major work of interpretation, Genovese had also written,

---

[72] Marx 1968, p. 239.
[73] Marx 1968, pp. 302–3.
[74] Marx 1971a, Volume 1, pp. 226–7; Marx 1976, p. 345.
[75] Preobrazhensky 1965, p. 185.
[76] Kautsky 1970, p. 205.
[77] Lenin 1964b, pp. 30, 50; italics in original.
[78] Genovese 1970, p. 69.

this time with reference to the American plantations, 'the planters were not mere capitalists [sic.], they were pre-capitalist, quasi-aristocratic landowners who had to adjust their economy and ways of thinking to a capitalist world market...'.[79]

In a review of the Frank-Laclau debate, Jay Mandle thought the plantations were 'intensely profit-oriented commercial enterprises' and the plantation owners 'profit-maximizing entrepreneurs', i.e. capitalists as we normally understand them, but added, to be on the safe side, that their exploitation of slave-labour made it 'impossible by Dobb's definition to classify them as capitalist'.[80] In fact, as we know, with the single exception of Lenin, the major argument proposed by all other writers against classifying the slave-plantations as a form of capitalist enterprise was precisely that 'by Dobb's definition', by virtue of his 'virtual identity', they could not be so because they exploited *slave*-labour.[81] Lenin himself proposed a quite different argument, and one which, as we shall see in a moment, contained a substantial insight, namely, that the level of technique and the extensive character of such an enterprise were sufficient to preclude their characterisation as 'capitalist' in the strict sense in which the various other types of agricultural enterprise in other

---

[79] Genovese, 1966, p. 23. This confusion or ambiguity is found outside Marxist writings as well: with reference to Mexico, François Chevalier described the coastal sugar-plantations of New Spain as 'the first great feudal estates' which, as early as the sixteenth century, 'anticipated the classical Mexican hacienda' (Chevalier 1963, p. 81ff.). On the other hand, to Lewis Gray, in a major work on the economics of American slavery, the plantation was a '*capitalistic* type of industrial organization' based on a mass of unfree labourers (Gray 1933, p. 302; italics in original). Dunn states in his sensitive social history that, when the English planters of Barbados turned to sugar-production, 'their prime goal was to make money, not to become seigneurs...' (Dunn, 1973, p. 65). To the 'new economic historians' of the USA, the econometric study of Conrad and Meyer was a decisive blow against 'the attempt to portray slaveowners as a "pre-capitalist" or "acommercial" class which failed to respond to modern business incentives' (cf. Fogel and Engerman 1971, p. 326). Finally, Samir Amin refers to the plantations as a 'slave owning mode of production' but adds that it should not be confused with the 'true' one (Amin 1974, Volume 2, p. 361).

[80] Mandle 1972.

[81] In other words, it is taken for granted, as I said earlier, that no form of forced labour can mediate capitalist relations of production. Cf. M.V. Freyhold, 'The Rise and Fall of Colonial Modes of Production': 'When the representatives of early capitalism started looking around the world for chances of appropriating the surplus-labour of other peoples, they soon realized that "free labour" was not available outside Europe. Any exploitation elsewhere would have to be based on forced labour of some kind. *Capitalist production was out of the question*'. The characterisation of the mode of production as 'colonial' which I myself accepted earlier, much too hastily, suspends the problem even more than either of the traditional characterisations.

zones of America were 'capitalist'. It would have made practically no sense for Lenin to have argued that the prevalence of slave labour as such made the plantations 'precapitalist', because, quite apart from his early descriptions of the various 'medieval' forms of capitalism prevalent in the Russian countryside, he also wrote, in that period: 'Our literature frequently contains too stereotyped an understanding of the theoretical proposition that capitalism requires the free, landless worker...'; this was true, Lenin argued, as 'indicating the main trend' (cf. Section 2.3.1 above where I referred to wage-labour in its simple determination, i.e., free labour, as the necessary basis for capitalism as the *generalised* form of social production), but agrarian capitalism was compatible with unfree labour at specific stages in its evolution.[82]

To indicate only briefly, and entirely by way of hypothesis, the framework for a more rigorous Marxist understanding of the slave-plantations: we argued earlier that the analysis of a given historical form of production treats its constituent enterprise basically as a unit of production, an entity governed by specific economic laws, and regards the emergence of its specific form of organisation of the labour-process, the process which corresponds to its laws of motion, only as a moment of its 'crystallisation'. The slave-plantations were commodity-producing enterprises characterised by speculative investments ('centres of commercial speculation') in the production of *absolute* surplus-value *on the basis* of landed property. Production was carried on in such enterprises at low, 'capital-specific' techniques which posited enlarged simple cooperation subject to economies of scale.[83] Accumulation in this form of speculative capitalist enterprise asserted itself only in the long run, as a relatively slow and mainly sporadic tendency dominated by feudal modes of consumption. The progress of such an enterprise would thus present the external aspect of a series of simple reproduction-cycles expanding slowly to higher levels according to a discontinuous and bunched rhythm of investments. At the level of all enterprises, this purely quantitative character of accumula-

---

[82] Lenin 1956, pp. 178–9.
[83] 'Economies of scale': in Barbados c. 1646 an average sugar plantation probably required an investment close to £2,500 (computed from data in Dunn 1973), which should be compared with Dobb's data on the scale of investment in seventeenth-century British industry (Dobb 1963 [1946], Chapter 4). In Jamaica, by the eighteenth century, the average value of such a plantation was £20,000 according to Sheridan 1965.

tion[84] and its 'natural' basis in the ownership of land (here, the capitalist and landlord being one and same person, as Marx indicated) would progressively convert the excess of commodity-values over prices of production inherent in the low *technical* composition of capital[85] into 'surplus-profits' appropriated *by the slaveowners themselves* as 'absolute rent'.[86] For we know that historically plantation land of a specific fertility would become, progressively a monopoly of only the most substantial or at least earlier-established slaveowners, and thus present a 'barrier' to the free investment of capital, as much as land incorporated as feudal property constituted such a barrier and thus generated 'absolute rent'. It follows that, even when cost-prices rose as the natural fertility of the soil declined through intensive exploitation at stagnant levels of technique, a crisis of profitability could be postponed indefinitely for a certain range of market-prices.

This specific form of enterprise therefore differs from the classical form of capitalist enterprise mainly in its lower intensity of accumulation and in the fact that accumulation is here compatible with a constant composition of capital, and therefore with stagnant or declining levels of labour-productivity. Increases in the rate of exploitation depend not on the conversion of necessary labour into surplus-labour, i.e. the production of relative surplus-value, but on an intensification of labour or on a lengthening of the working-day to the limits of physical endurance. The self-expansion of value no longer figures as an entirely autonomous and dominating force compelling each enterprise to reduce cost-prices to a minimum, but acquires a purely relative and sporadic existence as a function of feudally-dominated habits of consumption and display. Plantation-profits, we know, financed not only the (quantitative) expansion of the enterprise itself, but, probably to an even greater extent, peerages, marriage-alliances, seats in parliament and the purchase of feudal

---

[84] Cf. Genovese 1966, p. 16, 'the greater part of slavery's profits find their way back into production (but) economic progress is quantitative...'.

[85] In Marx's chapter on 'Absolute Ground-Rent', Marx 1981, Chapter 45, it is the *technical* proportion of living labour to the conditions of labour that determines the relation of the price of production to value. Thus the problem of how the 'organic composition of capital' can be determined for a capitalist slave-economy does not affect the hypothesis proposed.

[86] This is *implied* by Marx when he writes that as long as 'the elemental profusion of land...offers no resistance to capital investment', 'nothing will stand in the way of cost-price regulating market-value': Marx 1968, p. 303. We know that this condition would apply only in the early stages of settlement.

properties.⁸⁷ In short, the slave-plantations were *capitalist* enterprises of a patriarchal and feudal character producing absolute surplus-value on the basis of slave-labour and a monopoly in land. This heterogeneous and, as it appears, disarticulated nature of the slave-plantation generated a series of contradictory images when the early Marxist tradition, not equipped with the same abundance of material available today, attempted its first characterisations.

2.5.2. *The nascent world-market*

The sugar produced by enterprises of this nature in the Caribbean and exported by them mainly to England, France and Holland, became the leading item of a major re-export trade within Europe itself in the course mainly of the seventeenth century.⁸⁸ Given the circumscribed and localised distribution of a specifically bourgeois class in Europe at that time, the growth of this re-export trade suggests that the demand for sugar and other types of plantation-produce was not confined exclusively to the established mercantile or incipient industrial-capitalist classes of England or Holland. Moreover, we know also that the period when English sugar displaced Brazilian sugar from the markets of northern Europe was itself a period of rapid English commercial expansion in the Baltic. The deeper meaning of this connection becomes evident when we note that, throughout this period, and in fact much earlier, Europe had been divided into three more-or-less distinct price-zones whose centres of gravity tended to fluctuate while preserving a certain basic uniformity. On the eve of the seventeenth century, according to the price-series constructed by Braudel and Spooner, the price of grain in England, France or Holland was 200–300% higher than the price of Polish grain.⁸⁹ The growing volume of grain-exports from the port of Danzig had become a crucial mechanism in stabilising grain-prices in those countries in the period of rapid demographic reconstruction and currency-depreciation which began around 1570. So intense was this integration of Polish grain into the economy of Western Europe that Pokrovsky wrote in the *History of Russia*: 'The price of rye in Danzig determined the cost of living in Madrid or Lisbon',⁹⁰ and

---

⁸⁷ Pares 1960; Sheridan 1965.
⁸⁸ Cf. Davies 1954.
⁸⁹ Braudel and Spooner 1967.
⁹⁰ Pokrovsky 1931, p. 261.

Marian Małowist tells us that 'every disturbance in the delivery of grain from the coasts of the Baltic, especially from Poland, produced a rise in the cost of living in Holland and other provinces of the Low Countries...'.[91] But how were the English, Dutch or Portuguese to pay for these imports? Before the export of English textiles to Portugal helped to balance England's trade with the Baltic by sucking bullion out of Portugal,[92] this role of payments-mechanism in the expanding grain-trade devolved partly on the export wool-trade, which required a massive drive to expropriate the domestic peasantry, and partly on the re-export of colonial produce to the feudal classes of Eastern Europe. From this, we can draw two conclusions. Firstly, the demand which sustained production in the capitalist slave-enterprises of the West Indies depended to some degree on the expansion of feudal incomes in the grain-exporting zones of Eastern Europe. Secondly, these enterprises were compelled to operate within a framework of mercantilist control because colonial produce, as an element of feudal consumption, became one important means of financing grain-imports from the feudal estates. In the seventeenth century, at any rate, the world-economy presented a vastly different picture from the industrially-dominated world-market of the nineteenth, which formed the basis for the early Marxist theories of imperialism. For, at that stage, the structure of world-exchanges linked the capitalist slave-plantations of the Atlantic to feudal estates in Poland through a complicated network of basically mercantile and financial interests centred in Amsterdam and London. Each of these enterprises fitted into this structure of the world-economy as specific autonomous units of production driven by their own laws of motion. If this is evident for the slaveowners, 'driven by motives of bourgeois production', it now has to be established for the Polish estates.

2.6. Feudal production

2.6.1. *The estate*

The feudal economy was an economy of consumption based on a level of technique that was so rudimentary that a single aristocratic household required

---

[91] Małowist 1959.
[92] Fisher 1971.

for its support a vast arable area. In the earliest period for which estate-inventories become available, the ratio of output to seed barely exceeded 2:1. In Europe, on the eve of the fourteenth century, after a long swing of slow agricultural progress connected with improvements in ploughing technique and a gradually expanding triennial rotation, maximum grain-yields oscillated around 4:1. Finally, as late as the eighteenth century, both in the fertile Po Valley of northern Italy and in the black-earth region of Russia, the major cereals gave a yield of 3–5:1.[93] For this low productivity of labour, the estate, the basic enterprise of feudal production, compensated by practising an extensive economy. As the level of technique progressed only slowly, over several centuries, as our figures indicate, the estate's output was a function of the surface in production, and the surface which the lord could bring into production in any given period was a function of the disposable mass of labour-power.[94] The limits to the mobilisation of this mass of labour-power, when not determined technically by the available quantity of draught-animals, were imposed socially by the relation of forces, the possibility of flight and the relative degree of 'overpopulation'. The average volume of output was thus determined ultimately by the socially disposable mass of labour-time.[95]

As a form of enterprise, the feudal estate normally consisted of separate manorial units related metabolically as parts of a single economic organism centred on the lord's household. The structure of these units varied from those in which demesne arable was of no significance and feudal incomes consisted mainly of monetary payments based on tithes and seigneurial rights [*seigneurie banale*], to others in which demesne economy based on slave- or serf-labour predominated. In the feudal epoch as a whole, the estate's economy generated two relatively distinct modes of organisation of the labour-process. The first of these, defined by the insignificance of demesne, posited a higher elasticity of surplus in the peasant-sector and a distribution of arable

---

[93] Data on productivity collected from: Duby 1968, pp. 101–2 ; Woolf 1964–5, p. 268ff.; Blum 1968, p. 329.
[94] Kula 1970.
[95] This point, emphasised by Kula, is already to be found in Richard Jones (Jones 1831) who, precluding the possibility of rapid technical advances under feudalism, argued that rent could only be increased 'by an increase in the total quantity of labour exacted, and in this case while the lands of the proprietor will be better tilled those of the serfs, from which labour has been withdrawn, all the worse' (cited Marx 1971b, p. 400).

between peasant-holdings and demesne, which conferred on the former the character of a sector of *small peasant-production*, with the peasants disposing of the whole of their labour-time; here the rate of feudal exploitation was not immediately evident in the ratio of the two arables. In the second mode of organisation of the labour-process, the peasant-holding was a 'subsistence plot' or 'wage in kind',[96] and the totality of these holdings a sector of simple reproduction;[97] here, the distribution of the peasants' necessary and surplus labour-time would tend to coincide directly with the distribution of arable between peasant-holdings and lord's demesne. Taking the feudal epoch as a whole, the peasant-holdings thus figured in two determinate forms and functions: as small peasant-farms capable of generating a more or less substantial surplus over the peasants' immediate requirements of consumption, and as subsistence plots adapted to the reproduction of labour-power. As the organisation of the labour-process became effective within the framework of the manor, and as most estates comprised several manors, the ratio of demesne arable to peasant arable would tend to fluctuate quite sharply between the different manors, estates and regions, and the size of peasant holdings [*manses*] to vary even more sharply at any given time. In general, a casual survey suggests that the area occupied by demesne varied between 13% and 45% of the total area of a given estate or manor, with a tendency to vary inversely with the size of these units; while peasant-holdings ranged from miniscule plots of 10 acres or less to substantial farms of 100 acres. If we now ask which of these forms constituted the classical or fully developed structure of the feudal enterprise, the answer should not be difficult: the enterprise only 'crystallised', that is, acquired its classical structure, when the ratio of the peasants' necessary to surplus labour-time was directly reflected in the distribution of arable between demesne and peasant-holding. In other words, the form of organisation of the labour-process specific to the feudal mode of production in its developed form would be one which permitted the lord to assert complete control over the labour-process itself – in which the peasant-holdings assumed the form of, and functioned as, a sector of simple reproduction.

---

[96] Lenin 1963b, p. 189; Lenin 1963a, pp. 450, 493.
[97] Kula 1970.

Within the framework of this type of economy, and regardless of the structure of the labour-process, the production of wealth was subordinated to habits of generosity, display and consumption. Pirenne maintained that, in the 'patriarchal' organisation of the big estates, the notion of 'profits' in the sense of value which expands itself, was utterly alien;[98] as we know, the only 'investments' which such an enterprise ever undertook were those which were strictly necessary for the requirements of simple reproduction (and mainly, the periodic reconstitution of manorial livestock). In this sense, the lord's consumption constituted the only 'motor-force' of expansion in the feudal economy.[99]

Yet Pirenne's conception of the estate as a 'patriarchal' organisation is misleading (and did, in fact, mislead Sweezy). The determining role of consumption did not imply an ideal of isolationism, or any basic economic irrationality. We know that, as the twelfth century progressed, a large number of agricultural treatises appeared which regarded agriculture as a 'mechanical art' worthy of scientific interest and capable of systematic improvement. We know that, in gradually going over to a triennial rotation, the estates spread the risks of a bad harvest more widely, for in years when excessive moisture destroyed the winter-crops, spring-grain would come to the rescue. Above all, of course, we know that when the demand for agricultural produce expanded, demesne-cultivation accounted for a major share of the marketed output. The fact that, in phases of rapid inflation, estates would tend to convert from fixed monetary payments to 'direct management' implies that some mechanism of 'opportunity-cost' calculation operated. But the spread of these 'business-like' attitudes, as they were characterised by Sweezy,[100] was not only compatible with the character of the feudal economy as an economy of consumption, but inseparably tied to it. In a sense, this compatibility and basic link between feudal consumption and business-like attitudes is the central point. The consumption-requirements of the nobility and the perpetual need to adjust the level of income to rates of consumption were the most powerful determinants in drawing both lord and peasant into production for the market: the lord directly through the consolidation of a demesne-economy, the peasant

---

[98] Pirenne 1969, p. 56.
[99] Duby 1973, p. 200.
[100] Sweezy 1954, p. 9.

indirectly through the expanding weight of monetary payments. In phases of ascending production for the market (England *c*. 1250, Poland and Hungary *c*. 1600) it is quite probable that most commodity-producing estates rarely sold less than half their net output. For example, on the 32 dependent manors of the Bishop of Winchester for which detailed time-series are available, in average years close to 80% of net output was sold; on 6 of the Duchy of Lancaster's manors in Wiltshire, 90%.[101] Even outside periods of high grain prices, the proportion of marketed output was fairly high: *c*. 1150 one of the manors of the abbey of Cluny was selling the whole of its wheat-output and 33% of its output of rye;[102] two hundred years later, when demesne-production was in partial decline in the West, but the full impact of the incipient recession had still to come, a small estate in Essex for which figures are available, reserved 21% of its total wheat-receipts for seed, paid 19% in wages to workers on the demesne, sent 23% to the lord's household for direct consumption, and sold the remaining 30%, which comes to 37% of net output (deducting seed).[103] If these preliminary examples do not suffice, a different order of evidence might be used. The 'maximisation of sales' became a major slogan of the various treatises addressed to the Russian nobility of the eighteenth century. According to Confino,

> the basic idea underlying the economic treatises of this period was the realization of profits and expansion of feudal incomes: these became the major goal of the estate's economic activity, the main obsession of the *pomeščik* and the chief duty of the bailiffs.... Ryckov's book of instructions to estate-managers began, 'Our main interest in this book is how the income and profits of the lord may be expanded'.[104]

In another treatise, Bolotov described the most competent estate-managers as those who could maximise the volume of sales at the best price, while ensuring the immediate consumption-needs of the household.[105]

---

[101] Duby 1968, p. 136.
[102] Duby 1968, p. 211.
[103] Britnell 1966.
[104] Confino 1963, p. 131.
[105] Confino 1963, p. 138.

Far from facing the 'alternatives' of producing for the market or producing for 'use',[106] most estates were organised according to a certain internal specialisation, with some manorial units producing mainly or entirely for the market and others for household-consumption. In both aspects, the organisation of the estate was a function of the socially determined consumption needs of the lords. In their consciousness, commercial production and feudal 'subsistence' were not separate, conflicting aspects of their social practice as a class, for, as one of the Russian treatises indicated, the production of feudal profits was geared to the goal of feudal consumption.[107]

This preliminary outline of the basic characteristics of the estate is sufficient to imply two conclusions. (i) Production for the market did not entail competition between the different enterprises. What was mainly important to this type of enterprise was the preservation of a certain proportionality between income and consumption, not the rapid expansion of incomes from one year to the next on the example of a capitalist firm. In a capitalist economy, the market exerts its domination over each individual enterprise by compelling it to produce within the limits of a socially average level of productivity. The existence of this social average posits a mechanism of cost-calculation which was absent in conditions of feudal production. To be more precise, for a bourgeois enterprise, the 'absolute limit of exploitation' is constituted by the average profit of capital; for the small-commodity producer who sells the whole of his output, the limit is set by the costs of simple reproduction, comprising mainly his 'wage'. In the medieval world, as feudal consumption became bound up with the expanding currents of circulation and implied progressively higher levels of monetary expenditure, a specifically feudal structure of accounting tended to crystallise: 'costs' were defined mainly as those items of expenditure which required an outlay of cash, and 'profits' as all items of monetary receipt. As items of expenditure, the elements of consumption and production were merged into a common category, something like the 'sum of all expenses', which was then deducted from receipts to obtain an apparently spurious 'net balance'.[108] This ratio of receipts to expenditure was calculated

---

[106] As Sweezy tended to imply they were, after correctly stating that his conception of feudalism as a 'system of production for use' did not preclude the possibility of estates producing for the market .
[107] A.L. Komarov, cited by Confino 1963, p. 141.
[108] Levett 1927.

as the ratio of two consolidated sums; even when, on the side of income, the proceeds from the sale of various crops figured as separate items of receipt, costs of production were distributed under various agricultural operations, so that no attempt was made to determine individual monetary costs of production, or even the monetary costs of crop production as a whole. As all items of cash-income were regarded as 'profits', independently of any mechanism of cost-calculation, crops were more or less 'profitable', not according to their monetary rate of profit but according to the volume of cash which they brought in.[109] Any increment in crop-production which increased the total volume of these receipts, however marginal its contribution, was therefore 'profitable'. That is to say, for a given distribution of productive forces, even if it made sense to sell a given output at the highest price, sales would nonetheless continue over a wide range of prices below this bound. In short, in an economy which dissociated production from the 'rational' calculation of costs and which regarded 'profits' not as a ratio but as a simple magnitude, the 'limit of exploitation' could only be a vague and elastic concept, and one which could assert itself only in the longer run in a sort of feudal 'scissor's crisis', as the hiatus between income and consumption widened over a number of years.

(ii) Once the estates established a certain connection with the market, the lord's income became a function of three variables: (a) the volume of gross output, which would tend to fluctuate sharply from one year to the next; (b) the coefficient of the marketable surplus, whose elasticity would vary more or less directly in proportion to gross output; (c) the current price of grain.[110] As no estate had any control over prices, an expansion of manorial incomes depended mainly on expanding the marketable surplus. As the level of internal consumption was more-or-less constant, the volume of this surplus, sold on the market, would vary proportionately to the volume of the harvest. At the existing level of technique, the average productivity over time was a function of the surface in production and therefore of the disposable mass of labour-time. It follows that, in these conditions, the 'maximisation' of feudal

---

[109] The point is stressed by Confino 1963, who sees in this a transposition, to the feudal estates, of the economic logic of small-peasant production.
[110] Kula 1970.

profits necessarily implied incursions into the sector of small-peasant production, from which the estates drew their sources of labour.

2.6.2. Peculiarities of the 'second serfdom'

The feudal mode of production prevailed in England, for example, in its period of 'high farming' *c.* 1230, as well as in Poland *c.* 1600, when most of Western Europe was becoming heavily dependent on Polish grain exports. In England in that period, as in Poland, the larger and better-organised estates were extensively involved in the production of grain for the market, selling up to 80% of net output. But a deeper comparison would reveal differences of some interest. Of England, we are told by Duby,

> to associate the tenants with the labour of the demesne in the thirteenth century was an anachronism.... The revival of forced labour seems, therefore, to have been very limited: it was only temporary, since it declined definitely on the monastic estates after 1275, and was restricted in scope, since labour-services were only used to reinforce those of manorial employees.[111]

Seventeenth-century Poland, on the other hand, was experiencing a substantial feudal offensive, with the nobility beginning to 'limit the area of their peasant's cultivation, and, in this way, enlarge their own land'.[112] If we take these cases as prototypes of the first and second serfdoms respectively, it is clear that the tendency of demesne-consolidation at the cost of peasant-production, which they both reveal, prevailed with varying degrees of intensity in these conjunctures. The extent to which it prevailed and the intensity of its effects were a function of broader economic factors. The possibility of expanding manorial incomes or safeguarding feudal consumption by means other than direct management depended mainly on the elasticity of the surplus in small-peasant production, while demesne farming could itself be organised mainly on the basis of paid labour. At any rate, whether estates converted to monetary payments or retained demesne-cultivation with the use of paid labour, both processes posited a certain level of currency-circulation. At a deeper level of analysis, therefore, the first significant contrast between the epoch of 'high farming' and the 'second serfdom', between the two extremities of Europe, is

---

[111] Duby 1968, pp. 262–3.
[112] Małowist 1959.

located here. In the West, the enormously expanding weight of the *seigneurie banale* on which Duby lays so much stress in his most recent work,[113] and the growing volume of monetary payments by the peasantry implied proportionate increases both in the stock of money and in the velocity of its circulation. The leasing of demesne-lands, the imposition of jurisdictional taxes, entry-fines and 'permanent rents', the movement of commutation and the growing volume of peasant-indebtedness – all cash-transactions or transactions based mainly on cash – make no sense on any other assumption. In relative terms, the level of currency-circulation was quite different in the East: in Poland, it actually diminished in the early part of the seventeenth century, compelling the nobility to adapt to this situation by intensifying the economic isolation of the estate and establishing in this way, as Kula remarks, a 'mechanism of closed monetary operations'.[114] In the second place, conversion to monetary payments required a peasantry capable of producing for the market; and these surpluses would tend to derive mainly from the more substantial households. Although, in the West, the expanding weight of population after the early phases of arable colonisation led to a spontaneous fragmentation of most peasant *manses*, both the gradual improvements in productivity and the relaxation of feudal pressures on the peasant's surplus had enabled this sort of peasantry to establish itself. Once the structure of feudal exploitation itself became more diversified and fluid, this sector of the peasantry, the real base of peasant commodity-production in the feudal social formations, could consolidate its position to an even greater extent. In the East, the whole process of differentiation was more or less repressed up until the nineteenth century. The peasants' share of the total volume of grain-sales was therefore never very significant – in late tsarist Russia, landlords accounted for 90% of the marketed output of grain, and the eventual conversion to monetary payments (*obrok* in the Russian countryside) required migrations of the peasantry in search of employment [*otchod*].[115] Finally, the momentary vigour of demesne-farming in England was supported by an extensive use of hired labour and consequently closely linked to the overpopulation of the English countryside. Earlier conditions connected with clearance-operations and the

---

[113] Duby 1973.
[114] Kula 1970, p. 109.
[115] The connection between *obrok* and *otchod* is drawn out by Confino 1963.

expansion of arable – viz. improvements in agricultural techniques; gradual increases in productivity; the shift to a grain-centred system of husbandry and the connected shifts in the peasant's diet; the conversion of slave-gangs into serf-households – all favoured a rapid growth of the serf-population. By the middle of the thirteenth century, as this movement of grain expansion came to a halt, a new phase of 'overpopulation' was becoming evident.[116] In England, the proportion of serf-households which at that time was living at or even substantially below subsistence was close to 80%. The emergence in these conditions of a village-proletariat expanded the supply of labour at a subsistence wage, promoted the use of such labour on the medium and small estates insufficiently provided with villeins, and attracted even the bigger estates by its greater seasonal flexibility. About a third of the English peasant-population worked for wages in this period.[117] This increasing use of paid labour was closely linked with the expansion of monetary payments and with expanding levels of currency-circulation. By contrast, in Poland, Ukraine, Lithuania, the low level of currency-circulation and the high level of wages made an extensive use of such labour practically impossible. Unlike the lower layers of the nobility in England, who depended largely on reserves of free labour, the smaller Russian landowners, the *svoezemtsi*, who were their counterparts, were compelled to work their own lands, aided by slaves.[118] 'The Russian landowners', wrote Marx, 'complain about two things: first, about the lack of money-capital.... The second complaint is more characteristic. It is to the effect that even if one has money, not enough labourers are to be had at any time'.[119]

In short, a dearth of cash, a more backward differentiation of the peasantry, and a scarcity of free labour were the basic conditions distinguishing the 'second serfdom' from the so-called 'classical' feudalism of the medieval West.

---

[116] Duby 1968, p. 286.
[117] The proportion 80% is calculated by combining Postan's data on the size-distribution of holdings (Postan 1972, p. 130) with Titow's calculation of the size of a 'subsistence plot' (Titow 1969). Conditions in the thirteenth-century English countryside would thus have been comparable to the condition of India's peasantry today, except that the possibilities of employment may have been greater.
[118] Blum 1968, p. 206.
[119] Marx 1971a, Volume 2, pp. 33–4; Marx 1978, p. 117.

2.6.3. *Commodity-feudalism as the pure form*

The greater intensity and more primitive character of the 'second serfdom' were thus closely conditioned by the real rhythms of economic activity implicit in the movement of population and currency. But this greater primitiveness should not be confused with a more backward development of feudal production. In this primitiveness of the 'second serfdom' we find, in fact, an important clue to the real logic of the feudal enterprise. In the West, which is generally characterised as the locus of a 'classical' feudalism, the estate attained its really classical structure, as defined earlier (p. 74 above), only sporadically, and then mainly in the period of 'high farming'; that is, as a temporary and even abrupt prelude to the long process of diversification which followed towards the close of the thirteenth century. Surveying the development of the feudal economy across the whole of this early epoch, it is undeniable that, as feudal enterprises, the estates in the medieval West possessed a far more fluid and diversified structure than those which sustained the second serfdom. There, labour-services were for at least two centuries (centuries central to the epoch of 'classical' feudalism), a less powerful pressure on the peasant's labour-time than the *seigneurie banale*, as Duby argues. Even in the brief outburst of high farming, when the estates turned to commodity-production and attempted to compress the sector of small-peasant production into totally subordinate reserves of serf-labour, the largest and best-organised estates, such as those of the Bishop of Winchester, continued to derive a major share of their income from more archaic monetary payments and from marriage and entry-fines. Thus, the form of organisation of labour based on the partial autonomy of small-peasant production persisted even in this phase of intensified labour-services. By contrast, in the central period of East-European feudalism, this distinction of forms was of practically no significance: the large mass of the peasantry were reduced to the position of 'serfs', i.e. bound by labour-services; and the character of feudal enterprise in these countries was typically far less fluid, far more bound up with the exploitation of 'serfs' than in the West some centuries earlier.

In other words, the feudal enterprise in the early epoch of so-called 'classical' feudalism *crystallised*, or acquired its truly classical form (with the labour-process reducing the sector of peasant-production to a reserve of simple reproduction), only sporadically; and then only rarely in its pure form. In the grain-exporting countries of the 'second serfdom', the predominant form of feudal enterprise was the developed form. The primitiveness and barbarity of their social relations were an expression of the maturity of feudal relations of production, of their relative purity.

The clue to this contrast lies in the origins of the 'second serfdom'. When the countries of Eastern Europe plunged into this epoch, a world-market was already in the process of formation. Merchant-capital had already established an important and expanding grain-trade, which, in the course of the fourteenth century, was progressively integrating the Baltic into a European division of labour.

Marx himself, and most later Marxists, assumed as a matter of course that 'feudalism' evolved by a simple progression from labour-services to monetary payments through an intermediate form of 'rent in kind'. But if, in order to explain the peculiar connection between the *purity* of the 'second serfdom' and its location in an emerging world-market, we return to the early patriarchal Europe of the Carolingian period, we find that labour-services were of practically no importance on the manors of Gaul, Germany, Flanders and Lombardy: in this vast region of early feudal Europe, the demesne utilised slave-labour, and the peasantry were exploited through payments in kind.[120] In a famous article, Kosminsky set out to show that the monetary payments which predominated in England much later were only partly the result of commutation, and that a certain proportion of these payments derived from a more archaic structure of money-rents.[121] In the debate on the 'transition', to make the point that market-relations did not accelerate the decay of forced labour in England, Dobb cited this article by Kosminsky; he argued that serfdom (labour-services) disappeared 'earliest' in the backward and commercially-remote regions of the north and west. But Kosminsky's thesis was different: in these backward regions, labour-services had probably never prevailed. Thus, both in England and on the Continent, there were substantial zones where labour-services had been of little importance originally, and where payments assumed the form of produce or money. In Kosminsky's terms, the structure of the manor evolved independently of any formative influence of payments in labour.

---

[120] Duby 1968, pp. 53–4; Duby 1973, pp. 51–2, 105.
[121] Kosminsky 1935.

Eastern Europe, in its own phase of backward patriarchal isolation, provides even clearer evidence. In Hungary, in the fifteenth century, the peasantry was exploited predominantly in the form of money-rents and produce-rents; Pach notes that a demesne-economy as such had barely developed at this stage.[122] Around this period, in Mecklenburg, Prussia, Bohemia, Poland and Russia feudal incomes derived, as in Hungary, mainly in the form of cash- and kind-payments.[123]

The significance of this fact is enormous. It suggests that not only did the *crystallisation* of feudal relations of production find its only true and widespread expression in the 'second serfdom' (i.e. the more backward eastern periphery of Europe); but the feudal estate only *crystallised* (i.e., acquired its developed, 'adequate' form) not in the relative isolation of a Europe cut off from markets and forced to depend on local production, but precisely when the estate itself assumed the character of a commodity-producing enterprise. Labour-services, Kosminsky had argued, were more strongly represented in the most populated and industrialised areas with the biggest markets.[124] That is to say, insofar as the feudal enterprise tended to *crystallise* in its pure form in the earlier epoch of feudalism, the context was an expanding market. The history of the 'second serfdom' substantiates this point, if only because the process of crystallisation here was neither held back nor obscured by the survival of a specifically small-peasant production, and by the correspondingly more fluid nature of the enterprise. As the countries of Eastern Europe were drawn into production for the emerging world-market or for an expanding domestic market (which was the case in Hungary), labour-services advanced rapidly against both earlier forms of payment. This type of exploitation was thus a later development, and it reached its maximum intensity in agricultural regions close to urban centres, (for example, the zones surrounding Moscow and St. Petersburg), or in the hinterland of the port cities and major trade-routes.[125] The chronological distribution of labour-services shows the same pattern. In the second half of the sixteenth century – to cite only one example – as cereal-prices in the port of Danzig increased on average by some 200% over

---

[122] Pach 1966.
[123] Blum 1957.
[124] Kosminsky 1935, p. 40.
[125] Confino 1963.

fifty years under the pressure of expanding exports, the volume of labour-time mobilised from a full-sized peasant-holding on the estates increased by over 400%. Every favourable price conjuncture intensified the drive to expand the demesne at the cost of small-peasant production and to increase the volume of disposable serf labour-time both directly by imposing heavier work obligations and indirectly by a policy of cutting the size of the peasant-plot. The process of evolution of the classical manor, which the countries of the West, in particular England, had experienced in a relatively mild and impure form, was destined to be repeated at higher levels of intensity, without the same impurities, in Prussia, Denmark, Poland and Hungary;[126] and, finally, Russia, in the period inaugurated by the 'revolution of the world-market' in the sixteenth century. Under the impact of successive commercial booms, the European dimensions of which were already evident as early as the fourteenth century,[127] the estates, formerly relying on produce in kind or, to a limited extent, rents in cash, converted small-peasant production into a reserve of simple reproduction: a process described by Pokrovsky as the serf-owner's leap into 'new and more complicated forms of production'.[128]

But this process was not peculiar to the countries of Eastern Europe: it had been known much earlier, not only, on a limited scale, in the West, but also in China; and was found at that time and later in the major countries of colonial Latin America. We know that in the major countries of Latin America the form which the feudal estate assumed was the *hacienda*. The *hacienda* was an enterprise 'always dependent on a fairly large market for its products'.[129] Both major phases of expansion of the *hacienda* in Chile, for example, coincided and were closely tied up with the expansion of demand for Chilean grain. The *hacendado* could expand his volume of sales in such periods only by transforming peasant production into feudally-subjugated simple reproduction. In the course of successive booms, the older *arrendatario* gradually disappeared from the countryside of central Chile, replaced by a new serf-population of *inquilinos* concentrated in the areas which produced for the wheat-market. Peasant-livestock rapidly disintegrated in this process, peasant-holdings degenerated into subsistence-plots, and the earlier more deeply differentiated structure of

---

[126] Kula 1970; Pach 1972.
[127] Bautier 1971, p. 192.
[128] Pokrovsky 1931, p. 116.
[129] Keith 1971, p. 435. Keith, however, sees the connection with the market as sufficient for calling the *hacienda* a 'capitalist institution'.

the peasant-population, separating more prosperous tenant-households from the remainder, collapsed into a more or less uniformly impoverished mass.[130] In China, the same tendencies are evident some ten centuries earlier. Here, already in the T'ang epoch, the big estate had become a common feature of rural economy; but, in that period, before the commercial boom of the eleventh century, the tenants [*tien-hu*] who worked these estates under the control of bailiffs were generally bound by payments in kind, equivalent to half the crop. On the Sung estates, especially those of the prosperous coastal provinces of the south where 'wheat was grown purely as a cash-crop for sale in the cities of the lower Yangtze area',[131] the same tenants were progressively bound by labour-services and their mobility restricted in law. A substantial number of Sung estates worked by these serf-households 'produced either regularly or intermittently for the market'.[132] The parallel between the condition of such Sung peasants and the serf-populations of Europe was sufficiently striking to make the Japanese Marxist historians who pioneered Sung economic history date the transition to feudalism in China precisely at this conjuncture, when the whole southern economy was transformed by the rapid growth of cities, expanding levels of monetary circulation, a vast boom in the grain-trade and the establishment of commercial links with Europe through the intermediary of Arab traders.

To summarise; we defined the classical or developed form of the feudal enterprise as one which necessarily implies the lord's complete control over the labour-process; that is, where small-peasant production no longer retains its former autonomy but now functions in the form of a sector of simple reproduction, sustaining surplus-production on the demesne. We argued that, both in Europe, and elsewhere through the vast epoch of feudal production, the estate acquired this developed structure only as a commodity-producing enterprise. When Frank witnessed the signs of this specific evolution in the colonial history of Latin America, where it was repeated in a definite series of cycles, he could understand it only by reconstructing the *hacienda* in the image of capital; thus entirely ignoring the specific laws of motion according to which such enterprises operated; laws deriving not from the compulsion

---

[130] Bauer 1971; 1972.
[131] Twitchett 1962, p. 31.
[132] Elvin 1973.

to accumulate, but from the compulsion to defend and improve social-consumption levels which rapidly lost their patriarchal (non-monetary) character, if they had had such a character to begin with. But, when Frank's critics quickly demolished this illusion, the formal-abstract premises from which they started led them to the conclusion that, 'on the contrary', the market was a factor of feudal 'consolidation'. This poses a final question, namely, the 'long duration' of this type of economy, or the problem of its decline.

2.6.4. *Modes of production as objects of long duration*

The 'long duration' is the least perceptible, and in a sense, the slowest of all forms of historical time. Its effectivity is staggered across centuries, and its reality only measurable on that scale. Insofar as Marx conceived of modes of production in a broader, more truly historical sense as 'epochs of production' or 'epochs in the economic development of society', he implied that they were objects of this order of magnitude.

Pirenne had argued that as commerce and the stock of money expanded, the old economy of subsistence and custom could no longer adjust to the new and more sophisticated levels of consumption; the nobles were forced to borrow and their régime disintegrated. Even earlier than Pirenne, Weber had posed the question in similar terms; for him, the 'immediate cause' of the breakdown of the 'manorial system' had been the development of market-operations and market-interests on the part of both lords and peasants, although the major impetus derived, in his view, from the nascent commercial bourgeoisie of the towns who promoted the dissolution of the manor because 'it limited their own market opportunities'.[133] As a collapse-theory, the Pirenne-Weber thesis was obviously wrong: over short conjunctures, most estates were clearly capable of adapting to the market and expanding incomes.[134] Expanding levels of demand and the growing weight of monetised consumption could be sustained over a cycle of short conjunctures by stepping up the rate of jurisdictional income; intensifying demesne-exploitation; substituting short-term leases or exacting entry-fines to siphon off the cash-holdings of more substantial peasants or to profit directly from inflation. Impressed by these short

---

[133] Weber 1961, p. 82.
[134] Cf. Painter 1943.

conjunctures in which the best estates in particular demonstrated their ability to prosper, Dobb concluded that the market was a factor of consolidation, and that the decline of feudalism lay 'within' the 'sphere' of production, in the static levels of labour-productivity which would eventually compel the lords to overexploit their serfs and reduce their rates of reproduction.[135] Neither Dobb nor Sweezy saw that, to make any sense at all, their respective 'theories' of feudal decline *posited each other*; and neither posed the question of the durational scale over which each position could hold true when integrated with the other. The 'market' and the 'overexploitation of serf-labour' were not relatively independent phenomena, or factors which simply 'interacted', as both Dobb and Sweezy conceded in their moments of generosity. They were *indissolubly linked* aspects of a single process, the 'long duration' of feudal production.

In large areas of Europe, and outside Europe, the feudal estate acquired its classical or developed form only as a commodity-producing enterprise. In countries such as Hungary, Poland, Russia, and later in certain parts of the colonial world, the expansion of a demesne-economy and labour-services which had formerly been of little or no significance, began directly with and under the pressure of an expanding demand for agricultural produce in local and international markets. This adjustment to the market suited both the serf-owners and the importers of grain. It suited the latter because, in the feudal economies, there was no specific limit of exploitation which posited a certain level of prices. The fact that any sale brought a 'profit' and the perpetual thirst for such 'profits' ensured an abundant supply of grain at low prices. The adjustment suited the serfowners because the expansion of the market itself implied higher levels of *monetised* feudal consumption. As feudal consumption inevitably lost its patriarchal character; as the lure of old models of consumption ceased or the civilising influences of an established nobility exerted a pressure of sophistication on the consumption-needs of cruder barbarian aristocracies; and as the monetary share of feudal consumption progressively expanded to a point where 'internal consumption' was of scarcely any importance – the thirst for cash became the dominant motive force of feudal production.

---

[135] Dobb 1963 [1946], p. 42.

This 'thirst for cash' in fact operated in all but the patriarchal periods of medieval history; those exceptional conjunctures where trade declined, towns reverted to villages, and consumption was predominantly of a natural character. Once a network of world commodity-exchanges was established, it became an even more pervasive, more powerful factor. Driven by this thirst for cash, which each fall in the value of currency intensified enormously, the nobility reacted to the market in two distinct phases. Initially, the slowly rising levels of grain-prices would have automatically adjusted the rate of exploitation in the peasants' favour, if, as was normally the case, the level of monetary payments which prevailed earlier tended to remain static. In this phase of slow inflation, the lord's first response would be a progressive readjustment of the level of payments to the level of prices. This was, for example, the initial reaction of most Russian landlords during the sixteenth century, when the Polish nobility not far away was already constructing the foundations of a demesne-economy. In Russia, 'the increase in cash *obrok* during this century just about kept pace with the fall in the purchasing power of the currency'.[136] But, even in these phases of a gradual upward movement of prices, there were more far-sighted serf-owners who, to preserve the level of their income, turned to production for the market. Feudal commodity-production might originate then as a purely defensive manoeuvre, as in England, where 'in the face of the tendency for prices to rise, a more or less static income encouraged borrowing in order to sustain a customary level of consumption.... The abandonment of leasing might be a step towards solvency and a means of safeguarding consumption standards'.[137] Then, as the inflation periodically accelerated, more and more estates would be drawn into production for the market; and this compulsion would be so much stronger where feudal rates of consumption, now expanding more quickly in money-terms, pushed against the limits of a low elasticity of surplus in peasant-production and a low velocity of circulation in local markets.

Under the pressure of successive inflationary conjunctures of this type, a new and distinct phase of feudal production would begin, a phase of crystallisation, with demesne-arable expanding by incursions into fallow, forests, pasture and grazing land. At low and generally static levels of productivity,

---

[136] Blum 1968, p. 221.
[137] Miller 1971, p. 11.

output was limited mainly by the extent of arable in cultivation; and the expansion of arable required a proportionate expansion of the disposable mass of labour-time. The construction of demesne-economy, the process through which the feudal enterprise acquired its adequate form, implied a series of sharp and brutal inroads into peasant-land and a vast project of mobilising labour-power from the surrounding villages. This unwritten history of the 'primitive accumulation' of feudal economy evokes its most striking expression in the 'second serfdom', only because in the countries of Eastern Europe and the Baltic, the relatively sudden nature of their integration into the emerging world-economy compacted the process into a matter of decades. Where labour-services had existed formerly, their specifically low weight, at most one day per week, implied a basic compatibility with small-scale production. In the phase of crystallisation, with the weight of these services rising by several hundred per cent over a few decades, small-peasant production would be more or less rapidly converted into pockets of simple reproduction. The division between the peasant's necessary and surplus labour-time would now be directly encapsulated in the distribution of arable, with the peasant's holding fluctuating around the limits of subsistence.

Within the framework of this classical feudal economy with its specifically feudal organisation of the labour-process, the basic obsession of estate-management remained as before the adjustment of rates of income to rates of consumption, but now magnified on the larger scale of a more labile monetary consumption. Where consumption had retained its patriarchal character, the rate of feudal income would have fluctuated sharply from one year to the next, because the level of technique was never sufficiently high to dominate and control the stochastic cycle of production. To overcome potentially vast disproportions, the productive capacity of the undeveloped patriarchal estate would have been organised to ensure outputs above the level of current (internal) consumption. Once the circulation of money impinged on the organisation of this patriarchal economy, the curve of the new monetised feudal consumption would show a slow upward trend punctuated by short spasms of expansion with every fall in currency-values. But with income dependent on commercial surpluses and computed as the product of price and output, the inverse movements of these variables such as characterised feudal conditions would tend to average out the rate of revenue from year to year.[138] As the

---

[138] Kula 1973, p. 76.

rate of productivity tended to constancy, prices were given exogenously and rates of consumption were inflexible downwards, the estate could respond to this growing crisis of profitability by heavy borrowings, by the liquidation of assets, or by increasing the volume of output, hence the surface in production and the mass of available labour-time. Yet each of these responses expressed tendencies of feudal disintegration, and the later they supervened in the long cycle of feudal-commodity economy, the more sharply were these tendencies revealed. When the consumption of the serfs already oscillated around a level of simple reproduction, that is, when the classical form of the feudal enterprise had already crystallised, every new drive to 'maximise sales' – that is, to push the level of serf-consumption *below* the existing limits of simple reproduction – would in the longer run radically shorten the periodicity of the old crises of subsistence and aggravate their intensity; it would thus depress the rate of reproduction of the serf-population to one degree or another.[139] The progressive indebtedness and bankruptcy of the lords, the liquidation and ever increasing mobility of feudal property (comprising, as one of its elements, the serf-population itself), the compulsion to expand the volume of output or to expand the field of feudal colonisation and the ever greater frequency of short-term subsistence-crises were basic long run *tendencies* of feudal production, the necessary expression of its specific laws of motion, present to one degree or another in all sectors of the feudal world.[140]

In this sketch of the long duration, it is impossible to produce an abstract separation between the 'market' and the 'process of production' as if these were 'factors' of decline. The inherent limits of the 'process of production' on which Dobb focussed in the debate were only revealed, i.e. only became effective

---

[139] Duby suggests that such a decline was already evident in Europe some four decades before the Plague. For further evidence of declining population well before the Plague, see Herlihy 1965.

[140] If we take the rural economy of Russia, for example, on the eve of the emancipation, it was characterised by (i) a predominance of landlords on the grain-market, (ii) a serf-population of which 70% had been mortgaged to government credit-bureaux, (iii) an absolute decline in the serf-population, (iv) a buoyant market in serf-labour; cf. Blum 1968, Chapters 20–1. It should be emphasised that the 'model' proposed *abstracts* from all supplementary and contingent factors in order to reveal the process in its essential form: notably, it abstracts from (a) the intervention of the state, which could radically modify or restrain this whole process, as in China or Byzantium, (b) the crises specific to the old biological time, e.g., the Black Death which inaugurated the decay of feudal economy in the West, (c) the territorial expansion of capitalist powers.

as *limits*, in the context of expanding commodity-production or its underlying thirst for cash. Moreover, if, as Sweezy argued, the market was a factor of feudal disintegration, it could become so on the basis of the specific laws of motion of feudal economy, and only in the long run. In this sense, the debate argued from false premises, because the question which it posed posited a 'process of production' divorced from the specific character of feudal consumption, and a process of exchange devoid of any compulsion to exchange.

2.6.5. *Two brief conclusions*

To relate this short discussion more closely to the themes mentioned earlier: (i) Although it is in some sense quite self-evident and banal, the distinction between 'modes of production' and 'social formations' that is generally drawn in most recent Marxist literature may actually obscure and mystify the mechanisms of modes of production. For it is a fact that, even in its crystallised form, the feudal enterprise was sustained by a variety of forms of labour, comprising domestic servants who were legally slaves and who often undertook the principal tasks, especially ploughing; day-labourers who were housed separately on the estate; part-time hired workers recruited from the impoverished peasantry, free tenants who performed seasonal or supplementary services; and the serf-population as normally understood, i.e. villeins bound by labour-services. The slaves and hired labourers who intervened in this type of economy were as much part of specifically *feudal relations of production* as the serf-population itself. Their intervention did not signify the persistence or emergence of other relations of production ('slavery'; capitalism), and did not therefore imply an 'articulation' of several distinct 'modes of production'. Consistent with the logic of his definitions, Dobb was, however, forced to argue on these lines; the fact, that, on the thirteenth-century English estates which turned to commodity-production, the lords made increasing use of hired labour, signified for him the emergence of a 'new', i.e., capitalist, mode of production. If Dobb had really believed this, the debate on the transition would have had to deal with a second problem: not only the decline of feudal economy, but the decline, in fact collapse, of the barely established capitalist one. For as we know, this phase of commodity-production with hired labour was rapidly superseded in the history of Western Europe; and, as Dobb himself argued, the feudal enterprise preserved its dominance, in progressively modified forms, for at least another two centuries. Relations of exploitation based on the dispossession of labour, on the commodity labour-power, become capitalist relations of production only when we can posit the capitalist enterprise in one of its varied forms. Marx makes the point indirectly when he writes: 'if a nobleman brings the free worker together with his serfs, even if he re-sells a part of the worker's product, and the free worker thus creates value for him, then this exchange takes place only... for the sake of superfluity, for luxury consumption'.[141] In other words, *hired labour functions in this economy as an expression of specifically feudal relations of production*, the motive-force of which lies in the social-consumption needs of the owners of the feudal enterprise; it functions in an economy in which the production of commodities is itself only a mediation of consumption. (ii) The idea of world-economy as already dominated from its inception by the requirements of capital-reproduction is a false abstraction. To put the argument in its crudest form: the initial impulse which sustained the vast network of world commodity-exchanges before the eighteenth century derived from the expanding consumption-requirements of the lords. Moreover, at its inception the colonisation of Latin America was a *feudal* colonisation, a response to the crisis of feudal profitability which all the landowning classes of Europe were facing down to the latter part of the sixteenth century. In the Baltic and Eastern Europe, this crisis was partly overcome by territorial expansion into contiguous areas, and then displaced by the production of grain for export; but, in the maritime periphery of Europe, in Spain and Portugal where this feudal crisis recurred with periodic sharpness, it expressed itself in a movement of *overseas*-colonisation. The Spain which launched this movement of expansion was a Spain dominated by feudalism, but a feudalism in crisis. This thesis is not, of course, new: it was proposed by Vilar many years ago, when he described Spanish imperialism as the highest stage of feudalism;[142] and intimated some years later by Marian Małowist, when he asked whether the Spanish colonisation was not, to a certain extent, 'the result of a depression in rural economy and a sudden drop in the revenues of the nobility'.[143] The forms which this widespread feudal crisis took in different sectors of Europe, its specific local intensity, and the means used to overcome it are

---

[141] Marx 1973, p. 469.
[142] Vilar 1971.
[143] Małowist 1972, p. 106.

matters for investigation by historians. Suffice it to say that the crisis of feudal profitability not only unleashed movements of internal colonisation in Europe itself, in the land-locked territories; but the first major 'imperialist' conquest; and, if we examine the question more closely, those bastardised forms of *capitalist* production which prevailed in the colonial plantations, the profits from which enabled many bankrupt noble families to re-establish their economic position.

2.7. Simple-commodity production: a 'determination of form'

2.7.1. *The peasant mode of production*

The historical roots of the varied forms of simple-commodity production lie in the patriarchal-subsistence mode of production based on small-scale parcellised property and the exploitation of family-labour.[144] This connection is important because when simple-commodity production arises, the economic logic of the more archaic patriarchal enterprise *continues to dominate this form of production*. The chief expression of this fact is that products are sold without regard to price of production. According to Marx,

> [The small peasant operating in this mode] regards the expenditure of labour as the indispensable prerequisite for the labour-product, which is the thing that interests him above all. But, as regards his surplus-labour, after deducting the necessary labour, it is evidently realized in the surplus product; and as soon as he can sell the latter or use it for himself, he looks upon it as something that cost him nothing, because it cost him no materialized labour.... Even a sale below value and the capitalist price of production still appears to him as profit.[145]

It follows that 'for the peasant owning a parcel, the limit of exploitation is not set by the average profit of capital.... The absolute limit for him...is no more than the wages he pays to himself, after deducting his actual costs. *So long*

---

[144] The form was variously called the 'rural-patriarchal system of production' by Marx 1970, p. 33; 'die Kleinproduktion in der Landwirtschaft' by Engels (letter to Danielson 15 March 1892, in Marx and Engels 1968, p. 304); and the 'peasant mode of production' by Kautsky 1970, p. 317.

[145] Marx 1971a, Volume 3, p. 690; Marx 1981, p. 829.

as the price of the product covers these wages, he will cultivate his land, and often at wages down to a physical minimum'.[146] 'It is not necessary, therefore, that the market price rise either up to the value or the price of production of his product. This is one of the reasons why grain prices are lower in countries with predominant small peasant landownership than in countries with a capitalist mode of production'.[147] In Kautsky's conception, based on these passages of Marx, this 'incomplete remuneration for the labour-power expended' was, as Lenin notes, 'the distinguishing feature of small production'. 'As long as the peasant remains a simple commodity producer, he can be satisfied with the standard of living of the wage-worker; he needs neither profit nor rent; he can pay a higher price for land than the capitalist entrepreneur'.[148] In short, simple-commodity production internalises the patriarchal logic of the subsistence mode of production, much as feudalism does in its own way. Outputs are sold as a function of subsistence, and dissociated from any mechanism of 'rational' cost-calculation. In this devalorisation of labour-time lies the specific advantage of all small-scale forms of production threatened with extinction by the capitalistically produced commodity. In the epoch of capitalism, as Kautsky argued in *Die Agrarfrage*, 'overwork' and 'underconsumption' become the twin slogans of the peasant-economy.

2.7.2. *The simple-commodity producer as wage-slave*

As a pure form, simple-commodity production is a form of economy of a purely subordinate and transitional character, in which: (i) the labour-process preserves its patriarchal character, with the predominance of the self-sufficient peasant family-labour farm as the basic enterprise of production. (ii) The producing households preserve not only their self-sufficiency, transforming only their surplus into commodities,[149] but their independence as the basic agents of the productive process, chiefly expressed in their freedom to allocate labour-time between commercial production and immediate consumption, and between the different types of commercial production. (iii) The system of accounting retains a specifically patriarchal, subsistence-based interpretation

---

[146] Marx 1971a, Volume 3, p. 805–6; Marx 1981, pp. 941–2.
[147] Marx 1971a, Volume 3, p. 806; Marx 1981, p. 942.
[148] Lenin 1964a, p. 124; Kautsky 1970, p. 365.
[149] Marx 1968, p. 302.

of 'costs' and 'profits', as noted above; here the 'limit of exploitation' is equal, in principle, to the costs of simple reproduction. (iv) Subsistence remains the goal of production, even in those limiting cases where the whole of household labour-time is absorbed in commercial production. (v) As the co-efficient of marketed output rises and the monetary components of the labour-income expand, the volume of sales will tend to vary inversely with the movement of prices (the 'backward-sloping supply-curve' thus typically characterises households in this position). (vi) Fluctuations of the market introduce a process of differentiation among simple-commodity producers, which, in the first instance, remains a differentiation of *wealth*, in other words, preserves its historical content as a differentiation of simple-commodity producers.[150]

As Marx and Lenin were aware, the subordination of the simple-commodity mode of production to the power of capital converts this mode into the embryonic basis of specifically capitalist production, but a capitalist production which retains the determinate organisation of labour specific to the 'precapitalist' enterprise. Marx describes this process perhaps more rigorously in the following passage than anywhere else:

> [The] exchange of equivalents proceeds; it is only the surface layer of a production which rests on the appropriation of alien labour *without exchange*, but with the *semblance of exchange*. This system of exchange rests on *capital* as its foundation, and, when it is regarded in isolation from capital, as it appears on the surface, as an independent system, then it is a mere illusion, but a *necessary illusion*.[151]

Let us examine this process more closely.

The subjugation of the simple-commodity form of production to capital proceeds inevitably within the limits imposed by the prevailing organisation of production. Capital's struggle to dominate the enterprise of simple-commodity producers – to determine the type, quality and volume of its commercial output – posits as its basis the limitations imposed on its own elasticity by a labour-process not determined by itself; in which, therefore the enterprise of small producers retains its independence, if only as a formal determination ('quasi-independence').[152] Domination over the labour-process becomes

---

[150] Lenin 1963a, pp. 482–3.
[151] Marx 1973, p. 510.
[152] Lenin 1956, p. 473, 'quasi-independent producers'.

impossible on this basis, within these limits of quasi-independence, without those mechanisms which uproot the patriarchal sufficiency of the small enterprise. The compulsory enforced destruction of the small producer's self-sufficiency figures here as the necessary foundations for the dominance of capital.[153]

It follows that in this articulation, except at the limit where the enterprise effectively ceases to exist, where its formal independence is converted into the complete dependence of free labour on capital, the capitalist's control over the labour-process retains a partial and sporadic character. Frequent adulterations of the crop, as with the cotton produced in western India in the 1860s; smuggling on the open market, as with poppy grown in Bengal much earlier; restrictions in the volume of output, such as the colonial bureaucracies persistently feared; and the switching to more 'profitable' cash-crops, reflect this partial and unstable character of the capitalist's control.

Yet, *within the limits* of such control, continually re-established on the basis of various coercive forms of exploitation, the relations of production which tie the enterprise of small-commodity producers to capital are already relations of *capitalist* production. Between the market and the small producer, capital intervenes with the determinate forms and specific functions of both merchant and industrial capital (as in the slave-plantations, two radically distinct 'determinate forms' merge). In this process, two enterprises are thus present, a quasi-mercantile capitalist enterprise,[154] which figures solely as a *unit of production* (as defined earlier) without the labour-process specific to its mode of production; and an enterprise of formally independent small producers functioning according to its own *labour-process*, inherited from the conditions of a patriarchal economy, and according to its own *economic conceptions*, also patriarchal in their determination, but no longer as a totally independent unit of production. The social process of production incorporating the immediate labour-process of the small-peasant enterprise is governed by the aims of

---

[153] Lenin derived the small producer's dependence from the inherently monopsonistic position of merchant-capital in conditions of large-scale marketing, Lenin 1956, p. 387. He spoke of 'a necessary causal connection between small production for the market and the domination of merchant capital', *ibid.*, p. 389.

[154] The now classic examples of this form of enterprise are: the Société Commerciale de l'Ouest Africain; the Compagnie Française d'Afrique Occidentale; the United Africa Company; The British East Africa Corporation; Ralli Brothers; the Assam Company; Binny & Co.; Boustead & Co.

capitalist production; namely, by the compulsion to produce surplus-value. Within this social process of production dominated by the capitalist enterprise, the economic conceptions of the small households, and their formal possession of a portion of the means of subsistence, enter as *regulating elements* only as a function of the law of *surplus-value production*. The patriarchal notions of accounting, which dissociate the range of acceptable market-prices from the price of production, and the autonomous internally subsidised reproduction of labour-power which, from the perspective of the process as a whole, ensures a sale of labour-power below its value, enable capital to depress wages 'in a fashion unequalled elsewhere', as Engels noted.[155]

When we regard the simple-commodity enterprise articulated to capital, no longer as an independent unit of production imposing its own laws of motion on the process of production, but as a quasi-enterprise with the specific social function of wage-labour (in the strict sense, value-producing labour); in other words, when following Marx's method, we have correctly 'determined its form',[156] some conclusions are immediately evident. In the first place, the 'price' which the producer receives is no longer a pure category of exchange, but a category, that is, a relation, of production, a concealed wage. Behind the superficial 'surface' sale of products, peasants under this form of domination sell their labour-power. Secondly, the monopsonistic determination of 'prices' under this system, or the fact that the contracts which fix this price may often also stipulate the volume of output required and its specific quality, are necessary expressions of the capitalist's 'command over labour power'.[157] The more perceptive colonial administrators regarded such contracts 'as of the same kind as one between a capitalist and a worker'.[158]

---

[155] Engels to Bebel, 11 December, 1884.
[156] Cf. Rubin 1972, p. 37ff., for this principle of *Formbestimmtheit* in Marx. Translating the central thesis of the essay into these terms, we could say: forms of exploitation derive their specific historical 'social forms' and 'functions' from the relations of production which they mediate or which are embodied in them. When simple abstractions are confused for concrete categories, when they are not yet subjected to a process of further abstraction which is a process of their concretisation, the specific forms and functions which compose their historical content in any given situation are left 'indeterminate'. We can see, therefore, that there is a close and essential connection between Marx's pages on the 'method of political economy' in the *Grundrisse* (where the notions of 'simple' and 'concrete' categories figure) and the principle of 'form-determination', which figures in a practical way in the analysis of money.
[157] Chowdhury 1964, pp. 129–34.
[158] Chowdhury 1964, p. 162.

Finally, subsistence-production now figures, under this system, as the specific *form of reproduction of labour-power* within a capitalist process of production. It becomes misleading, therefore, to regard it as a specific, separate mode of production (e.g., a 'domestic mode of production') in a system of modes of production dominated by capitalism. This was, after all, the illusion which Lenin polemicised against so vigorously in his earlier writings against Narodnism, repeatedly making the point that capitalism always takes the 'technical process of production' *as it finds it*. Yet this illusion is today widespread in the neopopulist currents of 'Third-World political economy' which paradoxically end up by reconstituting the thesis of 'dual economy' at the very centre of their analyses, now in a Marxist terminology and with slight modifications of the original premises.[159]

In the colonial period, capitalistically-subjugated simple-commodity production, or, more precisely, capitalist production which is mediated through an internalised 'simple-commodity producing' enterprise, accounted for a major share of colonial output, when the latter did not derive from commodity-feudal estates or capitalist slave-plantations. The economy of whole sectors of the colonial world – West Africa, Uganda, Mozambique, Bengal, Burma, Cambodia – was dominated by this backward form of capitalist production *at its various stages of crystallisation*.[160] In one of his very last references to colonial questions, Marx wrote that, with their integration into the world-economy, the earlier forms of production which had prevailed in India, China, Egypt disintegrated but that this process of disintegration was not initially 'apparent'.[161] The colonial peasants integrated into commodity-production by a process called 'forced commercialisation' entered capitalist relations of production behind the backs of their existing forms of production: here, capitalist production thus retained a 'surface layer', an 'appearance' of superseded forms of economy, the peasants 'retained the external attributes of independent

---

[159] There is no obvious reason why the 'dual-economy' thesis could not be modified to incorporate the image of a 'traditional sector' not simply coexisting with the 'modernising' one, but actually relating to it through various forms of dependence and domination. In this sense, Laclau's critique of Frank (Laclau 1971) and Arrighi's critique of Barber (Arrighi 1970) do not actually transcend the thesis, but only render it more sophisticated.

[160] For historically concrete analyses of this form, see Chowdhury 1964; Mamdani 1976.

[161] Marx 1971a, Volume 2, p. 36; Marx 1978, p. 120.

producers',[162] and the forms of reproduction of labour-power retained the appearance of distinct, even if 'dependent', forms of production.

Thus, late nineteenth-century colonialism acquired a paradoxical character. In the midst of societies of apparently 'ageless stagnation', those that Marx called 'peasant nations',[163] a form of capitalistic production had already begun to establish a fairly deep local penetration. The capitalism that evolved on the foundations of small-commodity production differed from the classical or adequate form of capitalist production in several fundamental ways. In the industrialising sectors of the world-economy, the rule of capital depended crucially on the dispossession of labour from all means of subsistence, or on the constitution of a *labour-market*. Wakefield, conscious of this, would advocate an identical programme for the white colonies. Even in the 'peasant nations' such as Egypt or India, there were sections of the bureaucracy that saw the proletarianisation of the peasantry as a certain and inevitable fate, as a process that had begun under its own rule and one that would proceed with the force of a natural law. This was one way of imparting a historical function to the famines that began to hit the peasantry more and more frequently towards the closing decades of that century.

But, in these 'peasant nations', capital followed a less obvious or more deceptive trajectory. As it happens, it was in a note to one of Wakefield's comments on the depressed condition of the Irish peasantry that Marx summed up this fundamental fact. He wrote, 'In this case profit is called rent, *just as it is called interest when, for example, as in India*, the worker (although nominally independent) works with advances he receives from the capitalist and has to hand over all the surplus produce to the capitalist'.[164] By 'worker' Marx meant, of course, the peasant himself, and by 'capitalist', the monied bourgeoisie of moneylenders and merchants through whom the small producer was brought into relation with the market.

In 1859, Marx already implied that this relation was basically a capitalist one, but then with some uncertainty. Referring to the 'advance system', he wrote, 'In these cases, however, money functions only in the familiar form of means of purchase and therefore requires no new definition'. But he added,

---

[162] Preobrazhensky 1965, p. 186.
[163] Marx 1971b, p. 487.
[164] Marx 1971b, p. 188.

'Of course, *capital too is advanced in the form of money and it is possible that the money advanced is capital advanced...*'.[165] It makes a lot of difference which of these conceptions we accept, for, as Marx himself says, the latter 'does not lie within the scope of simple circulation'. That is to say, the 'advance' which a moneylender makes to the peasant is an advance of *capital* in the form of an advance of a certain sum of money or of the material elements of circulating capital (e.g., seed) and thus bearing the deceptive or illusory appearance of a pure 'loan'. Within a few years, it was this conception that Marx came around to accepting. Under this system, he wrote later, 'the producer pays the capitalist his surplus labour in the form of interest', or the capitalist receives his profit in the form of interest, so that 'We have here the whole of *capitalist production* without its advantages...'.[166] That is, the labour-process, still being a process specific to the form of small-scale parcellised peasant-production, allowed no scope for a production of relative surplus-value or for the technical renovations presupposed therein. It follows also that domination by capital in this specific form (by a monied bourgeosie) would force capital outwards in its drive to self-expand, force capital to extend the sphere of its domination *laterally*, to draw into its network an ever-growing mass of peasant-households .

This would explain why so many of the peasant-struggles of this period (e.g., the Deccan Riots of 1875) were directed against the monied bourgeoisie and not against the colonial state, in which sections of the peasantry would in fact see a potential benefactor. But, again, because this was likewise a form of capitalist production that depended not on the constitution and automatic functioning of a labour-market, but on the coercive subjugation of the small-commodity producer, the later historical empiricism of the Marxist tradition would simply isolate and concentrate on these relatively superficial elements of coercion and entirely ignore the inner content of the relationships they sustained. The widespread myth of 'semi-feudalism' is one of the legacies of this illusion.[167]

[1977]

---

[165] Marx 1970, p. 140.
[166] Marx 1971b, p. 487.
[167] I shall argue this in detail elsewhere, on the basis of the superbly informative British sources that cover this period for India. (See Chapter 10 below.)

Chapter Three
Historical Arguments for a 'Logic of Deployment' in 'Precapitalist' Agriculture

To the memory of Dave Rosenberg (1940–84)

In this essay I produce historical arguments for 'suspending belief' in the hypothesis of discontinuity, by which I mean the conception that the real or alleged differences between economic régimes and historical periods are in some sense (never explicitly discussed) more fundamental to their historical interpretation than the factors which they share in common. Part One challenges the notion that the different economic epochs are each characterised by a predominant type of labour-relation, for example the ancient world by slavery. Part Two looks very rapidly at the work of some medieval historians to extract the general postulate that the agriculture of any given period is characterised by a complex and differentiated use of labour. Finally, in the concluding pages I take up sharecropping and permanent farm contracts, referring mainly to India. The logical next step, after an essay of this sort, would be to look at the issue of managerial control in agriculture but in this paper I have sedulously avoided this massive subject.

3.1. Part I

I shall begin with the sort of rural economy presumed by the Elder Cato in the early years of the second century B.C. His *De agricultura* is the earliest agricultural treatise to survive in full and must have circulated widely even if improving landowners would soon have access to a translated (Latin) version of the monumental twenty-eight volumes by Mago of Carthage.[1] The permanent labour force of the farm is composed, clearly, of slaves, subject to the authority of an estate-manager-cum-general supervisor called the *vilicus*. But the farm's supply of labour depends crucially on the buying and selling of labour-power. This is obvious at the very start because one of the factors which should influence the decision of a prospective buyer is the availability of local labour.[2] It is also evident in another way: for a middle-sized olive-plantation, Cato gives us a manning ratio of thirteen slaves to every 240 *iugera*, that is, one slave to about eleven acres. In the slave-economy of the Caribbean, slave densities were at least five times higher, since the standard ratio was one slave for every two acres.[3] The slaves are an overhead cost; to run the farm profitably thus requires close control over the level and distribution of work-loads. To formalise control, Cato recommends an early version of prime-cost accounting – a device which he calls *ratio operum operarumque* – that is, a balance-sheet concerned specifically with jobs, their requirements of labour, and the amount of work actually accomplished.[4] With slave-labour, the essential requirement is continuity. They are like the expensive fixed capital equipment of modern refineries – a form of value which demands continuous operation.[5]

The owner runs a commercial enterprise, therefore storage-capacity is crucial since prices fluctuate and he must always sell at the best possible price. The hiring of labour proceeds in at least two distinct forms – by subcontracting jobs which require large inputs of seasonal labour, so the owner does not deal directly with the work-force – and by hiring labourers on a casual or semi-

---

[1] Heurgon 1976, on translations of Mago's work.
[2] Cato, *De agricultura*, 1.3: *operariorum copia*.
[3] Dunn 1973, p. 89, 'The Barbadians held one slave for every 2 acres, the standard ratio for effective sugar production throughout the Caribbean in the seventeenth and eighteenth centuries'. Cf. Sheridan 1961, p. 343. Contrast Cato, *De agricult.*, 10.1.
[4] Cato, *De agricult.*, 2.2.
[5] Vatin 1987 is the best recent discussion of continuity (with reference to flow-processes).

permanent basis. For the subcontract, Cato even drafts a series of model-agreements to give the owner the best possible terms in the bargain. The agreement specifies that the owner reserves the right to supervise the operation, e.g. the harvesting of olives, that no payment will be made unless the employees swear that nothing has been stolen, that ladders must be returned in good condition, that the contractor will furnish the requisite number of gatherers and pickers, for example, fifty active workers, two-thirds of them pickers. One of the most interesting clauses in the draft agreement is the following: 'No one shall form a combination for the purpose of raising the contract price for harvesting and milling olives, unless he names his associate at the time.' Finally, Cato designs a bonus-scheme to stimulate work-effort.[6] The use of hired labour is a standard presumption in the sort of countryside described by Cato. He has at least three terms for casual labourers, two of which refer to day-labourers, while one refers to a type of wage-worker who, in later periods of Italian agrarian history, were usually called *compartecipanti* or *centisti*, that is, workers employed for a sequence of operations up to and including threshing and paid on an incentive or 'share' basis (not sharecroppers, however).[7] In a somewhat mysterious sentence, Cato seems to imply that landowners should as far as possible retain their casual labour on daily contracts. Since the *politor*, the worker hired for a succession of operations, is included in the list, the sentence obviously cannot mean that owners should as far as possible avoid hiring the same casual workers for longer than a day.[8]

To conclude: the commercialised estate-economy described by Cato is based on what a recent German dissertation calls 'a flexible combination of different labour systems'.[9]

Large reserves of free labour were available to employers in the ancient Mediterranean and there is really no basis for Max Weber's supposition that such labour declined in relative importance.[10] Weber was deeply committed

---

[6] Cato, *De agricult.*, 144.
[7] Cf. Dongus 1969, p. 197, discussing Venice and Ferrara. The permanent labourers, by contrast, were called *trecentisti*.
[8] Cato, *De agricult.*, 5.4: *Operarium, mercennarium, politorem diutius eundem ne habeat die*, translated as 'must not hire the same day worker (etc.) for longer than a day'.
[9] Oehme 1988.
[10] E.g., Weber 1924a, p. 244 where he says of the Republican period, 'Allen diese freien Arbeiter...schrumpften immer mehr an relativer Bedeutung zusammen' (see Weber 1976, p. 325). Contrast Brunt 1980.

to the view that slave-labour was the basis of classical culture and that its decline catastrophically hastened the evolution of a postclassical world. The idea of the predominance of a specific *type* of labour as the fundamental institution of an entire historical period is, of course, common to him and to Marx. Roman employers were more practical, however, and behaved not as Weberians and Marxists expect them to but exactly as employers tend to behave – adapting the use of labour to their requirements and to the conditions of the local labour-market. I shall characterise this sort of behaviour and its historical workings as a 'logic of deployment' and argue that the description of this logic is more fundamental to a history of agrarian relations than the alleged peculiarities of historical *mentalités*.

A famous passage in Varro is underpinned by a logic of this sort.[11] In the closing years of the Republic, he divided the rural labour-force of the Mediterranean into two essential types – slave-labour and free labour – and then subdivided free labour into three categories – impoverished family-farms, hired workers and people working under debt-contracts. He then suggested, 'With regard to these in general this is my opinion: it is more profitable to work unwholesome lands [districts infested by malaria, J.B.] with hired hands than with slaves; and even in wholesome places it is more profitable to carry out the heavier farm operations, such as the vintage or harvest, with hired labour'. In other words, in an agriculture characterised by sharp seasonal fluctuations in the demand for labour, it would make no economic sense for employers to maintain large reserves of permanent farm-labour, whether slaves or free workers, unless they were not going to find workers at all during the peak-seasons. As Peter Brunt says, 'it would have been wasteful to maintain slaves for industrial or commercial operations that did not provide continuous employment'.[12] Now the rationality at work here, one which determined the use of labour on hundreds of individual estates *and* the structure of the labour-force as a whole, is what I have called the 'logic of deployment'. As long as free labour existed, the ways in which landowners organised production were bound to reflect an essential flexibility. Within the limits imposed by the availability of free labour, *employers could shift back and forth between different types of deployment*. Yet the possibility of such 'reversible shifts' con-

---

[11] Varro, *Res Rusticae*, I.xvii.2–3.
[12] Brunt 1980, p. 93.

tradicts what one might call the theory of the fixed line of evolution whose essential idea is the notion that paid labour succeeds the other – unpaid – forms of labour in a specific sequence arising out of their dissolution.

3.2. Part II

Flexibility in the use of labour has been repeatedly documented in studies of individual estates. For example, in his work on the estates of Ramsey Abbey, Raftis wrote, 'The account rolls reveal that workers were necessary in large numbers on the arable manors of Ramsey.'[13] Among medievalists, Postan's work was by far the most compelling contribution to a logic of deployment, drastically undermining the dogmas of evolutionism.[14] His attack on the fixed line of evolution created enough conviction to win over Marxists like Kosminsky.[15] Flexibility was conceded in general terms even by the more orthodox students of manorial organisation. For example, Bloch agreed, 'In principle, a lord had three categories of labour to draw on, and in practice used them all...he might pay labourers to work for him, he might own slaves, and he might exact services from his tenants'.[16] Kosminsky, of course, was much less hesitant. A whole chapter of *Studies in the Agrarian History of England in the Thirteenth Century* is devoted to the issue of the 'supply of labour'. 'It is evident that wage labour played in the thirteenth century countryside a very important part, far more important than...historians have allowed.' Generalising from the use of paid labour on thirteenth-century manors, Kosminsky noted that here, in the heart of feudal England, in its most characteristic enterprises, 'we usually find a combination of several forms of labour', and pointed out that 'The agricultural treatises of the thirteenth century noted this coexistence of several systems of labour organization'.[17]

---

[13] Raftis 1957; Raftis continues, 'Indeed, these wage labour groups were not incomparable with the numbers found in regions with a negligible villeinage tradition'. In short, the supply of serf-labour made no discernible difference to the lords' demand for wage-labour.
[14] The classic essay is Postan 1937, reprinted with revisions in Minchinton 1968.
[15] Cf. Kosminsky 1956, p. 177f.
[16] Bloch 1973, p. 66.
[17] Kosminsky 1956, pp. 295, 308–9. The chapter in question is Chapter 6, 'The Supply of Labour on the English Manor in the Thirteenth Century'.

Now what Postan did was to use the more static picture of the distribution of labour-services between estates and parts of the country as a basis for building a more purely historical theory of their actual evolution over time. 'The Chronology of Labour Services' showed why one could no longer accept the usual assumption of the 'gradual disappearance of labour services under the pressure of an expanding money economy'. 'If services were disappearing with the growth of money economy, how is it that in the more backward parts of the country, farthest from great markets, above all in the north-west, labour services were shed first, while the more progressive south-east retained them longest?' Postan then suggested that the crucial variable behind the pattern of distribution was the scale of operations, since this directly influenced the demand for labour. In other words, 'labour services vary from manor to manor and...the variations reflect the differences in the relative sizes of the demesne'. He then added, 'But if this is the true logic of the labour services, it should account not only for differences between them, but also for their evolution'.[18]

Thus, the form of labour-organisation was decisively influenced by commercial decisions about the scale on which to operate and the possibility of doing so profitably with one type of labour or another. Behind the apparent determinisms of economic life, the inflexible evolution of whole forms of economy, were countless concrete decisions about the use of labour.

The increasing exaction of labour-services in the great 'reaction' of the thirteenth century need not, of course, imply that estates were reducing their dependence on paid labour, since the *total* demand for labour could increase sufficiently to allow for a growing and simultaneous employment of both types of labour. The mechanics of this decision-making process was a subject Postan came back to only after the war, in the famous essay on 'The *Famulus*: The Estate Labourer in the Twelfth and Thirteenth Centuries'. Disregarding exceptional types of manors where the entire labour-force might consist of wage-labourers (notably the grange-manors),

> on most ordinary manors...the two forms of labour were employed simultaneously. On such estates customary services of villeins and the labour of hired men were in a sense alternative, for on most of them the landlords

---

[18] Postan 1937, pp. 76, 78.

possessed a freedom of choice. The manner in which they in fact exercised this choice, i.e., the proportion in which they chose to employ their villeins and their servants, was bound to differ from estate to estate and from year to year....Yet behind all the local and periodical vagaries of the lord's choice, it is possible to discern a broad administrative principle.

The description which then follows is crucial to a logic of deployment. Postan disaggregates the use of labour by *groups of operations* and emphasises the peculiar requirements of each. Seasonal and discontinuous operations with large inputs of labour were sustained through the dues of customary tenants, that is, labour-services. Operations which demanded continuous application throughout the season and throughout the working week required permanent functionaries. Collective and seasonal occupations like threshing and winnowing were done by hired labourers working for day-wages or on piece-rates. 'Ploughing itself was of course a seasonal occupation, but the ploughing seasons were fairly long, and work during the seasons had to be as continuous as weather allowed...' and, for this, most estates employed a permanent nucleus of ploughmen throughout the year. Postan concluded, '[t]aken as a whole, the evidence of records creates a strong impression that the use of hired labour was more general than the superficial reading of surveys might suggest'.[19]

To summarise: the differentiation of types of labour depended crucially on the requirements and characteristics of the essential operations. If one can generalise this, one might say that in agriculture the use of labour is task-specific, and that substitutions between types of labour depend not only on the level of labour-costs but, even more fundamentally, on the task-composition of individual crops and on the actual or perceived appropriateness of particular types of labour to particular tasks. For example, a recent study of mechanisation in Punjab shows that 88% of the total female labour used in improved-variety wheat cultivation is deployed in harvesting, almost none in irrigation, and negligible amounts in sowing and threshing. Moreover, the bulk of these women are casual labourers. On the other hand, only a minority of wheat-farms actually made use of women's labour, and the total input of female labour in Punjab wheat cultivation was in fact less than 10%.[20] When

---

[19] Postan 1954, esp. pp. 2–3.
[20] Agarwal 1983, p. 56, table 10.

we turn to rice, the picture is dramatically different. Between 46% to 50% of the total labour-time is due to female casual labour (this is true of Andhra and Tamilnadu but not of Orissa where the proportion is only 17% because most of the work is monopolised by males), with the bulk of the labour spread between three groups of operations (sowing/transplanting, weeding and harvesting).[21]

The reaction of the estates to the commercial boom of the thirteenth century underlines the centrality of decisions on employment. Paid and unpaid labour were both complementary and alternative. To describe the option for one or the other as the sign of a more or less 'feudal' mentality badly underestimates the weight of purely economic reasoning in the calculations of the landowners. Let me look very rapidly at Hungary.[22] Hungarian landlords developed their manors in three distinct phases. Phase l, the latter half of the fifteenth century, was characterised by the near non-existence of labour services, a limited use of hired labour and the predominance of money-rents. In Phase 2, which started c.1520, landlords were stimulated to expand their demesnes, and Pach tells us that the 'evolution of the demesne system also led to the more or less widespread use of hired labour'. Scales of production were being expanded commercially, and 'the landlord needed paid labour for almost every kind of work'. Then, c.1580 and in the early decades of the seventeenth century, in a third phase, the various forms of paid labour began to be phased down and the demand for labour met by the increasing exaction of unpaid labour-services. So here is a paradigm-case of the 'reversible shift', with forced labour succeeding paid labour in a movement exactly contrary to the one expected. And, of course, the expansion of labour-services was rooted in a drive to reduce labour-costs, since redeployment converted paid into unpaid labour. In other words, the controlling influence was a purely economic rationality.

In reorganising labour to sustain bulk levels of commercial production, the landlords of Central and Eastern Europe were doing more than simply responding to the commercial incentives of Dutch capitalism, they were in the process of organising an effective labour-system with all the characteristics

---

[21] Agarwal 1984, esp. p. A40, Table 2.
[22] The following is based on Pach 1982 (a contribution of considerable importance).

of a factory. The best social historian of late Prussianism, Hans Rosenberg, described it as a 'tight, military-autocratic, centralised plant [*Betrieb*] where workers were personally ruled by the *Gutsherrn*'.[23] Only very gradually was this patriarchal community of interests dissolved and rationalised through the extension of money-wages, the mass employment of seasonal workers, the relocation of resident workforces, and the decline of share-payments. These were the great developments which dominated the labour-relations of Prussian agriculture in the nineteenth century and which were so lucidly described by Weber in his brilliant essay on the East-Elbian rural labourers.[24]

3.3. Part III

Now I would like to suggest that to gain a true perception of the entire range of possibilities confronting agricultural employers, we should extend the logic of deployment to cover all or at least most types of *tenancy*. We should, as far as possible, re-examine tenancy as an aspect of the deployment of labour.

In Egypt in Justinian's time, sharecroppers standardly referred to their share of the crop (usually wine) as 'the half share accruing to us for the work we do'; that is, they saw the share they were entitled to as a form of wages.[25] The Bengal landlords who responded to the questionnaire circulated by the Floud Commission in the 1930s consistently took the stand that their *bargadars* were simply wage-labourers. In the North-Bengal districts where the *jotedars* were quite powerful, there had already been a rapid increase in sharecropping in the early years of this century, coinciding with a movement reported elsewhere in the country, for example in the central districts of Punjab.[26] But the decisive evolution was the catastrophic effects of the Depression in the jute district, with the outright transfer of some 1.6 million acres of cultivated *raiyati* land. In the first phase of the Depression, between 1930 and 1934, the annual rate of transfer, in terms of the number of transfers, was over 300,000, in the late thirties over 400,000, in the early forties 965,000 – certainly one of

---

[23] Rosenberg 1978, p. 91, following Weber.
[24] Weber 1894, transl. by K. Tribe in Weber 1979.
[25] The references are collected in 'Wine Production in Byzantine Egypt', paper presented to the Oxford Byzantine Seminar, Trinity 1990.
[26] Bhattacharya 1983, p. 144.

the most colossal movements of land-transfer in recent history!²⁷ By 1939, in eastern and northern Bengal, at least 40% to 45% of the agricultural population worked wholly or partly as sharecroppers.²⁸

Here are the responses of the various local landholders' associations. 'The bargadar is not a raiyat but a hired labourer', said the Bengal Landholders' Association. 'At first sight it seems that bargadars should have the occupancy right as they actually cultivate the lands but they are really glorified hired labourers and it is not advisable to extend the right to that class. They are hired labourers and should be treated as such. The only protection he needs is that he should get the stipulated share of wages...'.²⁹ From Burdwan, 'The bargadars are practically agricultural labourers and are paid in kind by a share of the produce'.³⁰ From Jessore, 'It is highly unreasonable and unwise to give the bargadars, who are nothing but labourers paid in kind, any statutory right.'³¹ From Malda, 'They are merely labourers and they are amply remunerated'.³² From Mymensingh, 'The Amending Act of 1929 has not given the bargadars any statutory right, because the bargadars are not tenants but only hired labourers, who get generally a half of the produce of the land in lieu of labour'.³³ The landholders also made it quite plain what would happen if occupancy rights *were* extended to the sharecroppers. The Khulna landlords were most explicit: 'If protection be given to bargadars by legislation, landlords and other people holding khas lands will certainly cultivate their lands by servants and a large number of bargadars will be thrown out of employment'.³⁴ And this of course is precisely what did happen. In a recent work, Rudra and Bardhan reported,

> Our own surveys have yielded unquestionable evidence that tenancy is on the decline almost everywhere in the State.... The decline of tenancy is being caused by large-scale eviction of tenants.... In about 80% of the villages tenant cultivation is being transformed into self-cultivation with the help of hired labourers through forceful eviction of tenants.³⁵

---

²⁷ Cf. Goswami 1984, esp. p. 357, Table 11.
²⁸ Cf. the excellent synthesis in Mukherji 1986.
²⁹ Government of Bengal 1940, Volume 3, p. 80.
³⁰ Govt. of Bengal 1940, Volume 3, p. 405.
³¹ Govt. of Bengal 1940, Volume 4, p. 46.
³² Govt. of Bengal 1940, Volume 4, p. 106.
³³ Govt. of Bengal 1940, Volume 4, p. 294.
³⁴ Govt. of Bengal 1940, Volume 4, p. 87.
³⁵ Rudra and Bardhan 1983, pp. 48–9.

So the *jotedars* certainly did enforce their threats in the middle and late seventies when this survey was conducted.

To contrapose a landlord/tenant relationship to an employer/labour relationship, as one writer has done in noting the progressive abandonment of sharecropping in West Bengal,[36] is certainly misleading. It underestimates the economic rationality of the *jotedars*, whose reasons for using *adhiars* and other sorts of sharecroppers were of course linked to rational considerations of profitability. As the Bakarganj landholders told the Commission, 'Day labourers will not cultivate the land with that amount of interest and diligence with which a bargadar cultivates, and the result will be a reduction in the outturn of crops'.[37] Landlords agreed that it was more profitable to employ sharecroppers. 'Cultivation by paid servants is scarcely profitable nowadays.'[38] In short, while landowners might abandon sharecropping for *political* reasons, the decision to retain or extend it was primarily economic.

Let me turn to another sort of labour-contract. Describing conditions in Birbhum district c.1910, O'Malley wrote (in the *District Gazetteer*),

> There is a large class of field labourers who are permanent servants of the cultivators, being employed by the year to cultivate the fields and receiving in return one-third of the produce. During the year before the crop ripens, these labourers live on advances of grain given by the cultivator, which are deducted with 25 per cent interest from their share of the crop at harvest time.[39]

In the village of Suner in Ferozepur district in the 1930s, 'The *siri* is engaged by the landowner for the year and is given his daily food at the landowner's home and a share of the total grain produced....To induce a man to become a *siri* he is given an advance by his employer which is made generally without interest'.[40] Finally, take an extract from one of the numerous settlement reports of the late nineteenth century – from Fletcher, a revenue-official employed in the Khandesh collectorate in the 1880s.

---

[36] Dasgupta 1984, p. 144, 'The data from West Bengal clearly indicate a move away from tenancies and in favour of hired labour-based agriculture.'
[37] Govt. of Bengal 1940, Volume 3, p. 9.
[38] Govt. of Bengal 1940, Volume 3, p. 437, from Dinajpur.
[39] O'Malley 1910, p. 67.
[40] Dawar and Dayal 1936, p. 18.

> It is a very common practice among the larger landholders to hire their farm labourers by the year, and from Rs.50–55 is the usual sum paid, not unusually in advance. No clothes or food are provided in the agreement, but it is common for the employer to advance grain up to the amount of 1 big *map* (about 10 bushels) during the year, to be paid for, without interest, out of the next year's wages.[41]

I have chosen to juxtapose these passages, deliberately, because the juxtaposition shows that indebtedness was an inessential feature of the relationship described. By this I do not mean that labourers were not often or even generally forced into debt but that these were forms of wage-labour in which labour was recruited through an advance of wages and it was purely incidental whether the employer chose to confer on these advances the fictitious appearance of a 'loan' – since, strictly speaking, no loan was involved here. *Treating wage-advances as consumption-loans was simply a way of manipulating effort-standards*. Thus bondage and wage-labour are not contrasting systems but one simply the most reified form of the other. (If you like, in bondage the slavery inherent in wage-labour is *posited* as such.) In bonded labour, not only are wages conceived as loans but these so-called 'loans' are advanced on the security of the worker's labour-capacity (he mortgages his labour), so a double mystification is involved. Labour-mortgaging was widespread in nineteenth-century India. The *Thana District Gazetteer* refers to contracts ranging from 'five to twelve or even fifteen years'.[42] The *Nasik District Gazetteer* tells us that 'Suits are occasionally brought to enforce the terms of the contract, but the courts refuse to take cognizance of such agreements'.[43] Permanent farm-labour has been in decline for over a century now.

---

[41] W.M. Fletcher, Supt. RSA Poona and Nasik, to T.H. Stewart, S.S.C., 23/2/1886, in Bombay Government Records, 186 n.s., *Papers relating to the Revision of the Rates of Assessment on the Expiry of the First Settlement in the Savda Taluka of the Khandesh Collectorate*, Bombay, 1886, p. 13.

[42] *Gazetteer of the Bombay Presidency Volume XIII, part 1: Thana*, Bombay, 1882, p. 310, 'The servants of the many rich Brahman, Vani, and Kunbi moneylenders, who are scattered throughout the district, are almost all bound in writing to serve their masters for periods of from five to twelve or even fifteen years'.

[43] *Gazetteer of the Bombay Presidency Volume XVI: Nasik*, Bombay, 1883, p. 122. 'The custom of mortgaging labour prevails to a very large extent among field labourers' (p. 121). It is essential to distinguish the contractual *form* of a relationship and its economic substance. The Greek papyri from Egypt are full of contracts which exemplify the need for such a distinction.

To conclude: overall shifts in the composition of the labour-force are best regarded as reflecting changes in *hiring practices*. But these ground-level shifts in the deployment of agricultural labour (movements between different sorts of contracts and categories of labour) have less to do with the alleged precapitalist inefficiencies of feudal or semi-feudal employers than with the general state of the labour-market and, of course, the rationality peculiar to agricultural employers as such. That employers felt compelled to secure control over labour by using cash-advances and permanent farm-contracts reflects the historical conditions of the labour-market in the eighteenth and nineteenth centuries.[44] Today the Indian agricultural labour-market is massively dominated by casual workers. The decision of the Madras Presidency *mirasidars* to cut back drastically on their employment of permanent farm-servants – the so-called *pannaiyals* – and reorganise production on the strength of casual labour was caused by the 'extraordinary glut of labour from the depression years onwards'. As Baker explains,

> it became ever easier to rely on the supply of casual labour to cover the workload during the peaks of the cultivation system, and this made it possible to dispense with a large number of pannaiyals who were maintained under-employed for most of the year simply in order to ensure a labour supply at the critical times. By the mid 1930s there were well-organized gangs of casual labour who moved up to a hundred miles between different tracts in order to find work.[45]

But there was no abstract inevitability about employers' responses, for, in Bengal, the same conditions and the same period produced a phenomenal rise in the employment of sharecroppers and the transition to casual labour occurred only much later, and under the pressure of a political threat. More recently, in Gujarat the shift to labour-gangs has resulted from the spread of irrigated crops and the need felt by the Patidars to enforce high standards of work intensity in particular jobs. So we turn full circle, having started with

---

[44] The ambiguity permeates the whole of colonial literature, e.g. Grierson in his report on Gaya writes, 'A *kamiya* usually sells himself to a master for a lump sum of money down. Formerly, this was an actual sale of himself and his heirs for ever, but this having been declared to be illegal, he now hires himself, in consideration of a stated advance or loan, to serve for a hundred years...', Grierson 1893, p. 110. O'Malley repeats the passage in several *Gazetteers*.
[45] Baker 1984, p. 196.

Cato's enthusiastic espousal of subcontracting and his model agreements for employers using contract-labour. For, Breman's Gujarat Patidars deal with labour-gangs through the mediation of a contractor, since the strains of personal supervision are too much for them. Breman points out that 'Farmers prefer to use *udhad* [contract jobs] when a great deal of work must be accomplished within a short time, i.e. when the tempo is faster than that paid for by a daily wage'.[46] The implication of this is that agriculture, like industry, is underpinned by a process of 'effort bargaining'[47] and that workers will do only as much as they feel they are reasonably compensated for.

Finally, against the classical vision of agriculture fluctuating violently between modes of production, I have repeatedly assumed that the evolution of the categories of labour reflects *decisions on employment* and that these decisions express a 'rationality' which is common to different historical periods. What we desperately need is a more complex model of the use of labour in agriculture which can both clarify this decision-making process and explain the considerable observed variety in the terms and conditions of labour-contracts in agricultural work.[48]

[*1992*]

---

[46] Breman 1985, p. 278ff. Rutten 1986 describes an alternative form of subcontracting used by the *patidars* of Kheda district.

[47] Baldamus 1967.

[48] Martinez-Alier 1971, Chapter 2 'Decisions on Employment', and Chapter 7 'Decisions on Tenancy'; Rudra and Bardhan 1983; Bhalla 1976; Dreze and Mukherjee 1989; and Ramachandran 1990, Chapter 9 'Aspects of the Labour Process in Agriculture', are particularly good in their concentration on the use of labour and/or types of contracts. (An earlier version of this paper was presented to the Oxford Peasant Studies Group in June 1991. I would like to express my gratitude to all who contributed to the excellent discussion afterwards, including Barbara Harriss-White, Richard Smith and Gavin Williams.)

Chapter Four
Workers Before Capitalism

There is a fascinating passage in Dio of Prusa's discourses 'On Slavery and Freedom' where he says, 'Literally thousands of free-born persons sell themselves to work like slaves by contract, sometimes on the worst possible terms'[1] Dio wrote these discourses during his period of exile under the emperor Domitian, towards the end of the first century. Now, it might seem natural to construe this passage as a reference to a special form of contract such as indentured labour, but I think this would be a wrong interpretation. Dio, who was strongly influenced by Stoic ideas, was making a different and more basic point, or rather two points, first that wage-labour was widespread in the Roman economy (the reference to 'thousands' selling themselves), and second that wage-contracts entailed a form of servitude, that wage-labour was a kind of slavery, undermining the distinction between slaves and free persons, which is in fact the central theme of these discourses. In fact, this idea seems almost to have been commonplace in the second sophistic, that is, the great renaissance of Greek intellectual culture that flourished in the second century. In a tract called 'On Salaried Posts in Great Houses', which he was later forced to retract, the satirist Lucian, whose life straddles the main

---

[1] Dio Chrys. *Or.*, 15.23. The key phrase is δουλεύειν κατὰ συγγραφὴν.

part of the second century, even coined a term for it, *ethelodouleia* or 'voluntary slavery'.[2] The Roman upper classes looked down on wage-labourers precisely for this reason.[3] A famous passage in Cicero's *De Officiis* says, 'Again, all those workers who are paid for their labour and not for their skill [*quorum operae, non quorum artes emuntur*] have servile and demeaning employment; for in their case the very wage is a contract to servitude.'[4] In other words, subordination was the essence of wage-labour. Later in the same work, of the various possible reasons why people might 'submit themselves to the command and power of another [*subiciunt se homines imperio alterius et potestati*]', Cicero mentions employment for wages, adding, 'as we often see in this republic of ours [*ut saepe in nostra re publica videmus*]'.[5]

This is the first sense in which the ancients perceived the nature of wage-labour in a relatively straightforward or unmystified form. Secondly, Roman law and society worked with their own conceptual equivalent of abstract labour, expressed by the term *opera*, pl. *operae*. The contract of employment was construed in Roman law as a *locatio operarum*, that is, a hiring (not sale) of units of labour designated by the term 'operae', for which it is impossible to find a satisfying translation. Although *operae* could just mean workers, as in the description of the Emperor Vespasian's grandfather as *manceps operarum*, a labour-contractor, referring in this case to seasonal workers who moved from Umbria to the Sabine country on a regular basis,[6] *locatio operarum* was not a hiring of workers but of labour-power, hence 'services' is about the best translation in English, labour in some quantifiable sense.[7] Waged minework-

---

[2] Lucian, 'On Salaried Posts in Great Houses', Loeb ed. 1960, Volume 3, p. 412ff. (p. 420 for 'voluntary slavery').
[3] Brunt 1980, p. 99, 'Upper-class writers regarded wage-earning as servile'.
[4] Cicero, *De officiis*, 1.150, tr. Griffin and Atkins 1991, p. 58.
[5] Cicero, *De officiis*, 2.22, tr. Griffin and Atkins 1991, p. 70.
[6] Suetonius, *Vesp.* 1.4., '...was a contractor for the day-labourers who come regularly every year from Umbria to the Sabine district, to till the fields'.
[7] *Operae* could mean 'services', e.g., *Dig.*, 7.7.1 ('A service consists in the performance of some task'), 7.7.3 ('The usufruct of a slave includes his services and payments received as a return for such services'), 33.2.3 ('The services of a freeman can also be legated, just as they can be [hired] out and made the subject of a stipulation'), Augustine, *Ep.* 24*.1 (Lancel 1987, p. 384) (parents who 'sell' the *operae* = labour-power of their children for a definite period of years); 'work days', e.g., Columella, *RR* xi.1.24, *Dig.*, 40.7.20.5 ('ten workdays'); 'labour', e.g., Columella, *RR* ii.2.12 (*si suadebit operarum vilitas*, 'if the low cost of labour makes it attractive'), Pliny, *NH* xvii.192 (*operarum conputatio*, 'labour cost calculations'); and 'labourers', e.g., *Dig.*, 45.1.137.3 (*fabris et plurimis operis*, 'craftsmen and numerous labourers'), Suet., *Vesp.* 1.4 (n. 6 above).

ers signed contracts with the formula 'dixit se locasse et locavit operas suas'.⁸ (Incidentally, the Digest makes it clear that slave-owners often hired out the services [*operae*] of their slaves. This was paid labour, except that the payment of the worker was appropriated by the master. The distinction between this situation and the hiring out of one's own services was of no relevance legally. All that mattered was that wages were paid. But, to complicate matters, we should note that a slave could also hire himself out.)

It is a remarkable fact that the surviving sources, both textual and documentary, make repeated reference to occupational designations, and workers often refer to themselves, in contracts for example, by their occupation. Even less-skilled labourers would do this. For example, *P.Oxy.* 3933 is a late sixth-century contract with someone who calls himself a 'goldsmiths' helper'.⁹ The general implication is that, for large numbers of people, the *work* they did was part of their identity, or at least of the way they identified themselves to others. Even contract-workers retained specific occupational identities. In his manual on farm-management, Cato advises landowners to gather the olives as soon as possible once they are ripe and not leave them on the ground for long, adding, 'The gatherers [*leguli*] want to have as many windfalls as possible that there may be more of them to gather; and the pressers [*factores*] want them to lie on the floor a long time, so that they will soften and be easier to mill'.¹⁰ But these workers, gatherers and pressers, were supplied to farm-owners by contractors, following agreements that ideally specified the numbers actually required. They were contract-labour. Moreover, entire towns might come to be known for the occupational communities that resided in them. Strabo describes Panopolis in Middle Egypt as 'an old settlement of linen workers and stone workers',¹¹ and in one inscription a worker describes himself as a 'stone cutter, one of those from Syene', implying that the best ones came from there.¹²

Opera (sing.) could likewise have the more abstract sense of 'labour', as in Pliny, *NH* xviii.38 ('some crops are not worth harvesting when you calculate the cost of labour', *si conputetur inpendium operae*).
 ⁸ Berger 1948.
 ⁹ *P.Oxy.* 3933 (588).
 ¹⁰ Cato, *De agricult.* 64.1; 144.3–4.
 ¹¹ Strabo, xvii.1.41.
 ¹² *CIG* iii, 4716, cited Fitzler 1910, p. 137.

Paid labour was widespread in construction, mining, agriculture and domestic service, and presumably also in the numerous industrial workshops that manufactured a very wide range of goods for consumption. In a famous paper, Peter Brunt showed that 'free labour was extensively employed in public works at Rome'.[13] The Baths of Caracalla, built between 212 and 216, consumed roughly 2.38 million mandays of skilled labour and a further 2.06 million mandays of unskilled labour, according to the painstaking calculations of one scholar.[14] The striking fact here is the predominance of skilled workers. The fact that skilled workers outnumbered the unskilled was entirely due to the quality of Roman public architecture. In periods of strong demand for construction-labour, the masons and other skilled workers were in a strong bargaining position and often tempted to abandon jobs halfway. This prompted repeated imperial intervention to regulate a code of discipline for the industry. For example, in April 459, the building workers of Sardis were forced to take an oath agreeing that employers would be indemnified against any wilful obstruction of work.[15] Another industrial sector that worked under similar tensions was the mint. On Aurelian's accession to power in 271, there was a massive rebellion of the workers of the mint of Rome. Aurelian is said to have suppressed this with the utmost ferocity, bringing the army in. One source puts the number of dead (on both sides presumably) at 7,000.[16] Although there are conflicting accounts in the sources, they concur in the view that the quality of the coinage was the heart of the issue between the mint-employees and the authorities. These tensions survived into the late empire. In 363, during the fierce religious conflicts that erupted in Alexandria, the manager of the mint was lynched by a mob, together with the hated Arian bishop George.[17] In one anonymous tract of the mid fourth century, written to suggest ways of effecting efficiencies in administration, the author wrote,

> the workers of the Mint must be assembled from every quarter and concentrated in a single island so as to improve the utility of the coinage and the circulation of the solidi. Let them, in fact, be cut off for all time from

---

[13] Brunt 1980, p. 84.
[14] DeLaine 1997.
[15] *CIG* 3467, the best discussion of which is di Branco 2000.
[16] Aurelius Victor, *Caes.*, 35.6 (scale of conflict); Eutropius, *Brev.*, 9.14 (repression).
[17] Ammianus Marcellinus, xxii.11.8–9; *Hist. Aceph.*, 2.10.

association with the neighbouring land, so that freedom of intercourse...may not mar the integrity of a public service.[18]

It is doubtful if any emperor would ever have taken this kind of prescription seriously. At any rate, the production of the gold coinage was always highly centralised, and one imagines the leading mints as workplaces that concentrated substantial numbers of workers in a shopfloor-régime that turned out millions of *solidi* each year. The remarkably high quality of late-Roman gold shows how tightly controlled all of this labour in fact was.

At the other end of the spectrum from these large imperial projects and government enterprises were the thousands of smaller private enterprises – workshops, farms and estates – where workers had much less leeway in terms of sheer size or physical concentration and had to rely mainly on their individual skills. But, here, we are fortunate in having substantial documentation in terms of the thousands of papyri that survive mainly from Middle Egypt – the districts south of the Delta. Most published papyri are in Greek and, to a lesser extent, Coptic, but Vienna contains a substantial holding of Arabic papyri, from the early Islamic period, which are largely unpublished. It is the papyrological evidence that shows how extensively *free* labour was used in areas of the Mediterranean such as Egypt, how widespread wage-labour was, and certainly became by late antiquity, and the very diverse forms in which workers were recruited, paid and controlled. In the surviving wage-agreements or *Arbeitsverträge* cash wages are common, and since most of these agreements are from the later period, mainly the sixth and seventh centuries, a period of exceptional prosperity for the Eastern Empire, this means wages in gold-coin [*solidi*]. But wage-formulae varied according to the type of employment (and age and gender), and so, of course, did the amount of the wage. In one second-century agricultural account, the wage-differential between masons and their helpers is 7:4, that is, unskilled wages are a little over 50 per cent of skilled wages. The skill differential appears to have been remarkably stable – Diocletian's Prices Edict from over a century later shows an almost identical ratio, 2:1, for a wide range of occupations, with the agricultural workers at the bottom of the scale and skilled or highly skilled occupations receiving twice as much or more.[19] The ceiling prescribed for rural labourers in the Prices Edict

---

[18] Anonymous, *De rebus bellicis*, 3.2 (Thompson 1952, p. 95).
[19] Giacchero 1974.

was a cash wage of 25 *denarii*, equivalent to just over 1½ kg of wheat a day. In sixth and seventh century contracts, the less-skilled groups receive two to three *solidi* a year. Converting these figures to wheat-equivalents yields a roughly similar amount, less if the wage was two *solidi*, more if it was three. In fact, John Chrysostom tells us that self-employed artisans were better fed than wage-labourers, because, as he says, employers tended to cut a substantial part of the wages of the workers they employed.[20] John lived and preached in Antioch, where there was a substantial middle class by the later fourth century, and it is possible that many employers were drawn from this class. On the other hand, skilled workers had more control over the terms of their agreements, and, it seems, a strong preference for piece-rates. In a second-century contract, two stone-cutters list a schedule of rates according to the size and type of stone to be cut and then state, 'All the aforesaid stone we will cut, but no ornamentation shall be required of us'.[21] In harvest-contracts from the same period, workers reserve the right to inspect the area assigned to them, since their wages were calculated on a per-hectare basis.[22] The Sardis building workers I mentioned earlier were able to get the authorities to agree that, if a craftsman was forced to abandon work due to sickness, the employer would be required to wait three weeks before seeking a replacement.[23] Perhaps the most striking fact about late antique wage-agreements is that employees were actually able to introduce a 'reciprocal penalty' clause in the event that either side terminated the agreement for no good reason. In *P.Oxy.* 3641, a contract between a large estate and a millstone-cutter who was being given his job for life, the clause reads, 'If your Excellency, through your administrators, ejects me without reproach or inefficiency or any cause whatsoever, you too shall be subject to the same penalty'.[24] But, even more remarkably, the reciprocal penalty found its way into less-skilled contracts. The goldsmiths' helper could get his employers to agree that 'If you eject me without any cause, you are to suffer the loss of my whole wage'![25] Even sharecroppers could get landowners to agree to such a clause. In *SB* XII 11240, which is called a *misthōtikē homologia*,

---

[20] John Chrysostom, *In Ep. I ad Cor., Hom.* xliii, 3 (PG 61.372).
[21] *P.Oxy.* 498.28ff. (2 c.), tr. Hunt and Edgar 1932, Volume 1, pp. 58ff.
[22] Schwartz 1961, pp. 117–23.
[23] See n. 15.
[24] *P.Oxy.* 3641.17ff.
[25] *P.Oxy.* 3933.24ff. (588).

that is, a wage-agreement, the sharecropper agrees he will pay a fine of twelve *solidi* if he decides to quit prematurely, but conversely, 'if you decide to evict me from the job before the expiry of the contract [*misthōsis*], you will pay me the same amount as a fine'.[26]

The expansion of wage-employment in the late antique period led to a new kind of confidence among workers. Some, indeed many, professional groups like reapers, stone-cutters, canal-workers, masons and shipwrights formed mobile self-regulating groups whose conditions of work and life were the antithesis of the isolated domestic servants recruited on general service-contracts, who were called *paramonarioi*.[27] These workers worked in teams[28] and moved around between construction-sites,[29] farms, estates, quarries, and so on. Others were part of a wider urban community, hence stable, with sometimes a strong attachment to their local bishop. In his funeral oration for Basil, bishop of Caesarea, Gregory of Nazianzus recounts how, on one occasion, when the highest official of the Eastern Prefecture, a man called Domitius Modestus, was rumoured to have summoned Basil and was threatening him (the year was 371), a huge crowd gathered armed with anything they could find. Gregory says that the nucleus of this 'fused group' was formed by workers in the government-owned arms-factories and textile-mills or workshops. About them he says, 'in situations like this it is they who are especially hot-headed and daring in their outspokenness',[30] an interesting glimpse into the psychology of the more organised groups of workers.[31] We know little

---

[26] *SB* XII 11240.19ff. (6/7c.). Twelve *solidi* were equal to one-sixth of a pound of gold.

[27] *Paramonē* seems to have acquired the meaning of an annual or longer-term service-contract, usually annual, with no connotation of any special compulsion; e.g., *SB* XII 11239 (418), *P.Oxy.* 140 (550), *SPP* XX 219 (604), *SB* XVI 13016 (638), *SB* I 4490 (641 or 656). Adams 1964, p. 75ff. shows that δάνειον in these contracts was not a loan but an advance-payment of wages.

[28] Kraus and Röder 1962, esp. pp. 98–116.

[29] Tchalenko 1953–58, t.1, pp. 51–2; Mango 1966.

[30] Gregory of Nazianzus, *Or.*, 43.57 (SC 384, p. 246), *kai gar eisi peri ta toiauta thermoteroi kai to tolman ek tēs parrēsias echontes*.

[31] For example, note Athanasius' reference to the execution of ten workers from the arms-factory in Hadrianopolis (Edirne in western Turkey), Athanasius, *Hist. Arianorum*, 18, again a case of workers rushing to the defence of their bishop. The combativity of groups like these implies a concentration of workers in the labour-process, cf. Jones 1964, pp. 835–6, 'The *fabricae* [factories] must have been large establishments, for their personnel was a substantial element in the population of the towns in which they were situated'.

about the internal organisation of workers but it is possible that the *coniu-rationes clericorum* or unions of priests of the Merovingian period (sixth to seventh century) which the Church-hierarchy sought to suppress[32] had their roots in a more widespread tradition of voluntary associations among artisans and workers in the fourth to sixth centuries. The dockhands of Portus formed a cartel or 'closed shop' in the mid fourth century to which government extended public recognition.[33] The craftsmen in the building industry also had associations of their own, and Sozomen reports that the public-sector employees of Cyzicus were organised into two large 'guilds [*tagmata*]'.[34] This raises a final issue of whether one can discern the elements of a culture of radicalism among workers. I would like to suggest that the answer, tentatively, is yes and to cite two rather different examples of this.

The first concerns harvest-gangs in North Africa in the fourth century. They are only known to us through sources that were unrelentingly hostile to them, since they became involved in the religious conflicts of the fourth century. The Catholic sources and at least one imperial constitution refer to them as 'Circumcellions' – a name, it seems, that they rejected, preferring to be called 'Agonistici', that is, those who struggle, 'militants'.[35] The Circumcellions were strongest in Numidia (Algeria today) where the wheat- and olive-harvests generated a huge demand for seasonal labour, particularly in the fourth century when Africa dominated Mediterranean markets. Augustine, who was very hostile to them, as he was to the Donatists generally, accused them of spreading terror in the countryside. Their gangs certainly included

---

[32] See Oexle 1985.
[33] *CTh* 14.22.1 (364).
[34] Sozomen, *Hist. Eccl.* 5.15 (*PG* 67.1256f.). I take τάγματα to be Sozomen's reference to the *corpora* or associations that workers in the key industrial sectors were required to enlist in.
[35] Agricultural workers: *Gesta conlationis Carthaginensis, Edictum cognitoris* (= Lancel 1972–1975, t.3, p. 978), calling on landowners who 'find that they have squads of Circumcellions on their estates [*Hii autem qui in praediis suis circumcellionum turbas se habere cognoscant*]' to curb the 'insolence [*insolentia*]' of these workers! Migrant-workers: e.g., Augustine, *Contra Gaudentium*, 1.28.32 (*CSEL* 53/3, p. 231) where he says, 'they wander around between rural storehouses for the sake of their livelihood [*victus sui causa cellas circumiens rusticanas*]'; Augustine, *Enarratio in psalm. cxxxii*, 3 (*CC* 40, p. 1928), 'they are used to going here and there, since they have no fixed residence [*solent enim ire hac illac, nusquam habentes sedes*]'. 'Agonistici': Augustine, *Ep.* 108. 18 (410); *Enarratio in psalm. cxxxii*, 6 (*CC* 40, p. 1930); Optatus, 3.4 (*CSEL* 26, p. 81), Donatus, bishop of Bagai, sent his agents through the local markets 'to assemble the Circumcellion militants [*circumcelliones agonisticos nuncupans*]'.

women, since Augustine tells us so repeatedly, because he found it scandalous.[36] What makes the Circumcellions so fascinating is the repeated reference to their radicalism in writers who were appalled by it. Optatus tells us that when the movement first emerged in the 330s, loan-agreements became null and void, no moneylender had the freedom to recover his capital, and, when they were travelling, employers were forced out of their vehicles and forced to run 'like slaves' behind their own employees [*mancipia*]. In short, 'Under their domination and thanks to the ideas they held, the condition of master and slave was reversed'.[37] The Circumcellions formed the radical wing of the Donatist church and must have drawn much of their inspiration from the way this church projected itself. The constant reference to their 'leaders [*principes*]' should be explained by the internal organisation of the harvest in North Africa. According to Marçais, the Maghreb reapers divide the field into sections line by line, and place the most skilled worker on the right. He is the one who 'starts and directs the work'.[38] The reference to this worker as *sultan* recalls the description of the Circumcellion gang-leaders as *principes*.

A different kind of radicalism is embodied in my second example, which is from Egypt. In the Fayyum, in the late fourth century, a whole network of monasteries sent their monks out into part-time wage-labour, again mostly the harvest, and these monks/part-time workers then pooled their wages into a fund that was used to feed the poorest families in the district or despatched to Alexandria, in the form of food and clothing, for people in the jails there as well as migrants and persons in need.[39] To assess this example properly, we should recall that monasticism began among ordinary people as one response to the huge restructuring of state and economy that occurred in the early decades of the fourth century.[40] Pachomius founded the first cenobitic monastery on the site of a deserted village in Egypt. And, as with the Circumcellions, whose leadership was drawn from the Donatist clergy, if Augustine is to be believed, this remarkable enterprise in the Fayyum was led by a priest called Sarapion.

---

[36] E.g., Augustine, *Ep.* 35.2 (*CSEL* 34/2, pp. 28–9), *Contra litteras Petiliani*, 2.88.195 (*CSEL* 52/2, p. 120).
[37] Optatus, 3.4 (p. 82); supported by Augustine, *Ep.* 185.4.
[38] Marçais and Guîga 1925, t.1, p. 249.
[39] Rufinus, *Hist. monachorum in Aegypto*, 18 (Festugière 1961, p. 114).
[40] Mazzarino 1951.

The main conclusion to emerge from all this is that the working class is not a product of capitalism specifically, *unless* there is a sense in which class itself is peculiar to capitalism, so that workers before capitalism fail to constitute a class in the same sense as workers under capitalism. Marxists have radically underestimated the extent of wage-labour in so-called 'precapitalist' societies, for reasons I shall come to in a moment. Some of the evidence cited here was available to Marx, if he had had the time and inclination to look for it, but most of it was unavailable. Papyri, for example, only began to be discovered in substantial numbers in the 1880s, and it was not till 1950 that anyone put together a published collection of wage-contracts from the papyrological material.[41] However, attention to historical detail is only part of the story. The more fundamental reason for simply ignoring the existence of workers before capitalism is the strength of primitivism in the Marxist tradition. Wage-labour strikes us as a peculiarly modern institution, because the ancient world, indeed all periods of history before capitalism, are seen as intrinsically impervious to any of the institutions that characterise capitalism. Not all socialists subscribed to this view. Whether, like Otto Rühle, they were willing to believe that 'Under the dominion of the Roman Empire the economy had developed in Italy *almost* to the threshold of capitalism',[42] or, like Arthur Rosenberg, one spoke of capitalists and proletarians in the Greek and Roman worlds (Rosenberg was a Roman historian before he became an active Communist),[43] or, like Feliciano Serrao today, one speaks of a 'form of capitalism compatible with the historical conditions of antiquity',[44] there has always been a modernist

---

[41] Montevecchi 1950.

[42] Rühle 1924.

[43] Esp. Rosenberg 1997, a popular work which deals mainly with Greek history. Rosenberg clearly saw the dominant section of the Republican oligarchy as a 'small circle of capitalists', describing Rome herself as the world's 'first capitalist power' (p. 91). He referred to the 'amassing of huge capitals in the hands of the Roman banker-class' and to Sulla's victory over the Marians 'breaking the power of the capitalist party' (p. 92). The Roman empire itself was a 'capitalist class-state of the crassest form' but one built on hundreds of self-governing local communities (p. 94ff.). Yet this imagery falls away in the concluding chapter of *Demokratie und Klassenkampf im Altertum*, which deals, with breathtaking speed, with the late empire and its unbridled despotism and describes the ruling groups as 'large landowners, millionaires, bureaucrats and bishops' (p. 101). On Arthur Rosenberg, see Riberi 2001; Keßler 2003.

[44] Serrao 1971, p. 767: '[Q]uella certa forma di capitalismo compatibile con le condizioni storiche generali dell'antichità'. Serrao's main essays have been brought together in Serrao 1989.

strand in left-wing thinking which we desperately need to salvage. Marx's savage footnote on Mommsen in Chapter 6 of Volume One is deeply polemical. He attacked Mommsen for positing the development of capital in a world that made widespread use of slavery.[45] In *Römische Geschichte*, Mommsen characterised the late Republic as a régime of aristocrats and bankers, and the Republican economy as an 'agrarian-mercantile economy based on masses of capital and on speculation'.[46] These views were strongly influenced by his perception of American capitalism in the 1850s, which he described as a 'government of capitalists in a country based on slavery [*das Capitalistenregiment im Sklavenstaat*]'.[47] True, Mommsen was not Marx and may not have had even a rudimentary grasp of what Marx called the 'modern meaning of capital' – the sort of capitalism that Marx took as the object of his investigation. But Marx himself was willing to describe the American slaveholders as capitalists;[48] in Volume Three, there is a passing reference to the Elder Cato as both landowner and capitalist,[49] and he and Engels refer in *The German Ideology* to the 'vineyards and villas of Roman capitalists' in the age of Augustus.[50] None of this seems particularly exceptionable today. In any case, the text which generated the footnote in Marx is one of the least well constructed in *Capital*. After saying, '[i]n and for itself, the exchange of commodities implies no other relations of dependence than those which result from its own nature', Marx goes on to say,

> [o]n *this assumption*, labour-power can appear on the market as a commodity only if, and in so far as, its possessor, the individual whose labour-power it is, offers it for sale or sells it as a commodity. In order that its possessor may sell it as a commodity...he must be the free proprietor of his own labour-capacity, hence of his person.

---

[45] Marx 1976, p. 271.
[46] Mommsen 1866, pp. 488 (régime), 504 (masses of capital).
[47] Mommsen 1866, p. 516.
[48] See the references in Banaji 2003, p. 81.
[49] Marx 1981, p. 923, n. 42a.
[50] Marx and Engels 1965, p. 58, 'in the Campagna of Rome he [Feuerbach] finds only pasture lands and swamps, where in the time of Augustus he would have found nothing but the vineyards and villas of Roman capitalists'; cf. 'Roman capitalists, proconsuls, etc.' at p. 151.

This is followed by the footnote on Mommsen.⁵¹ But, if the predominance of free labour is merely an assumption, what sense does it make to drag history into the picture and contest a historical depiction of reality? Moreover, even the statement 'On this assumption, labour-power can appear on the market as a commodity only if, and in so far as, its possessor, the individual whose labour-power it is, offers it for sale or sells it as a commodity' fails to be a valid deduction because it ignores slavery. Labour-power *can* appear on the market as a commodity, indeed did, even when free labourers are scarce or non-existent. Appian tells us that a major reason why the rich who had monopolised the public land and carved huge estates out of it preferred the employment of slaves was that the peasantry was subject to conscription and the supply of labour unstable.⁵²

The point of these remarks is not to deny the centrality of 'free labour' to the accumulation of capital in the modern economy (modern forms of capitalism) but to undermine the particular way Marx attempts to construe the link between wage-labour and capital. In Chapter 6, Marx tends to argue as if the use of free labour is a logical presupposition of capital, when it is clear that individual capitalists exploit labour in a multiplicity of forms, and this not just when capital exists as manufacture and domestic industry. *Marx was aware of this*, because he wrote

> Machinery also revolutionizes... the contract between the worker and the capitalist. Taking the exchange of commodities as our basis, our *first assumption* was that the capitalist and the worker confronted each other as free persons, as independent owners of commodities.... But now the capitalist buys children and young persons.... [The worker] sells wife and child. He has become a slave-dealer.⁵³

It is fascinating to see Marx referring back to Chapter 6 here, over 200 pages later, and re-emphasising the hypothetical nature of the assumption about

---

⁵¹ Marx 1976, p. 271.
⁵² Appian, *BC* 1.7 (White 1964, Volume 3, p. 15f.): 'for the rich...came to cultivate vast tracts instead of single estates, using slaves as labourers and herdsmen, lest free labourers should be drawn from agriculture into the army. At the same time the ownership of slaves brought them great gain from the multitude of their progeny, who increased because they were exempt from military service'.
⁵³ Marx 1976, p. 519.

the free worker. But it was that assumption that prompted his attack on Mommsen.

More fundamentally, Mommsen can be defended in terms of his characterisation of the economy of the Roman Republic as 'based on masses of capital and on speculation'.[54] That Marx was the first to expound the nature of capital in a scientific way does not mean that capital in general was a complete mystery to all earlier generations. The idea that a sum of value ceases to be capital unless it is constantly active and self-generating is found in both Basil and Gregory of Nyssa.[55] Ambrose, a member of the late Roman aristocracy, has a vivid passage on the restless nature of capital, and tells us that the capitalist [*faenerator*] has no interest in holding back his money but only in deploying it actively.[56] This is not the place to explore the background to these ideas

---

[54] See n. 46. Cf. Runciman 1995, p. 37, 'Rome's mode of production *was* capitalist in every respect except the dominance of a formally free labour force' (Runciman's italics!). Marx himself referred to the formation of 'big money capital' in the late Republic (in his response to Mikhailovsky). Weber and Hintze stressed the agrarian side of Roman capitalism, Hintze 1964, p. 312 even claiming that the ancient economy 'remained stuck in an agrarian capitalism based on slave-labour [*im Agrarkapitalismus mit seiner Sklavenarbeit*]'. Today this seems too restrictive. Commercial partnerships, branch-businesses, the governance of liability in Roman law (including the limitation of liability by means of complicated enterprise structures that used slaves in key managerial positions, see Di Porto 1984; Serrao 1989, p. 27ff.; Földi 1996), the decomposition of individual crafts and use of specialised workers which Marx saw as typical of manufacture, and the widespread activity of wholesale merchants with links to an impressive array of *industrial* enterprises in metalworking, textiles, ceramics, and so on, *all* seem like solid evidence that we can posit a more broad-based 'capitalistic sector' in Rome almost as much as we can in Islam. This is meant to *pose* a problem for historical materialists, not resolve one. On labour-processes typical of Marx's manufacture, cf. Augustine, *De civitate Dei*, vii.4 = Dyson 1998, p. 273, 'like workmen in the street of silversmiths, where one vessel passes through the hands of many craftsmen before it emerges perfect, although it could have been perfected by one perfect craftsman. But *many craftsmen are employed in this way only because it is thought better for each part of an art to be learned by a single workman quickly and easily*', with which cf. Marx 1976, pp. 456–8. The structuring of control over production varied even within industries, e.g., textiles in Drinkwater 1977–78; Robinson 2005.

[55] Basil, *Hom. in illud Lucae 'Destruam etc.'*, 5 (PG 31.269); Greg. Nyss., *Contra usurarios*, 16; 20 (PG 46.437), with images like 'money begetting itself' or 'working' for its owner. Gregory of Nyssa refers to the usurer's aversion to leaving his money 'idle and inactive'.

[56] Ambrose, *De Tobia*, 5.16 (Giacchero 1965, p. 95); 13.43 (p. 121); written c.389. Ambrose claims that capital [*pecunia faeneratoris*] simply cannnot 'stand still in one place for long, since it is its custom to circulate through numerous hands...it demands active use [*usus*] so that interest [*usura*] accrues. It is like the waves [*fluctus*] in the sea, not like the crops [*fructus*]' we harvest. 'Capital is never at rest [*pecunia numquam quiescit*]'. Another passage berates the arcane terminology used in business circles, e.g., 'They talk about the principal but call it "capital" [*sors dicitur, caput vocatur*]'.

(the vast accumulations of money-capital that formed the mainstay of the aristocracy).[57] Suffice it to say that, by late antiquity, both wage-labour and capital (the basic *elements* of the capitalist mode of production) were fully formed but that their conjunction was much less obvious. It took another five centuries before something like a capitalist system began to emerge in the Mediterranean.[58]

[2006]

---

[57] Banaji 2007a.
[58] Cracco 1967; Banaji 2007b.

Chapter Five
The Fictions of Free Labour: Contract, Coercion, and so-called Unfree Labour

For Jan Breman

5.1. Premises: the elusive reality of consent*

When is a contract 'voluntary'? The answer is, probably never. The underlying assumption in the claim that some or most contracts are 'voluntary' is that we can *'descriptively* identify domains of freedom and distinguish them from domains of choicelessness'.[1] The conception of contracts as the outcome of a free choice generalises to all sorts of contracts, including contracts of employment. Through contract (the general theory/classical law of), the nineteenth century sanitised wage-labour in the sanguine images of individual autonomy, private volition, free will, and free agency. There was, of course, a long pre-nineteenth-century tradition, going back to antiquity, that had seen wage-labour (contracts for the hiring of labour; 'service' in an earlier terminology) in terms of the subordination of the employee to

---

* Michael Anderson, Sebastian Budgen, Barbara Harriss-White, Karl Klare, Marcel van der Linden, and Pritam Singh supplied me with useful material when I was drafting this paper, and Tom Brass sent me a copy of his book. I am grateful to all of them.

[1] Kelman 1987, p. 87.

the employer.² In one formulation of this, what the worker sells is the 'right to control his labour-power'.³ Since labour-power is never disembodied, what employers buy when they 'buy' 'labour-power' is command over the use of workers' bodies and their persons. In other words, 'The worker and his labour, not his labour power, are the subject of contract'.⁴ Liberal legalism, or the 'pure' or 'general theory' of contract that developed in the nineteenth century, grounded the almost limitless subordination of the wage-labourer in the anodyne fictions of consent. For example, it was possible and consistent for the US courts to maintain that 'a servitude which was knowingly and willingly entered into could not be termed involuntary'.⁵ Here, 'willingly' meant no more than that 'No person is required to enter into such a contract unless he chooses to do so'.⁶ The voluntary sale of labour-power was not the antithesis of servitude but its precondition.⁷ Contracts were made to be enforced, and it was convenient to assume that 'enforcement of contracts was all about implementing the free wills of the parties'.⁸ Marx had no quarrel with this, describing the contract of employment or voluntary sale of labour-power as a

---

² For example, Cicero, *De Officiis*, II.22, 'And there are persons who even subordinate themselves [*subiciunt se*] to the control and power of others for various reasons. [Among those induced to behave in this way are] finally persons who are hired for wages [*mercede conducti*], a situation that is frequently seen in our society.' In I.150 the wage [*merces*] is described as 'remuneration for servitude [*auctoramentum servitutis*]'. Note Tom Paine's description of wage-labour in the late eighteenth century: 'By servitude I mean all offices or employments in or under the state, voluntarily accepted, and to which there are profits annexed', cited Steinfeld 1991, p. 131.

³ Marx 1976b, p. 1060: 'The worker sold the right to control his labour-power in exchange for the necessary means of subsistence'; cf. Batt, 1967, 'The master must have the right to control the servant's work, either personally or by another servant or agent. It is this right of control or interference, of being entitled to tell the servant when to work (within the hours of service) or when not to work, and what work to do and how to do it (within the terms of such service), which is the dominant characteristic in this relation...'.

⁴ Pateman 1988, p. 151. Pateman suggests that the 'disembodied fiction of labour power' buttresses the illusion that *workers themselves* are not commodities under capitalism. In the *Critique of Dialectical Reason*, Sartre uses the expressions 'selling labour-power'/'selling oneself' interchangeably, for example, he refers to the worker 'selling himself as a material object [se vendre comme un objet materiel]' and to the 'worker-commodity [l'ouvrier-marchandise]'.

⁵ Justice Brown in *Robertson v. Baldwin*, 1897, cited in Steinfeld 2001, p. 271.

⁶ From a state Supreme Court ruling cited by Steinfeld 2001, p. 268.

⁷ See Orren 1991, pp. 94–5.

⁸ Dalton 1985, p. 1027.

'formality',[9] while undermining the underlying sense that it had anything to do with the 'ultimate development of human freedom'[10] or with the kinds of transactions equally-placed capitalists struck between themselves.[11] The will theory of contract was a construct of the legal formalism of the nineteenth century and was accepted for precisely what it was,[12] hence the perfectly non-ironic assertion in Volume I of *Capital* that 'the wage-labourer...is *compelled to sell himself of his own free will*'.[13]

At another level, however, it is possible to argue that *no* contract is free because economic coercion is pervasive under capitalism. (This is as true for 'many capitals' as it is for the individual worker.)[14] This is certainly what Marx had in mind in characterising wage-labour as 'voluntary in appearance',[15] and, presumably, also the sense of Sartre's characterisation of the contract of employment as a 'pseudo-contract'.[16] However, *this* sense of constraint – as the 'diffused violence' of the practico-inert (the labour-market conceived as a 'collective' in Sartre's sense) or the 'dull compulsion of economic relations' – is signalled in Marx *less* by any obvious desire to contest the language of voluntarism than by repeated references to the free worker as a 'free' worker.[17] Whatever the common-law doctrine of duress, Marx and Engels clearly did not see the isolated wage-earner as a *free* agent or the wage-contract as a *free* contract.[18] The issue here is not that of the

---

[9] Marx 1976a, p. 724, n. 20: 'It will not be forgotten that, where the labour of children is concerned, even the formality of a voluntary sale vanishes'.
[10] Marx 1973, pp. 651–2: 'Hence, on the other side, the insipidity of the view that free competition is the ultimate development of human freedom'.
[11] Hence the reference in Marx 1976b to the 'deceptive *illusion* of a transaction' (p. 1064; Marx's emphasis), and in Marx 1976a, p. 520, to the 'appearance of a contract between free persons'.
[12] This is especially clear in Marx 1976a, p. 178 ('a relation between two wills'); p. 280 ('Their contract is the final result in which their joint will finds a common legal expression').
[13] Marx 1976a, p. 932; my emphasis.
[14] For example, Miranda 1982, pp. 26ff. On 'many capitals', note Marx's references to the 'coercive' force of competition, Marx 1976a, pp. 381; 433; 436.
[15] Marx 1976b, p. 1028; cf. Marx 1981, p. 958: '...forced labour, however much it might appear as the result of free contractual agreement'.
[16] de Beauvoir 1981, p. 455.
[17] For example, Marx 1976a, pp. 382; 412; 612; Marx 1978, p. 117; Hobbes rejected the common-law doctrine of duress, treating contracts as equally binding whatever their origins, see Thomas 1965, pp. 185–236, esp. 232ff.
[18] For example, Engels, in a review of *Capital*, Volume I, meant for *The Fortnightly Review*: 'The contract, on the part of the labourer, is not a free contract...it is merely the opposition of the labourers, as a mass, which forcibly obtains the enactment of

plasticity of legal reasoning,[19] of *where* one draws the line between free and unfree labour,[20] but of the *incoherence* of the concept of free labour under capitalism. Coercion is everywhere, because the 'outcomes [of bargaining] are heavily conditioned by the legal order in effect at any given moment'.[21] The line between freedom and coercion is impossible to draw, 'either as a matter of logic or as a matter of policy'.[22] Indeed,

> In *every* contract...it is an open question both whether the more informed party ought to have shared more of his information with his trading partner (that is, a question of 'fraud' arises, in some sense, in every case) and whether the contract would have been made had each party had other physically imaginable though socially unavailable options available to him (that is, a question of 'duress' arises in every case).[23]

5.2. A Marxism of liberal mystifications?

In a monograph published in the late 1970s, a young economist Sudipto Mundle made the interesting move of describing the evolution of bondage in Palamau, a district of South Bihar in India, as an instance of what Marx called the 'formal subsumption' of labour into capital. Mundle argued that 'the bonded labour system was a product of capital's penetration into agriculture' and was evolved by landowners in response to a massive exodus

---

a public law to prevent them from selling themselves and their children, by a "free" contract, into death and slavery' (in Marx and Engels 1985, p. 255).

[19] Kennedy 1998.
[20] Steinfeld 2001.
[21] Kennedy 1976, pp. 1685ff., and Kennedy 1998, p. 260.
[22] Dalton 1985, p. 1031.
[23] Kelman 1976, p. 21; cf. Wightman 1996 arguing that

[I]f consent is to retain its justifying power, the law must be able to distinguish when consent is real. But once the veil is pulled aside and the reality of consent is examined, all kinds of everyday economic pressure or necessity clamour for attention as potentially undermining consent. And since the law of contract has traditionally adopted an objective theory of agreement, where what counts is the appearance of agreement, it is not well equipped to begin to identify real consent. Thus the problem that legal writers face is one of confinement: how to define pressure in a way which will allow the victim to say the consent was not real without thereby undermining doctrines which depend on a much more restrictive conception of consent, the consequence of which would be the unravelling of all manner of contracts which are commonly entered into or modified without any real choice by one party. (p. 19)

of labour, in a bid to hold wages down.[24] Over a decade passed without any substantial theoretical discussion of these issues, till V.K. Ramachandran published *Wage Labour and Unfreedom in Agriculture* in 1990. Ramachandran displayed considerable condescension towards Mundle. To view the most backward forms of bonded labour as capitalist exploitation was only possible 'by means of something of a definitional trick'.[25] Bonded labour cannot be part of capitalism, it was alleged, because workers' choice is central to the nature of capitalist exploitation. Surprisingly, Ramachandran's own position has received scarcely any critical comment. In retrospect, it seems that if there was any juggling with definitions, it was his own curious assertion on the very first page of his book that whereas hired labour *was* compatible with 'unfreedom', wage-labour was not.[26] The distinction stated there is obviously arbitrary. For most of us, hired labour and wage-labour are interchangeable terms, and there is certainly no lexicon of social-science vocabulary that assigns these particular distinctions to them. What Ramachandran was obviously keen to do was preserve a model of wage-labour that would make the institution unintelligible outside its conventional description in the language of voluntarism. That this language came to us suffused with the premises and dichotomies of classical individualism – suffused, in other words, with ideology in the strongest sense – was, ostensibly, beyond Ramachandran's interest in the issue. Since I would define ideology as a system of beliefs/representations that naturalise social relations (particularly those of domination), the unreflexive stance vis-à-vis the individualist construction of wage-labour as free labour seemed to do little to confront the illusion of naturalness wrapped up with this notion.

Accepting the individualist construction of wage-labour as a free bargain, Ramachandran then faced the problem of the value to assign to this freedom. Thus, *Wage Labour and Unfreedom* characterises the freedom of the free worker both as 'formal' and as 'positive'. Not much is said about either of these notions or the contradiction implicit in using both characterisations.

---

[24] Mundle 1979, pp. 92ff., taking up Banaji 1977a.
[25] Ramachandran 1990, p. 18.
[26] Ramachandran 1990, p. 1: '...wage labour must be distinguished from the general category of hired labour. A wage labourer or proletarian is a hired labourer who is propertyless and is free to sell his or her labour power to the employer of his or her choice. This is in contrast, for instance, to a bonded labourer, who, though a hired labourer all right, is unfree to choose his or her employer'.

Free wage-labour is often referred to as 'free' wage-labour, implying adherence to the first description. But Ramachandran also speaks of the 'basic self-dignity and freedom from servitude that the freedom to choose employers implies'.[27] At any rate, one interesting consequence of this line of reasoning is that bondage precludes capitalism, since capitalism is based on wage-labour and wage-labour excludes bondage.

For Ramachandran, the polarity is one between wage-labour and unfreedom, because wage-labour is, by definition, free, and 'free' is construed here as substantially the opposite of 'unfree'. Tom Brass replaces this with the general polarity between free and unfree labour because, unlike Ramachandran, he seems to be unsure whether wage-labourers can be unfree. There is only one passage in his book where he uses the expression 'unfree wage-labour',[28] against many more where wage-labour is routinely described as 'free wage-labour' and numerous others where he speaks of 'unfree labour' *tout court*. Indeed, the index to *Towards a Comparative Political Economy of Unfree Labour* contains no item for 'wage-labour'! Measured against the reams of confident polemic on the issues of free and unfree labour, the least this suggests is a lack of clarity about where wage-labour itself fits into a conceptual schema built around the mesmerising contrast between 'free' and 'unfree' labour. Brass constructs a rigorously Manichean universe where workers are either free or unfree, and the scholars who write about them either realise that or function as apologists of bonded labour. He argues that debt-bound labour is unfree (i.e. not free labour dominated through debt), that employers use debt and bondage to 'decommodify' labour (re-incorporate labour into the means of production?), and, finally, that this tendency (of the forcible exclusion of workers from the labour-market) increases as individual employers 'restructure' the composition of the workforce to stave off growing 'class consciousness' (since 'unfree' workers are unlikely to organise). Brass has a peculiar notion of 'proletarianisation'. He defines it not in terms of the dispossession of labour but, evidently, as the formation of an organised working class. This enables him to speak of the factors which impede the formation of organised groups of workers as '*de*proletarianisation'. Bonded labourers may or may not

---

[27] Ramachandran 1990, p. 250.
[28] Brass 1999, p. 151, replicating parts of his joint 'Introduction' to Daniel, Bernstein, and Brass (eds.) 1993.

be wage-labourers (Brass leaves this unclear) but they are *not* a proletariat (in the idealised, Lukácsian sense used by Brass). Agrarian capitalists use bondage to deprive workers of an incipient proletarian subjectivity.

The upshot of their stark dualities is that Brass and Ramachandran both subscribe to a liberal-individualist notion of wage-labour as essentially free labour, labour based on the 'consent' of the individual worker and the free bargain that embodies that 'consent'. This is in sharp contrast to Marx whose references to free labour have a profoundly delegitimating intent. There are two aspects to Marx's handling of free labour: in Marx, free labour is both defined historically and contested ideologically. These are different levels of abstraction, and, while both are significant, my interest in this paper is in the second. I want to argue that his contestation of free labour makes Marx the first significant thinker to have adumbrated the critique of contract which emerged in the critical legal traditions of the twentieth century, starting with the Legal Realists. To abstract the references to free labour from the framework of this critique is to run the risk of imparting a naturalness to the notion of freedom which it does not possess. Not only did it take the *modern* world a long time to define a model of employment based on contract,[29] but when such a model did emerge, finally, in the nineteenth century, wage-labour was shrouded in a legal mysticism that remains with us to this day.

The famous passage in *Capital*, Volume I, which describes the sphere of circulation as a 'very Eden of the innate rights of man' is a succinct and sardonic statement of the nineteenth-century liberal-individualist ideology of contract. 'Freedom', 'Equality', and 'Property' are symbolic of the abstractions of classical individualism (core individualist concepts), while the references to natural rights, free will, and Bentham resonate with ideological imagery.[30] The implication is that 'freedom' is understood strictly in terms of the ideology of contract and the abstractions of individualism. Later, in Volume I, Marx characterises the employment contract as a 'legal fiction' which, with the mobility of labour, sustains the 'appearance of independence'.[31] Later still, the 'free contract' between capitalist and worker is described as an 'illusion'.[32] The perspective framing these sorties against individualism is the conception of the

---

[29] See Kahn-Freund 1977, pp. 508ff.
[30] Marx 1976a, pp. 280.
[31] Marx 1976a, pp. 719.
[32] Marx 1976a, pp. 935.

individual (free) worker from the standpoint of capital as such, that is, of the *total* social capital. Thus,

> In reality, the worker belongs to capital before he has sold himself to the capitalist. His economic bondage is at once mediated through, and concealed by, the periodic renewal of the act by which he sells himself, his change of masters, and the oscillations in the market-price of his labour.[33]

Again, the individual worker's 'enslavement to capital is only concealed by the variety of individual capitalists to whom [she] sells [herself]'.[34] Finally, 'the relation of exchange between capitalist and worker becomes a mere semblance belonging only to the process of circulation, it becomes a mere form, which is alien to the content of the transaction itself, and merely mystifies it'.[35]

All of this is summed up in a fascinating passage of the famous 'Appendix' where free contract is described as a 'formality', though one essential to capitalism, 'one of the essential *mediating forms* of capitalist relations of production' which is nonetheless a *mystification* of the 'essential nature' of wage-labour, an 'illusion' or 'deceptive appearance'.[36]

In other words, the 'essential' nature of wage-labour cannot lie in any of the ideological representations which *legitimate* the oppression of workers. To counterpose free labour to unfree labour the way Brass does is to ignore 'contract law's role in making actual domination appear free, natural, and rational'.[37] As Feinman and Gabel argue,

> The rise of capitalism...generated a dramatic and dislocating social upheaval....How could people have been persuaded or forced to accept

---

[33] Marx 1976a, pp. 723–4.
[34] Marx 1976a, pp. 763–4.
[35] Marx 1976a, pp. 729–30.
[36] Marx 1976a, pp. 1063–4.
  It follows that two widely held views are in error: There are firstly those who consider that wage-labour, the sale of labour to the capitalist, and hence the *wage form*, is something only *superficially* characteristic of capitalist production. It is, however, one of the *essential* mediating forms of capitalist relations of production, and one constantly reproduced by those relations themselves. Secondly, there are those who regard this superficial relation, this *essential formality*, this *deceptive appearance* of capitalist relations as its true *essence*. They therefore imagine that they can give a true account of those relations by classifying both workers and capitalists as *commodity owners*. They thereby gloss over the essential nature of the relationship, extinguishing its *differentia specifica*. [italics in original.]
[37] Mensch 1981, p. 767, reviewing Atiyah 1979.

such massive disruptions in their lives? One vehicle of persuasion was the law of contracts, which generated a new ideological imagery that sought to give legitimacy to the new order. Contract law was one of many such forms of imagery in law, politics, religion, and other representations of social experience that concealed and denied the oppressive and alienating aspects of the new social and economic relations. *Contract law denied the nature of the system by creating an imagery that made the oppression and alienation appear to be the consequences of what the people themselves desired.*[38]

Marx's conception of the wage-contract can thus be summed up in the words used by Friedrich Kessler to describe standardised contracts or contracts of adhesion in modern capitalism: the worker's 'contractual intention is but a *subjection more or less voluntary to terms dictated by the stronger party*'.[39] That is, nothing in the nature of free labour prevented employers from imposing the harshest possible terms on their employees, including restrictions on their mobility. If this seems paradoxical, that is only so because contract entails the 'general irony of coercion imposed in the name of freedom'.[40] Freedom of contract enables capitalists to 'legislate by contract', and to legislate in a 'substantially authoritarian manner without using the appearance of authoritarian forms'.[41]

Brass construes unfree labour in terms of mechanisms of control which tie labour down. The key mechanism is debt. The explanation lacks nuance (perhaps deliberately), and attachment, debt, and bondage become interchangeable expressions of an undifferentiated coercion = unfreedom.[42] Marx himself defined free labour primarily in terms of the dispossession of labour, and then, of course, its ability to make valid contracts. Since subordination (obedience, subjection to the employer) is the essence of wage-labour, it would have made no sense to allow the control of labour, in the labour process and/or the employment relation, to cancel freedom all the way through. Discussing the feudal remnant in the governance of American labour in the late

---

[38] Gabel and Feinman 1998, p. 501.
[39] Kessler 1943, p. 632.
[40] Mensch 1981, p. 767.
[41] Kessler 1943, p. 640.
[42] This looks like a caricature but cf. Brass 1996, p. 237: 'I tend to use all these four concepts interchangeably (attached labour = unfreedom = debt bondage = deproletarianisation)'.

nineteenth century, the remarkable fact that 'the law of master and servant was at the foundation of capitalist development and industrialism', Karen Orren writes,

> [W]hatever the public rights and private aspirations of the worker, he or she was in reality a free person against everyone except his or her employer. That does not mean there were no rights the servant could assert against the master, but they were severely restricted by the processes and content of the law, and by the practicalities that stemmed from the master's own – absolute – right to terminate the employment at any time.[43]

In the majority of instances discussed by Brass, contract is always the background against which coercion operates. But this is contract *imbued with a profound sense of inequality*, the hierarchy of master and servant, a 'medieval' remnant, even if the relations of production are certainly capitalist.

To repeat, in both Brass and Ramachandran, the critique of unfree labour is secured at a price, namely, endorsing the liberal mystification of a 'free' bargain,[44] against Marx's conception of the labour market as an instrument of coercion and the 'Realist' undermining of the premises of liberal legalism. On the other hand, their problematics diverge. The issue for Brass is whether labour that he construes as 'unfree' is compatible with capital/capitalism; the issue underlying the formalist orthodoxy on wage-labour (Ramachandran) is a different and more substantial one though, namely, whether 'unfree' labour can ever be construed as *wage*-labour, and here Brass is on the whole curiously silent, although he does, at one point, allow for the characterisation of unfree workers as unfree wage-labour.

The condescension with which Ramachandran dismissed Mundle would be less tenable today. In the diary of his travels in South India, Francis Buchanan refers repeatedly to 'hired servants' who were held in *bondage* by their masters. Unaffected by the formalisms that would later swamp the world of

---

[43] Orren 1991, pp. 70, 92.
[44] Brass attacks Pranab Bardhan for construing attached labour relationships in India as 'voluntaristic action by choice-making individuals' (Brass 1999, p. 224) but how else does one characterise his own model of free labour? The bland assertion that 'in economic terms the concept "market" is actually an *antithesis* of coercion.' (p. 262; his emphasis) forgets that 'the freedom of the "market" [is] essentially a freedom of individuals and groups to coerce one another, with the power to coerce reinforced by agencies of the state itself' (Dawson 1947, p. 266).

labour, he saw no obvious incongruity in juxtaposing what appear to us to be sharply conflicting images. To quote one of several possible passages from the travel diaries, he wrote, about southern Canara, 'The cultivation is chiefy carried on by *Culialu*, or hired servants'.

> At the end of the year the hired servant may change his service, if he be free from debt; but that is seldom the case. When he gets deeply involved, his master may sell his sister's children to discharge the amount, and his services may be transferred to any other man who chooses to take him and pay his debts to his master. In fact, he differs little from a slave.[45]

The bonding of migrant workers discussed by Breman in *Footloose Labour* describes a form of wage-labour in which employers 'use force and oppression as tools with which to increase their hold on the workers'.[46] Here, again, there is no abstract antithesis between bondage and the hiring of labour, even if the context is vastly different, with a massive erosion in the legitimacy of upper-caste dominance and workers less willing to accept domination. That workers did fight back even in much earlier periods is shown by the repeated litigation brought by Indian labourers before the General Indian Court of colonial Mexico for most of the seventeenth and eighteenth centuries. Borah describes the form of exploitation involved, so-called debt-peonage, as 'the recruitment of wage labor bound by debt', describing the workers themselves as 'coerced but not enslaved'.[47] Again, Martin Murray shows that the European rubber plantations of northern and eastern Cochinchina used a contract system that 'legally bound wage-labourers to the point of production for periods that almost always exceeded the initial three-year agreement'.[48] Finally, in a review of Byres's book on agrarian capitalism, Charles Post argues that 'capital is often compelled to rely on legally bonded wage-workers.... These workers are bound to a single employer or branch of production by laws restricting their ability to move geographically and enter short-term labour contracts'.[49]

---

[45] Buchanan 1870, Volume 2, pp. 227–8.
[46] Breman 1996, p. 168.
[47] Borah 1983.
[48] Murray 1992, p. 52, and the ref. to 'bonded forms of hire' at p. 59.
[49] Post 1999, p. 289, noting that 'Unlike slaves and serfs, coerced wage-workers are separated from both the means of production and subsistence'.

Stating all this in a more general form, employers have *repeatedly subjected free workers to repressive forms of control*. The massive deployment of Polish seasonal labourers on the East Elbian estates during the First World War and under Nazism,[50] the forced recruitment of wage-labourers in French and British Africa,[51] and the position of nineteenth-century English wage-earners who faced criminal sanctions for breach of contract[52] all exemplify situations where the 'boundary between compulsion and free will...was neither distinct nor of any great interest' to the authorities and employers.[53] Likewise, if 'attachment' is basically a means of *control* over labour, there is no reason why debt servitude cannot be a means of controlling *wage*-labourers. The advance payment of wages is manipulated to intensify the domination of labour.[54]

This at least partly deals with the orthodoxy that restrictions on freedom undermine the nature of wage-labour. Regarding the related issue of whether capital can exploit workers who are truly unfree (who represent bondage in Kant's sense),[55] the major problem with Brass's way of handling this thesis, apart from his definition of unfree labour, is that the needs of individual and social capital are conflated throughout his argument. Brass conceives capitalism *entirely* from the standpoint of individual capital, ignoring the fact that the logic that regulates capitalist economy is, necessarily, that of the *total* social capital. Thus, the real issue of theory here is whether we can sensibly visualise the accumulation of capital being founded on unfree labour (in the strict sense just noted) at the level of the expansion of the total social capital. And the obvious response is, no, since the mobility of labour is essential to the mechanism of capital at *this* level. That individual capitals are indifferent

---

[50] Herbert 1997.
[51] Cooper 1996.
[52] Steinfeld 2001, Chapter 2, linking the proliferation of stronger contract remedies to the evolution of 'freer labour markets'.
[53] Herbert 1997, p. 59, on German indifference to the Polish seasonal labourers.
[54] See Bolland 1981, especially p. 608: 'Central to effective control of the labor force was the practice of paying wages in advance', on the use of debt to trap free labourers in Belize.
[55] In the *Metaphysics of Morals*, published in 1797, Kant produced one of the most interesting classifications of the forms of labour when he distinguished between bondage, service, and pure wage contracts. Bondage [*Leibeigenschaft*] was his generic term for all types of slavery and serfdom, while 'service' was discussed under the rights pertaining to the heads of households or family heads and seen essentially as a form of wage-labour subject to patriarchy; see Kant 1996, pp. 431ff., 471–2, 496.

to the nature of the labour force and have no special concern for the rights of workers was argued at length in my paper in *Capital & Class* in 1977.[56]

5.3. Forms of exploitation based on wage-labour

Expanding on the argument developed in that paper, capitalist accumulation may involve any of the following 'methods':[57]

(i) more-or-less coerced/more-or-less 'free' forms of wage-labour;
(ii) unfree labour in the strict sense;
(iii) the integration of peasant family labour into the capitalist production process.

There is scarcely any doubt that Marx came around to seeing the Southern plantations (based on slavery) as *capitalist* enterprises. Thus the overworking of slaves in the Southern states of the American Union was, he tells us in Volume I, a question of the 'production of surplus-value itself'.[58] In the *Grundrisse*, he refers to '[t]he fact that we now not only call the plantation owners in America capitalists, but that they *are* capitalists'[59] and implies that these 'anomalous' forms of capitalist enterprise *could* exist because capitalism as a whole was based on free labour. (My interpretation of this is: the American slave-owners *are* capitalists because they are *part* of the total social capital.) In *Theories of Surplus Value*, he writes that the 'business in which slaves are used is conducted by *capitalists*', though this is qualified by saying that here the capitalist mode of production 'exists only in a formal sense'.[60] Finally, in Volume III of *Capital*, he writes, 'Where the capitalist conception prevails, as on the American plantations, this entire surplus-value is conceived as profit',[61] and, in Volume II, slaves are described as 'fixed capital'.

It is worth noting that, among later Marxists, Henryk Grossmann saw no incongruity in accepting Sombart's description of the seventeenth-century

---

[56] Banaji 1977b; Chapter 2 above.
[57] Cf. Hilferding 1981, p. 320: 'methods of capitalist accumulation'.
[58] Marx 1976a, p. 345.
[59] Marx 1973, p. 513.
[60] Marx 1968, pp. 302–3.
[61] Marx 1981, p. 940.

plantations as the 'first [exemplars of] truly large-scale *capitalist* organization'.⁶²
Indeed, Grossmann argued that

> in the first hundred years following the discovery of America, the whole character of Spanish and Portuguese colonisation was already capitalist in nature, characterised as it was by a drive for surplus-value, even if the plantations were run on the basis of slave labour.⁶³

At the level of *individual* capitals, it is accumulation or the 'drive for surplus-value' that defines capitalism, not the presence or absence of 'free' labour. Yet a majority of Marxists are probably still reluctant to abandon the comforting idea that slavery precludes capitalism 'because' capitalism is founded on free labour.

Ad iii), capitalist integration of the peasantry is best illustrated by the use of the advance system in nineteenth-century Indian agriculture. 'Advances' were especially widespread in the production of indigo, cotton, and sugarcane. Thus, the speculative capitalism of the Agency Houses that controlled the Bengal indigo trade in the early nineteenth century was based on a system of advances through which planters sought to 'bind' the peasantry to the factory.⁶⁴ The Report of the Indigo Commission noted that 'the contract for the growth and production of the plant, so far from being voluntary, is forced upon the ryot, who is compelled by more or less pressure to accept advances...'.⁶⁵ About the squaring of accounts that began in October, one respondent told the Commission, 'There are some individuals who could clear themselves, if we would let them, but *we would not clear them on principle, inasmuch as it would be tantamount to closing the factory*'.⁶⁶ Indeed, Chowdhury

---

⁶² Grossmann 1970, p. 406, citing Sombart 1917, ii/2, p. 1011. In the first volume of *Modern Capitalism*, Sombart described the slave plantations as the 'first large enterprises of a capitalist nature [*die ersten kapitalistischen Großbetriebe*]'.
⁶³ Grossmann 1970, p. 408.
⁶⁴ See Chowdhury 1964. Chowdhury writes, 'The peasant had to sign a properly stamped contract by which he agreed to do whatever was necessary to cultivate indigo and to deliver the plant to the planter.... The primary allurement in cultivating indigo was the advances. [A]ccording to Walters (1830), "If a ryot once received an advance, he could very seldom or never clear himself and thus becomes little better than a bond-slave to the factory"' (pp. 130–3). Walters was the then Magistrate of the City of Dacca.
⁶⁵ *Report of the Indigo Commission* 1860, § 16.
⁶⁶ *Report of the Indigo Commission* 1860, § 492 my emphasis.

reports that 'Macaulay looked upon the contract between the planter and the peasant as of the same kind as one between the capitalist and a worker'.[67]

In short, *historically*, capital-accumulation has been characterised by considerable flexibility in the structuring of production and in the forms of labour and organisation of labour used in producing surplus-value. The liberal conception of capitalism which sees the sole basis of accumulation in the individual wage-earner conceived as a free labourer obliterates a great deal of capitalist history, erasing the contribution of both enslaved and collective (family) units of labour-power.[68]

To take this further, it would surely represent an advance in Marxist theory to think of capitalism working through a *multiplicity* of forms of exploitation *based on* wage-labour. In other words, instead of seeing wage-labour as *one* form of exploitation among many, alongside sharecropping, labour tenancy, and various kinds of bonded labour, these specific individual forms of exploitation may just be ways in which paid labour is recruited, exploited, and controlled by employers. The argument is not that *all* sharecroppers, labour-tenants, and bonded labourers are wage-workers, but that these 'forms' may reflect the subsumption of labour into capital in ways where the 'sale' of labour-power for wages[69] is mediated and possibly disguised in more complex arrangements. The prototype of this kind of analysis is Waszyński's conception of the Byzantine sharecropper as a wage-labourer. Analysing Egyptian agricultural leases of the sixth and seventh centuries, Waszyński argued, '[the γεωργός of the sixth-seventh centuries] is basically no longer a tenant...he has become a hired worker [*Mietling*] or wage-labourer [*Lohnarbeiter*] whom the landlord can dismiss at any time'.[70] 'To form a proper assessment of these contracts, we should, instead of seeing the share accruing to the landlord in the division

---

[67] Chowdhury 1964, p. 162 (about indigo).
[68] Yann Moulier Boutang 1998 argues that capitalism has typically been founded on 'dependent' labour (rather than wage-labour specifically) and that the central issue for employers has always been some set of restrictions on the mobility of the worker (i.e., of living labour). More interestingly, he accepts that wage-labourers may work under diminished degrees of freedom, referring to 'salariat non libre' (e.g., p. 378).
[69] Marx 1976b, p. 1005: '...wage-labour (it is thus we designate the labour of the worker who sells his own labour-power)'; Marx 1972, p. 271: '...wage-workers, that is, workers who must sell their labour-power because their conditions of labour confront them as alien property'.
[70] Waszyński 1905, p. 92.

of the crop as rent, view the portion received by the γεωργός as a wage.'⁷¹ In Bengal in the 1930s, the various landholders' associations consistently took the stand that their *bargadars* (sharecroppers) were 'mere' labourers, that is, workers paid in kind, arguing that landowners preferred sharecropping due to its greater intensity of labour.⁷² In the US, most Southern states drew a legal distinction between croppers and tenants. 'Because the landlord supplied all necessary means of production, the sharecropper was a *wage worker whose form of wages was a share of the crop*'.⁷³ Angelo characterises Southern sharecropping (or at least the legal construction of it) as a 'disguised wage work contract'.⁷⁴ Francesco Maria Gianni described the Tuscan sharecroppers of the late eighteenth century as 'workers [*operai*] recruited by their respective landowners to hire out their labour not by the day or for any precise and definite daily wages but for at least a year and for half the crop produced by them'.⁷⁵ Yet P.J. Jones showed how, even as early as the late fourteenth/fifteenth centuries, when *mezzadria* expanded on the estates in Tuscany, it embodied a form of 'wage-type tenancy', with leaseholds akin to labour-contracts.⁷⁶ With renewed commercialisation in the late nineteenth century and the introduction of the new industrial crops, the *mezzadri* were subjected to further waves of proletarianisation, as farm sizes were drastically cut, work controls tightened, and eviction formally conceded to employers as their 'sole means of restoring discipline'.⁷⁷ Snowden refers to the 'emergence in sizeable numbers from the end of the century of a variety of new sub-categories of semi-proletarianised *mezzadri* – *camporaioli, logaioli, vignaioli*, and *mezzaioli*.... The new sharecroppers did not live on their plots.... Instead, they commuted to the land from neighbouring villages or from labourers' barracks'.⁷⁸

Labour-tenancy is susceptible to a similar analysis. Lenin described this form of exploitation as the 'capitalist system of providing the estate with agricultural workers by allotting patches of land to them' and characterised the

---

⁷¹ Waszyński 1905, p. 157.
⁷² Government of Bengal 1940, vols. 3–4.
⁷³ Angelo 1995, p. 594; italics in original.
⁷⁴ Angelo 1995, p. 595.
⁷⁵ Gianni, cited in Giorgetti 1977, p. 231.
⁷⁶ Jones 1968, who says, 'It [*mezzadria*] represented a "proletarization" of the peasantry' (at p. 225).
⁷⁷ Snowden 1979.
⁷⁸ Snowden 1979, p. 157.

allotment itself as 'wages in kind'.[79] He referred to labour being 'hired' on a 'labour-service and bonded basis'. Moreover, 'the latter form of labour always presupposes the personal dependence of the one hired upon the one who hires him, it always presupposes the greater or lesser retention of "other than economic pressure"'.[80] The less developed forms of agrarian capitalism made extensive use of labour-tenancy.[81] In South Africa, black families 'without the resources to work the land themselves entered labour-tenancy agreements'.[82] Labour tenants were thus worse off (less independent) than sharecroppers. Yet labour-tenancy staved off total dispossession. The form of payment was at least as strongly infuenced by tenants' aspirations to regain access to land and accumulate cattle as by the shortage of cash among landowners. In fact, 'obtaining pastures was far and away the most important reason for surrender to tenancy by homestead heads.... Typically, the negotiation of labour tenant contracts centred around cattle and children, with landlords grudgingly trading off grazing for the first in exchange for sufficient labour from the second'.[83] If employers preferred wages in kind,[84] so clearly did tenant households, for whom the 'cash proceeds of their labour contracts were of little or no economic significance'.[85] But white farmers lobbied aggressively to have labour-tenants placed under the jurisdiction of the Master and Servant Acts.[86] The general point to emerge from these struggles is that, as employers are driven to increase their control over these forms of labour (sharecroppers included), the contracts and means of compulsion used by them are progressively modified to diminish the rights of workers and their families and *proletarianise them further*.[87]

Similarly, Buchanan's reference to hired servants who were held in bondage by their masters forms the prototype for the analysis of bonded labour as

---

[79] Lenin 1972, pp. 200–203.
[80] Lenin 1972, p. 203.
[81] For Egypt, see Owen 1981; for Peru, Jacobsen 1993, Chapter 8; for Prussia, Perkins 1984.
[82] Keegan 1987, p. 77.
[83] Bradford 1987, pp. 37–8.
[84] Keegan 1987, pp. 122ff.
[85] Kanogo 1987, p. 23.
[86] See Williams 1996; for Kenya, Kanogo 1987, pp. 37ff.
[87] For Italy, see Snowden 1979; for Mexico, Bazant 1977, pp. 74ff. So, too, with the replacement of the *Instleute* by the *Deputatisten*, cf. Perkins 1984, p. 12: 'The confined labourer was far more of an economic object than the cottager'.

a further distinction of form within wage-labour.[88] The key mechanism here is debt, but the failure to disentangle 'industrial profit' (in Marx's sense),[89] from its fetishistic representation in the consciousness of employers generates endless confusion, even in the work of Marxists like Brass. 'Interest is a relationship between two capitalists, not between capitalist and worker'.[90] That employers choose to treat wage-advances (part of their variable, i.e. productive, capital) as 'loans' has nothing to do with the real nature of the relationships, which are those between wage-labourers and the functioning capitalist. The contrast between these levels (or forms) of reality is recurrent in Marx. Thus, 'Interest is just another name for surplus-value', Marx says of the advances made by usurers (money capitalists) in India.[91] Profit is 'called *rent*, just as it is called *interest* when, for example, as in India, the worker (although nominally independent) works with advances he receives from the capitalist and has to hand over all the surplus produce to the capitalist'.[92] Where profit is 'acquired in the form of interest' (is *called* interest), the capitalist 'appears as a mere usurer'. When this form of capitalism operates to control the labour of peasant producers who are both free and formally independent, '[w]e have here the *whole of capitalist production* without its advantages', namely, the development of the social forms of labour and of the productivity of labour that these generate.[93] In each of these passages, Marx implies a distinction between the actual nature of production, which is capitalist, and the forms in which those relations of production and exploitation are portrayed or 'represented' in the consciousness of its agents. To take these forms of representation at face value – for example, to divide the cash advances made by employers to their workers into a 'wage' component and a 'loan' component, as Brass does – is to move *within* the fetishised appearances that dominate the 'everyday

---

[88] See n. 45 above.
[89] Marx 1972, p. 490: '*Industrial profit*, in contradistinction to *interest*, represents capital in the [production] process in contradistinction to capital outside the process, capital as a process in contradistinction to capital as property; it therefore represents the capitalist as functioning capitalist...as opposed to the capitalist as...mere owner of capital'.
[90] Marx 1981, p. 506. Cf. Marx 1981, p. 503: '[I]nterest-bearing capital as such does not have wage-labour as its opposite but rather functioning capital.... Interest-bearing capital is capital *as property* as against capital *as function*' (emphasis in original).
[91] Marx 1976b, p. 1023.
[92] Marx 1972, p. 188.
[93] Marx 1972, p. 487, adding, 'This form is very prevalent among peasant nations' affected by market-relations. The italics are mine.

notions of the actual agents of production'.[94] Thus, wage-advances are characterised as 'loans', employers described as 'creditors', and workers transformed into 'debtors'.[95] The advances themselves are described *both* as 'wages for future employment' and as 'a loan for work yet to be done' – in the same paragraph![96] What this does is to conflate a component of productive capital (namely, wages) with a form of interest-bearing capital. It also fails to see that when employers *advance* wages, they actually *buy* labour 'instead of simply paying for it later'.[97]

Suppose that the use of cash/kind advances represents not the actual buying of labour-power (which is what it is) but simply the accumulation of claims to unrealised labour. There is still an issue about the nature of those claims. Conceived as interest-bearing capital, the claims to future labour would be fictitious capital, in the sense that 'the creditor cannot recall his capital from the debtor but [at best] can only sell the claim, his title of ownership'.[98] 'The capital itself has been consumed, spent by the [worker]. It no longer exists.'[99] In other words, conceived as debt (in the *strict* sense), the capital laid out in advances to the worker would be fictitious in exactly the sense in which the national debt represents 'fictitious capital'.[100] What the creditor possesses is simply a promissory note (a 'bond') equivalent to the state's promissory notes when creditors buy government bonds. But the advances are not securities at all, there is no proper market for the circulation of such paper assets,[101] and the analogy is as absurd as that between the usurer's interest and the modern

---

[94] Marx 1981, p. 969. Brass 1999, p. 82.
[95] Brass 1999, p. 297: 'Essentially, each consists of a relationship whereby cash or kind loans advanced by a creditor (usually – but not necessarily – a landlord, a merchant, a moneylender, a labour contractor, or a rich peasant) are repaid in the form of compulsory labour-service by the debtor personally etc.', about *enganche* in Peru and attached labour in India.
[96] Brass 1999, p. 225. Yet, Brass has a vague sense that one is dealing here with ideology, not with the actual nature of the transactions themselves, e.g., '*In ideological terms*, therefore, a bonded labourer works to pay off a debt rather than for a wage' (at p. 12); or, 'This sum was *regarded by the employer* as a debt contracted by the tribal' (at p. 84); my italics.
[97] Marx 1978, p. 295.
[98] Marx 1981, p. 595.
[99] Marx 1981, p. 595, where the sentence reads, 'The capital itself has been consumed, spent by the state. It no longer exists'.
[100] Marx 1981, pp. 595ff.
[101] For example, McArdle 1978, p. 118, 'Peasant indebtedness formed gigantic paper assets', about the Medici estates in Tuscany.

interest-rate decried by Marx.¹⁰² 'Debt', that is, the depiction of wages as loans, is simply a device to control labour in conditions where the competition for labour is likely to drive up the bargaining power and wages of workers.¹⁰³ It is a legal or pseudo-legal fiction used by employers to manoeuvre workers into a system of forced labour (which is still *wage-labour*) or contain their mobility and manipulate effort-standards.¹⁰⁴ Some employers clearly believed in the sanctity ('legality') of this fiction, others were (and have been) under no illusion.¹⁰⁵

5.4. 'Free contract' in Sartre's *Critique*

Vulgar Marxists have worked with a rigid dichotomy between free and unfree labour, suggesting that lack of coercion is a defining feature of wage-labour. This bright-line approach camouflages the fact that *all* wage-labour is subject to compulsion, both in the general and widely accepted sense that workers are compelled to sell their labour-power and subject, at this level, to a general market or economic coercion, and more directly, insofar as the exchange involved in wage-labour is one of 'obedience for wages'¹⁰⁶ and employers have to find ways to enforce contracts.¹⁰⁷ Given that all wage-labour is subject to constraint in this double sense, it follows that the 'freedom' of free labour is best construed in a *minimalist* sense to mean, *primarily*, the legal capacity ('autonomy') required to enter a labour agreement.¹⁰⁸ Construed in this way,

---

¹⁰² Marx 1981, p. 730.
¹⁰³ For example, McCreery 1983, p. 746: '*Habilitadores* [labour contractors] and employers competed fiercely among themselves for labor'.
¹⁰⁴ Fiction: cf. Chaudhuri 1969, p. 245, citing the words of a nineteenth-century district official: '[T]he fiction is usually kept up that the labourer is in his master's debt'. Forced labour: e.g., Daniel 1972. Marx characterised peonage as a form of slavery (Marx 1976a, pp. 271ff., n. 3), but see Zavala 1988, pp. 35ff. for the argument that *peonaje* involved a form of wage-labour, and his interesting comment on the footnote in *Capital*.
¹⁰⁵ Cf. Breman 1974, p. 236: '[landlords] know that repayment is practically impossible for the farm servants and are under no illusion in this respect'. Elsewhere, Breman writes: 'Employers present such arrangements as "advances" on wages that will be repaid through the labour of the borrower. However, such "advances" are solely intended to appropriate labour, whether immediately or at a later date. *Neither party views the transaction as a loan that will be terminated on repayment*' (in Parry et al. (eds.) 1999, p. 419; italics mine).
¹⁰⁶ Fox 1985, p. 113, citing J.S. Mill, 'obedience in return for wages'.
¹⁰⁷ See Steinfeld 2001.
¹⁰⁸ Cf. Orren 1991, p. 95. This is certainly how Marx understood free labour.

Marx's references to successive Tudor governments driving the propertyless into free labour in a process he calls the 'forced labour of free workers [*Zwangsarbeit der freien Arbeiter*]'[109] seem much less paradoxical than they might otherwise, as does Sartre's parallel reference to 'free forced labour [*le travail librement forcé*]' as typical of the repressive liberal capitalism of the early nineteenth century.[110] In particular, Sartre's expression refers to the methods used by English employers to break the recalcitrance of skilled workers and produce a subjugated labour-force. If labour subjected to 'repressive practices within factories'[111] was nonetheless 'free', this is because 'freedom', in *this* context, refers, minimalistically, to the mystified/mystifying moment of the wage-contract and the freedom-of-contract rhetoric of nineteenth-century liberal individualism.[112]

Sartre's references to free labour in the *Critique* work in terms of an implicit contrast between the real freedom of the worker, identified as the worker's *human* reality, and the abstract or mystified freedom of the wage-contract. Contract 'mystifies' freedom, both because the 'form' (of a free contract) disguises the dictatorial power of the employer[113] and makes the worker's domination appear 'free, natural, and rational',[114] and because the worker's freedom is in fact complicit in its own crushing. The wage-contract belongs to the practico-inert field of exploitation, whereas employment and labour – the search for work and work itself – presuppose the human freedom of the worker, or free individual *praxis*, insofar as these are forms of human activity. *Thus freedom is present in two guises* – as the mystification of 'free labour' (the inert 'idea' of liberal ideology)[115] and as the *real* freedom of the practical organism,

---

[109] Marx 1973, p. 736; Marx 1974, pp. 623f. ['Also noch *Zwangsarbeit* zu einem bestimmten Lohn der freien Arbeiter. Sie müssen erst *gezwungen* werden zu den vom Kapital gesetzten bedingungen zu arbeiten'].

[110] Sartre 1960, p. 694 (Sartre 1976, p. 742).

[111] Sartre 1960, p. 694 (Sartre 1976, p. 742); e.g., criminal restraints for breach of contract, cf. Steinfeld 2001.

[112] Sartre 1960, p. 269 (Sartre 1976, p. 207) defines the free worker as 'an exploited man whose exploitation resides entirely in freedom of contract'. At p. 697 (p. 746) he refers to 'liberal atomism', at p. 699 (p. 748) to 'liberal ideology'.

[113] Neumann 1936, p. 10.

[114] Mensch 1981, p. 767, cf. Klare 1998, p. 554: '[T]he alluring rhetoric of free contract [makes] it appear as though this control and domination of employees occur[s] by their own consent'.

[115] Sartre 1960, p. 644 (Sartre 1976, p. 679), 'la mystification du libre-contrat'; cf. Trotsky 1969: '[F]reedom was reduced to a legal fiction, on the basis of freely-hired slavery. *We know of no other form of free labor in history*' (p. 140; italics mine).

which is *praxis* itself conceived not as an abstract force traversing the heterogeneous moments of dialectical intelligibility[116] but as the 'free actions of individuals',[117] the free activity which 'in its freedom will *take upon itself* everything which crushes it',[118] which is *masked* by collective representations and the coerciveness of industrial routine,[119] and without which alienation (that is, the *impotence* of freedom or the impossibility 'inside' freedom)[120] would cease to have any meaning since there would be nothing to *be* alienated.[121] Thus, to say that the worker freely sells his labour-power is *not* tantamount to the claim that the worker's action is unconstrained or uncoerced but, rather, that the 'sale' of labour-power, like work itself and all human activity, requires the sovereign freedom of a practical agent. As Sartre says,

> It is true that he has no other way out; the choice is an impossible one; he has not the ghost of a chance of finding better paid work and in any case he never even asks himself the question: what is the point of it all? He goes and sells himself at the factory every morning...by a sort of sombre resigned *hexis* which scarcely resembles a *praxis*. And yet, in fact, it is a *praxis*: habit is directed and organized, the end is posited, the means chosen...; in other words, the ineluctable destiny which is crushing him passes right through him.[122]

One of the great strengths of the *Critique of Dialectical Reason* is its clarification of this issue. A Marxism untouched by the insights of the *Critique* conflates the real freedom of the worker (as a practical agent) – the freedom that wage-labourers *share* with all workers and all kinds of workers throughout history – with the mystified freedom projected in the rhetoric of liberal legalism and the common-law doctrine of the private right of free contract. More importantly, Sartre recovers the legal-realist insight that 'constraint does not

---

[116] Sartre 1960, p. 359 (Sartre 1976, p. 319): 'it would be absurd or idealistic to imagine that individual *praxis*, inert activity and common action are the three moments of the development *of a single force* conceived as *human praxis*'.
[117] Sartre 1960, p. 370 (Sartre 1976, p. 332).
[118] Sartre 1960, p. 364 (Sartre 1976, p. 325); emphasis mine.
[119] As Sartre would tell Simone de Beauvoir many years later, de Beauvoir 1981, p. 455.
[120] Sartre 1960, p. 367 (Sartre 1976, pp. 328–9).
[121] Sartre 1960, p. 180 (Sartre 1976, p. 97): 'if human relations are a mere product, they are in essence reified and it becomes impossible to understand what their reification really consists in'.
[122] Sartre 1960, p. 364 (Sartre 1976, p. 325).

eliminate freedom (except by liquidating the oppressed)'.[123] Coercion is not an 'overpowering of the will'. 'A victim of duress *does* normally know what he is doing, *does* choose to submit, and does intend to do so.'[124] Conversely,

> The fact that he [the victim] exercised a choice *does not indicate lack of compulsion*. Even a slave makes a choice. The compulsion which drives him to work operates through his own will power.... [T]hough he exercises will power and makes a choice, still, since he is making it under threat, his servitude is called 'involuntary'.[125]

It follows that the moment of the free contract between employers and wage-earners is, in Sartre's words, 'both the most shameless mystification and a reality'.[126] And it is a *reality* not because freedom of contract implies or entails that labour recruited by contract is free in the sense of being uncoerced, but because 'everything is sustained by individual praxis'.[127]

5.5. Summary

An uncritical deployment of the free/unfree labour antithesis valorises one of the most powerful fictions of possessive individualism, namely, the notion that the 'freedoms of circulation inherent in contract' are an expression of individual freedom[128] and that free labourers have some measure of control over their working lives *because* they can choose who to work for. This contrasts sharply with Marx's conception of the wage-contract as a legal fiction that both mediated and masked the domination of labour by capital. Brass

---

[123] Sartre 1960, p. 690 (Sartre 1976, p. 737), 'la contrainte ne supprime pas la liberté (sauf en liquidant les opprimés)'.
[124] Atiyah 1982, p. 200, against the traditional view of duress as a coercion of the will that 'vitiates consent'. The contemporary view is that a party's will is never actually overborne in the sense of losing control, for example, Feinman 1987, pp. 1537ff., reviewing Collins 1986.
[125] Hale 1943, p. 606; my emphasis.
[126] Sartre 1960, p. 364 (Sartre 1976, p. 325).
[127] Sartre 1960, p. 257 (Sartre 1976, p. 193). At p. 362 (p. 323) Sartre writes, 'it must be pointed out both that the practico-inert field *exists*, that it is *real*, and that free human activities are not thereby eliminated, that they are *not even altered* in their translucidity as projects in the process of being realized.'
[128] Haag 1999, p. 36. Haag's book is a brilliant critique of conflicting liberal constructions of women's sexual agency/oppression and makes repeated reference to the fictions of the free labour-contract.

deploys a discourse of freedom and unfreedom as if these terms had an obvious meaning. He identifies free labour with the free circulation of labour, and this is clearly also how Marx understood the expression. The crucial difference, however, is that that is all free labour meant for Marx – he did not view the worker as a free agent – whereas, for Brass, free labour resonates with its opposition to unfree labour, evoking subliminal images of freedom from bondage, oppression, and coercion, as if free labour was exempt from violence, much less from subtler forms of bondage and coercion. In short, *the fiction of the free labour-contract is renaturalised in an uncritical antinomy of free and unfree labour*. Secondly, I have argued that, while the organisation of labour under capital-accumulation implicates forms of exploitation beyond the presumptively normative free labour-contract (notably, slavery and the centralised field labour of slaves), the *wage-contract itself can be organised in different ways* (under different labour systems), for example, as sharecropping, labour tenancy, or various forms of bondage, once we extend the notion of wages to include payments in land, housing, etc.[129] Finally, free labour is a construct of liberal ideology, the lived experience of oppression under capitalism mystified as an 'outcome of ordinary principles of freedom of contract',[130] and the only real freedom workers possess under capitalism or any system of domination is their power of resistance, that is, the capacity they have as individuals to act on the world, both individually and through the common action of groups.

---

[129] Cf. Marx 1976, p. 820, 'They receive cottages and coal for firing "for nothing" – i.e. these form part of their wages, paid in kind', about miners in Britain.
[130] Stokes 1994, p. 90, about the legitimation of managerial power in the contract version of the traditional legal model of the company.

Chapter Six
Agrarian History and the Labour-Organisation of Byzantine Large Estates

6.1. Introduction

Although the emergence and consolidation of the new provincial aristocracies of Late Antiquity meant a considerable development of large estates and their exploitation as jointly owned consolidated holdings, not much has been written about the organisation of estates. Indeed, till today the only focused monograph is a study published in 1931.[1] Jean Gascou's thesis showed little interest in the internal administration and labour-arrangements of the large estates, and his basic argument was in any case hostile to such a perspective, since the estates, for him, were essentially public institutions, with the aristocracy working largely within a fiscal régime.[2] Kaplan's recent book systematically avoids Egypt, and bases its survey of the earlier centuries (sixth–seventh) on a kind of source-material that can tell us little about the actual functioning of estates.[3] This is all the more surprising, as the new estates reflect the characteristics of the late empire in a particularly lucid form, from the social origins and character of their owners to the managerial options they preferred, and the

[1] Hardy 1931.
[2] Gascou 1985.
[3] Kaplan 1992.

extraordinary sense of submission they imposed on a labour-force which was, after all, both free and structured and controlled essentially through contracts. Papyri from Egypt reflect a better image of these processes than any other body of evidence, as they stem directly from the operations of rural economy, but their dispersed and difficult character is possibly one reason for the neglect of aristocratic economy. However, the most important reason is probably the influence of minimalist views of the ancient economy – the idea that precapitalist classes lacked both sophistication and basic economic rationalism, and that large landowners, in particular, were simply *rentiers*, with no interest in labour-processes or the broader organisation of production.[4]

My interest in this paper is in the status of the peasantry in the late antique world, which very roughly spans the period from the fourth to the seventh centuries. This was an epoch of rapid social change, of new cultural dynamisms, and of a large-scale restructuring of both economic and political life.[5] For generations, however, the vitality and innovation of this period (a *post-classical* one) were simply ignored, and these prior proto-medieval centuries were seen as an age of unrelieved gloom and decay. When this sweeping orthodoxy was later relaxed, the assumptions scholars had made about the agrarian life of the period were merely inverted and, consequently, one is left today with two contradictory models which no longer seem particularly useful (see below). Neither of these models is tenable, as each fails to capture the peculiarity (and sophistication) of late antique economy and culture, which, with their deep-rooted and multiplex hierarchies, were nonetheless more fluid and democratic than the world from which they emerged. The parochial and human slaveries of the classical world were superseded by more metaphysical subordinations – servility to the emperor and to God, but both assumed freely by subjects conscious of themselves as loyal and/or devout individuals. At the economic level, more and more labour-power was repulsed from the fabric of the old economy and absorbed in the creative environment of monasteries[6] and large estates. Jördens' work shows that there was a long-

---

[4] E.g. Goffart 1974, p. 76 for a remarkably forthright statement of this view.
[5] Brown 1971 is still the best general introduction. Millar 1993 is a remarkable account of the cultural complexities of the Near East. On the demography of the East-Mediterranean countryside, Tate 1992 is now fundamental. For Egypt see Bowman 1996.
[6] E.g. Tchalenko 1953–8, t. 1, p. 20, on the Syrian monasteries, '...chaque monastère constitue une entreprise agricole autonome, très vaste, et très bien organisée'; also Wilfong 1999.

term expansion of wage-employment,⁷ and Susan Harvey's study of asceticism emphasises its profound links with the growing insecurities of a world repeatedly ravaged by warfare and scarcity.⁸ These wider or deeper contexts are naturally presupposed here, but they are important, for the economy of the late empire is, at one level, incomprehensible without them.

6.2. A historiography of abstractions

When a recent study of Egypt in the fourth to early fifth centuries gives historians the option of choosing between the 'feudalism' of the large estates and the 'unchanging centrality of the small family farm',⁹ the contrast is badly conceived, for feudal economies of a purer type have always presupposed what one historian calls the 'primacy of peasant economy'.¹⁰ Bagnall clearly did not intend agrarian historians to choose between peasant-proprietorship and tenancy, for these could easily have co-existed, as they frequently have done,¹¹ but between statuses – were peasants free or were they bound to large estates? That they may have been both free and worked for large estates, is not an option he considers, for he, like the traditionalists whose conclusions he rejects, automatically identifies large estates with the exercise of coercion. To reject the idea of widespread or universal coercion, he feels he must reject the view that large estates were an important element in the rural economy of the late Empire. Thus *Gutswirtschaft* and *Grundherrschaft* are both effectively swept away in one massive sweep of iconoclasm, and the issue of how large estates were actually organised is left in limbo.

There has, of course, been a long tradition of defining the peasants working on such estates as 'serfs', influenced, clearly, by the general conception of the colonate as an essentially medieval or feudal type of institution which coerced an unwilling peasantry into service on the large estates. The assumption here should be that landlords extracted labour by force, but, in fact, proponents of

---
⁷ Jördens 1990.
⁸ Harvey 1990. There is more than metaphorical irony in the fact that the first monastery founded in Egypt occupied the site of an abandoned village, cf. *S. Pachomii Vitae Graecae*, *Vita prima*, 54, referring to the site as a 'deserted village called Pabau', see Halkin 1932, p. 36.
⁹ Bagnall 1993, p. 115.
¹⁰ See Confino's review of Kolchin, Confino 1990, p. 1119ff., esp. pp. 1126–7.
¹¹ For centuries Persia had both peasant-proprietors and crop-sharing peasants, but they were, on the whole, quite distinct groups, see Lambton 1953.

this view do not see 'serfdom' in terms of the actual organisation of labour but as a more diffuse or abstract juridical relation. The economic forms in which estates exploited these juridical serfs (the so-called *coloni*) were the usual types of tenancy. As Clausing put it, the '*colonus* is revealed by the Codes as a small tenant whose most noticeable characteristic was his legal attachment to the soil. He cultivated his own land....As a payment for the use of the land he owed a yearly rental to the landlord. The rent was ordinarily paid in kind.'[12] The legal evidence, however, and the problems of its historical interpretation were too complex to sustain such lucid simplicities, and the thesis of a late Roman serfdom was largely given up.[13] The postwar revisionism was led by Johnson and West in an influential work published in the 1940s. They rejected the view that the peasants who worked on the large estates were serfs of some kind. 'The law did not bind the tenant to the soil....We suggest that the *enapographoi georgoi* were free tenants.'[14] Since 'free' clearly refers to the lack of any definite legal restrictions on the mobility of the peasantry, one or two qualifications might be useful. The juridical status of the so-called 'tenants' is no indication of how much pressure landlords actually applied to secure the submission or even complete dependence of their work-forces, and certainly not proof that they did not apply such pressure.[15] Secondly, they themselves admit that the 'position of the tenant seems to deteriorate in the sixth century'.[16] This was especially true of sharecroppers. Thus the legal freedom enjoyed by the Byzantine tenantry was no guarantee that their actual economic conditions might not deteriorate and make them more vulnerable to domination by landowners. However, it is worth retaining the idea that the 'tenants' recruited by large landowners were free peasants, for this tends to discredit the notion that they in particular depended on either servile or semi-servile labour of the sort that sustained production on the estates of the Russian *pomeshchiki*.[17]

---

[12] Clausing 1925, pp. 23–4.
[13] It is still argued, with some rigour, by de Ste Croix 1983, p. 244ff.
[14] Johnson and West 1949, p. 31.
[15] Cf. Jones 1964, p. 817 ('it was at the demand of landlords that the system was maintained and extended'), and now see the new letter of Augustine, *Ep.* 24.1, asking whether landowners had the right to transform their *coloni* into slaves.
[16] Johnson and West 1949, p. 77.
[17] Kolchin 1987.

One consequence is obvious: whichever view one adopts of the freedom of lack of freedom of the late antique peasantry, the majority of scholars seem to concur in the belief that large-estate peasants, the peasants of the Apions, for example, were small tenants, and that estates parcellised their land into smallholdings which were then leased out for payments in cash and/or kind.[18] With the exception of Mickwitz, I am not aware of a single dissenting view in this matter.[19] This consensus is even more impressive when we consider that both Johnson and West and Jean Gascou took the trouble to note that no leases actually survive in the relatively abundant documentation of the Apion estate.[20]

It is the aim of this paper to reject this view and substitute a more complex model. I shall argue that the organisation of the Byzantine large estate was fundamentally similar to the organisation of Egyptian large estates in the late nineteenth and twentieth centuries. To be able to establish this, however, we have to do several things: (1) look at the terminology for rural classes without making apparently commonsense assumptions as to who the *georgoi* were likely to have been (they are normally thought of as 'peasants' but the issue is who or what was a 'peasant' in the late antique context?); (2) re-argue the case for permanent labour; (3) pay more attention to the details of our evidence, referring especially to a few recently published papyri; and (4) 'correlate' all this evidence with whatever one has begun to learn about the organisation of estates in the more recent period, relying mainly on the work of Roger Owen and Alan Richards, and the sources they have used.[21]

6.3. Rural stratification: *geouchountes*, *ktetores* and *ergatai*

In his recent book, *The Pasha's Peasants*, Kenneth Cuno has drawn attention to the 'existence of a highly stratified rural society before 1800'.[22] The gap

---

[18] For this view of the Apion peasantry, cf. Banaji 1997a, n. 19.
[19] Mickwitz 1965, esp. p. 141ff. Jördens 1992, p. 269 is also against the mainstream in referring to the 'Eigenwirtschaft des Grundherren'.
[20] Johnson and West 1949, p. 60, 'Although no contracts are preserved between Apion and his tenants...'; Gascou 1985, p. 9, n. 9, 'Je ne connais chez les Apions que deux cas, à vrai dire douteux, de location' (emphasis mine).
[21] See below, esp. n. 90.
[22] Cuno 1992, p. 199, cf. also p. 148 ('Eighteenth-century peasant society was highly stratified.'), 67, 85, and Cuno 1984.

between the smallholding and landless strata and the wealthy peasantry increased in the course of the nineteenth century,[23] but it is clear that it preexisted the reforms of Muhammad 'Ali. In general, this stratification may be summed up by referring broadly to the wealthier peasant stratum, smallholders, and the landless. Clearly, much of the fiscal proletarianisation which Baer describes as characteristic of the régimes of Sa'id and Isma'il was borne overwhelmingly by the middle group, those described as smallholders.[24] Of course, above these various groups were the large landowners drawn mainly from the ruling family, high officials, army-officers, wealthy merchants, and the land-companies controlled by foreign and local investors.[25]

Now, similar divisions characterise the late antique rural situation in Egypt. The Egyptian peasantry of the sixth century was a deeply stratified mass, with divisions which broadly correspond to the three tiers mentioned above. The papyri from Aphrodito show that villages [*komai*] were run by a small circle of the leading village-families,[26] who described themselves as *ktetores* or *syntelestai*. 'Ktetor' was the term most often used for small and middling landowners who stood between the aristocracy and the mass of the more humble peasantry, regardless of whether they were urban or village-based.[27] The aristocracy, a purely urban class, were *geouchountes*, by contrast with these middling landowners,[28] and better structured and more elaborately graded than their nascent counterparts of the nineteenth century. What is significant, however, is that the leading village-families, a group with all the characteristics of a wealthy peasant stratum,[29] never called themselves *georgoi*, and this despite their largely Coptic cultural affinities with the rest of the 'peasantry'. Even the more substantial lessees described themselves as *misthotai* rather than *georgoi*.[30]

---

[23] Cuno 1992, p. 148.
[24] Baer 1962, p. 29ff.
[25] Baer 1962, p. 39ff.
[26] The expression is apt and used by Cuno 1992, p. 67.
[27] *P.Cairo Masp.* II 67130.4 (557), I 67110.8–11 (565), *P.Vatic.Aphrod.* 1.6–7 (598), *P.Cairo Masp.* III 67283 ii (before 9.11.547), *P.Amst.* I 85 (6th–7th century), and *P.Oxy.* XVI 2058.36 (6th century), all involve the village-based landed group, mostly owners of medium-sized properties, such as Flavius Dioscorus or the descendants of Apa Sourous, founder of a monastery which amassed a considerable amount of property locally.
[28] The terms *geouchon* and *ktetor* appear together in *P.Strasb.* I 40 (569), lines 7, 15, with *BL* 1.406, and it is certain that they designate different classes of landowners.
[29] Cuno 1980, p. 253, 'wealthy peasant stratum'.
[30] *P.Vatic.Aphrod.* 1 (598).

Indeed, these lessees hired labourers whom they ordinarily referred to as 'georgoi'.[31] The implication of all this is that the *georgoi* were not primarily a landed class, or, more accurately, not seen as one, which explains why they were in fact frequently counterposed (in imperial legislation, literary sources, etc.)[32] to the class of landowners as a group defined less by their ownership of land or other resources than by their physical labour on it, whether as smallholders, lessees, or rural labourers. Finally, it is possible to find documents where the *georgoi* and the *ergatai* are distinct categories,[33] reflecting situations where smallholders or lessees or permanent workers were distinguished from casual labourers. *Ergates* was the normal term for a casual worker, agricultural or other, but in late antiquity it came to be used of permanent labourers as well.[34] Since the most common way of referring to full-time workers was actually *georgos*, it was possible for these terms [*georgos/ergates*] to acquire broadly similar connotations, as in a novel of Justinian I which defines a particular category of *georgoi* we shall be concerned with as *oiketores ton chorion kai ton agron ergatai*, i.e., rural workers permanently resident on estates.[35]

6.4. The case for permanent labour

The argument for permanent labour flows directly from this. The assertion that 'hired labourers seem very rarely to have been employed on a permanent basis'[36]

---

[31] *P.Mich.* XIII 666.15–16 (512 or 527), τὴν πᾶσαν ἐργασίαν ποιήσασθαι ἐκ τῶν ἰδίων μου γεωργῶν, 'to get the whole job done with my own georgoi'; *P.Vatic.Aphrod.* 1.18, ἰδίοις μου κτήνεσιν καὶ γεωργοῖς, 'with my own cattle and georgoi'; *P.Cairo Masp.* III 67300.10–11 (526 or 527); *P.Michael.* 46.12 (559), *PHamb.* 1 68.11–12 (549/50 or 564/5), *P.Apoll.* 57.1–2.

[32] Procopius, *HA* 23.16, τοῖς τε κυρίοις καὶ τοῖς γεωργοῖς; 26.17ff., γεωργούς τε καὶ χωρίων κτήτορας καὶ κυρίους; *Nov.Justin II*, 1 a (*Jus Graecoromanun*, t. 1, p. 2) (566), ὥστε οὐδὲ γεωργοί οὐδὲ μισθωταί οὐδὲ ἐμφυτευταί οὔτε μὴν οἱ κεκτημένοι εἰσπραχθήσονται κτλ.; *Nov. Tiberius*, 11α (*Jus Graecoromanum*. t. 1, p. 18) (575), τὴν ἐπὶ τοῦ παρόντος δωρεὰν δι' ἧς concedimus γεωργοῖς τε καὶ συντελεσταῖς ἅπασι (ταὐτὸν δέ ἐστιν εἰπεῖν τοῖς τῶν χωρίων κυρίοις) integrum unum canonem, etc.

[33] *SPP* X 251(b) (7th century, prob. 626), lines 4ff., cash wages for casual labourers paid through a *georgos*; from a large Fayyum estate. *P.Apoll.* 98.21, disbursement of foodgrains τῷ γεωργῷ (καὶ) τοῖς ἐργάταις.

[34] See notes 35, 52 below, and cf. *P.Ross.-Georg.* V 71 (? 8th century), from the Fayyum, esp. Γνῶ(σις) ἐργ(ατῶν) φυγ(όντων) τῆς οὐσί(ας) Πκομ, 'list of workers who have fled from the estate at Pkom'.

[35] *Nov. Justinian I*, 162.2 (*Corpus Iuris Civilis*, 3.748).

[36] Jones 1964, p. 792f.

is not supported by the evidence of the papyri.[37] Indeed, there are at least three levels at which one might respond to this or to the view that permanent labour was not used because it was inefficient.[38] First, there is Egyptian evidence from other periods of the country's agrarian history. Then there is the general evidence of agrarian historians, which shows that permanent labour was the structural basis of large-estate agriculture in numerous and diverse historical settings until the agrarian restructuring of the late nineteenth century and the massive casualisation of rural labour-markets.[39] Two Chinese historians who have dealt with the organisation of large estates in late-imperial China use the term 'managerial landlords' to describe landowners who based their production on the work of long-term labourers.[40] I shall retain this phrase as an apt description of the Egyptian aristocracy of the fifth to seventh centuries. Finally, there is the evidence, sporadic though it may appear, of the papyri themselves, which ranges from the third to the seventh centuries.

I shall concentrate for the moment on levels one and three. In *Feudalism in Egypt, Syria, Palestine, and the Lebanon* Poliak describes the peasantry dominated by the Mamluk houses of the eighteenth century as 'permanent tenants' of the *multazims*.[41] All the references are to al-Jabartī's chronicles. However, the term which he seems to translate in this way, *muzāri'un*, simply has the more general meaning of 'peasants' or 'farmers',[42] and al-Jabartī frequently refers to 'their peasants' when he describes the domination of the multazims. That peasants [*fallāhīn*] in the *iltizam* system were 'permanent tenants' thus seems to be a description not of the way the labour-process was organised but of their juridical or quasi-juridical status, and it is therefore worth ignoring this passage. Lancret is in fact much more informative about the way the *multazims* organised production on their *usya* lands, and mentions leases to the village *shaykhs*, paid labour, and forced labour as the chief methods

---

[37] See Banaji 1997b for similar arguments.
[38] Bagnall 1993, p. 121, ignoring the recent literature on inter-seasonal labour-tying arrangements.
[39] This is even more true if plantation capitalism, serf estates, etc. are seen as based on forms of permanent labour, but even otherwise, see Richards 1979, and much of the work on Mexico, Chile, Peru, Prussia, China, and so on.
[40] Jing Su and Luo Lun 1959, studying Shandong *c*. 1900.
[41] Poliak 1939, p. 72.
[42] E.g., Wehr 1952, I, p. 341, مزارع, *muzāri'*, 'Landmann', 'Landwirt', 'Ackerbauer', 'Farmer'.

used to exploit such land.⁴³ It is unlikely that these were sharply contrasting systems of production, for each of these methods must have involved some degree of coercion. The fact is that exploitation by the *multazims*, whether on their own land or on peasant-land [*arḍ al-filāha*] created a general impression that the Egyptian peasantry of the neo-Mamluk period was a highly vulnerable and destitute group. For instance, when Volney wrote that 'the peasants are hired labourers to whom no more is left than barely suffices to sustain life',⁴⁴ he surely could not have meant that paid labour in some formal sense was the regular form in which peasant-labour was exploited, but only that, whatever the particular form of exploitation, the peasants were as good as labourers. More specific evidence is found, again, in Girard, who investigated the costs of production in rice-growing in the province of Damietta. Girard refers to 'les ouvriers attachés pendant l'année aux travaux de l'exploitation' and distinguishes them from 'les journaliers' who were clearly casual labourers employed in weeding, transplanting, and cleaning of canals.⁴⁵ In short, there is certainly some evidence for the use of permanent paid labour in the period before the full development of the *ezba* system, though its actual extent and precise forms remain unknown. Perhaps the most valuable contribution of the late-Ottoman sources is simply the general impression they convey of peasants who could be treated, and seen by others, as labourers, that is, of a peasantry without the resources, legal or material, to withstand coercion into 'coerced wage' or 'serf' labour. The sharecroppers mentioned by Poliak (again on the basis of al-Jabartī) would undoubtedly have belonged to this category, being mostly labourers paid in kind.⁴⁶

Again, the ancient evidence is largely concordant with this. As I noted earlier, Egyptian and other ancient sources tend not to treat the *georgoi* as

---

⁴³ Lancret 1809, p. 243 (cf. *DE*² XI, 481ff.). About the second of the three methods, he says, 'Dans le second cas, le moultezim a, dans chacun de ses villages, deux hommes principaux chargés de la culture et de la récolte de ses terres d'ousyeh: l'un est khaouly, ou surveillant; l'autre est oukyl, ou procureur. Le khaouly, de concert avec le cheykh, *distribue la terre aux divers fellâh, selon leurs besoins ou leurs demandes.* C'est lui, ou tout autre homme de confiance, qui est dépositaire des *fonds nécessaires au paiement des fellâh*' (*DE*² XI, p. 482).
⁴⁴ Volney 1787, t. 1, p. 188 ('Les paysans y sont des manoeuvres à gages, a qui l'on ne laisse pour vivre que ce qu'il faut pour ne pas mourir').
⁴⁵ Girard 1799–1800, pp. 237, 239, and in his general survey in Volume 2 of the *DE*¹, *État Moderne*, II, p. 578f., cf. Cuno 1980, p. 255.
⁴⁶ Poliak 1939, p. 72, noting that they could be evicted at any time.

a landed class but as a class living by its labour on the land. On the other hand, the question of permanent labour concerns the more specific issue of whether and how frequently such 'peasants' worked as full-time rural labourers on large estates with the resources (in land, grain, and cash) to employ them on this basis. Rathbone's study of the Fayyum estate of Appianus shows that at least some third-century large estates used the system of permanent labour, though his work also suggests that in terms of actual labour-inputs, such estates remained massively dependent on the supply of casual workers.[47] Mexican wheat-estates of the late nineteenth century tend to confirm this pattern, showing that estates with resident work-forces consistently required large numbers of seasonal labourers.[48] Mertens characterises such *haciendas* as 'wage-labour enterprises',[49] and, in a strict sense, the same description might be used of the Appianus estate. The significant point here is that the formation of an aristocracy did not preclude, and may even have stimulated, patterns of labour-use dependent largely on wage-labour. The next piece of evidence is also from the third century, this time from the estates of Calpurnia Heraclia, who came from an extremely wealthy Alexandrian family.[50] In *P.Oxy*. XLII 3048, dated 17–18 March 246, we have an absolutely unique snapshot of the labour-force of a large aristocratic estate in the mid-third century. Five groups are listed, two at managerial and three at work-force level. Of the non-managerial categories, it is clear that the mainstay of her estates were the *georgoi*. They, however, were not tenants (in the ordinary sense), as the document specifically tells us that the *georgoi*, like other sections of the labour-force, received monthly salaries [*meniaiai syntaxeis*] in grain.[51]

---

[47] Rathbone 1991, Chapter 3 and p. 149ff.
[48] Mertens 1983, p. 194ff.
[49] Mertens 1983, p. 195, 'Die Haciendas arbeiteten als Lohnarbeitsbetriebe'.
[50] Her father, C. Calpurnius Aurelius Theon, was a 'former member of the Museum' and himself the son, probably, of another Alexandrian landowner, Calpurnius Aurelius Horion, who turns up in early third-century documents, see *P.Oxy*. L 3564.1n.
[51] *P.Oxy*. XLII 3048 (246) 11.19–21, ἀπὸ δὲ τῶν προκ[ειμ]ένων δίδονται μηνιαῖαι συντάξεις πραγματευταῖς τε καὶ φροντισταῖ[ς καὶ] γεωργοῖς καὶ παιδαρίοις καὶ καταμηνείοις, 'Out of the above-mentioned [amounts], monthly allowances are given to the general managers. local managers, labourers, boys and monthly paid'. The other non-managerial groups were thus *paidaria*, 'boys', probably the sons of the *georgoi*, and more specialised workers whose wages were calculated on a monthly basis and who were therefore called *katamenioi*. *Paidarion* is often taken to mean 'slave' but in *SPP* XX 222 (6th/7th century), cf. *BL* 1.421, the *paidaria* are clearly the sons of peasants or rural labourers.

Moving into the fourth century, we have one document, the quarterly accounts of a fairly large estate at Hermonthis for one quarter in the year 338.[52] Here, the disbursements listed in col.xv show that wheat rations of 2 *artabas* per month were paid to a group of workers called *ergatai*. They were probably permanent labourers, as twenty are named individually for the month of Pharmouthi, and the payments must have been at least partly designed to sustain the family's consumption. The more specialised workers on this estate were called *opsoniastai*, *opsonia* being regular wage-payments in cash or kind. From the fifth century (possibly), a short account from the Hermopolite nome carries a heading which may be translated as 'Account of the wheat (disbursed as) wages of our *georgoi* for the 12th indiction'.[53] These labourers[54] were certainly permanent, as their wages are said to be for the whole year, although the amounts vary. Finally, a much later account from the archive of Papas, pagarch of Edfu, disbursed 132 *artabas* of barley *hyper misthou georgon*.[55] Divided by a standard ration of 12 *artabas*, this would yield a full-time labour-force of eleven workers [*georgoi*]. The least this establishes is that rural wage-labourers were used in Egypt not just on a casual or seasonal basis but as permanent or resident work-forces. The next issue is whether we can determine a form of exploitation (a labour-system) characteristic of the deployment of these workers.

Certainly, the most fascinating section of the Appianus labour force are the *epoikiotai*.[56] They are described by Rathbone as 'tenant labourers' or 'tenants with labour dues',[57] and their crucial function seems to have been the supply of peak-season labour at lower wage-rates, for a payment determined partly in cash and partly in the form of accommodation on the estate. Whereas casual workers were paid 4 *drachmas* a day for harvest work, these labourers received the substantially lower wage of 2 *drachmas* 6 *obols*.[58] In the growing literature on labour-tenancy, the usual term for such workers is 'labour-tenants'.[59]

---

[52] *P.Lips.* 97 (338).
[53] *P.Amh.* II 155 (5th century).
[54] They are so described by the editor.
[55] *P.Apoll.* 98.38.
[56] Literally, 'people from the *epoikia*', on which see below.
[57] Rathbone 1991, pp. 146, 150, 182–3.
[58] Rathbone 1991, p. 159, cf. the *terrasgueros* or cash-tenants on Mexican estates, Mertens 1983, p. 119.
[59] See Bradford 1987; Keegan 1987; Kanogo 1987; Loveman 1976; and most recently, Jacobsen 1993.

Another large third-century estate that made systematic use of labour-tenancy was the *ousia* of Valerius Titanianus at Theadelphia in the Fayyum. This was a large wine-producing operation owned by a former high official who was part of the Alexandrian aristocracy.[60] Accounts for the year 239 show that his estate extracted part of its labour-supply by charging a rent for accommodation on the estate, in the settlements called *epoikia*, and computing part of the rent in labour days [*ergatai*].[61] Since the basic rent included twelve days of labour every half-year, the estate obviously used this system to secure 'a substantial quantity of free casual labour from its tenants'.[62] However, at the imputed wage of 2 *drachmas*, there was no difference in the rates paid to these workers and to ordinary day-labourers. These two examples show that large landowners were consciously structuring their supplies of labour in forms that gave them maximum flexibility, and that forms of labour-tenancy were certainly in use by the third century.

6.5. Restructuring in the later empire

It is doubtful if the Alexandrian aristocracy of the third century ever completely succeeded in forming a coherent and stable class. Their purely economic influence was, in any case, limited, as much of the land was controlled by the municipal landed families who ran the town councils in the different districts or *nomes* of Egypt. In this largely municipal milieu, only the bigger landowners could have replicated the forms of management characteristic of the Alexandrian families. The majority undoubtedly relied on leasing as the dominant method of management, recruiting lessees from the considerable mass of landless or near-landless peasants for whom tenancy was a regular form of employment. In fact, it was this stratum of municipal landholders which would eventually suffer a near eclipse, as their properties were relentlessly sundered in the process of subdivision, and the deeper dynamisms of the late empire (economic, social, political) unleashed a prolonged restructuring of agrarian society, with the emergence of new landowning groups, such as the nascent aristocratic families of the fifth century, the Church, the

---

[60] On his background see Gilliam 1974.
[61] *P.Mich.* 620 (239–40). The accommodation consisted of single and double rooms [*kellai*].
[62] Rathbone 1991, p. 178.

monasteries, and the middling bureaucracy of the provincial towns.[63] Above these groups were the massive possessions of the imperial household (including the estates of various members of the imperial family) organised in the *Domus Divina*,[64] and below them, in the villages [*komai*], a rich peasantry who are remarkable counterparts of the village *shaykhs* of the nineteenth century. Thus, the agrarian landscape was both stratified and complex, and, of course, there is no reason to suppose that the forms of agrarian management characteristic of the élite-aristocracy were found at most other levels – other than the *Domus Divina* itself. Emerging 'from the upper ranks of the services', as Ostrogorsky in fact wrote of the Byzantine aristocracy of a later period,[65] the new landed aristocracy comprised mostly high officials, who, like the Russian *pomeshchiki* of the later eighteenth century,[66] were great believers in the careful management and bureaucratic administration of their properties, influenced, no doubt, by their Imperial background. These, then, were directly managed properties, with owners investing heavily in the 'infrastructure of administration'. By contrast, leasing was widespread on most other types of properties, though by itself the term conceals a great variety of content, both as to the type and duration of the lease and the type of lessee. In the countryside around Hermopolis, much of the land was leased to *georgoi* who resided in the town itself; the lessors were affluent middle-class landowners, many of them women, or ecclesiastical holders, such as the Holy Church of the Resurrection, whose lands were situated to the east of the town and leased out in tiny parcels (1–2 *arouras*) for durations of two years.[67] In the village of Aphrodito further south, middle-class landholders dealt with a similar stratum of peasants, though we also have leases of substantial farms (or 'gardens') to a group of obviously wealthier lessees.[68] Church and monastic properties were often exploited on perpetual leases, and the holders of these were again likely to be substantial lessees or persons of the aristocracy.[69]

---

[63] I have analysed these social changes in more detail in Banaji 1992.
[64] Delmaire 1989.
[65] Ostrogorsky 1971, p. 7.
[66] Confino 1963.
[67] P.Strasb. V 470 (497), 472 (533 or 534), 473 (537), 475 (6th century), with Bureth's introduction, p. 205ff.
[68] See n. 31 above, and see Keenan 1984; 1985.
[69] P.Lond. II 483 (p. 323ff.) (615 or 616); P.Cairo Masp. III 67299 (6th century); SB XII 10805 (7th century); P.Lond. III 1072(b) (p. 274) (6th century), with BL 1.299, and for the date BL 9.138.

Finally, some large estates were leased out to commercial farmers, who were probably similar to the Italian *massari* of more recent times.[70]

It should be clear, then, that the argument which follows is not intended to characterise the agrarian economy as a whole but only the organisation of aristocratic estates administered in the complex and bureaucratic forms characteristic of the sixth and seventh centuries. Nor should the contrast between direct management and leasing be exaggerated, both because the more humble lessees were often simply labourers and the lease more like a labour-contract (this was especially true of sharecroppers), and because 'tenancy' could be integrated into a régime of direct management, as I shall now try to show.

6.6. The new estates

In his monograph *The Large Estates of Byzantine Egypt*, Hardy says almost nothing about leasing, although, curiously, his account of the Apion estate assumes that it was organised on the basis of rents extracted from a peasantry which, while bound to the soil,[71] nonetheless leased its land from the proprietors. In a similar vein, the Italian scholar Segrè could write,

> The conditions under which the *coloni* rented the estates [sic] from the managers...are rather obscure. Tenancy at will is frequent in the leases of the fifth and sixth centuries. Apparently the *coloni adscripticii* remained on the estates for generations and cultivated the soil under rather permanent conditions.[72]

To add to the confusion, Segrè then went on to draw an analogy with Mexican estates and described the colonate, in more general terms, as a 'form of organisation of agricultural labour'. The sheer incongruousness of these accounts should have warned later scholars that something was seriously wrong, and that it might be worth probing the organisation of estates with fewer preconceptions. It is worth noting, however, that the first editors of the

---

[70] *P.Merton* I 49 (7th century) is certainly a lease of this sort; for the *massari*, cf. Snowden (1986).

[71] Hardy 1931, p. 75 ('The fundamental fact about the condition of coloni was that they were bound to the soil').

[72] Segrè 1947, p. 122.

Oxyrhynchus Papyri thought that the *georgoi* working on large sixth-century estates were labourers (of some sort), for 'labourers' was how they usually translated 'georgoi'.[73]

The Oxyrhynchite material relates predominantly to large and very large estates. Unfortunately, it is easier to form some impression of how the aristocracy was structured in what was then a fairly dynamic part of Middle Egypt, capital of the province of Arcadia, than to know how the different layers organised estates which clearly differed greatly in size.[74] The overwhelming bulk of the evidence derives from a single estate, that of the Apion family, though, of course, important isolated documents survive from other aristocratic, ecclesiastical, and medium-sized properties. By contrast, the Fayyum material is much more dispersed, and the evidence less easy to reconstruct.

The new aristocratic estates which emerged in the main part of the fifth century to reach their 'classical' form in the sixth, were called *oikoi* ('houses') to emphasise their structured and permanent character. From the Apion Archive, it is certain that these estates were held in joint ownership and thus immune to the devastating fragmentation of partible inheritance.[75] At the economic level, the most important fact about them is their considerable integration into monetary economy and their ability to generate substantial revenues in gold.[76] Finally, irrigation was widespread on the new estates,[77] and hired labour was used extensively.[78] The rapid diffusion of water-wheels in the countryside of the later fifth and sixth centuries reflects the willingness of owners to make substantial investments in the spread of summer-irrigation

---

[73] *P.Oxy.* I 135.15 (p. 210, 212), 136.18 (p. 216), XVI 1842 (p. 25), 1894.15 (p. 108), 1896.13 (p. 111), 1900.11 (p. 119), etc.

[74] *P.Oxy.* XVI 2020, 2040, from the 580s and 560s respectively.

[75] The Apion properties are attested from some time before 460 to the year 620, when the Oxyrhynchite was under Persian occupation and Flavius Apion III known to be dead, giving a span of over 160 years. See, however, *P.Oxy.* LXIII 4389, which could push the beginning of the archive back to 439, if the Strategius who appears in there is the aristocrat who turns up in mid-fifth-century documents as managing the Oxyrhynchite estates of Aelia Eudocia, wife of Theodosius II, i.e. the father of Flavius Apion I. (I am grateful to John Rea for having allowed me access to this and other documents in *P.Oxy.* LXIII in advance of publication.)

[76] For the background see Banaji 1996 and 1994.

[77] *P.Oxy.* XIX 2239.14, τὰς γεουχικὰς μηχανάς, see nn. 104, 105 below, and cf. the appearance of a new kind of accounting on fifth-century estates, *P.Med.* I² 64 (441), *P.Oxy.* XXXIV 2724 (469), XVI 1899 (476), 1982 (497).

[78] *SPP* III 86; *P.Oxy.* XVI 1911.157–159 (with *BL* 9.191), 1913.16–18, 19, 21–23, XVIII 2195.134–136; *SB* VI 9284 (553); *P.Grenf.* I 58 (561); also n. 116 below.

and implies a larger Byzantine legacy in the agricultural revolution of the Islamic period than Watson seems to allow for.[79] In particular, the stimulus of an expanding wine-industry encouraged producers to structure these investments carefully. For example, in the Apion Archive, the average turnover of an axle was put at seven years, and the issue of spares administered from a central office in Oxyrhynchus.[80]

The implicit rationalism of the new estates would, no doubt, have extended to their deployment of labour. The Apion Archive contains a series of accounts listing receipts in cash and kind, and, at first sight, this type of accounting seems like strong evidence in favour of the theory that estates based their revenues on the leasing of land to small tenants. But a closer scrutiny of the accounts suggests that, insofar as the estate drew revenues from rent-payments, the bulk of these revenues derived from the payments of substantial-looking tenants who bear a certain resemblance to the better-off *arrendatarios* on Mexican haciendas of the early nineteenth century.[81] Moreover, the analogy of these *haciendas* shows that estates which drew part of their income from cash rents, for example, might still be predominantly based on the exploitation of permanent labourers.[82]

The crucial fact about the Apion holdings is that the basic constituents of the estate were not villages but the smaller settlements known as *epoikia*. Since these are a decisive clue to the organisation of labour, they seem like an obvious starting-point for the argument. The *epoikia* were privately owned settlements, unlike villages, and were mostly controlled by the largest landowners, including the estates of the *Domus Divina*.[83] The régime of direct management was structured around the *epoikia*, and, consequently, they had a largely 'industrial' character, in the sense that their sole function was the concentration of groups of workers in residential sites in close proximity to the

---

[79] Watson 1983, esp. pp. 104 and 191, n. 15, substantially the same view as in Watson 1974.
[80] *P.Oxy.* I 137.23, XVI 1911.160–2.
[81] This is shown by an analysis of accounts such as *P.Oxy.* XVIII 2195 (576–7), XIX 2243(a) (590), and LV 3804 (566). The exercise consists in stratifying payments into levels, expressing wheat in cash or vice versa, and then seeing how much of the gross revenue from individual settlements is accounted for by the largest payments (defined, say, as rents of 4 *solidi* or more). For the *arrendatarios*, see Brading 1978, pp. 74, 110 ('substantial farmers'); his cut-off point seems to be a rent of 30 *pesos* = c. 46 bushels (of maize).
[82] On the combination of these forms see also Hoppe and Langton 1994, pp. 116, 121.
[83] *P.Oxy.* L 3585.4 (before 20.10.460); *P.Med.* I² 64.4; *P.Oxy.* L 3582.3 (442).

fields where they actually worked. Now this has been a universal feature of large estates of a certain kind, and one imagines that accommodation on these estates would have had a certain similarity to the *bohíos* in the larger, geometrically structured, sugar plantations of Cuba,[84] or the *galpones*, barracks or dormitories, of the north-coast plantations in Peru,[85] or the *calpanerías* on Mexican *haciendas* where resident workers were housed in shacks [*chozas*].[86] Of course, at another level, the more obvious analogy is with Egypt itself in the nineteenth and twentieth centuries, and I shall deal with this below. The unit of accommodation was the *kellion* (room?), and, in one Apion account, the implication seems to be that some settlements were built to a standard model of 100 rooms [*kellia*].[87] Peasants residing in such settlements were described – in the Oxyrhynchite anyway – as 'registered' employees of the estate,[88] meaning that the estate paid their taxes. The *epoikia* contained arable, orchards, and vineyards, and there are repeated references to *mechanai* watering various types of fields. They were heavily supervised, and the bulk of the peasants residing in them seem to have been partly or even very largely dependent on wage-employment,[89] that is, to have been mostly landless workers, though some families could afford to rent substantial holdings.

To historians familiar with the agrarian history of the nineteenth century, these privately owned settlements bear an obvious resemblance to the *ezbas* – so striking, indeed, that the homology is worth pursuing in more detail. This, I want to argue, lies in a set of labour-arrangements which gave owners both flexibility and control.[90] One of the earliest references is from the 1870s, by McCoan, who was editor of the *Levant Herald*, and wrote of the 'estates of the large owners, the wealthier Pashas and Beys' that they either employed

[84] Moreno Fraginals 1978, Volume 2, pp. 66–75.
[85] Gonzales 1985, pp. 97, 148.
[86] Nickel 1988, pp. 308f., 419.
[87] P.Oxy. XVI 1917.56, 98. Lozach 1935, p. 254, refers to 'l'esprit industriel, presque mathématique, que revêt cette exploitation', about the newer *ezbas* in the reclaimed areas of the northern Delta.
[88] I.e. *Enapographoi georgoi*.
[89] P.Köln II 102 = SB XII 11239 (418); P.Cairo Masp. I 67093 (553), γεωργὸς μισθωτὴς ἀπὸ ἐποικ[ί]ο(υ) Ψινίο(υ); P.Oxy. I 134 (569); BGU IV 1039.3–5 (Byz.); SPP III 86; P.Flor. I 70 (see n. 116); SB XVI 13016 (638); and cf. PSI III 165.2 (546?), τοῖς ἐργαταῖς διαφόρων ἐποικίων, 'to the labourers from the various *epoikia*'.
[90] Roger Owen and Alan Richards have valuable descriptions of the *ezba* system in various publications, see especially, Richards 1978; 1979, pp. 500–4; Owen 1981a; 1981b, pp. 146–8, 228–30; Richards 1982, pp. 58–68, 172–4; 1993, pp. 96–8.

'mourabain [*murābi'un*]', labourers who were paid a share of the crop (usually a fourth) or were worked by 'sub-letting small plots of ground at a fixed rental of so many days' field labour per feddan'.[91] In other words, the evolution of the new private estates had already generalised a kind of labour-tenancy, with owners using the labour of 'tenants' as labourers rather than tenants. In 1898, Nour Ed-Din described this system a bit more fully, explaining that owners attracted labour by offering workers substantially reduced rents, whose actual payment was then adjusted against any wages they earned, the important point being that the 'tenant' was entirely at the owner's disposal (as a wage-labourer).[92] Nour Ed-Din also described another group of workers who were generally paid a one-fifth share of most crops as wages, and often depended on consumption-loans.[93] In 1901, Nahas published a slightly more detailed account of these arrangements in a chapter of his thesis, and was the first to emphasise a crucial feature of the system, namely, that in hiring workers on this basis, landowners had access to the labour of women and children as well.[94] Contracts were verbal, labour intensely supervised, and the volume of labour adjusted to the requirements of the estate.[95] Nahas noted that in assigning subsistence-plots, landowners took account of the size of the tenant-household, and that the latter in turn contracted 'to furnish a specific number of workers' as potential wage-labourers, with the usual adjustment of wages against rent.[96] Nahas described these groups as workers permanently attached to the estate by contrast with the less privileged and more miserable

---

[91] McCoan 1877, p. 183.

[92] Nour Ed-Din 1898, pp. 5–6. The passage is worth reproducing: '3° Chaque ouvrier peut recevoir en location de un à deux feddans, suivant ses moyens et ses aptitudes au travail. Cette location est réduite de 50% sur le prix normal du fermage. Ainsi le feddan, qui se loue d'ordinaire 500 P.E. (130 fr.) par an, lui est loué 250 P.E. (65 fr.). Cette remise de moitié constitue son salaire. Au prix de cet avantage, l'ouvrier est, pendant l'année de fermage, à l'entière disposition du propriétaire, qui, en cas de nécessité, peut l'employer à la journée à raison de 1 à 2 P.E. (50 centimes). Le montant du salaire à lui dû est imputé sur le prix du fermage qu'il paie.'

[93] Nour Ed-Din 1898, p. 5, saying that they were usually paid a quarter-share of the maize crop, which was their staple.

[94] Nahas 1901, pp. 134, 137–8, 140.

[95] Nahas 1901, pp. 134, 141, 142.

[96] Nahas 1901, p. 141, esp. 'À chaque famille d'ouvriers, le propriétaire donne un ou plusieurs feddans de terre en fermage, en tenant compte du nombre des personnes qui composent cette famille; elle s'engage, en revanche, à fournir un nombre déterminé d'ouvriers qui devront, quand ils en seront requis, aller travailler le champ propre du propriétaire.'

migrant-labourers who were drawn chiefly from Upper Egypt. It was also his impression that labour exploited on this basis was less costly than the alternative system of paying workers in a share of the crop, despite the considerable enforcement-costs of what he called 'veritable brigades' of supervisors.[97] This, of course, is contrary to the thinking of most economists on this issue.[98]

To sum up: the details of these arrangements would have varied from one estate to the next,[99] but, in essentials, large landowners recruited workers by paying them either in a share of the crop or under some type of labour-tenancy. In either case, the *fallāh* was simply a wage-labourer.

6.7. The labour-organisation of sixth-century estates

To return to the Byzantine evidence, the model offered by the *ezbas* can and does help to elucidate the corresponding organisation of labour on the sixth-century estates. Two recently-published papyri are of special interest here, though I shall start by recalling the general characteristics of the labour-force on large properties in late antiquity. As I noted earlier, our only explicit definition of the kind of peasants who were called *enapographoi georgoi* treats this kind of labour-force as resident on estates and as mere labourers.[100] Moreover, this Novel and a great deal of other legislation was concerned specifically with problems arising out of claims over the progeny of such resident-labourers, thus implying that it was not uncommon for workers to reside on estates from one generation to the next, as for example on nineteenth-century Mexican *haciendas* studied by Bazant.[101] In fact, this is shown by two documents of the Apion Archive, with the *georgoi* stating in both that they had served the Apions or resided in their *ktema* (that is, the epoikion) *ek pateron*

---

[97] Nahas 1901, p. 142, 'En somme, l'exploitation à la journée exige plus de surveillance et un personnel dirigeant plus nombreux. Mais elle est souvent employée parce que, quand il s'agit de vastes domaines, elle est moins couteuse que le travail à la part, en raison meme de l'étendue du domaine.'
[98] E.g. see Majid 1994, for a discussion of supervision constraints and rationales for sharecropping.
[99] See Owen 1981b, pp. 229–30 for other examples.
[100] See above, on Justinian's Novel 162.
[101] Bazant 1975, p. 163, noting that on the *hacienda* de Bocas, in 1872, most *peones* were sons of the *peones* of 1852.

kai progonon ('from the time of our fathers and our ancestors').[102] Thus, the labour on these estates was, to a large extent, resident. Secondly, it was also intensively supervised. In *P.Oxy.* XIX 2239 (598) the aristocrat Flavius John recruited an *epikeimenos* or field-boss to take charge of general supervision of his *georgoi*.[103] The new manager, Jeremias, undertook to

> employ every care and efficiency in the cultivation of your estate with regard alike to the new plantation and to the large estate plants. Furthermore, I acknowledge also that I will cause all the labourers of your honour in every place and every holding of the same estate to sow the irrigated fields of the estate [*speirai tas geouchikas mechanas*],[104] to plant acacias, and to be ready to show every zeal in bringing your landed estates into better condition.[105]

Finally, it is clear that some or even many of the *georgoi* attached to large estates had livestock of their own,[106] and I suggest that this may have been the main factor which compelled them into forms of labour-tenancy, as with the Kikuyu squatters employed by white settlers on plantations and estates in the Rift Valley Province of the White Highlands in Kenya.[107]

What, then, of the actual deployment of these workers? Estate labour-forces included many groups of specialist workers, maintenance-staff, such as the carpenters who kept the *mechanai* in repair or actually fabricated them, using acacia-wood supplied or bought from the estate, millstone-cutters, smiths,

---

[102] *P.Oxy.* I 130.9 (563/564, contrast *BL* 8.232), 'I have been in [your] service as my fathers and forefathers were', *PSI* I 58.7 (566–568). This was not a peculiarity of the East Mediterranean, for *Nov.Justin* II, 6 (*Jus Graecoromanum*, t. l, p. 10) (570) tries to stop *coloni* from 'abandoning the estates in which they were born [*non posse eos dimittere praedia, in quibus nati sunt*]' and describes these birthplaces as the 'settlements [*vici*]' where they were born, clearly meaning estate-settlements. The reference is to 'Africana provincia', which means most of what is today Tunisia.

[103] The substantial salary he was paid shows that this sort of general supervisor was at a much higher level than the minor supervisory staff of such estates, similar in fact to the *mayordomo* on the Cortés plantation studied by Barrett 1970 or the *khawli* mentioned by Lancret (n. 43).

[104] I have added 'irrigated' to the translation.

[105] *P.Oxy.* XIX 2239.11–16. In l.12 one should probably read εἰς τέ τὰ [σ]ὺν '[θ(εῷ)]' νεόφυτα. The abbreviation is rare but found in *P.Oxy.* LVIII 3942.29 (606), and much more frequently in 7th-century documents from the Fayyum, e.g., *BGU* II 675.1; *SPP* VIII 1044.1, 1048.1.

[106] The best indication of this is *P.Oxy.* XVI 1913.4–5, where at the end of l.4 the photograph clearly shows κτήνων, not κτημάτων. Possession of livestock is also implied in *P.Oxy.* I 130 (n. 102), XVI 1912.148, 150, XVIII 2195.140.

[107] Kanogo 1987, p. 23.

stone-masons, etc., but few contracts are preserved and it is likely that their employment was not characterised by a standard type of contract. These workers reflected the workings of a free labour-market, with agreements signed for specific jobs,[108] or lifetime contracts, such as one with the aforementioned millstone-cutter who even got the estate to agree that it would pay a substantial fine if his employment was unreasonably terminated.[109] However, the remarks which follow do not apply to these workers, obviously, but to the main groups of the labour-force, such as *georgoi, ampelourgoi,* and *pomaritai.*

The system emerges especially clearly in *P.Oxy.* I 192 and 206, at one level, and *P.Wash.Univ.* II 102, at another. In their 'descripta' form in Volume I of *The Oxyrhynchus Papyri* (pp. 242–3), *P.Oxy.* 192, 194, and 206 were all described as 'loans', and in the first two of these documents, the 'loans' were said to be 'for' a *mechane*, whatever that might mean. It is now clear, however, that the term actually used in *P.Oxy.* 192 and *P.Oxy.* 206 (and almost certainly also in 194, which has still not been fully transcribed), is *prochreia*[110] which, more precisely, is an advance of wages.[111] Thus, all three contracts deal with wage-advances, paid, as it happens, in *solidi*. Secondly, in both *P.Oxy.* 192 and *P.Oxy.* 206, the recipients of these cash-advances are *georgoi*, and closer attention to the way they are described can allow us to make these documents a key to the interpretation of the labour-system on the whole estate. For in *P.Oxy.* 192 the worker Aurelius Apasion is called *enapographos georgos*, the term used for the vast majority of *georgoi* resident in the *epoikia*, and was himself from the *epoikion* of Kineas. In his receipt, the advance is associated with his responsibilities for an irrigated farm [*mechane*] called 'Western'.[112] In *P.Oxy.* I 206, some seven decades earlier, the worker John, from the *epoikion* of Leon, is described as '*georgos* of the *mechane* called Small Peso and of the *mechane* of

---

[108] *P.Oxy.* I 134 (569), contract for transport of stones.
[109] *P.Oxy.* LI 3641 (544). esp. lines 17–19.
[110] *P.Oxy.* I 192.8–9 (600/615), *P.Oxy.* I 206.2 (535), both published in Montserrat, Fantoni, and Robinson 1994, pp. 56f., 70f., but still described as 'loans'.
[111] For the proper sense of *prochreia* in employment-contracts and job-related documents such as *P.Oxy.* I 192, etc., see Jördens 1990, pp. 277ff., esp. 283, 'προχρεία auch die übliche Bezeichnung eines normalen Lohnvorschusses ist', and Jördens 1988, esp. p. 165.
[112] *P.Oxy.* I 192.2–6, 8–10, esp. λόγ[ῳ προ]χρείας τῆς ὑπ' ἐμὲ γεουχ(ικῆς) [μη]χανῆς, 'by way of the advance (received for) the estate's irrigated farm (which is) under my charge'.

Path (?)'.¹¹³ The expression *georgos mechanes* is crucial, as we have at least two other documents – among the longest in the Apion Archive – with the same or a similar expression. The first of these, *P.Oxy.* XIX 2244, repeatedly describes labourers from the various *epoikia* by the term *georgos mechanes*, meaning the worker assigned to such and such irrigated farm (and even refers to John son of Paleus from the *epoikion* of Leon, the worker in *P.Oxy.* I 206, though assigned to a different *mechane*),¹¹⁴ while *P.Oxy.* XVIII 2197, dealing with the consumption of bricks on the estate, refers repeatedly to the farms themselves [*mechanai*] as 'under' or '(in the care) of' such and such *georgos*, meaning the plot assigned to this or that individual. Thus *P.Oxy.* I 206 can be generalised to a large section of the Apion labour-force through these more detailed documents and the system of work-allocation they imply. The strong implication is that *georgoi* or other agricultural labourers such as those tending gardens¹¹⁵ or vineyards were assigned to individual irrigated plots or farms (or gardens or vineyards), or vice versa, usually paid cash-wages (in the prevalent gold-currency), and entitled to advances out of them. That these advances [*prochreiai*] were in fact wage-payments is especially clear from a Hermopolite document dated 627, where the concluding formula is the standard clause promising to pay back the advance should the employee abandon or cut short his or her assignment.¹¹⁶

It is likely, though we cannot prove it, that advances of the sort found in *P.Oxy.* I 192 were recorded in accounts pertaining to individual labourers, on the pattern described by Rathbone for the Appianus estate.¹¹⁷ Three of the

---

¹¹³ *P.Oxy.* I 206.1, Ἰ[ω]άννῃ ἀπὸ ἐποικ(ίου) Λέοντος γεωρ(γῷ) τῆς τε μηχ(ανῆς) καλουμ(ένης) Μικρ(οῦ) Πέσω κτλ. John's full name was John son of Paleus.
¹¹⁴ *P.Oxy.* XIX 2244.34, Ἰωάννῃ πιῷ Παλεοῦτος ἀπὸ ἐποικ(ίου) Λέοντος γεωρ(γῷ) μηχ(ανῆς) τοῦ νέου λάκκου κτλ. Thus the sixth indiction of *P.Oxy.* 2244 is either 527/8, 542/3, or 557/8, most probably the second of these dates.
¹¹⁵ Cf. *P.Amh.* II 149 (6th century), which shows the same relationship at work in the case of a gardener [*kepouros*] vis-à-vis the garden assigned to him. This man, Aurelius Anoup, was also from an estate settlement, was a 'registered' employee, and received his wages in cash. The expression *grammateion prochreias* (l.18) recurs in a series of receipts in *P.Oxy.* LVIII 3943–3946, showing that advance payment of wages was standard on the estate.
¹¹⁶ *P.Flor.* I 70 (27.11.627), esp. 10ff, with BL 8.125 for the date proposed by Harrauer (not 'arab. Zeit', as in BL 1.145). Cf. *P.Köln* II 102 (n. 89), and *P.Graec.Vindob.* 26252 = SB VI 9284.8–9, λόγῳ προχρείας τῆς [ἀ]ρδείας τοῦ κτή[μα]τος καλου(μένου) τοῦ Βάνου, and the clause in lines 11–12; correctly described by Gerstinger as 'Vorschußquittung für Arbeitslohn'.
¹¹⁷ Rathbone 1991, pp. 112, 319, etc.

many 'waterwheel receipts' in the Apion Archive refer to the *pittakia* of individual employees [*enapographoi georgoi*],[118] and these, I suggest, were employees' individual accounts with the estate.[119] The wider analogy here is with the systems of wage-accounting which characterised the Mexican *haciendas* till well into the twentieth century, a general term for which might be *ajustes de cuentas* or account adjustments.[120]

At another level entirely, *P.Wash. Univ.* II 102 shows individual settlements supplying an agreed number of workers for sowing operations on the *autourgia* of the Apion estate.[121] It is possible that, in this document, the term *ergates* simply meant casual labourer and that the casual labour-supply was normally organised through the *epoikia*, which acted as labour-brokers. It is equally possible, however, that the reference was to services required from permanent labourers, and that it did not particularly matter which families or individual family-members were finally sent out into the fields. The fact that workers living in these settlements were normally paid wages (in cash and/or kind) makes it more attractive to conceptualise this exaction of labour on the *ezba* model (as an exchange of labour against wages) and not simply as forced labour. Much of this is speculation, of course, and apart from straining at the limits of our knowledge, documents like *P.Wash. Univ.* II 102 emphasise the important methodological point that, in ancient history above all, the interpretation of individual items of evidence depends crucially on our building a larger and workable model of how estates actually functioned, and of the kinds of labour-régimes and systems they evolved.

6.8. Conclusion

In *L'habitat rural en Égypte* Lozach and Hug describe a complex defined by cash-crops, irrigation, the formation of large properties, and the concentration of workers in dispersed settlements controlled by the estates. For them,

---

[118] *P.Oxy.* I 137.19 (584), XVI 1988.23ff. (587), 1989.17ff. (590), called *entagia* here (for the equivalence of these terms, see *P.Oxy.* LVIII 3958.25–6n.).
[119] Cf. Preisigke, *Wörterbuch*, 1.311, s.v. πιττάκιον, 1 e) Abrechnungsbuch, Kontobuch.
[120] Carmen Velázques 1983; Nickel 1991; and cf. Van Young 1981, p. 255.
[121] *P.Wash. Univ.* II 102 is certainly from the Apion estate; of the six places mentioned, two (Nike and Maiouma) were Apion settlements, cf. *SB* XII 11231 = *P.Oxy.* XVI 1986 descr. (549), *P.Oxy.* LVIII 3952 (before 29.8.610), XIX 2244.14, 16, for Nike, and VI 999 (616/7) for Maiouma.

this landscape was a product of the evolving agrarian capitalism of the late nineteenth century, with its formation of large privately-held estates and the spread of perennial irrigation.[122] I have suggested, however, that this pattern was at least partially replicated in the history of the sixth-century estates. It is, of course, likely that the reordering of labour-relationships in the Egyptian countryside of the nineteenth century, with large landowners orchestrating campaigns *against* the *corvée* and the *ezbas* materialising new methods of labour-control, reflected the spread of summer-irrigation and a new set of labour-requirements on estates subject to the rationalising imperatives of nineteenth-century capitalism.[123] Nonetheless, in a longer perspective, these changes appear less revolutionary than they might otherwise seem. For example, in *Colonising Egypt* Timothy Mitchell has argued that the *ezba*'s 'regime of spatial confinement, discipline and supervision' was emblematic of the much larger emergence of new mechanisms of power, a new 'principle' of order, through which a quintessentially modern state (and its colonial agencies) pursued the systematic dissolution and synthetic *re*totalisation of societies and communities unstructured by the geometries of capital.[124] All of these are valuable and even obvious perspectives on the changes in the nineteenth century which reintegrated Egypt into a more modern world-economy shaped by the evolution of British industrial capital.[125] But, at a deeper level, they contain a major problem, or at least a paradox. If the *ezbas* were in some sense the revival or re-enactment of social forms, methods of organisation characteristic of Egyptian large estates in earlier centuries and, above all, in the period marked by the greatest development of private landownership prior to the nineteenth century (namely, the fifth to seventh centuries), then surely we must, again in some sense, extend these characterisations to the rural society of the sixth century and see in the large estates of that period a curious prefiguration of something intrinsically modern. Agriculture was history's first theatre of capitalism, but because our notions of the latter have been irreducibly shaped by modern large-scale industry and the profound

---

[122] Lozach and Hug 1930, pp. 195ff., esp. 204, 'La dispersion par 'ezbahs...est le produit de l'irrigation pérenne, de la grosse propriété et du capitalisme agraire' (in the section written by Hug).
[123] See especially Brown 1994.
[124] Mitchell 1988, pp. 43, 92, and *passim*.
[125] Owen 1969.

analysis that Marx developed in *Capital*, we only seem to be able to grasp the history of agrarian capitalism through a sort of palimpsest. The whole debate between the 'primitivists' and the 'modernists' is essentially a misunderstanding caused by this fact, for what the primitivists clearly do is measure economic behaviour by the revised edition of capitalism, so to speak.

Secondly, it is also worth emphasising that the Egyptian peasantry in particular has a strangely elusive quality. Our only detailed study, in English, of the agrarian structure of a country in the Middle East draws a useful distinction between peasant-proprietors, crop-sharing peasants, and landless labourers.[126] Even more interestingly, Lambton also pointed out, 'The vast majority of the peasant population of Persia is...composed not of peasant proprietors, who are a small minority, but of crop-sharing peasants or tenants and "landless" labourers', and noted that the sharecroppers 'too, strictly speaking, are landless'. Ancient historians who have dealt with Egypt have been too ready to assume that the situation Lambton seemed to see as characteristic of the Persian countryside, at least in the recent period, could not have been true of Egypt in antiquity, and that a large and stable class of 'peasant-proprietors' existed which was not drastically undermined even by the renewed expansion of large estates in late antiquity. However, this assumption has little basis in the evidence and seems to rest on what one might call terminological impressionism. I have suggested in this paper that the Egyptian peasantry was a less stable group than this convention assumes, that there was more landlessness in the ancient countryside than we seem willing to allow for, and finally that the organisation of the large estates could well have reflected this fact.

[1999]

---

[126] Lambton 1953, p. 295.

Chapter Seven
Late Antiquity to the Early Middle Ages: What Kind of Transition?

7.1. Introduction: Marxist uncertainties

A Marxist characterisation of late antiquity and the early middle ages (the whole period from 300 to 800, *grosso modo*) involves at least two sets of issues. First, what would a coherent Marxist characterisation of the economic structure of late antiquity look like? In sharp contrast to Stalin's theory of the final extinction of classical slavery in a 'slave revolution', slavery was widespread and entrenched in the post-Roman West. It had certainly not disintegrated under the hammer blows of a revolution, much less one carried through by slaves. But does the persistence or revival of slavery mean that a slave *mode of production* dominated the class-relationships of this period? Something like this was argued by Pierre Bonnassie from his seminal work on Catalonia. Bonnassie suggested that 'Catalan society in the ninth and tenth centuries was still a slave society'.[1] Serfdom emerged from the violent and dramatic rupture, the crisis of public authority, that characterised the eleventh century, and in this classic, late-feudal sense it was *not* a feature of the early middle ages.[2]

---

[1] Bonnassie 1991, p. 108.
[2] See the excellent survey in Freedman 1996.

On the contrary, 'The persistence of a slave economy constitutes one of the chief features of Visigothic Spain'.³ However, no Marxist historians have gone as far as this, and if anything they have done the opposite, projecting either serfdom or feudalism back into late antiquity. Thus A. Barbero and M. Vigil refer to the 'feudalisation' of Spain under the Visigoths, arguing this at length,⁴ and, among British Marxists, Geoffrey de Ste Croix could even suggest that serfdom was the 'predominant mode of production [sic.]' in the later Roman empire.⁵ This bears some resemblance to Rodney Hilton's view that late antiquity had seen large landowners 'creating the production relations characteristic of feudal society'.⁶ 'From at least as early as the crisis of the third century town life had been contracting, and *self-sufficient serf-worked estates had begun to dominate the social structure of the Empire*'.⁷ Hilton was clearly referring to the institution known to Roman historians as the colonate, but, at a deeper level, his views reflected a tradition of late Roman historiography shaped less by anything Marx himself had written than by Max Weber's famous lecture of 1896.⁸ The paradigm, which Weber himself did more to define than most, was one of widespread economic recession and a ruralisation of the life of the empire. The identification of the colonate with serfdom (common to most historians of the early twentieth century; Ste Croix was its last great representative) was clearly what underpinned the half-baked conception of late antiquity as a precursor of feudalism.

Today almost no serious scholar accepts this view, if only because feudalism itself is still so contested.⁹ So where does this leave us in terms of a general characterisation of the late antique world? A more solid Marxist characterisation can surely only come from the conjunction of new perspectives within

---

³ Bonnassie 1991, p. 71.
⁴ Barbero and Vigil 1978.
⁵ Ste Croix 1983, p. 155.
⁶ Hilton 1976, p. 112.
⁷ Hilton 1976, p. 110. Cf. Hilton 1973, p. 91 referring to the 'replacement of slavery by serfdom, *which was characteristic of the late Roman economy*...'. Contrast this with Marc Bloch who was emphatic that serfdom was a 'strictly personal bondage' which had *nothing* to do with 'attachment to the soil'. 'Definitions of serfdom arrived at by courts or jurists have survived in some quantity: *none* before the fourteenth century include "attachment to the soil" among its characteristics in any shape or form', Bloch 1973, p. 86. Bloch called serfdom 'the *most specifically medieval* of all existing institutions' (p. 105).
⁸ Weber 1924.
⁹ Reynolds 1994.

the historiography itself and simultaneous attempts to map out the *conceptual* landscape in new ways (for example, John Haldon, Manuel Acién, Eduardo Manzano).[10]

The second set of issues relates to our notions of feudalism and of the transition from late antiquity to the early middle ages. How well does the theory of modes of production work for this transition? Do Marxists have a coherent understanding of the feudal mode of production?[11] If a *fully* articulated feudal economy only emerged in the central or even later middle ages, what do we make of the early middle ages? What do we mean by 'serfdom' and when did it evolve? There is scarcely an integrated Marxist position on these issues. For example, Ste Croix implied that there was *no* integral link between serfdom and feudalism[12] and seemed to think that serfdom could form a mode of production *sui generis* (since it was, as he said, the 'predominant mode of production' in late antiquity). In contrast, Hilton, with more sense of historical specificity, had always seen serfdom as central to feudalism. But Hilton also believed that serfdom should not be defined by labour-services alone, whereas Marx himself had done precisely that, claiming in one passage that 'Serf labour... has this in common with wage-labour, in respect of rent, that the latter is paid in *labour*, not in *products*, still less in *money*'.[13] Not only was serfdom, for Marx, the 'broad basis of social production' in the middle ages[14] but its pure form involved the exaction of labour-services, a position that is clearly at odds with Hilton's view that 'labour rent was not an essential element in the feudal relations of production'.[15] In even greater contrast (to Marx), in Wickham's recent book the lord's *lack* of control of the labour-process is

---

[10] Acién is a Spanish Marxist historian whose major contribution was a study of the Andalusi rebel 'Umar ibn Ḥafṣūn, Acién 1997. Manzano writes within a broadly left-wing tradition (cf. Manzano 1998b) and recently published an excellent synthesis on al-Andalus (Manzano 2006).

[11] From a passage in the *Grundrisse*, it is arguable that Marx himself saw feudalism emerging as a 'synthesis' of the 'concentration of landed property' characteristic of the later Roman empire and the bondage peculiar to the Germanic peoples, Marx 1973, pp. 97–8.

[12] Ste Croix 1983, p. 136: 'there is evidently in some people's minds a groundless connection between serfdom and "feudalism"' (!).

[13] Marx 1971, p. 401.

[14] Marx 1981, p. 970; and of course the terms in which Marx criticised Kovalesky, see Marx 1879, p. 67 (= Krader 1975, p. 383), with Krader 1975, pp. 201ff.; Anderson 1974a, p. 406.

[15] Hilton 1976, p. 15.

(almost?) built into his definition of feudalism,[16] which emerges here in the more abstract structuralist guise of any system of 'coercive rent-taking' that pits landlords on one side against peasants on the other.[17] It was this kind of abstractionism, depleted of historical content, that Anderson had blasted in some of the best pages of *Lineages*,[18] even if his own conception of the feudal mode was a haphazard conglomeration of features that failed to have any significant impact on the historiography.[19] The best work by medievalists working in a left-wing tradition has been decidedly discontinuist, underlining the *novelty* of the middle ages.[20] The paradox of Wickham's conceptual choices is that, however one sees that novelty, it is not definable at the level of the mode of production, since his notion of the feudal mode is construed so loosely that it covers both the Roman empire and (probably) the whole medieval world and much else besides! The tendency to *dehistoricise* categories such as 'serfdom' (Ste Croix) and 'feudalism' (Wickham, Haldon) in order to be able to extend their application to Antiquity is surely a retrograde one. It stems as much from the lack of a more sophisticated Marxist theory of the feudal mode as it does from any conception of late antiquity as a precursor of feudalism.

---

[16] So too in Wickham 2000, p. 33, where *limited* landowner control over production is stated to be part of the 'economic logic' of feudalism: 'landowners could only influence production by indirect methods [*potevano solo influenzare la produzione con metodi indiretti*]'. This has been a long-standing belief of Wickham's and one which almost certainly stems from Hindess and Hirst. With characteristic disregard for the actual complexity of history, they believed it was a universal feature of precapitalist forms of agricultural production that 'direct producers' had 'effective possession of the means of reproduction of their own labour-power' (Hindess and Hirst 1975, p. 189). One of the strangest passages in *Pre-Capitalist Modes of Production* is the one where, after quoting Kosminsky to the effect that feudalism as a mode of production presumed 'a class of basic producers with a special connection with the land – *which remained, however, the property of the ruling class of feudal lords*' (Kosminsky 1956, p. vi), Hindess and Hirst conclude that feudalism presumes 'direct producers who *own* the means of reproduction of their labour-power' (1975, p. 191)!

[17] Contrast Anderson 1974a, p. 409, referring to the nobility's 'organizing role in production itself, whose typical form in Europe was the manor'.

[18] Anderson 1974a, p. 407ff., a strong defence of the 'specificity' of feudalism that starts with Marx's critique of Kovalevsky.

[19] Anderson 1974b, esp. pp. 147ff. Anderson himself called this a 'synthesis of elements' whose key markers included natural economy and the dispersal of political sovereignty. But surely neither is *central* to feudalism. If the former is scarcely credible today (e.g., Wickham 2005, pp. 291–2, 796–805), the latter fails to explain how a 'recharged apparatus of feudal domination' (Absolutism) could emerge within a mode of production *defined by* its dispersion of sovereignty.

[20] For example, Karol Modzelewski, Bruno Andreolli and Massimo Montanari, Manuel Acién, Paul Freedman...

But Chris Wickham's book is certainly the best starting-point for a discussion of these issues.

7.2. Background to the late empire

In Roman history, the 'late empire' refers in general to the period between the fourth and the seventh centuries, the fourth and early fifth if the focus is western, since the western empire fell apart in the fifth, and the sixth and early seventh as well if we look at the East. The fourth century is thus the watershed that divides Roman from *late* Roman history. Yet the basic *elements* of the fourth-century empire were established in the third, with the sweeping reorganisation of the army and the emergence of a new command-structure, on one side, and, on the other, the sustained expansion, throughout the late second and third centuries, of a network of provincial, mainly African, families who would later form the core of the western aristocracy under Constantine (306–37). Reform of the army excluded senators from military command and signified a major break in the traditional pattern of upper-class dominance. If this was a *democratisation* of the Roman army, as Lopuszański suggested in a seminal paper, it certainly paved the way for the evolution of a professionalised officer-corps and the consolidation of an *esprit de corps* in the higher ranks that dominated much of the political history of the late empire.[21] By the fourth century, senators were marginal to the composition of the army-leadership, which came, increasingly, to incorporate a strong Germanic component. The key result of all this was that, from the main part of the third century, emperors were drawn overwhelmingly from non-senatorial/military backgrounds. The *politically* relevant élite was not the senatorial class but a military élite whose upward mobility found renewed resonance in the civilian side of the administration, as bureaucracies were expanded and professionalised and a new value set on legal and related forms of expertise. *The social fluidity of the late empire was the key to its sudden effervescence.* The senate itself was transformed and expanded early in the fourth century and the equestrian order subsumed wholesale into the senatorial class, infusing administrative and business-skills. The consolidation of the western aristocracy meant, crucially, an *adjustment* with the state, the ability

---

[21] Lopuszański 1938.

to manoeuvre and as far as possible dominate. By contrast, in the East, state and aristocracy were much more closely integrated, since the aristocracy was itself of bureaucratic origin and the bedrock of the state's apparatus. These differences would become a major part of the story of why the empire survived so spectacularly in the East when it fell to pieces in the West.

The key innovation of the late empire that broke with centuries of tradition was Constantine's monetary reform. Just as the military revolution of the third century was decisive in defining the 'style' of the late empire, vesting state-power in the hands of the military, Constantine's creation of a new *gold*-currency provided the pivotal foundation that sustained the expansion of the governing class as a whole (both senators, new and old, and bureaucracy). As one contemporary commented, the aristocratic élites of the fourth century accumulated vast quantities of gold, so that 'the houses of the powerful were crammed full of it'. In the West, the countryside scaled new peaks of activity as the owners of these vast hoards of money-capital expanded productive capacities and upgraded their fixed-capital investments – a process which is best documented, archaeologically, for the Spanish countryside, most spectacularly in the very rich fourth-century villas of the northern Meseta. To ensure efficiency, the state intervened to pin labour down to the large estates, contriving new definitions that were antithetical to the purism of classical law. In short, the fourth century dramatically *re*configured law, society and economy in ways that were a disaster for the lower classes. For the Italian historian Santo Mazzarino, all this was a major part of the *crisis* of the western empire, in the sense that 'the peasant masses felt themselves crushed under the weight of the new economy'[22] and sought protection with the aristocracy against the state. 'The small peasant-proprietors turned themselves into *dediticii* of the rich, or as it was called in Celtic *vassi*'. 'These', Mazzarino claimed, 'are the first hints of the economic system of vassalage which marks the Middle Ages'. To offset the crisis government unleashed a prolonged deflation which 'in conditions of insufficient productivity brought the society nearer to a natural economy'. 'Thus', that is, with 'vassalage' on one side and natural economy on the other, both rooted in the conditions of the late empire, 'they set off toward the Middle Ages'.

---

[22] Mazzarino 1966, p. 154.

This framing of the 'transition', of the resilience of an empire undermined by *social* crisis, is conspicuously absent in Wickham's book. Indeed, it will be striking to his colleagues in Italy that there is no reference to their great mentor Mazzarino, not even in the bibliography! Wickham charts a very different course, abandoning the speculative-looking constructions of the 1950s and its textual tools in favour of a wider range of sources and considerable emphasis on the archaeological work, late Roman and medieval, of the last two decades. For Mazzarino's uncomplicated trajectory from late antique *patrocinium* to medieval vassalage, a model of almost appealing simplicity, Wickham substitutes a more involved and densely textured history – of landscapes, exchange-networks, aristocracies and urbanism, and of the fragile autonomy of the peasantry, all moving in complex and uneven ways in a fragmenting world whose sinews were being remorselessly severed throughout this period. The *collapse of the state* and the fragmentation that flowed from it are the structuring principles of Wickham's discussion of these diverse trajectories. Unlike Pirenne, who saw the disintegration of the western empire as a 'political fact' with minimal implications for the continuity of *'Romania'*, postponing the great catastrophe that ended it to the Islamic expansion of the later seventh century,[23] Wickham ascribes momentous significance to the *crisis of the state*. In particular, the breakdown of taxation, by which he means taxation in kind, had major long-term impacts in the West: a crisis of the urban traditions of antiquity, with major changes in the scale and quality of urbanism, a general weakening and impoverishment of the aristocracy, and the slow but inexorable disintegration of the Mediterranean world-system. All of this happened unevenly, of course, and Wickham tracks the changes with a strong sense of their local peculiarities, mapping their real or hypothetical evolution by region and subregion, and constructing a transition model of considerable complexity.

I have dealt elsewhere with what I regard as the major analytical weakness of the model, namely, its failure to integrate money into an overall account of the transformation, so here I shall deal with a different set of issues.[24] It is a tribute to the profoundly stimulating character of Wickham's book that it throws up a whole lot of issues which are *still largely unresolved*.

---

[23] Pirenne 1968.
[24] Banaji 2007, App. 5.

7.3. Unresolved issues

Chief among these unresolved issues are the following:

Firstly, how do we characterise the dynamic of the late empire? Wickham has clearly moved away from the model of 'The Other Transition' where state and aristocracy were seen as distinct and rival claimants to the 'surplus' and the system as a whole was *driven by the state*, so that the break-up of the western empire was a *victory* for the aristocracy. In *Framing* the aristocracy is a major *casualty* of the dissolution of the empire,[25] and aristocracy and state no longer embody rival modes of production. Yet the new picture is no less problematic. At least the model of 'The Other Transition' drew attention to an *internal* conflict – the aristocracy sabotaged the state, abandoned or deserted it and left the western empire to its fate. (Numerous historians have argued this, from Sundwall to Peter Brown.) In *Framing*, the model lacks any internal dynamic. The decline of taxation, triggered by the invasions and the break-up of the empire, unfolds like a huge tidal wave that drags the senatorial élites along, shattering the structures of their dominance – interregional networks, urban prosperity, the economic unity of the Mediterranean, and so on. Second, why use the imagery of *modes of production* to characterise the transition from the late empire to the middle ages, if, as Wickham claims, the feudal mode of production was the 'normal economic system of the *ancient and medieval* periods'?[26] The timelessness of this image contrasts sharply with the momentous changes that transformed the ancient world into a medieval one.

Secondly, how widespread was slavery in late antiquity?[26a] A *concentration* of slave-labour in mass-producing workshops based on an intensive rationalisation of labour-processes had sustained massive exports of Italian fine wares down to the Augustan age.[27] This was a type of Roman industrial slavery with striking resemblance to more recent forms of work-organisation (repetitive work-cycles, job-simplification and tight control over labour). With the rapid expansion of rural estates ('villas') following the bloody civil wars of the early

---

[25] Wickham 2005, pp. 255, 534.
[26] Wickham 2005, p. 535; my emphasis.
[26a] The best recent work is by Kyle Harper: see Harper 2008; 2011.
[27] Morel 1990, p. 404ff.

first century BC, an agrarian version of this 'slave mode of production' came to underwrite Italy's domination of related Mediterranean markets for wine and olive-oil.[28] It would make more sense to call these economic régimes 'slave-capitalism', following Max Weber and Otto Hintze,[29] than anything as vague as a 'slave mode of production', since it is far from obvious that there is a commonly agreed definition of the latter. In any case, this régime had more or less ended by the second century, whereas slavery continued and was even widespread in late antiquity. Wickham discounts its significance, however, because for him the 'numerous slaves of the late Empire or the period following it...were [not] for the most part anything other than tenants'.[30] This, I shall argue, vastly simplifies the actual transition from Roman to medieval relations of production ('slavery to serfdom' in the conventional metanarrative), which it would be more accurate to describe as involving a *mutation* of slavery than its outright supersession.

A third issue relates to our characterisation of the rural labour-force in the post-Roman West. Wickham wants to see the early middle ages as a low point in the general curve of aristocratic dominance. Whether that translates into reduced domination of the peasantry in the earliest middle ages, as he wants to argue,[31] is less certain. Surely this will depend on how we characterise the labour-force at the base of the rural economy in the post-Roman world and whether we see the slaves and freedpeople provided with plots of land as *workers*, as Ros Faith has argued,[32] convincingly in my view, or *peasants*, as Wickham would want. One of Wickham's most insistent leitmotifs is the triumph of the realities of tenure over legal distinctions.[33] The point can be accepted but it certainly does not rule out other models of greater

---

[28] Rathbone 1977; Giardina 2004, p. 233f.
[29] E.g., Hintze 1975, p. 434, argued that Max Weber has demonstrated 'how the unlimited economic exploitation of slave labor on plantations and in mines corresponded to the merciless political oppression of conquered peoples. Victory in the wars of the Greek city-states and the Roman Republic regularly led to a plundering of men and land, thus giving *slave capitalism* constant new nourishment...'.
[30] Wickham 1988, p. 188.
[31] E.g., Wickham 2005, p. 570.
[32] Faith 1997, p. 69.
[33] Wickham 2005, p. 563.

complexity, such as Faith has constructed for the 'inland' labour-organisation of Anglo-Saxon England.

Finally, and, for Marxists, most fundamentally, is the schema of 'modes of production' helpful in characterising the major transformations of the period Wickham deals with? If so, how would we have to formulate the transition, given that serfdom did not replace slavery in any obvious way? And does Wickham's own handling of historical-materialist concepts such as 'mode of production' help or hinder a materialist analysis of this?

In what follows, I shall suggest that the legacies of the Roman world and of late antiquity were more subtle than any straightforward debate about continuity makes them out to be, and that key among these were 1) the *pervasive influence of Roman law* in defining the condition of the medieval peasantry[34] and 2) the tradition of *direct management* which the Merovingian aristocracy, in particular, inherited from their late Roman counterparts. On the other hand, the aristocracy itself and the organisation of estates show major changes that mark a break with antiquity. The *relations of production* of the early middle ages were thus shaped by a complex set of influences that owe as much to subliminal legacies (law, management-traditions) as to the 'will' of the Frankish sovereign and his magnates in developing a new kind of rural enterprise.[35]

7.4. The reshaping of relations of production

What the post-Roman world inherited from the massive legal edifice of the late Roman state was a legacy of *oppression*. In other words, central to any characterisation of the form of Roman society that emerged in the fourth century must be the increasingly repressive legislation of the late empire, which eroded the rights of farm-workers in particular. In the words of Moses Finley, 'there was a gradual erosion in the capacity of the lower classes to resist working for the benefit of others under conditions of less than full "freedom of contract"'.[36] It is this that explains the paradox of why, despite the disintegration of the western empire and the dissolution of its aristocracy,

---

[34] This argument has been most forcefully developed by Wulf Eckart Voß in a much neglected paper cited below.
[35] '"Will" of the Frankish sovereign' from Devroey 2001, p. 120.
[36] Finley 1980, p. 143.

there was no visible change in the economic position of most or many rural inhabitants. Indeed, the post-Roman labour-force was in one respect at least *worse off*, in the sense that the sharp division between 'slave' and 'free' that was intrinsic to classical law was progressively abandoned, in practice anyway, as a uniformly servile tenantry evolved by the early part of the sixth century. This, I suggest, is why we need to take the colonate more seriously than Wickham does. It is next to impossible to account for the transition from the relatively open labour-markets of the third century[37] to the mixed servile labour-forces of the sixth and seventh centuries and later, without the decisive historical mediation of the colonate.[38] The key assumption behind the system was that resident-workers were part of the 'capital assets of the estate on which they lived and worked',[39] hence part of the estate's tax-liability. A rapid turnover of labour would undermine the stability of the system, and to ensure such stability both government and landowners concurred in *tying* workers to estates. The lawyers who drafted the legislation of the late empire rationalised this peculiar subordination of free labour with the legal fiction that tied labourers [*coloni*] were 'slaves of the land to which they were born',[40] in other words, attached to estates and not landowners, but, of course, in practice the colonate simply reinforced the power of employers over labour. That it did so explains why, in the Roman-controlled parts of the Mediterranean, this agrarian system survived down to the end of the sixth century,[41] if not later, certainly long after its fiscal origins and function had been forgotten.

7.4.1. *The legacy of the colonate*

Wickham's handling of the colonate is the least satisfying part of his superb book. The successor-states inherited a labour-force that included large numbers of former *coloni*, many of whom were or were still *regarded* as unfree

---

[37] Rathbone 1991; Banaji 1997.
[38] Cf. Davies 1996, p. 234, 'Tying the agricultural labour force to the land is one of the keys to the establishment of the condition of the later medieval peasantry'.
[39] Ros Faith's expression in *The English Peasantry and the Growth of Lordship*, Faith 1997, p. 84.
[40] *CJ* xi.52.1 (392-395), *servi terrae ipsius cui nati sunt aestimentur*, after (and despite!) the qualification that *coloni* were, legally, free-born persons.
[41] E.g., Gregory, *Ep.* 4.21 (594) which even refers to a *ius colonarium*!

workers/tenants. Did these groups fare differently in the different kingdoms or did they share an essentially similar fate? And if they did, what fate was that? In other words, what difference did the dissolution of Roman power make to the condition of these workers or peasants? There are scarcely any references to 'the' colonate in a post-Roman context, and it seems likely that the system had disintegrated in its classic late Roman form.[42] But what became of the *coloni* themselves? Some historians argue that the distinction between the main groups of the labour-force simply disappeared, as late Roman *coloni* were absorbed *en masse* into a more or less undifferentiated post-Roman servile class and from now on treated no differently from slaves.[43] For example, Finley asked, 'Were the *servi* of the Germanic codes all chattel slaves? The Visigothic laws, for example, ignore *coloni*, yet we know that they certainly existed, and were important in the Visigothic kingdom'.[44] This is not a position Wickham would want to identify with, in part because he thinks that legal, hence also servile status mattered less and less as one moved into the middle ages and partly because he sees the independent peasantry expanding as the western empire disintegrated. It is possible that there is room for *both* positions, depending on how things played out in the post-Roman West, but it would certainly have helped to have started with a clear conception of what the *colonatus* itself was, something Wickham does not do, both because he is (I think unduly) sceptical about the value of legal sources and because of his at least tacit support for Jean-Michel Carrié's own iconoclasm on this subject.

To take just two examples from the legal evidence, one late fourth-century constitution confers on estate-owners the authority to control their workers 'with the care of patrons and the *power of masters*'.[45] The 'power of masters' was, of course, the power masters exercised over slaves. Another, earlier one stipulates that workers [*coloni*] who run away from estates should be dragged back in chains.[46] On any straightforward reading of this sort of evidence most historians would conclude, and many still do, that government massively reinforced the power of large landowners over rural workers and did so in

---

[42] So too Bloch 1963, p. 232; De Martino 1986, p. 37.
[43] King 1972, pp. 160–1; Nehlsen 1972, p. 167; García de Cortázar 1988, p. 11.
[44] Finley 1980, p. 124.
[45] *CJ* xi.52.1 (392–5).
[46] *CTh* 5.17.1 (332).

sweeping ways. But the point is one Wickham is (for a Marxist, curiously!) unwilling to concede. The reasoning seems to be something like this: the *coloni* were not serfs but tenants. If coercion was applied to them, this was largely from the standpoint of the state and its need to ensure the regular payment of taxes, hence stable labour-forces. How far government succeeded in tying down these workforces must have varied enormously in practice. The laws may not have been effective. In any case, the colonate had more to do with the technicalities of taxation than the realities of exploitation and control of labour.

By way of a response, let us begin with the first proposition, about *coloni* not being serfs. In some influential work from the eighties, Carrié mounted a strong attack on the back-projection of feudal characteristics to the late Roman period – not just 'serfdom', but labour-services and manors as well. None of these were handed down to the middle ages from late Rome, especially not serfdom. A medieval reading of late Roman institutions is profoundly misleading. This part of Carrié's critique is of course unproblematic and few historians would disagree with it today. It stems in fact from the positions of Marc Bloch, except that Bloch saw things in the reverse perspective. He had denounced the assimilation of the serf to the *colonus* as a contrived anachronism, tracing its roots to the late thirteenth/early fourteenth century when it emerged under the influence of the kind of legal erudition that had led the way in the reception of Roman law in Europe.[47] *But the colonate itself raised no issues for Bloch*, it was, as the law-codes said it was, an institution that tied the peasantry to the soil and even invented a special vocabulary to express that. Indeed, in the chapter Bloch wrote for the *Cambridge Economic History of Europe*, he took the *colonatus* sufficiently seriously to call it 'the fundamental institution of the late Empire'![48] Carrié's argument moves in a very different direction. He suggests that the conventional view of the colonate as a coercive labour-system lacks *any* foundation in the sources, in other words, that it stems solely from the false assimilation that Bloch was the first to expose. A careful reading of the Roman legal sources shows that considerations of fiscality were the only ones paramount in the late Roman discussion about *coloni*. There was no institution like 'the' colonate if by that we mean that

---

[47] See Bloch 1921.
[48] Bloch 1963, p. 229.

the legislation of the late empire created a *special* status between slavery and freedom and imposed this on a large if indeterminate part of the rural population. The Roman law of persons recognised only two categories, free and slave, and that division remained axiomatic even later. It was never breached by the creation of a third category like 'half free'. True, the legislation of the fourth and fifth centuries refers repeatedly to servitude, comparing the tied tenantry [*coloni*] to slaves [*servi, mancipia*], calling them 'slaves of the land', and prescribing slave-like treatment for those who fled their estates, but Carrié suggests that these references were *purely metaphorical*,[49] and that the laws themselves had no intrinsic connection with labour or with labour regulation, only with the registration of tax-payers on the tax-rolls. If rural workers ended up being 'tied' to estates, this was part of a wider fiscal subjection that affected all sorts of groups and tied all of them equally to their places of origin or professions. The *adscripticii* whom the Emperor Justinian could not help comparing to slaves[50] were never actually reduced to a state of 'semi-slavery',[51] at least not in the fourth and fifth centuries (so Carrié more recently),[52] since no such condition could exist in Roman law.

Now, the view that the laws on the colonate had 'largely fiscal aims' is scarcely controversial. A.H.M. Jones argued for it convincingly way back in the 1950s, suggesting that it was 'primarily a fiscal measure'[53] *when it was first introduced*. Jones made it plain that he was referring to the *origin* of the measure that first led to the tying of labour to the land, and not characterising the institution as it worked, collusively no doubt, over some two or three centuries. Thus he repeatedly emphasised the considerable stake that substantial landowners had in the working of the colonate. 'If the tying of the agricultural population was in origin a measure dictated by public policy, it proved a great boon to landlords'.[54] '*It was at the demand of landlords that the system was maintained and extended*'.[55] And, of course, the system itself had drastic implications for the position of a large part of the labour-force.

---

[49] Carrié 1983, pp. 207, 220, 224.
[50] *CJ* xi.48.21.1 (530), cf. Ste. Croix 1983, p. 252.
[51] Carrié 1983, p. 213.
[52] Carrié 1997, p. 124.
[53] Jones 1958, p. 4 = 1974, p. 298.
[54] Jones 1958, p. 5 = 1974, p. 299.
[55] Jones 1964, p. 817; emphasis mine.

Between this view, which has no problem with a fiscal origin for the colonate but attaches equal importance to its actual historical function (e.g., Bloch's description of it as 'class legislation')[56] and Carrié's *lecture iconoclaste*, Wickham, as I said, inclines to the latter. Thus he refers to the laws on *coloni* as a set of 'laws about free taxpayers',[57] undeterred by the nebulousness of this conception. And he prefers to think that even as a set of legal arrangements the laws about it may have had little practical significance, that is, in the way things worked on the ground. Law is a dimension of reality, not a picture of it, and there is no reason to suppose either that people were fully aware of what the laws actually were (Augustine's hesitations about the way landowners treated their labourers is a good example)[58] or even that they were ever widely enforced.

Wickham does not deny that the laws prescribed the tying of labour to the land. Indeed, both he and Carrié seem to think that the whole rural population was tied in this way, including the free peasants, something for which there is in fact much less evidence, as Jones realised. But given that the *tying* of labour is not denied, at least as legal intent, there are two debates here: first, *did* the laws make any material difference to the position (status, civil rights, etc.) of the free working population? Did they entail a worsening of status for those sections, a *Statusverschlechterung* as the German legal historians call it? And second, were the late Roman *coloni* simply tenants in Wickham's sense, that is, rent-paying peasants in control of their own labour-process? (At times, Wickham seems to identify the colonate with tenancy per se: for example, he refers to 'the sea of the "colonate"',[59] meaning simply the prevalence of rent-paying tenancies.)

It is abundantly clear that the laws treat tied labourers (workers described by Pope Gregory as *ex condicione ligati*, 'bound by their legal position')[60] as not fully in control of their own lives. Not only were they attached to estates by law, but when they fled and worked elsewhere as sharecroppers or wage-labourers, they were regarded as behaving *quasi sui arbitrii ac liberi*, 'as if they

---

[56] Bloch 1963, p. 230.
[57] Wickham 2005, p. 526.
[58] Augustine, *Ep.* 24*.1, where he asks a lawyer friend whether landowners could simply transform their *coloni* and *coloni*'s children into slaves.
[59] Wickham 2005, p. 272.
[60] Gregory, *Ep.* 9.129 (599).

can make their own decisions and are free'.[61] The least this implies is that as *coloni*, workers bound to estates, they were *not* so regarded. Again, it was commonplace to describe such workers as being 'owned' by their employers or in their possession.[62] Although not formally incorporated into the law of persons, there is no doubt that the legal traditions of late antiquity did eventually acknowledge diminished degrees of freedom broadly approximating an intermediate status like 'half free'. References like 'a kind of servitude'[63] were not metaphors but attempts to reconcile a new social reality with the unyielding framework of classical law.[64] This is strikingly obvious in the legislation on 'mixed' marriages. These were marriages between persons of different class-backgrounds and the late Roman laws about them (about which unions were 'valid' and which were not and what consequences that had for the legal status or *condicio* of spouses and children) were *destined to have a profound influence on the conditions of the peasantry in medieval Europe*, indeed down to the final abolition of serfdom in the eighteenth and nineteenth centuries. For the 'general rule', the transmission of status through the mother, cf. *CTh* 14.7.1 (397), 'When the marriage is between persons of unequal status [*ubi non est aequale coniugium*], the children shall follow the mother [*matrem sequatur agnatio*]'. In other words, estate-owners had automatic rights of control over the progeny of female labourers even if their husbands were free persons. But what if male workers [*coloni*] married women who were free? According to the general rule, the children born of these unions were technically free, and landowners stood to lose a younger labour-force if they could not have the law amended to stop such individuals from pursuing their freedom, that is, migrating from estates that would otherwise hold them down as tied labourers. Hence *repeated* complaints, in the sixth century, that Justinian's legislation was depleting estates of their workers, and the conundrum Justinian himself faced in trying to reconcile established legal principles with the labour-needs of the aristocracy. (Interestingly, the key references here are to landowners in Africa and the Balkans.)[65] All of this has been discussed in detail in a very

---

[61] *CJ* xi.48.8.1.
[62] E.g., *Nov. Val.* xxvii.6 (449); *CJ* i.3.36 *praef.* (484); *Nov. Just.* 156 *pr.*; 157.1 (542); *Nov. Tib.* xii.2 (578–82).
[63] *CJ* xi.1.2.*pr.*(396)
[64] So too Lepelley 1983, p. 335, who refers to 'une inadaptation des catégories classiques à cette réalité nouvelle'.
[65] See Jones 1958, p. 10 = 1974, pp. 305–6; Voß 1985, p. 160ff.

substantial paper by Wulf Eckart Voß which Wickham, inexplicably, ignores.[66] The general point to make here is that the *post-Roman West was strongly influenced by these late Roman legal traditions* and that they came to form a decisive link between late antiquity and the middles ages.[67]

Were the *coloni* simply 'tenants'? That the supply of *labour* was seen as their chief social function is clear from the legal evidence: e.g., *CJ* xi.53.1 (371) about landowners who take in fugitive *coloni* having to compensate previous owners for the loss in labour-power or services [*in redhibitione operarum et damni, quod locis quae deseruerant factum est*]; *CTh* 5.6.3 (409), assignment of Sciri captives as a tied but non-servile labour-force: '*opera autem eorum terrarum domini libera [utantur]*...'; *CJ* i.12.6.9 (466), which refers to *obsequia*, 'services'.[68] In fact, the only explicit definition of terminology that we have comes from the sixth century, when Justinian tells us in so many words that the term *colonus* refers to 'those who live on estates and work as rural labourers'.[69]

To sum up, even if 'imperial laws were concerned with tax-paying, not labour relations', as Wickham claims,[70] there is certainly enough evidence, both in the legal sources and elsewhere, to suggest that late antique large estates depended on a *tied* labour-force. Certainly, serfdom was not a replication much less a survival of the colonate, but it does not follow that the *colonatus* was not itself a form of bondage. What distinguished late Roman forms of bondage from their medieval counterparts was that they, crucially, were buttressed and mediated by the state. We can, in this sense, speak of the *construction* of the colonate as opposed to its organic or spontaneous evolution. Marxists can surely generate more *specificity* than Geoffrey de Ste Croix managed to do by defining the colonate as a form of exploitation of labour *built on the legal fiction that the worker [colonus] was attached to the estate and not the landowner.*[71] This was obviously a fiction since no one can, literally, be the slave of an object. Even though this restricted the flexibility of owners in

---

[66] Voß 1985.
[67] See Voß 1985, p. 166ff.
[68] Cf. *Oxford Latin Dictionary*, p. 1221, s.v. 'obsequium', 2.
[69] *Nov. Just.* 162.2 (539), cited Banaji 2007, p. 182.
[70] Wickham 2005, p. 526.
[71] Bloch 1963, p. 229, 'But a sturdy fiction made him slave of a thing...'. Ste. Croix simply *equated* the colonate with serfdom, rejecting what he described as the 'groundless connection between serfdom and "feudalism"'; also p. 162, '[W]e must not take the use of the words "serf" and "serfdom" to imply any necessary connection with feudalism, even if we regard feudalism as necessarily involving forms of serfdom'.

the sense that they could not transfer labour between enterprises or sell land without the workforce,[72] in practice everyone understood that tying workers to the soil meant attaching them to their employers. E.g., *CJ* xi.51.1 (386) states straightforwardly that rural workers in the provinces of Palestine be bound to their landlords [*domino fundi teneatur*]. When even that restriction (workers tied to estates and not landowners) was abolished, as it was under Theoderic, the ground was cleared for a model of bondage closer to *servage*.[73]

7.4.2. *Slavery and the post-Roman labour-force*

Wickham works, indeed has always worked, with a stark opposition between the slave *mode* and tenant-labour, ignoring the intermediate agrarian organisations that are more likely to have characterised the general ('epochal') transition from slavery to serfdom.

> What makes the slave mode special...is the systematic subjection of slaves to the control of their masters in the process of production and reproduction; put them on a family plot as a *servus quasi colonus*...and they organize their own farming practices and family structures....The combination between a greater autonomy for what can now be called peasants...and the end of effective intervention by landlords in the procedures of production, transform[s] the whole logic of the economic system, or, as Marx called it, the mode of production.[74]

He adds, 'When the Romans abandoned the slave mode, they went *straight over* to rent-paying tenants'.[75] But Bloch was surely more correct in viewing the slave's holding as a form of salary and slave-tenancies as *labour-tenancies*. In his famous essay 'How and Why Ancient Slavery Came to an End', he suggested that estates needed reserves of labour-power, and that the land granted to slaves 'was like their salary'.[76]

The irony here is that this completely explodes what Susan Reynolds calls 'Marxist feudalism', a model which, by the way, she is sympathetic to! Reynolds 1994.
   [72] *CTh* 13.10.3 (357).
   [73] Cf. Bloch 1965, p. 257, citing *LRV* 5.10.1 on *coloni* being returned to their masters.
   [74] Wickham 1988, p. 187.
   [75] Wickham 1984, p. 31.
   [76] Bloch 1975, pp. 5–6.

The most incisive formulation of the distinction implied here comes in Ros Faith's account of the labour-organisation of the 'inland' in Anglo-Saxon England. She argues that freed slaves were more like workers and serfs more like peasants. Because of its importance, the passage is worth quoting in full:

> It was probably common to provide slaves and freedpeople with small plots of land when they were housed....This process, for which French provides the useful term *alotissement*, has often been seen as the main agent which transformed the slavery of the ancient world into the serfdom of the medieval. However, it is important to make some distinctions here. The housing of slaves brought into being a class of smallholders who were completely dependent on, and tied to, the inland....But the category of peasants who came to be called serfs in post-Conquest England mostly came into being by quite a different route. *The essential distinction is between worker and peasant*. The freed slave was a worker who in return for selling his labour as a commodity received a 'wage in land' from the lord, who was his employer and sole purchaser of that labour. The lord, in his capacity as employer, was essential to him. By contrast, the serf was a peasant with a holding, which, however small, supported him and his family and provided a surplus which was transferred to the lord in rent paid in cash, kind or labour (or in all these). This transfer of the serf's surplus was only made possible because the lord had control of the land: the lord was not as economically essential to his existence as he was to that of the slave.[77]

In short, 'slavery did not simply fade away but had a longer life than was previously supposed....Nor was serfdom, at least the serfdom of the tenth century its natural successor'.[78] There was a more complex set of relationships between slavery and serfdom than a simple 'transition', if by this we mean that one was simply substituted for the other. Even less credible is the model of a dramatic and *compacted* transition between them such as that posited by

---

[77] Faith 1997, pp. 69–70; italics mine. Postan 1954 is the classic essay on the transition from demesne slave to manorial labourer, and makes the more general point that 'At all times in the history of agriculture in Western Europe and elsewhere "tied cottages" or smallholdings attached to labourers' dwellings have been similarly used by landlords and farmers as a safeguard against the shortage or "turnover" of agricultural labour' (p. 26). For examples of this kind of worker, cf. Bloch 1965, p. 269 (on the German *Tageschalken*) and Faith 1997, pp. 209–10 (on the cottars).
[78] Faith 1997, p. 60.

Bonnassie[79] and Bois[80] for parts of Europe around the 'year 1000'. Wickham, of course, does not subscribe either to a linear transition (the famous metanarrative of vulgar Marxism) or to a compacted one. His favourite image is the conversion of slaves into self-managing peasants, which is really equivalent to the thesis that Roman landowners *abandoned direct management*. Thus, in *Framing*, he endorses the very substantial position that 'Most *servi/mancipia* in our period...were tenants who *controlled their own holding* and could keep its fruits after rents were paid'.[81] This is highly unlikely. *Mancipia* included former *coloni*, bound tenants, and *servi* were still slaves in Francia, Visigothic Spain, etc., and it is doubtful if these groups in particular were ever thought to 'control their own holdings', whatever other groups may actually have done so. A substantial part of the rural labour-force of the sixth to eighth, or even ninth, centuries comprised groups who, like Faith's inland-workers or worker-tenants,[82] were *more proletarian than peasant-like*, and often unmarried. In the Middle Rhine region studied by Franz Staab, these groups were still called *mancipia* in the eighth century, this in contrast to the *servi* who, like Wickham's self-managing tenants or Faith's serfs, were a better model of the peasantry, that is, autonomous even if subaltern.[83] Staab suggests that this 'special sense of *servus* already goes back to the Merovingian period',[84] but terminology evolved in different ways in different parts of Europe. The Domesday *servus* was a slave;[85] so too in Catalonia, where the 'lawyers never used the word *servus* except to deny that attached peasants were *servi*, a word used only for slaves'.[86] Finally, in Italy, the word used to describe slaves who 'had no habitation in which to lead a separate family life but who were lodged in outhouses in the courtyard'[87] was *praebendarii*, from *praebere*, 'to provide', which underscores their dependence on the doles provided by the employer.

---

[79] E.g., Davies 1996, p. 230.
[80] See Verhulst 1991, p. 195ff.
[81] Wickham 2005, p. 560. Cf. Wickham 1984, p. 9, 'those slaves had been turned into tenants, *and thus controlled the land and their own work process*'; my italics.
[82] Faith 1997, p. 60.
[83] Staab 1975, pp. 332, 342ff.
[84] Staab 1975, p. 342.
[85] Maitland 1960, p. 52.
[86] Freedman 1986, p. 296.
[87] Duby 1968, p. 38.

Thus Wickham's reiterated thesis of the 'general dominance of tenant-production' throughout the period that he covers is too much of an abstraction to give us any sense of the subtle ways in which relations of production changed.[88] Slavery was widespread in late antiquity and continued to be so in the kingdoms that followed the empire. What we have to try and reconstruct are the estate-structures that used the labour of both slaves and *coloni* in a legal and economic context where the differences between those groups became increasingly irrelevant. Wickham does not confront the issue of late-antique/early-medieval slavery in any serious way beyond the formal acknowledgement that it survived as a legal condition. The implied conclusion is that the survival of slavery in this more abstract sense had no implications for the way landowners *used* labour or *organised* production. It is hard to believe that, when the Spanish Church fought to retain control over manumitted slaves (*mancipia* who had been freed by a previous bishop, for example), it was seeking to retain control of tenants who, on manumission, were likely to migrate elsewhere! Why would tenants in control of their own holdings and work-process wish to leave in the first place? A closer reading of the conciliar legislation shows that what these *mancipia* or *servi* owed the Church, before and after manumission, were *obsequia*, that is, 'services', in other words, their labour-power.[89] Toledo IV, can. 73 (633) is especially revealing because it shows that lay landowners used the same mechanisms to retain control over the labour of freedpeople. The Council ruled that slaves who were freed by masters who chose not to retain control of their services [*obsequium*] were free to become clerics, but those who were still bound to employment [*servitute obnoxii*] even after manumission because employers chose to 'retain control of their services' could not be admitted.[90] Throughout the sixth century, in fact, the term *mancipium* was progressively extended to include former *coloni*.[91]

---

[88] Wickham 2005, p. 286.
[89] Vives, *Concilios Visigóticos*, pp. 127, 151, 214ff., 303, 339–40.
[90] Vives, *Concilios Visigóticos*, p. 216.
[91] *LBurg.* 54 (501–516), about the seizure of *mancipia* and lands in the Burgundian kingdom of Gaul, cf. Goffart 1980, p. 127ff., translating *mancipia* by 'bondsmen' and arguing, correctly in my view, that they 'can hardly be thought not to have numbered a sizable proportion of *coloni*' (p. 136); *Ed. Theod.* 142, which refers to *rustica utriusque sexus mancipia, etiamsi originaria sint*, proof that the term covered *coloni* as well, cf. Nehlsen 1972, p. 125ff.; *Test. Aredii*, in Pardessus 1969, t. 1, p. 136ff. at 139, *mancipia quae colonaria appellantur*, 'the *mancipia* who are called *coloni*', from the will of Aridius of Limoges, dated 572 or 591.

One upshot of this was that the word lost its strictly classical meaning (chattel-slave; in fact, the most reified expression for a slave) to function as a *generic* description for a labour-force characterised by looser forms of bondage. That the *mancipia* are consistently associated with *domus* (houses or dwellings) in the seventh-century Merovingian charters[92] suggests that this increasingly undifferentiated labour-force were provided with allotments which, as Faith remarks, 'were of a size *well calculated to prevent them becoming self-sufficient*'.[93] In the will of Aridius (late sixth century) these allotments are called *peculiaria* (from *peculium*, the assets managed by a slave) and what is interesting is that these small plots of land cannot be sold or gifted away by their occupants.[94]

Thus the labour-force of the early middle ages is probably best characterised in the expression Faith uses for the late Anglo-Saxon inland, viz., a mixed servile labour-force.[95] Wickham exaggerates the degree of control that peasants had either in the Roman countryside or in the early middle ages. To equate the colonate with tenancy[96] when we know that, for Wickham, 'an agrarian system based on tenancy is also one whose basic productive processes are under peasant, not landlord, control'[97] is to leave the reader with a strangely anodyne picture of the late Roman world. Who would dream of proposing a similar argument for the Anglo-Saxon *gebur* or the Castilian *collazos*, both close medieval counterparts of the late Roman *coloni*, even if not actually descended from them?[98] Again, to describe the Visigothic *servi*

---

[92] E.g., Weidemann 1986; Pardessus 1969, t. 1, No. 241; Busson and Ledru 1901, p. 158ff.; *Chart. Lat. Ant. xiii–xiv*, passim.
[93] Faith 1997, p. 70.
[94] Pardessus 1969, t. 1, p. 138, which states that the *mancipia* just listed should be free to enjoy possession of their *peculiaria* 'on condition that they do not presume to sell or alienate them [*ea vero conditione ut nec vendere nec alienare praesumant*]'.
[95] Faith 1997, p. 252.
[96] Wickham 2005, p. 272.
[97] Wickham 2005, p. 264.
[98] Faith 1997, pp. 76–84, esp. 80–1, on the *gebur*; Guglielmi 1967, esp. p. 100ff. on the *collazos*. Aston 1958 took Ine 67 ('If a man takes a yard of land or more, at a fixed rent, and ploughs it, [and] if the lord requires service as well as rent, he [the tenant] need not take the land if the lord does not give him a dwelling...', Attenborough 1922, p. 59) as evidence for the existence of the manorial system in seventh-century Wessex. By contrast, Faith considers it 'vital and early evidence of the status of the inland population'. 'The peasant with a yardland who is housed and tied to the estate corresponds in several respects to the *gebur*', Faith 1997, p. 76. The *geburs* were semi-free or bound tenants who formed part of the estate's labour-force. Interestingly, Anglo-Saxon legal works took them to be their nearest equivalent of the late-Roman *colonus*; this was a recreation of forms, since no actual ancestry was implied here.

as 'unfree tenants'[99] elides the strictly Roman, classical-law meaning that *servus* retained in the barbarian law-codes with the more purely medieval sense which the word acquired only later, in the eighth century.[100] Post-classical slavery was not a purely legal determination. *Leges Visigothorum* ix.2.9 refers to estates being cultivated by *servorum multitudines* ('masses of *servi*'), an odd expression if all these *servi* were was a scatter of autonomous tenancies.[101] It is much more likely that the *servi* were 'simple farm-labourers on a home farm', as P.D. King suggested,[102] Visigothic equivalents of Faith's 'farm servants huddled on the inland'. Under the Ostrogoths, the Italian (*coloni*) *originarii* were reclassified as *mancipia*, and their masters were now free to transfer them between estates,[103] again suggesting that if these were simply peasant families, they certainly had little control over their working lives. Of course, it does not follow that the typical post-Roman large estate was organised in terms of gang-slavery, as Anderson supposes.[104] What it does imply is that the post-Roman élites in Francia and Spain inherited a tradition of direct management of the land which they saw no compelling reason to abandon. This, arguably, was Rome's most substantial economic legacy, next to the vibrant monetary economy that the Umayyads inherited in the eastern provinces.

7.4.3. *The legacy of direct management*

The *direct management* of the early middle ages[105] was certainly a Roman legacy.[106] The contrary view, viz. that Roman landowners gave up direct management when they abandoned the slave-mode (Wickham himself and, for example, Pasquali)[107] stems chiefly from Domenico Vera, but it is crucial to note that Vera's reconstructions lack any *documentary* base even vaguely

---

[99] Wickham 2005, pp. 231 and 526–7, n. 17.
[100] E.g., Goetz 1993, p. 35.
[101] Zeumer 1902, p. 374.
[102] King 1972, p. 169.
[103] Nehlsen 1972, p. 125ff.
[104] Anderson 1974, p. 110.
[105] Duby 1973, pp. 50, 100.
[106] Cf. Modzelewski's repeated insistence on this; the extinction of the Roman aristocracy did *not* entail the dissolution of its estates, Modzelewski 1978, p. 41; also pp. 42–3, 50.
[107] Pasquali 2002, p. 10, 'Quasi del tutto assente sarebbe la gestione diretta, in vario modo esercitata (con schiavi, con manodopera salariato, con lavoro coatto)'; and this about the organisation of estates in late antiquity!

comparable to the papyrological archives, Merovingian charters or Carolingian inventories. (Reconstructing estate-management from a collection of letters, even those of an aristocrat, is a bit like trying to grasp the structure of the labour-process in a large manufacturing firm from the correspondence of its shareholders.)

Having said this, it is, of course, equally clear that the stereotype of slave-run *latifundia* being turned into serf-worked estates[108] is no longer credible. As the preceding pages suggest, and much of Wickham's own argument shows, the 'transition' was obviously much less straightforward. *The continuity in traditions of direct management did not imply a continuity of estate-structures.* The manor was a Frankish innovation, as were labour-services.[109] Yet, the serfdom of the central middle ages was shaped by and evolved out of the 'long continuities' that were bound up with late Roman traditions of labour-management[110] – the drive to create a tied labour-force, the increasing stigmatisation of those workers, the peculiarly repressive laws regulating 'valid' marriages and the transmission of status, the more or less rapid emergence of a servile labour-force where workers who were technically free (under Roman law) were simply reclassified as *servi/mancipia*, something close to slaves, in the barbarian law-codes. *All* of this flowed, with other, later developments (the expansion of peasant-tenures which began in the seventh century, the evolution of labour-services in the eighth, as well as the huge political changes of the tenth and eleventh centuries) into creating the *historically specific* kind of servitude known as 'serfdom'. Equally important here was the retrieval of Roman law in the twelfth century and the role it played in constructing, 'encouraging the definition of', serfdom, both ideologically and legally,[111] one product of which was the late Roman *colonus* as an abstract prototype of the medieval serf. (This 'autonomous' history of law is a superb example of what Marx described, with a sense of wonder, as the problem, the 'really difficult point', of 'how relations of production develop unevenly as legal relations'.)[112]

---

[108] Notably Hilton 1976, p. 113, 'the Roman nobility have been undergoing the process of transformation into feudal nobles since the third century. Their slave-run latifundia have been turned into serf-worked estates...'; about aristocrats in Italy and parts of Gaul.
[109] Verhulst 1966 (seminal); Rouche 1990; Rösener 1989; Andreolli and Montanari 1983.
[110] Davies 1996, p. 238 for the expression.
[111] Freedman 1991 and 1986.
[112] Marx 1973, p. 109.

None of this suggests that serfdom 'descended' from the colonate,[113] and acknowledging these manifold and converging trajectories is *not* equivalent to writing a linear history. Given this framework, of the subtle interplay of subliminal legacies, long continuities, historical innovation and political rupture, it should be possible to go back to strands of a less complex continuist history, such as that written by Pirenne for the 'Merovingian epoch' and weave those strands into a history that is more densely textured *à la* Wickham. Pirenne saw the survival of the large estate as a decisive link between the post-Roman world and the middle ages proper. 'Thanks to the domain, *the economic basis of the feudal system already existed*'.[114] Here, Pirenne identifies the element of continuity with the survival of Roman traditions of estate-management, suggesting that they formed the 'basis' of the system that emerged later. Now, in the period covered by Wickham's study (400–800), most aristocratic estates were organized on three basic models – *villae, massae,* and manors. (The East had its own forms and is not considered here.) Of these, the manor was a specifically medieval creation, so that Roman traditions of direct management were chiefly embodied in the types called *villae* and *massae. Massae* were substantial blocks of land, 'consolidated estates'[115] that were usually leased to *conductores* who are best described as 'entrepreneur[s] engaged in short-term financial speculation who assumed the management of the estate' for the period of the lease,[116] and whose ranks might include members of the aristocracy.[117] They were more dominant in southern Italy and the islands than anywhere else. A late fifth-century *massa* that we know about contained the standard 'mixed servile labour force' that I have argued was typical of the post-Roman West, in this case, *inquilini* (here, simply another name for *coloni*) and *servi*.[118]

---

[113] Cf. Shaw 1998, p. 40, stating that most recent scholarship is 'even more dismissive than he [Finley] was of any continuity between the "tied *coloni*" of the later Roman empire and the "serfs" of western European feudal labor regimes'.
[114] Pirenne 1968, p. 79; italics mine.
[115] Finley 1975, p. 112.
[116] Taken from Snowden 1986, p. 14, describing the *massaro* of early twentieth-century Apulia.
[117] The *clarissimus* John was willing to pay 10,000 *solidi* to lease Crown estates [*praedia*] in Apulia in the 520s, Cassiodorus, *Var.*, 5.6 (ed. Mommsen, *MGH, Auct. Ant.* xii/1, p. 147).
[118] *P.Ital.* 10–11, iv.1 (p. 292) (489). For *inquilinatus* = *colonatus* cf. Sidonius Apollinaris, *Ep.*, 5. 19 (Loyen, t. 2, p. 207). The *inquilinus* was otherwise a labour-tenant, cf. Krause 1987, p. 272, and viewed as a kind of wage-labourer, Paulinus, *Ep.*, 24.3.

The *villae* were the crucial transmission-belts of agrarian continuity. The substantial Merovingian estates of the seventh century were called *villae* because they were built on essentially Roman traditions of landholding and management. Bishop Bertram of Le Mans owned over 74 *'villae'*, c. 57 of these in undivided ownership.[119] From the general description of their features it is clear that these were physically *compact* or integrated estates, not dispersed properties interspersed with the estates of others; for example, the expression *cum termino suo* occurs repeatedly, referring to the outer boundaries of the *villa*. As consolidated spaces, *villae* were susceptible to division (fragmentation) but also *re*consolidation.[120] Adriaan Verhulst describes this typically Merovingian form as an 'estate...directly *cultivated by slaves, who had no holding* and lived on or near the centre of the estate. We may call it a "demesne-centred" estate (Germ. *Gutsbetrieb*)'.[121] My only quarrel with this would be to prefer 'slave and ex-slave farm servants',[122] since manumission was widespread by the seventh century and employers often retained control of their freedpeople.[123] The main point, however, is that the typical Merovingian estate exploited a *landless* workforce.[124] In England, the counterpart of this estate structure, the inland, was only finally superseded in the twelfth century, in a late and brutal development of the manorial system. By contrast, the *villa*-form was distinctly archaic by the ninth century in large parts of the Continent[125] and probably disappeared earliest in the core-regions of Frankish control between the Loire and the Rhine, where the manor came to embody a new form of labour-organisation, better resourced, bigger and more efficient.

That the Merovingian estates of the late sixth and seventh centuries were not structural innovations but rooted in the cultural and economic continuities of the successor-states would, in turn, have to be argued by constructing a model of the late Roman *villa*-estate. Like the Merovingian estate, the late Roman *villa* was sufficiently physically coherent or compact to have a name[126]

---

[119] Weidemann 1986, p. 102.
[120] Ibid.
[121] Verhulst 2002, pp. 34–5.
[122] Faith 1997, p. 209.
[123] E.g., Finberg 1972, p. 435.
[124] Sprandel 1968, p. 41; Verhulst 1966, p. 146.
[125] Verhulst 1991, p. 202.
[126] *Actes de la Conférence de Carthage*, t. 2, p. 822f., referring to the dozens of named estates in North Africa as *villae vel fundi* .

and, if it was substantial enough, to appear on maps or similar documents.[127] Both textual and archaeological evidence for the grouping of workers in settlements within the estate shows that these enterprises were based on a resident labour-force.[128] These settlements were called *vici* or *casas*, for example the Anicii, destined to be one of the richest families of the fourth-century aristocracy, owned several estates [*villae*] in the olive-growing regions along the Libyan coast already by the third century, one of these called *Casas villa Aniciorum*.[129] This was a region characterised by massive flows of migrant-labour, much of which may have been tribal. Large African estates retained 'squads' of seasonal workers for the harvest.[130] Estates that handled their own harvest were obviously 'directly managed'. And it is clear from the archaeology of the Spanish villas (villas here in an architectural and archaeological sense) both that much of the labour-force was housed within the estate[131] and that, in Spain at least, there was a 'substantial continuity' in the organisation of estates between the late Roman and Visigothic periods.[132]

A major part of Wickham's argument relates to the crisis of the villas, meaning their progressive disappearance throughout the former provinces of the western empire. Villas, in this archaeological sense – of the actual structures identified on the ground – disappear soonest in the northern parts of the empire and last of all in the core Mediterranean regions that remained under Roman control. In Italy, the fifth/sixth century is the period of the 'definitive dissolution of the villa system',[133] part of a much larger and complex transformation of the landscape that happened between the third or fourth and seventh centuries. Wickham downplays the catastrophist potential of this image of the withering away of the villas, proposing a cultural explanation for their demise. In another discussion of his book, I have suggested that all it reflected was the *crisis* of the western aristocracy, the progressive loss of control of the countryside and its overall disintegration as a unified imperial

---

[127] *Itin. Ant.* 59–63, where six estates are named.
[128] E.g., *CTh* 9.42.8, listing *mancipia, casarii, coloni*. The *casarii* were probably freed slaves who were given land as wages.
[129] *Itin. Ant.*, 61.2 (Cuntz, *Itineraria romana*, vol. 1, p. 9).
[130] *Actes*, t. 3, p. 978, where they are called *turbae*.
[131] Chavarría 2004, p. 70.
[132] Chavarría 2005, p. 280.
[133] Francovich 2002, p. 150.

class.[134] Villas survived best where the established late Roman aristocracy also survived, for example Sicily, and simply disappeared elsewhere. But, clearly, the emergence of new élites also had a cultural context and the two explanations are easily complementary.

This raises a final issue, one which is central to Wickham's analysis and the most solid part of his book, viz. the considerable evidence for a *crisis of the aristocracy* as a major part of the transition to the early middle ages. This, too, should really come under the 'reshaping of relations of production', so that is where I shall discuss it, briefly this time.

7.4.4. What happened to the aristocracy?

In Wickham's reconstruction of the evidence, one major trend that runs across the whole period from the fifth to the seventh centuries is the erosion of the aristocracy. The late Roman aristocracy survived longer in some places than in others, but the late sixth/early seventh century was a watershed in most places as the remnants of the senatorial class were finally absorbed, exterminated, or dispersed, and a new kind of aristocracy stabilised (as in Francia) or began its gradual, in England *very* gradual, emergence after 600. The best case of this hiatus is Italy itself, for, as Wickham notes elsewhere, 'even if it is possible to track senatorial families down to the time of Gregory the Great, this is no longer so in the seventh century, not even in Rome'.[135] In other words, the Italian aristocracy suffered large-scale disruption in the sixth century. This is *one* model of what happened to the late Roman aristocracy, but there are at least three or four others, which shows how uneven the transition was and why Wickham's approach, grounded in an acute sense of local peculiarities, is fundamental. This is a case where some degree of schematism may actually be helpful.

Model (1): *large-scale disruption* is best attested by the fate of Italy's aristocracy, partially exterminated and otherwise destroyed by war and fragmentation at various times throughout the sixth century. The Gothic war, started by Justinian, was a disaster for the landed aristocracy.

---

[134] Banaji 2007, p. 261.
[135] Migliario and Wickham 1998, p. 680.

Model (2): *aristocratic mutation*, the emergence of a new *kind* of aristocracy, more 'medieval' than late antique. Francia is by far the best example, because it is so well documented, not so much in Gregory of Tours's sixth-century narrative as in Book Four of the *Chronicle* of Fredegar, where the focus is the early part of the seventh century and the intrigues of powerful factions of the new Frankish ruling class.[136] These precocious medieval nobilities (of the subkingdoms or *Teilreiche*) were in place by 600,[137] the products largely of royal benefactions and of the considerable circulation of estates [*villae*] within the ruling establishment (the Church included). Especially striking here is the sheer mobility of landed property, related to the rapid reversal of political fortunes in a landscape where rival kings fought to expand control and consolidate support, but the result also of an intense competition for land and a resilient land market. The Lombards and Visigoths have their own (weaker) counterparts of these processes, except that we know much less about them. Tom Brown's work shows that the same model can almost certainly be extended to the Byzantine-controlled parts of peninsular Italy. Here, the Church remained the only element of continuity, as an administration dominated by military officials spawned new landed groups drawn from the military class; a new *kind* of élite, in other words, whatever we choose to call it.[138]

Model (3): *survival*. Sicily and Sardinia are the pure examples of this pattern, microcosms of a late Roman world frozen in time, the remnants of a 'Western' aristocracy basking in the protective gaze of the Eastern Empire. Here, probably *well* into the seventh century, all the basic institutions of late Roman civilian life – the colonate, money-taxes, the substantial circulation of a gold-currency, and villas in the architectural late Roman sense continued with no discernible break; a model that would, in modified form, apply to North Africa as well, I think.[139]

Finally, model (4): *flight*. A dispersion of the aristocracy which is best exemplified by the fate of the families who had dominated the East Mediterranean down to the Sasanian and Arab invasions of the seventh century (roughly,

---

[136] Wallace-Hadrill 1960.
[137] James 1982, pp. 135–7; Sprandel 1961, p. 43; Lebecq 1990, p. 138ff.
[138] Brown 1984.
[139] Agnellus, *Liber pontificalis ecclesiae Ravennatis*, 111 (MGH, *Script. Rer. Langobard.*, p. 350) and Orsi 1910, pp. 64–5 (money); Gregory, *Ep.* 9.129 (599) (colonate); Gregory *Ep.* 4.23 (594) (aristocracy); Molinari 1995, pp. 224–5 (sites).

610–42). For example, emigration was a widespread response of the Greek-speaking upper classes of the coastal towns of Syria.[140] Or, again, on the eve of the Arab invasion of Alexandria, several thousand of the wealthiest families are reported to have fled by sea. When Carthage was besieged by Ḥassān b. al-Nuʿmān al-Ġassānī in 695, the *last* late-Roman aristocracy of the Mediterranean again fled, some to Sicily, others to Spain.[141] Thus Model (4) is best reflected in the Byzantine-controlled parts of the Mediterranean that fell to the Arabs, that is, the east and the south.

These are the broad patterns, then, at least outside the core-regions of the empire that did survive, though it is still hard to say what happened in England in the fifth century. Wickham's impression of a dramatic pullout seems likely, though on one reading of the Welsh evidence that seems to have been much less true of south-east Wales, where Roman legacies (massive estates and charter-writing) may have suffered less dilution.[142] On balance, I would be less continuist than Wickham is for the East Mediterranean (he downplays the flight of the aristocracy,[143] as well as the massive disruption it suffered in the Arab invasions), and less fixated on aristocratic impoverishment; after all, the Umayyad élite was fabulously wealthy, North African landowners could pay substantial sums to buy off the Arabs in 647, decades after the economic involution of Tunisia is supposed to have begun, and the top *échelon* of the late Roman aristocracy had in any case comprised a tiny fraction even of the governing class.

7.5. Final comments: Wickham and modes of production

A key issue is how we characterise the *dynamic* of the late empire. For Wickham, the fiscal motor is central to this characterisation. Moreover, this was a fiscality where taxation in money was less important than taxes in kind. The coherence of the wider economy thus depended crucially on the transport of bulk goods for fiscal needs and the infrastructures this threw up. On its own, this fails to explain how it was possible for the Mediterranean

---

[140] Caetani, *Annali dell'Islam*, iii, p. 803 ff.; Balty 1984, p. 500; Balty 1989, pp. 94–5.
[141] Ibn al-Athīr, *Al-Kāmil fī al-taʾrīkh*, ed. Tornberg, t. 4, p. 300 = Ibn al-Athīr 1898, p. 28; Ibn Khaldūn 1968–9, t. 1, p. 213; with the date in Ṭāha 1989, pp. 69–70.
[142] Davies 1978a, Chapter 3, and 1978b.
[143] E.g., Wickham 2005, p. 241.

to see such a substantial growth in the money supply in late antiquity. Since Wickham has no obvious explanation for this, he tends to ignore it as well as the whole tradition of historiography that made the monetisation of taxes central to the conflicts of the fourth century. The accumulation of vast sums of gold in private hands suggests a more complex set of relationships between the aristocracy and the state, one where the neat division between them is less obvious. Tension, clearly (the state was not *reducible* to the aristocracy and their interests were often in collision) but also control and collusion. The colonate is an excellent case of the last, cf. Peter Brown's perceptive query about the extent to which the bureaucracy's 'regulations on the colonate colluded with the needs of the great landowners'.[144] My own analysis highlights other features of aristocratic dominance: huge monetary expansion and a tax-system less dominated by payments in kind than Marx believed or Wickham supposes;[145] a widespread use of free labour coupled with more rigorous forms of subordination that gave the aristocracy well-nigh absolute control over the lives of their employees; and the fact that government was defeated on the crucial issue of *patrocinium*.

Much of the analysis in 'The Other Transition', Wickham's first mapping of these issues, breaks down if we see state and aristocracy as integrated with each other and not distinct groups in competition; in other words, if we see the late Roman state as essentially an *aristocratic* form of state, staffed and controlled by an imperial aristocracy and the site of recurrent struggles between different factions of the ruling class (rather than a 'dominate', 'monarchy', etc., the ideological representations it had of itself). Consider the role played *by the state* in encouraging the expansion of aristocratic properties and the emergence of new élites; and consider the integration of functions like 'tax' and 'rent' through institutions such as the the *domus divina* (the state as landholder) and the pagarchy (the aristocracy as tax-collector), and the drive to tie labour to estates. None of this suggests the kind of gap (in *class*-terms)

---

[144] Brown 1967, p. 337 = 2007, p. 62 (from Peter Brown's review of Jones).
[145] Marx 1973, p. 103, 'in the Roman empire, at its highest point of development, the foundation remained taxes and payments in kind. The money system actually completely developed there only in the army'; yet he also states, correctly, that 'the full development of money, which is presupposed in modern bourgeois society, appears only in the period of their dissolution', referring to the Hellenistic monarchies and later Roman empire.

that rival modes of production would presume, which may be why both tax and rent are now seen as 'sub-types of the same mode of production'.[146]

Wickham's characterisation of the feudal mode is unrepentantly structuralist. There is no perceptible change in the stand taken in 'The Other Transition': 'Hindess and Hirst...show, rightly in my view, that feudal relations are represented simply by tenants paying rent to (or doing labour service for) a monopolistic landowner class'.[147] One disconcerting upshot of this is that much of *Roman* history is brought under the 'feudal mode'. It was, as he says in *Framing*, 'the normal economic system of the ancient and medieval periods'.[148] The 'economic shift from the slave to the feudal mode' occurs 'well before 400, in particular in the second and third centuries'.[149] Here, the feudal mode refers simply to the expansion of tenancy; in this perspective, it would make no sense to talk of a transition *between* modes of production, since the 'feudal mode' is seen as expanding in a gradual, piecemeal fashion.

The trouble with Wickham's use of these categories is that they lack any sense of historical dynamism. There is nothing in the way they are constructed that accounts for historical *change*. For Wickham, 'mode of production' can have any of three distinct senses – i) as a form of *exploitation* (slaves/tenants/wage-labourers), ii) as a form of *organisation of labour* (labour-service/slave-plantations), and iii) as an economic *system*. At p. 284 of his book, 'cultivated by the slave-mode' simply means cultivated by slaves, so too with 'slave-mode exploitation' at p. 301. At p. 273, 'modes of production' = 'labour relations' and refer clearly to forms of organisation of labour, different ways of organising the demesne.

For the feudal mode of production, Wickham prefers sense i), for the slave-mode sense ii); this enables him to stretch the feudal mode as widely as possible, on p. 535, or in his paper 'El fin del Imperio Carolingio', and conversely to restrict the slave-mode of production to a specific time and place, for example on p. 276 of *Framing*. Slaves 'do not have to be organised according to the

---

[146] Wickham 2005, p. 60.
[147] Wickham 1984, p. 6.
[148] Wickham 2005, p. 535.
[149] Wickham 2005, p. 262.

slave mode'¹⁵⁰ but Wickham prefers to *avoid calling them 'slaves'* if and when they are not!

The form of exploitation seems to have the capacity to generate an entire economic system through the kind of 'economic logic' embodied in it, for example in his essay on the end of the Carolingian Empire,¹⁵¹ which is why Wickham can equate modes of production with relations of exploitation, as in the passage just cited where 'estas distintas relaciones de explotación *representan distintos modos de producción*'.

It would be foolish to deny that Marx's handling of these categories was far from finished. He never left us with a developed or mature theory of modes of production, and a whole strand of his thinking on these issues can easily be mobilised to support the sort of equations that Wickham works with. But Marx also had a profoundly historical vision of what the different epochs or periods or modes of production were, which is, of course, best demonstrated in his analysis of capitalism. It is this second strand in his work that should form the point of departure for us. Clearly, by the capitalist mode of production, Marx meant more than the domination or widespread use of wage-labour, he meant the *laws of motion* that are summed up in the accumulation and competition of capitals. Since most of *Capital* was left unfinished, we do not have a proper or complete description of the interaction of 'many capitals', the *most dynamic part of the system*, and we tend to reduce the model to his description of individual capital in Volume One, which is one of its most abstract moments! In other words, 'relations of production', in Marx's sense at least, are just *not* reducible to the relations of exploitation depicted in Volume One. They would have to include competition, credit, share-capital, moments that each had an *Abschnitt* in the 1857 plan, as well as the 'world-market' and 'crises' to which he planned to devote the final book, all of which were

---

¹⁵⁰ Wickham 2005, p. 261.
¹⁵¹ Wickham 1995, p. 18, in a passage that resonates with the imagery of different modes of production or forms of exploitation (for Wickham, the same thing) co-existing in competition, e.g., in the third, fourth and fifth centuries, exaction of the peasant-surplus by landlords ('feudal exploitation') was supplemented by, and partly in competition with, fiscal exactions from both landowners and peasants alike. 'In another paper, I have suggested that *these distinct relations of exploitation represent distinct modes of production*, insofar as each is defined by a different economic logic...[En otro estudio he propuesto que *estas distintas relaciones de explotación representan distintos modos de producción*, por cuanto tienen una lógica económica diferente...]'; emphasis mine.

concrete determinations that Marx must, presumably, have lumped together in the general heading 'shapes of the total process' that was the proposed subject matter of 'Book Three' in the 1865/6 plan.[152] The point here is that, by 'capitalist relations of production', Marx clearly meant *all* of this and not just the general form of exploitation described with such lucidity in Volume One.

[2007–8]

---

[152] Rosdolsky 1974, p. 24ff.

Chapter Eight
Aristocracies, Peasantries and the Framing of the Early Middle Ages

8.1. Introduction

In this chapter, I would like to develop a general contrast between the West and the East Mediterranean/Near East which has its roots in the classical world, especially the period known as late antiquity. By, say, 600, the West was defined by a tradition of tied labour inherited from the late Roman world and shaped both by the strength of slavery in the *post*-Roman tradition and by the legacy of the colonate. By contrast, in the East, much of the rural labour-force is best described as a landless peasantry that survived on short-term leases or by labour-tenancy on the large estates, where these existed. The eastern provinces of the Roman empire were characterised by a disciplined aristocracy, a thriving monetary economy and densely populated countrysides.[1] A new aristocracy emerged in the late fifth century, and one of its most striking features was its ability to build substantial estates and ensure that these properties remained intact over generations.

---

[1] Banaji 2007. A preliminary draft of this chapter was written for the *JAC* conference in London in May 2008. I am especially grateful to Henry Bernstein and Terry Byres, for their support and friendship, and their remarkable achievement in forging a whole discipline and sustaining it through some of the direst decades of British intellectual and political life.

Thus, the Apion estates in Egypt are attested from the 430s down to the 620s, when the last known member of the family, Flavius Apion III, was killed by the Persians.[2] Both Peter Sarris and I have described the main features of estate-organisation characteristic of this late antique aristocracy, viz. the direct management of substantial estates which grouped their workers into settlements that were both structurally and topographically sharply demarcated from the villages [*kōmai*].[3] It is these workers whom I started by defining as a landless peasantry. The usual term for them was *georgoi*, but it is important to realise that, in their case, the term referred not to a smallholding peasantry but to rural households of whom the majority were clearly dependent on the estate for employment. In the more densely-settled eastern provinces, landlessness was endemic, and large estates were major employers of such labour.[4] But the East Mediterranean was also characterised by a diversified labour-market with considerable fluidity in the forms of employment and types of contracts that wage-earners settled for. Sharecropping was widespread, and sustained the expansion of the wine industry, but so was casual labour and a host of more skilled employments/trades, some regulated to impede collusive wage-agreements[5] or wage-inflation.[6]

Now, some of these features of the late antique East Mediterranean would have been true of the West as well. For example, Procopius tells us that the *majority* of Rome's population in the 530s consisted of artisans and casual labourers.[7] Also, there was no dramatic *de*-escalation of monetary economy in the West but rather a gradual decline. The crucial difference, of course, was that, by the sixth century, the late Roman aristocracies no longer ruled the state in the various 'kingdoms' that replaced the empire, since the imperial system had ceased to exist and their survival depended on adjustments with the Barbarian rulers in the regions where they regrouped. In other words, when the western empire fell apart in the fifth century and the former Roman

---

[2] *P. Oxy.* LXIII 4389 (439) for an early document; LVIII 3959 (12.1.620) and LXVIII 4703 (22.5.622) for the latest ones.
[3] Sarris 2006, esp. Chapter 2; Banaji 2007, Chapters 6–7.
[4] Banaji 1997, p. 93ff.
[5] *CJ* 59.2.1 (483), where the Emperor Zeno bans collusive agreements in the skilled building trades, calling such behaviour *monopolium*.
[6] *Nov. Just.* 122.1 (544), clearly reflecting a scarcity of labour of all types in the aftermath of the plague.
[7] Procopius, *BG* 1.25.11 (Dewing, *History of the Wars*, Volume 3, 240–2).

territories were taken over by the Franks, Burgundians and Goths, the western aristocracy ceased to exist as a unified imperial class, surviving now only as fragmented regional groupings, of which the most substantial, by the sixth century, were those in Rome, southern Italy and the south of France. In Chris Wickham's recent *magnum opus*, the general weakening and impoverishment of the aristocracy that was bound up with the fragmentation of the late empire is a major theme, rightly so, and a decisive part of the transition to the early middle ages.[8] By the *end* of the sixth century, the late Roman aristocracy had effectively ceased to exist in the West. Now, Wickham himself identifies this process, that is, the crisis of the western aristocracy, with a certain emancipation of the peasantry, in the sense that the huge fiscal machinery of the late Roman state had disintegrated so that peasants were less intensively taxed or not taxed at all, and the rural population faced a much less powerful group of landowners. In other words, the post-Roman West saw a recovery of control by peasants, an advance that was finally only reversed with the reassertion of aristocratic dominance that followed later, and unevenly, between the seventh and the tenth century.[9] As he argued in an earlier work, the peasantry was the 'chief social group that benefited from the fall of the Roman state', and a 'not insignificant class of peasant owners [...] had survived the wars and patronage agreements of the fifth century'.[10]

Of the two theses just delineated, that of a *crisis of the imperial aristocracy* (in the West) and of a *reassertion of peasant control* during much of the early middle ages, the former can scarcely be contested. The late Roman aristocracy disappeared, unevenly but, in the end, with finality. No historian has ever argued the opposite, despite the obsession with continuity peculiar to some historians in France. The second thesis, however, is much less obvious and substantially at odds with my own reading of the evidence. Wickham construes the advance of the peasantry in the earliest middle ages as an expansion of the 'peasant mode of production' which came to be juxtaposed with the feudal mode in a vast patchwork of *microregions* that reflected the extreme economic fragmentation of the post-Roman West. The main evidence for this view is the sharp differences in the scale and sophistication of exchange-networks

---

[8] Wickham 2005.
[9] Wickham 2005, p. 576ff.
[10] Wickham 1984, p. 30.

reflected in the ceramic evidence, at least as archaeologists currently construe this. This thesis, which I shall call the 'microregionality of modes of production', has its own share of problems, of course (here, modes of production become descriptive of a set of local economic structures), but my main interest at this stage is in Wickham's use of the written evidence. Wickham believes that the late Roman and the post-Roman West were both characterised by a feudal mode of production. This is (1) because he defines the feudal mode in a general way as the 'exploitative relationship between tenant and landlord', any tenant and any landlord (a definition that is, presumably, consciously ahistorical),[11] and (2) because he thinks that 'When the Romans abandoned the slave mode, they went *straight over* to rent-paying tenants',[12] and this long before the advent of the late empire.

These are substantial conceptual and historical claims, and I shall come back to them later. To begin with, however, I would like to try and use Wickham's book as a springboard for some reflections of my own about the West, and to start by mapping out a set of contrasts between aristocracies in the late antique world. I shall then propose a hypothesis about the nature of the seventh century, and devote the remaining part of the discussion of the West to a critique of Wickham's model of the transition from Late Antiquity to the early middle ages. Thus, the first part of the paper (about the West) deals with the three separate sets of issues just described, which, though distinct, are clearly interrelated. The third of these levels involves a much closer consideration of the whole issue of the deployment of labour. Wickham's model of the transition is premised on general categories that are unreconstructed or lack any further analysis. One upshot of this is that there is no serious engagement with documentary sources and no analysis of the actual vocabulary used in those sources, of crucial terms like *mancipium, mansus, colonica,* and so on. When Ganshof wrote in the 1950s and 60s, his confusing description of the Merovingian *villa* as a manor attracted no comment, because the whole issue of the origins of the bipartite estate still awaited the decisive clarification that it received in the work of Adriaan Verhulst.[13] Verhulst, of course, argued, convincingly in my view, that the classic manorial régime was a purely medieval

---

[11] Wickham 1985, p. 170.
[12] Wickham 1984, p. 31.
[13] Ganshof 1949, esp. pp. 33–4, 39.

creation, discontinuous with the Roman traditions of Gaul and an expression of the dynamism implicit in the Merovingian economy.[14] One of the theses I would like to propose in this chapter is that much of that dynamism was bound up with the kind of aristocracy that the Merovingians succeeded in establishing – unique for the post-Roman West. To see this, it may be useful to discuss the first of my topics (the contrasting nature and histories of aristocracies) in terms of the three distinct sets of issues that seem to be implicit in it, namely, first, of the *kinds* of aristocracies that dominate the main part of late antiquity, before the decisive evolution of the seventh century (we might call this the problem of morphology); second, of the fate or fortunes of the aristocracy in the huge upheavals that dominate the history of the empire in the fifth and sixth centuries when the Roman imperial state disintegrated bit by bit and eventually ceased to exist except as a pervasive cultural legacy; and third, of the dramatically different ways in which Franks and Visigoths, their nobilities in particular, reacted to rule by a hereditary monarchy, an issue which surprisingly has received little attention.

8.2. Aristocracies

To begin with the morphological problem; take the western empire in the fourth, fifth and early sixth centuries, Egypt or the East Mediterranean more generally between the later fifth and early seventh centuries, and Sasanian Iran. Iran under the Sasanids was ruled by powerful regional barons who were firmly wedded to the Sasanian dynasty but also largely in control of royal succession. Among late antique aristocracies, they were the least well-integrated into something we might call a state. Their unswerving commitment to dynastic rule is a striking feature and suggests that this was the key factor of cohesion in a class defined otherwise by strongly centrifugal tendencies. When Hormozdān, the powerful aristocrat who dominated south-western Iran at the time of the Arab conquest, was asked by 'Umar, 'From which territory ['*arḍ*] are you?', he replied, 'I am a Mehrajāni'.[15] Regional identities were clearly quite strong even and perhaps precisely at these levels

---

[14] Verhulst 1966.
[15] Al-Ṭabarī, *Ta'rīkh*, ser. i, pp. 2559 l.13–2560 l.3 = Al-Ṭabarī 1989, p. 140; asked through an interpreter.

of Sasanian society. At the opposite end of the spectrum to them is the early Byzantine east Mediterranean aristocracy that emerges with some vividness in the Egyptian papyri of the later fifth, sixth and early seventh centuries.[16] This aristocracy was typically a *Dienstadel*, its roots firmly embedded in service to the late Roman state, a concept for which there is no obvious Sasanian counterpart. Their trajectory runs from the main part of the fifth century to the early seventh, when they were destroyed or dispersed in the Sasanian and Arab invasions that followed in quick succession in the years 610–40. The little we know about the origins of this group suggests that it was the creature of a coherent, culturally sophisticated and economically affluent state, the east Roman empire which reached the pinnacle of its strength under Justinian in the sixth century.[17] Finally, the western aristocracy was an intensely traditionalist group or ensemble of groups more loosely integrated into the imperial state, dominating it as much as it served it and as subversive of imperial unity as the Iranian *bōzōrgān* were of rulers they disliked. An important aspect of this domination was the fact that the leading senatorial families (or more correctly 'clans') established a significant measure of control over the fiscal system through the offices they monopolised.[18] There is a tradition of late Roman historiography that argues that the Italian aristocracy more than any other sabotaged the coherence of its own state and bears a major share of the blame for the downfall of the empire in the West.[19] Whatever one thinks of this, the fact is that 'western aristocracies long outlived the Imperial government', seeking their own accommodation with Barbarian rulers.[20] If the disintegration of the western empire sounded the death-knell of an integrated imperial aristocracy of the kind that had emerged under Constantine, transforming the senate into a purely Italian

---

[16] Banaji 2007, Chapters 5–6.
[17] Most recently, Sarris 2006.
[18] This is best illustrated by Petronius Probus's repeated control of the praetorian prefecture in the years 364–83 and the devastating comment by one contemporary (the historian Ammianus Marcellinus) about the powerful lobby behind him and their 'countless instances of avarice', Amm. 27.11.3.
[19] Sundwall 1915, Chapter 5, esp. pp. 158–61, concluding, 'Economic relationships were what drove the Western empire to its catastrophe. The State became progressively poorer and the landed aristocracy ever more wealthy'; also Stein 1959, pp. 337ff., esp. 341–2.
[20] Wormald 1976, p. 224; Werner 1984, p. 302; Chastagnol 1966, pp. 48–56.

body and choking off the sources of renewal of a living senatorial tradition,[21] it *also* reflected the dispersive tendencies of aristocratic networks that had never been more than loosely integrated into a shifting imperial centre. The rapid consolidation of the western upper classes in the fourth century was followed by their gradual but sustained erosion in the fifth and sixth, as a unified state disintegrated under the pressure of barbarian migrations, settlement and conquest. This crisis was most obvious in sixth-century Italy, but reflected, of course, throughout the western provinces, to unequal degrees. For the moment, the point I wish to make is that late antique aristocracies show major differences in the nature of their integration into the state and that these differences are in some sense more fundamental than the civilian/military divide that Wickham concentrates on in discussing the transformation of the aristocracy.[22]

A quintessential late Roman aristocracy had more or less disappeared by the turn of the sixth century, but its surviving networks followed very different paths into limbo. The Italian aristocracy was decimated by the Gothic wars and the violence of the Lombard invasion that followed.[23] Unlike the Franks and the Burgundians, the Lombards did not seek the collaboration of the Roman aristocracy.[24] Thus large estates survived but the aristocracy was eliminated or fled.[25] By contrast, the Merovingian kingdoms and especially that of Neustria saw the evolution of an ethnically-integrated aristocracy based on a fusion of the surviving Roman families and their Frankish counterparts. Bertram, bishop of Le Mans from 586 to 616, is a superb example of the new kind of aristocracy that would dominate the political history of the seventh century, more powerfully and obviously in Francia than elsewhere in

---

[21] Chastagnol 1978.
[22] Wickham 2005, pp. 174–7, 200ff., 257.
[23] Moorhead 2000, pp. 384–6; Noyé 2000, p. 252; Bognetti 1968, pp. 75, 78; Jarnut 1982, pp. 49–50; Jarnut 2002, pp. 14ff., 323; and Tabacco 1989, p. 94f. The key passages are in Paul the Deacon, *Hist. Langobardorum*, ii, 31; 32 (ed. Waitz, 90), hinting at the liquidation/expulsion of the aristocracy.
[24] Modzelewski 1978, p. 31: 'Al contrario degli ostrogoti, i conquistatori longobardi non ricercarono la collaborazione dell'aristocrazia romana e non si sforzarono di difendere l'antico ordinamento istituzionale' (Unlike the Ostrogoths, the Lombard invaders did not seek the collaboration of the Roman aristocracy and made no attempt to preserve the old institutional order).
[25] Modzelewski 1978, p. 41: 'la fine dell'aristocrazia romana non abbia comportato la liquidazione fisica dei suoi beni' (the demise of the Roman aristocracy did not entail the physical liquidation of its estates).

the West.[26] My own feeling is that, if we want a zone of rupture between late antiquity and the early middle ages, it must lie here in the formation of the precocious nobilities that dominated the Frankish *Teilreiche* already by the first quarter of the seventh century.[27] They were the first purely medieval nobilities of Europe, a peculiarly Merovingian achievement, thanks largely to the conscious policy of Chilperic and his son Chlothar II, Neustrian rulers, in seeking the active support of regional élites throughout Francia, in Austrasia, Burgundy and Aquitaine, and integrating them into a pan-Merovingian Frankish ruling class.[28] This evolution is important for the agrarian history of the West, because it was in Francia that a new kind of enterprise and organisation of labour first emerged.[29] The continuity with Rome lay in the survival of large enterprises; the rupture in the rapid evolution of powerful new aristocracies by the late sixth century, unlike any previous ruling class that had dominated the West. In Spain, too, the old aristocracy passed rapidly into limbo. A surviving Roman aristocracy is much harder to track than it is in Gaul.[30] But the Visigothic aristocracy itself was deeply divided and permanently embroiled in conflict with the Crown. The repeated assassination of Visigothic rulers is striking testimony to this. The chronicler Fredegar or his seventh-century source called it the *morbum Gothorum*, the 'Visigothic addiction for dethroning their kings'.[31] Here, the Merovingian pattern of a strong dynasty and stable aristocratic élites could not have been more radically reversed. This raises a final issue about aristocracies.

I would like to suggest that the dynastic principle favoured the interests of the aristocracy. The weaker the monarchy, the less held together it was by the

---

[26] For example, in Rome itself the extinction of the old aristocracy left a vacuum in the seventh century, cf. Marazzi 2001, p. 46: 'È difficile parlare, per questo periodo (per il VII secolo in particolare), di una nuova aristocrazia urbana in senso stretto...'.

[27] Ewig 1976, pp. 169f., 172f.

[28] Sprandel 1957, Chapter 2.

[29] Verhulst 1966.

[30] Stroheker 1963 failed to come up with more than a handful. Thompson 1969, p. 115 suggests, 'The class of large Roman landowners had *in some measure* survived the storms of the fifth century'.

[31] Fredegar, iv. 82 (Wallace-Hadrill 1960, p. 70): 'One of the magnates named Chindaswinth was chosen king of Spain. When he had dethroned Tulga he had him tonsured; and then, having made sure of his power throughout the Spanish kingdom, and knowing the Gothic weakness for dethroning their kings (for he had been involved with them in such conspiracies), he ordered the killing, one by one, of all those whom he knew to be compromised in rebellion against kings who had been dethroned'.

common bond of a ruling family, the sharper the conflicts *within* the aristocracy. Unregulated succession to the throne reflected lack of cohesion among aristocrats and repeated attempts at usurpation, suggesting unmanageable levels of conflict and considerable fragmentation. This, as I just said, is best exemplified in Spain, where royal succession was characterised by chronic and often violent instability and there was deep factionalism within the aristocracy.[32] A succession of rulers were either deposed or overthrown. Leovigild was the only ruler to be followed on the throne by his son and grandson, and he, characteristically, had the reputation of having executed or exiled much of the aristocracy.[33] The contrast with his late sixth-century Frankish counterparts could scarcely be greater. Chilperic and his son had pursued a far-sighted policy of seeking the support of élites in Austrasia, Burgundy and Aquitaine and the net result was the rapid evolution of powerful aristocracies in the crucial decades around the later sixth and early seventh century. In Francia, where the dominance of the Merovingians was never actually contested, the dynastic principle worked in a complex form that necessitated the division and re-division of territories to preserve some balance between the competing Merovingian claimants. Whereas Spain saw an unstable monarchy pitted against a fractious and fragmented aristocracy, in Francia, conflict had tended to run between different members or branches of the ruling dynasty, and the division of territory between them almost certainly helped to reduce the level of conflict within the aristocracy. One reason may have been that it allowed for strong regional control, a principle formally embodied in the famous Edict of 614 in which Chlothar explicitly restricted the holding of office to families within the region.[34] This, as Sprandel emphasised repeatedly, was not equivalent to some form of Frankish regionalism.[35] On the contrary, what Chilperic and Chlothar managed to create was a *Reichsaristokratie* with firm local roots. Of the three main Germanic kingdoms that emerged from the ruins of the western empire, the *regnum Francorum* was far and away the most stable, whereas the muted struggle between the Visigothic nobility

---

[32] Thompson 1969, Chapters 8–9; García Moreno 1975, p. 140ff.; Reilly 1993, p. 39ff. García Moreno notes that the cohesion of the aristocracy was a major concern of the Spanish bishops, 1975, p. 161.
[33] Thompson 1969, p. 157; Isidore, *Hist. Goth.*, 51 = Wolf 1999, p. 102.
[34] *Chlotharii II Edictum*, 12 (*Capit. Merow.*, 22) = Murray 1999, p. 565ff. at 567, cf. Sprandel 1961, p. 61ff.
[35] Esp. Sprandel 1961, pp. 64–5.

and the crown that runs through much of the history of Spain in the seventh century culminates, of course, in the Arab conquest of the peninsula. The final episode in the internal factionalism of the Visigothic aristocracy was also a fatal one. Tradition claims that the sons of the deceased king Witiza actively conspired against Roderic, the last Visigothic king, to ensure his defeat in the decisive battle that ended his reign and the kingdom.[36] These divisions were so obvious to contemporaries that the *Chronicle of 754* links them directly to the success of the Arabs in overthrowing the Visigothic kingdom.[37]

8.3. The agrarian watershed of the seventh century

My hypothesis about the seventh century is that it forms an agrarian watershed in the history of the West. The seventh century, in the West, was crucial in two ways. First, it saw a reassertion of aristocratic control, and second it involved, I believe, the beginnings of a new agrarian expansion. These features would, of course, be linked if a strong case can be made for the view that the aristocracy financed much of that expansion. I do not propose to do that here, but it may be worth indicating briefly some clear signs that such a connection existed. One of the most striking features of the Merovingian charters is the sheer frequency of references to the purchase of land that appears in them. Here is a typical example from the will of Hadoind, bishop of Le Mans, dated 643. Among numerous donations listed in the will, Hadoind says he donates to the church of St Victor of Le Mans 'the estate [*villa*] called Aceruco, which I purchased for money, together with the houses, *mancipia*, vineyards, forests, meadows and pastures [*dono tibi villa nuncupante Aceruco, quam dato pretio comparavi, cum domibus, mancipiis, vineis, silvis, pratis et pascuis*]'.[38] There are dozens of references of this kind in the private charters of the Merovingian period and the least this tells us is that

---

[36] E.g. Montenegro and del Castillo 2007.
[37] *Chronicle of 754*, 52; 54 (Wolf 1999, pp. 131–2), and the reference to Oppas, King Egica's son, collaborating actively with Mūsā b. Nuṣayr as the latter moved against remnants of Toledo's nobility in the summer of 712. Barbero 1992, p. 216 and Barbero and Vigil 1978, pp. 209, 229 argued that the bulk of the Spanish aristocracy came to terms with the Arabs (struck deals with them) and that a substantial section converted to Islam. Manzano 2006 has the best discussion of those treaties and their role in integrating sections of the Visigothic aristocracy with the (Syrian) Arab military élite of al-Andalus.
[38] *Test. Hadoindi Cenomanensis episcopi*, in Busson and Ledru 1901, p. 157ff., at 158.

the new aristocracy of the seventh century made substantial investments in the acquisition of land, usually whole estates [*villae*]. They did the same in the great movement of land clearance that began in the seventh century, the 'vaste mouvement de défrichement' that Verhulst described as a key feature of the 'evolution' from the Merovingian estate to the Carolingian manor;[39] and the same again in the construction of water-mills, as Dietrich Lohrmann has pointed out in an important paper on Neustria.[40] Here, the crucial point is that the elements of a new organisation of labour began to be laid out as landowners encouraged the expansion of peasant-tenures as part of their reclamation of arable. This process must have thrown up hundreds of new settlements and I suggest that one term for these settlements was *colonica*. If the term *colonica* could refer *both* to the '"new settlements" located on the fringes, boundaries, or "appendages" of estates, suggesting an origin in the colonization of the wasteland'[41] *and* to the individual tenures that made up those settlements, this would explain why the word shows a mystifying semantic ambiguity, fluctuating between usages that manifestly refer to entire settlements, as in Bertram's will, where Margarete Weidemann explains the term as 'Ausbausiedlung im Bereich einer villa',[42] and other uses where *colonica* is undoubtedly a designation for farms, as when Abbo refers to various freedpeople of his holding *colonicae* 'in beneficio', this in Provence in the early eighth century.[43] One imagines that these new settlements were the first proper signs of the emergence or re-emergence of a peasantry in Europe, and that the *accolae* who appear with increasing frequency from the later seventh century (they are there already in Hadoind's will of 643)[44] were

---

[39] Verhulst 1966, p. 152.
[40] See Lohrmann 1989, especially the statement at p. 396 that monasteries were simply adding to or renovating equipment they inherited from previous owners.
[41] Herlihy 1960–1, pp. 86–7.
[42] Weidemann 1986, p. 109). The *colonicae* in Verf. 6; 9; 20; 25; and 35 are all substantial, not just small farms, much less 'tenant plots', as in Wickham 2005, p. 282.
[43] Geary 1985, e.g. 20 (p. 52), 24 (p. 54), 25 (p. 54), etc.; translated 'farms'. The fact that Merovingian *colonicae* often had proper names suggests that many were settlements, e.g. Kölzer 2001, Volume 1, no. 7, p. 29ff. at 31 (colonica Curtleutachario in Childebert I's donation to the monk Carilephus, dated 515, but 'unecht'); *Test. Remigii*, p. 478 (colonica Passiacus); Weidemann 1986, Verf. 6 (p. 13), 20 (p. 19), 25 (p. 21), 35 (p. 28); *Test. Hadoindi*, in Busson and Ledru 1901, p. 160; *Test. de saint Vigile*, ed. Quantin 1854, p. 17ff., at 20.
[44] *Test. Hadoindi*, in Busson and Ledru 1901, p. 160. *Accolae* are much commoner in late seventh-century charters, e.g. CLA xiii 560 (657/88), estates in the Beauvaisis; 564 (673); 570 (688); CLA xiv 577 (694).

essentially free peasants attracted to estates as part of their drive to expand cultivation. The 'colonization of the wasteland' was the seventh century's major contribution to the history of the countryside in this part of Europe.

By contrast, another key term *mansus*, which is almost invariably explained in the same way or referred to the same context, in other words, the creation of peasant-tenures, may well have had a more complex origin, the proper starting-point for which must be our notions of Merovingian estate-organisation. New estates for a new aristocracy? The answer, as almost always in history, is yes and no. In a typically fascinating aside, Marc Bloch once suggested that the best historical analogy for the early medieval estate is the Latin-American *hacienda*. What Bloch himself meant by this was that the régime of the *hacienda* was never so dense that it completely excluded the presence of 'small independent landowners'.[45] The more general point of the analogy, I take it, is that early-medieval estates, or let us say the typical Merovingian estate, exploited a landless workforce comparable in this respect to the *gañanes* in Mexico. This emphasises continuity with the late Roman world, if, unlike Wickham and the ancient historians he follows,[46] we see the Late Roman estate as an enterprise still based on direct management and not pulverised into semi-autonomous farms or holdings.[47] And again, that continuity is one of form

---

[45] Bloch 1963, p. 228.

[46] Notably Vera (1983), who describes the typical late-Roman aristocratic estate as a 'latifondo parcellizzato', operated essentially in terms of rent-tenancies.

[47] This has to be argued systematically. Cf. Procopius, *BG* 3.6.5 (Dewing, Volume 4, 198) which assumes that the incomes of large Italian estates will be in money. Also, Palladius, *Opus agriculturae*, 1.6.3 ('A standardised calculation of labour costs isn't possible when soil characteristics vary so much') only makes sense on the premise of direct management. The dominance of tenant-labour is one of Wickham's most firmly held beliefs about the organisation of estates in late antiquity and the early middles ages. But, in one instance at least, it involves a manifest misreading of the evidence. The famous passage in the (lost) history of Olympiodorus of Thebes which tells us that the richest senatorial families in the West drew 'a yearly income from their estates of 4,000 lbs of gold apart from grain, wine and other goods in kind the marketable value of which was equal to one-third of the cash income' (tr. Thompson 1944, p. 50) is taken as saying that 'annual income *in rents* for many aristocratic families...in Rome amounted to 5,000-plus pounds of gold...three-quarters of it from *rents in money*' (Wickham 2005, p. 162, repeated at p. 271, 'major Roman senators got three-quarters of their huge *rents* in money, a quarter in kind'; my emphasis). But Olympiodorus makes no reference to 'rents' anywhere in this passage. He says that the *estates* of the top aristocracy yielded (possibly gross) cash *incomes* of 4,000 lbs of gold, apart from the stocks of wine, grain, etc. which they *retained in kind*; had they sold these stocks as well they would have grossed a further third of that amount, bringing the total to just over 5,300 lbs of gold. E.A. Thompson's translation captures

rather than substance in the sense that the disappearance of the Roman aristocracy and the rise of new medieval nobilities signified a major rupture in the social and economic history of the West. Thus the best context to discuss the meaning of the term *mansus* surely has to be the way we visualise the transition from late Roman to purely medieval forms of organisation in terms of the way landowners structured the management and use of labour and of the kinds of workforces they deployed. Again, the Merovingian charters are our best clue to the nature of the rural labour-force in the sixth and seventh centuries. If the will of Remigius dated *c*. 533 is any indication, slavery was still widespread in Gaul in the early sixth century. In fact, Remigius' farms were based on a mixed labour-force of *servi* and *coloni*, and the *coloni* clearly were tied labourers inherited from the late empire, still called by that name and referring in the will itself to half-free or unfree rural labourers distinct from slaves; for example, they could be bequeathed with the land, transferred between owners, manumitted ('Vitalem colonum liberum esse iubeo'; 'Cispiciolum colonum liberum esse precipio'), and their families could likewise be bequeathed.[48] One of them had even owned a *servus*, and at least one of Remigius' *coloni* was still called *originarius*. Moreover, Remigius's *servi* also had families. Again, in 538 and roughly contemporary with Remigius' will, a Gallic church-council legislates that 'no person bound by the *condicio* of a *servus* or *colonus* should be admitted to ecclesiastical office'; the precise expression used is *Nullus servilibus colonariisque conditionibus obligatus*.[49] At any rate, neither slaves nor *coloni* disappeared with the disintegration of the western empire; both were present in large numbers and merged indiscriminately into the labour-force. The integration of these diverse categories of labour into an increasingly indiscriminate labour-force also found a precise expression in the way Latin terminology evolved. The strict Roman legal term for a slave, *mancipium*, became the standard generic description for a labour-force now characterised by looser forms of bondage, where the precise legal condition of the workers mattered less and less; for example, Remigius's will is decisive

---

the sense of the passage exactly and shows that the ratios Olympiodorus cites are those for the breakup of *income* between cash and kind, *not* for the amount of rent received in one form or the other.

[48] *Test. sancti Remigii* (CCSL 117/2, pp. 473ff.), 474 (bequeathed; transferred), 477, 478 (manumitted).

[49] *Conc. Aur.* (538), can. 29.

proof that many families were of mixed legal status, that is, members of the same family could be of different legal *condiciones*. These distinctions were not rigid therefore. *Mancipia* included both slaves and freedpeople, but postclassical slaves and freedpeople still subject to domination, and the expression *mancipia quae colonaria appellantur* from the will of Aredius, dated 573 or 591, shows that former *coloni*, tied labourers, were included as well.[50]

Now, the Merovingian charters refer standardly to *domus* and *mancipia* among the appurtenances of the estate [*villa*] in formulae such as *cum domibus, mancipiis, agris*, etc. In the will of Bishop Bertram, the most substantial document of its kind from the seventh century, which has a wonderful edition and commentary by Weidemann, *ipsam villam cum domibus, mancipiis*, and so on is about the most common expression used. I may be wrong but it is my strong impression that, in the seventh-century charters, *domus* are never mentioned without *mancipia*, which suggests that they were the dwellings of the labourforce. Bertram had some 74 estates [*villae*] and they were almost all equipped in this way, together with land, of course, and land of various descriptions such as vineyards, arable and pasture, as well as more substantial constructions called *aedificia*. There is also repeated reference to forest-land. Occasionally, Bertram refers to *colonicae*, but these were on the boundaries of his estates and, as Weidemann suggests, most probably the cutting edge of an expanding régime of arable.[51] At one point, Bertram refers to buying a villa or a portion of one, the estate of Brossay, where he 'constructed homes and settled labour [*ubi domus aedificavi et mancipias stabilivi*]'.[52] There is a fascinating passage in Gregory of Tours which shows that the drive to expand cultivation in this way was equally true of the first generation of the new Merovingian aristocracy, for Gregory describes a certain Chrodin, 'a man of great virtue and piety', almost certainly a Frank, deceased by 582, 'often creating estates from scratch, laying out vineyards, building homes, and clearing the land [*Nam sepe a novo fundans villas, ponens vinias, aedificans domus, culturas eregens*]'.[53] About a century later, Vigilius, bishop of Auxerre, donated vineland to his church

---

[50] The will can be found in Pardessus 1969, t. 1, pp. 136–41, the expression at 139; for the date cf. Kölzer 2001, Volume 2, p. 522.
[51] Weidemann 1986, p. 109.
[52] Weidemann 1986, Verf. 1 (p. 8), cf. Verf. 17 (p. 18), *ubi…mancipia posuimus*, 25 (21), *cum servientibus quos inibi posui*.
[53] Gregory of Tours, *LH* 6.20.

cum mancipiis quos ibidem stabilivi. The remarkable feature of the will of Vigilius, dated c. 680, is the repeated reference to *mansi* and *servi*.[54] Medievalists generally agree that the term *mansus* is largely an innovation of the seventh century,[55] but the precise agrarian function they tend to assign to it is as a kind of peasant-tenure, the role it has within the economic framework of the bilateral estate.[56] But bilateral estates were not a feature of the seventh century, they were a Carolingian innovation, and we have to explain the Merovingian *mansus* differently. One striking clue to its meaning is that while *mansi* appear repeatedly in the will just mentioned, there is no reference to *domus*! As Tits-Dieuaide suggested in an important paper, '*mansus* est utilisée ici à la place de *domus*'.[57] In other words, the Merovingian *mansi* were not primarily peasant tenures but allotments created for the *mancipia* (= *servi* in Vigilius's testament). Unlike the peasant-tenures of a later period, notably the central middle ages, these allotments were still an integral part of the Merovingian *Gutswirtschaft* and their occupants a class of workers, both slaves and freedpeople, endowed with service-holdings rather than self-sufficient farms.[58] The most substantial argument along these lines is, perhaps paradoxically, Ulrich Weidinger's excellent analysis of the ninth-century inventory material from Fulda, the *Güterverzeichnisse*, whose drafters used vocabulary rather differently from the people who drew up the purely economic documents.[59] Weidinger shows at length that the *mansi* which figure in the Fulda inventories did not include the surrounding fields and meadows. They were *kleine Hofstellenbetriebe* that functioned as reserves of labour for a still largely integrated estate, the *Gutswirtschaftssytem*, and their holders were a class of farm-workers, still servile of course, who were subject to almost unlimited exploitation.[60] Weidinger also argues that estate-owners would have carved out these plots with a view to

---

[54] *Test. de saint Vigile*, ed. Quantin 1854, p. 17ff.

[55] Ganshof 1958, p. 83; Verhulst 1966, pp. 154–5; Duby 1973, pp. 45–6. *Mansi* appear to have been widespread by 650, cf. the will of Leodebod, abbot of St-Aignan d'Orléans, in Prou and Vidier 1900, p. 5ff.

[56] E.g. Ganshof 1958, p. 84; Verhulst 1995, p. 493: 'From the middle of the seventh century, the term *mansus* is used as a technical term for a holding in a bipartite manor in the region of Paris'.

[57] Tits-Dieuaide 1985, p. 43.

[58] Just under 4 acres ('buonaria xv') in a deed dated 639–49/50, the earliest Neustrian document to refer to a *mansus*: Kölzer 2001, Volume 1, no. 75, p. 190ff., at 191, line 4.

[59] Weidinger 1991, pp. 23–54.

[60] Weidinger 1991, p. 41ff.

preserving or creating some symmetry, either square or rectangular, in their home-farms, which is why the *mansi* tended to fluctuate in size.⁶¹ In this sense, and in all these respects, then, the *mansi* were radically different from the peasant farms known as *hubae* (Bede's 'hide'), which, of course, did include fields, meadows and the like, and were of a size consciously calculated to yield the normative subsistence of a peasant-family, hence more standardised.

There are two points I would like to draw attention to in this analysis. First, Weidinger offers a model, at least implicitly, of the gradual dissolution of the post-Roman *Gutswirtschaft*, if the carving-out of service-holdings for allotment to the various groups of *mancipia* can, and it surely can, be construed as a mechanism that eroded the integrity of the classic late-Roman estate. A passage in the *Vitas sanctorum patrum Emeretensium*, a piece of Spanish hagiography written possibly in the 630s, suggests that it was standard practice to make such allotments when slaves were freed. When the bishop Masona 'wrote out documents of manumission for the slaves who had given him faithful service', he 'in confirmation of their liberty gave them a little sum of money and even little parcels of land [*exiguas possessiunculas*]'.⁶² In Italy, such allotments were probably called *casae* or *casales/casalia*,⁶³ and in the Lombard parts of Italy the *massarii* were initially overwhelmingly of servile origin. They were *servi massarii* and only slightly more exalted than the completely landless slaves.⁶⁴ My second comment is that Weidinger's distinction between *mansus* and *huba* chimes remarkably well with the kind of model Ros Faith has developed for the Anglo-Saxon 'inland' and her sharp distinction between worker-tenants and the self-sufficient small peasantry that came to form the true backbone of serfdom in the great feudal reaction of a later period. 'The inland', Faith writes, 'was an area likely to have been crowded with the dwellings of the workers and tenants who lived there', which reflects a very different topography of power from the bilateral estate.⁶⁵ In fact, it is the Anglo-Saxon material

---

⁶¹ Weidinger 1991, p. 40.
⁶² *Vitas sanctorum patrum Emeretensium*, 13.4 (ed. Garvin, p. 249); *Lives of the Visigothic Fathers*, 13.4 (Fear 1997, p. 101).
⁶³ *Casa*: Pelagius, *Ep.* 84 (c. 561). The *casales* in the estate-lists known as the *Casae Litterarum* (of Italian provenance and late antique) look like land-parcels on the boundaries of estates [*fundi*], cf. Migliario 1992, p. 373ff., calling them *appezzamenti*. Roth Congès 2005 is now the fundamental study of the surveyors' lists.
⁶⁴ They were widespread by the mid-seventh century, when Rothari refers to them in his 'Edict' of 643; the best recent edition is Azzara and Gasparri 2005.
⁶⁵ Faith 1997, p. 69.

that shows us how finely graded the early medieval labour-force *could* be, yet bound together by their common condition of landlessness and servility, and Faith's description of the inland workforce as a 'mixed servile labour force' strikes me as the best characterisation we have of the rural labour-force in the centuries between the fall of the western empire and the imposition of serfdom in the great feudal transformation in the decades around 1000. Faith refers to the 'slave and ex-slave farm servants with their cottages huddled on the inland round the curia',[66] which may well be how we should imagine the Merovingian labour-force, the *mancipia* in contrast to the *accolae*, that is, as farm workers and a class distinct from the peasantry.

8.4. Critique of Wickham

To turn now to *Framing the Early Middle Ages*, Wickham's image of the transition is completely different in this respect. It is an image dominated by a simple dialectic, the disintegration of something he calls the 'slave mode of production' and its more or less direct replacement by tenancy. This is supposed to have happened well before 400, 'in particular in the second and third centuries', and can, Wickham argues, be construed as an 'economic shift from the slave mode to the feudal mode'.[67] Thus, the feudal mode of production is seen as expanding in a gradual, piecemeal fashion, as tenancy expands, and it now covers a vast stretch of history from the second or third century to, presumably, the later middles ages, a period of well over 1,000 years, a view that should baffle Marxists, at least! This model, simple as it is, has several obvious and even massive implications for the way we construct the agrarian history of these periods. In the first place, it implies that Roman landowners gave up direct management when they abandoned the slave-mode. Secondly, it denies, ignores or hugely underestimates the persistence of slavery in late antiquity and the early middle ages. Thirdly, it construes the *colonatus* of the late empire simply as a system of rent-paying tenancies,

---

[66] Faith 1997, p. 209.
[67] Wickham 2005, p. 262: 'Actually, plantations had never been frequent outside central Italy, Sicily, and parts of Greece, and even there the basic economic shift from the slave to the feudal mode had already taken place well before 400, in particular in the *second and third centuries*. Throughout our period the slave mode was only a minor survival, everywhere marginal to the basic economic structure, the landlord-peasant relationship (where there were landlords at all)'; my emphasis.

with minimal implications for the actual subordination and control of labour. Finally, and most substantially, Wickham sees the tenancy of these historical periods as a type of self-management in which peasants 'controlled the land and their own work process', or *'controlled their own holding* and could keep its fruits after rents were paid'.[68] In other words, there was, as he says, limited landowner control over production, indeed limited interest in it,[69] at least till the emergence of manorialism in the Carolingian period.

I would like to suggest that Wickham's handling of both slavery and the colonate are among the weakest parts of his excellent book. The sheer scale of manumissions that followed in the seventh century (e.g. Spain, England) shows how widespread slavery was, still, in late antiquity. Legal sources, both late Roman and barbarian, provide one indication of this. Wickham's wholesale disregard of the legal evidence is not credible and has rightly been characterised, by Andrea Giardina, as a sort of reductionism.[70] There are *numerous* constitutions in the *Theodosian Code* which either deal with or refer to slavery, both rural and urban, though this clearly is not the place to rehearse the details. The standard legal term for a slave was *mancipium*, the neuter signifying conscious reification. In *CTh* 2.25.1 (possibly 325), Constantine stipulated that the children of slaves employed on imperial estates in Sardinia should not be separated from their parents when those estates were handed over to private individuals or divided in some way. In *CTh* 9.42.7 (369), a detailed inventory was prescribed for estates confiscated from private landowners convicted of criminal offences. This *plena descriptio* would have to indicate 'how many slaves, either urban or rural, are contained on the seized estate...how many cottagers and *coloni* there are, how many oxen are employed in working the land, etc.' It is hard to see why the potential evidence of constitutions like these should be discounted on the general prejudice that law has a normative function. In any case, 'Numerous sources refer to rural slaves'.[71] The Greek life of the younger Melania refers to the slaves [*douloi*] on her suburban estates [*proasteia*] near Rome, while the author of the 'Lausiac History', who knew

---

[68] Wickham 1984, p. 9; 2005, p. 560; italics mine.
[69] Wickham 2000, p. 33.
[70] Giardina 2007b, p. 28.
[71] Whittaker 1999, p. 699.

Melania, reports that she manumitted 8,000 of them![72] When Alaric besieged Rome in 408–9, 'many slaves, especially those of barbarian origin, deserted to join him'.[73] Augustine's polemic against the Donatists is full of references to recalcitrant slaves [*servi*], and, in the fifth century, one chronicle tells us that 'nearly all the slaves of the Gallic provinces [*omnia paene Galliarum servitia*] conspired in [the] Bacaudic movement'.[74] As E.A. Thompson remarked, 'Our sources seem to suggest that these revolts were due *primarily to the agricultural slaves*, or at any rate that slaves played a prominent part in them'.[75] In short, the balance of evidence supports Finley's conclusion that 'Slavery survived on a considerable quantitative scale'.[76] But this was equally true of the sixth and seventh centuries. According to Tom Brown, 'slaves were widely used in cultivating the patrimony of the Roman Church'.[77] Indeed, in Italy, it was not till the ninth century that slavery began to fade away.[78] In Spain, the Visigothic legislation is full of references to slavery. Thompson tells us 'No subject interested the legislators of the sixth and seventh centuries more than the recovery of escaped slaves'.[79] It is not surprising, then, that Werner Rösener should claim, as he has done in a recent paper, 'Slavery was still widespread in the transition from Late Antiquity to the middle ages' and 'The Germanic kingdoms of the early middle ages are scarcely different from the late empire in terms of the actual prevalence of slavery'.[80]

Why labour the point, however? First, because slavery was widespread in the *post*-Roman West and this surely was, at least partly, a Roman legacy.[81] Second, because the early middle ages were not a period of serfdom, if we understand the latter historically, but rather one of *servility*, that is, of *mixed* labour-forces where slaves, former *coloni* and freedpeople were conjointly deployed on large estates that were still structured on late Roman lines and

---

[72] *Vita Mel. graec.* 11 (*douloi*), Palladius, *Hist. Laus.* 61.5 (*andrapoda*): slaves, not 'unfree dependants', as in Innes 2007, p. 53. Cf. Symmachus, *Rel.* 28.3 for *mancipia* (strictly slaves) on a suburban estate [*suburbana villa*] of the aristocrat Olybrius, abducted from the holdings of a lesser aristocrat.
[73] Olympiodorus, fr. 7.5 (Blockley, p. 160), Sozomen, 9.6.3.
[74] *Chron. min.* i, 660, s.a. 435.
[75] Thompson 1952, p. 11.
[76] Finley 1980, p. 147.
[77] Brown 1984, p. 203.
[78] Cammarosano 2001, p. 185.
[79] Thompson 1969, p. 271.
[80] Rösener 2006, p. 79.
[81] Nehlsen 1972; Grieser 1997; King 1972.

indeed designated by an essentially late Roman vocabulary (*villae, mancipia, servi*, etc.). Thus, the 'metanarrative' of a transition from slavery to serfdom which Wickham himself rejects, correctly of course, breaks down because it is too much of an abstraction. It simply merges the late Roman world into a medieval one, as Rodney Hilton did when he spoke of 'late ancient society' 'creating the production relations characteristic of feudal society';[82] but, more than that, it eliminates the historical distinction between a middle ages dominated by a diversified servile labour-force exploited by estates which are not strictly bilateral and one characterised by manorial estates, labour-services and a renewed assault on the peasantry. Without the Roman background of slavery, the servile relations of production of the sixth to ninth centuries would be like Athena emerging from Zeus's head!

The other strand in this argument relates to the heated issue of the *colonatus*. A minor orthodoxy has emerged in late antique studies which consciously seeks to downplay the element of coercion that characterised the subordination of these workers. *Coloni* were a category of permanent farm-labour which the government sought to tie to estates in the general interests of fiscal efficiency. They were free persons in the legal sense that they were not slaves,[83] but restricted in their movements and subject increasingly to social downgrading and the control of their employers, for example estate-owners had automatic rights of control over the progeny of female labourers even if their husbands were free persons unconnected with estates. In the only formal definition to survive, the Emperor Justinian in the sixth century defined them as 'farm workers' who were permanently resident on the estates they worked for.[84] The issue here is not how widespread this category of labour

---

[82] Hilton 1976, p. 112.
[83] In his recent contribution to *The Cambridge Economic History of the Greco-Roman World*, Andrea Giardina reproaches me with failing to see that the late-Roman *coloni* were unfree (Giardina 2007a, p. 748, n. 19). Surprisingly for a scholar of Giardina's stature, this confuses two totally separate issues: (1) the fact that *coloni* were free individuals under Roman law (not slaves), hence my reference to 'free labour' (i.e. not slave-labour; the standard contrast in historical materialism), and (2) the kinds of coercion that the régime of the colonate subjected these particular workers to. If they were 'unfree' to begin with (in some essentialist way), the tensions and paradoxes created by the *gradual* imposition of the laws relating to them would simply evaporate and the fascination of the subject (for scholars anyway) would be a pure enigma.
[84] *Nov.Just.* 162, cited Banaji 2007, p. 182; see n. 119. Savigny assumed that most *coloni* were landless, cf. von Savigny 1850, p. 32, and certainly landlessness is strongly implied in Just., *Nov.* 128.14, which contains the expression 'Even if [the *coloni*] should

was in the imperial territories – it existed presumably wherever large estates did – but what happened to them when the empire disintegrated in the West. On my reading of the evidence, *coloni* continued to exist into the sixth century but were increasingly absorbed into a less and less differentiated labour-force that I have characterised as 'servile'. This is why, in one of the earliest pieces of post-Roman legislation we have, the Edict of Theoderic, there are repeated references to *servus aut colonus*, 'slaves or coloni', distinct but not vastly different in status (more or less the same legal provisions apply to both groups),[85] whereas, in barbarian law-codes of a later date, such as the Visigothic legislation of the seventh century, there are no references to them as a separate category but to *servi* and *mancipia*, that is, servile classes that undoubtedly included former *coloni*.[86] Indeed, it is fascinating to be able to map this crucially important extension in the meaning of the term *mancipium* from its strict Roman sense of 'chattel-slave' to the much looser post-Roman and early-medieval meaning of an unfree/ servile labourer through the *whole* of the sixth century, when this evolution first begins. Burgundian legislation already subsumes tied labourers under the more general description *mancipia*.[87] And, in Theoderic's 'Edict', the expression *servus sive colonus* is used interchangeably with *mancipium*, showing that the latter term could now embrace both groups, slaves as well as *coloni*.[88] By the later sixth century, and certainly by the seventh, it was absolutely standard to use *mancipium* as a generic description that included workers descended from former *coloni* who might themselves, still, be called by this name, as, for example, in the will of Aredius which I cited earlier, or in Dagobert's donation of the estate of Etrépagny to the abbey of

---

happen to have farms of their own'. For the survival/re-emergence of the *colonatus* in the Byzantine parts of Italy, cf. Pelagius, *Ep.* 64 (559); Gregory, *Ep.* 4.21 (594).

[85] *Ed. Theod.* (FIRA², ii, p. 684ff.) 21; 84; 98; 104; 109; 121; 148, all have *servus aut colonus*. In *Ed.Theod.* 80 we have *servus aut originarius*.

[86] King 1972, pp. 160–1; Nehlsen 1972, pp. 166–7; Voss 1985, p. 168, n. 239; p. 170, n. 252.

[87] *LBurg* 54, issued by Gundobad between 501 and 516, refers to the Burgundian élite seizing one-third of the labour-force on Gallic estates where they had been settled 'by the rule of hospitality'. The term used for these workers is *mancipia* and, as Goffart 1980, p. 127ff., esp. 135–6, argues, it is inconceivable that the word should have referred *only* to slaves; so too Whittaker 1987, p. 109.

[88] Nehlsen 1972, p. 131 notes, '...der Kolone, der nunmehr zu den *mancipia* gezählt wird'. Cf. *Ed. Theod.* 142, which has the expression *rustica utriusque sexus mancipia, etiamsi originaria sint*, 'agrarian *mancipia* of either sex, even if they happen to be *originarii*', that is, happen to be the tied labourers technically known as *coloni originarii* because the estate was their *origo*, the place where they were enrolled for tax-purposes.

Saint-Denis, dated 628, which has the expression *cum omni integritate et soliditate, hoc est domibus, edificiis...mancipiis, colonis, inquilinis, accolabus, libertis, servis tam ibidem oriundis quam et aliundis translatis.*[89] Indeed, one will of 632, that of the bishop Eligius, even contains the expression *originarii*.[90]

Wickham disregards all of this evidence to bolster the impression that a more or less self-managing peasantry had emerged from the ruins of the Roman empire and the crisis of its aristocracy, and that words like *servus* and *mancipium* described a purely formal dependence which could barely counter the economic reality that most rural labourers were now actually tenants who, as he says, 'controlled the land and their own work process'.[91] In *Framing*, he endorses the very substantial position that 'Most *servi/mancipia* in our period...were tenants who controlled their own holding and could keep its fruits after rents were paid'.[92] But the written evidence just does not support this. As I have said, in the early sixth-century will of Remigius, bishop of Reims, *colonus* is a term for half-free or unfree rural labourers, distinct from slaves, who could be bequeathed with the land, transferred between owners, and even manumitted, and whose families could likewise be bequeathed. These peasants can scarcely be construed as controlling the land. Again, throughout the later sixth and seventh century, the Spanish Church fought hard to retain control over the 'services' of freedpeople [*liberti*] who had once been their slaves, and refused to acknowledge their freedom unless it had such control.[93] And Merovingian charters are full of references to *mancipia* who, given the nature of the typical Merovingian estate [*villa*], still rooted in Roman traditions of *Gutswirtschaft*, were not a loose collection or dispersed mass of rent-paying tenancies but, at best, allotment-holders retained by the estate as a captive labour-supply and otherwise simply landless slaves domiciled 'in the outbuildings of [their] master's farm'[94] or near the estate-centre. The huge wave of manumissions that transformed the landscape of medieval

---

[89] Kölzer 2001, Volume 1, no. 31, p. 85ff. (628); Tits-Dieuaide 1985, p. 32.
[90] *Test. Eligii*, 2, ed. Krusch, *MGH Script. rer. merow.* t. 4, p. 746.
[91] Wickham 1984, p. 9.
[92] Wickham 2005, p. 560.
[93] Toledo III, *can.* 6 (Vives 1963, p. 127), Sevilla I, *can.* 1 (pp. 151–2), Tol. IV, *can.* 68, 70, 73 (pp. 214–16), and Conc. Mérida, *can.* 20 (pp. 339–40), dated 589, 590, 633 and 666 respectively, all dealing with *mancipia ecclesiae* who had been 'manumissa' but over whom the Church still wanted control [*patrocinium, obsequium*]. Also *LV* 4.5.7 (Zeumer, 205f.), a law of Wamba that refuses to allow these *liberti* to marry freeborn women.
[94] Finberg 1972, p. 431.

Europe, re-assembling what would later and only gradually become a peasantry proper, threw up a vast array of intermediate categories between pure slaves and pure peasants, and it is this mass of servile labour that formed the backbone of élite-agriculture down to the feudal reaction of the eleventh to thirteenth centuries and the imposition of serfdom.[95] Thus, on the one hand, slaves and slavery remained a substantial part of Lombard, Anglo-Saxon and other early medieval societies, while, on the other hand, large numbers of them were settled on the land with the allotments called *mansi*, described legally as their *peculium, peculiaria* or *res peculiares* (the usual vocabulary for the assets managed by a slave).

The general point I wish to make is that the post-Roman/early-medieval world was characterised by a great deal more complexity in the structuring and composition of its rural labour-force than suggested by Wickham's simplified image of 'tenants who controlled their own holding and could keep its fruits after rents were paid'.[96] The best generic description, as I suggested earlier, might be a 'mixed servile labour force'[97] where families themselves might be of mixed legal status, and where the great movement of manumission was creating reserves of labour still integrated into centralised estates rather than the independent farm complexes called *hubae*, also known, confusingly, as *mansi* when the latter term acquired its more expansive sense in the central middle ages. That a more substantial or autonomous peasantry existed or was emerging is incontrovertible (the feudal reaction would be incomprehensible without it), but to understand its emergence we have to describe the context of the relations of production within which it developed with less abstraction and certainly less schematically than either Wickham or an earlier generation of Marxists have tended to do. The metanarrative of the transition from slavery to serfdom which Wickham rejects *cannot* be replaced by the equally abstract idea that 'When the Romans abandoned the slave mode, they went straight over to rent-paying tenants',[98] or by the notion that the 'economic shift from the slave to the feudal mode had already taken place well before

---

[95] The Anglo-Saxon bordars and cottars, German *Tageschalken*, Italian *servi prebendari*, etc. There is a rough analogy in the 'bondsmen' used by modernising Prussian estate-owners of the nineteenth century, cf. Conze 1969, p. 67.
[96] Wickham 2005, p. 560.
[97] Faith 1997, p. 252.
[98] Wickham 1984, p. 31.

400'.[99] It is bizarre to call the Roman empire 'feudal', unless one is determined to deplete the category of all historical content. And slavery did not simply disappear. It would be altogether more correct to refer to its 'mutation', as Georges Duby does.[100] Wickham's simple dichotomy between legal condition and economic form (slavery persisting at the first level, 'tenancy' widespread at the second) lacks the subtlety needed to characterise the transition, *even if* legal status mattered less and less and, as Innes says, 'there was no real social gulf between free and unfree' by the Carolingian period.[101]

Now, viewed teleologically, in terms of some inexorable evolution towards the manor and its eventual triumph, the allotment-holders of the post-Roman/early-medieval countryside may seem like a transitional type, a sort of station between two terminals, one called Antiquity, the other Feudalism; or, if you prefer, between Slavery and Serfdom. But this, I suggest, is absolutely the wrong way of approaching the issue. Between the 'demesne-slave' or *servi praebendarii* and the peasant-families in possession of substantial tenements (viz. 10-acre holdings at the lower end) lay a whole series of intermediate categories who are surely better defined as farm-workers than as peasants: the *Tageschalken* in Germany, the *geburs*, *bordars* and *cottars* in Anglo-Saxon England, and so on. They were 'a substantial proportion of the rural population of Anglo-Saxon England'[102] and doubtless the same is true of most countries on the Continent. If we choose to call them tenants, then *worker-tenants* is a better description of these groups than the tenants that Wickham seems to have in mind. Wickham discusses their legal status as largely irrelevant on the grounds that the distinction between free and unfree was typically and increasingly fuzzy. This is true, but the diminished legal condition of most or all of these groups was surely not unrelated to the fact that, taken as a whole, they formed a tied labour-force on a model familiar to late-Roman landowners and their free but tied *coloni*. Indeed, the laws on the colonate were themselves a major influence on the social condition of the medieval peasantry,

---

[99] Wickham 2005, p. 262.
[100] Duby 1973, p. 51: 'une lente mutation de l'esclavage'.
[101] Innes 2000, pp. 78–80. Of course, by the same token, Bonnassie's thesis of the persistence of a slave-*economy* down to the 'feudal mutation' of *l'an mil* is equally untenable (Bonnassie 1991). There is a great deal of value in Bonnassie's work, but the best critiques of his main thesis are Freedman 1996; Freedman 2002; and Verhulst's discussion of Bois, Verhulst 1991, p. 195ff.
[102] Faith 1997, p. 85.

insofar as the successor-kingdoms absorbed them selectively and enforced them against their own dependent populations.[103] The *mancipia* who appear in Merovingian charters were certainly not slaves in the strict Roman sense,[104] but the fact that they *were* described in this way was not unrelated to the way large estates saw themselves using the labour of these workers.

To sum up, early-medieval relations of production were defined by considerable complexity, not so much in terms of legal status, which mattered less than it did in the Roman world, as economically, in the nature of the labour-force, which was typically mixed but in general characterised by the kind of servility that was distinctive of postclassical slavery[105] and best conveyed by the term *mancipium*. This was a late antique legacy, but one which the post-Roman kingdoms transformed, insofar as a common condition of servility now engulfed both slaves and former tied labourers, manumissions were widespread but freedpeople still subject to domination [*obsequium*], and new aristocracies were bringing land into cultivation by creating peasant-tenures of a kind previously unknown. Large-scale enterprise and direct management were crucial parts of the legacy late Rome passed on to the Carolingians. Both tied labour and the direct management of estates were integral features of the Carolingian world and of the new energies manifested in the evolution of bilateral estates by the eighth century. *Yet the continuity in traditions of direct management did not imply a continuity of estate-structures*. However we construe serfdom, whether economically in terms of labour-services or socially in terms of the characteristics Marc Bloch emphasised, it was *not* a feature of the period between 400 and 750 or even 800.[106] The spread of slave-tenancies created a captive labour-supply in the form of reserves of labour-power. As Bloch himself indicated, 'The land that had been granted to them [slaves]...was like their salary'.[107] This was closer in nature to labour tenancies than to the more archetypal feudal institution of labour-services. Finally, as Faith writes,

---

[103] See Voss 1985, the most substantial treatment of the subject.
[104] Panero 1999, p. 89.
[105] Davies 1996, p. 231.
[106] 900, if serfdom is construed in the full-bodied sense used by Bloch, e.g. 1975, Chapter 2.
[107] Bloch 1975, p. 6.

The freed slave was a worker who in return for selling his labour as a commodity received a 'wage in land' from the lord, who was his employer and sole purchaser of that labour. The lord, in his capacity as employer, was essential to him. By contrast, the serf was a peasant with a holding, which, however small, supported him and his family and provided a surplus which was transferred to the lord in rent paid in cash, kind or labour (or in all these).[108]

What this suggests is the more general distinction between *labour-services*, bound up with the expansion of the manorial régime from the eighth century, and *labour-tenancies*, still rooted in late-antique models of estate-organisation.

8.5. The East: vulnerability

In his book *The Islamic Law of Land Tax and Rent*, Baber Johansen argues, in a chapter strikingly entitled 'The "Death of the Proprietors"' that the small-holding peasantry of the Islamic world began to disappear from the second half of the tenth century, with the evolution of the *iqṭāʿ* system. (*Iqṭāʿ*, in this later sense, referred, of course, to the holding of revenue-assignments on specified lands in lieu of a cash-salary and thus presupposes a more-or-less centralised state. The system was widely used throughout the Islamic world, including India, where it went by a variety of names, such as *muqasa, jāgīr*, and so on.) In later centuries, Johansen argues, the trend was consolidated as large estates were formed through the privatisation of these tax-assignments, capital-investments in the purchase of land and the outright grant of private ownership to members of the élite.[109] Much of the political economy of Islam might be seen as an unstable equilibrium between the fiscal supremacism of the state and the capitalist tendencies of members of the élite who defended claims to private property and the rights of pious foundations (*waqf* rights), especially on arable lands where these were sometimes fiercely contested. In these struggles, the jurists of the Mamluk and Ottoman periods tended to support the latter.[110] In the fifteenth century, the Hanafi mufti Ibn al-Humām exclaimed in bafflement, 'Can't you see that the land is not the property of

---

[108] Faith 1997, pp. 69–70, a superb passage.
[109] Johansen 1988, p. 81.
[110] Johansen 1988, p. 81ff.

the cultivators [*zurrā*']? This is so in spite of what we said about the lands of Egypt being *kharāj* lands'.[111] In other words, it no longer mattered that the peasants paid taxes [*kharāj*]; the legal fiction that the payment of taxes [*kharāj*] was proof of one's title to the land was now effectively defunct. 'For Ibn al-Humām the notion of the "death of the *kharāj* payer" served to explain and legalise the tenant status of peasants and the fact that they no longer enjoyed property rights with regard to their lands in spite of their paying their levies to the *muqtā'* and the ruler'.[112] In the following (sixteenth) century, Ibn Nujaym's defence of the property-rights of the landed classes against the incipient Ottoman drive to transform all land back into state-property rationalised those claims by arguing that peasants too poor to pay taxes or cultivate the land would lose the disposition of their property and that the ruler was entitled to sell such land on their behalf. But, once sold, the government was no longer entitled to an extra payment for the use of the land, that is, such land would count as tax-exempt.[113] In an odd piece of reasoning, Ibn Nujaym then went on to argue that whether land was tax exempt or not could be ascertained from how much buyers had paid for it, since no one would pay a high price for land that attracted taxes. Tax-exemption was seen as a sign of the status of the landowner as a member of the ruling class. When high prices were paid, the buyer 'becomes an exclusive proprietor [*mālik^{un} lahā 'alā l-khuṣuṣ*] of the land and he is not a share-cropper [*muzāri'*] or a peasant [*fallāḥ*]'.[114]

Now, what is interesting in the convoluted argument used to justify the dispossession of the peasantry is not just the conceptual landscape that lies at the back of the argument, viz. that the rural world is divided into landowners and peasants, and that they are sharply distinct classes, but the strong sense of the vulnerability of the peasantry itself. As Johansen notes, 'Private landed property no longer comes into being through the confirmation of the primordial rights of the peasants by the ruler',[115] referring here to the doctrine that the conquest had confirmed the peasantry in its ownership of the land,

---

[111] Cited Johansen 1988, pp. 84–5.
[112] Johansen 1988, p. 85.
[113] Johansen 1988, pp. 88–9.
[114] Cited Johansen 1988, p. 90: *fī hādhihi l-ḥālati mālik^{un} lahā 'alā l-khuṣuṣi laisa bi-muzāri'^{in} wa-lā fallāḥ*.
[115] Johansen 1988, p. 91.

in southern Iraq at any rate, and in the general sense that *kharāj* was a tax on private property, so that *kharāj*-payers were proprietors in a full-bodied sense.[116] Whatever one thinks of the notion that the conquest entailed a sort of emancipation of the peasantry (to me, it seems unlikely), Johansen's book is a good starting-point for the general argument I would like to propose in this part of the chapter, namely, that we have to think of the peasantry in the Middle East in very different terms from the situation in the West. I concluded a paper published in 1999 with the claim that it is 'worth emphasising that the Egyptian peasantry in particular has a strangely elusive quality'.[117] I now believe that this is true of the Middle-East peasantry as a whole, even if the Egyptian material makes it easier to establish for that country. I would like to lay out *three* arguments for this general thesis, which are, respectively, about class-structure, sharecropping, and the meaning of 'estate'. Taken together, these arguments suggest that the peasantry in these parts of the world, that is, everywhere from the Maghreb to Sind, lived permanently in a twilight-zone of near-landlessness. Johansen's discussion of Ibn Nujaym has demonstrated one form of this and I shall now look briefly at each of the three topics just mentioned.

By late antiquity, there is almost no evidence of a *substantial* stratum that might be called small and middle peasants, except in isolated regions and ecological niches where they were less vulnerable to the depredations of large landowners. In the Byzantine East, summary descriptions of the chief rural classes comprise only two groups, *hoi tōn choriōn despotai* and *hoi geōrgoi*, or *hoi kyrioi* and *hoi geōrgoi*, or some variation on these couplets such as *hoi ta chōria kektēmenoi* and *hoi geōrgoi*,[118] that is, landowners on one side, peasants on the other. But, from the way these terms are deployed, it is clear that the *geōrgoi* were not mainly a landed class. It was not the ownership of land that defined their identity in the eyes of the members of the élite who drafted the laws or wrote histories. What defined them collectively was the fact of rural labour. This is why it was standard to use the term *georgos* when referring to *coloni* in the East, although Justinian himself took the trouble to explain that the Latin word designated a class of workers who were 'residents of large estates and

---

[116] Johansen 1988, Chapter 1.
[117] Banaji 1999, p. 213; see p. 179 above.
[118] Procopius, *HA* 23.16, 26.17ff., *Nov.Just.* 157 (542), *Nov.Tib.* 11 (575), etc. In *Nov. Just.* 8, praef. (535) *ktētores* and *geōrgoi* are the only rural groups listed.

farm workers'.[119] On one third-century estate, *geōrgoi* were included among the groups who received monthly wages (in grain),[120] and going even further back, el-Abbadi describes the *dēmosioi geōrgoi* or peasants on former royal (that is, Ptolemaic) land as 'the great mass of landless public peasants', adding that at this time (the first century) the word *georgos* 'usually indicate[s] a farmer who owned his own land'.[121] In short, the first thing agrarian historians have to do is reconstruct the meaning of words instead of allowing words to dominate their perception of the flow of history.

In the Sasanian Near East, we know next to nothing about agrarian relations, beyond the fact that much Iranian history revolved around the tensions or conflict between the ruler and powerful regional aristocracies. There is one fascinating reference in Ammianus to the Sasanian upper class wielding 'the power of life and death over their slaves and *plebeii obscuri*'.[122] *Bandag* was the standard Middle-Persian term for 'slave' or 'servant', but how we should (reverse) translate the latter expression is anyone's guess; perhaps it was Ammianus's Latin equivalent of *driyōšān*.[123] It referred, presumably, to the mass of commoners who survived through employment for the rich, and probably also to the kind of social groups from which the revolutionary priest Mazdak drew his support early in the sixth century. These are described in the (much later!) Arabic sources by a profusion of terms, of which the most telling denote utter destitution.[124] Patricia Crone, in a justly famous paper, argued that Mazdak drew his support from the peasantry, especially in the aftermath of fiscal reforms that introduced a fixed monetary tax.[125] But this, of course, begs the question whether such a group (a peasantry) existed on

---

[119] *Nov.Just.* 162.2, *tous oikētoras tōn chōrion kai tōn agrōn ergatas*. Note that *ergatēs* was the usual Greek term for an unskilled wage-earner.

[120] *P. Oxy.* XLII 3048 (246).

[121] el-Abbadi 1967, p. 219.

[122] Ammianus, 23.6.80: *vitae necisque potestatem in servos et plebeios vindicantes obscuros*. Note that Ammianus had travelled into Sasanian territory with Julian's army.

[123] Sunderman 1976, esp. p. 179.

[124] The most evocative are *al-muqillīn* (the destitute) and *al-fuqarā'* (the poor), both in al-Ṭabarī, *Ta'rīkh*, ser. i, p. 886 = al-Ṭabarī 1999, p. 132. Al-Tha'ālibī, *Ghurar akhbār mulūk al furs* (Zotenberg) p. 600 describes Mazdak's social base as 'the poor [*al-fuqarā'*], the low-class [*al-sifla*] and the rabble [*al-ghaughā'*]'. *Al-ḍu'afā'* (the powerless) was another common description. It seems very likely that the Arabic tradition was trying to render the sense of the Middle-Persian terms *driyōš* and *škōh*, on which see Sundermann 1976 and Colditz 2000, pp. 177ff., 190ff.

[125] Crone 1991, esp. p. 32ff.; Frye 1984, p. 323.

any substantial scale by the sixth century. What does seem clear is that, *if* Mazdak's supporters were rural, they were landless, but, on balance, it is more likely that Mazdak attracted the urban poor, groups who had no access to food in times of scarcity, *and*, it seems, no access to women and a family-life either. At any rate, the picture of late-Sasanian society is one of a deeply divided formation where the antagonism between rich and poor was a constant source of anxiety for the ruling groups,[126] and one of the most valuable survivals of an authentic Middle-Persian text (via Arabic) shows a ruler, probably Khusro I, strongly advocating the attachment [*ilḥāq*] of the poor to their closest aristocratic neighbours to reduce class-antagonisms and ensure the continued submission of those stricken by poverty.[127] The scale of destitution implied in all this fits remarkably well with the kind of agrarian picture reflected in a major work of agronomy written, almost certainly, in Syriac, in late antiquity, and translated by Ibn Waḥshiyya at the start of the tenth century.[128] Here, as Gunnar Lehmann points out in a review of a recent study of the massive redaction attributed to Ibn Waḥshiyya, 'In the rural masses of the *kitāb al-filāḥa an-nabaṭīya* we are dealing with "free" agricultural workers in Marx's sense. The population depicted there is *employed solely by the large estates, it has no share in landed property*'.[129] That, at the time of the conquest of southern Iraq, the Arabs did not in fact find a substantial smallholding peasantry but villages ruled by *dehqāns*, a minor gentry, and estates cultivated by mainly Aramaic-speaking 'tenants',[130] is suggested by a tradition reported in Abū Yūsuf's *Kitāb al-kharāj*, viz. "Umar b. al-Khaṭṭāb first wanted to distribute [the lands of] al-Sawād amongst the Muslims and ordered a census. It was found that each of them would receive two or three tenants (*al-ithnain wa-l-thalātha min al-fallāḥīn*) with their lands' and he decided eventually not to pro-

---

[126] E.g. *Dēnkard* 6.147 (Shaked, p. 60), which refers to the poor having contempt [*tarmenišnīh*] for the rich and powerful [*tawānīgān*].

[127] Grignaschi 1966, p. 99, with Sundermann 1976, p. 175.

[128] For recent studies, see El Faïz 1995, and Hämeen-Anttila 2006; on the Arabic translator, see Fahd, 'Ibn Wahshiyya', *Enc. Islam.*, 2nd ser., vol. 3, p. 963ff.

[129] Lehmann, review of El Faïz (n. 126), *JESHO* 40 (1997) p. 117ff., at 119; my italics. Fahd points out that the Leiden manuscript of the *Kitāb* runs into 1264 pages!

[130] In al-Ṭabarī, *Ta'rīkh*, ser. i, p. 2426, l.13ff., Shirazadh, *dehqān* of Sābāṭ, describes the peasants as '*ulūj* of the Persians, with the general sense, perhaps, of mere servants. Al-Ṭabarī's use of the generic *al-fallāḥīn* for the remnants of the Sasanian peasantry is scarcely a clue to how estates were structured or labour organised, hence the significance of this particular passage!

ceed with the division.¹³¹ In short, an independent peasantry was not a major feature of the core regions of the Sasanian Empire, and, both here and in the Byzantine-controlled East Mediterranean, landlessness and dependence on large and medium-scale landowners was widespread. Thus, *proletarianisation took very different forms in the East and West*, flowing from the gradual dissolution of bondage and the structured creation of reserves of labour (labour-tenancies) in one case, the West, and from the widespread landlessness of the peasantry, in the other, the East, where the threat of eviction was a more powerful means of control.

Staying with the East, the second remarkable feature is the kind of sharecropping that prevailed there and its sheer ubiquity. Noting the frequency of indefinite durations in the Egyptian leases of the sixth to seventh centuries, Stefan Waszyński had concluded, correctly in my view, that the Byzantine sharecropper had become a pure and simple wage-labourer whom the landowner could evict at any time.¹³² No modern papyrologist has registered any serious disagreement with this view, because it is so obvious that tenants-at-will are entirely at the mercy of their landlords. Thus, whether the *geōrgoi* were 'bound' to large estates as *coloni* or permanent farm-workers (see n. 119) or worked as sharecroppers and tenants-at-will, they were united by their common condition of landlessness and total dependence on the employer. It is *this* feature of East-Mediterranean sharecropping that comes to the fore in the Islamic period. Here are two passages illustrative of this. Discussing a category of land called the *'arḍ al-ḥauz* or lands that have come into the possession [*ḥauz*] of the ruler and been appropriated by him, the ninth-century Iraqi jurist al-Khaṣṣāf writes, 'the *ḥauz* is something that the Sultan takes possession of [*ḥāzahu*]. He brings the sharecroppers [*muzāri'ūn*] to it, so that they may cultivate it. In this way they become farm-hands [*akara*] of the Sultan, whom he may oust at any time he pleases'.¹³³ And Abū Yūsuf in his discussion of different types of agricultural contracts describes two in particular which are relevant to our theme. One of them is called *muzāra'a* and defined as an

---

¹³¹ Abū Yūsuf, *K. al-kharāj*, p. 21 (1885 edn), tr. Ben Shemesh 1969, Volume 3, p. 97.
¹³² Waszyński 1905, p. 92, esp. 'im Grunde genommen ist dieser demütige *georgos* kein Pächter mehr...er ist zum Mietling, zum Lohnarbeiter geworden, den der Grundherr nach Belieben hinauswerfen kann'; about the *eph'hoson chronon boulei* ('for any period you choose') clause.
¹³³ Cited Johansen 1988, p. 14.

agreement where the tenant receives a third or fourth share of the crop.[134] The other, not called *muzāra'a*, is described as follows: 'A landowner hires a peasant to cultivate some land and bears all the expense, promising the peasant a sixth or a seventh of the crop as wages'.[135] From al-Khaṣṣāf it is clear that sharecropping [*muzāra'a*] was widespread on large estates, even though it was rejected by jurists like Abū Ḥanīfa and Shāfi'ī[136] on the substantial legal grounds that the 'rent' was non-existent and unknown at the time the contract was made. The jurists who defended its validity did so on the practical grounds that it was part of the way business [*ta'āmul*] was conducted in their countries. These later Ḥanafī models of sharecropping draw a clear distinction between labour and capital, basing the landowner's claim to a share of the crop on his need to expand his property (i.e. the seed) and the worker's claim on the contract alone.[137] The fact that in most parts of the Islamic world *muzāra'a* typically involved shares varying from one-fourth to one-seventh is, I suggest, linked to an underlying conception of these contracts as a hiring of labour. Their sheer tenacity across the most diverse periods of the history of the Middle East is one indication of the peculiarly fragile nature of the peasantry in this part of the world. As Alan Richards says, 'Since the peasants often had little to supply but their labor power, it is not surprising that they usually received only one-fourth or one-fifth of the cotton harvest'.[138] In Nabulsi's Egypt (thirteenth century), the *murābi'ūn* or one-fourth croppers ranked lower than other sorts of tenants, hence Sato's description of them as 'a class of agricultural labourers'.[139] *Murāba'a* was widespread in the Levant, *khammāsa* more common in North Africa.[140] In his monumental study of Algeria under French occupation, Albert Nouschi included the *khammès* [*khammās*] under 'proletarians'.[141]

---

[134] Abū Yūsuf, *K. al-kharāj*, p. 52, l.1: *muzāra'a bi-l-thulth wa-l-rub'*, wrongly translated by Ben Shemesh as 'the owner gets a third or fourth of the yield', 1969, Volume 3, p. 115, contrast Haque 1977, p. 327.

[135] Abū Yūsuf, *K. al-kharāj*, p. 52, 1.4ff., with Ben Shemesh 1969, Volume 3, p. 116, though *fa-yad'uu akkār^{an}* is better translated 'hires a labourer'.

[136] Johansen 1988, pp. 52–3.

[137] Johansen 1988, p. 63; Haque 1977, p. 325.

[138] Richards 1982, p. 68, about the period 1890–1914.

[139] Sato 1997, p. 219.

[140] Firestone 1975, p. 8, who also states, 'in view of the low value attaching to his labour, the cropper cannot really exercise any control in the association. Accordingly, some jurists hold cropping to be a share-wage contract and hence basically illicit'. The *khammès* received a fifth of the crop as his/her share.

[141] Nouschi 1961, p. 154.

On the other hand, what the influx of European settlers brought from the 1840s was a different kind of *prolétarisation* of Algerian society, an organised dispossession that disintegrated entire tribes and uprooted wider sections of the peasantry, creating a new kind of landless worker. (Land confiscations affected one third of Algeria's population, once the *colons* decided that impoverishment was the best means of pacification.)[142] The vulnerability I have been at pains to stress is different from the organised creation of labour-markets that characterises much nineteenth and early twentieth century colonialism. It is better reflected in Iran, which never knew colonialism in this sense and where, as Ann Lambton points out in her book,

> The *vast majority of the peasant population of Persia is...not composed of peasant proprietors, who are a small minority, but of crop-sharing peasants or tenants and 'landless' labourers*. It is with the former that this chapter is concerned. They, too, strictly speaking are landless, but by virtue of a contract, written, or more often merely verbal, a certain area of land is handed over to them on a crop-sharing basis for a specified or unspecified period of time, the peasant providing the seed, draught animals, and agricultural implements, or only one or two of these in addition to the labour, whereas the *landless labourer, although he may be also paid by a share of the crop, is differentiated from the crop-sharing peasant by the fact that he provides only labour and can be dismissed at will*.[143]

Since the division between the two groups described here cannot have been a rigid one, this is a lucid summary of the general argument I have made about the nature of the peasantry in the Middle East, conceived historically and in contrast to the West, where the legacies of late antiquity combined a tied labour-force with the later expansion of peasant-tenures.

The third and final plank of my argument concerns the meaning of the word 'estate' in much of the Near East. Like its sharply polarised agrarian structure, this too is a legacy of late antiquity that survived best in the Muslim world, but one which drew more on Armenian and Sasanian traditions of landholding

---

[142] Nouschi 1961, pp. 306, 448–9, 403ff.; *prolétarisation* at 511. Cf. Sartre 1960, pp. 674–88, arguing that the inert violence of the *system* was rooted in concrete operations (massacres, legal interventions, etc.) designed to shatter an existing society and create [*réaliser*] a mainly agrarian 'sub-proletariat of the destitute and chronically unemployed'.

[143] Lambton 1953, p. 295; my emphasis.

than on any Byzantine or late Roman equivalents. The form of landholding I have in mind involves the ownership of villages (usually entire villages and often many more than one) and contrasts sharply with the Byzantine large estate that turns up in the papyri of the later fifth to seventh centuries. The latter, as I suggested at the start of this paper, grouped its workers into estate-settlements that were visibly distinct from villages and never confused with them. Since these settlements were called *epoikia*, I have described this kind of estate as '*epoikion*-type'.[144] It corresponds exactly to the *ezba*-estates that proliferated in Egypt in the nineteenth century, as land was increasingly re-privatised and the ruling groups invested massively in cotton. The striking feature of the papyrological evidence is the singular absence of anything vaguely resembling the ownership of villages in late antique Egypt. In sharp contrast to this, Procopius refers to an Armenian collaborator persuading the emperor Justinian (in the early 530s) to 'present him with certain villages [*kōmai*] of Armenia'. He became, Procopius says, the 'owner' [*kyrios*] of these estates [*chōrion*].[145] When this man was assassinated by the pro-Sasanian faction, Justinian handed the same villages over to his nephew Amazaspes.[146] Now this, it seems to me, was primarily a Sasanian tradition, as Michael Morony has argued in a paper that describes this type of landholding as 'village estates'.[147] Thus Hormozdān owned a village which 'Uthmān later granted to Sa'd b. Abī Waqqāṣ as his *iqṭā'* (in its classical meaning, any concession of land).[148] In the mid fifth century, another equally powerful Sasanian figure Mihr Narseh is described as 'founding' four villages and laying out orchards around them,[149] and even earlier, in the fourth century, Shapur II is described as 'building' the village of Vardāna near Bukhārā.[150] Indeed, in Bukhārā, where a minor Iranian aristocracy survived down to the Sāmānid period, the tradition is abundantly attested in Narshakhī's *History of Bukhara*, a tenth-century work of which the

---

[144] Banaji 2007.
[145] Procopius, *BP* 2.3.1–2 (Dewing, *History of the Wars*, Volume 1, p. 270).
[146] Procopius, *BP* 2.3.3 and *PLRE* IIIa 54.
[147] Morony 1981.
[148] Balādhurī, *Futūḥ al-buldān*, p. 272 = Hitti 1916, p. 431; Abū Yūsuf, *K. al-kharāj*, p. 35, Ben Shemesh 1969, Volume 3, p. 77.
[149] Al-Ṭabarī, ser. i, p. 870 = Al-Ṭabarī 1999, pp. 104–5, which ends, 'These villages, with the gardens and the fire temples, have remained continuously in the hands of his descendants, who are well known till today'; here 'today' is almost certainly taken from al-Ṭabarī's Sasanian source and does not refer to his own period.
[150] Narshakhī, *Tārīkh-i Bukhārā*, pp. 44–5; Narshakhī 1954, p. 32.

only exemplar is the Persian translation made in the early twelfth century. This refers to the buying and selling of villages, and in one passage to 75 'private' villages [*dīhe khās*] 'on the river of Bukhara and the Upper Farāvāz'.[151] It is *this* tradition, I suggest, that survived both in Iran where, even in the late 1940s, the typical 'large landed proprietors' were described by Lambton as owners of villages, the *'umdeh mālikīn* whose 'estates range from single villages to several villages, the number of which, in certain exceptional cases, is alleged to run into three figures',[152] *and* in those *zamindari* villages of the Mughal period which, though confusingly also known as *dehāt-i-tāluqa*, were the big *zamindars' private* or exclusive possessions, as opposed to other villages, obviously the majority, over which, technically at least, their rights were essentially fiscal and the model of 'ownership' less full-blooded and closer to a hierarchy of shared claims.[153] Ownership of villages also seems to have been widespread in Egypt in the nineteenth century,[154] and as the term *'uhda* suggests, evolved at least partly from Muḥammad Ali's forced restoration of the *iltizām* system (which he had abolished in 1814) and the tendency of the *muta'ahhidūn* or tax-farmers (more correctly, 'tax-guarantors')[155] to treat villages whose liabilities they assumed as their private property.[156] Thus, Baer points out that 'a number of observers at the time of Muhammad 'Alī simply stated that the system turned the fellahs into labourers working for the *'uhda* recipient. Artin asserts that 'Abbās granted full ownership rights to some *muta'ahhidūn'*.[157] Moreover, the ruling family's *çiftliks* also consisted of villages which the peasantry had abandoned. Some of these were enormous; for example, 'Sa'īd's at al-Khazzān near Alexandria covered 20,000 feddans'.[158] What the Egyptian example suggests is that a model that was predominantly Iranian/Sasanian was taken over and generalised after the expansion of Islam, almost certainly through the practice of granting *villages* to members of the ruling élite, either as pure

---

[151] Narshakhī, *Tārīkh*, pp. 18, 21, 22, 75; Narshakhī 1954, pp. 13–16, 54.
[152] Lambton 1953, p. 266, and in fact the whole of Chapter 13.
[153] E.g. Grover 1965, esp. p. 266ff.
[154] Baer 1962.
[155] Alleaume 1999, p. 336.
[156] *'Uhda* = contractual obligation of some type; *muta'ahhid* = contractor, guarantor; also, by the evolution just described, estate-holder.
[157] Baer 1962, p. 15, discussing *al-'uhda* as a renewed 'basis for the creation of large estates'.
[158] Baer 1962, p. 18.

land-concessions [*iqṭā'āt, qaṭā'i'*] or, later, in lieu of cash-salaries, and later still as tax-farms.

The general point about this form of landholding is that effectively it abandoned the mass of the peasantry to the arbitrary power and domination of a range of large landowners who came to be called by a wide variety of names. Typically, 'estate' in this Near-Eastern/Islamic sense meant control (and often ownership) of villages and not the compact and discrete blocs of land that were inherited from late Rome and transformed into bilateral estates or manors under the Carolingians. Again, this reinforces my general point that, in these parts of the world, the peasantry, or a considerable part of it, always lived on the verge of dispossession, shadowed by landlessness. A final qualification, however; this model of the elusive boundary between peasants and landlessness does not preclude the existence of a wealthy peasantry; on the contrary, it explains why this village-élite tended to be a small, highly concentrated group, possibly endogamous and even stable over generations,[159] and, secondly, it allows room for the evolution of estates in the more 'western' sense, as Egypt demonstrates with the *ezbas* and Sasanian Iran with the *dastgird*.

[2009]

---

[159] E.g. Cuno 1984.

Chapter Nine
Islam, the Mediterranean and the Rise of Capitalism

9.1. Historiographies of capital

Our conception of capitalist origins has been so heavily dominated by the so-called 'transition' debate that Marxists are apt to forget that the first debate on origins actually began with the publication of the first edition of Sombart's *Modern Capitalism* and the various responses to its major argument that agrarian wealth or the accumulation of ground-rent provided the chief source of the fortunes that financed capitalist expansion in Europe. For Sombart, the aristocracies of Europe played the leading role in the evolution of industrial capitalism, and even *Kolonialkapitalismus* was to a large extent the work of these 'aristocratic entrepreneurs'.[1] The earliest systematic response to Sombart's thesis was Jakob Strieder's seminal and, in some ways, still unsurpassed book *Studien zur Geschichte kapitalistischer Organisationsformen* (1914). Strieder strongly believed that the first large-scale capitalist enterprises in industry, particularly mining, were financed and controlled by merchants, and this could be shown for the South-German mining industry of the fifteenth and sixteenth centuries.[2] Three aspects of Strieder's argument are worth noting:

---

[1] Sombart 1916, p. 865.
[2] Strieder 1914.

first, that the mining industry played a seminal role in the evolution of modern capitalism; second, that merchants *created* large enterprises, that is, involved themselves in the organisation of production and industry; and, finally, the more general thesis that commercial capitalism lay at the origin of the so-called capitalist spirit several centuries earlier, in Venice, Florence and other centres of 'early capitalism'. The last of these theses became the focus of a subsequent paper which Strieder published in 1929, called 'Origin and Evolution of Early European Capitalism'. Here, he argued that, in a whole series of industries (the woollen goods, silk weaving, linen export and metal industries), 'the merchant who organized the export trade, and made advances in one form or another to the workman, gained control over industries which had previously been in the hands of independent craftsmen'.[3] This evolution was, of course, particularly advanced in Italy, where 'the forms of money and credit economy, inherited from the ancient world, had *kept their vitality*'.[4] This is a particularly interesting idea because the legacies of late antiquity are seen here as unmediated. There is, if you like, an unbroken line of descent from the ancient world to medieval capitalism, and the story is purely European.

In the same year, Earl Hamilton proposed his now famous argument that while many 'factors' contributed to the rise of modern capitalism, chief among these were the discoveries and the 'vast influx of gold and silver from American mines'.[5] His main thesis, of course, was that trans-Atlantic flows boosted profitability for employers by triggering a price inflation, but Hamilton also suggested a causal connection between American treasure and the East India trade, arguing that Portugal, Holland, England and France were able to finance their trade expansion in the east thanks to the vast influx of precious metals from Mexico and Peru and the ability of those countries to attract the largest share of this metallic mass.[6] Unlike Strieder, however, all of these developments were simply seen as 'factors' in the rise of 'modern capitalism', that is, presuppositions of capital rather than movements or enterprises ('concerted praxes')[7] *presupposing* capital.

---

[3] Strieder 1929, p. 3.
[4] Strieder 1929, p. 5.
[5] Hamilton 1929, p. 344.
[6] Hamilton 1929, p. 347.
[7] Sartre 1960, pp. 235–45, using the work of Braudel and Hamilton.

The close connection between the East India trade and American treasure and the rise of modern capitalism has been overlooked or neglected largely because Portugal, the first nation to profit from trade with the Spice Islands by the Cape route, and Spain, the recipient of American gold and silver, showed no significant progress toward capitalism.[8]

When Hamilton says, 'no significant progress toward capitalism', he clearly means *industrial* capitalism. Yet Hamilton's main contribution was to draw attention to the Atlantic. By 1932, Portuguese historians could suggest that the countries of the Atlantic seaboard were the 'true founders of modern capitalism'.[9] The great centres of modern capitalism were Lisbon and Antwerp. In a deeply provocative formulation, Veiga-Simoes wrote, 'the whole of the new commercial life and even the capitalist system stem fundamentally from Portuguese economic policy at the end of the 14th and beginning of the 15th centuries'.[10] I shall argue that this is *basically* correct and the speculative core of a more internationalist historiography of capitalism than that implied in the 'transition' debate.

Portugal straddled two phases of commercial capitalism, subordinating the Atlantic to the Mediterranean, and then the Mediterranean to the Atlantic.[11] Yet Portugal's imperial adventure began as a confrontation with the commercial networks of Islam, an attempt to undermine those networks internationally. In his brilliant and much neglected book *O Capitalismo monárquico Português (1415–1549)*, subtitled 'Contribution to a Study of the Origins of Modern Capitalism', Manuel Nunes Dias argued that 'with the conquest of the Dark Sea, Europe overthrew the Mediterranean frameworks that had shackled her progress. In the great Ocean lay the engine that drove her capitalism'.[12] Behind the capture of Ceuta in 1415 lay the whole weight of the 'incipient commercial capitalism of the later Middle Ages' and its relentless fascination with the spectre of African gold.[13] The political victory of the bourgeoisie in 1440, raising Dom Pedro to the throne of Portugal, inaugurated a period

---

[8] Hamilton 1929, p. 356.
[9] Veiga-Simoes 1932, p. 291.
[10] Veiga-Simoes 1932, p. 295.
[11] To a 'northern, Atlantic, international capitalism', as Braudel called it, Braudel 1975, Volume 1, pp. 510; 228; the phrase is from p. 640.
[12] Dias 1963, Volume 1, p. 37.
[13] Dias 1963, Volume 1, p. 57ff, especially p. 65.

of intense activity along the Atlantic coast of Africa, signifying the strategic triumph of maritime expansion over territorial imperialism and enabling Henry the Navigator to implement his policy of deflecting the Sudan-Sahara traffic from the desert routes to the Atlantic. Through its progressive 'capture' of the Atlantic, Portugal emerged as the most 'active representative of the nascent commercial capitalism of the Christian West'.[14] By the time Dom João II ascended the throne in 1481, Portugal was Europe's first colonial power, the 'driving force of a capitalist revolution' of far-flung trading establishments [*feitorias*, 'factories'] buttressed by military fortresses. The Portuguese became 'pioneers of the modern colonial system', harnessing the Crusader tradition of a marginalised aristocracy within the peculiar fusion of Crown and commercial capitalism which Dias calls 'monarchical capitalism', with its chief international centre at Antwerp, the 'headquarters' of modern capitalism. The gold shipped from São Jorge da Mina raised Portugal's credit rating and consolidated the power of the monarchy, creating the crucial basis for expansion to the East.[15]

This is hardly a fair summary of a book that runs into 1,097 pages and one which even Braudel seems largely to have ignored. What is striking in Dias is not just the sense that capitalism was a thoroughly international system *from its inception* and that the problems confronted by Portugal were problems that *all* of European capitalism was keen to solve (above all, the scarcity of gold), but the much less obvious idea that Portugal's Atlantic expansion began in fact as an assault on Islamic commercial supremacy, both its domination of the Sahara gold trade and its monopoly of the Indian Ocean. The legacies of late antiquity were retrieved in different ways by Islam and the Italian city republics, and the dynamics of European capitalism are incomprehensible without some attempt to understand *those* totalisations. Here, the late 1960s saw two significant contributions. In *Società e stato nel medioevo veneziano (secoli xii–xiv)*, Giorgio Cracco developed a brilliant analysis of the power of commercial capital in the Venetian republic of the twelfth and thirteenth centuries, the fierce domination of the commune by an oligarchy of capitalists whose fortunes were tied up with international trade. The Venetian republic was a *stato*

---

[14] Dias 1963, Volume 1, pp. 148–98.
[15] Dias 1963, Volume 1, pp. 211–12, 218–25; Volume 2, pp. 260–7.

dei mercanti, a *stato dei grandi capitalisti*,[16] based, by the middle decades of the thirteenth century, on a huge concentration of capital that narrowed the social and political base of the mercantile economy, and on the relentless subordination of all sectors not directly bound up with the Levant traffic. Finally, in a paper published in 1969, Subhi Labib argued that 'capitalism was able to develop much earlier in the Islamic regions than in the Occident', largely because the Muslim Mediterranean could build on the continuing traditions of late antiquity (unlike the West?).[17] Labib referred to 'Islamic capitalism', 'the medieval capitalistic trade of Islam', to 'trading companies', bills of exchange, big business, etc., and thought that the failure of the state to sustain these structures led to their progressive unravelling by the later Middle Ages.

9.2. Towards a Marxist theory of commercial capitalism

Marx's *Capital* is premised on the primacy of industrial capital. This means that, with the evolution of industrial capitalism,

> the other varieties of capital which appeared previously...are not only subordinated to it and *correspondingly altered in the mechanism of their functioning*, but they now move only on its basis, thus live and die, stand and fall together with this basis.[18]

The merchant or 'merchant capitalist'[19] is simply a 'circulation agent' of industrial capital,[20] a 'form' or 'branch' of industrial capital, lacking any independent existence. Marx also seems to suggest that, under industrial capitalism, commercial capital is increasingly 'stripped of all the *heterogeneous functions that may be linked to it*, such as storage, dispatch, transport, distribution and retailing, and confined to its true function of buying in order to sell'.[21] Thus 'commercial capital' is simply a specialised form of the circulation functions of industrial capital, and no independent system can be construed for it. But *this* conception of commercial capital is clearly inapplicable to the

---

[16] Cracco 1967, p. 201f.
[17] Labib 1969, p. 80.
[18] Marx 1978, p. 136, emphasis mine.
[19] Marx 1981, p. 406.
[20] Marx 1981, p. 403.
[21] Marx 1981, p. 395, emphasis mine.

historical trajectories associated with the international traders or merchant-financiers who dominated the earlier history of capitalism. It is a definition of the nature and functions of commercial capital that presupposes the circuit of industrial capital or the dominance of large-scale industry, a situation that was only finally realised as late as the nineteenth century. And it seems logically absurd to me to imagine that a history of capitalism can be written using a notion of commercial capital that was developed by Marx for the kind of capitalist economy that evolved only in the nineteenth century. In practice, of course, this is largely what has tended to happen. The most striking case of this is Maurice Dobb, who referred sneeringly to the 'Pokrovsky-bog of "merchant capitalism"',[22] conceived of capitalism in essentially national terms, and sought to understand origins in terms of factors peculiar to England. There is a methodological impasse at work here, a staggering confusion of history and logic that accounts for the singular inability of Marxists influenced by Dobb to confront the past of capitalism beyond such manifestly untenable assertions as: 'The capitalist system was born in England. Only in England did capitalism emerge, in the early modern period, as an indigenous national economy';[23] or: 'By its very nature, merchant-capital must attach itself to a system of production...'.[24]

Dobb was evidently mesmerised by the distinction between 'production' and 'exchange', generalising this into an alleged contrast between capitalism as a 'commercial system' and capitalism as a 'mode of production'. Central to the latter was 'productive activity on the basis of a wage-contract'. 'Men of capital, however acquisitive, are not enough: their capital must be used to yoke labour to the creation of surplus-value in production'.[25] Methodologically, there were at least two interesting responses to this kind of reasoning. Reviewing *Studies* in the very year that saw Sweezy and Dobb publish their exchange in *Science and Society*, Tawney suggested that the 'restricted' sense of capitalism which Dobb favoured eliminated a great deal of the history of capitalism, and even led 'at times' to a 'misconception of the significance of the part played by capitalist interests in periods when an industrial

---

[22] Dobb 1976, p. 62.
[23] Wood 1991, p. 1.
[24] Fox-Genovese and Genovese 1983, p. 7.
[25] Dobb 1963, pp. 7–8.

wage-system was, in this country [England], in its infancy'.[26] Dobb underestimated the strength of capitalist interests in the century before the English Civil War. Georges Lefebvre's excellent contribution to the 'transition' debate sidestepped the antithesis by suggesting that, even in England, the merchants played a more decisive role in the evolution of capitalism than Dobb was willing to allow for, and ended with a plea for renewed interrogation of the sources.[27] The *dominant* sector of capital 'had no thought of overturning the social and political order'. Indeed, it was the 'collusion between commerce and the State [that] promoted the development of capitalism'.[28] The methodological step forward in Lefebvre's critique is the explicit move away from the wholly abstract opposition between production and circulation, or merchants and manufacture. 'The merchant created manufactures; his interests coincided with those of [the] State, and of the great landowners who were enclosing estates and evicting tenants, to transform agriculture.'[29]

The general implication of these critiques is that we need a model of commercial *capitalism* that allows for the reintegration of production and circulation, so that one is no longer fixated on the idea that merchant-capital is always and inherently external to production. For this to be possible, we have to see Marx's definition of commercial capital as specific to the framework of his analysis of industrial capital, and construct a circuit of commercial capital that would explain the movement of the kinds of capital exemplified by the Dutch and English East India Companies, for example. They dominated world trade for a period of centuries and brought about the kind of capitalist world economy that large-scale industry took for granted when it began its own expansion in the nineteenth century. But, when these joint-stock companies were formed on the eve of the seventeenth century, they in turn built on the legacies of earlier and possibly less internationalised forms of merchant capitalism whose origins lie in Europe around the twelfth century, and elsewhere – in the Islamic world and China – even earlier. As a broad periodisation, I would suggest that we see the twelfth to fifteenth centuries as the period of the growth of capitalism in Europe ('Mediterranean capitalism') and

---

[26] Tawney 1950, p. 311.
[27] Lefebvre 1976, p. 124ff.
[28] Lefebvre 1976, p. 125.
[29] Lefebvre 1976, p. 126.

the sixteenth to eighteenth centuries as the period of Company-capitalism, marked by more brutal methods of accumulation and competition.

9.3. From corporate capitalism to the earliest capitalist forms of association

The institutional framework of industrial capitalism only emerged towards the end of the nineteenth century with the so-called 'corporate revolution'.[30] Industrial capitalism *became* corporate capitalism with the spread of free incorporation, limited liability, and the legal doctrine of separate personality. These were developments underpinned by a huge expansion in the scale of enterprise, the evolution of investment banks, and the financing of investment by the capital-market. When Hilferding wrote *Finance Capital*, he described a particular (national) form of this development, but he was the first Marxist to do so, that is, to come to terms with the new era of corporate capitalism.

Now, as Paddy Ireland has shown, the doctrine of separate personality evolved against the background of legal changes that reconceptualised the share as an autonomous form of property, a 'separate and distinctive form of money capital'.[31] This process was more or less complete in Britain by the third quarter of the nineteenth century.[32] If shareholders had 'no direct interest, legal or equitable, in the property owned by the company, only a right to dividends and the right to assign their shares for value',[33] the company, by contrast, was now seen as the owner of its own assets. Separate personality severed the link between the assets of joint-stock companies and their shares, 'externalising' shareholders and depersonifying the company.[34] In other words, *before* these changes and throughout

> the seventeenth, eighteenth and early nineteenth centuries, shares in joint stock companies, incorporated and unincorporated, were consistently conceptualised as equitable interests in the assets of the company. Shareholders were regarded as owners in equity of the company's property

---

[30] One of the best accounts is Roy 1997.
[31] Ireland 1996; 1999; Ireland, Grigg-Spall and Kelly 1987.
[32] Ireland 1996, p. 53ff.
[33] Ireland 1999, p. 41.
[34] Ireland 1996, p. 60, Ireland, Grigg-Spall and Kelly 1987, p. 152.

and shares as an equitable right to an undivided part of the company's assets.³⁵

What this means is that *there was no distinction in law between companies and partnerships*.

> [T]he first English partnership law treatise, written in 1794 by William Watson, differentiated partnerships and companies on a purely economic basis. In the second edition of the book, published in 1807, the distinction was drawn with particular clarity. In England, Watson wrote, the 'first great division' was into 'public and private partnerships'. Public partnerships were 'usually called companies or societies' and 'generally consist[ed] of many members' carrying on 'some important undertaking for which the capital and exertions of a few individuals would be insufficient'. These companies were sometimes incorporated, sometimes not.... [J]oint stock companies 'not confirmed by public authority' were, legally speaking, mere partnerships, distinguishable only by the fact that 'the articles of agreement between [their members were] usually very different'. Other treatise writers followed Watson's classifications.³⁶

In short, partnerships remained the most common and dominant form of capitalist organisation down to the nineteenth century.³⁷ For example, the wealthy merchants who dominated the Glasgow tobacco trade in the eighteenth century – among the most successful capitalists of their time – came to form massive syndicates which basically consisted of interlocking partnerships. According to Devine, three such groups of interlocking partnerships handled over fifty per cent of the tobacco in the 1770s.³⁸ Scottish partnerships were exceptionally conducive to accumulation, since 'partners were only allowed 5 per cent interest on the value of their shares [and] the vast proportion of company earnings were ploughed back'.³⁹ '[T]he larger Glasgow firms were miniature prototypes of later private joint-stock organisations', notes

---

³⁵ Ireland 1996, p. 49.
³⁶ Ireland 1996, p. 44, citing Watson, *A Treatise of the Law of Partnership*, 2nd edition, 1807.
³⁷ For example, Angeli 1982, p. 107f., on the organisation of the business firms that controlled the silk industry.
³⁸ Devine 1975, p. 74.
³⁹ Devine 1975, p. 92.

Devine.[40] The same, of course, has been said about the colonial companies of the seventeenth century, and, before them, of the great Augsburg family firms of the sixteenth, which Strieder was so impressed by.[41]

All of these enterprises were owned and controlled by merchants. It was *merchant* capitalism which innovated the unlimited partnership and the whole spectrum of forms of association that flowed from it. The large Italian mercantile and banking houses of the thirteenth to fifteenth centuries were relatively permanent associations ('companies') with international operations, sophisticated systems of accounting and control, branch organisations, and the division of capital into shares.[42] The Bardi of Florence had overseas representatives at Avignon, Barcelona, Bruges, Cyprus, Constantinople, Jerusalem, London, Majorca, Marseilles, Nice, Paris, Rhodes, Seville and Tunis.[43] Although maritime trade was generally based on the single-venture agreements called *commenda/colleganza*, by the fourteenth century even Venetian large-scale trade was dominated by *compagnie*. One of these, floated by the Corner brothers, involved a capital of 83,275 ducats in 1365.[44] Federico Corner acquired the concession on massive sugarcane plantations in the south of Cyprus, with the aim of exporting refined sugar. His son Giovanni estimated some five to six thousand ducats would be needed annually to keep this business running.[45] By the fourteenth century, Venice was an economy *dominated* by capital, with the same families controlling trade, transport, finance, and industry.[46] More or less the same was true of Genoa in the fifteenth century. Here, the largest of the stock companies, an enterprise set up to extract and import alum from the East, controlled a capital of 280,000 ducats in 1449. Like the Corner enterprise in Cyprus, this one enjoyed a veritable monopoly.[47] Genoese companies [*societates*] divided their capital into 24 shares ('carats') or multiples thereof, and were run by a close-knit board of governors. More generally,

---

[40] Devine 1975, p. 79.
[41] The description 'great Augsburg (etc.)' is from Trevor-Roper 1967, p. 34.
[42] de Roover 1999, Hunt and Murray 1999, and the wide-ranging discussion of Italian merchant capitalism in Jones 1997, Chapter 3.
[43] Sapori 1952, p. xxxvi.
[44] Luzzatto 1961, p. 93.
[45] Luzzatto 1954, pp. 117–23.
[46] Luzzatto 1961, p. 72, referring to the 'supremazia che il capitale esercita a Venezia su tutte le attività economica...'
[47] Heers 1961, p. 201.

shares were transmissible within the lifetime of the company without breaking up the partnership. They were held not only by members of the families of the founders of a company, and by its principal employees, who were encouraged to put their own savings into their own company, but also by other rich men. These were investors not at all concerned with the actual running of the company. In addition to the *corpo*, that is, the capital raised by the shareholders when a company was formed or re-formed, additional capital could be put in later, by shareholders, by employees and by outsiders. Such *denari fuori del corpo* carried fixed rates of interest, like modern debentures. The sedentary merchant at home was no longer a simple individual capitalist....[48]

Thus, the evolution of the corporate form in the course of the thirteenth century signified an expansion in the scale of enterprise. Yet, throughout the thirteenth and early fourteenth centuries, the dominant form of association by far was the *commenda* or single-venture agreement in which an investor (the capitalist) advanced or entrusted capital to a second party, the merchant or factor, to be used in an overseas commercial venture and returned together with an agreed share of the profit, usually three-fourths.[49] Luzzatto notes that the capital was generally advanced in commodity form, that is, was commodity capital.[50] The *commenda* was the chief mechanism of the capitalist expansion of trade which began in the eleventh century, and the widespread recourse to it from that time presumes substantial liquidity, an accumulation of money-capital looking for investment. I shall argue that at least some of this was 'primitive' accumulation from the raids and plundering expeditions that were common across the Mediterranean in the later eleventh and twelfth centuries, against the background of the Crusades.[51] The *commenda* broadened the investor base and vastly expanded the scope of accumulation. It was thus typical of the more egalitarian and expansive maritime capitalism of the earliest period, when, as Cracco argues, substantial sectors of the population had a stake in the expansion of trade (indeed, trade expansion was Europe's only way out of the growing demographic impasse, Cracco claims)[52] and 'many merchants

---

[48] Spufford 1988, p. 253.
[49] Lopez and Raymond 1955, p. 174ff.
[50] Luzzatto 1961, p. 84.
[51] An argument first advanced by Lopez 1959.
[52] Cracco 1967, p. 16, n. 1.

were both investors and factors', that is, switched roles within the *commenda* contract.⁵³ The main part of the thirteenth century was characterised by a renewed stratification of capital, as the bigger merchants [*grossi mercanti*] preferred to form associations only between themselves and took decisive steps to regulate the competition of capitals in the Levant trade.⁵⁴

A final link: whether or not Lopez was right in saying, 'La *commenda* a une origine islamique et peut-être plus ancienne [the *commenda* has Islamic origins and may be even older]',⁵⁵ the fact is that 'the *commenda* constituted one of the most widespread tools of commercial activity' in the Islamic world.⁵⁶ Islamic commercial law and business practice knew both *commenda* agreements [*muḍāraba, qirāḍ*] and investment partnerships [*mufāwaḍa*], and, as Udovitch says, 'virtually *all* the features of partnership and *commenda* law are already found fully developed in the earliest Hanafite legal compendium, Shaybānī's *Kitāb al-Aṣl*, composed toward the end of the 8th century'.⁵⁷ Thus, the major institutions of long-distance trade were firmly in place, certainly well before the end of the eighth century. But even more interesting, is the implication that the capitalism of the Mediterranean was *preceded* by (and could *build on*) an earlier tradition of capitalist activity which has so far received considerably less attention.

9.4. The Arab trade-empire

Concepts of profit, capital, and the accumulation of capital are all found in the Arabic sources of the ninth to fourteenth centuries. For example, al-Shāfi'ī (d. 204/820) defines the function of partnership as the 'expansion of capital [*namā' al-māl*]'.⁵⁸ *Al-māl* was primarily capital not money, and whenever it is translated as 'money' it means capital in money-form or money-capital. Again, discussing the discretion allowed to agents under *commenda* agreements, al-Sarakhsī (d. 483/1090) writes, 'the investor's aim in handing over

---

⁵³ Krueger 1962, p. 42, about the twelfth century.
⁵⁴ Cracco 1967; Luzzatto 1954, pp. 73–9.
⁵⁵ Lopez 1970, p. 345.
⁵⁶ Udovitch 1970a, p. 49.
⁵⁷ Udovitch 1970a, pp. 41–2. Shaybānī died in 189/805.
⁵⁸ Udovitch 1970b, p. 81, 'augmentation of the capital investment'. (I am grateful to Avrom Udovitch and Mohamed El Mansour for discussing some of these texts with me.)

the capital to him [the agent] is the achievement of profit'.[59] In another passage where he defends the usefulness of such contracts, Sarakhsī says the contract is allowed

> Because people have a need for this contract. For the owner of capital [ṣāḥib al-māl] may not find his way to profitable trading activity [al-taṣarruf al-murbiḥ], and the person who can find his way to such activity may not have the capital. And profit cannot be attained except by means of both of these, capital and trading activity.[60]

A later writer Kāsānī (d. 1191) distinguishes the 'creation' of capital from its further expansion, arguing 'The need for the creation of capital [taḥṣīl aṣl al-māl] takes precedence over the need for its augmentation [ilā tanmiyyatihi]'[61] and defining partnerships as a 'method for augmenting or creating capital [ṭarīq namā' al-māl aw taḥṣīlihi]'.[62]

That this vocabulary was part of the wider cultural world of Islam and not confined to the legal schools is shown by other writings. Thus, the tenth-century geographer al-Iṣṭakhrī describes the traders of Fars in southern Persia as having a 'passion for the accumulation of capital [maḥabbat jam'a al-māl]'.[63] In the Kitāb al-ishāra ilā maḥāsin al-tijāra, 'Handbook on the Beauties of Commerce', a manual on trade probably written in the eleventh century, the author refers repeatedly to the capitalist as ṣāḥib al-māl (literally 'owner of capital').[64] It is clear from this manual that merchants involved in international trade normally relied on commenda agreements and that the muqāraḍ or factor usually received a share of the profit [ribḥ].[65] Finally, in Ibn Khaldūn (d. 1405), there is even a clear resonance of the labour theory of value (or a labour theory of value). In the Muqaddima, he states clearly that 'labor is the cause of profit [sabab al-kasb]'. '[H]uman labor is necessary for every profit and capital accumulation', while gold and silver are the only socially acceptable measures of value 'for all capital accumulations'.[66] He also defines profit [ribḥ]

---

[59] Udovitch 1970b, pp. 205–6.
[60] Udovitch 1970b, p. 175.
[61] Udovitch 1970b, p. 82.
[62] Udovitch 1970a, p. 55.
[63] Al-Iṣṭakhrī 1870, p. 138, repeated by Ibn Ḥauqal 1938, Volume 2, p. 290.
[64] Ritter 1917, for extracts in German.
[65] Ritter 1917, p. 58.
[66] Ibn Khaldūn 1958, Volume 2, pp. 280, 313.

as the 'extent by which capital increases' (or is increased), and commerce as the 'striving for profit by means of the expansion of capital [*muḥāwala ilā al-kasb bi-tanmiyyat al-māl*]'.[67]

The Arabs inherited the intensely urban and – by the seventh century – very largely monetised territories of late antiquity, Roman and Sasanian, and integrated them into a powerful and strikingly cosmopolitan civilisation whose economic resources and stability were unrivalled, except for those of China.[68] Whatever the initial impetus behind the conquests, there is little doubt that further expansion was to some degree motivated by financial and commercial considerations. Al-Balādhurī reports that the conquest of Sind in 711 brought the Arabs a *net* profit of 60 million dirhams by the reckoning the famous Umayyad governor al-Ḥajjāj (d. 95/714) is supposed to have made.[69] Sind was also commercially strategic, a major *entrepôt* in the Far-Eastern trade, which the Sasanians had traditionally dominated. The early eighth-century expansion to the East was like a pincer movement, driving northwards to the wealthy oases beyond Khurāsān and south to control of the Indian Ocean.[70] That the Arabs were seeking to dominate *existing* networks of trade, as the Portuguese would do centuries later, is proved by al-Ṭabarī's fascinating reference to 'ships from China' frequenting the harbour of al-Ubulla in 633, on the eve of the conquest of southern Iraq.[71] Trade with the Far East was conceivably the most lucrative sector of accumulation in the eighth to tenth centuries, generating the kind of wealth that was famously associated with Gulf ports like Baṣra and Sīrāf. In the West, the corresponding movement was Islam's commercial expansion across the Sahara, to the sources of gold in the western Sudan. This happened in the eighth century, when the Arabs broke the Berber monopoly of the trans-Saharan routes and sparked a long period of unbroken prosperity for the towns of Morocco. Ya'qūbī's geography, completed in 891, describes Fez as a 'splendid city and immensely

---

[67] Ibn Khaldūn 1958, Volume 2, p. 336. Cf. al-Fārābī 1961, § 72 (p. 153 Ar. = p. 53 Eng.), '[The virtuous man's anxiety about death is like] the anxiety of one who thinks that what he loses is not his capital but a gain which he was measuring and hoping for [*laisa ra's-mālihi bal ribḥ kāna yuqaddiruhu wa yarjūhu*]', playing on the distinction between 'capital [*ra's-māl*]' and 'profit [*ribḥ*]'.
[68] Lombard 1971, esp. pp. 7–17.
[69] Al-Balādhurī 1924, p. 223.
[70] See Maclean 1989, p. 67, referring to the 'two-pronged Arab expansion,' and p. 68, to an 'Arab trade empire'.
[71] Al-Ṭabarī 1881–2, p. 2384.

prosperous'.⁷² Sidjilmasa, according to Ibn Ḥauqal, who went there in 951, enjoyed 'uninterrupted trade with the Sudan' which brought in 'huge profits [arbāḥ mutawāffiratun]'.⁷³ At Awdaghost he saw a letter of credit [ṣakk], a private transaction, to the tune of 42,000 dinars, something he had never seen in the East. It is hardly surprising that the major dynasties that ruled this sector of North Africa in the eleventh to thirteenth centuries sprang from the Islamised Berber populations of southern Morocco, and that Tlemsen, Fez, and Āghmāt were described (by the Spanish geographer al-Idrīsī) as the wealthiest cities of the Maghreb.⁷⁴ Indeed, 'North Africa with its supply of gold...became the driving force of the entire Mediterranean' in the fourteenth and fifteenth centuries,⁷⁵ showing us how unconvincing it is to look at the growth of capitalism in Europe without the significant ways in which this powerful commercial background shaped its evolution. The Muslims created a vigorous monetary economy based on expanding levels of circulation of a stable high-value coinage (the dinar) and the renewed integration of monetary areas that had been distinct and indifferent to each other.⁷⁶ This was an enormous achievement, both for the kind of economy it allowed for (the sheer extent of the monetary sector) and for its role in enabling Europe to 'return' to gold.⁷⁷ However we characterise that economy, it was certainly not just some loose ensemble of feudal régimes. Trade was fundamental to its structure. The growth of cities and expanding urban markets, the diffusion of new crops⁷⁸ and *explosive* growth of cash-cropping (rice, flax, hemp, sugarcane, raw silk, indigo, cotton)⁷⁹ are all general indications of the remarkable commercial vitality of the eighth to eleventh centuries. We know little about the 'market systems' that sustained this huge expansion on the ground⁸⁰ but the tenth-century geographers refer repeatedly to substantial concentrations of capital in the port towns and numerous inland centres that acted as *entrepôts* or wholesale markets at the intersection of converging trade routes. Towns

---

⁷² Al-Jakûbî [Ya'ḳūbī] 1892, p. 358; al-Jakûbî [Ya'ḳūbī] 1937, p. 223.
⁷³ Ibn Ḥauḳal 1938–9, Volume 1, p. 99.
⁷⁴ Jaubert 1975, p. 27; al-Idrīsī 1866, p. 80.
⁷⁵ Braudel 1975, Volume 1, p. 467.
⁷⁶ The classic reference is Lombard 1947.
⁷⁷ Watson 1967.
⁷⁸ Watson 1983.
⁷⁹ See al-Muqaddasi 1994, with detailed descriptions of each locality.
⁸⁰ See Harriss-White 1996, Chapters 5–6 for the first proper discussion of how such systems work.

like Siraf, Nishapur and Narmasir[81] in Iran, Baikand near Bukhara,[82] Daybul in Sind, Mahdia (al-Mahdiyya) in the Sahel, and Cordoba, Almeria and Ceuta in the western Mediterranean were all consistently described in these terms by the geographers. For example, Ibn Ḥauqal's description of Nishapur refers to the huge market complexes called 'fonduks [Ar. *funduq*, Italian *fondaco*]' which were 'occupied by wealthy merchants specialising in a single branch of commerce, with huge quantities of commodities and large capitals [*ahlu al-baḍā'i' al-kibār wa'l-amwāl al-ghizār*]'.[83] The cloth merchants [*bazzāzīn*] were especially active here, as Nishapur was a manufacturing centre exporting silk and cotton fabrics as far away as Europe. Sīrāf with its densely packed multi-storied teak houses was a purely commercial site, the point of access to China, after 'Umān, in al-Muqaddasī's description. 'I have not seen in the realm of Islam more remarkable buildings or more handsome; they are built of teakwood and baked brick. They are towering houses, and a single house is bought for more than 100,000 dirhams'.[84] According to al-Iṣṭakhrī, the merchants of Siraf spent lavishly on their homes, over 30,000 dinars in some cases. 'In my time, one of them acquired assets worth 4,000,000 dinars, yet his clothes were scarcely distinguishable from those of a labourer [*ajīr*]'.[85] Daybul, too, on the barren coast of Sind just west of the Indus was consistently described as a 'place of merchants'.[86] Al-Muqaddasi, who visited Sind some time before 985, writes, 'Daybul is on the sea.... The water beats against the walls of the town. It has an entirely merchant population, speaking both Sindī and Arabic. It is the port of the area, giving rise to a considerable income'.[87] In the Medi-

---

[81] Al-Muqaddasī 1994, p. 407, referring to 'substantial merchants'; 'I heard some of them say that every year, between dates and costly Indian merchandise, about one hundred thousand [camel] loads are transported', p. 412.

[82] [Narshakhī] 1954, p. 18, 'The people of Baikand were all merchants. They traded with *Chīn* and the sea and became very wealthy'; also Ibn Khordādhbeh 1889, p. 19, who calls it *madīnat al-tujjār*.

[83] Ibn Ḥaukal 1938–9, Volume 2, p. 432; 1964, Volume 2, p. 418.

[84] Al-Muqaddasi 1994, p. 378.

[85] Al-Iṣṭakhrī 1870, pp. 127, 139; cf. Mordtmann 1845, p. 69ff. Oman may have been even wealthier, cf. the late tenth-century Persian geographer in Minorsky 1937, p. 148: 'Merchants are numerous in it. It is the emporium [*bārkadha*] of the whole world. There is no town in the world where the merchants are wealthier [*tuvangartar*] than here'.

[86] *The Chachnama, an Ancient History of Sind*, an early thirteenth-century Persian translation of a ninth-century Arabic narrative of the conquest of Sind, which says, 'The people of Debal [Daybul] were mostly merchants' (about the year 632); al-Iṣṭakhrī 1870, p. 35, *majma' al-tujjār*; Minorsky 1937, p.123, 'the abode [*jāygāh*] of the merchants'; Ibn Ḥaukal 1938–9, Volume 2, pp. 322–3; Ibn Ḥaukal 1964, Volume 2, p. 316.

[87] Al-Muqaddasi 1994, p. 420.

terranean, the late tenth-century Persian geographer of the *Ḥudūd al-'Ālam* described Cairo as the 'wealthiest city in the world, extremely prosperous'.[88] The records of the Cairo Geniza show that in that century and the following much of Cairo's commercial life was controlled by merchant-houses, like that of Ibn 'Awkal, working through a network of agents spread across the Mediterranean. Ibn 'Awkal's firm exported large quantities of flax to Mahdia in the Sahel.[89] This was both a flourishing international port and a textile centre, and, in the twelfth century, al-Idrīsī refers to its 'wealthy and generous-minded merchants'.[90] Even further west, Almeria with its 'bustling shipyards, vessels, and silklooms'[91] was described by al-Idrīsī as unmatched, in Spain at least, for the 'wealth, industriousness and commercial inclinations of its people', and said to include 970 hostels for merchants from all parts of the world.[92]

Finally, *scales* of business: these were huge. Ships which entered the Gulf ports laden with goods from China could contain cargoes worth 500,000 dinars![93] Ibn Ḥauqal notes that Kābul was a major wholesale market for indigo, and tells us,

> The indigo that is sold every year from what is produced in the town and the surrounding countryside amounts to *over 2 million dinars*, according to what their merchants report [*'alā mā yadhkuruhu tujjāruhum*], not including the stocks left with the traders at the end of the year.[94]

Again, in the second half of the eleventh century, Alexandria was exporting well over 5,000–6,000 tons of raw flax to markets in the Mediterranean.[95]

Thus, Islam made a *powerful contribution to the growth of capitalism in the Mediterranean*, in part because it preserved and expanded the monetary economy of late antiquity and innovated business techniques that became the staple of Mediterranean commerce (in particular, partnerships and *commenda* agreements), and also because the seaports of the Muslim world became a rich

---

[88] Minorsky 1937, p. 151.
[89] See Stillman 1973, p. 28ff., and now Gil 2004.
[90] Jaubert 1975, p. 257 (port), 259 (merchants); al-Idrīsī 1866, p. 107, 109, *tijār mayāsīr nubalā'*.
[91] Braudel 1975, Volume 1, p. 118.
[92] Jaubert 1975, Volume 2, p. 44.
[93] Stern 1967, p. 10, citing the anonymous twelfth-century abridger of Ibn Ḥauqal.
[94] Ibn Ḥauqal 1964, Volume 2, p. 436; 1938–9, Volume 2, p. 450; note the fascinating reference to the testimony of the merchants themselves!
[95] Udovitch 1999, p. 270f.

source of the plundered money-capital which largely financed the growth of maritime capitalism in Europe. Indeed, Mandel stated this with unabashed bluntness when he wrote: 'The accumulation of money capital by the Italian merchants who dominated European economic life from the eleventh to the fifteenth centuries originated directly from the Crusades, an enormous plundering enterprise if ever there was one'.[96]

9.5. From Genoa to Portugal

The 'Fourth' Crusade (1204) secured Venetian dominance over the East Mediterranean[97] and consolidated the hold of the purely capitalist element in the ruling oligarchy.[98] In the case of Genoa, it was Lopez who argued that the ability of a largely agrarian élite to finance trade expansion and set off a chain reaction of rapid accumulation through trade and shipbuilding derived, *in the first instance*, from the huge quantities of cash acquired by the Genoese in Crusading expeditions and raids on the Spanish and North African coasts.[99] It was the war with the 'Arabs' that gave Genoese enterprise its first decisive push. Thus Portuguese expansion *started* on a classically Mediterranean model, even if its consequences were destined to end the centrality of the Mediterranean (and 'Antiquity') forever. To begin with, there was a long and peculiarly Mediterranean background to the Portuguese assault on Ceuta (1415). In 1087, the Genoese led a massive raid on Mahdia, seized the commercial quarter, and extracted the huge sum of 100,000 dinars.[100] Caesarea in Palestine was sacked in 1101 and 15 per cent of the vast booty reserved for Genoa's captains and offcers.[101] In 1148, Sfax and other Sahel ports were seized by the Normans.[102] In 1234, the Genoese laid siege to Ceuta, demanding vast sums in reparation for losses sustained in the harbour, and in 1260 the Castilians attacked Salé on the Atlantic coast. Clearly, by the twelfth century, the Christians had recovered control of the seas, indeed one aim of these expeditions was to secure dominance of the sea, but linked to that and driving

---

[96] Mandel 1968, Volume 1, p. 103.
[97] Luzzatto 1961, p. 29; Cracco 1967, pp. 56–7.
[98] Cracco 1967, p. 58.
[99] Lopez 1959, especially pp. 304–7.
[100] Ibn Khaldoun 1969, Volume 2, p. 24.
[101] Bautier 1971, p. 100.
[102] Jaubert 1975, p. 257.

many of these attacks were the commercial interests at stake, above all the drive to gain access to the 'gold of Ghana'. The shortage of gold affected the European economies in waves all the way down to the mid-fifteenth century. By the last quarter of the twelfth century, the Genoese were heavily involved in northwest Africa, dominating the region's external trade and directing the third largest share of their investments to the Moroccan port of Salé in a carefully concealed bid to open an Atlantic gold route.[103] As Watson notes, it was probably 'this African gold reaching the shores of Italy which allowed Genoa to issue her precious gold coins at the end of the twelfth century or the beginning of the thirteenth'.[104] From the 1250s on, 'the gold which flowed into Europe from the ports of North Africa and Spain *largely remained in Europe*'.[105] In the following decades and centuries, Genoese commercial exploration of the Atlantic expanded hugely, with major spin-offs for the problem of long-distance shipping.[106] By the late thirteenth and fourteenth centuries, Genoa was receiving 'enormous quantities of gold', and during the whole of the fifteenth century 'the "gold of Ghana" still reached Italy *mainly* through the port of Genoa'.[107]

Thus Genoa *prefigures* Portugal in interesting ways; indeed, it was Portugal that put a halt to Genoese expansion in Morocco in a veritable struggle for control of the gold routes.[108] The capture of Ceuta was a calculated move to subvert the entire balance of power in the Straits of Gibraltar, undermining the competition of the main Iberian powers (Aragon and Castile) as well as the Genoese,[109] without the clear perception at this stage of an 'Atlantic' strategy. The 'calculated imperialism' of the Portuguese monarchy which crystallised with Dom João II (1481–95) and his successor Dom Manuel was more a result than a cause of decades of exploration which were largely driven by private and commercial interests, such as those of the big Lisbon merchant Fernão Gomes or the Lagos merchants who organised the earlier expedition to the

---

[103] See Lopez 1936, especially p. 34ff.
[104] Watson 1967, p. 14.
[105] Ibid., my emphasis.
[106] Lopez 1936, p. 48.
[107] Watson 1967, p. 16, 19, also Heers 1961, pp. 67–8, 477–9.
[108] Heers 1961, p. 480f., adding the importance to Portugal of Morocco's grain markets.
[109] This is argued by Unali 2000, p. 209ff.

Rio Grande[110] and, of course, the private interests of the Infante Dom Henrique, who carved out a substantial maritime estate in the Azores, a strictly commercial enterprise, in the 1440s.[111]

9.6. Company-capitalism and the advance system

Portuguese maritime expansion *transformed* the nature of commercial capitalism, subsuming the legacies of the Mediterranean in a coherent imperial project of the expansion of capital as the 'basis of a nation's power and predominance in modern society'.[112] It was the Dutch and English Companies that embodied the new kind of (commercial) capitalism in its pure forms, but the *Estado da India* was not fundamentally different (*pace* Steensgaard), and Portuguese enterprise was clearly the frontrunner in this field. On the other hand, it was the Dutch company that embodied the logic of accumulation in it purest form, for only here, in the early seventeenth century, was there a conscious attempt to build a 'permanent circulating capital', that is, generate suffcient reserves for further expansion of the business.[113] By 'permanent circulating capital' Coen meant the permanent and expanded circulation of capital mainly in the form of commodities extracted from one end of Asia to the other and circulating *between* the different Asian markets where the VOC had factories.[114] He had visualised this quasi-multilateral trading system as based formally on barter, as a great deal of international commerce was at the time,[115] but, in reality, the Dutch required vast quantities of precious metals to

---

[110] Dias 1963, p. 168.

[111] The best analysis of the evolution of Portuguese policy is Thomaz 1989, arguing that the Atlantic strategy emerged with considerable hesitation. Note Zurara's comment in the *Crónica da Guiné*, 'merchants only sail to places where they know the profit is sure', cited Thomaz, p. 223.

[112] Marx 1981, p. 921, 'The national character of the Mercantile System is therefore not a mere slogan in the mouths of its spokesmen. Under the pretext of being concerned only with the wealth of the nation and the sources of assistance for the state, they actually declare that the interests of the capitalist class, and enrichment in general, are the final purpose of the state.... At the same time, however, they show their awareness that the development of the interests of capital and the capitalist class, of capitalist production, has become the basis of a nation's power and predominance in modern society' – a remarkable characterisation of mercantilism.

[113] Steensgaard 1974, pp. 136–41, arguing that the English, by contrast, were interested in 'quick returns'.

[114] Steensgaard 1974, p. 406.

[115] For example, Davis 1967.

sustain the Europe-Asia trade.¹¹⁶ By the late seventeenth century, they dominated the trade in Spanish silver, so that Amsterdam was the world's leading centre in the trade in precious metals.¹¹⁷

Now, given that the age of Company-capitalism (sixteenth to eighteenth centuries) was one of ferocious commercial rivalries and repeated recourse to violence and the annexation of territories, it seems unreal to suppose that the self-expansion of commercial capital was simply grounded in some simplistic formula like 'buying cheap and selling dear'. *The stronger the competition of commercial capitals, the greater is the compulsion on individual capitals to seek some measure of control over production.* Marx was clearly aware of this when he referred to the 'colonial system' and the VOC in particular as a 'striking example' of the 'manner and form in which commercial capital operates where it *dominates production directly*'.¹¹⁸ Here, the abstract antithesis between circulation and production is abandoned in a realisation that mercantile companies might be involved in production in ways that contradict the concept of merchant capital as a mere mediation between extremes. But, of course, today it is not suffcient to limit ourselves to a general characterisation of this kind, we need a more precise morphology of the possible ways in which 'merchant entrepreneurs'¹¹⁹ have sought control over production or organised the production of capital, that is, of the forms in which circulation has dominated production. Here, it is crucial not to confuse scale with centralisation. 'Scale' refers to the volume of capital deployed by the individual capitalist, not the degree of dispersal or centralisation of the labour force.¹²⁰ The mercantile houses which dominated the trade of colonial India in the late eighteenth and nineteenth centuries were relatively large units of capital, but typically the mass of labour-power which they exploited was hugely dispersed. The 'advance system' was the crucial mechanism which allowed this paradoxical and seemingly fragile combination of large-scale enterprise and dispersed

---

¹¹⁶ Om Prakash 1985.
¹¹⁷ Van Dillen 1923.
¹¹⁸ Marx 1981, pp. 446–7.
¹¹⁹ Mandel 1968, Volume 1, p. 112.
¹²⁰ The distinction derives from Sombart 1891, the best discussion of 'domestic industry' akin to Marx's own understanding (e.g. Marx 1976, Volume 1, pp. 462–3; Marx 1978, pp. 318–19).

labour-power, and Bengal in particular provides us with some fine research on how it worked for commodities like indigo[121] and cotton piece-goods.[122]

Thus the 'circulating capital' visualised by J.P. Coen as the basis of the Dutch commercial capitalist system would to a certain if not very large extent have involved the circulation (investment) of capital in the form of advances. Van Santen has shown this for Dutch exports of indigo from northern India in the 1620s and 1630s, when, according to an English estimate, the VOC had 100,000–150,000 rupees invested each year in the variety known as Bayana indigo, that is, in the advances [*voorschotten*] themselves.[123] It was through a system of advances that commercial capital controlled almost every commodity within Europe or outside in which it had substantial business interests. The chief exceptions to this pattern were those enterprises, relatively centralised, where merchants integrated vertically through direct ownership of fixed assets, as happened in the Cuban sugar mills in the mid-nineteenth century.

Our intellectual prejudice against commercial capitalism is so deeply rooted that whole swathes of the history of capitalism are ignored by Marxists, with the result that there *is* no specifically Marxist historiography of capitalism. This must surely count as one of the strangest intellectual paradoxes of all time, but it was not one that Mandel contributed to. *Marxist Economic Theory* is one of those rare texts that attempts to integrate history in an understanding of Marx's economic theory. Mandel was thoroughly familiar with some of the best work in medieval and early-modern economic history, citing a very wide range of sources including writers like Armando Sapori, Robert Lopez, and Raymond de Roover. His chapter on the development of capital is one of our best short histories of early capitalism and assigned a major role to the 'expansion of trade from the eleventh century onward'. Certainly, Mandel did not subscribe to the schematic contrast between 'exchange' and 'production' that so fascinated Dobb, and because he was too well-read in European history he refused to minimise the role of commercial capitalism. That much of this history was seen as a 'primitive accumulation' of capital stems, of course, from the almost universal orthodoxy that writes the history of capitalism as a genealogy of industrial capital. That this is not necessarily the best perspective to

---

[121] See Chowdhury 1964.
[122] Hossain 1988.
[123] Van Santen 1982, Chapter 4.

adopt is suggested by the history of industry itself. Thus *traders* dominated the English coal industry in the seventeenth century, one of the most heavily capitalised sectors of the British economy in that period.[124] They invented the 'factory-system' by concentrating labour in the large silk mills of northern Italy in the same century. That was itself only possible because of technological changes in silk spinning and the more advanced technology of the Bologna silk mills.[125] They controlled the very advanced forms of enterprise found in South-German mining in the sixteenth century,[126] and were responsible for the 'dramatic technological revolutions' that sparked the Central-European mining boom of the fifteenth century.[127] Finally, they floated agricultural holding companies in Cuba in the mid-nineteenth century and moved actively into the production of sugar through the rapid accumulation of mills, plantations and labour forces at a time when international competition made technological advances imperative.[128]

9.7. Concluding note: merchant-capitalism and labour

In short, the contrast between capitalism as a 'commercial system' and capitalism as a 'mode of production' is schematic and overstated, and a major reason why Marxists have paid so little attention to merchant-capital. In the more developed forms of commercial capitalism, circulation dominates production in the sense that production is controlled by a class of capitalists who *remain* merchants and cannot properly be classified as 'industrialists'. The subsumption of labour into merchant-capital is thus irreducible to any single formula, even though Marx tended to associate it primarily with the 'stage' of manufacture. Merchant-capitalists controlled a variety of enterprises from putting-out networks and peasant agriculture to slave plantations and factories in the modern sense. The North-Italian silk mills of the seventeenth century were among the earliest embodiments of the factory-system, based on fourteen-hour shifts and a tight regulation of labour.[129] On the plantations, the rapid

---

[124] Neff 1929, p. 422ff.
[125] Poni 1976, esp. pp. 467–71 on the leadership of the *grandi mercanti*.
[126] Strieder 1914; Braudel 2002, pp. 321–5.
[127] Munro 1998, pp. 35–50, underlining the role of the 'German merchant-financiers'.
[128] Bergad 1990, esp. pp. 132ff., 170ff.
[129] Poni 1976, pp. 483ff.

depreciation of slave-labour-forces ensured that resident planters piled up mountains of debt, financed, again, by merchants.¹³⁰ As Braudel said about the Brazilian sugar-plantations, 'It was European trade that commanded production and output overseas'.¹³¹ If we understand this literally, it means that the subsumption of slave-labour into capital involved both merchants and planters. Merchant-capital *shared* in the economic exploitation of slaves through 'merchant economic control over the planters', for example, through the *refacción* contracts which financed the Cuban sugar industry of the second quarter of the nineteenth century, before the spate of acquisitions which put the Havana merchant houses in more direct control.¹³² The 'articulated' nature of merchant-capitalism is even more evident in the forms in which it typically established control over the labour of artisans and small peasants. Under Company-capitalism, the circuit of merchant capital acquired its moment of reality when the money-capital financing the 'investment' (the annual list of orders sent out by the company's directors) circulated in the form of *advances*. Since these were usually disbursed by the company's commercial agents through local capitalists (merchants or, less often, commission-agents),¹³³ the organisation of production acquired the appearance of a chain, a hierarchy of capitals connecting a dispersed mass of labour-power to the company across a series of 'intermediate agents'.¹³⁴ When the free merchants (i.e. European private traders) intruded into this system, they operated on exactly the same basis, merely intensifying competition and the drive to enforce tighter control on the 'producers'.¹³⁵

Analysing the relationship between merchants and weavers in a system roughly comparable to this, Marx wrote that this method of exploitation 'simply worsens the conditions of the direct producers, transforms them into mere wage-labourers and proletarians under worse conditions than those directly subsumed by capital'.¹³⁶ In other words, he saw merchant-capitalism trans-

---

¹³⁰ Pares 1960, pp. 38–40.
¹³¹ Braudel 2002, p. 273, about the export merchants of Lisbon.
¹³² Bergad 1990, pp. 65–6.
¹³³ Om Prakash 1985, p. 102f., describing the Dutch procurement of textiles in Bengal.
¹³⁴ Marx 1978, p. 319.
¹³⁵ For the methods used to bind Bengal weavers to their contracts, see Mitra 1978, pp. 66ff, 78ff.
¹³⁶ Marx 1981, p. 453, about the French silk industry, etc.; it is possible that Marx was less convinced by his earlier suggestion (in the 'Appendix', Marx 1976, p. 1023)

forming whole swathes of rural workers[137] into *wage-labourers*. So, too, in the *Grundrisse*, where he wrote,

> The way in which money transforms itself into capital often shows itself quite tangibly in history; e.g. when the merchant induces a number of weavers and spinners, who until then wove and spun as a rural, secondary occupation, to work for him...but then has them in his power and has brought them under his command as wage labourers.[138]

In short, the *dispersal* of production was no indication that these forms of domestic industry were not part of a network of *capitalist* enterprises.[139] For Marx, the crucial mechanism in the subsumption of labour was the merchant's ability to undermine the independence of small producers by restricting them 'little by little to one kind of work in which they become dependent on selling, on the *buyer*, the *merchant*, and ultimately produce only *for* and *through* him'.[140] For Sombart, this was possible because the key 'production factor' which merchants controlled was not so much the means of production as the market.[141] The attractive feature of this conception is that it yields a model applicable to both the *Verlagssytem* and peasant agriculture. The *Verlagssystem* was the dominant organisational form of early capitalism,[142] and characterised by an almost exclusive predominance of circulating capital, severe competition between capitalists, domestically dispersed labour, and the sustained use of piece-rates. It was almost certainly as widespread in the Islamic world as it became in Europe.[143]

Referring to the 'well-known form of advance-payment', Marx seemed to define the standard case as one where, in the transaction M-C, 'money

---

that merchant domination of production was still not tantamount to the formal subsumption of labour under capital.

[137] Marx 1978, pp. 318–19, about the merchant-controlled cottage industries of Russia.
[138] Marx 1973, p. 510.
[139] See Braudel 2002, p. 316ff.
[140] Marx 1973, p. 510; Marx's emphasis.
[141] Sombart 1891, p. 117.
[142] Cf. the title of Fridolin Furger's study, *Zum Verlagssytem als Organisationsform des Frühkapitalismus im Textilgewerbe* – Furger 1927.
[143] Note al-Dimashqī's term for the export merchant, the third of his three kinds of merchants, viz. *mujahhiz*, 'supplier of equipment' (noted by Rodinson 1970, p. 25) and his reference to advance payments [*salaf muʿajjal*, lit. 'prepaid advance'] as one of the three main forms of contract used by merchants, cf. Ritter 1917, p. 58.

functions only in the familiar form of means of purchase', adding, 'Of course capital, too, is advanced in the form of money and it is possible that the money advanced is capital advanced'.[144] I have argued that, under commercial capitalism, advances were the major form in which capital circulated, and that the transactions between merchants and artisans, etc. surpassed the scope of simple circulation. The dynamic at work was one that Marx himself outlined in the *Grundrisse*:

> He [the merchant] bought their labour originally only by buying their product; as soon as they restrict themselves to the production of this exchange value and thus must directly produce *exchange values*, must exchange their labour entirely for money in order to survive, then they come under his command, and at the end even the illusion that they *sold* him products disappears.[145]

By analysing the advance system as a circulation of capital, we can extend this to the way in which capital took hold of agriculture. Take India for example. If we exclude the more substantial sections of the peasantry and the purely proletarianised strata, such as the sharecroppers of Sind or the lower tenantry of the United Provinces, much of the remaining agricultural population conforms to this model of a class subject to capitalist domination by a *multitude* of commercial interests, from the export houses and large wholesalers [*mahajans*] to the primary merchants and local moneylenders.

[2007]

---

[144] Marx 1970, p. 140 and note; cf. Marx 1971, p. 188, '[profit] is called *interest* when, for example, as in India, the worker (although nominally independent) works with advances he receives from the capitalist and has to hand over all the surplus produce to the capitalist'; so too in Marx 1976, p. 1023, 'The exorbitant interest which it [the capital of the usurer]...extorts from the primary producer is just another name for surplus-value', also about India.

[145] Marx 1973, p. 510; Marx's emphasis.

Chapter Ten
Capitalist Domination and the Small Peasantry: The Deccan Districts in the Late Nineteenth Century

10.1. The 'subordination of labour to capital'

There is a widespread notion that the Indian countryside is still to a large extent dominated by 'pre-capitalist' relationships of a 'semi-feudal' variety. What is this 'semi-feudalism' supposed to consist of? According to one of the clearest exponents of this tendency, A. Bhaduri, its basic features are: '(1) An extensive non-legalised sharecropping system, (2) perpetual indebtedness of the small tenants; (3) [rural exploiters] operating both as landowners and lenders to the small tenants; (4)... tenants having incomplete access to the market'.[1] Bhaduri describes a system of production in which the power of money is clearly of fundamental importance: the small producer who may, for example, be a sharecropper, is 'indebted' to his landlord, who extorts surplus-labour from him on the basis of a relationship that is fundamentally one of economic dependence. The 'consumption loans', through which the small producer is bound to his landlord-moneylender, form advances for the reproduction of his labour-power. The small producer bears no direct relationship

---
[1] Bhaduri 1973.

to the market, because his landlord-moneylender intervenes in the process of production to realise the surplus-labour extorted from him on the market. Why is this system 'semi-feudal'? Because, obviously, Bhaduri starts with a conception of capitalist relations of production in which none of those features would be compatible with these relations. For example, 'sharecropping' would not be compatible with capitalist production, no more than 'moneylending', 'bondage', etc. The same basic assumption underlies Utsa Patnaik's more recent arguments. She refers to '*feudal-type* exploitation such as leasing-out, usury, etc.'. Here again, the prevalent notion is that the specific institutional forms of production-relations, e.g., sharecropping, are in some sense integral to the definition of such relations.

Patnaik, however, bases her positions on a more specific idea, common to many Marxists.

> Certain persons with no direct control over land, such as traders and moneylenders, can nevertheless acquire a claim on a part of the peasant's surplus-labour and appropriate it *in the form of trading profit and interest, respectively*. The reason that the trader and moneylender do not figure in our chart is because they represent *essentially capital in the circulation process*, and not in the production process.[2]

The two major categories here are 'trading profit' (or 'interest') and 'capital in the circulation process'. Obviously, Patnaik wants to argue that the surplus-labour extorted by these 'traders and moneylenders' does not take the form of surplus-value, but represents rather 'mercantile profit' or 'interest', depending on the case.

But what is 'mercantile profit'? (a) In the sense of *commercial profit*, it would represent a redistribution from the mass of social surplus-value. That is, it would presuppose the prevalence of the bourgeois mode of production in its developed form, under which merchant's capital and commercial capital represent only functionally-specialised forms of that portion of the total social capital which is 'in circulation'. Each individual (industrial) capital assumes, within its total life-cycle, the form of 'capital of circulation', in the

---

[2] Patnaik 1976, emphasis mine. I have isolated Bhaduri and Patnaik for criticism in this paper only because their respective essays are among the most sophisticated expressions of the positions that either deny the development of capitalism completely or date this development basically to the last thirty years.

specific shapes of commodity-capital and money-capital. Commercial capital is then only a 'transmuted form' of commodity-capital, i.e., ultimately a function of the circulation-process of industrial capital. From the point of view of industrial capital, 'mercantile' or 'commercial profits' represent costs of circulation. Insofar as mercantilist illusions ascribed the value-creating property (of industrial capital) to merchant's capital, it was necessary for Marx to stress their 'distinction of form' or economic specificity.[3] If 'trading profit' were meant by Patnaik in this specific sense (i.e., what Marx calls 'commercial profit'), then she would have to assume the prevalence of the capitalist mode of production already in those periods of India's development when 'traders and moneylenders' played a decisive role in town and countryside. But this is not an assumption that Patnaik would want to make, obviously.

(b) In the sense of purely 'mercantile profit', i.e., representing stages of social economy in which merchant's capital functions as mediator in the exchange of commodities between separate enterprises, regardless of their social character, 'trading profit' would presuppose the prevalence of these other modes of production, and it would itself 'largely originate' from 'outbargaining and cheating', and from the ability to exploit long-term price-differentials.[4] In this case, 'capital in the circulation process' would be merely a vulgar and misleading way of referring to merchant's capital in its precapitalist forms and functions, and here the basic assumption would have to be that the peasants whose surplus-labour these traders and moneylenders extorted were, in fact, autonomous simple commodity-producers.

This essay attempts to show why a dilemma of this sort represents only a choice between the devil and the deep blue sea. It attempts to argue that the positions of Bhaduri and Patnaik, and many others of a similar tendency, rest on an erroneous conception of 'intervention in the process of production', on a failure to explore and understand properly Marx's views of the relationships in question and, finally, on a failure to analyse concretely the system of production that actually prevailed in various parts of the country as early as the nineteenth century. The nucleus of this essay consists, therefore, of

---

[3] Marx established the determinateness of form of 'commercial capital' mainly in *Capital*, Volume III, pt. IV.
[4] Marx 1971a, Volume 3, p. 330. This can be the only source of mercantile profits, for the premise of its operation in the precapitalist epoch is the domination of modes of production other than capital.

precisely one such analysis – of the disintegrating small-production economy of the Deccan in the period shortly before and after the cotton boom (the 1860s). Let me begin, however, with Marx's fundamentally important remarks on the two forms of 'subsumption of labour into capital', because these will figure centrally in the analysis later.

These remarks are contained in a hitherto unpublished 'Appendix', intended to form part of Volume One of *Capital*. Here, Marx distinguishes two basic stages in the historic process of the subordination of the small producer to capital, that is, in the long-term evolution of the bourgeois mode of production. The first of these he calls the '*formal* subsumption of labour into capital', the second 'the *real* subsumption of labour into capital'. Both forms imply capitalist relations of exploitation, i.e., the category of 'surplus-value'. That is, both forms imply the extortion of surplus-labour *as surplus-value*. However, the *formal* subordination of labour to capital presupposes a process of labour that is 'technologically' continuous with earlier modes of labour. It is the form that crystallises when capital confronts the small producer, invades his process of production and 'takes it over' without subjecting it to technical transformation.[5] These relations – of the formal subsumption of labour into capital – may thus develop *outside* the framework of a specifically capitalist mode of production. They do not presuppose the bourgeois mode of production in its advanced or developed form, under which labour is subordinated to capital no longer merely 'formally', but 'really'. This 'real' subsumption-process entails a suspension of all inherited or existing labour-processes, alien to the pure motion of capital itself. It presupposes the production of capital in the form of *relative surplus-value*, hence a process of *labour* that is *specifically capitalist*.

The formal subsumption of labour into capital implies that, while the labour-process remains continuous with earlier modes of labour, 'the process of production has become the process of capital itself', i.e., of the self-expansion of value, of the conversion of money into capital. This in turn implies that capital is here 'the immediate owner of the process of production' and

---

[5] Marx 1976 (in the new translation by Ben Fowkes, which is a vast improvement on the Moscow version), pp. 1019–38, from the 'Appendix: Results of the Immediate Process of Production', and covering the two modes of subordination of labour.

that the immediate producer is merely 'a factor in the production process and dependent on the capitalist directing it'.[6]

The formal subsumption of labour into capital was, for Marx, the *general* form of every capitalist process of production in so far as it implied (1) the extortion of surplus-labour in the form of surplus-value, and (2) the intervention of capital as the 'immediate owner' of the production-process. This general form, however, is not the developed or adequate form of the process of capitalist production, because the labour-process remains external to the movement of capital, and therefore the individual capitals are not bound together by any objective social interconnection. The labour-process remains technically fragmented, or decentralised, whereas the pure movement of capital posits a centralisation of the social means of production and labour-power. In its developed form, the capitalist mode of production presupposes not simply the compulsion to perform surplus-labour, hence not merely the category of 'surplus-value', but the constitution of the forces of labour as social forces, or the shedding by capital of its 'individual character'.[7] In a system based on the formal subordination of labour, capital retains its small-scale individual character, or it is embodied mainly by 'small capitalists who differ only slightly from the workers in their education and their activities'.[8]

It is obvious that Marx's distinction of the two forms of surplus-value – relative and absolute – corresponds exactly to the distinction between the real and the formal subordination of labour to capital. In the latter, based on absolute surplus-value, increases in the rate of exploitation of labour-power can only be a function of those mechanisms that produce *absolute* surplus-value: mainly, of course, a lengthening of the working-day, or a greater intensification of labour.

Before proceeding further, it is important to investigate this form more closely. The first characteristic of such a system – i.e., the extortion of surplus-labour as surplus-value, is *not* sufficient to constitute this type of subordination. Thus, a monied capitalist (for example, a merchant, moneylender) may dominate the small producer on a *capitalist* basis, he may, in other words, extort surplus-value from him, without standing out as the 'immediate owner

---

[6] Marx 1976, pp. 1020, 1023.
[7] Marx 1976, p. 1035.
[8] Marx 1976, p. 1027.

of the process of production'. In this case, his domination will be based on control of *only portions* of the means of subsistence and production of the small producer. For example, he may advance to him his raw materials or tools without exerting any specific control over, or pressure on, the small enterprise. Clearly, such a system, a 'preformal' subordination of labour to capital, would tend to lead in the vast majority of cases to the system of formal subordination – i.e., over time, the monied capitalist would gain control over the entire means of subsistence and production of this enterprise, so that reproduction of its process of production from one cycle to the next would now come to depend entirely on the 'advances' he makes. This is the initial and rudimentary sense in which his *intervention* in the process of production would be established.

A very important conclusion follows from all this: there might be historical situations where *in the absence of a specifically capitalist mode of production on the national scale, capitalist relations of exploitation may nonetheless be widespread and dominant*. Such relations would then take either of two forms – (a) In a 'preformal' sense, the small producer retaining control to one extent or another over his means of subsistence, would nevertheless be subjected to exploitation by capital, in so far as the monied capitalist, e.g., the usurer 'advances raw materials or tools or even both to the immediate producer' and extorts surplus-value in the form of 'interest'; (b) in the formal sense that the small producer, completely expropriated, is nonetheless retained in his former process of production and subjected to exploitation by capital on a more continuous or intense basis, i.e., with capital disposing of the power to reconstitute the process of production from one cycle to the next. There are passages in which Marx assimilated cases of type (a) to type (b), that is, did not regard the distinction as particularly important.[9]

---

[9] The contrast is drawn by Marx in the Appendix, in Marx 1976, p. 1c23 (with reference to India). It is completely disregarded by him in Marx 1971b, which I shall quote later.

10.2. Commodity-expansion in the Deccan districts, 1850–90[10]

Even before the chronological divide separating the two halves of the nineteenth century, the weight of commodity-economy in the life of the Deccan peasantry had made itself felt in a peculiarly retrograde form. Is a good year always 'good'?[11] The prolonged and severe depression that hit the small-production economy of the Deccan districts on the decline of Peshwa power leaves no doubt on this score. It is true that, in the central area of the Deccan, in a district like Ahmednagar, for example, one out of every two years in that twenty-seven year period (1821–47) was a year of poor harvests or famines. But there were some unusually fine harvests in this period and they were all disastrous. The lack of any easy means of transporting grain meant that, in these years when harvests were good, local markets were glutted and prices fell ruinously low. With rates of assessment worked out in relation to earlier price-conjunctures, every long-term decline in the level of prices, such as set in around 1822, or every abrupt and sharp fall in the level, such as occurred periodically in 'good' years, would only intensify the degree of exploitation of the peasantry by the state. By the mid 1830s, at the height of this depression, the original rates of assessment had thus automatically 'doubled' according to a district collector who witnessed 'serious and widespread suffering' in Ahmednagar.[12] The alternation of good and bad years thus formed a series of bad years, a prolonged depression or a crisis that the Deccan would emerge from only much later. This was a period in which large tracts of arable land lay waste or uncultivated, villages were deserted, and the smaller towns fell into decay.

---

[10] Abbreviations used in this essay:
BGR: Selections from the Bombay Government Records, New Series (containing mainly papers relating to the assessment and revision of assessment of various *talukas*).
DRC: Deccan Riots Commission (which published its report on the riots of 1875 in five volumes, including one quite superb statistical appendix).
GBP: *Gazetteers of the Bombay Presidency* (only the detailed early series published in the 1880s has been used).
RD: Revenue Department (containing, in manuscript-form, reports submitted by the Assistant Collectors to their Collectors, and by them to the Revenue Commissioners).
[11] For a brief discussion of the nature of crises within a small-production economy, and of the impact of good and bad years on peasant welfare, see Abel 1973.
[12] GBP, Volume XVII, *Ahmednagar*, Bombay 1884, p. 467.

It was in the early 1850s that this crisis began to pass. The declining or stagnant curves of cultivated area break and ascend swiftly around this point. With the introduction of the 'Survey Settlement', a systematic overhauling of the interim revenue-system began in the Deccan. The new layers of the bureaucracy who argued out these revisions on paper – proponents of a system of peasant-capitalism that had yet to emerge – established more precise criteria of 'classifications' in the revenue-scale, separating out the different components of differential rent, in an effort to reallocate the burden of revenue demand.

One of these officials, George Wingate, dated the 'turning of the tide' to 1852–3. Ten years removed from that date, on the eve of the cotton-boom, he was writing, 'in all parts suitable for the production of exportable products', i.e., commodities, 'such as the Southern Maratha Country and Khandesh, these are promptly raised to meet the wants of the market, as shown by the rapid growth of the export trade of Bombay. The peasantry are becoming comparatively wealthy, independent, and enterprising'. But Khandesh was the only district in the Deccan to become structurally integrated into the cotton-economy that dominated the districts further east, outside the limits of the Presidency, in Berar. What about the districts further south, where the staple foodgrains (*jowar, bajra, nachni*) dominated the cropping patterns? Wingate replied:

> It has been, without due consideration, remarked of other parts of the country, and more especially of the collectorates of Poona, Ahmednagar, Sholapur and Satara, that the cultivators there continue the old round of grain crops, and do not turn their attention to the raising of valuable products suited for export. The observation, however, is most unjust to them, for, with the great populations of Bombay and Poona to feed within easy distance, it so happens that grain crops in the arid climates of those collectorates *pay better than cotton* or other exportable products, and this is the reason why they are so extensively grown.[13]

In short, the peasantry was responsive to the market, Wingate argued, and if it continued a traditional crop-distribution, then this was so mainly for eco-

---

[13] G. Wingate, 2 May, 1862, in BGR, No CVII, *Papers Relative to the Revision of the Assessment of the Indapoor Talooka*, Bombay 1868, p. 192.

nomic reasons – in the districts south of Nasik, grain was a more 'profitable' commodity.

This special pleading on behalf of the responsiveness of the peasantry to the 'civilising' mission of imperialism contains some important clues. To start with, Wingate was writing before the cotton-boom had started; that is to say, the expansion of commodity-economy had already begun, it was in motion, at least ten years before the whole level of commodity-prices was jerked sharply upwards by the boom in international cotton-prices. In this conjuncture of commodity-expansion, moreover, the staple foodgrains were, supposedly, increasingly produced as commodities. And, finally, Wingate identified, implicitly, a basic structural contrast within the Deccan districts when he isolated Khandesh. For, while Khandesh, like Berar, produced largely for world-markets, the districts further south, in the heart of the Deccan, derived the impetus of their commodity-expansion from the growing regional demand for foodgrains and other produce. That is, the division of labour was changing within the Deccan economy. The extent of arable land in cultivation did indeed pick up through this conjuncture, and the whole pace of commodity-circulation quickened perceptibly. By the seventies and eighties, a district like Ahmednagar was exporting Rs 3.5 million worth of basically agricultural produce. By the nineties, further north, isolated *talukas* like Chalisgaon could export produce worth over Rs 5 million annually. When the bureaucracy later reflected on this whole period, it saw in it a commercial revolution that had qualitatively transformed the conditions of the old economy.

A basic index of this transformation is the level of commodity-production which prevailed, on average, through these decades. In the eighties, Ahmednagar exported, that is, sold outside the district, 'large' quantities of wheat to Sholapur, Poona and Bombay, in order to import 'large' quantities of the basic foodgrains along the the opening afforded by the Dhond-Manmad railway. The trade in these staples was dominated by wealthy Bhatia and Marwari merchants, based in the district itself. Immediately to the south, Poona imported the basic staples in even larger quantities: in 1873, the railway-traffic registered a *net* import of 17,000 tons of 'grain', in 1878 of 34,300 tons, in 1880 of 45,500 tons. Further south, Kolhapur was a major exporter of paddy to the markets of the eastern Deccan and other parts of Bombay Karnatak. In the Konkan, Ratnagiri, devoting most of its crop-pattern to the 'inferior' cereals, depended crucially for its consumption of rice on the exports of Kolaba district.[14]

More local in expansion were commodities that generally required irrigation or relatively large outlays of capital. In the Satara villages, along the Krishna, sugarcane and groundnut had begun to expand rapidly. 'The latter are exported in very great quantities to Bombay and thence to Marseilles and Italy, where it is stated they are largely used in the manufacture of olive-oil'.[15] Poona exported cabbages, potatoes, and other fresh vegetables 'in considerable quantities to Bombay'.[16] In Ahmednagar, the *talukas* around the town itself witnessed a considerable expansion of irrigated acreage due to 'the large demand for garden produce'. Vineyards covered the best soil around the major local market, their crop destined for sale to merchants from Bombay.[17] In Khandesh, the cultivation of linseed was spreading fast, 'owing to the Bombay demand',[18] that is, to European demand which absorbed 170,000 tons on average in the 1890s.

That a more tightly integrated market was in the process of emerging over this conjuncture is suggested quite strongly by the behaviour of commodity-prices. For the country as a whole, and for a much longer period which includes the late nineteenth century, Hurd has established the effect of railway-expansion in bringing about a progressive equalisation of market-prices.[19] When one examines the early segments of local price-curves, generally before 1860, the discrepancies between local prices, even within the same district, are perfectly apparent. The period from the cotton-boom to the famine of 1876 then forms a sort of transition, during which the local series rapidly move closer into line. During the famine itself, for obvious reasons, and in its aftermath, the series tend to merge into a thick line. Apart from this distinct con-

---

[14] GBP, *Ahmednagar*, pp. 267, 343, 345, 685; GBP, Volume XVIII/2, *Poona*, Bombay 1885, pp. 167, 172; GBP, Volume XXIV, *Kolhapur*, Bombay 1886, p. 165; RD, Volume 8, 1874.

[15] *Report on the Administration of the Bombay Presidency for the Year 1892–3*, pt. 2, Bombay 1893, p. 110.

[16] GBP, *Poona*, pt. 2, pp. 55, 170.

[17] GBP, *Ahmednagar*, pp. 274–5: irrigated acreage expanded by around 5 per cent per annum over some thirty years.

[18] GBP, Volume XII, *Khandesh*, Bombay 1880, p. 152. Linseed export-figures from *Report on the Administration* covering the years in question, Appendix IV, D (2) of each report.

[19] Hurd 1975.

vergence-impact, however, the commodity-expansion of those years tended to reduce the annual amplitude of price-fluctuations, that is, to modify the purely local determination of price-movements that characterises the least developed commodity-markets. All of this would have meant that neighbouring prices were, in most cases, sufficiently strong to influence a given local price, as when the poor harvests reaped by the southern and central *talukas* of Khandesh in 1874–5, following several years of scarcity and floods, were combined, in predictably disastrous fashion, with low prices due to the bumper crops in Nimar and Berar close by.[20]

These processes of price-convergence and of the lower amplitude of fluctuations imply, moreover, not just a greater specific mobility of commodities due to improvements in the means of communication which took place over that period, but the emergence and development, side by side with the expansion of railways and metalled roads, of a whole number of depots and wholesale-markets in various parts of the Deccan. Apart from the major commercial centres such as Poona or Jalgaon, a large number of smaller towns and big villages come into prominence in this specific function. The population of such towns and villages – Kharda, Vambhori, Karad, Tasgaon, Sowda, Faizpur, Lasalgaon, etc. – would tend to vary between 5,000 and 10,000 persons, and their 'mercantile' sector to account generally for anywhere between four and ten per cent of those populations. It is these smaller centres that mediated the local, inter-district and external trade of the Deccan. The monied capitals, whose intervention in this trade was absolutely decisive, resided mainly in such centres, connecting links between the larger capitals of the major local wholesale-market and the *taluka* peasantry. The emergence of such centres specifically would tend to even out discrepancies between local price-movements, enable the big peasantry to relate more easily to the 'open' market, and facilitate the operation of a chain of 'mercantile' transactions whose structure we shall come to shortly.

But probably the most revealing single index of the specific weight of the commodity-economy in the life of the peasantry is the fact that the whole system of state-exploitation of the peasantry – the system of 'assessment' and

---

[20] A detailed examination of the commodity-price series and their behaviour over time will be taken up elsewhere. Regressions between local series in general suggest a very high degree of correlation.

revenue-demand – depended crucially on the estimated level of commodity-prices at the time of introduction of a settlement, and on the access of groups of villages to local markets, wholesale centres, or railway-stations. Both the Survey and its Revision based their classifications of such village-groups in the revenue-scale on the level of 'exports' that any given group was considered capable of sustaining – apart from the more general circumstances determining differential rent.[21] Thus the commodity-economy was the basic premise of the revenue-system, just as the expansion of the market formed, in a broader sense, the nucleus of its programme of 'civilising' the country, that is, introducing the bourgeois mode of production into it.

The general process of commodity-expansion described above would imply, moreover, that labour-power is itself, increasingly, a commodity. It would imply the conversion of the small producer into a wage-labourer, even if not necessarily into a 'productive worker', i.e., one employed by capital.[22] This, too, formed an essential dimension of the economic liberalism of the colonial bureaucracy – a conception that vacillated between the moderately blithe optimism that India was fast reconstructing itself in the image of more advanced nations, and the disenchanted rebuttals of this conception by those who sought to protect and strengthen the big peasantry against the monied capitalists. By and large, it was the sense of optimism that prevailed – even the famines demonstrated the inexorable laws of liberal political economy, the inevitable destruction of the 'thriftless' small producer, and the rise of

---

[21] This is a striking characteristic of practically every *taluka* settlement report reprinted in *Bombay Government Records (New Series)*. Characteristically, the settlements or revised settlements introduced in the sixties extrapolated from the very high prices prevailing in the boom, with the consequent fixing of rates that peasants found impossible to pay in the price-depression that followed.

[22] In the debate on the 'mode of production' some of the contributors, and notably Paresh Chattopadhyay, who put a lot of weight on the proletarianisation of the small producer and the expansion of labour-power as a commodity, tended to argue straight from this to the development of capitalism. This is obviously too abrupt because 'wage-labour' and 'productive labour' are not the same. Regardless of how important the distinction remains within the developed bourgeois mode of production, in earlier periods when a large number of 'wage-workers' would have been employed out of revenue rather than capital, i.e., for purposes not productive of surplus-value, it *is* important to make this distinction. With this specific qualification, and the further one that Chattopadhyay based his argument for the emergence of capitalist relations almost totally on processes of *commodity*-expansion, I would now *repudiate completely* my critique of him (1973) as badly misdirected. Chattopadhyay was in general absolutely correct to emphasise that capitalist relations are not a novelty in India.

'the English agricultural system of large landlords, capitalist farmers of large farms, and peasant-labourers for wage'.[23]

What made this optimism credible was the quite perceptible process of decay of the smaller peasant-households. In Poona, many of them had, by the 1880s, following the devastating impact of two continuous famine years, 'given up husbandry and taken to be messengers, constables, grooms and day-labourers'.[24] During a famine, the first option of most peasant-households would be emigration: those who stayed behind would generally have to subsist on relief-works, and the fact that they stayed behind would indicate that most of these were households without livestock, or deprived of their livestock. A census taken in Poona at the height of the famine of 1876 shows that, of the total number of workers on 'relief' – close to 50,000 – exactly half were 'holders or underholders of land' by occupation. A quarter of the district's emigrant-population 'never returned', i.e., they abandoned agriculture or moved elsewhere to restart cultivation. The contrast with Khandesh is striking. The powerful currents of emigration that swelled up over those years took a large number of cultivating households precisely into areas like Khandesh and Berar. Here, during the famine, cultivating households formed only 22 per cent of those compelled to subsist on 'relief' – mild indication of the more independent condition of the Khandesh peasantry. Yet, even here, in a relatively favoured zone of the Deccan with a still expanding land-frontier, a process of proletarianisation was under way well before the famine.

> There can be no doubt that the number of persons in Khandesh subsisting on their labour [on the sale of their labour-power] has much increased of late years. This is owing to the fact of many cultivators having lost their

---

[23] 'Improvidence' and 'thriftlessness' were the most frequent explanations that the bureaucracy had for the condition of the small-production economy. Supporters of the programme of peasant-capitalism did, however, register their disagreements with that majority view. See T.C. Hope in BGR, No CLVII, *Papers and Proceedings Connected with the Passing of the Deccan Agriculturists' Relief Act, XVII of 1879*, Bombay 1882, p. 143ff. at p. 148. Hope had a much better understanding of the internal dynamics of a small-production economy than most officials, something quite close to the view proposed by Marx himself in *Theories of Surplus-Value*. Thus he wrote: 'It is obvious that where there is a peasant-proprietary, though the stimulus to individual exertion is considerable...the individual capital cannot be great and misfortunes comparatively small will throw even a thrifty and industrious person into the hands of the moneylenders for temporary loans' (pp. 149–50).

[24] GBP, *Poona*, pt. 1, p. 288.

lands either from the action of the Civil Courts or from inability to pay the government demand; while again the establishment of cotton-presses and other factories has added largely to the demand for working hands.[25]

Khandesh wage-rates would have formed a strong incentive to many small peasants to 'forsake their fields for the railway, the workshops, the cotton and spinning mills', especially in a period of recurrent scarcities such as Khandesh went through over the whole of the seventies, and at a time when the average daily wage a small peasant would have earned from 'subsidiary' occupations fluctuated around 9½ annas.[26]

Drought, scarcity, and famine played a major role in the proletarianisation of the small producer only because of the already exhausted and decrepit condition of the Deccan small-production economy. This condition was ascribed in the first instance to the persisting pressure of revenue-demands on peasant-incomes. Even the more 'scientifically' based classifications of the Survey and its Revision had in a greater number of *talukas* only increased the general average rate of exploitation, straining to breaking-point the resources of the poorer districts and *talukas*. In Sholapur, a district of this sort, a junior official wrote: 'I see no reason to doubt the fact stated to me by many apparently trustworthy witnesses and which my own personal observation confirms, that in many cases the assessments are only paid by selling ornaments or cattle'.[27] A household without cattle was a household on the verge of extinction – either in the direct form of having to desert the *taluka* and abandon cultivation, or in the less direct form of sinking into 'indebtedness'. For, 'land and bullocks are the principal organs of our body, in the same way as hands and feet are', the peasants said.[28]

It followed that, against this background of intensified exploitation by the state, the famine of 1876–7 'irretrievably ruined a large number of the smaller cultivators' in Sholapur, against whose *khatas* arrears would have been accumulating year after year, or who, to pay off the assessment, were forced to

---

[25] RD, Volume 6/1, 1875, W. Ramsay to the Revenue Commissioner Northern Division, §9.
[26] Ibid., H. Woodward to Ramsay, §11.
[27] RD, Volume 9/1, 1875, J. Davidson to J.H. Grant, §11.
[28] Petition dated 5/7/1875 from the *ryots* of Mirajgaon, taluka Karjat in Ahmednagar, cited DRC, Appendix C. *Notes of Evidence, Statistics and Other Papers*, pp. 206–7.

sell portions of their means of subsistence.[29] In neighbouring Satara, of a total of 46,000 labourers 'on relief', 53 per cent derived from the peasantry. They would have represented obviously the most impoverished strata, the slightly better-off small peasants choosing to migrate 'with their pair of bullocks and a cow or two'.[30] In Nasik, a 'considerable' number of persons were supposed to have 'sunk from the status of landholders to that of labourers'.[31]

Thus the proletarianisation of the small producer was a process common to all districts of the Deccan regardless of their specific rates of commodity-production. It formed part of a longer, less visible cycle extending back into the early decades of the nineteenth century. Take the ruinous year of 1847–8, when in Ahmednagar, *talukas* like Rahuri, Nevasa, and Sangamner were compelled to disburse over half their grain-output on the market. In Rahuri, at that time, 'to pay his rent', that is, the government demand, 'a ryot had frequently to part with a bullock or other property'.[32] Prices had fallen lower and lower under the pressures of a market overstocked with local grain. Wingate described the mechanism at work over that season: 'The assessment was always too heavy to be defrayed in full, but in a good season', such as 1847–8, 'the remissions given were of a less amount and the demand on the ryot consequently greater than in less favourable years. He was, in consequence, obliged to bring forward to market a larger amount of produce than in ordinary seasons to meet this additional demand [for revenue], and by thus forcing sales prices were lowered, and more and more produce had to be sold in order to raise the money he required to meet the extra demand...until the market became so glutted and prices so ruinously low' that many households would either sink further into debt or alienate their means of production in distress sales. Thus in Nevasa 'many of the ryots...had to resort to the moneylenders and in many cases to dispose of their farming stock'.[33] This is how even a year of general abundance could, like a year of famine, accelerate both the proletarianisation of the small producer and the rate of expansion of the monied capitalist.

---

[29] RD, Volume 28, 1879, A. Spry and J. Davidson.
[30] GBP, Volume XIX, *Satara*, Bombay 1885, p. 174.
[31] RD, Volume 23, 1879, W. Ramsay, §14.
[32] BGR, No CXVII, *Report on the Assessment of the Rahooree Talooka in the Ahmednuggur Collectorate*, Bombay 1870, p. 7 (written by Anderson in 1849).
[33] *Ibid.*, G. Wingate to E. Townsend, 15 December, 1849, p. 50.

Beyond the countryside proper, in the Deccan towns, a similar movement was in progress. Here, rising subsistence-costs and the competitive pressure of machine-based commodities were jointly driving many artisan families either deeper into debt or into the more obvious forms of wage-labour. In Kolhapur, many weavers had come to 'work as labourers',[34] in Nasik further north they had 'to take a field or even to work as day-labourers'.[35] Given the specific nature of the relation of 'indebtedness', which we shall examine later, it is possible to understand why even the falling costs of raw materials supplied by machine-production would scarcely have improved the fortunes of the majority of weavers, and only increased the profits of their capitalist exploiters. Again, many artisan-households would have joined the currents of emigration during famine-years. In the town of Yeola in Nasik, where weavers formed 57 per cent of the total population, large numbers were compelled to migrate 'in the hope of employment' elsewhere.[36]

These, then, were among the basic phenomena of the process of commodity-expansion that occurred over the late nineteenth century. How far, within this context, did capitalist relations of exploitation crystallise or evolve? From the commodity we move to capital.

10.3. Structure of capital in the Deccan

Only the less developed forms of capital, which, within the framework of the capitalist mode of production in its developed sense, would form subordinate types – pure functions of the circulation-process of industrial capital – had evolved in the colonial economy. Thus, in most Deccan districts, 'merchants' and 'traders' formed the numerically dominant sector of capital, ranging from 60 to 75 per cent of all persons with 'positions implying the possession of capital'. The other groups consisted of rentiers, moneychangers, shopkeepers, bankers, etc.

In the more backward world of the Deccan, 'banking', 'mercantile', and 'usurer' capital were, in most cases, inseparable. For example, in Khandesh it was asserted that as a general rule 'the same man is often a merchant, a mon-

---

[34] GBP, *Kolhapur*, p. 95.
[35] GBP, Volume XVI, *Nasik*, Bombay 1883, p. 53.
[36] RD, Volume 16, 1877, H.R. Cooke; RD, Volume 14, 1878, Cooke.

eylender and a broker'. Why was this? Bureaucrats trained in the rudiments of nineteenth-century 'political economy' understood the underlying cause. 'At Jalgaon alone is there trade enough to allow of firms confining themselves to fixed branches of business'.[37] In other words, *scales* of production and circulation were just not sufficient to generate an elaborate division of labour. Or take the example of one of the 'biggest capitalists' in Nasik district. This man deployed a capital of between Rs 300,000 and 400,000 – which compares quite favourably with the larger capitals in Gujarat at that time. But who was he? 'A well known Brahman *banker and moneylender*' from Chandor *taluka*.[38] Banker or moneylender? The fact is that it is impossible to answer questions like that. The bureaucracy directly encountered the difficulty. It wrote: 'The trading group is the most difficult of classification on account of the vague terms used, meaning often simply merchant or trader'.[39] The more obvious case of this lack of differentiation or specialisation was the almost total fusion of the twin categories of 'mercantile' and 'usurer' capital – there was scarcely a 'merchant' who could not also be classified as a 'moneylender', and *vice versa*.

But it would be wrong to conclude, conversely, that such 'merchants-cum-moneylenders' were pure agents of the circulation-process (in the sense in which merchant's and commercial capital are within the developed bourgeois mode of production). Precisely because the 'occupational' classifications of capital did *not* reflect a strict division of labour of the sort that prevails where industrial capital predominates, the concomitant distinction, between purely 'parasitic' and basically 'productive' types of capital, becomes somewhat misleading. The system of production that prevailed within the Deccan will explain why.

In Kolhapur, the total estimated volume of capital available for 'loans' amounted to the substantial sum of Rs 3.1 million already by the early 1850s.[40] Further north, Satara twenty years later was the site of a total capital *of this sort* equal to Rs 15.3 million. Fairly good data are available for Tasgaon *taluka*

---

[37] GBP, *Khandesh*, p. 191.
[38] GBP, *Nasik*, p. 114; GBP, *Satara*, p. 184, 'Traders whose dealings are on a large scale are almost always also large moneylenders'.
[39] *Report on the Administration... 1892–3*, p. 133. This is why the Census-data on the distribution and weight of the various 'occupational' groups has to be used with some caution.
[40] BGR, No VIII, *Statistical Report on the Principality of Kolhapur, Compiled by Major D.C. Graham*, Bombay 1854, p. 273.

in the south of the district. Here, the total (*taluka*) capital was estimated at Rs 900,000 – 'exclusive of the capital of the great banking house of Jog, which may be set down at several lakhs additional'. This size of capital was roughly equal to the total value of the *taluka's* exports over four years. Over half of this sum was concentrated in Tasgaon town itself, and most of the rest in only about nine villages. The official who assembled all this data from what he thought were reliable sources estimated the number of big capitalists in the *taluka* at 20 to 30 – from a total of over 300 *sowcars*.[41] This implies a fairly high degree of concentration, so that most of these 300 *sowcars* would have deployed capital sums of Rs 1,000 and Rs 2,000. The same data show that 38 per cent of all Satara district *sowcars* had started business 'within the last 20 years', that is, since 1855. In fact, throughout the Deccan, and even more so in the districts further north, where Marwari capital tended to predominate, the emergence and expansion of these *smaller* moneylenders was a relatively *recent* phenomenon. Between the commodity-expansion of those years (1852 on) and the general expansion and multiplication of the class of monied capitalists, there was a close, intimate, inseparable link, which we must turn to now. For there is one fact that the bureaucracy never tired of mentioning, and around which it structured some of its best social investigations. This was that the vast majority of households in the Deccan countryside were, to one degree or another, 'indebted'. The aggregate estimates, which indicate only an order of magnitude, would be 66–90 per cent of such households across the Deccan as a whole.

To grasp the deeper significance of these twin phenomena – the expanding monied capitals on one side, and indebtedness on the other – we can start with the chain-like structure of operation of 'mercantile' capital. Viewed vertically, the structure of this capital could be envisaged in the following way:

> The capitalist classes are first and most numerous the small traders and moneylenders *of the villages*, chiefly Marwaris and Guzars. *These advance grain for seed and subsistence*.... The second class are the rich bankers or traders of *large towns* (including a good many Brahmins). Those Kulkarnis who are moneylenders are generally *closely affiliated to these Brahmin bankers*.... They

---

[41] The man was a hard working '2nd Assistant Collector' called A. Wingate. His report on Tasgaon *taluka* (dated 4/8/1875) is among the best descriptions of any *taluka* available for these years. See RD, Volume 8, 1875, pp. 239–90 (§11 of the report).

deal much less in advance of grain than the traders of lower caste and have a much greater taste for *getting land into their own hands and names*.... As the Kulkarnis are connected with these [the second 'class'], so are the small [moneylenders] of the villages mentioned in the first class *mere jackals to their richer caste-fellows in the towns*. The third class consists of *cultivators who have kept out of debt*.[42]

This account allows one to regroup the three 'classes' of capitalists into two basic types:

(1) Merchant-moneylending-banking businesses organised on a caste-basis, *divided internally* into a larger, town-based capital, more widespread in its range of operations, and a small 'sponsored' capital, operating locally, resident in the village itself, generally controlling a portion of its retail-trade, started with capital borrowed from kinsmen, and directly in contact with the peasantry.
(2) Moneylenders sprung from the mass of the peasantry itself, by and large big peasants, a lot of them of the Kunbi caste.

In India, with businesses of this or a higher sort organised on a *caste-basis*, the smaller, local capitals would, in many cases, have functioned only as elements of a collective grouping with its main base in the towns and wholesale centres. Thus it would make no sense to see the town 'merchants' or 'bankers' and the village 'moneylenders' as entirely distinct agents personifying separate social functions. The point can be put differently: when the Commission met to investigate the Deccan Riots, it found that the 'smaller class of *sowcars*, who are also the most unscrupulous, have increased very considerably during the last ten years', that is, since 1865. But this very rapid expansion of the small *sowcars* would to a large extent have signified only the general expansion, and deeper entrenchment, of many of the larger, town-based capitals already constituted before the boom. The crucial mechanism here would have been the 'sponsoring' of new capitals on a family or caste-basis, by way of an extension of the general (individual) scale of business of the firm in question. This would hold especially for the smaller Marwari and Gujarati moneylenders

---

[42] DRC, *Report of the Committee on the Riots in Poona and Ahmednagar 1875*, Bombay 1876, pp. 24–5, citing W.F. Sinclair, Asst Collector of Ahmednagar, emphasis mine.

who 'usually begin business as clerks or servants of one of the established *sowcars*'. Even in the districts further south, for example, Satara where this layer was less well developed, the class of 'small lenders' were thought to 'have little or no capital' and to 'borrow from wealthy firms', i.e., from those 'traders whose dealings are on a large scale' and who 'are almost always also large moneylenders'.[43] The major exception to this pattern were the big peasants who turned to moneylending.[44]

The deeper significance of this sort of stratification of capital is brought out by the fact that, during the riots of 1875, 'in villages where *sowcars* of the Brahmin and other [local] castes shared the moneylending business with Marwaris, it was usual to find that the latter only were molested'.[45] The faster rates of expansion of the sponsored capitals would imply, on the one hand, a gradual erosion of the sphere of activity of the indigenous monied capitalists, and on the other, an increasing expropriation of the small peasantry. The riots would then have been a sort of united front of these classes against capitalists who had settled in the district or *taluka* in the recent past.

All this views the structure of such capital vertically. Across the district, so to speak, the interconnections would take the form of a *chain of operations* extending from the peasantry at one end to the Bombay and international markets at the other. Take Ahmednagar cotton.

> The cotton dealers, who are Marwar and Gujarat *vanis*, advance *money to the landholders* and buy their crops often before they are ready for picking. They pack it in bundles or *dokdas* of about 120 pounds and send it to *their agents* in Ahmadnagar, of whom there are about twenty.... From these agents the cotton-dealers receive advances and draw bills or *hundis* to the extent of 70 or 80 per cent of the value of the cotton. After the cotton has come, the Ahmadnagar agents sell it to *Bombay merchants*.... The cotton bought by the agents of the Bombay firms is either offered for sale in Bombay or is pressed and shipped to Europe.[46]

---

[43] GBP, *Satara*, pp. 182–4.
[44] In Nasik, according to GBP, *Nasik*, p. 142, 'village shopkeepers' were said to be 'almost entirely dependent on borrowed capital'.
[45] DRC, *Report of the Committee on the Riots in Poona and Ahmednagar*, p. 5.
[46] GBP, *Ahmednagar*, p. 343; italics mine.

The same sort of chain operated in field-produce generally, further south in Poona. Here

> the merchants that deal direct with Bombay and other large markets are generally Marwar *vanis*.... They export grain and other produce, principally garden-crops.... Field produce passes through several hands before it leaves the district. It goes to market generally through the village shopkeeper, who passes it on to a dealer in some large town, who sends it direct to Bombay or to some export merchant in Poona.... The village shopkeeper generally gathers articles of export *in exchange for money advanced or lent*.

He was 'usually a Gujarat or a Marwar *vani*' connected with the 'large towns with which he has business relations, and where probably the moneylender, on whom he is often dependent, lives'.[47] In Khandesh, the same structure of business covered most commodities apart from cotton. 'As a rule, the husbandman has received advances from, or mortgaged his crop to, some village moneylender, who, in turn, has borrowed from some larger capitalist'.[48] In Khandesh cotton, the big Bombay firms had, to a large extent, succeeded in modifying this standard pattern. 'Many of the native merchants resident in the towns of Sowda, Faizpoor, and Ravere, purchase cotton in the Hoosingabad districts under consignment for houses in Bombay'.[49] Further west, in Amulnair,

> the native merchants of the district...simply purchase the articles for exportation from the ryots and resell them almost immediately to some agents of Bombay native merchants, several of whom reside in Amulnair and whose sole business appears to be the purchase and exportation to Bombay of cotton, linseed, tillee and coriander seed.[50]

In the period we are concerned with, European firms had not made much headway, and the cotton-trade of Khandesh was 'still almost entirely in native hands'. 'According to the common practice, from September to the end of April, growers and petty dealers go to the exporters, and contract to deliver a

---

[47] GBP, *Poona*, pt. 2, p. 164.
[48] GBP, *Khandesh*, p. 217.
[49] BGR, No XCIII, *Papers Relative to the Introduction of Revised Rates of Assessment into Eight Talukas and Two Pettas of the Khandesh Collectorate*, Bombay 1865, p. 8, A.F. Davidson.
[50] *Op. cit.* p. 278, P.A. Elphinstone.

certain quantity of cotton within a given period'.⁵¹ The dominance of Indian capital was destined to decline, however, for, in the early part of this century, in Dhulia and Jalgaon, the chief Khandesh markets, 'foreign firms' accounted for 50–75 per cent of all upcountry-sales.⁵²

The variation afforded by Khandesh cotton was probably an expression of the more independent character of the peasantry there. *Jalap*, which formed the main system on which cotton-contracts operated, was already in a state of near-disintegration by the late nineties, when in *talukas* such as Chalisgaon only the 'poor ryots' consented to such arrangements.⁵³ Outside the Deccan, but still in the Bombay Presidency, in the much more prosperous Gujarat district of Broach, this independence was apparent as early as the sixties. There, ever since Broach became a 'field for the investment of European capital', the course of its cotton trade had changed considerably.

> Cotton is now bought in one of two ways, either by the local agents of Bombay firms, or by the owners of ginning-factories in Broach. The local agents, when ordered to buy, sometimes send out their own broker to the villages to purchase direct from the grower. But they generally do business through the dealer, who, as in former times, gets the cotton into his hands by making advances to the cultivators.... The nature of the dealings between the cultivator and the *wakharia* would seem to have somewhat changed since 1850. The advance is now said to be earnest-money, to bind the cultivator to his bargain, rather than the mortgage of his crop by the cultivator to tide over the hard months on to harvest.⁵⁴

Thus, the penetration of European commercial capital into the cotton-trade of districts such as Broach and Khandesh did not imply a tighter domination of the peasantry. The evidence seems to suggest that the reverse – the growing independence of the peasantry vis-à-vis local monied capitalists and the deeper entrenchment of European firms – were phenomena that coincided in time, though their internal connection cannot be traced out here.

The more typical form that the chain assumed further south, in the heart of the Deccan, reflected the far more dependent character of the peasantry in

---

⁵¹ GBP, *Khandesh*, p. 221.
⁵² Cf. Dantwala 1937, p. 40ff.
⁵³ This has been shown by Guha 1977.
⁵⁴ GBP, Volume II, *Gujarat: Surat and Broach*, Bombay 1877, p. 429ff.

those districts – the greater intensity of domination over the peasantry by local monied capitalists. This was the zone in which peasant resentment against the intrusions of monied capitalists was chiefly concentrated, the general area within which most of the known assassinations of moneylenders actually occurred. There is a simple statistical index of this pattern: in 1891, according to the Census-figures, over 55 per cent of the total Marwari population of the Presidency resided in the three districts of Nasik, Ahmednagar, and Poona – districts whose share of the total Presidency-population was roughly ten per cent.[55]

As an illustration of the specific weight of the more expansive Marwari capital resident in the core districts of the Deccan, one might take Parner *taluka* in Ahmednagar.[56] Here, the biggest moneylenders were, almost without exception, Marwaris. In the village of Parner itself, of a total of fifty local moneylenders only six, all of them Marwaris, accounted for over one-third of the total acreage that had passed into the *khatas* of moneylenders generally in the previous forty years. The biggest of them, Tularam Karamchand, controlled, at least on paper, 659 acres, transferred into his *khata* through fifty-five separate transactions. Tularam's father, Karamchand, had settled in the *taluka* even before 1820. In the thirties, Tularam, his eldest son, had joined him as his 'agent'. By 1875, Tularam's accumulation of 660 acres represented an annual income of Rs 3,600. Chandrabhan Bapuji, the second biggest moneylender in Parner, controlled 520 acres, transferred through thirty-one separate transactions. His father, likewise, had come to Parner around the time that the British took over the Deccan districts, and like Tularam, Chandrabhan had started off in a 'small' way.

The Parner data also illustrate the expansion, side by side with the larger capitals, of the smaller, predominantly indigenous capitals. Around half the number of moneylenders had built up *khatas* of generally less than 20 acres. The chronological distribution of the individual transactions through which Parner moneylenders built up their 'estates' of varying sizes shows a quite definite and interesting pattern: of a total of 271 such transactions, one-third belong to the early sixties and slightly over one-third to the early seventies,

---

[55] Census of India 1891, Volume VII, *Bombay and Its Feudatories, Part 2, Imperial Tables*, Bombay 1892, Table XVIA.
[56] The Parner data are taken from DRC, *Report Appendix C. Notes of Evidence, Statistics, and Other Papers*, pp. 180–97.

when the boom had broken and prices were declining rapidly. The mass of small moneylenders, many of them sprung from the peasantry itself, would have expanded their *khatas* basically in the second phase, or within five years of the date of the Commission enquiry. Thus, in Kolgaum village of Shrigonda, 'twelve kunbi *sowcars* examined state that they have all commenced business within the last five years'.[57] It is this very recently emerged layer that would have experienced the crises of 1875–7 as a severe limit to its further rapid expansion, even if, in the aftermath of the riots, the bigger moneylenders such as Tularam and Chandrabhan were hauled up before the criminal courts on charges of forgery and extortion.[58]

Finally, an examination of the data collected by the Commission from various villages of Poona suggests that, over the longer period from 1854–5 to 1874–5, the monied capitalists tended to withdraw from the smaller villages and relocate their activities in the faster-expanding large villages. Thus, in the big villages of Indapur or Talegaon, each with a total of 370–80 *khatedars*, both the number of *sowcars* in operation and the total assets controlled by them tended to expand fairly rapidly. In Talegaon, for example, there were only three *sowcars* in 1854–5 and they controlled, in their own names, only 122 acres; ten years later, in the middle of the boom, their number had expanded slowly to eleven, and their total acreage to 556; another ten years later, over the crest and decline of the boom, their number had shot up to forty-six and the total acreage controlled by them to 3,110. On the other hand, in the very small villages both their numbers and their control tended to decline – there was Nimgaon Khedki, for example, where by 1874–5 only one *sowcar* was left, controlling half the amount that he and others had controlled earlier.[59] How does one explain this movement? By modifying the structure of differential rent, the commercial expansion of those twenty years would have exerted strong pressures on the relocation of such capital. Small *sowcars* who started off in the 1850s in the smaller villages of a *taluka* would, over time, shift to the bigger villages, closer to the nerve-centres of commodity-expansion. Among the

---

[57] DRC, *Report Appendix C*, p. 84.
[58] RD, Volume 12, 1881, T.S. Hamilton, stationed in Parner and the neighbouring *talukas*, wrote, 'I believe I am correct in saying that the race of small moneylenders has been utterly crushed'.
[59] DRC, *Report Appendix C*, p. 200ff.

sowcars jailed after the riots was one Hariram Bubhan who had shifted from Panodi in Parner to Parner itself, 'requiring', as he says, 'a large sphere'.[60]

10.4. 'Interest' as surplus-value: increasing formal subsumption of labour into capital

Abstracting from differences internal to the structure of this class, it is not difficult to see that this sector of capital and of society as a whole would have been the 'greatest beneficiary' of British rule. The penetration of the monied capitalist into the small-production economy of the Deccan coincided with, and sheltered behind, the take-over of these districts by the British bureaucracy. Despite the systematic attacks to which they were continually subjected in writing, these capitalists were never seriously threatened by the state, and even the effort to modify the impact of their domination, with the passing of the Agriculturists Relief Act, only subdued the pace of their expansion, shifting their preferences from mortgages to direct sales. The reason for this contradictory behaviour lies, of course, in the structural role that this class played within the framework of colonial domination. State-exploitation of the peasantry was premised on the expansion of commodity-production. But, however 'responsive' the Deccan peasantry may have appeared to men like Wingate, the peasantry as a whole was in no position to sustain this effort. Commodity-expansion thus came to be *mediated through* the interventions of the monied capitalists.

One concrete piece of evidence is enough to demonstrate their role in this process. In 1850–1, the last year of the old revenue-system in that *taluka*, eleven villages of Tasgaon paid Rs 40,373 into the Treasury on account of 'revenue'. Of this sum, no less than 48 per cent was 'raised by loans from *sowcars*'![61] If Tasgaon were a typical case, then this would mean that the whole system of state-exploitation of the peasantry depended crucially on the monied capitalist, just as the control he came to exercise over the peasantry found one of its deepest sources in that very system of exploitation.

---

[60] DRC, *Report Appendix C*, p. 248.
[61] RD, Volume 11/2, 1876, where Moore, collector of Satara, wrote, the moneylenders 'are the class who profit most by our administration'. The example of Tasgaon from BGR, No CCIV, *Papers Relating to the Revision Survey Settlement of Thirty-Six Villages of the Tasgaon Taluka of the Satara Collectorate*, Bombay 1888, p. 9.

Why would peasant-households have 'borrowed'? When the Commission asked the collector of Poona, he replied, 'The ryots generally attribute their embarrassments to the weight of the assessment and also to the operation of the civil courts...'.[62] In the poorer *talukas* of Sholapur, further east, the basic cause of indebtedness was 'that the rates are so high'.[63] This underlying pressure would not necessarily be expressed directly in the more immediate causes that led groups of households into the hands of moneylenders. A Tasgaon *sowcar* thought the *ryots* borrowed 'chiefly to buy cattle and to marry'; this was the opinion of 'a man who has occasion to go into the Civil Courts upwards of 50 times in a year'.[64] Among the various immediate causes of indebtedness listed by peasant-households interviewed by the Commission, four basic categories stand out. Subsistence-costs or consumption-loans, normally on a running grain-account basis, formed the prevalent type, 25 per cent of all instances. The need to purchase bullocks was likewise important, 23 per cent. Another 23 per cent of cases derived from what one might call the social costs connected with kinship and marriage. Finally, the pressure of assessment was itself listed as an immediate cause in 14 per cent of all cases. This establishes that, in close to half the total number of cases (in this sample) *shortage of means of production and subsistence* was listed as the immediate pressure compelling households to 'borrow'. We shall see later, when we come to the structure of the Deccan peasantry, that this was a compulsion specific to the lower strata of the peasantry, and that the social costs of kinship would normally involve strata of the middle peasantry not otherwise compelled to meet subsistence-costs from 'loans'.[65]

On contracting a debt, the household would in most cases find itself incapable of reimbursing it unless, as happened occasionally, a good harvest coincided with a year of high prices. Years of scarcity and famine, of which there were several, would drive these households only further into debt, so

---

[62] DRC, *Report Appendix A. Papers Relating to the Indebtedness of the Agricultural Classes in Bombay and Other Parts of India*, Bombay 1876, p. 244. The fact that the transactions between peasant and moneylender were *legally enforceable* was regarded almost universally, by state and peasantry alike, as one of the chief causes of the oppression of the *ryot*. Thus, Hope (n. 23) called it 'the *arming* of the moneylender', and G. Wingate wrote, 'this antagonism of classes and degradation of people, which is fast spreading over the land, is the work *of our laws* and our rule', DRC, *Report Appendix A*, p. 88 (to the Registrar of the Court of Sadar, Bombay, 24/9/1852).

[63] RD, Volume 9/1, 1875, J. Davidson.

[64] RD, Volume 8, 1875, reported to A. Wingate by Venkaji Gopal Kinkar.

[65] DRC, *Report Appendix C*, passim (interviews with indebted households).

that finally they would often have to confront several creditors. Over time, a household in this position would find itself subsisting 'at the mercy of' its creditor, who would in this way come to establish *control over its reproduction process* from one cycle to the next. Elements of the production-process would be 'advanced' to the peasant either in money-form or directly in material form, and the peasant would then surrender the whole of his crop by way of 'interest'-payments. Where these payments included those portions of the means of production over which the small producer still retained control, e.g., bullocks, which was frequently the case, this would only intensify the dependence of his process of production on the advance of elements required for its reconstitution.

This is the initial approximation, and it is the hallmark of vulgar empiricism that it sticks fast to this surface appearance. When the *Gazetteers* describing the chain of 'mercantile' operations discussed earlier wrote, 'The local dealers would advance money to the grower and *buy his crop* before it was ready for picking' (emphasis mine), then the surface appearance here is definitely that of a transaction between sellers and buyers. In other words, this superficial appearance belongs strictly to the sphere of *simple circulation,* and within this sphere and its 'appearance' the household figures as a simple owner (and producer) of commodities. As far as the Civil Courts, i.e., bourgeois law, was concerned, only this appearance mattered, for in law all commodity-owners are equal.

The crucial point comes now. Marx, describing the case where buyer and seller become creditor and debtor, respectively, where the price of the commodity has been realised in advance, before the commodity is handed over, cited the example of the 'advance payments' prevailing in other parts of India in the purchase of opium. We know today that the opium-trade was hardly as simple as this, and that very few of the households producing poppy could validly be called 'simple-commodity owners'. Marx himself was aware that in the transaction M–C, M might represent not simply money in its functional form of 'means of purchase', but *capital* being advanced (as it almost always is) *in the form of money.* 'Of course, capital, too, is advanced in the form of money and it is possible that the money advanced [in the transactions in opium] is capital advanced'.[66] To simplify matters and somewhat schematically, the 'advances' could be seen in one of two quite distinct ways.

---

[66] Marx 1970, p. 140 and footnote.

(*a*) According to the laws of simple circulation, the advances would represent payments for the commodity, or a realisation of the price of the commodity before the commodity itself is handed over. In this case, money would function as 'means of purchase'.

(*b*) According to the laws of capital circulation, the advances would represent advances of capital in money-form.

That is to say, here, in case (*b*), the advances would *reconstitute the process of production* by enabling the reproduction of labour-power (the peasant's subsistence) and reproduction of the means of production (his seed, bullocks). Whereas in (*a*) the crop 'sold in advance' would represent the peasant's commodity, in case (*b*) it would represent the commodity-capital of the capitalist who has made the advances, that is, the capital he advanced at the start of the cycle, now expanded to include surplus-value, but emerging at the end of the labour-process in commodity-form.

To which of these schematically distinct cases would the relations of the Deccan economy conform? We have already seen that the peasantry of the Deccan 'borrowed' in most cases to meet its *subsistence-costs* and other *simple reproduction-costs*, i.e., to reconstitute their process of production from one year to the next. This is *not* a situation that fits well with case (*a*), where the agents of the production process are independent simple commodity-owners and producers. That a system of *capitalist* exploitation was in fact embodied in the 'advances' emerges more clearly when we turn back to the historical sources.

In Poona 'the husbandman, when his crops were reaped, threshed and garnered, carted them in lump to his creditor's house or shop....As he had parted with all his crop, the husbandman had to borrow fresh sums in cash or grain to meet the instalment of land-revenue, or his own support and for seed'.[67] So, here, the basic circulating elements of the process of production derived entirely from the 'advances'. In Khandesh, 'Both town and village moneylenders often advance grain and money for seed and to support the cultivator's family during the rainy season. These advances are repaid at harvest-time...with the addition of 50 per cent to the sum advanced'.[68] But why would such 'repayments' not have disentangled the household from the grip

---

[67] GBP, *Poona*, pt. 2, p. 132.
[68] GBP, *Khandesh*, p. 195.

of its creditor? The answer is interesting: the small producer's dependence on the monied capitalist would not necessarily continue because the 'account' still remained open, or because the household still had to pay off its 'debts'. Thus, in Sowda *taluka*,

> when the produce of the land has been gathered into the *kullee* and the grain ready for market, the *sowcar closes his account* for presentation, to be liquidated either by money-payment or in grain. By a mutual arrangement contracted at the commencement of the season, the accumulated debts of the year are *for the most* part disbursed in grain...[69]

In other words, even if the 'debts' were 'repaid', the small producer would be left with absolutely no means of subsistence for the coming season – his dependence on the capitalist would thus continue from one cycle to the next, even where at the close of every cycle the 'payments' covered the accumulated debts for the previous year.

It is this domination of the small producer by the capitalist that accounts for the fact that the small cotton-growing peasantry of *talukas* such as Dhulia gained absolutely nothing from the boom of the 1860s. 'The sudden and excessive rise in the price of cotton has given a great stimulus to the cultivation of this crop; but as yet the ryots do not appear to have profited much by this change, the native merchants being the only parties who are really the gainers'.[70] If the cotton-crop represented to a large extent the commodity-capital of monied capitalists rather than the commodities of the small producer, then the rise of commodity-prices would leave the small producer quite untouched. In *talukas* where relationships of this type prevailed, the monied capitalists controlled the bulk of the local produce. Again, in Sowda, 'the *sowcars* hold direct control over the greater portion of the produce raised'; and it was in this sense that Davidson, who witnessed this system in the sixties, wrote, quite correctly: 'the cultivation of the entire district is conducted' by the monied capitalists.

---

[69] BGR, No XCIII, *Papers Relative to the Introduction of Revised Rates of Assessment into Eight Talukas and Two Pettas of the Khandesh Collectorate*, p. 17 (from Davidson's excellent account of Sowda).
[70] BGR, No LXXII, *Papers Relative to the Introduction of Revised Rates of Assessment into the Dhoolia and Chalisgaon Talookas*, Bombay 1863, p. 5.

Translated into Marx's terms, this statement would read: the process of production of the entire district is controlled by monied capitalists.[71]

There were, of course, a few officials in the bureaucracy who did manage to separate the surface appearances from the inner content of such relations. One of them, an assistant collector stationed in the eastern *talukas* of Poona shortly before the famine, wrote:

> The *Sowkar* gives the ryot sufficient to eat and takes the remainder of the produce as part payment of the interest of the debt. This is what actually takes place though of course on the surface the facts look somewhat different, the ryot borrowing cash from the *Sowkar* and paying Government, while the *Sowkar* debits him the cash and credits him with the produce.[72]

Here, Macpherson came very close to understanding the purely capitalist nature of the relationship between the peasant and moneylender. The *surplus-value* extorted from the small producer would be called 'interest', but this would only express the specific form in which relations of production entered the consciousness of its agents. Commenting on Wakefield's description of the depressed condition of the Irish tenantry, Marx wrote: 'In this case [Ireland] profit is called rent, *just as it is called interest*, when, for example, *as in India*, the worker (although nominally independent) works with *advances* which he receives from the capitalist and has to hand over all the surplus produce to the capitalist'.[73] Commodity-relations of production are never directly reflected in consciousness – their forms of appearance mediate their reception into consciousness.

In fact, it would be quite wrong to suppose that these superficial appearance-forms of the basic relations of production represented nothing but 'pure show', something illusory or unessential. They represented the necessary forms of appearance of capitalist relations in the conditions of a small-

---

[71] BGR, No XCIII, *Papers Relative to the Introduction of Revised Rates of Assessment into Eight Talukas and Two Pettas of the Khandesh Collectorate*, p. 17 (Davidson).

[72] RD, Volume 7, 1875, C.G.W. Macpherson, citing his own letter of 16 March 1875. The notions of 'surface layer' and 'necessary illusion' figure in an important passage in Marx 1973, pp. 509–10, where he describes the merchant's control over the small producer. Cf. esp. 'This system of exchange rests on *capital* as its foundation, and when it is regarded in isolation from capital, as it appears on the surface, as an *independent* system, then it is a mere *illusion*, but a *necessary illusion*' (Marx's emphasis).

[73] Marx 1971b, p. 188. Elsewhere, both in this book and in the *Grundrisse*, Marx refers to the 'interest' that the monied capitalist extorts as 'including' his 'profit'.

production economy where the process of labour remained the process of the small producer. This is the specific situation that Marx described at some length in *Theories of Surplus-Value*.[74] 'The third of the older forms of interest-bearing capital is based on the fact that capitalist production does not as yet exist'. That is, its premise is the absence of the specifically capitalist mode of production in its developed form of relative surplus-value production. 'This implies: first that the producer still works independently with his own means of production and that the means of production do not yet work with him'. In other words, it implies that the process of labour remains that of the small-production economy. 'Secondly, that the means of production belong only nominally to the producer; in other words, that because of some incidental circumstances *he is unable to reproduce them* from the proceeds of the sale of his commodities'. Thus the second characteristic of this form – apart from its technological continuity with earlier modes of labour – is the latent crisis of simple reproduction which the small-production economy is thrown into either under the pressures of a series of bad years ('incidental circumstances') or for more basic structural reasons, such as state-exploitation of peasant-production. This crisis of simple reproduction – the hopeless inability of small producers to renew their process of production from one cycle to the next – is precisely what was expressed on the one hand in the proletarianisation of the small producer in the Deccan, on the other hand, in the rapid incursions of the monied capitalist. If the small-production economy of the 1850s already contained such latent defects, then the crises of the period that followed only intensified those defects through the massive and staggering devastation of livestock, and by forcing sales of land and other means of production, crippling reserves of labour-power and pushing up subsistence costs in general. Marx continues that in this form 'The producer pays the capitalist his surplus-labour *in the form of interest*'. That is to say, the capitalist extorts surplus-value

---

[74] Marx 1971b, p. 487. The only other extensive passage which is as explicit comes from the *Grundrisse*, Marx 1973, p. 853, which already contains the germ of the idea developed in the passage in *Theories of Surplus-Value*. There Marx writes, 'The most odious exploitation of labour still takes place...without the relation of capital and labour *here carrying within itself any basis whatever for the development of new forces of production*....What takes place is exploitation by capital without the mode of production of capital'. These passages may be seen as Marx's early attempts to work out the distinction between the formal and the real subsumption of labour into capital. They can be dated quite exactly to the years 1858–63.

in the form of interest, for, as Marx writes elsewhere, 'the exorbitant interest which the capital of the usurer attracts... is *just another name for surplus-value*'.[75] It follows, and this is Marx's own conclusion: 'We have here', in the 'form' just outlined, '*the whole of capitalist production* without its advantages – the development of the social forms of labour and of the productivity of labour to which they give rise'. Thus the 'third of the older forms of interest-bearing capital' would compose a system of capitalist exploitation but *outside* the framework of the specifically capitalist mode of production based on machinery, continuous revolutionising of the process of labour, and the production of relative surplus-value. It would compose the form which we encountered earlier as the 'formal subsumption of labour into capital'. 'This form is very prevalent among peasant nations who already have to buy a portion of the necessaries of life and means of production as commodities'. India was one such 'peasant nation' in Marx's day, as were Egypt, China and Peru.

It is now possible to detect the fault underlying so many of the arguments that downgrade the development of capitalist relations in India. Arguments of the sort that Bhaduri or Patnaik propose confuse the capitalist's intervention in, or control over, the *process of production* with the specifically capitalist form of the *labour*-process. When the process of production of a small-peasant household depends from one cycle to the next on the advances of the usurer – when, without such 'advances', the process of production would come to a halt – then in this case the 'usurer', i.e., the monied capitalist, exerts a definite *command over* the process of production. This control or command is established and operates even when, as in this case, the labour-process remains technologically primitive, manually operated, and continuous with earlier, archaic, modes of labour. The purely formal and stereotyped conceptions of 'capitalist production' that see in its basic relations only the glitter of technological advance (machinery, fertiliser, and so on) have very little in common with Marx's understanding of capitalism, and derive, in large part, from the formalism promoted by Marxists like Dobb.

Let me pose the question more sharply. Is the domination of capital over the small producer – that is, the extortion of surplus-value from small peasants, artisans, etc. – compatible with the forms of the process of labour specific

---

[75] Marx 1976 p. 1023. (Marx is here describing that phase of the process of subordination that I have called 'pre-formal'.)

to those households? Both Marx and Lenin answered, quite clearly, 'yes'. For, 'the fact is that capital subsumes the labour process as it finds it, that is to say, it takes over an existing labour process, developed by different and more archaic modes of production.'[76] This is a theme that Lenin had to constantly emphasise against the Narodniks in Russia, even at the cost of coining terms like 'medieval forms of capitalism'.[77] It follows that, in these forms, based on the 'formal subsumption of labour into capital', the small peasant is a 'simple commodity owner' only by way of his *external* attributes.[78] In Ahmednagar, on one report,

> 75 per cent of the cultivators may be said to be overwhelmed with debt. I have never spoken to one of the poorer class who did not admit that he was completely in the hands of the *sowcar*. I have often seen the *sowcar* sitting in the field while the crop was being reaped, which shows that, in such cases, at least, the cultivator is not a free agent but is compelled to part with his crop, at whatever price the *sowcar* thinks proper.[79]

Again, the sort of compulsion that Norman witnessed around 1874 was a compulsion specific to capitalist relations. The peasants whom Norman saw were not 'bonded labourers' of any variety. Labour-mortgaging was common in various parts of the Deccan from Satara to Khandesh, but the compulsion or element of unfreedom that this assistant collector saw pertained *specifically to*

---

[76] Marx 1976, p. 1021.

[77] Lenin 1963a, pp. 380, 414 ('semi-feudal forms of appropriation of surplus-value'), 485. Cf. his description of the pottery-industry of Moscow *gubernia* in Lenin 1963b, p. 216ff. Lenin's neologisms stem from the fact that the important pages of the Appendix had not been read by him, since they were published for the first time only in 1933.

[78] Preobrazhensky 1965, p. 186: 'As the last transitional stage to genuinely capitalist surplus-value, we may cite the work of handicraftsmen in their homes, for a buyer-up, when they work up the customer's raw material, with tools belonging to him, and are in essentials already actual wage-workers, *even though they retain the external attributes of independent producers.*' The whole conception of peasant households as wage-labour has been developed quite superbly, and with deep empirical reference, by Mike Cowen in Cowen 1976a and 1976b. Cowen's work is distinguished from the general run of Marxist writings by its *combination* of empirical content and theoretical sophistication. Marxists who are interested mainly in the 'theoretical' problems raised by historical materialism are generally quite ignorant of real historical processes (the best case of this is Hindess and Hirst 1975), whereas, conversely, Marxist historians do not feel the need to develop the categories of historical materialism and thus rarely intervene in the purely theoretical debates. The work represented by Marxists such as Cowen is, therefore, especially important.

[79] RD, Volume 3, 1874, H.B. Boswell, citing the Acting Collector G. Norman.

the fact that the small peasants of Ahmednagar were not free to dispose of their crop as they chose, so long as they were bound by a capitalist who year after year paid their subsistence-costs (their wages) and, to one extent or another, controlled their means of production. That is to say, in these relationships, there was 'no fixed political and social relationship of supremacy and subordination' of the sort that characterised the feudal economies of Europe.[80] The person appropriating surplus-labour and the persons surrendering it were bound together by 'the pure money relationship'; the process of exploitation was here 'stripped of every patriarchal, political or even religious cloak'.[81] The coercive power of the moneylender was the coercive power of *capital in its general form*, the form in which it is common to the more advanced forms of capitalist production.

10.5. The big peasantry of the Deccan

The social formation that became involved in this complex and uneven process of the formal subordination of small producers to monied capitalists was one whose internal social morphology was changing rapidly in the nineteenth century. There is a fair amount of evidence which shows that indebtedness as such was not a condition peculiar to the class of small producers. The traditional local ruling classes of the Deccan had likewise to one degree or another become bankrupt and financially dependent on the bigger banking houses and moneylenders. Economically, at least, the *sowcar* was often the wealthiest individual in a given village or small town. The most opulent house there would belong to his family, even if they had moved in only a generation back.

The *sirdars* of Kolhapur formed a tiny and in general wealthy fraction of the district's population. But, of the 600-odd *sirdars*, 'all are in debt, and half of the annual revenue is gathered into the coffers of the bankers'. These *sirdars* continued to live in 'sufficient ease', many of them maintaining retinues of 50 to 80 servants, but their 'estates' were 'heavily mortgaged' to a stratum of bankers who likewise lived in 'very comfortable circumstances'.[82] In neighbouring

---

[80] Marx 1976, p. 1026.
[81] Marx 1976, p. 1025ff.
[82] BGR, No VIII, *Statistical Report on the Principality of Kolhapur*, pp. 160, 166.

Ratnagiri, the picture was even bleaker: 'many of the original *khot* families have now passed away and the *khot* estates are now either held by *sowcars* or by impoverished *khots* who are entirely in the hands of *sowcars*'.[83] So, in the southern periphery of the Presidency, the sector of big agrarian property had fallen into fairly deep financial dependence on the monied capitalists. Like the *taluqdars* of the United Provinces, their fortunes were fast declining in the nineteenth century. Further north, in the central Deccan area, many *patil* families had fallen into similar circumstances. In Haveli taluka of Poona, 'the Patel Vittoojee affords a good instance of the old-fashioned debtor. He has recently mortgaged the whole of his large garden-lands and well to Suddoo Bapoo for a debt of Rs 900'. What makes this case striking is that Suddoo was a *kunbi* by caste.[84] A more typical case comes from Parner village. 'The Kowray family held the patelship of Parner two generations back, when the office was one of great dignity. There is not now one yoke of bullocks or acre of land in Parner village held by the Kowrays'. Raoji Sukraji Kowray's father had owned some 60 acres 'which is all gone into the hands of money-lenders', mainly those of a Marwari who started his business in that area only in the late sixties and over seven years had accumulated 108 acres.[85] There was the patel of Khirdi village in Sowda, whose father had owned '70 acres of the best land'; by the seventies, a series of debts incurred mainly to finance the costs of marriage, coinciding with the price-depression, left this man in the position of a 'day labourer'. 'My eldest son is also a day-labourer'.[86] Or there was the aged patel of Yelavi in Tasgaon, a rich and independent man who, under British rule, had 'descended from the position of a *jagirdar* patil to what he is pleased to term a day-labourer'.[87]

In the sharpest possible contrast to this declining curve of encumbered traditional 'estates', a big peasantry was slowly entrenching itself in the Deccan. This was a layer of the peasantry that based its expansion on that very mobility of agrarian property signified by the decline of *sirdars*, *patels*, *khots*, *jagirdars*, *inamdars*, and so on. These were the peasant-households whom the bureaucracy called, quite impressionistically, 'well-to-do husbandmen', or

---

[83] RD, Volume 1, 1875, Todd.
[84] DRC, *Report Appendix C*, p. 65.
[85] DRC, *Report Appendix C*, p. 66.
[86] DRC, *Report Appendix C*, p. 258f.
[87] RD, Volume 8, 1875, A. Wingate.

occasionally 'small capitalists'. A 'well-to-do' husbandman was defined, in the first instance, precisely in relation to the system of capitalist exploitation that was crystallising across the Deccan. That is to say, he too was engaged in lending money, or in exploiting the labour of other peasants on a basis scarcely different from the one described earlier, even if on a smaller scale. The following picture of such households emerges from the descriptions of the bureaucracy – they generally sold their produce directly on the market, they 'saved' a considerable part of their incomes, they possessed sufficient reserves to last out one or two very bad seasons, they owned a better quality of livestock and could afford to feed their cattle much better, they would generally cultivate *bagait* land to which they applied large quantities of manure, and finally, apart from hiring day-labourers, they could afford to maintain a reserve of permanent farm-labour probably to meet peak-season demands in areas of labour-shortage such as Khandesh. In Ahmednagar, households of this sort could be found in the immediate periphery of the town or in *talukas* like Nevasa where the soil was generally good. In this *taluka*, 'a few husbandmen hold farms of over 200 acres and have 20 to 30 bullocks, and a good many are free from debt and have grain pits of their own'.[88] What would have been the significance of this stratum in a district so tightly dominated by professional moneylenders? 'About 60 per cent of all money-lenders [in the district] are traders...and 40 per cent are husbandmen and others'.[89] In other words, even here, a fairly large proportion of moneylenders were of peasant-stock and occupation. They would have formed part of the smaller, local layer of monied capitalists that entered its process of expansion only in the depression following the boom. In Poona, such households of 'rich landholders' or 'small capitalists', as they were called here, 'themselves bring their produce to the large markets of Poona and Junnar'.[90] This better class of cultivators generally 'had stocks of their own' to weather the bad seasons and, of course, to lend out as grain for the subsistence of the smaller peasantry. Here, thirty per cent of moneylenders were 'husbandmen'. Further south, in Satara, such households exported their produce directly to Poona and Chiplun. In the south and

---

[88] BGR, No CXXIII, *Papers Relating to the Revision of Assessment in Six Talookas of the Ahmednagar Collectorate*, Bombay 1871, p. 12.
[89] GBP, *Ahmednagar*, p. 299.
[90] GBP, Poona, pt. 2, p. 164. They were called 'small capitalists' by J. Francis, BGR, No CVII, *Papers Relative to the Revision of the Assessment of the Indapoor Talooka*, p. 50.

southwest portions of the district 'large and well-to-do husbandmen' regularly utilised permanent farm-labourers on the labour-mortgage system.[91] In Sholapur district to its east, 'substantial farmers' could be found 'in every village of any size' as early as the fifties.[92] They were in most cases 'patils and the higher classes of farmers who always carried on their field operations by means of hired labour'.[93] In Kolhapur, the big peasantry could afford the cost of growing sugarcane, probably the most expensive crop next to grapes, and would generally crush the cane in their own *ghanas*.[94] (This was, of course, before the main period of expansion of cane-cultivation in districts like Kolhapur.) The 'saving classes' of the district included, among others, 'a few rich cultivators'.

It was, however, in the more intensely commercialised north, in Nasik and Khandesh, that this layer of the peasantry was more obvious or prominent. In Nasik, where they combined moneylending with husbandry, such households would deploy minimum capitals of Rs 2,000. Here, 'village headmen and rich cultivators frequently, but on a small scale, lend money and advance seed-grain'.[95] In Dhulia *taluka* of Khandesh, 'we find a great number of very substantial farmers all over the district'.[96] Only these big peasants could afford to 'give their cattle anything like proper sustenance', or only they were 'able to manure their fields properly'.[97] The control of a better quality of livestock, and more of it, meant, moreover, that 'almost all well-to-do husbandmen sell clarified butter', or *ghee*, mainly for local consumption. In all the districts of western Khandesh, close to the Gujarat border, the assistant-collectors generally encountered 'substantial men with plenty of cattle and large holdings'. 'In one or two instances', wrote one of them, 'I have noticed that the lands belonging to Bhils in the Shahada villages are now falling into the possession of *kunbi* farmers' (this dated 1880).[98] These would have been the

---

[91] GBP, *Satara*, p. 189.
[92] BGR, No IV, *Report on the Collectorate of Sholapore*, Bombay 1854, p. 2; the statement was made in 1850.
[93] RD, Volume 22, 1881, A.H. Spry. Because of a labour-shortage that season, these big peasants were forced to watch and harvest their own crops.
[94] GBP, *Kolhapur*, pp. 176, 158.
[95] GBP, *Nasik*, p. 116.
[96] BGR, No LXXII, *Papers Relative to the Introduction of Revised Rates of Assessment into the Dhoolia and Chalisgaon Talookas*, p. 6; GBP, *Khandesh*, p. 364.
[97] GBP, *Khandesh*, pp. 28, 147.
[98] RD, Volume 17, 1880, J. Davidson.

poorer Bhil cultivators who were said to have 'been much impoverished during' the seasons of 1872–4 and reduced to even more desperate circumstances in the famine that followed.[99] Annual wage-contracts were common in this part of Khandesh, where labour was scarce. Further east, in Sowda, 'The peculiarity of the moneylending system in this part of Khandesh is that the capitalists who lend are of the cultivating class themselves.... They are not of the Marwari and Guzar classes'.[100] Thus the *sowcars* who, in this *taluka*, controlled almost its entire process of production, on Davidson's description, derived to a large extent from the peasantry itself. This becomes especially significant when one considers that Sowda witnessed much faster rates of expropriation of the peasantry than most *talukas* of the Deccan would have done. Excluding the few villages along the Satpura range, in most other areas of the *taluka* between seven and nine per cent of the total village arable was transferred either on mortgage or through 'sales' over three years in the early eighties. (It was at this time, moreover, that the expropriation of the Bhil peasantry further west was just beginning.) The beneficiaries of this transfer-process would, therefore, be the big peasants themselves.[101]

One striking expression of the behaviour of this group in the famine is provided by the large sums of private capital invested in the construction of wells both during the famine and in its aftermath. In Nasik, 'it was astonishing to see how many fresh wells...were sunk'. Baines assembled figures to show that in one year of the famine the total number of ordinary wells expanded over 17 per cent in the two *talukas* of Sinnar and Nasik.

> Looking at the comparatively small amount advanced for wells by Government to the ryots in 1876–7, it is clear that the amount of private capital sunk is considerable.... Whenever I have been encamped at the river valley at Sinnar deepening and sinking wells has been going on all round.[102]

---

[99] RD, Volume 6, 1874, R.B. Worthington.
[100] BGR, No CLXXXVI, *Papers Relative to the Revision of the Rates of Assessment on the Expiry of the First Settlement in the Savda Talooka of the Khandesh Collectorate*, Bombay 1886, p. 204 (T.H. Stewart).
[101] Based on an analysis of the 1,099 sales-transactions listed in BGR, No. CLXXXVI.
[102] RD, Volume 14, 1878, J.A. Baines.

In Satara, it was

> obvious that many among the cultivators must be in easy circumstances and able to save. For more than half of the whole amount expended [on well construction, viz. Rs 40,361] was obtained by the ryots from their own resources....It is clear that a considerable class of persons exist, who are bent on effecting improvements on their land.[103]

In Poona, 'the low rate of wages at which labourers were obtainable during the prevalence of the drought in Sirur taluka...caused an extraordinary impetus to private expenditure on garden-wells'. Here, over 1876–7, 193 wells were repaired and another 140 wells newly constructed entirely from private funds. If we take the average cost of digging a well in this period as Rs 400, then, in that year alone, Rs 56,000 of private capital was sunk in the construction of wells in just this one *taluka*,[104] where, in an average year before the seventies, a *taluka* of this size would not have expended more than Rs 6,000.

If we now take the big peasants and the big moneylenders together as a bloc, what picture of their investment-behaviour emerges over this period? In Ahmednagar and Poona, 'traders spend much of their savings in *adding to their business* and in house property....Cultivating classes, especially village headmen, spend their savings in *buying cattle, sinking wells, and adding to their holdings* or building houses'.[105] The 'house property' that the Nagar moneylenders invested in would comprise, for example, the 'small mud-walled and flat-roofed houses' in which the poorer urban classes towards the north of the town lived at rents that could absorb ten per cent of their annual wages. In Satara, 'traders use their increased capital *to extend their business*....In some cases, in which the possession of land has been transferred...especially to husbandmen, the new holders have *invested money in the land* and taken steps to improve it'.[106]

Now the general expansion of commodity-economy, the connected expansion of railways and the general rise of commodity-prices would have boosted the demand for land over this period. The Satara *Gazetteer* tells us

---

[103] RD, Volume 21, 1881, C.H. Jopp.
[104] RD, Volume 17, 1877, E.C. Ozanne.
[105] GBP, *Ahmednagar*, p. 296; *Poona*, pt. 2, p. 100, emphases mine.
[106] GBP, *Satara*, pp. 179, 189.

that 'land is perhaps the favourite investment with all classes possessed of a substantial surplus.... Even among traders, all who are natives of the district are glad to own land.... The fondness for land-investment has undoubtedly increased under British rule'. The first cause listed was the 'increased price of field produce'.[107] So commodity-expansion would have entailed not just faster rates of expansion of monied capitals, but a faster rate of expropriation of the small producer. The 'demand' for land would find its specific reflection not in the ordinary transactions of 'buying and selling', but precisely in the pressure exerted by monied capitalists for mortgages against the small producer's land.

The railways alone would have completely shattered the existing structure of differential rent, so that land would be most in demand in areas with easy access to the market. A detailed and careful analysis of some 2,000 transactions involving land-'sales' in Sowda *taluka* over the early eighties shows that the great majority of villages with the highest rates of land-transfer, alternatively the highest rates of expropriation, fall east of a line drawn vertically down the *taluka* and bisecting it roughly at Faizpur in the centre. Such villages lay, in other words, very close to the railway-stations and within easy access of the Raver and Sowda markets; towards Yaval, moving away from the railway-line, the rates of land-transfer show a distinct drop. The majority of villages in which the process of expropriation was most intense were distinctly 'sub-urban' in character, lying within a 5-mile radius of the local towns. In such villages, the general average rates would exceed 3.33 per cent per year; at this rate, the whole village arable would be transferred in one generation.[108] At the other end of Maharashtra, in Tasgaon, the highest rates of transfer were concentrated in the centrally-located groups of villages around the Krishna River and near Tasgaon market.

Investment in land thus took a specific and more complicated form conditioned by the prevalence of the small-production economy. Moreover, it was not just a general 'mania' for the ownership of land from the point of view of factors like 'prestige', but determined specifically by *economic* motives connected with the process of commodity-expansion. It follows also that an 'investment' in moneylending was not simply a process of extortion of surplus-labour as surplus-value, but also a process of expropriation of the small

---

[107] GBP, *Satara*, p. 179f.
[108] Based on the sales-transactions in BGR, No CXXXVI, App. K, pp. 27–57.

producer, and thus part of the concentration of the means of production as capital. Relating this back to the more general remarks on 'how traders spend much of their savings', it is possible to see that much of the investment-behaviour of big moneylenders and big peasants related to an accumulation and concentration of capital, but within the specific limits imposed by labour-processes continuous with those of the small-production economy.

10.6. Peasant-differentiation

The descriptions provided by various revenue-officials suggest that we can posit the following 'classes' of the Deccan peasantry:

(1) A *big* peasantry – exploiting small peasants as *monied capitalists* and employing hired labour in cultivation;
(2) A *small* peasantry, differentiated internally into:
    (i) an independent middle peasantry that incurred loans to meet occasional expenses of an economic or social nature;
    (ii) a more depressed and dependent middle peasantry regularly exploited by monied capitalists, from whom it derived much of its means of subsistence and production;
(3) A *semi-wage-labour* peasantry – structurally dependent on hiring out its labour-power and not generally 'creditworthy'.

Davidson, in his account of the Sowda and Yaval *talukas*, writes,

> I would divide [the cultivators] into three classes: 1) Individuals holding land, either *deshmouks, patels, choudries,* or *koolkurnies,* who being possessed of considerable wealth, lend it out at interest to the poorer cultivators, besides which they purchase largely the produce both for consumption within the district and for export. 2) Individuals who are in comfortable circumstances, and can farm their lands without applying to the *sowcars* for capital. 3) The larger portion of the cultivators are included in this grade who are absolutely in the hands of the wealthier class, to whom they apply for money in the the first instance to enable them to purchase their seed grain, also sufficient to support existence while their crops are in the ground.[109]

---

[109] BGR, No XCIII, *Papers Relative to...Eight Talukas and Two Pettas of the Khandesh Collectorate*, p. 16 (A.F. Davidson, 23 December 1854).

Thus here, in a sector of the Deccan defined by very high rates of commodity-production, the combination would be 1 + 2(i) + 2(ii). Further east, in the *talukas* where a Bhil peasantry was more common, the general combination would include them as 3 (a class dependent on wage-employment). South of Khandesh, in Nasik, Ramsay classified the peasantry on a similar model: 'My own opinion briefly put is that about one-third of the cultivators are hopelessly in debt', that is, would depend on advances for their annual subsistence, 'another third more or less so, and the remaining third free from serious encumbrances. I allude here to the better portions of the district', namely, the *deshi* villages as opposed to the peasantry in the hills.[110] Here, a similar combination prevailed, with the important difference that 2(i), the independent middle peasantry was in a state of far deeper dependence on the monied classes. This is confirmed by Baines, who made a statement that is otherwise difficult to comprehend: 'The greater portion of the middle class cultivators of the *deshi* villages exist by the favour of their creditors in a state of fairly well-to-do solvency; that is, they mostly owe a good deal more than they ever...are able to pay'.[111] This is the sort of layer within the general stratum of small peasants that would experience a quite perceptible decline in its position in the event that the rates of assessment were enhanced, or in periods of scarcity and famine. Households of this sort would be compelled to intensify their labour-activity and/or cut down their level of consumption under pressures of this type.

The decision to intensify labour-activity might mean deeper dependence on the *sowcar* by way of an application for the money with which to construct wells. Thus, in Nasik, 'the recent scarcity has, of course, increased the burden thus thrown upon them but they will pass it over to their sons'.[112] The Commission investigating the riots found that, for a large number of households, indebtedness was an inherited or 'ancestral' condition, reflecting debts incurred by the previous generation. In 1875, these households would have formed a depressed middle peasantry, but its origins would lie in the disintegration of a more independent layer that had been forced into the hands of monied capitalists over the previous thirty years. In Sholapur, the collector

---

[110] RD, Volume 14, 1878, W. Ramsay.
[111] RD, Volume 23, 1879, J.A. Baines.
[112] Ibid., Baines.

thought not much pressure for recovery of arrears should be applied to the middle strata of the peasantry 'whose resources have been crippled by the famine'.[113] An abrupt recovery of arrears that had accumulated over four or five years would mean, even supposing it were possible, a wholesale disintegration of the independent middle peasantry into the ranks of a depressed and capitalistically exploited lower-middle peasantry, or into the labour-market. Against a background of high rates of assessment, this layer, 2(i), would emerge out of every conjuncture of price-depression or famine with a progressively *weaker base for the process of reproduction*. It would find it increasingly difficult to reconstitute its process of production from one year to the next, and would generally end up as a depressed and completely dependent stratum.

Further south, in Satara,

> Husbandmen may be roughly divided into four classes: 10 per cent with good credit, 25 per cent with fair credit, forty with scanty credit, and 25 per cent with little or no credit. The ten per cent of first class husbandmen are well-off.... First class husbandmen also occasionally lend small sums to the poorer husbandmen of their own village. The 25 per cent of second class husbandmen are fairly off. They are generally in need of no loans either for food or seed, but they often borrow to pay the Government assessment and to meet the extraordinary expenses of marriages and other family events.... The 40 per cent of third class husbandmen are well off for a few months after harvest. During the rest of the year...they have to borrow for food as well to pay the Government assessment. In poor seasons their condition is generally miserable.... The 25 per cent of the fourth class are badly off during the greater part of the year. Besides tilling small plots of land they work as field labourers.[114]

Thus, the structure of the Deccan peasantry mirrored the different phases of the long-run process of formal subsumption of labour into capital. The domination of capitalists in the specific form described earlier would extend over the vast mass of the small peasantry as I have defined this. But, within this mass of small peasants, the two layers distinguished earlier would reflect

---

[113] RD, Volume 22, 1881, Spry.
[114] GBP, *Satara*, p. 185.

different degrees of subordination of labour to capital, or different moments of the actual process of formal subsumption. To repeat, under formal subsumption, the capitalist stands out as the immediate owner of the process of production, whether this 'ownership' has been legally sanctified or not. The reconstitution of the production-process depends on the advances of capital that he makes in the form of 'loans' or 'advance-payment'. Now, this degree of domination would cover only those households who depended precisely on such 'advances' for their annual subsistence-costs and means of production. It would cover, in other words, specifically that layer which was described above as a *depressed and dependent middle peasantry*.

It follows that, between the general condition and levels of welfare and consumption of *this* stratum of the peasantry, on one side, and of the proletariat, on the other, there would be scarcely any difference at all. In fact, referring to this specific group of households, Bapu Purshottam, a district deputy-collector based in Dhulia, thought that 'the condition of some of the landholders has been *actually worse than that of day labourers*'.[115] An official based elsewhere in Khandesh made the same point: 'in very many cases the condition of the independent *khatedar*', independent in the sense of being nominally in control of his means of production, 'is *far worse* than that of the poorest *saldar*'.[116] When we grasp the underlying relations of production that such *khatedars* were involved in, that is, their exploitation *by capital*, statements of this kind become easier to understand.

Now, in this whole argument, one further notion is implicit. The formal subsumption of labour into capital implies and entails a process of expropriation of the small producer. Thus a further conclusion from the analysis presented above is that precisely these middle-strata of the peasantry suffered the process of expropriation especially severely. This is a conclusion strikingly confirmed by the data on land-transfers. The most complete data that I have analysed pertain to Tasgaon for the nine years from 1866 to 1874, and

---

[115] RD, Volume 6, 1874, Bapoo Purshottam, emphasis mine.
[116] RD, Volume 6/1, 1875, J. Pollen, emphasis mine. A *saldar* family would have consumed around 300 litres of grain a year, which compares with the *lowest* rates of consumption that we know from classical antiquity. In Cato's day, slave-rations were in fact considerably higher. For 'labour-intensification' and the economic logic of small-peasant production, see the model proposed tentatively in Banaji 1976.

the further five years from 1881 to 1885.¹¹⁷ Data on individual transactions are available only for the latter period. The analysis of this shows that of a total of 121 transactions over those five years, 40 per cent involved land-pieces of 10–20 acres in extent, and another 21 per cent land-pieces from 20 to 30 acres. The *khatas* from which these land-pieces derived would normally be somewhat bigger in size, as households would not have sold off the whole *khata* but only specific portions of it. It follows that *at least* two-thirds, and probably much more, of the total number of transactions involved layers of the peasantry operating *khatas* of more than ten acres. In Satara, ten acres in fact formed the critical divide between a household that could support itself 'in decent comfort' and one that could not.¹¹⁸ The 'fourth class' of households who in this district were said to be largely dependent on wage-labour would tend to fall on one side of this divide, and the 'second' and 'third' classes, or the small peasantry proper, on the other.

If we contrast the ratios in which these various groups figured in the overall distribution of holdings for the *taluka* with the ratios of their participation in the list of land 'sales', as shown in Table 1, it is obvious that the *middle*-strata of Tasgaon's peasantry suffered the process of expropriation more severely than the other groups. In Tasgaon the movement of expropriation was concentrated in the years 1866–74, the aftermath of the cotton-boom, and barely six or seven years later it had lost its impetus. For villages with generally high transfer-rates, those in the Krishna valley and around Tasgaon itself, the average annual rate of transfer in that early period was 4.4 per cent: at this rate, had it been sustained, the entire arable land of these villages would have changed hands in just twenty-two years. In Tasgaon, the expropriation of the small producer thus coincided mainly with a period of declining prices and recurrent scarcities. Already by 1875, only about 100 of the *taluka*'s 900 families of landowners were thought to be 'entirely independent of debt'.¹¹⁹

---

¹¹⁷ Data for the early period is available in A. Wingate's description of Tasgaon in RD, Volume 8, 1875, pp. 239ff.; the later period was covered by H.K. Disney in BGR, No CCIV, *Papers Relating to...Tasgaon Taluka of the Satara Collectorate*, Bombay 1888.
¹¹⁸ GBP, *Satara*, p. 150. Of course, this would form the dividing line only in the more fertile Krishna villages.
¹¹⁹ From A. Wingate's report, see n. 117.

Table 1. Land-transfer in Tasgaon by classes of peasantry.

Social type	Acreage group	Overall %	% selling out
3	0.1–10	33.8	31.4
2 (ii)	10–20	26.6	40.5
2 (i)	20–30	16.8	21.5
1	30+	22.8	6.6

If middle peasants were exploited in the ways described above, poor peasants with *khatas* of less than ten acres in the more fertile areas or less than thirty in the barren eastern *talukas* of the Deccan depended on wage-employment. Even here, the employers of hired labour were often the monied capitalists, for a large proportion of small peasants were involved in transporting grain for moneylenders who, by extortion of their surplus-labour, had built up these reserves of grain. In Ahmednagar, 'in January, when the busy season is over, many with their bullocks are *hired by* Marwaris and other traders to carry grain and oil-seeds to Ahmednagar and Poona in the traders' carts from Jamkhed, Karjat, Parner and Shrigonda'.[120] Alternatively, these and other lower strata of the peasantry would 'go for a time to Bombay and other places to work as labourers and carriers'.[121] In Poona, 'during the eight months from October to June... a considerable proportion of the *kunbi* or cultivating classes go to Bombay where they earn a living as palanquin-bearers, carriers, grass-cutters and labourers'.[122] In Kolhapur, 'the poorer husbandmen work also as field labourers, chiefly in weeding and harvesting'.[123] In Sangli, 'the poorer husbandmen, when freed from field work, are employed as day labourers'.[124] These patterns of annual labour-migration, implying a structural dependence on wage-labour, would characterise only the lower groups of the peasantry. In contrast to them, 'in years of local scarcity the people scatter in search of subsistence to all parts of the Presidency, to the Berars' and to Marathwada.[125]

---

[120] GBP, *Ahmednagar*, p. 241; BGR, No CXXIII, *Papers Relating to the Revision of Assessment in Six Talookas of the Ahmednagar Collectorate*, p. 15.
[121] GBP, *Ahmednagar*, p. 241.
[122] GBP, *Poona*, pt. 1, p. 98.
[123] GBP, *Kolhapur*, p. 154.
[124] GBP, *Kolhapur*, p. 337.
[125] GBP, Poona, pt. 1, p. 98; BGR, No CXVII, *Report on the Assessment of the Rahooree Talooka*, p. 6; BGR, No CXXIII, *Papers Relating to... Six Talookas of the Ahmednagar Collectorate*, p. 107.

These were more random cyclical migrations that would involve a large proportion of the middle peasantry that found itself unable to survive in years of famine.

Seasonal dependence on wage-labour was more intense in the poorer regions of the Deccan, where alternative sources of income such as the production of livestock, the sale of firewood or timber or grass, could not substitute adequately. The Man *taluka* in Satara was one such region. It was 'subject to constant droughts....Every year, large numbers of people are forced to leave in search of work'.[126] Bhimthadi in Poona is another example. Here 'the deficit which frequently exists [in the peasant budget] is made up by the produce of stock and of the dairy and by the [wage-] labour of the *kunbi* and that of his family and his cattle'.[127] 'This exported labour must be looked upon as maintaining the solvency of the district, for little else is exported'. Thus wage-labour was crucial to Bhimthadi. It was likewise important in Sholapur where large numbers would migrate annually, 'even in the best of years'.[128]

The most dramatic case is of course the Konkan district of Ratnagiri, which supplied the bulk of the labour-force for the nascent textile-industries of Bombay. Ratnagiri was by universal consent the most impoverished district of the Presidency, characterised by 'overpopulation', brutal quit-rent exploitation, permanent grain-deficits, and large currents of outward migration. Here 'the poorer class of cultivators maintain themselves by cutting every stick they can lay their hands on'.[129] At the opposite pole of the Presidency, Khandesh affords a case of the exception proving the rule – endowed with a better quality of soil, less prone to drought, and devoting a large proportion of his arable to commodity production, the Khandesh *kunbi* had 'seldom to leave his family-holding in search of work'.[130] In Khandesh, hired labourers were recruited mainly from the Bhil tribal peasantry.

---

[126] GBP, *Satara*, p. 435.
[127] DRC, *Report of the Committee on the Riots in Poona and Ahmednagar*, p. 40.
[128] RD, Volume 28, 1879, Spry.
[129] RD, Volume 7, 1875, J. Elphinstone.
[130] GBP, *Khandesh*, p. 179.

10.7. The stage of evolution of capitalism in the nineteenth-century Deccan

The same form of capitalist exploitation that prevailed in the countryside worked in the small towns in relation to the smaller artisans. 'As a class handloom weavers are entirely in the hands of moneylenders. The moneylenders advance all the yarn and silk required and take possession of the article'.[131] In Satara, artisans generally procured their raw materials 'from the traders at high credit rates'. The cotton-weavers of this district were internally differentiated into a group that owned capital and employed wage-labour, and a larger mass that 'borrow money from Gujars and Marwaris to buy the yarn and pay for it by the articles they weave'.[132] Thus, in this branch of production as well, surplus-value would be extorted from the small producer in the form of 'interest'. This transitional and backward form of capitalist production was generally prevalent throughout the artisan-economy of the Deccan. In Khandesh, 'very few artisans, not more than 10 per cent, are free from debt.... *Koshtis* are, as a rule, in the hands of moneylenders, who advance money or yarn and in return get the goods when ready'.[133] Such weavers were said to 'work under the orders of' their creditors. As in Satara, so in Khandesh, the weaving community was internally differentiated into a group of 'small capitalists' who would 'lend money', i.e., exploit artisan-labour on a capitalist basis, and a large mass of proletarianised artisans 'employed by men of capital'. 'Both men and women weave, keeping not more than 30 holidays in the year, and working, except for about an hour's rest at noon, from morning to night, so long as they have light to see'. In this district the proletarianised weavers would thus have worked a minimum of 12 hours a day. A 'good' workman might earn Rs 200 a year, most of this in the busy season from May to October. An artisan more tightly dominated by the capitalist would earn at most Rs 140, and on average Rs 90.[134] The family as a whole would have to subsist on these rates of pay, and that in a period when subsistence-costs were rising in the Deccan towns with the expansion of the railway-lines,[135] when demand-recessions inevitably followed periods of scarcity and famine, as

---

[131] GBP, *Ahmednagar*, p. 302.
[132] GBP, *Satara*, pp. 184, 222.
[133] GBP, *Khandesh*, p. 198.
[134] GBP, *Khandesh*, pp. 224, 229 and for factory wage-rates p. 231.
[135] GBP, *Ahmednagar*, p. 348, with reference to town labourers and artisans.

they did in earlier epochs of production, e.g., in late-medieval Europe, and when, finally, the monied capitalists would be compelled to intensify the rate of exploitation of household-labour, producing more absolute surplus-value, under the competitive threat of large-scale industries. In Nasik, the silk-industry was composed of a small group, around ten per cent, who 'have capital and work up and dispose of their own silk', and a majority-group of 'skilled labourers employed by capitalists and paid by the piece'. The average annual earnings of a proletarianised silk weaver in Nasik would be around Rs 80.[136] Finally, in Kolhapur, the more dependent goldsmiths, also skilled workers, were employed by 'some rich bankers...on daily wages to make ornaments for sale'; they earned around Rs 90.[137]

The capital/wage-labour relationship was thus widespread throughout the Deccan, in both town and countryside, at a time when it was expanding fast, in more modern forms, in Bombay itself. This bears directly on the recent debate on 'the mode of production' which, by general agreement, has been quite inconclusive so far.

In this debate, (1) one tendency entirely denies the development of capitalist relations in the country. It argues that India is even today a 'semi-feudal' country and that no bourgeois revolution, even of the 'passive' type analysed by Antonio Gramsci,[138] has occurred here. Yet precisely the political activists of this tendency have for the last ten years struggled against *capitalist* forms of exploitation in the countryside, and, for this, they have been subjected to brutal repression by the bourgeois state.

(2) A centrist current agrees that bourgeois relations have developed to a limited extent, but it argues that this development has taken place mainly since Independence. In the conclusion, I shall concentrate on this tendency.

(3) Finally, there is a Gunder-Frankian tendency that sees in India's historical integration into the capitalist world-economy sufficient proof of the prevalence of bourgeois relations within the country. Because the dominance of capitalist relations on the world-scale is a more-or-less obvious fact, this tendency has never seriously undertaken the task of actually demonstrating in what forms capitalist relations evolved within the country. At best, and

---

[136] GBP, *Nasik*, pp. 161, 168.
[137] GBP, *Kolhapur*, p. 207.
[138] Gramsci 1976, pp. 106–7, referring to 'the current phenomenon of Gandhism in India'.

this would apply to Paresh Chattopadhyay, tendencies of this type appeal to a series of more-or-less isolated phenomena internal to the country's development, which relate, however, almost entirely to the processes of *commodity*-expansion and, therefore, only establish that the framework for the evolution of bourgeois relations had emerged internally.

An assessment of the debate – which I do not propose here – would have to start with the pure historical impressionism that has characterised most of the contributions. Arguments were hardly ever related to the very concrete historical data comprised in countless numbers of volumes that are today only gathering dust in various record-offices throughout the country. However, the method and understanding of theory that underlies the contributions are far more significant. Take the extreme formalism that attempts to classify households of the peasantry according to the 'labour-exploitation criterion'.

To start with, Bhaduri and Patnaik reflect a widespread tendency when they identify labour-arrangements and forms of organisation of the labour-process implied by sharecropping and other types of tenancy with 'pre-capitalist' or 'semi-feudal' *relations of production*. Now, big peasants of the sort that we encountered in the nineteenth-century Deccan would be 'capitalist entrepreneurs in agriculture who as a rule employ several hired labourers' (Lenin) but who do not necessarily confine themselves to labour-arrangements involving only day-workers or casual labour. They might, for example, maintain a reserve of 'permanent' farm-labour, as they did in Khandesh, or they might base their labour-arrangements on one of several types of tenancy. If a big peasant (or a big landowner) chooses to substitute tenant-labour for wage-labour, then this could relate to a permanent shortage of labour in the area, or to fact that wage-costs have been rising (both true of Khandesh in the nineteenth century), or it could relate to the fact that 'tenancy is more profitable than wage-labour', and not 'because small-scale farming is more efficient but because self-employed labourers make a fuller use of available labour'.[139] Again, which particular form of tenancy a big peasant or landowner decides to organise will depend on the type of cultivation, its specific technical requirements, a possible preference for piece-work in an attempt to minimise costs,

---

[139] Martinez-Alier 1971 analyses labour-arrangements and labour-contracts on the Spanish *latifundia* to show how capitalist relations of production are compatible with forms such as tenancy and sharecropping. See also his polemic against Warriner in Chapter 8.

the degree of managerial control that this or that type allows, and so on and so forth.

None of this affects the social character or content of the *production-relations* that these labour-arrangements embody. The big peasantry, personifications of capital in the rudimentary forms in which capital exists within a small-production economy where the specifically capitalist mode of production is absent, do not change their social forms and functions as small capitalists merely according to the types of labour-arrangements they deploy, or the labour-contracts that they enforce. Lenin was quite aware of this and, therefore, delivered a warning. He wrote, 'our literature frequently contains too stereotyped an understanding of the theoretical proposition that capitalism requires the free, landless worker.... The allotment of land to the rural worker is very often done in the interests of the rural employers themselves.... The type assumes different forms in different countries' – forms that Lenin correctly thought were historically conditioned.[140]

However, Patnaik is quite consistent. Starting from the erroneous identification of (a) the particular labour-arrangements and labour-contracts deployed by employers in the countryside, with (b) the relations of production as such, she forces herself to split up the capitalist peasantry into a 'proto-feudal rich peasantry' and a 'proto-bourgeois rich peasantry'. Verbal contortions of this type only indicate the complete lack of clarity into which her approach inevitably leads.[141]

Bhaduri's empiricism is identical in content: all the superficial forms of the formal subordination of labour to capital are converted into independent, substantive features that express entirely different production-relations. To start with, indebtedness as such is not a hallmark of 'pre-capitalist' relations, if only because it is precisely through the *power of money* that the *despotism of capital* is initially established. In the second place, when Bhaduri distinguishes 'usury' and 'property rights in land' as two separate 'modes of exploitation' of labour-power, he only grasps the distinction of form *within capital itself*: for, both money and land are simply used as capital, i.e., for the extortion of surplus-value. The tying of labour to this or that individual capital (landowner)

---

[140] Lenin 1956, pp. 178–9.
[141] Patnaik 1976. The very absurdity of the term 'feudal peasantry' should have suggested to Patnaik that something was seriously wrong with her whole approach. 'Protos' and 'semis' will not help us either.

does not in the least alter the content of the social relation as one of capitalist domination. For such forms of bondage are precisely a characteristic of the *formal* subordination of labour to capital, that is, of a system in which capital retains its individual character.

All of these points could be summed up if we return to the specific way in which Lenin understood the development of bourgeois relations in the so-called 'domestic industries', in this case, the pottery-industry around Moscow.

> The *relations* in this industry too – and similar examples could be quoted indefinitely – are bourgeois.... We see how a minority, owning larger and more profitable establishments, and receiving a 'net' income from the labour of others...accumulate 'savings', while the majority are ruined.... It is obvious and inevitable that the latter should be enslaved to the former – inevitable precisely because of the capitalist character of the given production relations. These relations are: the product of social labour, organised by commodity economy, passes into the hands of individuals and in their hands serves as an instrument for oppressing and enslaving the working people, as a means of personal enrichment by the exploitation of the masses. And do not think that this exploitation, this oppression, is any less marked because relations of this kind are still poorly developed, because the accumulation of *capital*, concomitant with the ruination of the producers, is negligible. Quite the contrary. This only leads to cruder, serf forms of exploitation, to a situation where capital, not yet able to subjugate the worker directly, by the mere purchase of his labour-power at its value, enmeshes him in a veritable net of usurious extortion, binds him to itself by kulak methods, and as a result robs him not only of the surplus-value but of an enormous part of his wages too'.[142]

Thus, here is a case of the development of bourgeois relations necessitating 'crude serf forms of exploitation'. The position would obviously have been no different in the Deccan countryside and towns, and is no different in many parts of India today where the subordination of labour to capital remains 'formal'.

---

[142] Lenin 1963b, p. 216, emphasis in original.

As I suggested earlier, Bhaduri, Patnaik, and others of a similar tendency, simply confuse the capitalist's command over the process of production with the specifically capitalist form of the labour-process. At the first level, the command or intervention of capital summarises a value-relationship pure and simple, a relationship of surplus-value production, or of the process of production as a 'valorisation-process'. All that is necessary to the constitution of this command is that a relationship of *pure economic dependence* prevail between the producer and the owner of capital, and that on this basis he compels the production of surplus-labour.

This general social despotism of capital over labour may find its *adequate expression or shape* within the specifically capitalist form of the labour-process (relative surplus-value production) based on machinery and the increasing predominance of fixed capital. There remains, all the same, an important distinction between the two, and it is this that Bhaduri, Patnaik and others have yet to grasp. For, even where the labour-process remains external to the movement of capital as a process of centralising social means of production and labour-power for the more effective extortion of surplus-value, capital may, can, and does extort surplus-labour in the form of surplus-value. This brings us directly to a central underlying premise of the whole debate, one common, in different ways, to all sides.

Positions downgrading the development of capitalist relations in India automatically supposed that, if you denied that a specifically capitalist mode of production prevailed in India, or does prevail today, then you would be denying the prevalence of capitalist forms of exploitation of whatever type, however undeveloped the stage of bourgeois production that they express. This is a premise that totally contradicts Marx's whole effort to distinguish the specific modes of subordination of labour to capital. It contradicts the view proposed by Marx himself that the 'formal subsumption of labour under capital...can be found as a *particular* form alongside the specifically capitalist mode of production in its developed form, because although the latter entails the former, the *converse does not necessarily obtain*'.[143] That is to say, the formal subsumption of labour under capital can be found even in the absence of the developed form of the capitalist mode of production positing large-scale

---

[143] Marx 1976, p. 1019; Marx 1973, p. 853, emphasis mine.

industry, social forces of production, etc. This essay has attempted to demonstrate precisely this thesis within a concrete frame of reference. It shows that:

(1) The capitalist mode of production in its developed or 'adequate' structure was neither dominant nor widespread within the country, that, in this sense, India remained a 'backward' nation that had yet to witness a process of large-scale industrialisation.
(2) But capitalist relations of exploitation signifying the less advanced forms of capitalist production[144] had emerged within a conjuncture of expanding commodity-production, and were widespread and in some districts dominant.

Under this system, the monied capitalists of the Deccan exerted a definite *control* over the process of production, even if the process of labour as such remained technologically continuous with the labour-process of the small-production economy. A greater proportion of the small peasantry and town-based handicraftsmen were in no position to reconstitute the process of production from year to year. The capitalist advanced them their wages and means of production as 'loans', and recovered his surplus-value as 'interest'. These relations did not, of course, transcend the limits of the production of *absolute* surplus-value, so that increases in the rate of exploitation of labour-power were purely a function of the most primitive forms of labour-intensification and a lengthening of the working day.

This stage of development, called by Marx the formal subordination of labour to capital, was the specific stage the Deccan districts had reached towards the final decades of the nineteenth century. What is wrong, then, with the position that argues that relations within the backward countries were capitalist from their very inception as components of world-economy (tendency 3)?

When we locate the national-economic forms that crystallised in various parts of the country within the deeper context of an expanding capitalist world-economy, then it is immediately apparent that the nationally-dominant forms of subsumption of labour into capital were merely 'a *particular* form alongside the specifically capitalist mode of production'. For, the determina-

---

[144] 'More and less advanced forms' in Marx 1976, p. 1054.

tion of capital as a social reproduction-process or of capital as social capital reflects itself most adequately in the form of world-capital, and this composed the deeper framework of the process of commodity-expansion that started in the Deccan around the 1850s. Well before the cotton-boom, every poor cotton-harvest in America, for example in 1836, 1838, 1845, 1846, 1849, had revived and stimulated the interest of British capitalists in an Indian cotton-supply. After 1848, the Manchester Chamber of Commerce began a systematic and concerted campaign to secure Government interest in a supply from India. This agitation occurred against the background of a steady rise in the price of the standard American quality. By 1861 the programme of the Cotton Supply Association included as its major objectives the conversion of land into a commodity, the establishment of effectual courts of law with the power to enforce contracts, and massive state-expenditure in public works that would link the cotton-districts to the port of Bombay.

It was around this time, on the eve of the boom, that an interesting debate broke out on the specific mechanisms through which an expanded supply of cotton could be procured. On one side were men like Sir Charles Wood, Secretary of State for India, who thought that a 'fair and remunerative price' was a sufficient basis for an expansion of the supply; that is, that the small peasants of the cotton-districts had direct access to the market and would allocate their means of production in response to the movement of market-prices. On the other side, J.B. Smith, orthodox Free Trader and President of the Manchester Chamber of Commerce argued that the Indian peasant was not a 'free agent' but in thrall to moneylenders so that 'demand according to our European notion is not comprehended in India'.[145] Of course, both sides were both right and wrong – the Chamber of Commerce in believing that the small producer was not a 'free agent', that is, a simple-commodity producer, was fundamentally correct, but as the boom would show them in only one or two years, the movement of market-prices *was* a basic determinant of the level of supply, if only because the economic agents who had come to control the process of production of the small producer, those who dominated him as a wage-slave, found nothing incomprehensible in the 'European' conception of profitability.

---

[145] All this based on two detailed studies: Silver 1966; Harnetty 1972.

The commodity-expansion of those years was thus rooted, quite specifically, in the world-demand for commodities like cotton, wheat, oilseeds and foodgrains generally. It was rooted, in other words, in the expansive rhythms of the world reproduction-process of capital, and, in this sense, the specific form of capitalist production that evolved within the local commodity-framework composed a *subordinate and transitional system* within the bourgeois mode of production in its *world*-extension.

Now, the Gunder-Frankian tendency sees only this general or abstract determination – the pressures of the world reproduction-process of capital and their mediation through the state. This general determination becomes its *idée fixe*, its peculiar obsession, so that it then supposes that it is sufficient to point to the dominance of the specifically capitalist mode of production on the world-scale to establish the prevalence of capitalist relations in India. Thus, whereas positions of the second type combine a formalist *apriorism* with crude empiricism, positions of the third type directly subordinate the concrete to the abstract in the manner of Ricardo's understanding of the value-relation. Here, the real process that unifies essence and appearance, that makes them parts of a single process, is completely ignored. The concrete processes by which capitalist relations evolved in various parts of world economy are simply dissolved in the abstract identity of world-capitalism.

[1977]

Chapter Eleven
Trajectories of Accumulation or 'Transitions' to Capitalism?

The late nineteenth century was the watershed of agrarian capitalism, the first age of discernibly modern forms of agriculture and their rapid evolution. Founded in 1866 by a group of powerful progressive landowners, the Sociedad Rural Argentina would see its membership expand some two decades later. The rapid transformation of livestock-farming in the 1880s was dominated by powerful *estancieros* and made Argentina's landowners 'the most prestigious and dynamic sector of the Argentine bourgeoisie'.[1] 'By the turn of the century, the pampean *estancia* had become the most efficient meat-producing enterprise in the world'.[2] Because rural wages in the pampas were the highest in Latin America, 'Argentine landowners were compelled to use labour more efficiently than any other Latin American rural employers'. The typical big *estancias* could comprise several thousand hectares 'but employ no more than a few dozen labourers'.[3] In Ferrara, the vast reclamation-schemes of the 1870s and 1880s and the involvement of limited companies aiming at the exploitation of enormous tracts of land[4] were the symbols of this

---
[1] Hora 2001, p. 64.
[2] Hora 2001, p. 224.
[3] Hora 2001, p. 94.
[4] Corner 1975, pp. 1–2.

burgeoning capitalism.[5] The estates formed out of those schemes were divided into huge blocks of several hundred hectares each and worked mainly by gangs of casual labourers drawn from the massified labour-forces of Emilia and the lower Po valley.[6] The specialised, intensive horticulture that emerged in California in the 1880s and 1890s created a different kind of countryside, but one based, like the Emilian estates, on the low-wage mobility of impoverished migrant workers. As this orchard-capitalism engendered a radical simplification of landscapes, it brought about an explosion of insect-populations, and a whole network of scientists, agencies and industries sprang up to 'rescue fruit growing from the effects of its own expansion'.[7] And, in Cuba, the turn of the century paved the way for the restructuring of the Cuban sugar-industry as 'the older mills, known as ingenios, were dismantled and replaced by modern, large-scale central factories, known in Cuba as centrales'.[8] The large-scale sugar-factories that emerged in the aftermath of the Cuban War of Independence (1895–8) exploited economies of scale and were financed largely by North-American capital. 'By 1927, North American companies controlled about three-quarters of the Cuban sugar crop'.[9]

These were among the most advanced forms of capitalist agriculture c. 1900, heavily capitalised enterprises owned by the biggest landowners, and by banks and companies, that used substantial volumes of migrant-labour or even dispensed with labour to a very large degree. But the agricultural watershed of the late nineteenth century had been preceded by more sporadic and gradual histories of capitalism in the countryside. For example, for most of the nineteenth century itself, both Prussia and southern Italy embodied

---

[5] Cf. Seton-Watson 1967, p. 79, 'The most notable results were obtained between 1870 and 1890 in Emilia, where in the plains around Ravenna and Ferrara great tracts of waste land and marsh were reclaimed. Here wheat, sugar beet, hemp and other industrial crops were produced by modern capitalist methods on a scale hitherto unknown in Italy. Much land passed into the hands of a new rural middle class, or into those of banks and even industrial companies'.

[6] Roveri 1972, pp. 35–6; on the massification of workers, cf. Procacci 1970, p. 282, 'The labourers who worked in these places...constituted a human and social aggregate to which there was no parallel in the agricultural proletariat of the other European countries', adding 'they did not have behind them a past of subjection and resignation'.

[7] Stoll 1998, p. 94ff.

[8] Dye 1998, p. 87.

[9] Dye 1998, p. 63; North-American dominance was founded on the fusion between US banks and sugar-refining interests, cf. Ayala 1999, p. 94ff.

forms of agrarian capitalism dominated by their aristocracies.[10] And, in Tuscany where the *nobiltà* remained strong, capitalism had to struggle to emerge against the background of inherited relationships. There landowners had to *break down* traditional forms of sharecropping and undermine the sharecroppers' resistance to crops that required heavier outlays of capital. This they achieved through a tightening of contracts, drastic reductions in the average size of farms [*podere*] and the creation of new categories of 'semi-proletarianised mezzadri' who commuted to the land from neighbouring villages or farm-labourers' barracks.[11] In other words, the 'commercialisation of Tuscan agriculture followed a course radically different from the classical pattern of the Po Valley'. Frank Snowden suggested that Tuscan landowners, for political reasons, opposed the 'Emilian idea of restructuring the countryside through the establishment of large commercial farms worked by wage labour'.[12] Whatever the truth of this, it remains true that agrarian capitalism *could and did take radically different forms even within individual countries*. The entrenched orthodoxy that England's history supplies us with an archetype of capitalist agriculture is a myth. It is much less credible today as historians begin to map the very different ways in which capitalism evolved in agriculture and continues to do so. There *is* no 'pure' agrarian capitalism.

The advanced forms of agrarian capitalism that emerged in the late nineteenth century could make a head start on the rapid expansion of new tracts of land, an expanding internal frontier. (In Cuba, this included the eastern provinces, which became the preserve of the largest mills on the island.) However, Jan Bazant's seminal contribution that the Mexican *haciendas* were essentially capitalist enterprises, radically different from the *encomiendas* that had preceded them, even if characterised (often and in practice) by 'feudal survivals',[13] takes us back to a much earlier culture of agrarian capitalism, one that had evolved in the seventeenth and eighteenth centuries against the background of labour-practices that had been overtly coercive. That background had cast its shadow on the *hacienda*, hence the reference to 'survivals'. Bazant's paper had avoided the issue of labour and simply noted in passing that Zavala had characterised the *hacienda* as an enterprise based on *wage-labour*. In fact, the

---

[10] Schiller 2003; Montroni 1996.
[11] Snowden 1979.
[12] Snowden 1979, p. 150.
[13] Bazant 1950, p. 88ff.

beauty of Zavala's analysis was that it avoided any reference to a language of 'survivals'. In any case, both papers (Zavala's, published in 1944, and that of Bazant from the 50s) converged around the image of the *hacienda* as an institution that had little or nothing to do with 'feudalism' *per se*.

But, if the *hacienda* was emblematic of a kind of capitalism that was more typical of the seventeenth, eighteenth and early nineteenth centuries, there is scarcely any clarity about what kind precisely. Is it possible to describe these early forms of agrarian capitalism in ways that avoid the teleological charge of a 'transition'? If the more modern rural businesses that emerged in the late nineteenth century were characterised by their massive use of migrant-workers, the *haciendas* had always operated with a core labour-force of permanent workers, and estates would often seek to control that permanence by methods reminiscent of bondage. The workers, typically, were neither 'free' in the sense in which most industrial workers in the twentieth century were free nor 'unfree' in the sense of being purely bonded labourers. This suggests that we might try locating at least one general feature of these early forms of capitalism in their *hybridity*. This was a capitalism where the capitalists were often drawn from the nobility and one where production was often based on and shaped by asymmetric labour-contracts. For example, estates might use credit (wage-advances) to attract workers but various forms of compulsion to retain them. Operations could be structured to maximise profitability but profits from the estate or the enterprise as a whole could underwrite a purely aristocratic life-style in cities like Naples.[14] The hybridity of these forms has rarely been explored systematically (Petrusewicz is an exception), although it is so obvious that it tends to polarise scholars, especially on the Left, into defending manifestly one-sided positions.

The more general point here is that a more solid taxonomy of the forms of capitalism in agriculture would have to range more widely than Lenin's essentially political contrast between landlord- and peasant-dominated trajectories. It would have to include the *general forms of labour used* (e.g. the slave-based agricultural capitalism of the Old South), the specific *labour-systems* under which workers were deployed, the *circumstances in which large private estates emerged or consolidated* at various times in, say, the later eight-

---

[14] Petrusewicz 1996, p. 236.

eenth and nineteenth centuries,[15] including the *land-management policies* that defined the context within which large landowners worked and the kinds and amount of finance available to them, and the backgrounds from which they themselves emerged, and finally the kinds of *microecologies* within which estates functioned, which were obviously bound up with the crops they grew (cf. Dusinberre's account of South Carolina's 'rice kingdom' and its coastal swampland[16]). These are all basic variables in any passably comprehensive study of the landscapes of agricultural capitalism. In this chapter, however, I shall look strictly at one dimension, namely, labour or the nature of the workforce, that is, the particular ways in which capital integrated and transformed peasant-labour, which itself had a lot to do with the labour-market (the abundance or scarcity of labour) as well as the socially-determined resistance to wage-work.

At this level, the most useful distinction to start from is between systems that functioned in terms of *regular access to family-labour* and those that depended primarily on the massive seasonal deployment of a *casual labour-force* that was predominantly male *or* female but rarely mixed.[17] Frank Snowden's brilliant description of the Apulian *latifundia* illustrates one form of the casual labour model, for example 'the massive dependence on casual day labour set Apulia apart from the rest of the South of Italy. Nowhere else in the Mezzogiorno was the work force so homogeneous or so comprehensively proletarianized'.[18] Moreover,

> A rigid sexual division of labour was one of the props of the social order, isolating half of the population in the home and removing them from contact with nascent bonds of class solidarity.... The prevailing practice on the latifundia was simply stated by the mayor of Altamura in 1875, when he reported that 'Women are not employed in the cultivation of the land either as day labourers or as salaried personnel.'[19]

---

[15] Ghislaine Alleaume's description of the 'industrial revolution' in Egyptian agriculture is exemplary in this respect, Alleaume 1999.
[16] Dusinberre 1996.
[17] E.g., Snowden 1986, p. 67; Petrusewicz 1996, p. 154ff. On family-labour systems, see esp. Stolcke 1995.
[18] Snowden 1986, p. 20.
[19] Snowden 1986, p. 67.

By contrast, in the more diversified economy of rural Calabria, gang-labour embraced all groups of the family, men, women and children, but working separately in their own, gender-segregated gangs. In Apulia, the farmworkers were concentrated in towns, the so-called 'agro-cities', described by Snowden as classic company-towns, where workers lived 'without light or water, squeezed at the rate of ten people to a single squalid, windowless room five metres square that served at once as living room, kitchen, bedroom and lavatory'.[20] These desperately harsh conditions contrast interestingly with the *braccianti* on the massive Barracco estate in neighbouring Calabria, rapidly accumulated in the early nineteenth century, who were less 'comprehensively proletarianized', that is, drawn from the local small peasantry, and even more strongly of course with the rest of the wage-earners on that *latifondo* who were integrated into the rudimentary networks of social security that Petrusewicz calls the estate's 'guarantee system', including, crucially, job-security.[21]

Indeed, it is now clear that job-security was a key factor in consolidating the labour-forces of estates that needed a year-round supply of labour (unlike those in Apulia and more like the Barracco estate) and sought to attract workers with credit (wage-advances), land-allotments and access to grazing rights, or some combination of these. The classic form of this labour-régime is surely the *hacienda*, but there are strong variants or homologues elsewhere, notably in Egypt and South Africa. The *hacienda* was a 'commercial, profit-seeking enterprise'[22] that comprised a labour-force of *full-time* labourers attracted to the estate by advances (in Mexico the Indians refused to work without these)[23] and integrated into its operations through a series of fringe-benefits, if we can call them that, of which the most important were land-parcels and/or grazing rights. This core labour-force was then supplemented by substantial numbers of seasonal workers, so that hacienda-type estate-systems generated a two-tiered labour-force[24] and a stratified labour-market.[25] The general *form of exploitation* characteristic of *hacienda*-style estate-systems is best described as labour-tenancy, and there are two key points we need to make about it. First,

---

[20] Snowden 1986, p. 42.
[21] E.g., Petrusewicz 1996, p. 191.
[22] Bazant 1977, p. 80.
[23] E.g., Van Young 1981, p. 256, 'Even far into the eighteenth century laborers simply refused to work without advances'.
[24] Richards 1979, p. 500.
[25] E.g., Katz 1974, p. 21, 'a very complex hierarchy of social groups'.

as the great Mexican historian Silvio Zavala argued in a seminal paper from the 1940s, the *gañanes* were wage-labourers, 'workers attracted [to the *hacienda*] by means of a voluntary contract'.[26] Zavala made this crucial point to show that the *hacienda* did not evolve out of the *encomienda*, as a whole tradition of Mexican politics and historiography suggested.[27] In other words, the *hacienda* did not have *feudal* origins, even ones mediated by colonialism, and presupposed the mobility of the worker. Second, although 'debt-peonage' is widely seen as the hallmark of the Latin-American *hacienda* because it fits so neatly into the feudal stereotype, 'the *fact* of debt cannot be taken to imply bondage', as Alan Knight argued in a lucid paper.[28] To conflate debt with bondage is to ignore the compulsions that drove Indian workers into the *hacienda* in the first place. It was the predatory and often catastrophic effect of colonialism, and the cyclical crises that went with it, that ensured that in New Spain, for example, the 'many stresses of the sixteenth and seventeenth centuries' would work as 'inducements to Indians to seek employment in haciendas and in some instances to move completely from town to hacienda residence'.[29] As Gibson pointed out in his monumental book *The Aztecs under Spanish Rule* (1964), 'The hacienda was less overtly coercive in its policies of labor recruitment than any of the antecedent institutions'.[30] In fact, Gibson produced a major *Gestalt*-switch in the understanding of this issue by reconceptualising the debt as an advance of wages.

> It was impossible, [one late eighteenth century] writer stated, to find Indians who would work with a debt of only five pesos, at this time a legal limit.... [I]f an employer were to refuse to raise his offer over five pesos, the Indian would desert and move to another hacienda where conditions were more attractive. *Here the emphasis is reversed from the conventional interpretation of debt labour,* for it assumes relative freedom among the workers, whose objective was not to escape but to enlarge the indebtedness.... *In any case, the amount of the debt may be considered in some degree as a measure of the bargaining power*

---

[26] Zavala 1988 [1944], p. 56 (from the collected papers, *Estudios*): 'En la hacienda, el indio es un trabajador libre atraído por medio de un alquiler voluntario.... El amo debe pagar un salario al gañán a cambio del trabajo'.
[27] Zavala 1988 (orig. 1944), p. 35ff.
[28] Knight 1986, pp. 49–50; my italics.
[29] Gibson 1964, pp. 245, 248.
[30] Gibson 1964, p. 249.

of the worker. The relatively dense population of the Valley [of Mexico] may have reduced this bargaining power, and accordingly reduced the amount of indebtedness and the role of peonage.[31]

Gibson's reversal of perspective, in turn, was the basis for the kind of distinctions that Alan Knight went on to make in an essay that breaks with the 'superficial similitude of debt' to distinguish classic debt-servitude from other more 'proletarian' and certainly less coercive forms that are usually conflated with it.[32] Knight's paper contains a brilliant description of the fiercely repressive form of capitalism that prevailed in late nineteenth-century Yucatán, where the boom in fibre-production was met by a monocultural, quasi-industrial *hacienda*-régime based on extreme coercion (flogging, debt-servitude, etc.)[33] but also financed to a great degree by New York brokers and the banks they borrowed from.[34] As Wells points out, the expansion of the henequen industry was bound up with legal changes that stipulated that 'the *peón* who left work without paying the sums that he owed would be prosecuted before the courts'.[35] But Yucatán's 'classic' debt-servitude was part of a *capitalist* labour-régime where it functioned to reinforce the 'internal mobility and flexibility' of a tightly regulated labour-force where workers were transferred between tasks and in general piece-rated,[36] and it is worth emphasising that, in Mexico anyway, these types of extreme coercion ('comparable to chattel slavery') were more characteristic of quasi-industrial enterprises such as those in timber and tobacco than of the coffee-plantations of Chiapas or the purely agricultural *haciendas* of central Mexico.[37]

In Prussia, where the export-boom of the late eighteenth century was sustained initially by labour-services and feudal bonds sharpened to create an effective labour-system, this system already contained 'markedly capitalist features', by which Schissler means that the Prussian estate-owners used

---

[31] Gibson 1964, p. 255.
[32] Knight 1986, p. 46.
[33] Knight 1986, p. 61ff.
[34] Wells 1985, p. 34 (for the brokers and New York City banks).
[35] Wells 1985, p. 157, about the *Ley agrícola industrial del estado de Yucatán*, dated 1882.
[36] Wells 1985, p. 169, and the whole description in Chapter 6.
[37] Knight 1986, pp. 68–73; 'comparable to etc.' at p. 56. Even within Chiapas, a sector like coffee-production could show major differences in labour-régimes, see Washbrook 2007.

their traditional *Herrschaftsrechten* for purely economic ends and the ensuing labour-régime was one characterised above all by its hybridity, 'no longer feudal but not purely capitalist either'.[38] The interesting feature in Schissler's account is that the modernisation of the Prussian estates was financed by the money-market, with mortgage-companies encouraging the concentration of estates in the hands of magnates and large owners and deepening differentiation within the ranks of the landed class [*Gutsbesitzerschicht*].[39] By the 1860s, 1.5% of estates controlled sixty per cent of the land area.[40] As the demand for labour expanded, landlords 'settled laborers on their estates as *Insten*'.[41] The link between capitalist profitability and the new kinds of labour-contract is explicit in Thaer's advice that the use of *Instleute* would help landowners reduce wages to offset the impact of low grain-prices.[42] The *Instmann*, of course, was the Prussian counterpart of the labour-tenant and this is a good example of agrarian depression (1806–37) accelerating the rationalisation of estates, as the renovated landed élites of the early nineteenth century came to comprise a substantial layer of *Agrarkapitalisten* and, in the words of Hans Rosenberg, the *Gutsaristokratie* of the earlier period was transformed into a unified *Unternehmerschicht* by 1850.[43] Rosenberg himself describes this 'reorganized *Gutswirtschaft*' of the nineteenth century as a tightly controlled enterprise [*Betrieb*] whose autocratic forms of governance meant that its workers were personally ruled by the *Gutsherrn*.[44] If the East-Elbian aristocracy was a key factor in the support for German fascism,[45] as much as the *latifondisti* of Apulia were in the rise of Italian fascism and its suppression of the farmworkers' leagues,[46] then the agrarian relations of these hybrid forms of capitalism have something to do, certainly, with those political cultures and their

---

[38] Schissler 1978, pp. 59ff., 66–8. Conze 1969, p. 64 is surely correct in dating the Prussian 'conversion to capitalism' to the eighteenth century.
[39] Schissler 1978, p. 82ff.
[40] Schissler 1978, p. 162.
[41] Richards 1979, p. 487.
[42] Schissler 1978, p. 176.
[43] Rosenberg 1978, p. 90.
[44] Rosenberg 1978, p. 91, 'Die reorganisierte Gutswirtschaft war ein straff monarchisch-soldatisch zentralisierter Betrieb, dessen Arbeiter vom Gutsherrn persönlich beherrscht wurden'.
[45] Puhle 1975, p. 41.
[46] Snowden 1986, Chapter 10; but they simply followed the lead of their Northern counterparts.

undermining of the basis for a transition to true democracy.[47] At any rate, the capitalist manorialism of the Prussian East was sufficiently distinct to count as one reasonably well-defined model of agrarian capitalism; indeed, we all know that Lenin even dignified it with the general description 'landlord capitalism'. And again (as with southern Mexico and its integration into international markets), East Elbia supplied much of the grain and wool consumed by Britain, implying, here too, that the hybrid forms of capital that dominated much of the countryside in the nineteenth century flourished best within the circuits of a rapidly expanding industrial capitalism. (Gunder Frank's point surely was that their integration within *these* circuits conferred on countries like Mexico a different *kind* of capitalist history from any imagined archetype; the point is one that seems self-evident to me.)

Probably the best example of this is the transformation of the Egyptian countryside that was triggered in part by the growing British demand for cotton. As Roger Owen argued in his classic monograph, the large estates produced better cotton and obtained higher yields per acre.[48] The collapse of the boom in the late 1860s caused widespread dispossession among the mass of the peasantry (the fellaheen lost over 300,000 feddans during Isma'il's reign)[49] with no comparable effect on the biggest landowners, who came to control roughly fifty per cent of the land in private ownership by 1907.[50] Owen published *Cotton and the Egyptian Economy* in 1969. Since then, both he and Alan Richards have used the work of Nahas and others to reconstruct the kind of labour-organisation that prevailed on those large estates. This was the *ezba*-system, Egypt's version of labour-tenancy, constructed around estate-settlements (*'ezāb* in Arabic; *ezbas* if Anglicised) that housed a year-round labour-force of workers called *tamaliyya*, who were basically peasants who

> agreed to provide a regular amount of work on the estate in exchange for the right to rent a small plot of land for their own use.... [T]his system had been used on the royal *jiftliks* in the 1840s; later it became institutionalized

---

[47] So too Barrington Moore, Jr., Moore 1966, p. 433ff. and his suggestive link between 'labor-repressive agrarian systems' and the growth of fascism. But the distinction suggested there between the 'use of political mechanisms on the one hand and reliance on the labor market, on the other' (p. 434) does not seem so plausible to me.
[48] Owen 1969, pp. 75–6.
[49] Owen 1969, pp. 143ff., 148.
[50] Owen 1969, p. 239.

with the creation of agricultural settlements known as *izbas* in which the tenants were housed in mud dwellings grouped round the central stores and the residence of the owner.[51]

According to Richards, *tamaliyya*-labour was 'especially employed in cotton-cultivation'[52] and their parcels 'rotated with the crop rotation of the estate'.[53] In a seminal thesis, Nahas observed that in hiring workers on this basis, the estate had access to the labour of women and children as well,[54] and described one contract 'by which each peasant family was required to supply an agreed number of workers for the owner's fields at a daily wage to be determined in advance'.[55] Of course, the precise details of such arrangements varied between estates but the fact remains that the *ezba*-system 'was the most common mode of exploitation for large estates',[56] and expanded rapidly between the 1880s and the 1920s.[57]

It might seem paradoxical that it should be a Third-World country, Egypt, that best illustrates the purely capitalist rationality at work in the evolution and expansion of these enterprises. When two young French geographers, Lozach and Hug, students of Albert Demangeon, studied the landscapes of the Delta and the Fayyūm in the 1920s (basing this on 4,000 questionnaires to the fellahs), they saw the *ezbas concentrating* peasant-labour for more effective capitalist control.[58] The *ezbas* were inseparable from the dense network of canals that spread through Lower Egypt in the late nineteenth century and thus a product of land-management policies that set out to restore the infrastructure of the country, but they were also, typically, the outcome of a new 'agrarian capitalism',[59] capitalist settlements, as Hug called them, whose function was to facilitate closer surveillance of the workers and cut down on the time needed to travel to the fields.[60] And in a separate work published in

---

[51] Owen 1981b, p. 146.
[52] Richards 1982, p. 62.
[53] Richards 1979, p. 501.
[54] Nahas 1901, pp. 133–4, 137–8.
[55] Owen 1981b, p. 146, citing Nahas 1901, pp. 141, 143.
[56] Richards 1978, p. 508.
[57] Owen 1981a, p. 523.
[58] Lozach and Hug 1930, pp. 180, 202.
[59] Lozach and Hug 1930, p. 204, 'Elle [la dispersion par 'ezbahs] est la produit de l'irrigation pérenne, de la grosse propriété et du capitalisme agraire', and proof of the country's agricultural revolution (from the pages written by Hug).
[60] Lozach and Hug 1930, p. 202.

the 1930s Jean Lozach referred to the 'industrial, almost mathematical spirit' behind the construction of these settlements.⁶¹ Ghislaine Alleaume has recenty built on these conceptions to describe the *ezbas* as workers' villages and points out that the 'larger estates could hold several such compounds'. *'The parailels with industrial manufacturing are striking* at the formal level as well. 'Izbas were rural versions of the workers' compound', conceived in the experiments of French civil engineers linked to the Saint-Simonians, and took off in the 1880s when

> 'Ali Mubarak drafted a legal framework which laid out in precise detail the technical prescriptions for the width of roads, sanitation, building materials and so forth. Strongly influenced by French legislation promulgated in the aftermath of Blanqui and Villermin's social study of workers in large industry, the law was initially conceived for workers' suburbs in the cities.⁶²

It is hardly surprising then that nineteenth-/early twentieth-century Egypt should form such a solid base for the critique of the feudal stereotype suggested in the work of Roger Owen and Alan Richards.⁶³ This critique has Latin-American parallels, of course, and South-African ones as well,⁶⁴ and it is unlikely that many Marxists today would still want to adhere to the ruined orthodoxy of 'feudal' or 'semi-feudal' modes of production. But this critique has left a theoretical vacuum we still need to address. The key fact is that, in the estate-systems described or alluded to above (including those in parts of Italy which were based on sharecropping), 'the peasants had no claim whatsoever to the land' and sharecroppers and estate-workers could be dismissed at any time.⁶⁵ Eviction was, in the words of one Tuscan aristocrat, 'the sole means of restoring discipline among the sharecropping masses',⁶⁶ and its suppression was a key demand in the series of largely spontaneous sharecropper-strikes that broke out in central Tuscany in 1919. In fact, it has been suggested that because the Socialists wanted to abolish *mezzadria* rather than reform or regulate it, the Red Pact of 1920 allowed evictions, on 'fair'

---

⁶¹ Lozach 1935, p. 254ff.
⁶² Alleaume 1999, pp. 341–4.
⁶³ Esp. Owen 1981b, p. 147 and Richards 1979, p. 486ff.
⁶⁴ Martínez-Alier 1967; Mertens 1983; Taylor 1984; for S. Africa, cf. Bradford 1990 and her reference to the work of Beinart and others.
⁶⁵ Richards 1979, pp. 488–9.
⁶⁶ Snowden 1979, p. 162.

grounds, these including 'the takeover of the farm for the owner's own use', and 'transformation of the system of administration to capitalist methods', both amounting, presumably, to the more advanced forms of capitalist management which they preferred.[67] The point of all this is that eviction would have been 'no punishment for a serf',[68] which takes us back to the general distinction I drew in Chapter 8 between bondage (more characteristic of the post-Roman and medieval West) and landlessness (more typical of the East). Hybrid forms of agrarian capitalism (of the later eighteenth and nineteenth centuries) were *built on the dispossession and landlessness of the peasantry more than its bondage*, but always ready to use coercion to ensure minimal disruption to the supply of labour. For capitalists, this is perfectly rational behaviour, as long as it does not jeopardise the *social* mobility of labour, that is, the ability of workers in general to move between villages and estates or between different parts of the countryside including the estates themselves. There is no evidence that even the most extreme forms of debt-servitude ever had this particular effect of restricting the mobility of social labour or undermining the fluidity of the labour-market. On the contrary, even enterprises that made regular use of wage-advances and sought to retain labour in stronger ways used substantial numbers of seasonal workers, as Mertens' study of the Mexican *haciendas* shows at length.

In short, at least *one* sense of hybridity is this coupling of proletarianisation and compulsion, of an uprooted landless peasantry and the peculiar forms of domination, the whole battery of devices (including legal ones) used to ensure its submission. But, going back to Egypt for a moment, there is another aspect of hybridity worth noting, one that I alluded to briefly at the start. I referred there to aristocratic mentalities and noted the example of the South-Italian *latifondisti* as typical of this mixed behaviour.[69] In Egypt, the groups who embodied or 'personified' the agrarian capitalism of the nineteenth and earlier twentieth century were even more extreme in their diversity, thoroughly

---

[67] Gill 1983, p. 161.
[68] Martínez-Alier 1977, p. 152, 'the analogy with serfdom would be inappropriate, in that eviction would have been no punishment for a serf', about the threats of expulsion used on agricultural *haciendas* in Peru.
[69] E.g., Petrusewicz 1996, p. 234, '[A]utonomy from the dictates of the market enabled the latifondista to be at once a modern capitalist producer and an old-style lord of the manor'. At p. 9 she claims 'the latifondisti – the very agents of this agrarian entrepreneurship – were by origin and mentality neither feudal lords nor bourgeois'.

atypical of the canonical model of agrarian capitalism that many Marxists still subscribe to. The Egyptian capitalists who ruled the expanding countryside of the *ezbas* and gained the most from the massive dispossession of the fellahs were a small élite of government officials (including army-officers), merchants and, of course, members of the ruling family, coupled with numerous land-companies controlled by foreign and local investors, themselves from a huge diversity of ethnic backgrounds.[70] Now, the formalist orthodoxy of a 'pure' agrarian capitalism homogenises *both* capital and labour, ignoring the legacies that shaped the real evolution of capitalism in the countryside, above all, the backgrounds from which the capitalists themselves emerged and the striking anomalies of their existence. Frank understood that the history of world-capitalism was not an endless rehearsal of the *same* transition, but a considerably more complex process, as 'totalisations' generally are.

To sum up, 'hybrid forms of agrarian capitalism' is a possible description of wage-labour enterprises characterised by 1) low levels of capitalisation (relative to industry) but not immune to modernisation, much less to the use of modern technology and machinery;[71] 2) 'asymmetric labour-contracts' or coercive labour-régimes (usually but not always); and 3) considerable flexibility in the use of labour and systems of estate-management.[72] They were, quintessentially, products of liberalism, insofar as it was the liberal atomism of the nineteenth century that prised open markets for land and labour on historically unprecedented scales, both increasing the mobility of labour and sanctioning the use of coercion against workers. The expansion of these labour-systems against the background of a growing industrial demand for crops like cotton, sugarcane, rice and tobacco (and dozens of others!) is surely a sufficient and sufficiently strong explanation of the integration of bound labour into world-capitalism, the seeming paradox of which generated the debate between Frank and Laclau. The point here is that *it would be wrong to*

---

[70] All this is best documented in Baer 1962, esp. pp. 41ff., listing the various landed groups, 66ff. on foreign investors, 121ff. on the land companies. I have not referred, of course, to the *mushāyikh* or village-notables who normally engrossed most of the land in the villages they controlled and formed their own species of capitalist.

[71] There is no systematic investigation of this subject as far as I know; cf. Petrusewicz 1996, p. 241. On the issue of 'rationality', cf. Moreno Fraginals' acerbic comment about the French planters of the eighteenth century, 'Sin hipérbole, puede afirmarse que la contabilidad moderna ha agregado muy poco al antiguo sistema establecido por los plantadores esclavistas franceses', 1978, Volume 2, p. 18.

[72] E.g., Mertens 1983, p. 194ff., a detailed treatment.

think of the labour-systems themselves as 'modes of production', since they were constructed and driven by capitalists, or by a combination of capitalist classes, who themselves emerged from very different historical backgrounds. The trouble with Laclau's response to Frank was that he systematically confused relations of production with forms of exploitation of labour. This hardly needs to be demonstrated, as it runs through almost every page of his critique, and leads him, in the 'Postscript' that he added six years later, to a theoretical position that asserts the very opposite of Marx's own conception. Laclau summed up his view as follows:

> The concept of 'world capitalist system' is...the nearest approximation to the concrete which a merely economic analysis permits, and if what we have asserted in this essay is correct, it cannot be *derived* from the concept of 'capitalist mode of production' but must be *constructed* by starting from a theoretical study of possible articulations of the different modes of production.[73]

By contrast, Marx maintained (and tells us in the *Grundrisse*), 'The tendency to create the *world market* is directly given in the concept of capital itself'.[74]

Before a synthesis is possible, historians will have to map the various early-modern paths to agrarian capitalism in more detail, working not at the national but at the regional or sub-national level. It is not obvious that there are 'national' 'paths of transition', and it seems more useful therefore to concentrate on trajectories of accumulation of the kind alluded to, in passing, in the last few pages of this chapter. Whether these were also transitions, and if so, to what exactly, can obviously only be established once we have clear descriptions or reconstructions of the different trajectories themselves. In *Capitalism from Above and Capitalism from Below*, Terry Byres concludes by underlining the diversity in the forms taken by capitalist transformation.[75]

---

[73] Laclau 1977, p. 43, adding, 'The analysis of these [precapitalist modes of production, presumably] is thus a precondition of a *theoretical* study of the world capitalist system'. All italics Laclau's.

[74] Marx 1973, p. 408, which continues, 'Every limit appears as a barrier to be overcome. Initially, to subjugate every moment of production itself to exchange and to suspend the production of direct use values not entering into exchange, i.e. precisely to posit production based on capital in place of earlier modes of production, which appear primitive from its standpoint'.

[75] Byres 1996, p. 420.

I take this as a claim about *both* 'Agrarian questions', 2 as well as 3,[76] but if so, it means that Lenin's two paths cannot be a sufficiently strong basis to guide future work. 'Trajectories of accumulation' is a more flexible concept, in the sense that the chronological spans are variable, different trajectories can be at work simultaneously, and the outcome is not predetermined.

[2008–9]

---

[76] Bernstein 1996, for a clear distinction between the various senses of the 'Agrarian Question'.

Chapter Twelve
Modes of Production: A Synthesis

Marx's own sense of history was best encapsulated in the view that societies historically had assumed distinct economic forms, and that much of the history of Europe at least revolved around the differences between such forms, or modes of production, as he called them. In a broad historical perspective, the history of Europe was defined by an exuberance of economic forms, compared to what Marx saw as the monotony and stagnation of 'Asiatic' development (or non-development). Here, 'Asiatic' included Russia and embraced the most diverse cultural formations from the Islamic regions of the Near East to China. It was clearly a *residual* category, a sort of 'non-Europe' which Marx believed (or half-believed) embodied a common economic structure where the ruling class, *if* one could speak of such a class, was subsumed in the state, and the mainspring of the economy lay in the tenacity of unchanging village-communities. This model is usually called the 'Asiatic mode of production' and was a sort of default-category, the most sense Marx and Engels could make of societies whose history was largely inaccessible to them.

The two most general senses in which Marx used the term 'mode of production' are (1) as an *epoch of production*[1] or *economic formation of society*,[2] of which the best example is capitalism itself, and (2) as a 'mode of labour', 'labour-process' or 'form of production', that is, an *organisation of labour* based on the requirements of a given type of industry or branch of production such as agriculture. These are different senses of the term, one clearly more historical than the other and much broader in scope. The second, less historical sense is used repeatedly by Marx in 'Results of the Immediate Process of Production' (the only surviving part of the manuscript of the very first version of *Capital*, Volume I) when discussing the formal subsumption of labour under capital, and it is this subordinate sense that Marx retains when he refers to the 'specifically' capitalist mode of production, meaning by this the *real* subsumption of labour into capital, that is, the restructuring of labour-processes to generate relative surplus-value, the form best adapted to the nature of capital. This sense is exemplified in passages of the following type, 'The subordination of the labour-process to capital does not at first affect the actual *mode of production* and its only practical effects are these: the worker bows to the command, the direction and supervision of the capitalist . . .'.[3] Under formal subsumption, 'There is no change as yet in the *mode of production* itself. Technologically speaking, the labour process goes on as before . . .'.[4] By contrast, 'With the real subsumption of labour under capital a complete (and constantly repeated) revolution takes place in the *mode of production*'.[5] Again, 'Productive capital, or the *mode of production* corresponding to capital, can be present in only two forms: manufacture and large-scale industry'.[6] It is in this more technological sense that Marx refers to the 'mode of production of the guilds',[7] or to agriculture as a mode of production ('Agriculture forms a mode of production *sui generis*')[8] or refers, finally, to the 'mode of production' of small-holding peasants 'isolating them from one another'.[9]

---

[1] Marx 1973, p. 85, cf. Marx 1976, p. 286; Marx 1978, p. 120 ('economic epochs'); Marx 1973, pp. 97–8 ('period of production').
[2] Marx 1976, pp. 286, 345, 914.
[3] Marx 1976, p. 1010.
[4] Marx 1976, p. 1026.
[5] Marx 1976, p. 1035.
[6] Marx 1973, p. 585.
[7] Marx 1976, p. 1022.
[8] Marx 1973, p. 726.
[9] Marx, *Eighteenth Brumaire of Louis Bonaparte*, cited McLellan 1971, p. 163.

It is the first, more purely historical meaning that is celebrated as encapsulating Marx's view of the way we should visualise the general evolution of Europe from Antiquity to the modern world. References dispersed across Marx's writings have generated a canonical genealogy which sees Europe's past (more precisely, the past of *western* Europe) moving *from* slavery *to* feudalism *to* capitalism in a sort of inflexible succession spanning whole centuries. Yet Marx himself had to emphasise the contingency of that process when he referred to his description as a 'historical sketch of the genesis of capitalism in Western Europe', not 'the general path every people is fated to tread' ('Reply to Mikhailovsky', 1877). Marx paid scant attention to 'precapitalist' modes of production, and much of the subsequent literature on these reflects the uncertainties and formalism this engendered. How were modes of production to be understood? How much complexity should we attribute to them? Could one simply read them off some register of forms of *exploitation* of labour? Did the feudal mode of production mean much more than the prevalence of serfdom? How widespread was it historically? Which modes of production could best account for the evolution of societies outside western Europe? And, most crucially, because of its political implications, should Marxists see transitions to capitalism simply replicating some universal model or general sequence such as that implied in the metanarrative of Europe's development? On the last issue, Marx's own response was emphatically negative.

Marx and slavery. Marx thought that much of *pre*capitalist history could be mapped out in terms of just three basic modes of production: the slave-mode, the feudal mode, and the tributary (or 'Asiatic') mode. The Asiatic mode has been called the 'Loch Ness monster of historical materialism' because of the huge amount of controversy it generated, but the slave mode of production is no less problematic, unless all one means by it is any form of production based on the use of slave-labour (an ahistorical usage). In fact, Marx avoided the term, preferring alternatives like 'slave system', 'slave economy', and so on. At the very least, a slave *mode of production* would have to imply a concentration of slave-labour in enterprises other than households, for example, in the mass-production workshops that turned out highly standardised products for the ceramic- and building industries of southern Italy in the late Republic,[10] or, even more obviously, plantation-slavery. But the idea that the whole of the

---

[10] Morel 1990, p. 402ff.

ancient economy was characterised by these forms of production is no longer accepted today. Moreover, as Wendy Davies points out,

> Since it is axiomatic [within traditional Marxism] that the slave mode gave way to the feudal mode, Marxists have to deal with the gap between the end of classical Antiquity (and ancient slavery) and the fully fledged serfdom which characterised the feudal model of the late Middle Ages, *a gap of some six or seven hundred years.*[11]

It scarcely makes sense to see a transition between modes having a longer shelf life than the mode it supersedes! In fact, closer attention to the way Marx himself handled slave-production shows a considerably more sophisticated grasp of the nature of Roman slavery. In *Capital*, Volume 3, he writes:

> In the ancient world, the influence of trade and the development of commercial capital always produced the result of a slave economy; or, given a different point of departure, it also meant the transformation of a patriarchal slave system oriented towards the production of the direct means of subsistence into one oriented towards the production of surplus-value.[12]

It may seem odd to find the idea of *surplus-value* coupled with the slave-system, but Marx repeatedly reasoned in terms of the analogy with capitalism itself. In *Capital*, Volume 3, he described the agrarian economies of Carthage and Rome as showing the 'most analogy with the capitalist rural economy'.[13] In several passages, he suggests that the investment in slave-labour was a form of *fixed capital*, for example, 'In the slave system, the money capital laid out on the purchase of labour-power plays the role of fixed capital in the money form, and is only gradually replaced as the active life of the slave comes to an end',[14] or, more concisely, 'The slave-owner buys his worker in the same way as he buys his horse. If he loses his slave, he loses a piece of capital'.[15] When Marx deals with modern (plantation-) slavery, this aspect is even more pronounced. In the plantations, where 'production is intended for the world market, the capitalist mode of production exists, although only in

---

[11] Davies 1996, p. 231; my emphasis.
[12] Marx 1981, pp. 449–50.
[13] Marx 1981, p. 923.
[14] Marx 1978, p. 554.
[15] Marx 1976, p. 377.

a formal sense... the business in which slaves are used is conducted by *capitalists*'.[16] Again, 'The fact that we now not only call the plantation owners in America capitalists, but that they *are* capitalists...'.[17] Or, finally, 'Where the capitalist conception prevails, as on the American plantations...'.[18] However one characterises classical or Roman slavery, modern plantation-slavery was certainly a form of capitalism, and one implication of this is that modes of production are more complex sorts of entities than the labour-relations on which they are founded. Relations of production are not reducible to given forms of exploitation of labour.

12.1. Marxists and feudalism

A major theme to emerge from recent historiography is the persistence of slavery through late antiquity and the early middle ages down to about the ninth century. If the use or even widespread presence of slave-labour were sufficient to justify talk of a slave mode of production, this would mean having to posit the existence or survival of such a mode till fairly late into the middle ages, an option favoured by Bonnassie, who links the extinction of slavery to the agrarian expansion of the tenth century.[19] This strand of history sees feudalism emerging from a violent and dramatic rupture in the decades around the 'year 1000'. The general model has been extensively debated and subjected to considerable critique, but the least it establishes is that the degradation of peasant-status which we call serfdom was a *late* phenomenon; in Catalonia, which inspired the thesis of the 'feudal mutation', not much earlier than the thirteenth century.[20]

For Marx, serfdom was a central feature of the feudal mode and peculiar to that form of society (Engels had different views), so the problem raised by a belated serfdom is how we characterise the late empire and the early middle ages. In some general sense, there clearly *was* a transition from slavery to feudalism, but how or at what level do we grasp that? The kind of bond-

---

[16] Marx 1968, pp. 302–3; Marx's emphasis.
[17] Marx 1973, p. 513; Marx's emphasis.
[18] Marx 1981, p. 940. Perfectly *orthodox* Marxists like Henryk Grossmann saw no problem in describing the slave-plantations as capitalist enterprises.
[19] Bonnassie 1991, pp. 151–2.
[20] Freedman 1991.

age that defined serfdom evolved only gradually and much later,[21] so that the *mancipia* of the post-Roman world were not serfs in the strict (medieval) sense but a conglomeration of slaves and freedpeople, of whom the majority were provided with service-holdings and more like farm-workers than peasants. The manor, in contrast, was a purely Frankish innovation, a model actively propagated by the ruling classes of Frankish society and bound up with the active creation of peasant-tenures. Ros Faith's monograph on the Anglo-Saxon 'inland' is a model of how a newer Marxist historiography can tackle some of these issues,[22] while Chris Wickham's book offers a wide-ranging basis for discussing them, even if his own theorisations are scarcely convincing, especially the view that we should identify the feudal mode with 'coercive rent-taking' or that the feudal mode was the 'normal economic system of the ancient and medieval periods'.[23]

12.2. The tributary mode

Against the orthodoxy of several or even many modes of production in history, John Haldon has posited the dominance of a single precapitalist mode of production whose essential category was 'rent'.[24] However, rent in Haldon's sense *subsumes* tax, so that there is no fundamental difference between, say, an economic régime in which the state is confronted by cohesive peasant-communities, there is no significant aristocracy to speak of, and taxation is the main charge on peasant-labour (for example, al-Andalus in Guichard's description of Valencia),[25] and a régime in which the peasantry is dominated by a class of private landowners. Thus, feudalism and the tributary mode are variants of the same mode of production, despite the huge differences that Marx himself saw between western Europe and 'Asiatic despotism'. In this version of the tributary mode, not only are major structural differences eliminated, but the *organisation of labour* seems to lose any significance for a characterisation of the economy, so that, to take the most obvious example of

---

[21] 'The serf's hereditary attachment was to a man, not to a tenure', Bloch 1973, p. 86, contrasting serfdom with the *colonatus*.
[22] Faith 1997.
[23] Wickham 2005, p. 535.
[24] Haldon 1993.
[25] Guichard 1990–1; see Manzano 1998a, p. 348; 1998b, p. 894ff.

this, the nature of estates – the fact that the most dynamic estates of the central middle ages abandoned the use of slave-labour to reorganise production on the basis of demesnes and labour-services – ceases to have any meaning at all (contrast the approach of historians like Verhulst and Devroey, *more* materialist in this respect!), and class-relations are configured in ways that fail to convey any sense of why there has been a debate about the feudal revolution at all. On the other hand, Haldon's drive to innovate is as commendable as it is rare. For his part, Wickham, having started by defining 'tax' and 'rent' as the bases of distinct modes of production,[26] has now veered round to the view that a single, universal mode can sensibly span Asiatic-type régimes such as the Ottoman and Mughal Empires and West-European feudalism, except that he prefers a feudal nomenclature to Haldon's tributary one.

Marx would scarcely have agreed with any of this, since he thought that the absence of *private* property in land in Asiatic-style régimes was a crucial difference, strong enough to mark off their economic relations as substantially different, historically, from those prevailing in medieval Europe.[27] The distracting feature in Marx's model is his belief in the survival of almost pristine forms of communal property such as the *bhaiachara* communities of North India that were models of the kind of village-communes he had in mind. This was a misreading of the British land-revenue reports available to him,[28] just as it was possible for him to misconstrue the reconstructed clan-organisation of the Scottish Highlands as the relics of a much earlier, more communal mode of production.[29] However, if Marx's 'repeated assertion of the stagnation and immutability of the Oriental world'[30] has fallen out of favour (together with the Orientalism that inspired it!), there is still a problem about the proper Marxist characterisation of 'Asiatic' systems, Russia included, and Marx's loud thinking about 'Asian' history contains both sound insights and flashes of brilliance. He rejected Kovalevsky's characterisation of medieval India as feudal. 'Kovalevsky forgets, among other things, that serfdom – which represents an important element in feudalism – does not exist in India'.[31] The

---

[26] Wickham 1984.
[27] Marx in Avineri 1969, p. 451; Anderson 1974, pp. 473f., 482.
[28] Dumont 1966.
[29] Davidson 2001, pp. 312ff., 320.
[30] Anderson 1974, p. 476.
[31] Marx 1879, p. 383.

major category was serfdom, not rent. And, as early as 1853, Marx had suggested, 'It seems to have been the Mohammedans who first established the principle of "no property in land" throughout the whole of Asia'.[32] Even if this is not strictly true, it contains the important insight that the Ottomans and the Mughals configured class-relations around the legal fiction of the sovereign as the 'real' owner of all the land. My own view is that it is, paradoxically, a recast version of the tributary mode that can help resolve the problem of the Asiatic mode of production, both vindicating Marx's sense of history's peculiarities and superseding his own obsolete model. As an aside, we can add that it makes no sense for the Spanish Marxists who have been at the cutting edge of these debates (Manuel Acién especially) to radicalise the difference between Islam and feudalism *and* endorse the view (Haldon's) that feudal and tributary régimes are simply variants of the same mode of production.[33]

12.3. Periodising capitalism

Marx refers in the *Grundrisse* to the 'Mercantile system' as an 'epoch where industrial capital and hence wage labour arose in manufactures.... Industrial capital has value for them [the Mercantilists]...because it creates mercantile capital'.[34] When exactly was that? In *Capital*, Volume I, the sixteenth century is the watershed that inaugurates the 'capitalist era'.[35] '[In] the sixteenth century, and partly still in the seventeenth, the sudden expansion of trade and the creation of a new world market had an overwhelming influence on the defeat of the old mode of production and the rise of the capitalist mode...'.[36] Yet Marx was willing to allow for a sporadic capitalism in the Middle Ages. The clearest reference is *Capital*, Volume 1, '...we come across the first *sporadic traces of capitalist production as early as the fourteenth and fifteenth centuries in certain towns of the Mediterranean*'.[37] Or again, 'And yet the modern mode of production in its first period, that of manufacture, developed only where the conditions for it had been created *in the Middle Ages*'.[38]

---

[32] Marx in Avineri 1969, p. 457.
[33] See Acién's discussion of Haldon in Acién 1998.
[34] Marx 1973, pp. 327–8.
[35] Marx 1976, p. 876.
[36] Marx 1981, pp. 450–1.
[37] Marx 1976, p. 875f.
[38] Marx 1981, p. 450.

Indeed, the distinction implied in these passages can be theorised more than it has been. Marx himself argued, 'At the initial stages of bourgeois production, trade dominated industry'.[39] But what *were* the 'initial stages'? Rodinson grappled with the problem in *Islam and Capitalism*, suggesting that the Muslim world of the middle ages had a highly developed 'capitalistic sector', meaning one largely dominated by merchant- and 'financial' capital.[40] Because a specifically Marxist historiography of capitalist origins is so mesmerisingly Anglocentric and focused on developments from the sixteenth century onwards, there has been no systematic attempt (by Marxists anyway) to map the origins of capitalism on a wider Mediterranean canvas, using the hints given by Marx. Commercial partnerships, bills of exchange, transfer-banking, the widespread availability of money, the growing power of the merchants' guilds and the evolution of business-firms[41] were all signs of the emergence of a substantial business-economy (Sombart's expression)[42] by the thirteenth century, which it seems strange *not* to characterise as capitalist. But, of course, this was a form of capitalism dominated by monied capitalists (merchants and bankers above all) and drawing on traditions inherited in part from the Islamic world, where the partnership was a highly developed institution with a strong legal tradition. The *Annales* historian Frédéric Mauro suggested that the period between the Renaissance and the French Revolution should be seen as the 'era of commercial capitalism',[43] but the origins of this epoch go much further back, even if, like all origins, they are impossible to pin down with any precision. What can be argued with some plausibility is that the 'initial stages' that Marx referred to straddled a long history *from at least the twelfth century to the late eighteenth*. The powerful rivalries of the age of 'Company capitalism' were completely different in character from the banking and commercial capitalism of the thirteenth and fourteenth centuries. Portuguese expansion, driven by the commercial bourgeoisie and backed by the monarchy, marks off the fifteenth century as the true watershed. It was this phase that ended in the decline of Dutch commercial supremacy and the subordination of com-

---

[39] Marx 1987, p. 233.
[40] Rodinson 1966, p. 25 where he defines what he means by 'capitalistic sector', and Chapter 3.
[41] 'There were literally hundreds of such firms in each of the towns of thirteenth-century Italy', Hunt and Murray 1999, p. 62.
[42] Sombart 1899.
[43] Mauro 1955.

mercial to industrial capital, as Marx put it.[44] Commercial capitalism spawned the slavery of the Americas. The plantations were 'capitalist creations *par excellence*'.[45] The Dutch merchant-capitalism which Marx saw dominating the seventeenth century[46] was a capitalism founded, in large measure, on sugar. But, long before that, and indeed throughout the era of commercial capitalism, capital extended its sway over whole sectors of production (in iron-work, textiles, shipbuilding and the cottage-industries) through the *Verlagssystem*.[47]

In short, the theoretical distinction we need here is one between capitalism in this more general sense, a sense which allows for the commercial capitalism of the twelfth to eighteenth centuries, and what Marx himself called the 'capitalist mode of production'. The latter is only a historically developed form of capitalism in the more general sense which, in this way, acquires a wider purchase and helps resolve problems that continue to mystify Marxists. The model here is one of *combined* development, rather than the linear succession between modes of production familiar from the 'transition' debates. The 'initial stages', as Marx called them, threw up distinct configurations of capitalism, from the foundries of northern Kiangsu in the eleventh century[48] or the capitalist groups who dominated the economy of Venice in the thirteenth[49] to the 'massive syndicates' that controlled the Glasgow tobacco-trade in the eighteenth.[50] The slave-plantations of the seventeenth century and later were *one* configuration within this general landscape, *capitalist* enterprises but not quite of the form that Marx would see as typical of the 'specifically' capitalist mode of production, that is, industrial capitalism.

12.4. Articulation?

---

[44] Marx 1981, p. 451.
[45] Braudel 2002, p. 272ff.
[46] Marx 1976, p. 916.
[47] Braudel 2002, p. 316ff.; Marx 1978, pp. 318–19; Marx 1981, pp. 452–3.
[48] Hartwell 1996, p. 44ff.
[49] Cracco 1967.
[50] Devine 1975.

Whatever one thinks of the distinction just proposed, there is the separate issue of how capitalist production can integrate diverse forms of exploitation and ways of organising labour in its drive to produce surplus-value. This is particularly clear in agriculture, where it often accounts for an integration of household-labour into capitalism. The use of sharecropping and labour-tenancy on capitalist farms in the late nineteenth/early twentieth centuries is a striking example of a capitalism based on *family-labour systems*. The literature on agrarian capitalism displays an impressive variegation of labour-systems and general ways of controlling and exploiting living labour that capitalist landowners deployed according to the special requirements of different crops, landscapes and labour-processes. Indeed, agrarian studies is one area where Marxists or Marx-influenced scholars have turned out superlative work, which includes the rich South-African debate in which Tim Keegan and Helen Bradford were major contributors.[51] The upshot of all this work is that relations of production are not *reducible* to forms of exploitation of labour, since capitalist relations of production are compatible with a wide variety of forms of labour, from chattel-slavery, sharecropping, or the domination of casual labour-markets, to the coerced wage-labour peculiar to colonial régimes and, of course, 'free' wage-labour. Indeed, the widespread use, under fascism, of forced labour in large industrial concerns such as Daimler-Benz[52] shows how simplistic it is to read relations of production off some imagined register of labour-types. To construe the ways labour is exploited and controlled as distinct relations (and therefore *modes*) of production is to end with a model that sees the *capitalist* world-economy as structured by an articulation of different modes of production (usually 'feudalism'). But, historical materialism needs to move beyond this motionless paradigm to a construction of the more complex ways capitalism works. In fact, the huge commercial expansion of the nineteenth century very largely involved an integration of peasant agriculture into industrial capitalism, which, in turn, spurred the expansion of more local systems of commercial capitalism and a widespread dispossession of the peasantry. Thus what the world-economy of the nineteenth century threw up was an articulation of *forms of capitalism*

---

[51] Bradford 1987; Keegan 1987.
[52] Hopmann et al. 1994.

more than a combination of modes of production, in other words, economic changes driven by the gigantic expansion of industry and the rapid growth in demand for cotton, tobacco, silk, indigo and so on. The gravitational pull of European and American industry wrought changes in the distant countrysides they drew on through local trajectories of accumulation and dispossession.[53] The prehistories of a more fully developed capitalism and the struggles bound up with primitive accumulation[54] were only ways in which 'capitalist world trade', in Marx's expression, 'destroyed and dissolved all earlier forms of production', 'revolutionizing the entire economic structure of society' the world over.[55]

[2008–9]

---

[53] E.g., Owen 1981a.
[54] E.g., Keegan 1989.
[55] Marx 1978, pp. 119–20.

Publications of Jairus Banaji

Published

1970, 'The Crisis of British Anthropology', *New Left Review*, I, 64: 71–85.
1972, 'For a Theory of Colonial Modes of Production', *Economic and Political Weekly*, 7, 52: 2498–502.
1973, 'Backward Capitalism, Primitive Accumulation and Modes of Production', *Journal of Contemporary Asia*, 3, 4: 393–413.
1976, 'The Peasantry in the Feudal Mode of Production: Towards an Economic Model', *Journal of Peasant Studies* 3, 3: 299–320.
1976, 'Summary of Selected Parts of Kautsky's *The Agrarian Question*', *Economy and Society*, 5, 1: 2–49, repr. in Harold Wolpe, ed., *The Articulation of Modes of Production: Essays from Economy and Society* (London, etc., 1980) 45–92; and in Frederick H. Buttel and Howard Newby, eds., *The Rural Sociology of the Advanced Societies* (Montclair, NJ, 1980) 39–82.
1976, 'Chayanov, Kautsky, Lenin: Considerations Towards a Synthesis', *Economic and Political Weekly*, 11, 40: 1594–607.
1976, 'Marx, Ricardo and the Theory of the Value-Form: Prelude to a Critique of Positive Marxism', *Marxistisk Antropologi*, 2, 2–3.
1977, 'Modes of Production in a Materialist Conception of History', *Capital and Class*, 3: 1–44.
1977, 'Capitalist Domination and the Small Peasantry: the Deccan Districts in the Late Nineteenth Century', *Economic and Political Weekly*, 12, 33–4: 1375–404.
1977, 'The Comintern and Indian Nationalism', *International*, 3, 4: 25–41.
1979, 'From the Commodity to Capital: Hegel's Dialectic in Marx's *Capital*', in *Value: The Representation of Labour in Capitalism*, edited by Diane Elson, London: CSE Books.
1980, 'Gunder Frank in Retreat?', *Journal of Peasant Studies*, 7, 4: 508–21.
1990, 'Illusions About the Peasantry: Karl Kautsky and the Agrarian Question', *Journal of Peasant Studies*, 17, 2: 288–307.
1990 (with Rohini Hensman), *Beyond Multinationalism: Management Policy and Bargaining Relationships in International Companies*, New Delhi, etc., Sage.
1990, 'Review of Wim Jongman, *The Economy and Society of Pompeii*', *Journal of Roman Studies*, 80: 230–2.
1992, Translation and abridgement of Henryk Grossmann, *The Law of Accumulation and Breakdown of the Capitalist System, Being also a Theory of Crises*, London: Pluto Press.
1992, 'Historical Arguments for a "Logic of Deployment" in "Pre-Capitalist" Agriculture', *Journal of Historical Sociology*, 5: 379–91.
1995, 'The New Farmers' Movements: A Critique of Conservative Rural Coalitions', in *New Farmers' Movements in India*, edited by Tom Brass, London: Frank Cass.
1995, 'India: Multinationals and the Resistance to Unionised Labour', *International Union Rights*, 2, 2: 5–6.
1996, 'The Circulation of Gold as an Index of Prosperity in the Central and Eastern Mediterranean in Late Antiquity' in *Coin Finds and Coin Use in the Roman World*, edited by C.E. King and D.G. Wigg (Thirteenth Oxford Symposium on Coinage and Monetary History, 25.–27.3.1993), Berlin: G. Mann.

1996, 'Globalization and Restructuring in the Indian Food Industry', in *Agrarian Questions. Essays in Appreciation of T.J. Byres*, edited by Henry Bernstein and Tom Brass, London: Frank Cass.

1997, 'Modernizing the Historiography of Rural Labour: An Unwritten Agenda', in *Companion to Historiography*, edited by Michael Bentley, Routledge.

1997, 'Lavoratori liberi e residenza coatta: il colonato romano in prospettiva storica', in *Terre, proprietari e contadini dell' impero romano*, edited by Elio Lo Cascio, Rome: La Nuova Italia Scientifica.

1998, 'Discounts, Weight Standards, and the Exchange-Rate Between Gold and Copper', *Atti dell' Accademia Romanistica Costantiniana. XII Convegno Internazionale in onore di Manlio Sargenti*, Naples: Edizioni Scientifiche Italiane.

1999, 'Agrarian History and the Labour Organisation of Byzantine Large Estates', in *Agriculture in Egypt from Pharaonic to Modern Times* (Proceedings of the British Academy – 96), edited by Alan Bowman and E. Rogan, Oxford: Oxford University Press for the British Academy.

1999, 'Estates', in *Late Antiquity: A Guide to the Postclassical World*, edited by G.W. Bowersock, Peter Brown and Oleg Grabar, Cambridge, MA.: Harvard University Press.

2000, 'State and Aristocracy in the Economic Evolution of the Late Empire', in *Production and Public Powers in Classical Antiquity*, edited by E. Lo Cascio and D.W. Rathbone, Cambridge: The Cambridge Philological Society.

2001 (with Gautam Mody), *Corporate Governance and the Indian Private Sector*, QEH Working Paper 73, Oxford, available at: <http://www3.qeh.ox.ac.uk/pdf/qehwp/qehwps73.pdf>.

2001, *Agrarian Change in Late Antiquity: Gold, Labour and Aristocratic Dominance*, Oxford: Oxford University Press.

2001, 'Workers' Rights in a New Economic Order: The First Arvind N. Das Memorial Lecture from the Association of Labour Historians', *Biblio: A Review of Books*, 6, 1–2: 36–9.

2002, 'The Metamorphoses of Agrarian Capitalism', *Journal of Agrarian Change* 2/1: 96–119 (review essay on Daniel Thorner, *Ecological and Agrarian Regions of South Asia c. 1930*).

2003, 'The Fictions of Free Labour: Contract, Coercion and So-Called Unfree Labour', *Historical Materialism* 11, 3: 69–95

2004, 'Institutional Investors and Nominee Directors', in *Corporate Governance, Economic Reforms and Development*, edited by Darryl Reed and Sanjoy Mukherjee, New Delhi: Oxford University Press.

2005, 'Thwarting the Market for Corporate Control: Takeover Regulation in India', available at: <http://www.qeh.ox.ac.uk/dissemination/conference-papers/banaji.pdf/>.

2006, 'Precious Metal Coinages and Monetary Expansion in Late Antiquity', in *Dal Denarius al Dinar: l'Oriente e la moneta romana: atti dell'incontro di studio, Roma 16–18 settembre 2004*, edited by Federico De Romanis and Sara Sorda. Rome: Istituto italiano di numismatica.

2007, 'Islam, the Mediterranean and the Rise of Capitalism', *Historical Materialism*, 15, 1: 47–74.

2007, 'Mickwitz's Modernism: The Writings of 1932–36', in *Gunnar Mickwitz (1906–40) nella storiografia europea tra le due guerre*, Acta Instituti Romani Finlandiae, Volume 34, Rome: Institutum Romanum Finlandiae.

2007, *Agrarian Change in Late Antiquity: Gold, Labour and Aristocratic Dominance*, revised paperback edition, Oxford: Oxford University Press.

2008, 'Spätantike Agrarverhältnisse – Kontinuitat oder Umbruch? Einige Überlegungen zu Wickhams *Framing the Early Middle Ages*', in *Agrarrevolutionen. Verhältnisse in der Landwirtschaft vom Neolithikum zur Globalisierung*, edited by Markus Cerman, Ilja Steffelbauer and Sven Tost, Innsbruck, Vienna, Bozen: StudienVerlag.

2009, 'Aristocracies, Peasantries and the Framing of the Early Middle Ages', *Journal of Agrarian Change*, 9, 1: 59–91.

2010, 'Late Antique Legacies and Muslim Economic Expansion', in *Money, Power and Politics in Early Islamic Syria*, edited by John Haldon, Aldershot: Ashgate.
2010, 'The Ironies of Indian Maoism', *International Socialism*, 128: 129–48.
2011, 'Reconstructing Historical Materialism', *Humanities Underground*, 6–7 February, available at: http://humanitiesunderground.wordpress.com/2011/02/06/reconstructing-historical-materialism/.

Forthcoming

'On the Identity of "Shahralanyozan" in the Greek and Middle Persian Papyri from Egypt', in *Documents and the History of the Medieval Islamic World*, edited by Petra Sijpesteijn, Leiden, etc.: Brill.
'The Economic Trajectories of Late Antiquity', in *The Oxford Handbook of Late Antiquity*, edited by Scott Johnson, Oxford University Press.

References

Abel, Wilhelm 1973, *Crises agraires en Europe (XIIIe–XXe siècle)*, Paris: Flammarion.
Acién Almansa, Manuel 1997, *Entre el feudalismo y el Islam. 'Umar ibn Ḥafṣūn en los historiadores, en las fuentes y en la historia*, 2nd edition, Jaén: Universidad de Jaén.
—— 1998, 'Sobre el papel de la ideología en la caracterización de las formaciones sociales. La formacion social Islamica', *Hispania*, 58, 3: 915–68.
Adams, Bertrand 1964, *Paramoné und verwandte Texte. Studien zum Dienstvertrag im Rechte der Papyri*, Berlin: De Gruyter.
Agarwal, Bina 1983, *Mechanization in Indian Agriculture: An Analytical Study Based on the Punjab*, New Delhi: Allied.
—— 1984, 'Rural Women and High Yielding Variety Rice Technology', *Economic and Political Weekly*, 19, 13: A39–52.
Alam, Muzaffar 1986, *The Crisis of Empire in Mughal North India: Awadh and the Punjab, 1707–48*, Delhi: Oxford University Press.
'Alī b. Ḥāmid Kūfī 1900, *The Chachnama, an Ancient History of Sind*, translated by Mirza Kalichbeg Fredunbeg, Karachi: The Commissioner's Press.
Alleaume, Ghislaine 1999, 'An Industrial Revolution in Agriculture? Some Observations on the Evolution of Rural Egypt in the Nineteenth Century', in *Agriculture in Egypt from Pharaonic to Modern Times*, edited by A. Bowman and E. Rogan, Oxford: Oxford University Press.
Amin, Samir 1974, *Accumulation on a World Scale*, tr. Brian Pearce, New York: Monthly Review Press.
—— 1976, *Unequal Development*, tr. Brian Pearce, New York: Monthly Review Press.
Anders on, Perry 1974a, *Lineages of the Absolutist State*, London: NLB.
—— 1974b, *Passages from Antiquity to Feudalism*, London: NLB.
Andreolli, B. and M. Montanari 1983, *L'azienda curtense in Italia: proprietà della terra e lavoro contadino nei secoli VIII–XI*, Bologna: CLUEB.
Angeli, Stefano 1982, *Proprietari, commercianti e filandieri a Milano nel primo Ottocento: il mercato delle sete*, Milan: Angeli.
Angelo, Larian 1995, 'Wage Labour Deferred: The Recreation of Unfree Labour in the US South', *Journal of Peasant Studies*, 22, 4: 581–644.
Antoniades-Bibicou, Hélène 1969, 'Byzance et le mode de production asiatique', in *Sur le "Mode de production asiatique"*, Paris: Éditions Sociales.
Antrobus, Hinson Allan 1957, *A History of the Assam Company, 1839–1953*, Edinburgh: Priv. print. by T. and A. Constable.
Arrighi, Giovanni 1970, 'Labour Supplies in Historical Perspective: A Study of the Proletarianization of the African Peasantry in Rhodesia', *Journal of Development Studies*, 6, 3: 197–234.
Aston, Trevor Henry 1958, 'The Origins of the Manor in England', *Transactions of the Royal Historical Society*, 5th ser., 8: 59–83; repr. with 'Postscript' in *Social Relations and Ideas: Essays in Honour of R.H. Hilton*, edited by T.H. Aston et al., Cambridge, etc., 1983.
Aston, T.H. and C.H.E. Philpin (eds) 1985, *The Brenner Debate: Agrarian Class Structure and Economic Development in Pre-Industrial Europe*, Cambridge: Cambridge University Press.

Athar Ali, M. 1997, *The Mughal Nobility under Aurangzeb*, revised edition, New Delhi: Oxford University Press.
—— 2006, *Mughal India: Studies in Polity, Ideas, Society, and Culture*, New Delhi: Oxford University Press.
Atiyah, Patrick S. 1979, *The Rise and Fall of Freedom of Contract*, Oxford: Clarendon Press.
—— 1982, 'Economic Duress and the "Overborne Will"', *Law Quarterly Review*, 98: 197–202.
Attenborough, Frederick Levi 1922, *The Laws of the Earliest English Kings*, Cambridge: Cambridge University Press.
Avineri, Shlomo 1969, *Karl Marx on Colonialism and Modernization*, New York: Anchor Books.
Ayala, César J. 1999, *American Sugar Kingdom: The Plantation Economy of the Spanish Caribbean 1898–1934*, Chapel Hill: University of North Carolina Press.
Azzara, Claudio and Stefano Gasparri, 2005, *Le leggi dei Longobardi. Storia, memoria e diritto di un popolo germanico*, 2nd edn., Rome: Viella.
Baer, Gabriel 1962, *A History of Landownership in Modern Egypt 1800–1950*, London: Oxford University Press.
Bagnall, Roger S. 1993, *Egypt in Late Antiquity*, Princeton: Princeton University Press.
Bahro, Rudolf 1978, *The Alternative in Eastern Europe*, tr. David Fernbach, London: NLB/Verso.
Baker, Christopher John 1984, *An Indian Rural Economy 1880–1955: The Tamilnad Countryside*, Oxford: Clarendon Press.
al-Balādhurī 1924, *The Origins of the Islamic State (Kitāb futūḥ al-buldān)*, pt. 2, tr. F.C. Murgotten, New York: Longmans.
Baldamus, Wilhelm 1967, *Efficiency and Effort: An Analysis of Industrial Administration*, London: Tavistock.
Balty, Jean Charles 1984, 'Notes sur l'habitat romain, byzantin et arabe d'Apamée', in *Apamée de Syrie: bilan des recherches archéologiques, 1973–1979*, Brussels/Paris: Diffusion de Boccard.
—— 1989, 'Apamée au VIᵉ siècle. Témoignages archéologiques de la richesse d'une ville', in *Hommes et richesses dans l'Empire byzantin*, Paris: P. Lethielleux.
Banaji, Jairus 1970, 'The Crisis of British Anthropology', *New Left Review*, I, 64: 71–85.
—— 1976, 'Chayanov, Kautsky, Lenin: Considerations towards a Synthesis', *Economic and Political Weekly*, 11, 40: 1594–607.
—— 1977a, 'Capitalist Domination and the Small Peasantry: Deccan Districts in the Late Nineteenth Century', *Economic and Political Weekly*, 12, 33–4: 1375–404.
—— 1977b, 'Modes of Production in a Materialist Conception of History', *Capital and Class*, 3: 1–41.
—— 1979, 'From the Commodity to Capital: Hegel's Dialectic in Marx's *Capital*', in *Value: The Representation of Labour in Capitalism*, edited by Diane Elson, London: CSE Books.
—— 1992, *Rural Communities in the Late Empire AD 300–700*, 2 volumes, Oxford D.Phil. thesis.
—— 1994, 'State and Aristocracy in the Economic Evolution of the Late Empire', in *Production and Public Powers in Classical Antiquity*, edited by E. Lo Cascio and D. W. Rathbone, Milan: International Economic History Congress; repr. Cambridge Philological Society, Supplementary Volume 26 (Cambridge, 2000).
—— 1996, 'The Circulation of Gold as an Index of Prosperity in the Central and Eastern Mediterranean in Late Antiquity', in *Coin Finds and Coin Use in the Roman World*, edited by C.E. King and D.G. Wigg (*Studien zu Fundmünzen der Antike*, Bd. 10), Berlin: Mann.
—— 1997a, 'Lavoratori liberi e residenza coatta: il colonato romano in prospettiva storica', in *Terre, proprietari e contadini dell'impero romano. Dall'affitto agrario al colonato tardoantico*, edited by E. Lo Cascio, Rome: La Nuova Italia Scientifica.
—— 1997b, 'Modernizing the Historiography of Rural Labour: An Unwritten Agenda', in *Companion to Historiography*, edited by Michael Bentley, London: Routledge.

—— 1999, 'Agrarian History and the Labour Organization of Byzantine Large Estates', in *Agriculture in Egypt*, edited by A. Bowman and E. Rogan, Oxford: Oxford University Press for The British Academy.
—— 2003, 'The Fictions of Free Labour', *Historical Materialism*, 11, 3: 69–95.
—— 2007a, *Agrarian Change in Late Antiquity: Gold, Labour and Aristocratic Dominance*, 2nd edn., Oxford: Oxford University Press.
—— 2007b, 'Islam, the Mediterranean and the Rise of Capitalism', *Historical Materialism*, 15, 1: 47–74.
Barbero de Aguilera, Abilio 1992, *La sociedad visigoda y su entorno histórico*, Madrid: Siglo Veintiuno de España Editores.
Barbero, Abilio and Marcelo Vigil 1978, *La formación del feudalismo en la Península Ibérica*, 1st edn., Barcelona: Editorial Critica.
Barrett W. 1970, *The Sugar Hacienda of the Marqueses del Valle*, Minneapolis: University of Minnesota Press.
Batt, Francis Raleigh 1967, *The Law of Master and Servant*, Fifth Edition, by George G. Webber, London: Pitman.
Bauer, Arnold J. 1971, 'Chilean Rural Labor in the Nineteenth Century', *American Historical Review*, 76, 4: 1059–82.
—— 1972, 'The Hacienda *El Huique* in the Agrarian Structure of Nineteenth-Century Chile', *Agricultural History*, 46, 4: 455–70.
Bautier, Robert-Henri 1971, *The Economic Development of Medieval Europe*, London: Thames and Hudson.
Bayly, Christopher Alan 1983, *Rulers, Townsmen and Bazaars: North Indian Society in the Age of British Expansion, 1770–1870*, Cambridge: Cambridge University Press.
—— 1986, 'The Middle East and Asia during the Age of Revolutions, 1760–1830', *Itinerario*, 10, 2: 69–83.
Bazant, Jan 1950, 'Feudalismo y capitalismo en la historia económica de México', *El Trimestre Económico*, 17, 1: 81–98.
—— 1975, *Cinco haciendas mexicanas: tres siglos de vida rural en San Luis Potosí (1600–1910)*, Mexico City: Colegio de México.
—— 1977, 'Landlord, Labourer, and Tenant in San Luis Potosí, Northern Mexico, 1822–1910', in *Land and Labour in Latin America: Essays on the Development of Agrarian Capitalism in the Nineteenth and Twentieth Centuries*, edited by Kenneth Duncan and Ian Rutledge, Cambridge: Cambridge University Press.
Beinart, W. and P. Delius 1986, 'Introduction', in *Putting a Plough to the Ground: Accumulationn and Dispossession in Rural South Africa, 1850–1930*, edited by William Beinart, Peter Delius and Stanley Trapido, Johannesburg: Ravan Press.
Ben Shemesh, Aharon 1969, *Taxation in Islam Vol. III: Abu Yusuf's Kitab al-kharaj*, Leiden: E.J. Brill and Luzac & Co.
Bergad, Laird W. 1990, *Cuban Rural Society in the Nineteenth Century. The Social and Economic History of Monoculture in Matanzas*, Princeton: Princeton University Press.
Berger, A. 1948, 'A Labor Contract of A.D. 164', *Classical Philology*, 43, 4: 231–42.
Bernier, François 1916, *Travels in the Mogul Empire A.D. 1656–1668*, tr. Archibald Constable, 2nd editon revised by Vincent A. Smith, Oxford: Oxford University Press.
Bernstein, Henry 1996, 'Agrarian Questions Then and Now', in *Agrarian Questions: Essays in Appreciation of T.J. Byres*, edited by Henry Bernstein and Tom Brass, London: Frank Cass & Co.
Bettelheim, Charles 1972, 'Theoretical Comments', in A. Emmanuel, *Unequal Exchange*, London: NLB.
Bhaduri, Amit 1973, 'An Analysis of Semi-Feudalism in East Indian Agriculture', *Frontier*, 6, 25–7: 11–15.
Bhalla, Sheila 1976, 'New Relations of Production in Haryana Agriculture', *Economic and Political Weekly*, 11, 26: A23–30.
Bhattacharya, Neeladri 1983, 'The Logic of Tenancy Cultivation: Central and Southeast Punjab 1870–1935', *Indian Economic and Social History Review*, 20, 2: 121–70.

Bivar, Adrian David Hugh 1976, 'Trade between China and the Near East in the Sasanian and Early Muslim Periods', in *Pottery and Metalwork in T'ang China: Their Chronology and External Relations*, London: SOAS.
Bloch, Marc 1921, 'Serf de la glèbe: histoire d'une expression toute faite', *Revue Historique*, 136: 220–42; rééd. *Mélanges historiques*, t. 1, Paris: SEVPEN.
—— 1963, 'The Rise of Dependent Cultivation and Seigniorial Institutions', in *Mélanges historiques*, t.1, Paris: SEVPEN.
—— 1965, *Feudal Society*, tr. L.A. Manyon, 2 volumes, London: Routledge & Kegan Paul.
—— 1973, *French Rural History: An Essay on its Basic Characteristics*, tr. Janet Sondheimer, Berkeley: University of California Press.
—— 1975, *Slavery and Serfdom in the Middle Ages: Selected Essays*, tr. W.R. Beer, Berkeley: University of California Press.
Blum, Jerome 1957, 'The Rise of Serfdom in Eastern Europe', *American Historical Review*, 62, 4: 807–36.
—— 1968, *Lord and Peasant in Russia from the Ninth to the Nineteenth Century*, New York: Atheneum.
Bognetti, Gian Pietro 1968, 'La proprietà della terra nel passaggio dal mondo antico al Medioevo occidentale', in *L'età longobarda*, 4: 67–89, Milan: Giuffrè Editore.
Bolland, Nigel O. 1981, 'Systems of Domination After Slavery: The Control of Land and Labor in the British West Indies After 1838', *Comparative Studies in Society and History*, 23, 4: 591–619.
Bombay Government Records 1886, *Papers relating to the Revision of the Rates of Assessment on the Expiry of the First Settlement in the Savda Taluka of the Khandesh Collectorate*, Selections from the Bombay Government Records new series 186, Bombay: Printed for Govt. at the Education Society's Press.
Bonnassie, Pierre 1991, *From Slavery to Feudalism in South-Western Europe*, tr. Jean Birrell, Cambridge and Paris: Cambridge University Press and Editions de la Maison des Sciences de l'Homme.
Bowman, Alan K. 1996, *Egypt after the Pharaohs*, 3rd edn., Berkeley: University of California Press.
Bradford, Helen 1987, *A Taste of Freedom: The ICU in Rural South Africa 1924–1930*, New Haven: Yale University Press.
—— 1990, 'Highways, Byways and Culs-de-Sacs: The Transition to Agrarian Capitalism in Revisionist South African History', *Radical History Review*, 46–47: 59–88.
Brading, David A. 1978, *Haciendas and Ranchos in the Mexican Bajío: León 1700–1860*, Cambridge: Cambridge University Press.
Branco, Marco di 2000, 'Lavoro e conflittualità in una città tardo-antica. Una rilettura dell' epigrafe di Sardi *CIG* 3467', *Antiquité Tardive*, 8: 181–208.
Brass, Tom 1996, 'Yet More on Agrarian Change and Unfree Labour', *Economic and Political Weekly*, 31, 4: 237–40.
—— 1999, *Towards a Comparative Political Economy of Unfree Labour: Case Studies and Debates*, London: Frank Cass.
—— 2003, 'Why Unfree Labour is Not "So-Called": The Fictions of Jairus Banaji', *Journal of Peasant Studies*, 31, 1: 101–36.
Brass, Tom and Henry Bernstein 1993, 'Introduction', in *Plantations, Proletarians and Peasants in Colonial Asia*, edited by Val Daniel, Henry Bernstein, and Tom Brass (= *Journal of Peasant Studies* 19, 3–4, 1992), London: Frank Cass.
Brătianu, Gheorghe Ioan 1933, 'Servage de la glèbe et régime fiscal: Essai d'histoire comparée roumaine, slave et byzantine', *Annales d'histoire économique et sociale*, 5, 5: 445–62.
Braudel, Fernand 1972, 'History and the Social Sciences', in *Economy and Society in Early Modern Europe: Essays from Annales*, edited by Peter Burke, London: Routledge & Kegan Paul.
—— 1975, *The Mediterranean and the Mediterranean World in the Age of Philip II*, 2 volumes, translated by Siân Reynolds, London: Fontana.
—— 2002, *Civilization and Capitalism 15th–18th Century: Volume 2, The Wheels of Commerce*, London: Phoenix Press.

Braudel, Fernand and Frank Spooner 1967, 'Prices in Europe from 1450–1750', in *The Cambridge Economic History of Europe, IV: The Economy of Expanding Europe in the Sixteenth and Seventeenth Centuries*, edited by E. Rich and C.H. Wilson, Cambridge: Cambridge University Press.
Breman, Jan 1974, *Patronage and Exploitation: Changing Agrarian Relations in South Gujarat, India*, Berkeley: University of California Press.
—— 1985, *Of Peasants, Migrants and Paupers. Rural Labour Circulation and Capitalist Production in West India*, New Delhi: Oxford University Press.
—— 1996, *Footloose Labour: Working in India's Informal Economy*, Cambridge: Cambridge University Press.
Britnell, Richard H. 1966, 'Production for the Market on a Small Fourteenth-Century Estate', *Economic History Review*, 2nd ser., 19, 2: 380–7.
Brown, Nathan J. 1994, 'Who Abolished Corvée Labour in Egypt and Why?', *Past and Present*, 144, 1: 116–37.
Brown, Peter 1967, 'The Later Roman Empire', *Economic History Review*, 2nd ser., 20, 2: 327–43; repr. in *Religion and Society in the Age of St. Augustine* (Eugene, Oregon, 2007).
—— 1971, *The World of Late Antiquity: From Marcus Aurelius to Muhammad*, London: Thames and Hudson.
Brown, Thomas S. 1984, *Gentlemen and Officers: Imperial Administration and Aristocratic Power in Byzantine Italy, A.D. 544–800*, London: British School at Rome.
Bruckner, Albert and Robert Marichal 1981–2, *Chartae Latinae Antiquiores, Parts xiii–xiv: France I-II*, Dietikon-Zurich: Graf.
Brunt, Peter A. 1980, 'Free Labour and Public Works at Rome', *Journal of Roman Studies*, 70: 81–101.
Buchanan, Francis 1870 [1807], *A Journey from Madras through the Countries of Mysore, Canara and Malabar*, Second Edition, 2 vols., Madras: Higginbotham & Co.
Busson, G. and A. Ledru 1901, *Actus Pontificum Cenomannis in Urbe Degentium. (Archives historiques du Maine, II.)*, Au Mans: Au siège de la Société.
Byres, Terence J. 1985, 'Modes of Production and Non-European Pre-Colonial Societies: The Nature and Significance of the Debate', in *Feudalism and Non-European Societies*, edited by T.J. Byres and Harbans Mukhia, London: Frank Cass & Co.
—— 1996, *Capitalism from Above and Capitalism from Below: An Essay in Comparative Political Economy*, Basingstoke: Macmillan.
Calkins, Philip B. 1970, 'The Formation of a Regionally Oriented Ruling Group in Bengal, 1700–1740', *Journal of Asian Studies*, 29, 4: 799–806.
Cammarosano, Paolo 2001, *Storia dell'Italia medievale dal VI all' XI secolo*, Rome: Laterza.
Campbell, George 1852, *Modern India: A Sketch of the System of Civil Government*, London: John Murray.
Carmen Velázquez, M. del 1983, *Cuentas de sirvientes de tres haciendas y sus anexas del Fondo Piadoso de las Misiones de las Californias*, Mexico: Colegio de México, Centro de Estudios Históricos.
Carrère d'Encausse, Hélène and Stuart R. Schram 1969, *Marxism and Asia: An Introduction with Readings*, London: Allen Lane.
Carrié, Jean-Michel 1982, 'Le "colonat du Bas-Empire": un mythe historiographique?', *Opus*, 1: 351–70.
—— 1983, 'Un roman des origines: les généalogies du "colonat du Bas-Empire"', *Opus*, 2: 205–51.
—— 1997, '"Colonato del Basso Impero": la resistenza del mito', in *Terre, proprietari e contadini dell'impero romano: Dall'affitto agrario al colonato tardoantico*, edited by Elio Lo Cascio, Rome: La Nuova Italia Scientifica.
Cato, Marcus Porcius 1967, *On Agriculture*, tr. W. Hooper and D. Boyd, Cambridge, MA.: Harvard University Press.
CERM (Centre d'Études et de Recherches marxistes) 1969, *Sur le "mode de production asiatique"*, Paris: Éditions Sociales.
Chastagnol, André 1966, *Le Sénat romain sous le règne d'Odoacre. Recherches sur l'Épigraphie du Colisée au Ve siècle*, Bonn: Rudolf Habelt Verlag.

—— 1978, 'Sidoine Apollinaire et le sénat de Rome', *Acta Antiqua Academiae Scientiarum Hungaricae*, 26, 1–2: 57–70.
Chaudhuri, Binay Bhushan 1969, 'Rural Credit Relations in Bengal, 1859–1885', *Indian Economic and Social History Review*, 6, 3: 203–57.
Chavarría Arnau, Alexandra 2004, 'Interpreting the Transformation of Late Roman Villas: The Case of Hispania', in *Landscapes of Change*, edited by Neil Christie, Ashgate: Aldershot.
—— 2005, 'Dopo la fine delle ville: le campagne ispaniche in epoca visigota', in *Dopo la fine delle ville: Le campagne dal VI al IX secolo*, edited by G.P. Brogiolo, A. Chavarría, M. Valenti, Mantova: SAP.
Cheesman, David 1996, *Landlord Power and Rural Indebtedness in Colonial Sind 1865–1901*, Richmond: Curzon.
Chevalier, François 1970, *Land and Society in Colonial Mexico: The Great Hacienda*, tr. Alvin Eustis, Berkeley: University of California Press.
Cheynet, Jean-Claude 1990, *Pouvoir et contestations à Byzance (963–1210)*, Paris: Publications de la Sorbonne.
—— 2006, *The Byzantine Aristocracy and its Military Function*, Aldershot: Ashgate.
Chi, Ch'ao-ting 1963, *Key Economic Areas in Chinese History as Revealed in the Development of Public Works for Water-Control*, New York: Paragon Book Reprint Corp.
Chowdhury, Benoy 1964, *Growth of Commercial Agriculture in Bengal (1757–1900)*, Calcutta: Indian Studies Past and Present.
Clark, Hugh R. 2009, 'The Southern Kingdoms between the T'ang and the Sung, 907–979', in *The Cambridge History of China, Volume 5/1: The Sung Dynasty and its Precursors, 907–1279*, Cambridge: Cambridge University Press.
Clausing, Roth 1925, *The Roman Colonate. The Theories of its Origin*, New York: Columbia University.
Colditz, Iris 2000, *Zur Sozialterminologie der iranischen Manichäer. Eine semantische Analyse im Vergleich zu den nichtmanichäischen iranischen Quellen*, Iranica Bd. 5., Wiesbaden: Harrassowitz.
Colletti, Lucio 1972, 'Bernstein and the Marxism of the Second International', in *Rousseau to Lenin*, London: NLB.
Collins, Hugh, 1986 *The Law of Contract*, First Edition, London: Weidenfeld and Nicolson.
Confino, Michael 1963, *Domaines et seigneurs en Russie vers la fin du XVIIIe siècle*, Paris: Institut d'Études slaves de l'Université de Paris.
—— 1990, 'Servage russe, esclavage américain (Note critique)' (review of Kolchin, *Unfree Labor*), *Annales E.S.C.*, 45, 5: 1119–41.
Conrad, Alfred H. and John R. Meyer 1971, 'The Economics of Slavery in the Ante-Bellum South', in *The Reinterpretation of American Economic History*, edited by R.W. Fogel and S.L. Engerman, New York: Harper & Row.
Conze, Werner 1969, 'The Effects of Nineteenth-Century Liberal Agrarian Reforms on Social Structure in Central Europe', in *Essays in European Economic History 1789–1914*, edited by F. Crouzet, W.H. Chaloner and W.M. Stern, London: Edward Arnold.
Cooper, Frederick 1996, *Decolonization and African Society: The Labor Question in French and British Africa*, Cambridge: Cambridge University Press.
Corner, Paul 1975, *Fascism in Ferrara 1915–1925*, Oxford: Oxford University Press.
Coulson, N.J. 1978, *A History of Islamic Law*, Edinburgh: Edinburgh University Press.
Cowen, Michael 1976a, 'Notes on Capital, Class and Household Production', *IDS Miscellaneous Papers*, 84, Nairobi: University of Nairobi.
—— 1976b, 'Capital and Peasant Households', *IDS Miscellaneous Papers*, 91, Nairobi: University of Nairobi.
Cracco, Giorgio 1967, *Società e stato nel medioevo veneziano (secoli xii–xiv)*, Florence: Olschki.
Crone, Patricia 1991, 'Kavād's Heresy and Mazdak's Revolt', *Iran*, 29: 21–42. Repr. in *From Kavād to al-Ghazālī. Religion, Law and Political Thought in the Near East, c. 600–c. 1100*. Aldershot: Ashgate, 2005.
—— 2004, *Medieval Islamic Political Thought*, Edinburgh: Edinburgh University Press.

Cuno, Kenneth M. 1980, 'The Origins of Private Ownership of Land in Egypt: A Reappraisal', *International Journal of Middle East Studies*, 12, 3: 245–75.
—— 1984, 'Egypt's Wealthy Peasantry, 1740–1820: A Study of the Region of al-Manṣūra', in *Land Tenure and Social Transformation in the Middle East*, edited by T. Khalidi, Beirut: American University of Beirut.
—— 1992, *The Pasha's Peasants. Land, Society, and Economy in Lower Egypt, 1740–1858*, Cambridge: Cambridge University Press.
Dalton, Clare 1985, 'An Essay in the Deconstruction of Contract Doctrine', *Yale Law Journal*, 94, 5: 997–1114.
Daniel, Pete 1972, *The Shadow of Slavery: Peonage in the South, 1901–1969*, Oxford: Oxford University Press.
Dantwala, M.L. 1937, *Marketing of Raw Cotton in India*, edited by C.N. Vakil, Bombay: Longmans.
Dasgupta, Biplab 1984, 'Agricultural Labour under Colonial, Semi-Capitalist and Capitalist Conditions: A Case Study of West Bengal', *Economic and Political Weekly*, 19, 39: A129–48.
Davidson, Neil 2001, 'Marx and Engels on the Scottish Highlands', *Science and Society*, 65, 3: 286–326.
Davies, Wendy 1978a, *An Early Welsh Microcosm: Studies in the Llandaff Charters*, London: Royal Historical Society.
—— 1978b, 'Land and Power in Early Medieval Wales', *Past and Present*, 81, 1: 3–23.
—— 1996, 'On Servile Status in the Early Middle Ages', in *Serfdom and Slavery: Studies in Legal Bondage*, edited by M.L. Bush, London: Longman.
Davis, Ralph 1954, 'English Foreign Trade, 1660–1700', *Economic History Review*, 2nd ser., 7, 2: 150–66.
—— 1967, *Aleppo and Devonshire Square: English Traders in the Levant in the Eighteenth Century*, London: Macmillan.
Dawar, Lajpat Rai and Shiv Dayal 1936, *An Economic Survey of Suner, a Village in the Ferozepore District of the Punjab*, Lahore: C. & M. Gazette.
Dawson, John P. 1947, 'Economic Duress – An Essay in Perspective', *Michigan Law Review*, 45, 3: 253–90.
Degras, Jane 1971, *The Communist International 1919–1943: Documents*, 3 vols., London: Frank Cass & Co.
Delmaire, Roland 1989, *Largesses sacrées et res privata. L'aerarium impérial et son administration du IVe au VIe siècle*, Rome: École Française de Rome.
Devine, Thomas Martin 1975, *The Tobacco Lords: A Study of the Tobacco Merchants of Glasgow and their Trading Activities c. 1740–90*, Edinburgh: John Donald.
Devroey, Jean-Pierre 2001, 'The Economy', in *The Early Middle Ages: Europe 400–1000*, edited by Rosamond McKitterick, Oxford: Oxford University Press.
Dias, Manuel Nunes 1963, *O Capitalismo monárquico Português, 1415–1549. Contribuição para o estudo das origens do capitalismo moderno*, 2 vols., Coimbra: Faculdade de Létras da Universidade de Coimbra.
Dobb, Maurice 1954, 'A Reply', in Sweezy et al. 1954.
—— 1963, *Studies in the Development of Capitalism*, London: Routledge & Kegan Paul.
—— 1976, 'A Reply', in *The Transition from Feudalism to Capitalism*, intr. by Rodney Hilton, London: NLB.
Dongus, Hansjörg 1969, 'Gutsbetrieb und Bauernhof in den Marschen der östlichen Po-Ebene', *Zeitschrift für Agrargeschichte und Agrarsoziologie*, 17: 194–214.
Drèze, Jean and Anindita Mukherjee 1989, 'Labour Contracts in Rural India: Theories and Evidence', in *The Balance between Industry and Agriculture in Economic Development. Vol. 3: Manpower and Transfers*, edited by Sukhamoy Chakravarty, Basingstoke: Macmillan.
Drinkwater, John F. 1977–8, 'Die Secundinier von Igel und die Woll- und Textilindustrie in Gallica Belgica: Fragen und Hypothesen', *Trierer Zeitschrift*, 40/41: 107–25.
Duby, Georges 1968, *Rural Economy and Country Life in the Medieval West*, tr. C. Postan, London: Edward Arnold.

—— 1973, *Guerriers et paysans VIIe–XIIe siècle: Premier essor de l'économie européenne*, Paris: Gallimard.
Dumont, Louis 1966, 'The "Village Community" from Munro to Maine', *Contributions to Indian Sociology*, 9, 2: 67–89.
Dunn, Richard S. 1973, *Sugar and Slaves. The Rise of the Planter Class in the English West Indies, 1624–1713*, New York: W.W. Norton & Co.
Dusinberre, William 1996, *Them Dark Days: Slavery in the American Rice Swamps*, Oxford: Oxford University Press.
Dye, Alan 1998, *Cuban Sugar in the Age of Mass Production: Technology and the Economics of the Sugar "Central", 1899–1929*, Stanford: Stanford University Press.
Dyson, Robert W. 1998, *Augustine: The City of God Against the Pagans*, Cambridge: Cambridge University Press.
DeLaine, Janet 1997, *The Baths of Caracalla: A Study in the Design, Construction, and Economics of Large-Scale Building Projects in Imperial Rome*, Portsmouth, R.I.: Journal of Roman Archaeology.
De Martino, Francesco 1986, 'Schiavi e coloni tra antichità e Medioevo', *Studi Tardoantichi*, 2: 7–43; repr. in *Diritto, economia e società nel mondo Romano, Volume 3: Economia e società*, 1997.
Di Porto, Andrea 1984, *Impresa collettiva e schiavo "manager" in Roma antica (II sec. a.C.–II sec. d.C.)*, Milan: A. Giuffrè.
El-Abbadi, Mostafa 1967, 'The Edict of Tiberius Julius Alexander: Remarks on its Nature and Aim', *Bulletin de l'Institut français d'archéologie orientale*, 65: 215–26.
El Faïz, Mohammed 1995, *L'Agronomie de la Mésopotamie antique. Analyse du 'Livre de l'agriculture nabatéenne' de Qûtâmä*, Leiden: E.J. Brill.
Elvin, Mark 1973, *The Pattern of the Chinese Past*, London: Eyre & Methuen.
Engels, Frederick 1951, 'Ludwig Feuerbach and the End of Classical German Philosophy', in Marx and Engels 1951, Volume 2, pp. 324–64.
—— 1959, *Anti-Dühring*, Moscow: Foreign Languages Publishing House.
—— 1985 [1868], 'Unpublished Review of *Capital* Volume I', in Marx and Engels 1985.
Ewig, Eugen 1976, *Spätantikes und fränkisches Gallien. Gesammelte Schriften (1952–1973)*, edited by H. Atsma, 2 vols., Munich: Artemis Verlag.
Faith, Rosamond 1997, *The English Peasantry and the Growth of Lordship*, London: Leicester University Press.
Al-Fārābī 1961, *Fuṣūl al-Madanī. Aphorisms of the Statesman*, edited with an English translation, introduction and notes by D.M. Dunlop, Cambridge: Cambridge University Press.
Fear, Andrew Thomas 1997, *Lives of the Visigothic Fathers*, Liverpool: Liverpool University Press.
Feinman, Jay M. 1987, 'Contract after the Fall', *Stanford Law Review*, 39, 6: 1537–54.
Festugière, André-Jean 1961, *Historia monachorum in Aegypto: édition critique du texte grec*, Brussels: Société des Bollandistes.
Finberg, Herbert Patrick Reginald 1972, 'Anglo-Saxon England to 1042', in *The Agrarian History of England and Wales, I/ii, A.D. 43–1042*, edited by H.P.R. Finberg, Cambridge: Cambridge University Press.
Finley, Moses I. 1975, *The Ancient Economy*, London: Chatto & Windus.
—— 1980, *Ancient Slavery and Modern Ideology*, London: Chatto & Windus.
Firestone, Ya'akov 1975, 'Crop-sharing Economics in Mandatory Palestine – Part I', *Middle Eastern Studies*, 11, 1: 3–23.
Fisher, Harold Edward Stephen 1971, *The Portugal Trade: A Study of Anglo-Portuguese Commerce*, London: Methuen.
Fitzler, Kurt 1910, *Steinbrüche und Bergwerke im ptolemaïschen und römischen Ägypten*, Leipzig: Quelle & Meyer.
Földi, András 1996, 'Remarks on the Legal Structure of Enterprises in Roman Law', *Revue Internationale des Droits de l'Antiquité (Bruxelles)*, third ser., 43: 179–212.
Fox, Alan 1985, *History and Heritage: The Social Origins of the British Industrial Relations System*, London: Allen & Unwin.

Fox-Genovese, Elizabeth and Eugene D. Genovese 1983, *Fruits of Merchant Capital: Slavery and Bourgeois Property in the Rise and Expansion of Capitalism*, Oxford: Oxford University Press.
Francovich, Riccardo 2002, 'Changing Structures of Settlements', in *Italy in the Early Middle Ages: 476–1000*, edited by C. La Rocca, Oxford: Oxford University Press.
Frank, Andre Gunder 1969, *Capitalism and Underdevelopment in Latin America: Historical Studies of Chile and Brazil*, Harmondsworth: Penguin Books.
Freedman, Paul 1986, 'Catalan Lawyers and the Origins of Serfdom', *Mediaeval Studies*, 48: 288–314.
—— 1991, *The Origins of Peasant Servitude in Medieval Catalonia*, Cambridge: Cambridge University Press.
—— 1996, 'La servidumbre catalana y el problema de la revolución feudal', *Hispania*, 56, 2: 425–46.
—— 2002, 'Siervos, campesinos y cambio social', in *Señores, Siervos, Vasallos en la Alta Edad Media = XXVIII Semana de Estudios Medievales, Estella 16–20 julio 2001*, Pamplona: Gobierno de Navarra, Departamento de Educación y Cultura.
Freyhold, Michaela von [n.d.], 'The Rise and Fall of Colonial Modes of Production', Dar-es-Salaam: The Institute of Finance Management.
Frölich, Paul 1976, 'Ewigkeit totalitärer Regime? Gedanken zu einem aktuellen Thema', *Jahrbuch Arbeiterbewegung*, 4: 149–55.
Frye, Richard N. 1984, *The History of Ancient Iran*, Handbuch der Altertumswissenschaft 3/7, Munich: C.H. Beck.
Furger, Fridolin 1927, *Zum Verlagssystem als Organisationsform des Frühkapitalismus im Textilgewerbe*, Stuttgart: W. Kohlhammer.
Gabel, Peter and Jay Feinman 1998, 'Contract Law as Ideology', in Kairys (ed.) 1998.
Ganshof, François L. 1949, 'Manorial Organization in the Low Countries in the Seventh, Eighth and Ninth Centuries', *Transactions of the Royal Historical Society*, 4th ser., 31: 29–59.
—— 1958, 'Quelques aspects principaux de la vie économique dans la monarchie franque au VIIe siècle', in *Caratteri del secolo VII in Occidente (Settimane di studio 5)*, pp. 73–101.
García de Cortázar, José Angel 1988, *La sociedad rural en la España medieval*, Madrid: Siglo Veintiuno.
García Moreno, Luis A. 1975, *El fin del reino visigodo de Toledo*, Madrid: Universidad Autónoma.
Gascou, J. 1985, 'Les grands domaines, la cité et l'État en Égypte byzantine', *Travaux et Mémoires*, 9: 1–90.
Geary, Patrick J. 1985, *Aristocracy in Provence: The Rhône Basin at the Dawn of the Carolingian Age*, Philadelphia: University of Pennsylvania Press.
Genovese, Eugene D. 1966, *The Political Economy of Slavery: Studies in the Economy Society of the Slave South*, London: MacGibbon & Kee.
—— 1970, *The World the Slaveholders Made: Two Essays in Interpretation*, London: Allen Lane.
Giacchero, Marta 1965, *Ambrosii De Tobia: saggio introduttivo, traduzione con testo a fronte*, Genoa: Istituto di filologia classica e medioevale.
—— 1974, *Edictum Diocletiani et collegarum de pretiis rerum venalium*, Genoa: Istituto di storia antica e scienze ausiliarie.
Giardina, Andrea 2004, *L'Italia romana. Storie di un'identità incompiuta*, Bari: Editori Laterza.
—— 2007a, 'The Transition to Late Antiquity', in *The Cambridge Economic History of the Greco-Roman World*, edited by W. Scheidel, I. Morris and R. Saller, Cambridge: Cambridge University Press.
—— 2007b, 'Marxism and Historiography: Perspectives on Roman History', in *Marxist History-Writing for the Twenty-First Century*, edited by Chris Wickham, Oxford: Oxford University Press for The British Academy.
Gibson, Charles 1964, *The Aztecs under Spanish Rule: A History of the Indians of the Valley of Mexico, 1519–1810*, Stanford: Stanford University Press.

Gil, Moshe 2004, 'The Flax Trade in the Mediterranean in the Eleventh Century A.D. as Seen in Merchants' Letters from the Cairo Geniza', *Journal of Near Eastern Studies*, 63, 2: 81–96.
Gill, Desmond 1983, 'Tuscan Sharecropping in United Italy: The Myth of Class Collaboration Destroyed', in *Sharecropping and Sharecroppers*, edited by T.J. Byres, *Journal of Peasant Studies*, 10, 2–3: 146–69.
Gilliam, J. Frank 1974, 'An *ab epistulis Graecis* and *praefectus vigilum* from Egypt', in *Mélanges d'histoire ancienne offerts à William Seston*, Paris: E. de Boccard.
Giorgetti, Giorgio 1977, 'Agricoltura e sviluppo capitalistico nella Toscana del 1700', in *Capitalismo e agricoltura in Italia*, Rome: Editori Riuniti.
Girard, R.S. 1799–1800, 'Notice sur l'aménagement et le produit des terres de la province de Damiette', *La Décade Égyptienne*, t. 1, Cairo: L'Imprimerie Nationale.
Goetz, Hans-Werner 1993, 'Serfdom and the Beginnings of a "Seigneurial System" in the Carolingian Period: A Survey of the Evidence', *Early Medieval Europe*, 2, 1: 29–51.
Goffart, Walter 1974, *Caput and Colonate: Towards a History of Late Roman Taxation*, Toronto: University of Toronto Press.
—— 1980, *Barbarians and Romans A.D. 418–584: The Techniques of Accommodation*, Princeton: Princeton University Press.
Goitein, Shelomo Dov 1966, *Studies in Islamic History and Institutions*, Leiden: Brill.
Gonzales, Michael J. 1985, *Plantation Agriculture and Social Control in Northern Peru, 1875–1933*, Austin: University of Texas Press.
Goswami, Omkar 1984, 'Agriculture in Slump: The Peasant Economy of East and North Bengal in the 1930s', *Indian Economic and Social History Review*, 21, 3: 335–64.
Government of Bengal 1940, *Report of the Land Revenue Commission Bengal, Vols. 3–4, Landholders' Replies to the Questionnaire issued by the Land Revenue Commission and their Oral Evidence*, Alipore: Bengal Government Press.
Gramsci, Antonio 1976, *Selections from the Prison Notebooks*, London: Lawrence and Wishart.
Gray, Lewis Cecil 1933, *History of Agriculture in the Southern United States to 1860*, Volume 1, Washington: Carnegie Institution.
Grierson, George A. 1893, *Notes on the District of Gaya*, Calcutta: Printed at the Bengal Secretariat Press.
Grieser, Heike 1997, *Sklaverei im spätantiken und frühmittelalterlichen Gallien (5–7 Jh.): das Zeugnis der christlichen Quellen*, Stuttgart: Franz Steiner.
Griffin, Miriam T. and E. Margaret Atkins 1991, *Cicero: On Duties*, Cambridge: Cambridge University Press.
Grignaschi, Mario 1966, 'Quelques spécimens de la littérature sassanide conservés dans les bibliothèques d'Istanbul', *Journal Asiatique*, 254: 1–142.
Grossmann, Henryk 1970, *Das Akkumulations- und Zusammenbruchsgesetz des kapitalistischen Systems*, Reprint, Frankfurt: Verlag Neue Kritik.
Grover, B.R. 1965, 'Nature of *Dehat-i-Taaluqa* (Zamindari Villages) and the Evolution of the *Taaluqdari* System during the Mughal Age', *Indian Economic and Social History Review*, 2, 2: 259–90.
Guglielmi, Nilda 1967, 'La dependencia del campesino no-propietario (Leon y Castilla – Francia – siglos xi–xiii)', *Anales de historia antigua y medieval (Buenos Aires)*, 13: 95–187.
Guha, Ranajit 1996, *A Rule of Property for Bengal: An Essay on the Idea of Permanent Settlement*, Durham, NC.: Duke University Press.
Guha, Sumit 1977, 'The Peasantry and Commodity Production: Khandesh 1850–1930', Centre for Historical Studies, JNU, New Delhi [unpublished].
Guichard, Pierre 1990–1, *Les musulmans de Valence et la Reconquête, xie–xiiie siècles*, 2 vols., Damascus: Institut Français de Damas.
Haag, Pamela 1999, *Consent: Sexual Rights and the Transformation of American Liberalism*, Ithaca: Cornell University Press.
Haider, Najaf 1996, 'Precious Metal Flows and Currency Circulation in the Mughal Empire', *Journal of the Economic and Social History of the Orient*, 39, 3: 298–364.

Haldon, John 1993, *The State and the Tributary Mode of Production*, London: Verso.
Hale, Robert 1943, 'Bargaining, Duress, and Economic Liberty', *Columbia Law Review*, 43, 5: 603–28.
Halkin, François 1932, *Sancti Pachomii Vitae Graecae*, Brussels: Société des Bollandistes.
Hämeen-Anttila, Jaakko 2006, *The Last Pagans of Iraq: Ibn Waḥshiyya and his 'Nabatean Agriculture'*, Leiden: Brill.
Hamilton, Earl J. 1929, 'American Treasure and the Rise of Capitalism (1500–1700)', *Economica*, 9, no. 27: 338–57.
—— 1934, *American Treasure and the Price Revolution in Spain, 1501–1650*, Cambridge, MA.: Harvard University Press.
Haque, Ziaul 1977, *Landlord and Peasant in Early Islam: A Study of the Legal Doctrine of Muzara'a or Sharecropping*, Islamabad: Islamic Research Institute.
Hardy, Edward R. 1931, *The Large Estates of Byzantine Egypt*, New York: Columbia University Press.
Harnetty, Peter 1972, *Imperialism and Free Trade: Lancashire and India in the Mid-Nineteenth Century*, Vancouver: University of British Columbia.
Harper, Kyle 2008, 'The Greek Census Inscriptions of Late Antiquity', *Journal of Roman Studies*, 98: 83–119.
Harper, Kyle 2011, *Slavery in the Late Roman World, AD 275–425: An Economic, Social and Institutional Study*, Cambridge and New York: Cambridge University Press.
Harris, William V. 2006, 'A Revisionist View of Roman Money', *Journal of Roman Studies*, 96: 1–24.
Harriss-White, Barbara 1996, *A Political Economy of Agricultural Markets in South India*, New Delhi: Sage Publications.
Hartwell, Robert 1966, 'Markets, Technology, and the Structure of Enterprise in the Development of the Eleventh-Century Chinese Iron and Steel Industry', *Journal of Economic History*, 26, 1: 29–58.
—— 1982, 'Demographic, Political, and Social Transformations of China, 750–1550', *Harvard Journal of Asiatic Studies*, 42, 2: 365–442.
Harvey, Susan Ashbrook 1990, *Asceticism and Society in Crisis: John of Ephesus and the Lives of the Eastern Saints*, Berkeley: University of California Press.
Hasan, S. Nurul 1969, 'Zamindars under the Mughals', in *Land Control and Social Structure in Indian History*, edited by Robert Eric Frykenberg, Madison: University of Wisconsin Press.
Hay, Douglas and Paul Craven 2004, 'Introduction', in *Masters, Servants, and Magistrates in Britain and the Empire, 1562–1955*, edited by Douglas Hay and Paul Craven, Chapel Hill: University of North Carolina Press.
Heers, Jacques 1961, *Gênes au XVe siècle: activité économique et problèmes sociaux*, Paris: SEVPEN.-
Herbert, Ulrich 1997, *Hitler's Foreign Workers: Enforced Foreign Labour in Germany under the Third Reich*, Cambridge: Cambridge University Press.
Herlihy, David 1960, 'The Carolingian Mansus', *Economic History Review*, 2nd ser., 13, 1: 79–89.
—— 1965, 'Population, Plague and Social Change in Rural Pistoia, 1201–1430', *Economic History Review*, 2nd ser., 18, 2: 225–44.
Heurgon, Jacques 1976, 'L'agronome carthaginois Magon et ses traducteurs en latin et en grec', *Comptes Rendus des Séances de l'Académie des inscriptions et belles-lettres*, pp. 441–56.
Hilferding, Rudolf 1981, *Finance Capital: A Study in the Latest Phase of Capitalist Development*, translated by Morris Watnick and Sam Gordon, London: Routledge and Kegan Paul.
Hilton, Rodney H. 1969, *The Decline of Serfdom in Medieval England*, London: Macmillan.
—— 1973, 'Warriors and Peasants', *New Left Review*, I, 83: 83–94.
—— 1976, 'A Comment', in *The Transition from Feudalism to Capitalism*, introduction by R.H. Hilton, London: NLB.
Hindess, Barry and Paul Q. Hirst 1975, *Pre-Capitalist Modes of Production*, London: Routledge & Kegan Paul.
—— 1977, *Mode of Production and Social Formation: An Auto-Critique of 'Pre-Capitalist Modes of Production'*, Basingstoke: Macmillan.

Hintze, Otto 1964, *Soziologie und Geschichte: Gesammelte Abhandlungen zur Soziologie, Politik und Theorie der Geschichte*, edited by Gerhard Oestreich, expanded 2nd edition, Göttingen: Vandenhoech & Ruprecht.
—— 1975, 'Economics and Politics in the Age of Modern Capitalism', in *The Historical Essays of Otto Hintze*, edited by F. Gilbert, Oxford: Oxford University Press.
Hitti, Philip Khûri 1916, *The Origins of the Islamic State, being a Translation from the Arabic... of the Kitâb Futûh al-Buldân of... al-Balâdhuri*, New York: Columbia University.
Ho, Chuimei 2001, 'The Ceramic Boom in Minnan during Song and Yuan Times', in *The Emporium of the World: Maritime Quanzhou, 1000–1400*, edited by Angela Scottenhammer, Leiden: Brill.
Hobson, John Atkinson 1917, *The Evolution of Modern Capitalism: A Study of Machine Production*, London: Walter Scott.
Hopmann, Barbara et al. 1994, *Zwangsarbeit bei Daimler-Benz*, Stuttgart: F. Steiner.
Hoppe, Göran and John Langton 1994, *Peasantry to Capitalism: Western Ostergotland in the Nineteenth Century*, Cambridge: Cambridge University Press.
Hora, Roy 2001, *The Landowners of the Argentine Pampas: A Social and Political History 1860–1945*, Oxford: Clarendon Press.
Hossain, Hameeda 1988, *The Company Weavers of Bengal: The East India Company and the Organisation of Textile Production in Bengal, 1750–1813*, Delhi: Oxford University Press.
Hunt, Arthur S. and Campbell Cowan Edgar 1932, *Select Papyri*, 2 volumes, London: William Heinemann.
Hunt, Edwin S. and James M. Murray 1999, *A History of Business in Medieval Europe 1200–1550*, Cambridge: Cambridge University Press.
Hurd, John 1975, 'Railways and the Expansion of Markets in India, 1861–1921', *Explorations in Economic History*, 12, 3: 263–88.
Ibn al-Athīr 1898, *Annales du Maghreb et de l'Espagne, traduites et annotées par E. Fagnan*, Alger: Adolphe Jourdan.
Ibn Ḥauḳal 1938–9, *Opus geographicum auctore Ibn Ḥauḳal, etc.*, edited by J.H. Kramers, 2 volumes, Leiden: E.J. Brill.
Ibn Ḥauqal 1964, *Configuration de la terre (Kitāb ṣūrat al-'arḍ)*, translated by J.H. Kramers and G. Wiet, 2 volumes, Beirut and Paris: UNESCO.
Ibn Khaldûn 1958, *The Muqaddimah: An Introduction to History*, translated by Franz Rosenthal, 3 volumes, Princeton: Princeton University Press.
Ibn Khaldoun 1968–9, *Histoire des Berbères et des dynasties musulmanes de l'Afrique septentrionale*, tr. le baron de Slane, new edition by P. Casanova, 4 volumes, Paris: Paul Geuthner.
Ibn Khordādhbeh 1889, *Kitāb al-masālik wa'l-mamālik*, edited by M.J. de Goeje, Leiden: Brill.
al-Idrīsī 1866, *[Kitāb nuzhat al-mushtāḳ fi'khtirāḳ al-āfāḳ =] Description de l' Afrique et de l'Espagne par Edrîsî. Texte arabe avec une trad., des notes et une glossaire*, edited by Reinhart Dozy and M.J. de Goeje, Leiden: Brill.
Indigo Commission Bengal 1860, *Report of the Indigo Commission Appointed under Act XI of 1860, with the Minutes of Evidence Taken before Them; and Appendix*, 1860, Calcutta: [s.n.].
Innes, Matthew 2000, *State and Society in the Early Middle Ages: The Middle Rhine Valley, 400–1000*, Cambridge: Cambridge University Press.
—— 2007, *Introduction to Early Medieval Western Europe, 300–900: The Sword, the Plough and the Book*, London: Routledge.
Ireland, Paddy 1996, 'Capitalism Without the Capitalist: The Joint Stock Company Share and the Emergence of the Modern Doctrine of Separate Corporate Personality', *Journal of Legal History*, 17, 1: 41–73.
—— 1999, 'Company Law and the Myth of Shareholder Ownership', *The Modern Law Review*, 62, 1: 32–57.
Ireland, Paddy, Ian Grigg-Spall and Dave Kelly 1987, 'The Conceptual Foundations of Modern Company Law', in *Critical Legal Studies*, edited by Peter Fitzpatrick and Alan Hunt, Oxford: Blackwell.

al-Iṣṭakhrī 1870, *Kitāb al-masālik wa'l-mamālik*, edited by M.J. de Goeje, Leiden: Brill.
Isenburg, Teresa 1971, *Investimenti di capitale e organizzazione di classe nelle bonifiche ferraresi (1872–1901)*, Florence: La Nuova Italia.
Jackson, Peter 1999, *The Delhi Sultanate: A Political and Military History*, Cambridge: Cambridge University Press.
Jacobsen, Nils 1993, *Mirages of Transition. The Peruvian Altiplano, 1780–1930*, Berkeley: University of California Press.
al-Jakûbî [Ya'qūbī] 1892, *Kitâb al-boldân*, edited M.J. de Goeje, Leiden: Brill.
James, Edward 1982, *The Origins of France: from Clovis to the Capetians, 500–1000*, London: Macmillan.
Jarnut, Jörg 1982, *Geschichte der Langobarden*, Stuttgart: W. Kohlhammer.
—— 2002, 'Aspekte des Kontinuitätsproblems in der Völkerwanderungszeit', in *Herrschaft und Ethnogenese im Frühmittelalter. Gesammelte Aufsätze von Jörg Jarnut*, edited by Matthias Becher, Munich: Scriptorium.
Jaubert, Pierre-Amédée 1975, *La Géographie d'Édrisi traduite de l'Arabe*, Amsterdam: Philo Press.
Jing Su and Luo Lun 1959, *Landlord and Labor in Late Imperial China. Case Studies from Shandong*, tr. E. Wilkinson, Cambridge, MA.: Council on East Asian Studies, Harvard University.
Johansen, Baber 1988, *The Islamic Law of Land Tax and Rent: The Peasants' Loss of Property Rights as Interpreted in the Hanafite Legal Literature of the Mamluk and Ottoman Periods*, London: Croom Helm.
—— 2006, 'Le contrat *salam*. Droit et formation du capital dans l'Empire abbasside (xie et xiie siècle)', *Annales. Histoire, Sciences sociales*, 61, 4: 863–99.
Johnson, Allan Chester and Louis C. West 1949, *Byzantine Egypt: Economic Studies*, Princeton: Princeton University Press.
Jones, Arnold Hugh Martin 1958, 'The Roman Colonate', *Past and Present* 13, 1: 1–13; repr. in *The Roman Economy*, edited by P.A. Brunt (Oxford: Basil Blackwell, 1974).
—— 1964, *The Later Roman Empire 284–602: A Social Economic and Administrative Survey*, 2 vols., Oxford: Basil Blackwell.
Jones, Philip James 1968, 'From Manor to Mezzadria. A Tuscan Case Study in the Medieval Origins of Modern Agrarian Society', in *Florentine Studies: Politics and Society in Renaissance Florence*, edited by Nicolai Rubinstein, London: Faber.
—— 1997, *The Italian City-State: From Commune to Signoria*, Oxford: Clarendon Press.
Jones, Richard 1831, *An Essay on the Distribution of Wealth, and on the Sources of Taxation*, London: John Murray.
Jördens, Andrea 1988, 'P. Prag. I 34: Ein Arbeitsvertrag', *Zeitschrift für Papyrologie und Epigraphik*, 75: 164–6.
—— 1990, *Vertragliche Regelungen von Arbeiten im späten griechischsprachigen Ägypten*, Heidelberg: Carl Winter.
—— 1992, 'Μίσθωσις τῶν ἔργων. Ein neuer Vertragstyp', *Proceedings of the Nineteenth International Congress of Papyrology*, Cairo, 2–9 September 1989, Volume 2.
Kahn-Freund, Otto 1977, 'Blackstone's Neglected Child: The Contract of Employment',*The Law Quarterly Review*, 93, 4: 508–28.
Kairys, David (ed.) 1998, *The Politics of Law, A Progressive Critique*, Third Edition, New York: Basic Books.
Kanogo, Tabitha 1987, *Squatters and the Roots of Mau Mau, 1905–1963*, London: James Currey.
Kant, Immanuel 1996, 'The Metaphysics of Morals', in *Practical Philosophy*, edited by Mary J. Gregor, Cambridge: Cambridge University Press.
Kaplan, Michel 1992, *Les hommes et la terre à Byzance du VIe au XIe siècle. Propriété et exploitation du sol*, Paris: Publications de la Sorbonne.
Katō, Shigeshi 1952–3, *Shina keizai shi kōshō [Studies in Chinese Economic History]*, 2 vols., Tokyo: Toyo Bunko.
Katz, Friedrich 1974, 'Labor Conditions on Haciendas in Porfirian Mexico: Some Trends and Tendencies', *Hispanic American Historical Review*, 54, 1: 1–47.

Kautsky, Karl 1970 [1900], *La Question agraire*, Paris: V. Giard & E. Brière; Reprint François Maspero.
Keegan, Timothy J. 1987, *Rural Transformations in Industrializing South Africa: The Southern Highveld to 1914*, Basingstoke: Macmillan.
—— 1989, 'The Origins of Agrarian Capitalism in South Africa: A Reply', *Journal of Southern African Studies*, 15, 4: 666–84.
Keenan, James G. 1984, 'Aurelius Apollos and the Aphrodito Village Élite', *Atti del XVII Congresso internazionale di papirologia*, Naples: Centro Internazionale per lo Studio dei Papiri Ercolanesi.
—— 1985, 'Notes on Absentee Landlordism at Aphrodito', *Bulletin of the American Society of Papyrologists*, 22, 1–4: 137–69.
Keith, Robert G. 1971, 'Encomienda, Hacienda, and Corregimiento in Spanish America', *Hispanic American Historical Review*, 51, 3: 431–46.
Kelman, Mark 1987, *A Guide to Critical Legal Studies*, Cambridge, MA.: Harvard University Press.
Kennedy, Duncan 1976, 'Form and Substance in Private Law Adjudication', *Harvard Law Review*, 89, 8: 1685–778.
—— 1985, 'The Role of Law in Economic Thought: Essays on the Fetishism of Commodities', *The American University Law Review*, 34: 939–1001.
—— 1998, *A Critique of Adjudication: [Fin de siècle]*, Cambridge, MA.: Harvard University Press.
Kessler, Friedrich 1943, 'Contracts of Adhesion – Some Thoughts About Freedom of Contract', *Columbia Law Review*, 43, 5: 629–42.
Keßler, Mario 2003, *Arthur Rosenberg. Ein Historiker im Zeitalter der Katastrophen (1889–1943)*, Cologne: Böhlau Verlag.
King, Paul David 1972, *Law and Society in the Visigothic Kingdom*, Cambridge: Cambridge University Press.
Klare, Karl 1998, 'Critical Theory and Labor Relations Law', in Kairys (ed.) 1998.
Knight, Alan 1986, 'Mexican Peonage: What Was It and Why Was It?', *Journal of Latin American Studies*, 18, 1: 41–74.
Kolchin, Peter 1987, *Unfree Labor: American Slavery and Russian Serfdom*, Cambridge, MA.: Harvard University Press.
Kölzer, Theo 2001, *Die Urkunden der Merowinger nach Vorarbeiten von Carlrichard Brühl*, 2 vols., Hannover: Hahn.
Korsch, Karl 1963, *Karl Marx*, New York: Russell & Russell.
Kosminsky, Evgeny Alekseevich 1934–35, 'Services and Money Rents in the Thirteenth Century', *Economic History Review*, 1st ser., 5, 2: 24–45.
—— 1956, *Studies in the Agrarian History of England in the Thirteenth Century*, tr. R. Kisch, Oxford: Blackwell.
Krader, Lawrence 1972, *The Ethnological Notebooks of Karl Marx (Studies of Morgan, Phear, Maine, Lubbock)*, Assen: Van Gorcum & Co.
—— 1975, *The Asiatic Mode of Production: Sources, Development and Critique in the Writings of Karl Marx*, Assen: Van Gorcum & Comp.
Krätke, Michael R. 2007, 'On the History and Logic of Modern Capitalism: The Legacy of Ernest Mandel', *Historical Materialism*, 15, 1: 109–43.
Kraus, Theodor and Josef Röder 1962, 'Mons Claudianus. Bericht über eine erste Erkundungsfahrt im März 1961', *Mitteilungen des Deutschen Archäologischen Instituts, Abt. Kairo*, 18: 80–120.
Krause, Jens-Uwe 1987, *Spätantike Patronatsformen im Westen des römischen Reiches*, Munich: C.H. Beck.
Kreifelts, Reinhold 1995, 'Das System von Teetransport und – vertrieb in der Nördlichen Song-Zeit (960–1126)', in *Beamtentum und Wirtschaftspolitik in der Song-Dynastie*, edited by Dieter Kuhn, Edition Forum: Heidelberg.
Krueger, Hilmar C. 1962, 'Genoese Merchants, their Associations and Investments, 1155 to 1230', in *Studi in onore di Amintore Fanfani, I: Antichità e alto medioevo*, Milan: Giuffrè.

Kuhn, Dieter 2009, *The Age of Confucian Rule: The Song Transformation of China*, Cambridge, MA.: The Belknap Press of Harvard University Press.
Kula, Witold 1970, *Théorie économique du système féodale. Pour un modèle de l'économie polonaise 16e–18e siècles*, Paris: Mouton.
Labib, Subhi Y. 1969, 'Capitalism in Medieval Islam', *Journal of the Economic and Social History of the Orient*, 29, 1: 79–96.
Laclau, Ernesto 1971, 'Feudalism and Capitalism in Latin America', *New Left Review*, I, 67: 19–38; reprinted in *Politics and Ideology in Marxist Theory*, London: NLB.
—— 1977, 'Feudalism and Capitalism in Latin America: Postscript', in *Politics and Ideology in Marxist Theory*, London: NLB.
Lambton, Ann K. S. 1953, *Landlord and Peasant in Persia. A Study of Land Tenure and Land Revenue Administration*, Oxford: Oxford University Press.
Lancel, Serge 1972–5, *Actes de la Conférence de Carthage en 411*, 3 vols., Paris: Éditions du Cerf.
—— 1987, *Oeuvres de Saint Augustin 46B. Lettres 1*–29**, Paris: Études Augustiniennes.
Lancret, Michel-Ange 1809, 'Mémoire sur le système d'imposition territoriale et sur l'administration des provinces de l'Égypte, dans les dernières années du Gouvernement des Mamlouks', in *Description de l'Égypte. État moderne* (lst edn), t. 1, Paris: Imprimerie impériale.
Lau, Nap-yin and K'uan-chung Huang 2009, 'Founding and Consolidation of the Sung Dynasty under T'ai-tsu (960–976), T'ai-tsung (976–997), and Chen-tsung (997–1022)', in *The Cambridge History of China, Volume 5/1: The Sung Dynasty and its Precursors, 907–1279*, Cambridge: Cambridge University Press.
Lebecq, Stéphane 1990, *Les origines franques v^e-ixe siècle (Nouvelle Histoire de la France médiévale)*, Paris: Éditions du Seuil.
Lefebvre, Georges 1976, 'Some Observations', in *The Transition from Feudalism to Capitalism*, intr. by Rodney Hilton, London: NLB.
Lenin, Vladimir I. 1956, *The Development of Capitalism in Russia*, Moscow: Foreign Languages Publishing House.
—— 1963a, 'The Economic Content of Narodism and the Criticism of it in Mr. Struve's Book', in *Collected Works*, Volume 1, Moscow: Progress Publishers.
—— 1963b, 'What the "Friends of the People" are and How They Fight the Social-Democrats', in *Collected Works*, Volume 1, Moscow: Progress Publishers.
—— 1964a, 'Capitalism in Agriculture', in *Collected Works*, Volume 4, Moscow: Progress Publishers.
—— 1964b, 'New Data on the Laws Governing the Development of Capitalism in Agriculture. Part One', in *Collected Works*, Volume 22, Moscow: Progress Publishers.
Lepelley, Claude 1983, 'Liberté, colonat et esclavage d'après la Lettre 24*', in *Les Lettres de Saint Augustin découvertes par Johannes Divjak*, Paris: Études augustiniennes.
Levett, Ada Elizabeth 1927, 'The Financial Organization of the Manor', *Economic History Review*, 1st ser., 1, 1: 65–86; repr. in *Studies in Manorial History* (Oxford, 1938).
Lo, Jung-pang 1969, 'Maritime Commerce and its Relation to the Sung Navy', *Journal of the Economic and Social History of the Orient*, 12, 1: 57–101.
Lohrmann, Dietrich 1989, 'Le moulin à eau. Dans le cadre de l'économie rurale de la Neustrie (VIIe–XI siècles)', in *La Neustrie. Les pays au nord de la Loire de 650 à 850*, 2 vols, edited by H. Atsma, Volume 1, Sigmaringen: Jan Thorbecke Verlag.
Lombard, Maurice 1947, 'Les bases monétaires d'une suprématie économique: l'or musulman du VIIe au XIe siècle', *Annales ESC*, 2, 2: 143–60.
—— 1971, *L'Islam dans sa première grandeur (viiie–xie siècle)*, Paris: Flammarion.
Lopez, Roberto 1936, 'I Genovesi in Africa Occidentale nel medio evo', in *Studi sull' economia genovese nel medio evo*, Turin: S. Lattes.
—— 1959, 'Alle origini del capitalismo genovese', in *Storia dell'economia italiana: saggi di storia economica. Vol. 1, Secoli settimo-diciassettesimo*, edited by Carlo M. Cipolla, Turin: Einaudi.

—— 1970, 'Les méthodes commerciales des marchands occidentaux en Asie', in *Sociétés et compagnies de commerce en Orient et dans l'Océan indien: Actes du huitième colloque international d'histoire maritime*, Paris: SEVPEN.
Lopez, Robert S. and Irving W. Raymond 1955, *Medieval Trade in the Mediterranean World: Illustrative Documents*, New York: W.W. Norton.
Lopuszański, Georges 1938, 'La transformation du corps des officiers supérieurs dans l'armée romaine du Ier au IIIe siècle après J.-C.', *Mélanges d'archéologie et d'histoire*, 55: 131–83.
Loveman, Brian 1976, *Struggle in the Countryside: Politics and Rural Labor in Chile, 1919–1973*, Bloomington: Indiana University Press.
Lowry, Heath W. 2003, *The Nature of the Early Ottoman State*, Albany: State University of New York Press.
Lozach, Jean 1935, *Le Delta du Nil. Étude de géographie humaine*, Cairo: Société Royale de Géographie d'Égypte.
Lozach, Jean and Georges Hug 1930, *L'habitat rural en Égypte*, Cairo: Société Royale de Géographie d'Égypte.
Lukács, Georg 1966, 'Technology and Social Relations', *New Left Review*, I, 39: 27–34.
—— 1968, *Geschichte und Klassenbewußtsein*, Neuwied: Luchterhand.
Luxemburg, Rosa 1963, *The Accumulation of Capital*, tr. by Agnes Schwarzschild, London: Routledge and Kegan Paul.
—— 1972, 'The Accumulation of Capital – an Anti-Critique', in *Imperialism and the Accumulation of Capital*, edited by Kenneth J. Tarbuck, London: Allen Lane.
Luzzatto, Gino 1954, 'Capitalismo coloniale nel Trecento', in *Studi di storia economica veneziana*, Padua: CEDAM.
—— 1961, *Storia economica di Venezia dall' XI al XVI secolo*, Venice: Centro internazionale delle arti e del costume.
Maclean, Derryl N. 1989, *Religion and Society in Arab Sind*, Leiden: Brill.
Madariaga, Isabel de 1974, 'Catherine II and the Serfs: A Reconsideration of Some Problems', *Slavonic and East European Review*, 52, 1: 34–62.
—— 1995, 'The Russian Nobility in the Seventeenth and Eighteenth Centuries', in *The European Nobilities in the Seventeenth and Eighteenth Centuries, Volume 2: Northern, Central and Eastern Europe*, edited by H.M. Scott, London: Longman.
Maitland, Frederic William 1960, *Domesday Book and Beyond: Three Essays in the Early History of England*, London: Collins.
Majid, Nomaan 1994, *Contractual Arrangements in Pakistani Agriculture. A Study of Share Tenancy in Sindh*, Oxford D.Phil. thesis.
Malatesta, Maria 1989, *I signori della terra. L'organizzazione degli interessi agrari padani (1860–1914)*, Milan: Franco Angeli.
Małowist, Marian 1959, 'The Economic and Social Development of the Baltic Countries from the Fifteenth to the Seventeenth Centuries', *Economic History Review*, 2nd ser., 12, 2: 177–89.
—— 1972, 'Movements of Expansion in Europe in the Sixteenth and Seventeenth Centuries', in *Economy and Society in Early Modern Europe: Essays from Annales*, edited by Peter Burke, London: Routledge & Kegan Paul.
Mamdani, Mahmood 1976, *Politics and Class Formation in Uganda*, New York: Monthly Review Press.
Mandel, Ernest 1968, *Marxist Economic Theory*, translated by Brian Pearce, 2 volumes, London: Merlin.
Mandle, Jay 1972, 'The Plantation Economy: An Essay in Definition', *Science & Society*, 36, 1: 49–62.
Mango, Cyril 1966, 'Isaurian Builders', in *Polychronion: Festschrift Franz Dölgerzum 75 Geburtstag*, edited by Peter Wirth, Heidelberg: C. Winter.
Manzano Moreno, Eduardo 1998a, 'El problema de la invasión musulmana y la formación del feudalismo: un debate distorsionado', in *"Romanización" y "Reconquista" en la Península Ibérica: Nuevas perspectivas*, edited by Ma. José Hidalgo, Dionisio Pérez, Manuel J. R. Gervás, Salamanca: Ediciones Universidad de Salamanca.

―― 1998b, 'Relaciones sociales en sociedades precapitalistas: una crítica al concepto de "modo de producción tributario"', *Hispania*, 58, 3: 881–913.
―― 2006, *Conquistadores, emires y califas. Los omeyas y la formación de al-Andalus*, Barcelona: Crítica.
Marazzi, Federico 2001, 'Aristocrazia e società (secoli VI–XI)', in *Roma medievale*, edited by André Vauchez, Bari: Editori Laterza.
Marçais, William and Abderrahmân Guîga 1925, *Textes arabes de Takroûna: transcription, traduction annotée, glossaire*, 2 vols., Paris: Imprimerie nationale.
Mariátegui, José Carlos 1971, *Seven Interpretive Essays on Peruvian Reality*, tr. Marjory Urquidi, Austin: University of Texas Press.
Martínez-Alier, Juan 1967, 'El latifundio en Andalucía y en América latina. ¿Un edificio capitalista con una fachada feudal?', *Cuadernos de Ruedo ibérico*, 15: 3–53.
―― 1971, *Labourers and Landowners in Southern Spain*, London: George Allen & Unwin.
―― 1977, 'Relations of Production in Andean Haciendas: Peru', in *Land and Labour in Latin America*, edited by K. Duncan and I. Rutledge, Cambridge: Cambridge University Press.
Marx, Karl 1877a, 'Reply to Mikhailovsky', in McLellan 1971.
―― 1877b, '[Letter to *Otechestvenniye Zapiski*]', in Marx and Engels 1989.
―― 1879, 'Excerpts from M.M. Kovalevskij, *Obščinnoe Zemlevladenie*', in Krader 1975.
―― 1968, *Theories of Surplus-Value, Part II*, Moscow: Progress Publishers.
―― 1969, *Theories of Surplus-Value, Part I*, Moscow: Progress Publishers.
―― 1970, *A Contribution to the Critique of Political Economy*, Moscow: Progress Publishers.
―― 1971a, *Capital*, 3 volumes, Moscow: Progress Publishers.
―― 1971b, *Theories of Surplus-Value, Part III*, Moscow: Progress Publishers.
―― 1972, 'Notes on J. Phear, *The Aryan Village in India and Ceylon (1880)*', in Krader 1972.
―― 1973, *Grundrisse: Foundations of the Critique of Political Economy (Rough Draft)*, translated by Martin Nicolaus, Harmondsworth: Penguin Books.
―― 1974, *Grundrisse der Kritik der politischen Ökonomie (Rohentwurf) 1857–1858*, Second German Edition, Berlin: Dietz.
―― 1975, *The Poverty of Philosophy*, Moscow: Progress Publishers.
―― 1976, *Capital, Volume One*, translated by Ben Fowkes, Harmondsworth: Penguin Books.
―― 1978, *Capital, Volume Two*, translated by David Fernbach, Harmondsworth: Penguin Books.
―― 1981, *Capital, Volume Three*, translated by David Fernbach, Harmondsworth: Penguin Books.
―― 1987, *Economic Manuscripts of 1857–58*, in Marx and Engels 1987.
Marx, Karl and Friedrich Engels 1934, *Correspondence 1846–1895*, New York: International Publishers.
―― 1951, *Selected Works in Two Volumes*, Moscow: Foreign Languages Publishing House.
―― 1965, *The German Ideology*, London: Lawrence & Wishart.
―― 1985, *Collected Works Volume 20*, London: Lawrence & Wishart.
―― 1987, *Collected Works Volume 29: Karl Marx 1857–61*, New York: International Publishers.
―― 1989, *Collected Works Volume 24*, Moscow: Progress Publishers.
―― 1968, *Werke*, Berlin.
Mauro, Frédéric 1955, 'Pour une théorie du capitalisme commercial', *Vierteljahrschrift für Sozial- und Wirtschaftsgeschichte*, 42: 117–21.
Mazzarino, Santo 1951, *Aspetti sociali del quarto secolo. Ricerche di storia tardo-romano*, Rome: 'L'Erma' di Bretschneider; new edition by Elio Lo Cascio, Milan: Biblioteca Universale Rizzoli (2002).
―― 1966, *The End of the Ancient World*, tr. G. Holmes, London: Faber & Faber.

—— 1980, *L'impero romano*, 3rd edition, 3 vols., Bari: Laterza.
McArdle, Frank 1978, *Altopascio: A Study in Tuscan Rural Society, 1587–1784*, Cambridge: Cambridge University Press.
McCoan, James Carlile 1877, *Egypt As It Is*, London: Cassell, Petter & Galpin.
McCreery, David 1983, 'Debt Servitude in Rural Guatemala, 1876–1976', *Hispanic American Historical Review*, 63, 4: 735–59.
McGeer, Eric 2000, *The Land Legislation of the Macedonian Emperors*, Toronto: Pontifical Institute of Mediaeval Studies.
McLellan, David 1971, *The Thought of Karl Marx: An Introduction*, Basingstoke: Macmillan.
Meehan-Waters, Brenda 1982, *Autocracy & Aristocracy: The Russian Service Elite of 1730*, New Brunswick: Rutgers University Press.
Mensch, Betty 1981, 'Freedom of Contract as Ideology', *Stanford Law Review*, 33, 6: 753–72.
Mertens, Hans-Günther 1983, *Wirtschaftliche und soziale Strukturen zentralmexicanischer Weizenhaciendas aus dem Tal von Atlixco (1890–1912)*, Wiesbaden: Franz Steiner.
Metcalf, Thomas R. 1979, *Land, Landlords, and the British Raj: Northern India in the Nineteenth Century*, Berkeley: University of California Press.
Mickwitz, Gunnar 1965, *Geld und Wirtschaft im römischen Reich des vierten Jahrhunderts n. Chr.*, Amsterdam: Adolf M. Hakkert; reprint of 1932 edition.
Migliario, Elvira 1992, 'Terminologia e organizzazione agraria tra tardo antico e alto medioevo: ancora su *fundus* e *casalis/casale*', *Athenaeum*, 80, 2: 371–84.
Migliario, Elvira and Chris Wickham 1998, 'Continuità e fratture tra tardo-antico e alto Medioevo', in *Restaurazione e destrutturazione nella tarda antichità*, Milan: Teti.
Miliband, Ralph 1983, 'State Power and Class Interests', *New Left Review*, I, 138: 57–68.
Miliukov, Paul 1962, *Russia and its Crisis*, London: Collier-Macmillan.
Mill, James 1820, *The History of British India*, 2nd edition in six volumes, London: Baldwin, Cradock, and Joy.
Millar, Fergus 1993, *The Roman Near East 31 BC–AD 337*, Cambridge, MA.: Harvard University Press.
Miller, Edward 1971, 'England in the Twelfth and Thirteenth Centuries: An Economic Contrast?', *Economic History Review*, 2nd ser., 24, 1: 1–14.
Minchinton, Walter E. 1968, *Essays in Agrarian History*, Volume 1, Devon: David & Charles.
Minorsky, Vladimir 1937, *Ḥudūd al-'Ālam: The "Regions of the World". A Persian Geography 372 A.H. –982 A.D.*, London: Luzac.
Miranda, José Porfirio 1982, *Communism in the Bible*, London: SCM.
Mitchell, Timothy 1988, *Colonising Egypt*, Cambridge: Cambridge University Press.
Mitra, Debendra Bijoy 1978, *The Cotton Weavers of Bengal 1757–1833*, Calcutta: Firma KLM.
Modzelewski, Karol 1978, 'La transizione dall' antichità al feudalesimo', in *Dal feudalesimo al capitalismo (Storia d'Italia. Annali 1)*, edited by Ruggiero Romano and Corrado Vivanti, Turin: Giulio Einaudi.
Molinari, Alessandra 1995, 'Le campagne siciliane tra il periodo bizantino e quello arabo', in *Acculturazione e mutamenti. Prospettive nell'Archeologia medievale del Mediterraneo*, edited by E. Boldrini and R. Francovich, Florence: All'insegna del giglio.
Mommsen, Theodor 1866, *Römische Geschichte Bd. 3*, 4th edition, Berlin: Weidmannsche Buchhandlung.
Montenegro, Julia and Arcadio del Castillo 2007, 'Le règne de Rodéric, Akhila II et l'invasion musulmane de la péninsule ibérique', *Francia (Moyen Âge)*, 34, 1: 1–17.
Montevecchi, Orsolina 1950, *I contratti di lavoro e di servizio nell'Egitto greco romano e bizantino*, Milan: s.n.
Montroni, Giovanni 1996, *Gli Uomini del re: la nobiltà napoletana nell'Ottocento*, Catanzaro: Meridiana Libri.
Montserrat, Dominic, Georgina Fantoni, and Patrick Robinson 1994, 'Varia Descripta Oxyrhynchita', *Bulletin of the American Society of Papyrologists*, 31, 1–2: 11–80.

Moore, Jr., Barrington 1966, *Social Origins of Dictatorship and Democracy, Lord and Peasant in the Making of the Modern World*, Harmondsworth: Penguin Books.
Moorhead, John 2000, 'Totila the Revolutionary', *Historia*, 49: 382–86.
Mordtmann, Andreas David 1845, *Das Buch der Länder von Schech Ebu Ishak el Farsi el Isztachri*, Schriften der Akademie von Hamburg, Bd. 1, Abth. 2, Hamburg.
Morel, Jean-Paul 1990, 'La produzione artigianale e il commercio transmarino', in *Storia di Roma, 2/1. La repubblica imperiale*, edited by G. Clemente, F. Coarelli, E. Gabba, Turin: Einaudi.
Moreno Fraginals, Manuel 1978, *El Ingenio: complejo económico social cubano del azúcar*, 3 vols., Havana: Editorial de Ciencias Sociales.
Mori, Giorgio 1955, 'La mezzadria in Toscana alla fine del XIX secolo', *Movimento Operaio*, n.s., 7, 3–4: 479–510.
Morony, Michael G. 1981, 'Landholding in Seventh-Century Iraq. Late Sasanian and Early Islamic Patterns', in *The Islamic Middle East, 700–1900: Studies in Economic and Social History*, ed. A.L. Udovitch, Princeton: Darwin Press.
Mukherji, Saugata 1986, 'Agrarian Class Formation in Modern Bengal, 1931–51', *Economic and Political Weekly*, 21, 4: PE-11–27.
Mundle, Sudipto 1979, *Backwardness and Bondage: Agrarian Relations in a South Bihar District*, New Delhi: Indian Institute of Public Administration.
Munro, John H. 1998, 'Precious Metals and the Origins of the Price Revolution Reconsidered', in *Monetary History in Global Perspective 1500–1808*, edited by Clara Eugenia Núñez, Seville: Universidad de Sevilla.
al-Muqaddasī 1994, *The Best Divisions for Knowledge of the Regions: A Translation of "Ahsan al-Taqasim fi Ma'rifat al-Aqalim"*, translated by Basil Anthony Collins, Reading: Garnet.
Murray, Alexander Callander 1999, *From Roman to Merovingian Gaul: A Reader*, Peterborough, ON.: Broadview.
Murray, Martin J. 1992, '"White Gold" or "White Blood"? The Rubber Plantations of Colonial Indochina, 1910–40', *Journal of Peasant Studies*, 19, 3–4: 41–67.
Nahas, Joseph F. 1901, *Situation économique et sociale du fellah égyptien*, Paris: Arthur Rousseau.
Naitō Konan [Naitō Torajirō] 1983, 'A Comprehensive Look at the T'ang-Sung Period', tr. Joshua A. Fogel, *Chinese Studies in History*, 17, 1: 88–99.
Narshakhī, Muhammad b. Ja'far 1954, *The History of Bukhara, translated from a Persian Abridgement of the Arabic Original*, tr. Richard N. Frye, Cambridge, MA.: Mediaeval Academy of America.
Neff, John U. 1929, 'Dominance of the Trader in the English Coal Industry in the Seventeenth Century', *Journal of Economic and Business History*, 1: 422–34.
Nehlsen, Hermann 1972, *Sklavenrecht zwischen Antike und Mittelalter*, Göttingen: Musterschmidt.
Neumann, Franz 1936, *European Trade Unionism and Politics*, New York: League for Industrial Democracy.
Nickel, Herbert J. 1988, *Morfología social de la hacienda mexicana*, tr. A. Scherp, México: Fondo de Cultura Económica.
—— 1991, *Schuldknechtschaft in mexikanischen Haciendas*, Stuttgart: F. Steiner.
Nour Ed-Din, S. 1898, 'Condition des fellahs en Égypte', *Revue de l'Islam*, 3: 5–7.
Nouschi, Andre 1961, *Enquête sur le niveau de vie des populations rurales constantinoises de la conquête jusqu'en 1919. Essai d'histoire économique et sociale*, Paris: Presses Universitaires de France.
Noyé, Ghislaine 2000, 'Économie et société dans la Calabre byzantine (IVe–XIe siècle)', *Journal des Savants*, Juillet–Décembre: 207–80.
Oakes, James 1982, *The Ruling Race: A History of American Slaveholders*, New York: Alfred A. Knopf.
—— 1990, *Slavery and Freedom: An Interpretation of the Old South*, New York: Alfred A. Knopf.
Oehme, Marlis 1988, *Die römische Villenwirtschaft. Untersuchungen zu den Agrarschriften Catos und Columellas und ihrer Darstellung bei Niebuhr und Mommsen*, Bonn: Rudolf Habelt.

Oexle, Otto Gerhard 1985, 'Conjuratio und Gilde im frühen Mittelalter. Ein Beitrag zum Problem der sozialgeschichtlichen Kontinuität zwischen Antike und Mittelalter', in *Gilden und Zünfte: kaufmännische und gewerbliche Genossenschaften im frühen und hohen Mittelalter*, edited by B. Schwineköper, Sigmaringen: J. Thorbecke.

Orren, Karen 1991, *Belated Feudalism: Labor, the Law, and Liberal Development in the United States*, Cambridge: Cambridge University Press.

Orsi, Paolo 1910, 'Byzantina Siciliae', *Byzantinische Zeitschrift*, 19, 1: 63–90.

Ostrogorsky, Georges 1954, *Pour l'histoire de la féodalité byzantine*, tr. Henri Grégoire, Brussels: Éditions de l'Institut de philologie et d'histoire orientales et slaves.

—— 1956, *Quelques problèmes de l'histoire de la paysannerie byzantine*, Brussels: Éditions de Byzantion.

Ostrogorsky, Georg 1963, *Geschichte des Byzantinischen Staates*, 3rd rev. ed., Munich: Beck.

Ostrogorsky, George 1968, *History of the Byzantine State*, tr. Joan Hussey, Oxford: Basil Blackwell.

—— 1971, 'Observations on the Aristocracy in Byzantium', *Dumbarton Oaks Papers*, 25: 1–32.

Owen, Roger 1969, *Cotton and the Egyptian Economy, 1820–1914: A Study in Trade and Development*, Oxford: Clarendon Press.

—— 1981a, 'The Development of Agricultural Production in Nineteenth-Century Egypt: Capitalism of What Type?', in *The Islamic Middle East, 700–1900*, edited by A.L. Udovitch, Princeton: Darwin Press.

—— 1981b, *The Middle East in the World Economy 1800–1914*, London: I.B. Tauris & Co.

O'Leary, Brendan 1989, *The Asiatic Mode of Production: Oriental Despotism, Historical Materialism and Indian History*, Oxford: Basil Blackwell.

O'Malley, Lewis Sydney Steward 1910, *Bengal District Gazetteers. Birbhum*, Calcutta: Bengal Secretariat Book Depôt.

Pach, Zsigmond Pál 1966, 'The Development of Feudal Rent in Hungary in the Fifteenth Century', *Economic History Review*, 2nd ser., 19, 1: 1–14.

—— 1972, 'Sixteenth-Century Hungary: Commercial Activity and Market Production by the Nobility', in *Economy and Society in Early Modern Europe: Essays from Annales*, edited by Peter Burke, London: Routledge & Kegan Paul.

—— 1982, 'Labour Control on the Hungarian Landlords' Demesnes in the Sixteenth and Seventeenth Centuries', in *Grand Domaine et Petites Exploitations en Europe au Moyen Age et dans les temps modernes. Rapports nationaux*, edited by P. Gunst, T. Hoffmann, Budapest.

Painter, Sidney 1943, *Studies in the History of the English Feudal Barony*, Baltimore: John Hopkins University Press.

Palloix, Christian 1971, *L'économie mondiale capitaliste t.1: Le stade concurrentiel*, Paris: Maspero.

Panero, Francesco 1999, *Schiavi, servi e villani nell'Italia medievale*, Turin: Paravia Scriptorium.

Pardessus, Jean Marie 1969, *Diplomata, chartae, epistolae, leges aliaque instrumenta ad res Gallo-Francicas spectantia*, 2 vols. Reprint of Paris edition of 1843–9, Aalen: Scientia Verlag.

Pares, Richard 1960, *Merchants and Planters*, Cambridge: Cambridge University Press for the Economic History Review.

Parry, Jonathan P., Jan Breman, Karin Kapadia 1999, *The Worlds of Indian Industrial Labour*, New Delhi: Sage Publications.

Pasquali, Gianfranco 2002, 'L'azienda curtense e l'economia rurale dei secoli VI–XI', in *Uomini e campagne nell'Italia medievale*, edited by A. Cortonesi, Bari: Editori Laterza.

Pateman, Carole 1988, *The Sexual Contract*, Cambridge: Polity.

Patnaik, Utsa 1976, 'Class Differentiation within the Peasantry: An Approach to the Analysis of Indian Agriculture', *Economic and Political Weekly*, 11, 39: A82–101.

—— (ed.) 1990, *Agrarian Relations and Accumulation. The 'Mode of Production' Debate in India*, Bombay: Oxford University Press.

Patterson, Orlando 1979, 'On Slavery and Slave Formations', *New Left Review*, I, 117: 31–67.
Pavlov, Andrej P. 2005, 'Les réformes du milieu du XVIe siècle et l'évolution structurelle de la noblesse russe', *Cahiers du Monde russe*, 46, 1–2: 91–106.
Pecirka, Jan 1967, 'Discussions sovietiques', in *Premières sociétés de classes et mode deproduction asiatique = Recherches internationales à lumière du Marxisme*, 57–8, Paris: Éditions de la 'Nouvelle Critique'.
Perkins, John A. 1984, 'The German Agricultural Worker 1815–1914', *Journal of Peasant Studies*, 11, 3: 3–27.
Petrusewicz, Marta 1996, *Latifundium: Moral Economy and Material Life in a European Periphery*, tr. Judith Green, Ann Arbor: University of Michigan Press.
Pipes, Richard 1995, *Russia Under the Old Regime*, 2nd edition, Harmondsworth: Penguin Books.
Pirenne, Henri 1968, *Mohammed and Charlemagne*, tr. B. Miall, London: Allen & Unwin.
—— 1969, *Histoire économique et sociale du Moyen Âge*, Paris: Presses Universitaires de France.
Plekhanov, George 1969, *Fundamental Problems of Marxism*, New York: International Publishers.
Pokrovsky, Mikhail Nikolaevich 1931, *History of Russia, from the Earliest Times to the Rise of Commercial Capitalism*, tr. J.D. Clarkson and M.R.M. Griffiths, New York: International Publishers.
Poliak, Abraham N. 1939, *Feudalism in Egypt, Syria, Palestine, and the Lebanon, 1250–1900*, London: Royal Asiatic Society.
Poni, Carlo 1963, *Gli aratri e l'economia agraria nel bolognese dal xvii al xix secolo*, Bologna: Zanichelli.
—— 1976, 'All' origine del sistema di fabbrica: tecnologia e organizzazione produttiva dei mulini da seta nell'Italia settentrionale (sec. xvii–xviii)', *Rivista storica italiana*, 88, 3: 444–97.
Post, Charles 1999, 'Review of *Capitalism from Above and Capitalism from Below*, by Terence J. Byres', *Historical Materialism*, 4: 282–94.
Postan, Michael 1937, 'The Chronology of Labour Services', *Transactions of the Royal Historical Society*, 4th ser., 20: 169–94; reprinted with revisions in W.E. Minchinton (ed.), *Essays in Agrarian History*, Volume 1 (Devon, David & Charles, 1968).
—— 1954, 'The *Famulus*: The Estate Labourer in the XIIth and XIIIth Centuries', London: Cambridge University Press for the Economic History Society.
Prakash, Om 1985, *The Dutch East India Company and the Economy of Bengal, 1630–1720*, Princeton: Princeton University Press.
—— 1994, *Precious Metals and Commerce: The Dutch East India Company in the Indian Ocean Trade*, Aldershot: Variorum.
Preobrazhensky, Evgeny 1965, *The New Economics*, tr. Brian Pearce, Oxford: Clarendon Press.
Procacci, Giuliano 1970, *History of the Italian People*, tr. Anthony Paul, London: Weidenfeld and Nicolson.
Prou, Maurice and Alexandre Vidier 1900, *Recueil des chartes de l'abbaye de Saint-Benoit-sur-Loire*, t. 1, Paris: A. Picard et fils.
Psellus, Michael 1966, *Fourteen Byzantine Rulers: The "Chronographia" of Michael Psellus*, tr. E.R.A. Sewter, Harmondsworth: Penguin Books.
Puhle, Hans-Jürgen 1975, *Politische Agrarbewegungen in kapitalistischen Industriegesellschaften. Deutschland, USA und Frankreich im 20. Jahrhundert*, Göttingen: Vandenhoeck & Ruprecht.
Pulleyblank, Edwin G. 1955, *The Background of the Rebellion of An Lu-shan*, Oxford: Oxford University Press.
Quantin, Maximilien 1854, *Cartulaire générale de l'Yonne. Recueil de documents authentiques*, t. 1., Auxerre: Perriquet.
Raftis, J. Ambrose 1957, *The Estates of Ramsey Abbey: A Study in Economic Growth and Organization*, Toronto: Pontifical Institute of Medieval Studies.

Ramachandran, V.K. 1990, *Wage Labour and Unfreedom in Agriculture: An Indian Case Study*, Oxford: Clarendon Press.
Ransom, Roger and Richard Sutch 1988, 'Capitalists without Capital: The Burden of Slavery and the Impact of Emancipation', *Agricultural History*, 62, 3: 133–60.
Rathbone, Dominic 1983, 'The Slave Mode of Production in Italy', *Journal of Roman Studies*, 73: 160–8.
—— 1991, *Economic Rationalism and Rural Society in Third-Century AD Egypt: The Heroninos Archive and the Appianus Estate*, Cambridge: Cambridge University Press.
Ray, Rajat and Ratna Ray 1975, 'Zamindars and Jotedars: A Study of Rural Politics in Bengal', *Modern Asian Studies*, 9, 1: 81–102.
Reilly, Bernard F. 1993, *The Medieval Spains*, Cambridge: Cambridge University Press.
Reynolds, Susan 1994, *Fiefs and Vassals: The Medieval Evidence Reinterpreted*, Oxford: Oxford University Press.
Riberi, Lorenzo 2001, *Arthur Rosenberg. Democrazia e socialismo tra storia e politica*, Milan: Franco Angeli.
Richards, Alan 1978, 'Land and Labor on Egyptian Cotton Farms, 1882–1940', *Agricultural History*, 52, 4: 503–18.
—— 1979, 'The Political Economy of *Gutswirtschaft*: A Comparative Analysis of East Elbian Germany, Egypt, and Chile', *Comparative Studies in Society and History*, 21, 4: 483–518.
—— 1982, *Egypt's Agricultural Development, 1800–1980: Technical and Social Change*, Boulder: Westview Press.
—— 1993, 'Land Tenure', in *The Agriculture of Egypt*, edited by G.M. Craig, Oxford: Oxford University Press.
Richards, Donald Sidney (ed.) 1970, *Islam and the Trade of Asia: A Colloquium*, Oxford: Bruno Cassirer.
Richards, John F. 1975, *Mughal Administration in Golconda*, Oxford: Clarendon Press.
—— 1993a, *The Mughal Empire (The New Cambridge History of India, 1/5)*, Cambridge: Cambridge University Press.
—— 1993b, *Power, Administration and Finance in Mughal India*, Aldershot: Variorum.
—— 2004, 'Warriors and the State in Early Modern India', *Journal of the Economic and Social History of the Orient*, 47, 3: 390–400.
Ritter, Helmut 1917, 'Ein arabisches Handbuch der Handelswissenschaft', *Der Islam*, 7, 1: 1–91.
Robinson, Damian 2005, 'Re-thinking the Social Organisation of Trade and Industry in First Century AD Pompeii', in *Roman Working Lives and Urban Living*, edited by Ardle Mac Mahon and Jennifer Price, Oxford: Oxbow Books.
Rodinson, Maxime 1966, *Islam et capitalisme*, Paris: Éditions du Seuil.
—— 1970, 'Le marchand musulman', in Richards (ed.) 1970.
Rösener, Werner 1989, 'Strukturformen der adeligen Grundherrschaft in der Karolingerzeit', in *Strukturen der Grundherrscahft im frühen Mittelalter*, Göttingen: Vandenhoeck and Ruprecht.
—— 2006, 'Vom Sklaven zum Bauern. Zur Stellung der Hörigen in der frühmittelalterlichen Grundherrschaft', in *Tätigkeitsfelder und Erfahrungshorizonte des ländlichen Menschen in der frühmittelalterlichen Grundherrschaft (bis ca.1000). Festschrift für Dieter Hägermann*, edited by Brigitte Kasten, Stuttgart: Franz Steiner Verlag.
Roover, Raymond de 1999 [1948], *Money, Banking and Credit in Mediaeval Bruges: Italian Merchant-Bankers, Lombards and Money-Changers. A Study in the Origins of Banking*, London: Routledge.
Rosdolsky, Roman 1974, *Zur Entstehungsgeschichte des Marxschen "Kapital". Der Rohentwurf des Kapital 1857–1858*, 2 vols., Frankfurt: Europäische Verlagsanstalt.
Rosenberg, Arthur 1997, *Demokratie und Klassenkampf im Altertum*, Freiburg (Breisgau): Ahriman-Verlag.
Rosenberg, Hans 1978, 'Die Pseudodemokratisierung der Rittergutsbesitzerklasse', in *Machteliten und Wirtschaftskonjunkturen: Studien zur neueren deutschen Sozial- und Wirtschaftsgeschichte*, Göttingen: Vandenhoeck und Ruprecht.

Rostovtzeff, Michael Ivanovitch 1959, *The Social and Economic History of the Hellenistic World*, 3 vols., Oxford: Clarendon Press.
—— 1971, *The Social and Economic History of the Roman Empire*, 2 vols., 2nd edition, revised by P.M. Fraser, Oxford: Clarendon Press.
Roth Congès, Anne 2005, 'Nature et authenticité des Casae Litterarum d'aprés l'analyse de leur vocabulaire', in *Les vocabulaires techniques des arpenteurs romains*, edited by D. Conso, A. Gonzales and J.-Y. Guillaumin, Besançon: Presses Universitaires de Franche-Comté.
Rouche, Michel 1990, 'Géographie rurale du royaume de Charles le Chauve', in *Charles the Bald: Court and Kingdom*, edited by M.T. Gibson and J.L. Nelson, 2nd revised edition, Aldershot: Variorum.
Roveri, Alessandro 1972, *Dal sindacalismo rivoluzionario al fascismo. Capitalismo agrario e socialismo nel Ferrarese (1870–1920)*, Florence: La Nuova Italia.
Roy, William G. 1997, *Socializing Capital: The Rise of the Large Industrial Corporation in America*, Princeton: Princeton University Press.
Rubin, Isaak I. 1972, *Essays on Marx's Theory of Value*, Detroit: Black & Red.
Rudra, Ashok and Pranab Bardhan 1983, *Agrarian Relations in West Bengal: Results of Two Surveys*, Bombay: Somaiya.
Rühle, Otto 1924, *From the Bourgeois to the Proletarian Revolution*, available at: <http://www.marxists.org/archive/ruhle/1924/ruhle01.htm.>
Runciman, Walter Garrison 1995, 'The "Triumph" of Capitalism as a Topic in the Theory of Social Selection', *New Left Review*, I, 210: 33–47.
Rutten, Mario 1986, 'Social Profile of Agricultural Entrepreneurs: Economic Behaviour and Life-Style of Middle-Large Farmers in Central Gujarat', *Economic and Political Weekly*, 21, 13: A15–23.
Santen, Hans Walther van 1982, *De Verenigde Oost-Indische Compagnie in Gujarat en Hindustan, 1620–60*, Meppel: Krips Repro.
Sapori, Armando 1952, *Le marchand italien au moyen age: conférences et bibliographie*, Paris: A. Colin.
Sarris, Peter 2006, *Economy and Society in the Age of Justinian*, Cambridge: Cambridge University Press.
Sartre, Jean-Paul 1960a, *Questions de méthode*, Paris: Gallimard.
—— 1960b, *Critique de la raison dialectique t.1. Théorie des ensembles pratiques*, Paris: Gallimard.
—— 1976, *Critique of Dialectical Reason*, Volume 1, translated by Alan Sheridan-Smith, London: New Left Books.
Sato, Tsugitaka 1997, *State and Rural Society in Medieval Islam: Sultans, Muqta's and Fallahun*, Leiden: E.J. Brill.
Sayer, Derek 1987, *The Violence of Abstraction: The Analytic Foundations of Historical Materialism*, Oxford: Basil Blackwell.
Schiller, René 2003, *Vom Rittergut zum Grossgrundbesitz: Ökonomische und sociale Transformationsprozesse der ländlichen Eliten in Brandenburg im 19. Jahrhundert*, Berlin: Akademie Verlag.
Schissler, Hanna 1978, *Preußische Agrargesellschaft im Wandel. Wirtschaftliche, gesellschaftliche und politische Transformationsprozesse von 1763 bis 1847*, Göttingen: Vandenhoeck und Ruprecht.
Schwartz, Jacques 1961, *Les archives de Sarapion et de ses fils*, Cairo: l'Institut Francais d'Archéologie Orientale.
Sée, Henri 1927, *Matérialisme historique et interprétation économique de l'histoire*, Paris: Alcan.
Segrè, Angelo 1947, 'The Byzantine Colonate', *Traditio*, 5: 103–33.
Serrao, Feliciano 1971, 'Sulla rilevanza esterna del rapporto di società in diritto romano', in *Studi in onore di Edoardo Volterra*, six volumes, Milan: Giuffrè.
—— 1989, *Impresa e responsibilità a Roma nell'età commerciale. Forme giuridiche di un'economia-mondo*, Pisa: Pacini.
Seton-Watson, Christopher 1967, *Italy from Liberalism to Fascism, 1870–1925*, London: Methuen.

Shaw, Brent D. 1998, '"A Wolf by the Ears": M.I. Finley's *Ancient Slavery and Modern Ideology* in Historical Context', in M.I. Finley, *Ancient Slavery and Modern Ideology*, expanded ed., Princeton: Markus Wiener Publishers.
Sheridan, Richard B. 1961, 'The Rise of a Colonial Gentry: A Case Study of Antigua, 1730–1775', *Economic History Review*, 2nd ser., 13, 3: 342–57.
—— 1965, 'The Wealth of Jamaica in the Eighteenth Century', *Economic History Review*, 2nd ser., 18, 2: 292–311.
Sifonas, C. S. 1994, 'Basile II et l'aristocratie byzantine', *Byzantion*, 64: 118–33.
Silver, Arthur W. 1966, *Manchester Men and Indian Cotton, 1847–72*, Manchester: Manchester University Press.
Skocpol, Theda 1979, *States and Social Revolutions*, Cambridge: Cambridge University Press.
Smith, Mark M. 1998, *Debating Slavery: Economy and Society in the Antebellum American South*, Cambridge: Cambridge University Press.
Smith, Simon David 2006, *Slavery, Family, and Gentry Capitalism in the British Atlantic: The World of the Lascelles, 1648–1834*, Cambridge: Cambridge University Press.
Snowden, Frank 1979, 'From Sharecropper to Proletarian: The Background to Fascism in Rural Tuscany, 1880–1920', in *Gramsci and Italy's Passive Revolution*, edited by John A. Davis, London: Croom Helm.
—— 1986, *Violence and Great Estates in the South of Italy. Apulia, 1900–1922*, Cambridge: Cambridge University Press.
—— 1989, *The Fascist Revolution in Tuscany 1919–1922*, Cambridge: Cambridge University Press.
Sombart, Werner 1891, 'Die Hausindustrie in Deutschland', *Archiv für Gesetzgebung u. Statistik*, 4: 103–56.
—— 1899, 'Die gewerbliche Arbeit und ihre Organisation', *Archiv für soziale Gesetzgebung und Statistik*, 14: 1–52, 310–405.
—— 1916, *Der moderne Kapitalismus. Bd. 1 Die historischen Grundlagen des modernen Kapitalismus*, Munich: Duncker and Humblot.
—— 1917, *Der moderne Kapitalismus, Band 2: Das europäische Wirtschaftsleben im Zeitalter des Frühkapitalismus*, 2nd edition, Munich: Duncker und Humblot.
Sprandel, Rolf 1957, *Der merovingische Adel und die Gebiete östlich des Rheins*, Freiburg im Breisgau: E. Albert.
—— 1961, 'Struktur und Geschichte des merowingischen Adels', *Historische Zeitschrift*, 193, 1: 33–71.
—— 1968, 'Grundbesitz- und Verfassungsverhältnisse in einer merowingischen Landschaft: die Civitas Cenomannorum', in *Adel und Kirche: Gerd Tellenbach zum 65. Geburtstag...*, edited by Josef Fleckenstein and Karl Schmid, Freiburg: Herder.
Spufford, Peter 1988, *Money and its Use in Medieval Europe*, Cambridge: Cambridge University Press.
Staab, Franz 1975, *Untersuchungen zur Gesellschaft am Mittelrhein in der Karolingerzeit*, Wiesbaden: F. Steiner.
Stalin, Joseph 1941, *Dialectical and Historical Materialism*, London: Lawrence and Wishart.
Ste Croix, Geoffrey E.M. de 1983, *The Class Struggle in the Ancient Greek World from the Archaic Age to the Arab Conquests*, London: Duckworth.
Stedman Jones, Gareth 1972, 'History: The Poverty of Empiricism', in *Ideology in Social Science*, edited by Robin Blackburn, London: Fontana/Collins.
Steensgaard, Niels 1974, *The Asian Trade Revolution of the Seventeenth Century: The East India Companies and the Decline of the Caravan Trade*, Chicago: University of Chicago Press.
Stein, Ernest 1959, *Histoire du Bas-Empire, t.1. De l'état romain à l'état byzantin (284–476)*, tr. J.-R. Palanque. Paris: Desclée de Brouwer.
Steinfeld, Robert J. 1991, *The Invention of Free Labor: The Employment Relation in English and American Law and Culture, 1350–1870*, Chapel Hill: University of North Carolina Press.
—— 2001, *Coercion, Contract and Free Labor in the Nineteenth Century*, Cambridge: Cambridge University Press.

Stern, Samuel Miklos 1967, 'Rāmisht of Sīrāf, a Merchant Millionaire of the Twelfth Century', *Journal of the Royal Asiatic Society*, April: 10–14.
Stillman, Norman A. 1973, 'The Eleventh Century Merchant House of Ibn 'Awkal (a Geniza Study)', *Journal of the Economic and Social History of the Orient*, 16, 1: 15–88.
Stokes, Mary 1994, 'Company Law and Legal Theory', in *A Reader on the Law of the Business Enterprise: Selected Essays*, edited by Sally Wheeler, Oxford: Oxford University Press.
Stolcke, Verena 1995, 'The Labors of Coffee in Latin America: The Hidden Charm of Family Labor and Self-Provisioning', in *Coffee, Society, and Power in Latin America*, edited by W. Roseberry, L. Gudmundson, M. S. Kutschbach, Baltimore: John Hopkins University Press.
Stoll, Steven 1998, *The Fruits of Natural Advantage: Making the Industrial Countryside in California*, Berkeley: University of California Press.
Strieder, Jakob 1914, *Studien zur Geschichte kapitalistischer Organisationsformen: Monopole, Kartelle und Aktiengesellschaften im Mittelalter und zu Beginn der Neuzeit*, Munich: Duncker and Humblot.
—— 1929, 'Origin and Evolution of Early European Capitalism', *Journal of Economic and Business History*, 2: 1–19.
Stroheker, Karl Friedrich 1963, 'Spanische Senatoren der spätrömischen und westgotischen Zeit', *Madrider Mitteilungen*, 4: 107–32.
Subrahmanyam, Sanjay and C.A. Bayly 1988, 'Portfolio Capitalists and the Political Economy of Early Modern India', *The Indian Economic and Social History Review*, 25, 4: 401–24.
Sundermann, Werner 1976, '*Commendatio pauperum*. Eine Angabe der sassanidischen politisch-didaktischen Literatur zur gesellschaftlichen Struktur Irans', *Altorientalische Forschungen*, 4: 167–94.
Sundwall, Johannes 1915, *Weströmische Studien*, Berlin: Mayer & Müller.
Sweezy, Paul M. 1954, 'A Critique', in Sweezy et al. 1954.
Sweezy, Paul et al. 1954, *The Transition from Feudalism to Capitalism: A Symposium*, London: Fore Publications.
Tabacco, Giovanni 1989, *The Struggle for Power in Medieval Italy: Structures of Political Rule*, tr. R.B. Jensen, Cambridge: Cambridge University Press.
al-Ṭabarī 1881–2, [*Tarīkh al-rusul wa'l-mulūk* =] *Annales quos scripsit Abu Djafar Mohammed Ibn Djarir at-Ṭabari*, edited by M.J. de Goeje et al., Series one, Leiden: E.J. Brill.
—— 1989, *The Conquest of Iraq, Southwestern Persia and Egypt (The History of al-Tabari Volume xiii)*, tr. Gautier H.A. Juynboll. Albany: State University of New York Press.
—— 1999, *The Sasanids, the Byzantines, the Lakhmids, and Yemen (The History of al-Tabari Volume v)*, tr. C.E. Bosworth. Albany: State University of New York Press.
Ṭāha, 'Abdulwāḥid Dhanūn 1989, *The Muslim Conquest and Settlement of North Africa and Spain*, London: Routledge.
Tate, Georges 1992, *Les campagnes de la Syrie du Nord du IIe au VIIe siècle. Un exemple d'expansion démographique et économique à la fin de l'antiquité*, Paris: Paul Geuthner.
Tawney, Richard Henry 1950, 'A History of Capitalism', *Economic History Review*, 2nd ser., 2, 3: 307–16.
Taylor, Lewis 1984, 'Cambios capitalistas en las haciendas Cajamarquinas del Peru, 1900–1935', *Estudios Rurales Latinoamericanos*, 7, 1: 93–129.
Tchalenko, Georges 1953–8, *Villages antiques de la Syrie du Nord. Le Massif de Bélus à l'époque romaine*, 3 vols., Paris: P. Geuthner.
Thomas, Keith 1965, 'The Social Origins of Hobbes' Political Thought', in *Hobbes Studies*, edited by K.C. Brown, Oxford: Basil Blackwell.
Thomaz, Luís Filipe 1989, 'Le Portugal et l'Afrique au XVe siècle: les débuts de l'expansion', *Arquivos do Centro Cultural Português*, 26: 161–256.
Thompson, Edward Arthur 1944, 'Olympiodorus of Thebes', *Classical Quarterly*, 38, 1–2: 43–52.
—— 1952a, 'Peasant Revolts in Late Roman Gaul and Spain', *Past and Present*, 2, 1: 11–23.
—— 1952b, *A Roman Reformer and Inventor, being a New Text of the Treatise "De Rebus bellicis" with a translation and introduction*, Oxford: Clarendon Press.

—— 1969, *The Goths in Spain*, Oxford: Clarendon Press.
Thompson, Edward P. 1978, *The Poverty of Theory and Other Essays*, London: Merlin Press.
Titow, Jan Zbigniew 1969, *English Rural Society 1200–1350*, London: George Allen and Unwin.
Tits-Dieuaide, Marie-Jeanne 1985, 'Grands domaines, grandes et petites exploitations en Gaule mérovingienne. Remarques et suggestions', in *Le grand domaine aux époques mérovingienne et carolingienne/Die Grundherrschaft im frühen Mittelalter*, edited by Adriaan Verhulst, Ghent: Centre Belge d'Histoire Rurale.
Toulmin, Stephen and June Goodfield 1967, *The Discovery of Time*, Harmondsworth: Penguin.
Trapido, Stanley 1971, 'South Africa in a Comparative Study of Industrialization', *Journal of Development Studies*, 7, 3: 309–20.
Trevor-Roper, Hugh 1967, 'The Reformation and Economic Change', in *Capitalism and the Reformation*, edited by M.J. Kitch, London: Longman.
Trotsky, Leon 1967, *The History of the Russian Revolution*, 3 vols., London: Sphere Books.
—— 1969, *Terrorism and Communism: A Reply to Karl Kautsky*, Ann Arbor: University of Michigan Press.
—— 1972, *1905*, tr. Anya Bostock, London: Allen Lane.
Tuan, Yi-fu 1970, *China*, London: Longman Group.
Turner, Bryan S. 1978, *Marx and the End of Orientalism*, London: George Allen & Unwin.
Twitchett, Denis 1962, *Land Tenure and the Social Order in T'ang and Sung China*, Oxford: SOAS.
—— 1963, *Financial Administration under the T'ang Dynasty*, Cambridge: Cambridge University Press.
—— 1973, 'The Composition of the T'ang Ruling Class: New Evidence from Tunhuang', in *Perspectives on the T'ang*, edited by Arthur F. Wright and Denis Twitchett, New Haven: Yale University Press.
—— 1979, 'Introduction', in *The Cambridge History of China, Volume 3: Sui and T'ang China, 589–906, Part I*, edited by Denis Twitchett, Cambridge: Cambridge University Press.
Udovitch, Abraham 1970a, 'Commercial Techniques in Early Medieval Islamic Trade', in Richards (ed.) 1970.
—— 1970b, *Partnership and Profit in Medieval Islam*, Princeton: Princeton University Press.
—— 1999, 'International Trade and the Medieval Egyptian Countryside', in *Agriculture in Egypt from Pharaonic to Modern Times*, Proceedings of the British Academy 96, edited by Alan Bowman and Eugene Rogan, Oxford: Oxford University Press.
Unali, Anna 2000, *Ceuta 1415. Alle origini dell'espansione europea in Africa*, Rome: Bulzoni.
van der Linden, Marcel 2007, *Western Marxism and the Soviet Union: A Survey of Critical Theories and Debates since 1917*, Historical Materialism Book Series, Leiden: Brill.
Van Dillen, Johannes Gerard van 1923, 'Amsterdam als wereldmarkt der edele metalen in de 17de en 18de eeuw', *De Economist*, 72,1: 538–50, 583–98.
Van Young, Eric 1981, *Hacienda and Market in Eighteenth-Century Mexico. The Rural Economy of the Guadalajara Region, 1675–1820*, Berkeley: University of California Press.
Vatin, François 1987, *La fluidité industrielle*, Paris: Meridiens Klincksieck.
Veiga-Simões, Alberto da 1932, 'La Flandre, le Portugal, et les débuts du capitalisme moderne', *Revue économique internationale*, August: 249–98.
Vera, Domenico 1983, 'Strutture agrarie e strutture patrimoniali nella tarda antichità: l'aristocrazia romana fra agricoltura e commercio', *Opus*, 2, 2: 489–533.
Verhulst, Adriaan 1966, 'La genèse du régime domanial classique en France au haut moyen âge', in *Agricoltura e mondo rurale in Occidente nel Alto Medioevo (Settimane di Studio 13)*: 135–60.

—— 1991, 'The Decline of Slavery and the Economic Expansion of the Early Middle Ages', *Past and Present*, 133, 1: 195–203.
—— 1995, 'Economic Organisation', in *The New Cambridge Medieval History Vol. 2, c.700–c.900*, edited by R. McKitterick, Cambridge: Cambridge University Press.
—— 2002, *The Carolingian Economy*, Cambridge: Cambridge University Press.
Vilar, Pierre 1971, 'The Age of Don Quixote', *New Left Review*, I, 68: 59–71.
—— 1973, 'Marxist History, A History in the Making: Towards a Dialogue with Althusser', *New Left Review*, I, 80: 64–106.
Vives, José 1963, *Concilios Visigóticos e hispano-romanos*, Barcelona: Instituto Enrique Flórez.
Volney, Constantin-François 1787, *Travels through Syria and Egypt in the years 1783, 1784, and 1785*, 2 vols., London: Printed for G.G.J. and J. Robinson.
Von Savigny, Friedrich Carl 1850, 'Ueber den römischen Kolonat', in *Vermischte Schriften*, Volume 2. Berlin: Veit u. comp.
Voß, Wulf Eckart 1985, 'Der Grundsatz der "ärgeren Hand" bei Sklaven, Kolonen und Hörigen', in *Römisches Recht in der europäischen Tradition. Symposion aus Anlass des 75. Geburtstages von Franz Wieacker*, edited by O. Behrends, M. Diesselhorst, W.E. Voß, Ebelsbach am Main: R. Gremer.
Wallace-Hadrill, John Michael 1960, *The Fourth Book of the Chronicle of Fredegar, with its Continuations*, London; New York: Nelson.
Wallerstein, Immanuel 1974, *The Modern World-System: Capitalist Agriculture and the Origins of the European World-Economy in the Sixteenth Century*, New York: Academic Press.
Washbrook, Sarah 2007, '*Enganche* and Exports in Chiapas, Mexico: A Comparison of Plantation Labour in the Districts of Soconusco and Palenque, 1876–1911', *Journal of Latin American Studies*, 39, 4: 797–825.
Waszyński, Stefan 1905, *Die Bodenpacht: agrargeschichtliche Papyrusstudien*, Leipzig: B.G. Teubner.
Watson, Andrew M. 1967, 'Back to Gold – and Silver', *Economic History Review*, 2nd ser., 20, 1: 1–34.
—— 1974, 'The Arab Agricultural Revolution and its Diffusion, 700–1100', *Journal of Economic History*, 34, 1: 8–35.
—— 1983, *Agricultural Innovation in the Early Islamic World: The Diffusion of Crops and Farming Techniques, 700–1100*, Cambridge: Cambridge University Press.
Weber, Max 1894, 'Entwicklungstendenzen in der Lage der ostelbischen Landarbeiter', *Preußische Jahrbücher*, 77: 437–73; repr. in Weber 1924a; tr. by Keith Tribe in Weber 1979.
—— 1924a, *Gesammelte Aufsätze zur Sozial- und Wirtschaftsgeschichte*, Tübingen: Mohr.
—— 1924b [1896], 'Die sozialen Gründe des Untergangs der antiken Kultur', in Weber 1924a.
—— 1961, *General Economic History*, New York: Collier Books.
—— 1968, *Economy and Society: An Outline of Interpretive Sociology*, edited by Guenther Roth and Claus Wittich, 2 vols., Berkeley: University of California Press.
—— 1976, *The Agrarian Sociology of Ancient Civilizations*, tr. R.I. Frank, London: NLB.
—— 1979, 'Developmental Tendencies in the Situation of East Elbian Rural Labourers', *Economy and Society*, 8, 2: 177–205.
Wehr, Hans 1952, *Arabisches Wörterbuch für die Schriftsprache der Gegenwart*, 2 vols., Leipzig: O. Harrassowitz.
Weidemann, Margarete 1986, *Das Testament des Bischofs Berthramn von Le Mans vom 27. März 616*, Mainz: Verlag des Römisch-Germanischen Zentralmuseums.
Weidinger, Ulrich 1991, *Untersuchungen zur Wirtschaftsstruktur des Klosters Fulda in der Karolingerzeit*, Stuttgart: A. Hiersemann.
Wells, Alan 1985, *Yucatán's Gilded Age: Haciendas, Henequen, and International Havester 1860–1915*, Albuquerque: University of New Mexico Press.

Werner, Karl Ferdinand 1984, *Histoire de France t.1: Les origines (avant l'an mil)*, Paris: Fayard.
Whitcombe, Elizabeth 1971, *Agrarian Conditions in Northern India, Volume 1: The United Provinces under British Rule, 1860–1900*, Berkeley: University of California Press.
White, Horace 1964, *Appian's Roman History*, 4 volumes, (Loeb ed.) London: Willam Heinemann.
Whittaker, Charles Richard 1987, 'Circe's Pigs: from Slavery to Serfdom in the Later Roman World', in *Classical Slavery*, edited by M.I. Finley, London: Frank Cass.
—— 1999, 'Slavery', in *Late Antiquity: A Guide to the Post-Classical World*, edited by G.W. Bowersock, Peter Brown, Oleg Grabar, Cambridge, MA.: Belknap Press of Harvard University.
Wickham, Chris 1984, 'The Other Transition: From the Ancient World to Feudalism', *Past and Present*, 103, 1: 3–36.
—— 1985, 'The Uniqueness of the East', in *Feudalism and Non-European Societies*, edited by T.J. Byres and H. Mukhia, London: Frank Cass.
—— 1988, 'Marx, Sherlock Holmes, and Late Roman Commerce', *Journal of Roman Studies*, 78: 183–93.
—— 1995, 'El fin del Imperio Carolingio. ¿Qué tipo de crisis?', in *Las crisis en la Historia*, edited by C. Wickham et al., Salamanca: Ediciones Universidad de Salamanca.
—— 2000, 'Le forme del feudalesimo', in *Il feudalesimo nell'alto medioevo*, 2 vols. (Settimane di studio 47), Volume 1: 15–46.
—— 2005, *Framing the Early Middle Ages: Europe and the Mediterranean 400–800*, Oxford: Oxford University Press.
Wightman, John 1996, *Contract: A Critical Commentary*, London: Pluto Press.
Wilfong, Terry G. 1999, 'Agriculture among the Christian Population of Early Islamic Egypt: Practice and Theory', in *Agriculture in Egypt*, edited by A. Bowman and E. Rogan, Oxford: Oxford University Press.
Williams, Gavin 1996, 'Transforming Labour Tenants', in *Land, Labour and Livelihoods in Rural South Africa*, Volume 2, edited by Michael Lipton, Frank Ellis, and Merle Lipton, Durban: Indicator Press.
Wittfogel, Karl August 1929, 'Geopolitik, geographischer Materialismus und Marxismus', *Unter dem Banner des Marxismus*, 3: 1751, 485–522, 699–735.
—— 1931. *Wirtschaft und Gesellschaft Chinas*, Leipzig: C.L. Hirschfeld.
—— 1932, 'Die natürlichen Ursachen der Wirtschaftsgeschichte', *Archiv für Sozialwissenschaft und Sozialpolitik*, 67: 466–92, 579–609, 711–31.
Wolf, Kenneth Baxter 1999, *Conquerors and Chroniclers of Early Medieval Spain*, 2nd edn., Liverpool: Liverpool University Press.
Wood, Ellen Meiksins 1991, *The Pristine Culture of Capitalism*, London: Verso.
Worger, William H. 1987, *South Africa's City of Diamonds: Mine Workers and Monopoly Capitalism in Kimberley, 1867–1895*, New Haven: Yale University Press.
Wormald, Patrick 1976, 'The Decline of the Western Empire and the Survival of its Aristocracy', *Journal of Roman Studies*, 66: 217–26.
al-Ya'ḳūbī 1937, *Les Pays*, tr. Gaston Wiet, Cairo: Institut français d'archéologie orientale du Caire.
Zaidi, S. Inayat A. 1997, 'Akbar and the Rajput Principalities: Integration into Empire', in *Akbar and his India*, edited by Irfan Habib, New Delhi: Oxford University Press.
Zavala, Silvio 1988, 'Orígenes coloniales del peonaje en México', reprinted in *Estudios acerca de la historia del trabajo en México*, edited by Elias Trabulse, Mexico City: Colegio de México, Centro de Estudios Históricos.
Zeumer, Karl 1902, *Leges Visigothorum*, Hannover: Hahn.
Zwanenberg, Roger van 1971, *Primitive Colonial Accumulation: Kenya 1919–1939*, D. Phil, University of Sussex.

Index

'Abbasids 25
'absence' of private property in
  land 16, 18, 355
  as legal fiction 18–19, 356
  view abandoned by Marx 20
absolute surplus-value 69, 281, 325
abstraction
  formal 2, 48
  forced xi, 52, 61
  levels of 52–5
Abū Ḥanīfa 246
Abū Yūsuf 244, 245
Academy, Plato's 48–9
access to family-labour 172, 343
accolae 225–6, 231, 236
Acién Almansa, Manuel 22, 183, 356
adhiars 113
adscripticii 194
advances
  basis of mercantile capitalism 274, 276
advance system 100–101, 144–5, 271–2
  Marx on 275–6, 303
  as a circulation of capital 276, 304
  surface appearance 303
Africa 62, 63, 64, 142
African gold 253–4, 264, 269
Agency Houses 144
Agrarian capitalism 69, 147, 177–9, 333–348, 359
  no 'pure' model 335
  hybridity 336, 341, 345
  hybrid forms of 342, 346
  variables in a taxonomy 336–7
  capitalist manorialism 342
agro-cities 338
Ahmednagar cotton 296
Akbar 35, 36, 37
'Alā' al-Dīn Khaljī 35
Alaric 233
Alexandria 120, 125, 210, 267
Algeria 63, 124,
  under French occupation 246–7
Alleaume, Ghislaine 344

Almeria 266, 267
Althusser, Louis 15
Ambrose, bishop of Milan 129
American South 10–11, 57, 67, 143, 146, 336
Amin, Samir 64
Ammianus Marcellinus 243
Amsterdam 72, 271
al-Andalus 22, 354
Anderson, Perry xii, 7, 8, 9, 31, 184, 203
Angelo, Larian 146
Anicii 207
Annales 49
Antioch 122
Antwerp 253, 254
Aphrodito 160, 167
Apion family/estate 159, 168, 169, 170, 171, 173–4, 176, 177, 216
Appian 128
Appianus estate 164, 176
Apulia 337, 338
  latifondisti and fascism 341
Arab invasions/conquest 209–10, 220, 241–2
Arab trade empire 264–7
Aragon 269
Arcadia 169
'arḍ al-ḥauz 245
Argentina 333
aristocracies
  Late Roman/Western 25, 185–6, 207–8, 208–10, 216–7, 220, 221
  Byzantine 26, 34, 167
  Chinese 28, 33
  boyars 31–2
  Russia 34
  mansabdars 35
  Hindu chiefs 35
  jagirdars 17, 36–9
  late antique/early Byzantine 160, 162, 167, 215–16, 220
  Alexandrian 164, 166
  mutation 209

flight 209–10
  kinds of in Late Antiquity 219–21
  Sasanian 219–20
  Merovingian 221–2, 223, 228
  Visigothic 222, 223–4
  senatorial, incomes of 226 n.47
  East Elbian 341
Armenia 248
Arrighi, Giovanni 64
artisans 216
  better fed than wage-labourers 122
  proletarianisation of 292
  domination by capital 324–5
Asiatic mode of production 15, 17–18, 20, 21, 22, 24, 349, 351, 356
  village communities 355
Assam 63
Athar Ali, M. 17, 19
Atlantic 253, 269
Atlantic slavery 10–11
  capitalist nature of 67–71
  creation of commercial capitalism 358
Augsburg 260
Augustine of Hippo 124–5, 129 n.54, 195, 233
Aurangzeb 16, 37
Aurelian 120
Azores 270

'bad theory' 7–8
Baer, Gabriel 160, 249
Bagnall, Roger 157
Bahro, Rudolf 23 n.102
Baker, C.J. 115
al-Balādhurī, Aḥmad b.Yaḥyā 264
Balkans 35, 196
Baltic 71–2, 90
bandag 243
Barbados 63, 68 n.79, 69 n.83
Barbero, Abilio 182
Bardhan, Pranab 112
bargadars 111–12, 146
  compared with day-labourers 113
Bardi of Florence
  international spread 260
Barracco estate 338
Basil, bishop of Caesarea 123, 129
Basil II 34
Baṣra 264
Baths of Caracalla 120
Bayly, C.A. 38
Bazant, Jan 173, 335
Bengal 38, 39, 40, 97, 99, 111–13, 115, 146, 272
  indigo trade 144–5
Bernier, François 16–17, 26, 39

Bertram, bishop of Le Mans 206, 221, 225, 228
Bettelheim, Charles 64
Bhaduri, Amit 277–8, 308, 326, 327, 329
Bihar 134
Blackstone, William 13
Bloch, Marc 6, 107, 182 n.7, 193, 195, 198, 226, 239
Bohemia 84
Bois, Guy 199–200
Bolotov, Andrei 76
Bombay export firms 286, 296, 297, 298
bondage 15, 134, 140–1, 197, 198, 245, 328, 336
  Kant's definition 142
bonded labour 114, 134–5, 147–8
Bonnassie, Pierre 3, 181–2, 199–200, 353
Borah, Woodrow 141
bordars 238
braccianti 338
Bradford, Helen 4, 5, 359
Brass, Tom 14, 136–7, 138, 139, 140, 142, 148–9, 153–4
Brătianu, G.I. 34
Braudel, Fernand 46, 71, 254, 274
Breman, Jan 116, 141, 150 n.105
Brenner, Robert xii
British
  confused about *zamindars* 39
British capitalists and Indian cotton-supply 331
British revenue-system
  the Survey Settlement 284
  premised on the market 287–8
  pressure of revenue-demand 290, 291
  'arming of the moneylender' 302 n.62
Broach cotton trade 298
Brown, Peter 188, 211
Brown, T.S. 209, 233
Brunt, Peter 106, 120
Buchanan, Francis 140–1, 147
Bukhārā 248–9, 266
Bukharin, N.I. 65
bureaucracy
  as ruling group 25, 26, 27–8, 31
  service-class in Russia 33
Burgundians 217, 221
Burma 99
Byres, Terence J. 22, 141, 347
Byzantine East
  rural classes in Egypt 160–1
  class division in countryside 242–3
  diversified labour-market 216
Byzantium 19, 26, 37, 39

Cairo 267
Calabria 338
California 334
Callinicos, Alex xii
Cambodia 99
canals 343
capital
  serf-owning 57–8
  domination over small producers 96–9, 308–9
  notions of in Antiquity 129–130
  historiographies of 251–5
  notion in Arabic sources 262–4
  pure movement 281
  subsumes labour-process as it finds it 309
capitalism
  configurations of 9, 358
  slaveholding 10–11
  history of 12, 256
  early traces 12 n.49, 356–7
  in Sung China 29–30
  can intensify backward forms of exploitation 56
  backward forms of 99
  coercion pervasive under 133
  & bondage 136
  flexibility in structuring of production 145
  rationalising imperatives 178
  agriculture its first theatre 178
  origins 3–4, 251–3, 254–5, 257
  'monarchical' 254
  Mediterranean 257, 262
  Company 258, 270–2, 357
  no Marxist historiography of 272
capitalist relations of exploitation
  widespread when economy not fully capitalist 282
capitalist relations of production
  not reducible to *Capital*, Volume One 213–214
  'necessary forms of appearance' in less-developed economies 306–7
  compatible with tenancy, etc. 326–7
  compatible with debt-servitude 340
Caribbean 10, 67, 71, 104
Carolingians 239, 250
Carrié, Jean-Michel 192, 193–4, 195
Carthage 210, 352
casae 207, 230
casales 230
Castile 269
casual labour 337
  in Rome 105, 216
  in East Mediterranean 216
  dominant in paddy cultivation 110
  during Depression 115
  gangs 115, 124–5, 338
Catalonia 181, 200, 353
Cato the Elder 104–5, 116, 119
centisti 105
Ceuta 253, 266, 268, 269
Chattopadhyay, Paresh 288 n.22, 326
Ch'en Yin-k'o 28
Cheynet, Jean-Claude 26
Chiapas 340
Chile 85
Chilperic I 222, 223
China 25, 27–31, 34, 86, 99, 162, 257, 264, 267
Chinese ceramics 29
Chowdhury, Benoy 144–5
Chlothar II 222, 223
Chrodin 228
Cicero 118, 132 n.2
Circumcellions 124–5
Clausing, Roth 158
Cochinchina, rubber plantations 141
Coen, J.-P. 270, 272
coercion 134, 153
collazos 202
colonate 157, 168, 182, 191–8, 211, 234
  as subordination of free labour 191
  legal fiction behind 191
  Wickham on 193, 195, 197, 202
  Marc Bloch on 193
  Jones on 194
  legislation on mixed marriages 196
  impact on medieval peasantry 196–7
  landowner complaints 196
  possible Marxist definition 197
coloni 202, 234–6
  landowner power over 192
  slave-like treatment of 194
  legal position 195–6
  labourers more than tenants 197
  defined by Justinian 197, 234, 242–3
  bound to their employers 197–8
  mostly landless 234 n.84
  on Remigius' farms 227, 236
  absorbed into a servile labour force 235
colonica 218, 225, 228
colonialism 63, 100, 247, 339
colonial régimes 62, 99–100, 359
  agencies of a modern state 178
Comintern 58
commenda 260, 261–2
commercial capitalism 9–10, 29, 36, 37, 43–4, 252, 253, 270, 273, 276, 357–8
  for a Marxist theory of 255–8
  Dutch 12–13, 270–2, 358

commercial capitals, competition of 271
commercial partnerships 259, 357
compagnie 260
conductores 205
Confino, Michael 76
consent, reality of 134 n.23
Constantine I 25, 185, 220, 232
contract law, role of 138–9
contract of employment
 as legal fiction 137
 as mystification 138, 151, 153
contracts of adhesion 139
Corner brothers 260
corvée
 campaigns against 178
cottars 238
cotton 57, 58, 63, 67, 97, 144, 246, 248, 265, 266, 272, 284, 296, 297–8, 305, 324, 331, 343, 346
 collapse of boom 321, 342
Cowen, Mike 309 n.78
Cracco, Giorgio 254–5, 261
Craven, Paul 13
Crone, Patricia 243
Cuban sugar industry 63, 171, 272, 273, 274, 334, 335
 Havana merchant houses 9–10, 274
culialu 141
Cuno, Kenneth 159
Cyprus 260
Cyzicus 124

Daimler-Benz 359
Damietta 163
Danzig 71, 84
dastgird 250
Davidson, A.F. 314, 317
Davies, Wendy 352
Daybul 266
debt 114, 136, 139, 141
 no automatic implication of bondage 339
 as advance of wages 339–40
 as form of appearance 148
 how used by employers 150
 criterion of peasant stability 317, 319
Deccan in the nineteenth century
 contrasts within 284–5
 commercial expansion 284–7
 size of capitals available for loan 293–4
 most households in debt 294
 expansion of smaller moneylenders 294, 295, 299–300
 capitalist classes in 294–5
 big Marwari moneylenders 299–300
 moneylenders never seriously threatened by state 301
 financial state of local élites 310–311
 rich peasantry in 311–315, 326
 Bhil cultivators 313–314, 318, 323
 pattern of land-transfer 316, 320–2
 capital/wage-labour relationship widespread 325
dehqāns 244
Demangeon, Albert 343
demosioi georgoi 243
Denmark 85
deployment of labour 5–6, 41, 170, 218
 on medieval estates 107–9
 eviction of sharecroppers 112–113
 shift to casual labour 115–116
 decisions on employment 108, 116
 on Late Antique estates 175–7
Depression, 1930s
 impact of 111
Devine, T.M. 259–60
Devroey, Jean-Pierre 355
dialectic 48
 in *Capital* 59
 in Engels 59
Dias, Manuel Nunes 253–4
Digest 119
Dio Chrysostom of Prusa 117
direct management 167, 170, 190, 200
 Rome's legacy 203, 239
Dobb, Maurice 52, 54, 55, 64, 68, 83, 88, 91, 92, 256–7, 272, 308
Dom João II 254, 269
Dom Pedro 253
Dom Manuel 269
domestic industry 50, 271 n.120, 275
domus
 associated with *mancipia* 228
Domus Divina 167, 170, 211
Donatists 124, 125, 233
driyōšān 243
Duby, Georges 54, 79, 80, 82, 238
Dusinberre, William 11, 337
Dutch East India Company 13, 257, 270–1
dynastic rule
 Sasanian aristocrats committed to 219
 favoured aristocracy 222–4
 contrast between Visigoths and Merovingians 223

early middle ages
 relations of production 190, 202
 characterisation of 233–4, 237
 a self-managing peasantry? 236

Eastern Europe   63, 66, 72, 83, 84–5, 90, 93, 110
economic liberalism
  of colonial bureaucracy   288–9
  liberal atomism of nineteenth century   346
effort bargaining   116
Egypt   99, 111, 121, 125, 145, 155–180, 246, 248, 249, 338, 342–4, 345–6
  smallholders worst affected   160
Egyptian capitalists   346
El-Abbadi, Mostafa   243
Emilia   334
employers
  no inevitability about responses   115
enapographoi georgoi   173
encomiendas   335, 339
Engels, Friedrich   xvii, 42, 45–6, 47, 59, 98, 133, 353
England   252, 256
  re-export trade   71–2
  medieval estates   54, 76, 79, 80, 89
  Anglo-Saxon   190, 199, 202, 230–1, 237, 238, 354
  'inland'   199, 202, 206, 230–1
  strength of capitalist interests   257
  coal industry   273
  dependence on wages   81
English East India Company   257, 270
epikeimenos   174
epoikia   170, 248
epoikiotai   165
ergates   161, 177
estates
  in Sung China   86
  Ramsey Abbey   107
  Prussian   111
  East Elbian   142
  Egyptian in nineteenth century   171–2
  Mexican   170, 171, 177
  in Western empire   205, 206–7, 226
  Merovingian   206, 225, 226, 228–9
  bipartite   218, 229, 230
  Bishop Bertram's   228
  in Near East   247–250
  estancia   333
Europe's return to gold   265
eviction, threat of   245, 344–5
evolutionism   6, 107
ezba   171, 177, 178, 248, 250, 343–4
  ezba system   342–3

factory system   273
Faith, Rosamund   189, 199, 202, 203, 230–1, 239–40, 354

fallāḥ
  as wage-labourer   173
family-labour   337, 359
Far East, trade with dominated by Sasanians   264
farm management
  in the elder Cato   104–5
Fars   263
fascism   41, 341, 359
Fayyūm   343
  monasteries in   125
  estates   164, 166, 169
Feinman, Jay M.   138–9
Fernão Gomes   269
Ferrara   333–4
feudal enterprise/estates
  'crystallised' form of   74, 88
  economic rationality   75
  commercialisation   76
  organisation of   75–7
  methods of accounting   77–8
feudal mode of production   72–8, 79
  lord's consumption in   75
  contrast between western and eastern Europe   79–85
  Carolingian period   83
  long-term tendencies   87–92
  forms of exploitation in   92
  responses to crisis of   93–4
  in Wickham   3, 183–4, 212, 218, 237–8, 354
  in Dobb   52
feudal stereotype, critique of   344
feudalism   355, 356
  peasant-holdings under   74
  Marxists on   353–4
  coherent Marxist view?   183–4
Fez   264–5
fictitious capital   149
Finley, Moses   190, 192, 233
Flanders   83
flax   265, 267
Fletcher, W.M.   113
flexibility
  desired by Roman landowners   166
Florence   252
Floud Commission   111–112
'forced commercialisation'   99
'form determination'   98
formal subsumption   xiii, 134, 308, 309, 350
  possible outside a specifically capitalist mode of production   280, 329–30
  labour-process external to the movement of capital   281, 329, 350

entails expropriation 320
found as a 'particular' form alongside the capitalist mode of production 329
formalism 8, 61, 308, 346
France 16–17, 44, 71, 217, 252
Francia 200, 203, 209, 221, 222
  integrated ruling class 222
Frank, A.G. 62, 64, 65, 86, 325, 332, 342, 346, 347
Franks 217, 219, 221
Fredegar 209, 222
'free' labour 11, 13
  & liberal ideology 137, 140, 151, 154
  CLS critique of 133–4
  Marx's conception 137
  repressive forms of control 142
  how best construed 150
free/unfree labour dichotomy
  critique of 150–4
freed slaves/freedpeople 225, 229
  more like workers 199
  still subject to domination 201, 239
freedom of contract 139
Frölich, Paul 24
Fulda 229

Gabel, Peter 138–9
gañanes 226, 339
Ganshof, F.L. 218
Gascou, Jean 155, 159
Gaul 219, 222, 233
gebur 202, 238
Genoa 43, 260, 268–9
Genovese, Eugene D. 10, 67–8
georgoi 160–1, 163–4, 165, 168–9, 173, 216, 242–3
  could own livestock 174
  assigned to individual farms 176
georgos mechanes 176
Germany 83, 238, 251–2
Gianni, Francesco Maria 146
Giardina, Andrea 232, 234 n.83
Gibson, Charles 339–40
Girard, P.S. 163
Glasgow tobacco trade 259–60, 358
Goitein, S.D. 49
gold 7, 36–7, 121, 169, 186, 211, 226 n.47, 252, 254, 263, 264, 265, 269
Gothic wars, impact on aristocracy 208, 221
Goths 217
grain-prices in Europe 71–2
Gramsci, Antonio 325
Gregory of Nazianzus 123
Gregory of Nyssa 129
Gregory of Tours 209, 228

Gregory the Great 195, 208
Grossmann, Henryk xiv, 12, 143–4
Guichard, Pierre 22, 38, 354
Gujarat 115–116
Gulf 264, 267

Haag, Pamela 153 n.128
haciendas 4, 64, 85, 170, 171, 173, 177, 226, 335, 336, 338–40, 345
  as 'wage-labour enterprises' 164, 335
Hadoind, bishop of Le Mans 224
al-Ḥajjāj b. Yūsuf al-Thaqafī 264
Haldon, John 3, 22, 183, 184, 354–5, 356
Hamilton, Earl J. 49, 252–3
Hang-chou 29, 30
Hardy, E.R. 168
harvest 122, 124–5
Harvey, Susan 157
Hasan, Nurul 35
Ḥassān b. al-Nuʿmān al-Ġassānī 210
Hay, Douglas 13
Hegel, G.W.F. xiii
henequen 340
Henry the Navigator 254, 270
Hermopolis, leases in countryside around 167
Hilferding, Rudolf 258
Hilton, Rodney 49 n.19, 182, 183, 234
Hindess, Barry 8, 184 n.16, 212
Hintze, Otto 189
hired labour
  extensive on English medieval estates 80–1
  in feudal economy 93
  on Cato's model farm 104–5
  recommended for malarial land 106
  in thirteenth century 107, 109
  widespread in Rome 120, 121
  and bondage 140–1
  extensively used on Egyptian estates 169
Hirst, Paul Q. 8, 184 n.16, 212
historical materialism
  Stalinist vulgarisation of 48
history
  and Marx 46, 47
  and vulgar Marxism 46–7
  Marxist historians 49, 309 n.78
Hobson, J.A. 58
Holland 12, 71, 110, 252, 270–1
Hormozdān 219, 248
hubae 230, 237
Hug, G. 177–8, 343
Hungary 84, 85, 110
Hurd, John 286

Ibn Ḥauqal   265, 266, 267
Ibn al-Humam   240–1
Ibn Khaldūn   263–4
Ibn Nujaym   241, 242
Ibn Waḥshiyya   244
Ibrahim Halebi   20
al-Idrīsī   267
indebtedness
  widespread in nineteenth-century Deccan   294
  reasons cited for   302
India   37, 99, 134, 148, 240, 271, 355
  Delhi Sultanate   20–21, 35
  mode of production debate in   325–6
Indian Ocean   254, 264
indigo   144, 265, 267, 272
  value of trade at Kabul   267
Indigo Commission   144
individual capitals
  indifferent to form of exploitation   142–3
industrial capitalism   178, 258, 358, 359–60
Innes, Matthew   238
inquilini   205, 236
Instmann   341
interest as surplus-value   301–8
investment banks   258
iqṭāʿ   20–21, 240, 248, 249–50
Iran/Persia   18, 179, 247, 249, 263
  Sasanian   219–20, 243–5, 250
  bōzōrgān   220
Ireland, Paddy   258–9
Islam
  assault on Islam's commercial dominance   254
  capitalism more precocious in   255
  contribution to growth of capitalism   267–8, 357
Islamic world   6, 12, 257, 275
  ownership of land   19
  distinctive economic régimes   22, 38–9, 356
  'death of the *kharāj* payer'   240–1
  tension between state and élite   240
  arguments undermining peasant rights   240–1
  partnerships in   262, 263
  cash-cropping   265
  scales of business   267
  developed 'capitalistic sector'   357
al-Iṣṭakhrī   263
Italy   4, 5, 73, 126, 188–9, 200, 207, 208, 221, 230, 233, 252, 269, 273, 286, 344
  Byzantine   209
  mercantile houses   260

Italian Socialists, position on *mezzadria*   344–5

al-Jabartī, ʿAbd al-Rahman   162, 163
job security   338
Jördens, Andrea   156–7
Johansen, Baber   240–2
John Chrysostom   122
Johnson, A.C.   158, 159
Jones, A.H.M.   194, 195
Jones, Philip James   146
Jones, Richard   17, 18
jotedars   40, 111, 113
Justinian I   111, 161, 194, 196, 220, 242, 248

Kābul   267
Kahn-Freund, Otto   14
Kant, Immanuel   142
Kaplan, Michel   155
al-Kāsānī   263
Katō Shigeshi   49
Kaufman, I.I.   2, 46, 59,
Kautsky, Karl   57, 67, 95
Kazhdan, Alexander   19
Keegan, Timothy   359
Kelman, Mark   42
Kennedy, Duncan   15, 42
Kenya   63, 174
Kessler, Friedrich   139
Khandesh cotton   297–8
kharāj   35, 242
al-Khaṣṣāf   245–6
Khurāsān   264
Khusrō I   244
Kikuyu   174
Kimberley diamond mines   41
King, P.D.   203
Knight, Alan   339, 340
Kosminsky, E.A.   49 n.19, 83, 84, 107
Kovalevsky, M.M.   16, 20, 21, 355–6
Kula, Witold   2, 49, 80

Labib, Subhi   255
labour
  combination of forms   105, 107
  no shortage in ancient Mediterranean   105
  flexibility in the use of   107, 346
  reversible shifts   110
labour-markets   15, 43, 115
  concerted creation of   247
labour-mortgaging   114, 309
labour-services   340
  Kosminsky's argument about   83–4
  Frankish innovation   204
  influenced by scale of operations   108
  in Hungary   84, 110

labour-tenants/labour-tenancy 146–7, 165–6, 174, 205 n.118, 245, 338, 341, 359
  distinct from labour-services 239–40
  in nineteenth-century Egypt 171–3, 342
Labrousse, Ernest 49
Laclau, Ernesto 62, 64, 65–6, 67, 346–7
Lambton, Ann K.S. 18–19, 179, 247, 249
Lancret, Michel-Ange 162
land
  reclamation of 30, 333–4
  colossal transfer in Bengal 111–112
  clearance in seventh century 225–6
  'favourite investment' 315–316
landlessness
  in Byzantine and Sasanian Near East 245
Lascelles 10
Late Antique estates
  grouped workers into settlements 248
  labour forces permanent 165, 173–4
  organisation of 168–73
  investments 169–70
  labour-system 173–7
  close supervision 174
Late Antique peasantry
  serfs? 157–8
  tenants? 159
  internally stratified 160
Late Antiquity 264
  economic maturity of 129–30
  contrast with classical world 156
  Church as landowner 166–7
  problem of a Marxist characterisation 181–3
  precursor of feudalism? 182
  influence of legal traditions 197
  legacies for mercantile capitalism 252, 254, 255
later Roman empire
  Max Weber on 25
  Mazzarino's characterisation 25
  restructuring in 166–7
  feudalism projected back into 182, 193
  new governing class 185–6
  monetary reform 186
  problem of dynamic 188, 210–11
  eastern provinces 215–16
  senatorial class 185, 220–1
  disintegration 220–1
latifondisti 341, 345
Latin America 62, 63, 93, 344
law
  internal to relations of production 15, 42–3
  'autonomous' history of 204
  'laws of motion' 46, 58–60, 213
  historically determinate 47–8
  defining role 60
  of feudal economy 88–91
Lefebvre, Georges 49, 257
Legal Realists 137
Lenin, V.I. 4, 5, 21, 41, 50, 65, 95, 146–7, 309, 326, 336, 342, 348
  on the labour-service system 41
  on subordination of small producers 50–1
  on Moscow pottery industry 55, 328
  on plantations in the U.S. South 67, 68–9
  against formalist constructions of capitalism 327
Leovigild 223
Levant 246, 255, 262
Lisbon 71, 253
Lithuania 81
locatio operarum 118
'logic of deployment'
  complex in agriculture 6,
  in Roman agriculture 106
  in medieval agriculture 109
Lohrmann, Dietrich 225
Lombards 209, 221, 237
Lombardy 83
London 10, 72
Lopez, Robert 262, 268, 272
Lopuszański, Georges 185
Lozach, J. 177–8, 343, 344
Lucian of Samosata 117–118
Luxemburg, Rosa 12, 41, 57, 65,

McCoan, J.C. 171
Macpherson, C.G.W. 306
Macaulay, Thomas Babington 145
Madras presidency 115
Madrid 71
Maghreb reapers 125
Mago of Carthage 104
Mahdia (al-Mahdiyya) 266, 267, 268
Małowist, Marian 93
managerial landlords 162
Manchester Chamber of Commerce 331
mancipia 218, 235, 354
  post-Roman 200, 201, 203
  coloni included under 201, 228
  semantic evolution 201–2, 227–8, 235
  service-holdings or allotments of 202, 229, 230

in Merovingian sources 228–9, 231, 236, 239
Mandel, Ernest 268, 272
Mandle, Jay 68
manor 204, 205, 206, 225
  Frankish innovation 354
mansus 218, 226–30, 237
  innovation of seventh century 229
  in the Fulda inventories 229
  more expansive sense of 237
Manucci, Niccolao 36
manufacture 51, 129 n.54
manumission 201, 206, 236–7
Manzano Moreno, Eduardo 183, 224 n.37
Marçais, William 125
Mariátegui, José Carlos 58
Marseilles 286
Marx, Karl 106, 178, 182, 211, 213, 281, 282
  averse to an all-encompassing feudalism 20, 21
  on the tributary mode 38
  on landed interests in India 39
  plans for section on ground-rent 42
  on the slave plantations 57, 67, 143, 352–3
  on slavery in Antiquity 57, 352
  on the small peasant 94–5
  on the subordination of small producers 96
  attack on Mommsen 127–8
  on child labour 128
  on contract of employment 132–3, 137, 138
  on the category 'interest' 148
  on serf labour 183
  history of law 204
  definition of commercial capital 257
  on Dutch East India Company 271
  on merchant capitalism 274–5
  on moneylending capitalism 307–8
  on the world-market 347
Marx's *Capital* 59–60, 127–8, 137–8, 178, 255
massa 205
massarii 230
master & servant régimes 43, 139–40, 147
Mauro, Frédéric 357
Mazdak 243–4
Mazzarino, Santo 25, 186, 187
Mecklenburg 84
medieval companies, financial organisation 260–1
Mediterranean 253, 255
Melania, younger 232–3

Mendeleïev's Periodic Table 61
mercantile capitalism, examples 97 n.154
mercantilism 72, 270 n.112
merchants/merchant's capital 9–10, 13, 30, 43, 50, 51, 57, 58, 83, 97, 129 n.54, 160, 257, 259, 260, 261, 262, 263, 266, 267, 269, 271, 272, 273–6, 279, 285, 286, 292–3, 296, 297, 305, 346, 357
  controlled key economic sectors 273
  created large enterprises 251–2
  innovated the unlimited partnership 260
  value of cargoes from Far East 267
  chain-like structure 294–5, 296–9
  under industrial capitalism 255
Merovingian charters 202, 227, 228, 239
  purchase of land in 224
Merovingians 190, 219, 221, 223
  aristocracy financed expansion 224–6, 228
Mertens, H.-G. 164, 345
Metcalfe, Sir Charles 17
'methods' of capitalist accumulation 143
Mexico 226, 252, 338–40, 342
  General Indian Court of 141
mezzadri 5, 146
  semi-proletarianised categories of 335
Mickwitz, Gunnar 49, 159
middle ages, novelty of 184
Middle East
  peasantry in 242
  share levels in 246
migrant labour/workers 124 n.35, 207, 334
  massive use of 336
Mihr Narseh 248
Mikhailovsky, N.K. 2
Miliukov, Paul 33
minimalism/primitivism 126, 156
  strong in Marxist tradition 126
mining 251–2, 273
mirasidars 115
misthotai 160–1
Mitchell, Timothy 178
'mixed servile labour force' 202, 205, 231, 233, 237
mobility of labour-power 54, 86, 137, 139, 142, 334, 339, 345, 346
modernism among Marxists 126–7
modes of production 1, 4, 60,
  not deducible from labour-systems 346–7
  no fixed sequence 6, 351
  two meanings in Marx 50–52, 349–50
  and economic cycles 60–1

objects of the *longue durée* 87
articulation? 92, 359–60
  in Chris Wickham 212–213
  and post-Roman transition 188, 190
  'microregionality of'? 217–218
Modzelewski, Karol 221 nn.24–5
Mommsen, Theodor 127, 129
  description of American capitalism 127
monetary economy 7, 25, 29, 36–7, 80, 169, 210–11, 216, 265
money-market
  financed modernisation of estates 341
moneylenders
  expansion linked to commercialisation 294
  organisation of business 295–6
  assassinations of 299
  crucial to revenue-system 301
Moore, Jr., Barrington 58
Moreno Fraginals, Manuel 346 n.71
Morocco 264–5, 269
Morony, Michael 248
Mozambique 63, 99
Mughals 16, 34–7, 38, 39, 249, 355, 356
Muhammad Ali Pasha 249
multazim/iltizām 162–3, 249
Mundle, Sudipto 134, 140
al-Muqaddasi 266
murābiʿūn 171–2, 246
Murray, Martin 141
Muscovy 19, 23–4, 31–3
mutaʿahhidūn 249
muzāraʿa 245–6
muzāriʿ (pl. -ūn) 162

Nahas, J.F. 172–3, 342, 343
Naito Torajiro 27
Naples 336
Narodniks 55, 309
Narshakhī, Muḥammad b. Jaʿfar 248–9
Neustria 221, 222, 225
New York brokers 340
Nishapur 266
Normans 268
North Africa 124–5, 196, 209, 210, 246, 265, 269
  'driving force of the Mediterranean' 265
North India, *bhaiachara*
  communities 355
northern Kiangsu, foundries of 29–30, 358
Nour Ed-Din 172
Nouschi, Albert 246–7

O'Malley, L.S.S. 113
Oakes, James 10
obsequia 197, 201
Oikonomidès, Nicolas 19
opera (pl. *operae*)
  Roman equivalent of abstract labour 118
  different senses of 118 n.7
opsoniastai 165
Optatus 125
'Oriental despotism' 16, 24
originarii 203, 227, 235 n.88, 236
Orren, Karen 139–40
Ostrogorsky, George 26, 49, 167
Ostrogoths 203
Ottomans 19, 35, 241, 355, 356
Owen, Roger 159, 342, 344
ownership of villages 247–50
  generalisation of a Sasanian model 248–9

Pach, Z.P. 49, 84, 110
Pachomius 125
Palestine 198, 268
pannaiyals 115
Panopolis 119
papyri 121, 126, 156
paramonarioi 123
paroikoi 39
Pasquali, Gianfranco 203
Patnaik, Utsa 278–9, 308, 326, 327, 329
patrocinium 211
Patterson, Orlando 10
Pavlov, Andrej 32
peasant mode of production 94–5, 217
peasant/moneylender
  transactions legally enforceable 302 n.62
  capitalist nature of relationship 306, 309–10
'peasant nations' 100, 308
peasantry
  integrated into capitalist production 144–5, 359
  elusive line between it and landless labour 179, 242, 250
  on East Mediterranean estates 215
  chief beneficiary of fall of the Roman empire? 217
  re-emergence 225, 237
  farm-workers distinct from 231
  vulnerability of 241
  in sixth-century Iran 243–4
  and capitalist domination 276
  differentiation in Deccan 317

peasants
    under feudalism   74
    in the *iltizam* system   162–3
    as good as labourers   163
peculiaria   202, 237
peonaje   5, 141, 150 n.104, 339–40
permanent labour   113–114, 115, 161–5, 336
    ways of attracting   338
Peru   4, 58, 63, 65, 171, 252, 308
Peter the Great   33, 57
Petrusewicz, Marta   336, 338
Pipes, Richard   19
Pirenne, Henri   49, 75, 87, 187, 205
Plekhanov, G.V.   47
Po Valley   73, 334, 335
Pokrovsky, M.N.   57–8, 71, 85, 256
Poland   79, 80, 81, 84, 85, 89
    Polish grain   71–2
Poliak, A.N.   162, 163
politor   105
pomest'ye system   33
Poni, Carlo   5
Portugal   72, 93, 144, 252, 268, 269–70, 357–8
    seminal role in capitalism   253–4
positivism   47
possessive individualism   137, 153
Post, Charles   141
post-Roman *Gutswirtschaft*, dissolution of   230
Postan, M.M.   107–9
praebendarii   200
Preobrazhensky, Evgeny   57, 67,
prices, stimulus of   84–5, 89
primitive accumulation   43, 261, 272–3, 360
prochreia   175
Procopius   216, 248
production/circulation, abstract opposition between   257, 271
profit, disguised forms of   306
Provence   225
Prussia   63, 84, 85, 111, 334–5, 340–2
    landed class   341
Punjab   111

radicalism
    culture among workers   124–5
Raftis, J.A.   107
Ramachandran, V.K.   135–7, 140
Ramsay, W.   318
Ransom, Roger L.   11
Rathbone, Dominic   164, 165, 176
Ratnagiri, export of labour   323
real subsumption
    defines the 'specifically' capitalist mode of production   350
relations of production
    not reducible to forms of exploitation   4–5, 41, 58, 353, 359
    confused/conflated with relations of exploitation   2–3, 53, 347
    defined in terms of laws of motion   60
Remigius, bishop of Rheims   227–8, 236
rice   11, 110, 163, 265, 337
Richards, Alan   159, 246, 342–3, 344
Richards, John F.   36, 37
Roderic   224
Rodinson, Maxime   357
Rösener, Werner   233
Roman law
    retrieval of in twelfth century   204
    Law of Persons   194
Romanovich Slavatinsky, A.   33
Rome
    Roman Republic   7
    sophistication of finance   7
    management of labour   104–6
    occupational identities   119
    skilled workers in construction sector   120
    capitalist sector in   129 n.54
    R.'s industrial slavery   188–9, 351
    pervasive influence of Roman law   190
Rome, City of   216
Rosenberg, Arthur   126
Rosenberg, Hans   111, 341
Rostovtzeff, M.   49
Rudra, Ashok   112
Rühle, Otto   126
Rumania   34, 57
rural labour force
    on Mexican estates   164, 171, 173
    on third-century estates   164
    residential patterns   171
    on Late Antique estates   174–5
    in post-Roman West   189–90, 191, 200, 235–6
    landless on Merovingian estates   206, 226
    in Dagobert's donation of Etrépagny   235–6
Russia   7, 19, 21, 23, 25, 31–4, 37, 40, 41, 42, 57, 80, 81, 84, 88, 89, 91 n.140, 349, 355
    eighteenth-century nobility   76
    pomeshchiki   158, 167

Ste. Croix, Geoffrey de   182, 183, 184, 197
Safavids   18
Sahara   254, 264
salam contract   12 n.49
Salé   268
Saint-Simonians   344
Santen, H.W. van   272
São Jorge da Mina   254
al-Sarakhsī   262–3
Sardinia   209, 232
Sardis, building workers   120, 122
Sarris, Peter   216
Sartre, Jean-Paul   xviii, 133
  on freedom of contract and real freedom   150–3
Sasanian Iran
  power of upper-class   243
  social divisions   244
  village-estates   248
Schissler, Hanna   340–1
Scottish Highlands   355
'second serfdom'   63, 79–81, 90
  origins of   83
Sée, Henri   49
Segrè, A.   168
segregation of women   337
'semi-feudalism'   277–8
  myth of   101
separate corporate personality, doctrine of   258
serfdom   5, 12, 14 n.55, 41, 83, 53 n.36, 183, 190, 196, 197, 199, 230, 345 n.68, 352, 353, 354
  not caused by decline of slavery   6
  not a feature of the early middle ages   181, 233, 239
  Dobb's definition   52–3
  in Russia   33–4
  in late Rome?   157–8, 182
  'long continuities'   204
  not descended from colonate   205
  'does not exist in India'   355–6
Serrao, Feliciano   126
servi   205, 229, 235
  post-Roman   200, 201
  Visigothic   202–3
servi praebendarii   238
service-holdings   354
  Merovingian *mansi*   229
  in Spain and Italy   230
servility   233, 239
seventh century, agrarian watershed   224–31
Sfax   268
al-Shāfi'ī   246, 262
Shapur II   248

sharecroppers   5, 111–113, 122–3, 147, 158, 163, 179, 241, 276, 277, 335, 344
  as wage-labourers   145–6
  Byzantine   245
sharecropping   216, 335, 359
  more profitable   113
  in Islamic world   245–6
  rejected by Muslim jurists   246
  automatically semi-feudal?   277, 278
shareholders   258
shares, a distinctive form of money-capital   258
al-Shaybānī, Muḥammad   262
Shore, John   40
Sicily   208, 209, 210
Sidjilmasa   265
silk   43 n.251, 44 n.256, 50, 252, 259 n.37, 265, 266, 267, 273, 274 n.136, 324, 325
'simple categories'   54
simple commodity producers, subjugation by capital   95–9
Sind   264, 266, 276
Siraf   264, 266
siri   113
Skocpol, Theda   23
slave densities, Cato's farm compared with Caribbean   104
slave mode of production?   3, 10 n.38, 181, 189, 351–2, 353
slave-labour as fixed capital   143, 352
slave-plantations   12, 65, 66
  as form of capitalism   69–71, 143, 353, 358
  financed by merchants   273–4
slavery
  widespread in the later Roman empire/ Late Antiquity   9, 189, 201, 232–3
  widespread in post-Roman West   181, 201, 227, 233, 237
  post-Roman   198–203
  mutation in early middle ages   238
slaves   3, 11, 67, 81, 92, 128, 129 n.54, 199, 206, 230, 236, 243, 274
  on Russian estates   55
  on early-medieval estates   83
  rule of continuity   104, 106
  labour-power hired out   119
  use of by Church   233
slave-tenancies   198, 239
small capitalists   281
small peasantry   338
  decline in Deccan   289–91
  gain nothing from cotton-boom   305
  expropriation of   316–317
Smith, J.B.   331

Snowden, Frank M. 146, 335, 337–8
Sociedad Rural Argentina 333
solidi, production of 121
Sombart, Werner 12, 49, 143–4, 251, 275, 357
South Africa 147, 338, 344, 359
  gold mines 63
South Carolina 11, 337
South India 140–1
South-east Asia 62
Southern Iraq 242, 244, 264
Southern Italy 205, 334–5, 337, 351
Sozomen 124
Spain 93, 210
  Visigothic 182, 192, 200, 202–3, 207, 222, 223–4, 233, 235
  late Roman 186
  Church control over freedpeople 201, 236
  Arab conquest of 224
Spanish colonisation 65, 93, 144
Spanish villas 186, 207
Spooner, Frank 71
Sprandel, Rolf 223
Staab, Franz 200
Stalin, J.V. 47, 48, 181
Stalinism 48, 49
state, problem of the 23
Steensgaard, Nils 270
Steinfeld, Robert J. 14
Strabo 119
Strieder, Jakob 251–2, 260
subsumption of labour into capital 280–1
  into merchant's capital 273–6
sugar 10, 58, 63, 67, 69 n.83, 71, 104 n.3, 144, 171, 260, 265, 272, 273, 274, 286, 313, 334, 358
Sundwall, J. 188
Sutch, Richard 11
Sweezy, Paul 52, 54, 64, 75, 88, 92
Syene, famous for its stone-cutters 119
Syria 210

al-Ṭabarī, Muḥammad b. Jarīr 264
Tageschalken 238
tamaliyya 342–3
Tawney, R.H. 256–7
Taylor, Lewis 4, 5
tenancy/tenants 111–113, 166, 170, 202, 212, 244, 326
  eviction in West Bengal 112
  'wage-type tenancy' 146
Thaer, Albrecht 341
Theadelphia 166
Theoderic 198
Thompson, E.A. 226 n.47, 233

Thompson, E.P. 15
Tits-Dieuaide, M.-J. 229
tobacco 67, 259, 340, 346, 358
total social capital 138, 142, 143, 278
trajectories of accumulation 347–8, 360
transition to early middle ages 190, 199–200, 204
  zone of rupture 221–2
  new organisation of labour 225
tributary mode of production 22, 23–40, 354–6
  cash reserves under 25 n.114, 36
  forms of exploitation under 38–40
tributary régimes, vitality of 24–5, 30, 36
Trotsky, L.D. xi–xii, xvii, 21, 23, 25, 31, 32–3, 45
Tuscany 146, 335, 344
Twitchett, Denis 18, 27

al-Ubulla 264
Udovitch, A.L. 262
Uganda 99
Ukraine 81
ʿUmar b. al-Khaṭṭāb 244
Umayyads 25, 203, 210
United Provinces (India) 40, 276, 311
use of labour
  task-specific in agriculture 109
  in Punjab wheat 109–110
  captive supply on Merovingian estates 236
ʿUthmān b. ʿAffān 248

Varro 106
Veiga Simões, Alberto 253
Venice 252, 254–5, 260, 268, 358
  dominated by capital 260
Vera, Domenico 203–4
Verhulst, Adriaan 206, 218–219, 225, 355
Verlagssystem 275, 358
Vespasian 118
Vigil, Marcelo 182
Vigilius, bishop of Auxerre 228–9
Vilar, Pierre 49, 93
villae
  integrated estates 206
  obsolete by ninth century 206
  late Roman 206–7
  settlements on 207
  Merovingian 218
villas (in archaeological sense) 207–8
Visigoths 182, 209, 219
Volney, C.-F. 163
Voß, Wulf Eckart 196–7

wage-accounting, systems of   176–7
wage-advances   336, 338, 345
   in Indian countryside   113–114
   means of controlling wage-
      labourers   142
   how treated by employers   148
   proper analysis of   148–50
wage-employment
   poor peasant dependence on   322–3
wage-labour   13
   voluntarist model of   14, 131–3,
      135
   forced recruitment   41, 142
   as a simple category   53
   as capital-positing   54
   widespread in Roman economy   117
   a kind of slavery   117–118
   scale radically underestimated   126
   shrouded in legal mysticism   137
   'distinctions of form' within   145–50
wages
   of rural labourers under
      Diocletian   121–2
   skill differentials in Antiquity   121
   piecerates   122
   expansive notion of   154
Wakefield, Edward Gibbon   100, 306
Wales   210
Waszyński, Stefan   145, 245
water-mills   225
water-wheels (*mechanai*)   169–70
Watson, Andrew   170
Weber, Max   25, 27, 31, 32, 33, 87,
   105–6, 111, 182, 189
Weidemann, Margarete   225, 228
Weidinger, Ulrich   229–30
wells   314–315
Wells, Alan   340
West, L.C.   158, 159
West Africa   99
West Indies   10, 62, 66, 72

Wickham, Chris   xii, 2, 183–5, 187, 188,
   189, 191, 198, 200, 201, 202, 204, 205,
   207, 208, 210, 211–213, 217–218, 231–8,
   354, 355
will theory of contract   131–3
   Marx's critique   137–8
wine   111, 166, 170, 189, 216
Wingate, George   284, 285
   key mechanism described by   291
Witiza   224
Wittfogel, Karl A.   xii
Wood, Sir Charles   331
wool   72, 252, 342
work practices
   in Roman olive-harvest   119
workers
   nineteenth-century England   14, 142
   seasonal   118, 124–5, 142, 207
   Rome's construction sector   120
   Rome mint   120–1
   control over terms of agreement   122
   concentration in labour-process   123
      n.31
   self-regulating groups   123
   dock workers of Portus   124
   militancy in late Rome   123–5
   unwilling to accept domination   141
   real freedom of   152, 154
   forms of accommodation on large
      estates   171
worker-tenants   200, 230, 238
working-class   126
world-economy   65, 93, 359–60
   seventeenth century   72

al-Yaʿqūbī   264
Yucatán   340

zamindars   21, 39–40, 249
   recalcitrant   35–6
Zavala, Silvio   150 n.104, 335–6, 339

www.ingramcontent.com/pod-product-compliance
Lightning Source LLC
Chambersburg PA
CBHW071145070526
44584CB00019B/2661